GLENCOE
PHYSICS
Principles and Problems

Problems and Solutions Manual

Glencoe McGraw-Hill

New York, New York   Columbus, Ohio   Woodland Hills, California   Peoria, Illinois

GLENCOE
PHYSICS
Principles and Problems

Student Edition

Teacher Wraparound Edition

Teacher Classroom Resources

Transparency Package with Transparency
Masters
Laboratory Manual SE and TE
Physics Lab and Pocket Lab Worksheets
Study Guide SE and TE
Chapter Assessment
Tech Prep Applications
Critical Thinking
Reteaching
Enrichment
Physics Skills
Supplemental Problems
Problems and Solutions Manual
Spanish Resources
Lesson Plans with Block Scheduling

Technology

TestCheck Software (Win/Mac)
MindJogger Videoquizzes
Interactive Lesson Planner
Interactive Teacher Edition
Website at science.glencoe.com
Physics for the Computer Age CD-ROM
(Win/Mac)

**The Glencoe Science Professional
Development Series**

Graphing Calculators in the Science Classroom
Cooperative Learning in the Science Classroom
Alternate Assessment in the Science Classroom
Performance Assessment in the Science
Classroom
Lab and Safety Skills in the Science Classroom

Glencoe/McGraw-Hill

A Division of The McGraw·Hill Companies

Copyright © by the McGraw-Hill Companies, Inc. All rights reserved. Permission is
granted to reproduce the material contained herein on the condition that such
material be reproduced only for classroom use; be provided to students, teachers,
and families without charge; and be used solely in conjunction with the *Physics:
Principles and Problems* program. Any other reproduction, for use or sale, is
prohibited without prior written permission of the publisher.

Send all inquiries to:
Glencoe/McGraw-Hill
8787 Orion Place
Columbus, Ohio 43240

ISBN 0-07-825936-3
Printed in the United States of America.

2 3 4 5 6 7 8 9 024 07 06 05 04 03 02

Contents

To the Teacher

The *Problems and Solutions Manual* is a supplement of Glencoe's *Physics: Principles and Problems*. The manual is a comprehensive resource of all student text problems and solutions. Practice Problems follow most Example Problems. Answers to these problems are found in the margin of the *Teacher Wraparound Edition*. Complete solutions to these problems are available to the student in Appendix C of the student text. Chapter Review Problem and Critical Thinking Problem answers are found in the margins of the *Teacher Wraparound Edition*. Each Practice Problem, Chapter Review Problem, and Critical Thinking Problem with the solution is restated in this manual. Complete solutions for the Extra Practice Problems in Appendix B, as well as solutions for the Additional Topics in Physics in Appendix D, can be found at the end of this manual.

1 What is physics?

No Practice Problems.

Critical Thinking Problems

page 13

11. It has been said that a fool can ask more questions than a wise man can answer. In science, it is frequently the case that a wise man is needed to ask the right question rather than to answer it. Explain.

Both asking a question and answering a question are important. Often, however, the training, experience, and imagination necessary to know just what question to ask have provided the insight necessary to find the answer.

Copyright © by Glencoe/McGraw-Hill

2 A Mathematical Toolkit

Practice Problems

2.1 The Measures of Science
pages 16–23

page 20

1. Express the following quantities in scientific notation.

   a. 5800 m

   5.8×10^3 m

   b. 450 000 m

   4.5×10^5 m

   c. 302 000 000 m

   3.02×10^8 m

   d. 86 000 000 000 m

   8.6×10^{10} m

2. Express the following quantities in scientific notation.

   a. 0.000 508 kg

   5.08×10^{-4} kg

   b. 0.000 000 45 kg

   4.5×10^{-7} kg

   c. 0.000 360 0 kg

   3.600×10^{-4} kg

   d. 0.004 kg

   4×10^{-3} kg

3. Express the following quantities in scientific notation.

   a. 300 000 s

   3×10^5 s

   b. 186 000 s

   1.86×10^5 s

   c. 93 000 000 s

   9.3×10^7 s

page 21

4. Convert each of the following length measurements as directed.

   a. 1.1 cm to meters

   $(1.1 \text{ cm}) \left(\dfrac{1 \times 10^{-2} \text{ m}}{1 \text{ cm}} \right) = 1.1 \times 10^{-2}$ m

   b. 76.2 pm to millimeters

   $(76.2 \text{ pm}) \left(\dfrac{1 \times 10^{-12} \text{ m}}{1 \text{ pm}} \right)$

   $\times \left(\dfrac{1 \times 10^3 \text{ mm}}{1 \text{ m}} \right)$

   $= 76.2 \times 10^{-9}$ mm

   $= 7.62 \times 10^{-8}$ mm

   c. 2.1 km to meters

   $(2.1 \text{ km}) \left(\dfrac{1 \times 10^3 \text{ m}}{1 \text{ km}} \right) = 2.1 \times 10^3$ m

   d. 2.278×10^{11} m to kilometers

   $(2.278 \times 10^{11} \text{ m}) \left(\dfrac{1 \text{ km}}{1 \times 10^3 \text{ m}} \right)$

   $= 2.278 \times 10^8$ km

5. Convert each of the following mass measurements to its equivalent in kilograms.

   a. 147 g

   $1 \text{ kg} = 1 \times 10^3 \text{ g}$

   so $147 \text{ g} \left(\dfrac{1 \text{ kg}}{1 \times 10^3 \text{ g}} \right)$

   $= 147 \times 10^{-3}$ kg

   $= 1.47 \times 10^{-1}$ kg

   b. 11 Mg

   $1 \text{ Mg} = 1 \times 10^6 \text{ g and } 1 \text{ kg} = 1 \times 10^3 \text{ g}$

   so $11 \text{ Mg} \left(\dfrac{1 \times 10^6 \text{ g}}{1 \text{ Mg}} \right) \left(\dfrac{1 \text{ kg}}{1 \times 10^3 \text{ g}} \right)$

   $= 11 \times 10^6 \times 10^{-3}$ kg

   $= 1.1 \times 10^4$ kg

Copyright © by Glencoe/McGraw-Hill

Physics: Principles and Problems

5. (continued)

    c. 7.23 μg

$$7.23 \ \mu g \left(\frac{1 \text{ g}}{1 \times 10^6 \ \mu g} \right)$$
$$\times \left(\frac{1 \text{ kg}}{1 \times 10^3 \text{ g}} \right)$$
$$= 7.23 \times 10^{-6} \times 10^{-3} \text{ kg}$$
$$= 7.23 \times 10^{-9} \text{ kg}$$

    d. 478 mg

$$478 \text{ mg} \left(\frac{1 \times 10^{-3} \text{ g}}{1 \text{ mg}} \right)$$
$$\times \left(\frac{1 \text{ kg}}{1 \times 10^3 \text{ g}} \right)$$
$$= 4.78 \times 10^{-4} \text{ kg}$$

page 22

Solve the following problems. Write your answers in scientific notation.

  6. **a.** 5×10^{-7} kg $+ 3 \times 10^{-7}$ kg

$$= (5 + 3) \times 10^{-7} \text{ kg}$$
$$= 8 \times 10^{-7} \text{ kg}$$

    b. 4×10^{-3} kg $+ 3 \times 10^{-3}$ kg

$$= 7 \times 10^{-3} \text{ kg}$$

    c. 1.66×10^{-19} kg $+ 2.30 \times 10^{-19}$ kg

$$= 3.96 \times 10^{-19} \text{ kg}$$

    d. 7.2×10^{-12} kg $- 2.6 \times 10^{-12}$ kg

$$= (7.2 - 2.6) \times 10^{-12} \text{ kg}$$
$$= 4.6 \times 10^{-12} \text{ kg}$$

  7. **a.** 6×10^{-8} m^2 $- 4 \times 10^{-8}$ m^2

$$= 2 \times 10^{-8} \text{ m}^2$$

    b. 3.8×10^{-12} m^2 $- 1.90 \times 10^{-11}$ m^2

$$= 3.8 \times 10^{-12} \text{ m}^2 - 19.0 \times 10^{-12} \text{ m}^2$$
$$= (3.8 - 19.0) \times 10^{-12} \text{ m}^2$$
$$= -15.2 \times 10^{-12} \text{ m}^2$$
$$= -1.52 \times 10^{-11} \text{ m}^2$$

    c. 5.8×10^{-9} m^2 $- 2.8 \times 10^{-9}$ m^2

$$= 3.0 \times 10^{-9} \text{ m}^2$$

    d. 2.26×10^{-18} m^2 $- 1.8 \times 10^{-18}$ m^2

$$= 0.46 \times 10^{-18} \text{ m}^2$$
$$= 4.6 \times 10^{-19} \text{ m}^2$$

  8. **a.** 5.0×10^{-7} mg $+ 4 \times 10^{-8}$ mg

$$= 5.0 \times 10^{-7} \text{ mg} + 0.4 \times 10^{-7} \text{ mg}$$
$$= 5.4 \times 10^{-7} \text{ mg}$$

    b. 6.0×10^{-3} mg $+ 2 \times 10^{-4}$ mg

$$= 6.0 \times 10^{-3} \text{ mg} + 0.2 \times 10^{-3} \text{ mg}$$
$$= 6.2 \times 10^{-3} \text{ mg}$$

    c. 3.0×10^{-2} pg $- 2 \times 10^{-6}$ ng

$$= 3.0 \times 10^{-2} \times 10^{-12} \text{ g}$$
$$- 2 \times 10^{-6} \times 10^{-9} \text{ g}$$
$$= 3.0 \times 10^{-14} \text{ g} - 0.2 \times 10^{-14} \text{ g}$$
$$= 2.8 \times 10^{-14} \text{ g}$$

    d. 8.2 km $- 3 \times 10^2$ m

$$= 8.2 \times 10^3 \text{ m} - 0.3 \times 10^3 \text{ m}$$
$$= 7.9 \times 10^3 \text{ m}$$

page 23

Find the value of each of the following quantities.

  9. **a.** $(2 \times 10^4$ m$)(4 \times 10^8$ m$)$

$$= (2 \times 4) \times 10^{4+8} \text{ m}^2$$
$$= 8 \times 10^{12} \text{ m}^2$$

    b. $(3 \times 10^4$ m$)(2 \times 10^6$ m$)$

$$= (3 \times 2) \times 10^{4+6} \text{ m}^2$$
$$= 6 \times 10^{10} \text{ m}^2$$

    c. $(6 \times 10^{-4}$ m$)(5 \times 10^{-8}$ m$)$

$$= 30 \times 10^{-4-8} \text{ m}^2$$
$$= 3 \times 10^{-11} \text{ m}^2$$

    d. $(2.5 \times 10^{-7}$ m$)(2.5 \times 10^{16}$ m$)$

$$= 6.25 \times 10^{-7+16} \text{ m}^2$$
$$= 6.25 \times 10^9 \text{ m}^2$$

  10. **a.** $\dfrac{6 \times 10^8 \text{ kg}}{2 \times 10^4 \text{ m}^3}$

$$= 3 \times 10^{8-4} \text{ kg/m}^3$$
$$= 3 \times 10^4 \text{ kg/m}^3$$

    b. $\dfrac{6 \times 10^8 \text{ kg}}{2 \times 10^{-4} \text{ m}^3}$

$$= 3 \times 10^{8-(-4)} \text{ kg/m}^3$$
$$= 3 \times 10^{12} \text{ kg/m}^3$$

Copyright © by Glencoe/McGraw-Hill

10. (continued)

c. $\dfrac{6 \times 10^{-8}\ \text{m}}{2 \times 10^4\ \text{s}}$

$= 3 \times 10^{-8-4}\ \text{m/s}$

$= 3 \times 10^{-12}\ \text{m/s}$

d. $\dfrac{6 \times 10^{-8}\ \text{m}}{2 \times 10^{-4}\ \text{s}}$

$= 3 \times 10^{-8-(-4)}\ \text{m/s}$

$= 3 \times 10^{-4}\ \text{m/s}$

11. a. $\dfrac{(3 \times 10^4\ \text{kg})(4 \times 10^4\ \text{m})}{6 \times 10^4\ \text{s}}$

$= \dfrac{12 \times 10^{4+4}\ \text{kg} \cdot \text{m}}{6 \times 10^4\ \text{s}}$

$= 2 \times 10^{8-4}\ \text{kg} \cdot \text{m/s}$

$= 2 \times 10^4\ \text{kg} \cdot \text{m/s}$

The evaluation may be done in several other ways. For example

$\dfrac{(3 \times 10^4\ \text{kg})(4 \times 10^4\ \text{m})}{6 \times 10^4\ \text{s}}$

$= (0.5 \times 10^{4-4}\ \text{kg/s})(4 \times 10^4\ \text{m})$

$= (0.5\ \text{kg/s})(4 \times 10^4\ \text{m})$

$= 2 \times 10^4\ \text{kg} \cdot \text{m/s}$

b. $\dfrac{(2.5 \times 10^6\ \text{kg})(6 \times 10^4\ \text{m})}{5 \times 10^{-2}\ \text{s}^2}$

$= \dfrac{15 \times 10^{6+4}\ \text{kg} \cdot \text{m}}{5 \times 10^{-2}\ \text{s}^2}$

$= 3 \times 10^{10-(-2)}\ \text{kg} \cdot \text{m/s}^2$

$= 3 \times 10^{12}\ \text{kg} \cdot \text{m/s}^2$

12. a. $(4 \times 10^3\ \text{mg})(5 \times 10^4\ \text{kg})$

$= (4 \times 10^3 \times 10^{-3}\ \text{g})(5 \times 10^4 \times 10^3\ \text{g})$

$= 20 \times 10^7\ \text{g}^2$

$= 2 \times 10^8\ \text{g}^2$

b. $(6.5 \times 10^{-2}\ \text{m})(4.0 \times 10^3\ \text{km})$

$= (6.5 \times 10^{-2}\ \text{m})(4.0 \times 10^3 \times 10^3\ \text{m})$

$= 26 \times 10^4\ \text{m}^2$

$= 2.6 \times 10^5\ \text{m}^2$

c. $(2 \times 10^3\ \text{ms})(5 \times 10^{-2}\ \text{ns})$

$= (2 \times 10^3 \times 10^{-3}\ \text{s})(5 \times 10^{-2} \times 10^{-9}\ \text{s})$

$= 10 \times 10^{-11}\ \text{s}^2$

$= 1 \times 10^{-10}\ \text{s}^2$

13. a. $\dfrac{2.8 \times 10^{-2}\ \text{mg}}{2.0 \times 10^4\ \text{g}}$

$= \dfrac{2.8 \times 10^{-2} \times 10^{-3}\ \text{g}}{2.0 \times 10^4\ \text{g}} = 1.4 \times 10^{-9}$

b. $\dfrac{(6 \times 10^2\ \text{kg})(9 \times 10^3\ \text{m})}{(2 \times 10^4\ \text{s})(3 \times 10^6\ \text{ms})}$

$= \dfrac{(6 \times 10^2\ \text{kg})(9 \times 10^3\ \text{m})}{(2 \times 10^4\ \text{s})(3 \times 10^6 \times 10^{-3}\ \text{s})}$

$= \dfrac{54 \times 10^5\ \text{kg} \cdot \text{m}}{6 \times 10^7\ \text{s}^2}$

$= 9 \times 10^{-2}\ \text{kg} \cdot \text{m/s}^2$

14. $\dfrac{(7 \times 10^{-3}\ \text{m}) + (5 \times 10^{-3}\ \text{m})}{(9 \times 10^7\ \text{km}) + (3 \times 10^7\ \text{km})}$

$= \dfrac{12 \times 10^{-3}\ \text{m}}{12 \times 10^7\ \text{km}}$

$= \dfrac{12 \times 10^{-3}\ \text{m}}{12 \times 10^7 \times 10^3\ \text{m}} = \dfrac{12 \times 10^{-3}\ \text{m}}{12 \times 10^{10}\ \text{m}}$

$= 1 \times 10^{-13}$

2.2 Measurement Uncertainties
pages 24–29

page 27

State the number of significant digits in each measurement.

15. a. 2804 m

   4

b. 2.84 km

   3

c. 0.0029 m

   2

d. 0.003 068 m

   4

e. 4.6×10^5 m

   2

f. 4.06×10^{-5} m

   3

16. a. 75 m

   2

b. 75.00 m

   4

Copyright © by Glencoe/McGraw-Hill

16. (continued)

    c. 0.007 060 kg

      4

    d. 1.87×10^6 mL

      3

    e. 1.008×10^8 m

      4

    f. 1.20×10^{-4} m

      3

page 28

Solve the following addition problems.

17. **a.** 6.201 cm, 7.4 cm, 0.68 cm, and 12.0 cm

      6.201 cm
      7.4   cm
      0.68 cm
      <u>**12.0 cm**</u>
      26.281 cm

      = 26.3 cm

    b. 1.6 km, 1.62 m, and 1200 cm

      1.6 km = 1600   m
      1.62 m =   1.62 m
      1200 cm = <u>   12   m</u>
      1613.62 m

      = 1600 m or 1.6 km

Solve the following subtraction problems.

18. **a.** 8.264 g from 10.8 g

      10.8   g
      <u>**−8.264 g**</u>
      2.536 g

      2.5 g (rounded from 2.536 g)

    b. 0.4168 m from 475 m

      475   m
      <u>**− 0.4168 m**</u>
      474.5832 m

      475 m (rounded from 474.5832 m)

Solve the following multiplication problems.

19. **a.** 131 cm $\times$ 2.3 cm

      3.0×10^2 cm^2 (the result 301.3 cm^2 expressed to two significant digits. Note that the expression in the form 300 cm^2 would not indicate how many of the digits are significant.)

    b. 3.2145 km $\times$ 4.23 km

      13.6 km^2 (the result 13.597335 km^2 expressed to three significant digits)

    c. 5.761 N $\times$ 6.20 m

      35.7 N · m (the result 35.7182 N · m expressed to three significant digits)

Solve the following division problems.

20. **a.** 20.2 cm $\div$ 7.41 s

      2.73 cm/s (the result 2.726045 . . . cm/s expressed to three significant digits)

    b. 3.1416 cm $\div$ 12.4 s

      0.253 cm/s (the result 0.253354 . . . cm/s expressed to three significant digits)

    c. 13.78 g $\div$ 11.3 mg

      13.78 g $\div$ 11.3 $\times$ 10^{-3} g

      1.22 $\times$ 10^3 g (the result 1.219469 . . . $\times$ 10^3 g expressed to three significant digits)

    d. 18.21 g $\div$ 4.4 cm^3

      4.1 g/cm^3 (the result 4.138636 . . . g/cm^3 expressed to two significant digits)

2.3   **Visualizing Data**
      pages 30–36

page 36

21. The total distance a lab cart travels during specified lengths of time is given in the following data table.

Copyright © by Glencoe/McGraw-Hill

21. (continued)

TABLE 2-4	
Time (s)	Distance (m)
0.0	0.00
1.0	0.32
2.0	0.60
3.0	0.95
4.0	1.18
5.0	1.45

a. Plot distance versus time from the values given in the table and draw the curve that best fits all points.

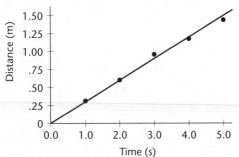

b. Describe the resulting curve.

straight line

c. According to the graph, what type of relationship exists between the total distance traveled by the lab cart and the time?

linear relationship

d. What is the slope of this graph?

$$M = \frac{\Delta y}{\Delta x} = \frac{1.5 - 0.60}{5.0 - 2.0} = \frac{0.90}{3.0}$$

$$= 0.30 \text{ m/s}$$

e. Write an equation relating distance and time for this data.

$$d = 0.30(t)$$

Chapter Review Problems

pages 39–41

page 39

Section 2.1

Level 1

30. Express the following numbers in scientific notation:

a. 5 000 000 000 000 m

    5×10^{12} m

b. 0.000 000 000 166 m

    1.66×10^{-10} m

c. 2 003 000 000 m

    2.003×10^{9} m

d. 0.000 000 103 0 m

    1.030×10^{-7} m

31. Convert each of the following measurements to meters.

a. 42.3 cm

$$\frac{42.3 \text{ cm}}{1}\left(\frac{1 \times 10^{-2} \text{ m}}{1 \text{ cm}}\right) = 0.423 \text{ m}$$

b. 6.2 pm

$$\frac{6.2 \text{ pm}}{1}\left(\frac{1 \times 10^{-12} \text{ m}}{1 \text{ pm}}\right)$$

$$= 6.2 \times 10^{-12} \text{ m}$$

c. 21 km

$$\frac{21 \text{ km}}{1}\left(\frac{1 \times 10^{3} \text{ m}}{1 \text{ km}}\right) = 2.1 \times 10^{4} \text{ m}$$

d. 0.023 mm

$$\frac{0.023 \text{ mm}}{1}\left(\frac{1 \times 10^{-3} \text{ m}}{1 \text{ mm}}\right)$$

$$= 2.3 \times 10^{-5} \text{ m}$$

e. 214 μm

$$\frac{214 \text{ } \mu\text{m}}{1}\left(\frac{1 \times 10^{-6} \text{ m}}{1 \text{ } \mu\text{m}}\right)$$

$$= 2.14 \times 10^{-4} \text{ m}$$

f. 570 nm

$$570 \text{ nm}\left(\frac{1 \times 10^{-9} \text{ m}}{1 \text{ nm}}\right)$$

$$= 5.70 \times 10^{-7} \text{ m}$$

32. Add or subtract as indicated.

a. 5.80×10^{9} s $+ 3.20 \times 10^{8}$ s

    5.80×10^{9} s $+ 0.320 \times 10^{9}$ s

    $= 6.12 \times 10^{9}$ s

32. (continued)

b. 4.87×10^{-6} m $- 1.93 \times 10^{-6}$ m

    $= 2.94 \times 10^{-6}$ m

Copyright © by Glencoe/McGraw-Hill

c. 3.14×10^{-5} kg $+ 9.36 \times 10^{-5}$ kg

$= 12.50 \times 10^{-5}$ **kg** $= 1.25 \times 10^{-4}$ **kg**

d. 8.12×10^{7} g $- 6.20 \times 10^{6}$ g

8.12×10^{7} **g** $- 0.620 \times 10^{7}$ **g**

$= 7.50 \times 10^{7}$ **g**

Level 2

33. Rank the following mass measurements from smallest to largest: 11.6 mg, 1021 μg, 0.000 006 kg, 0.31 mg.

$$\frac{11.6 \text{ mg}}{1}\left(\frac{1 \times 10^{-3} \text{ g}}{1 \text{ mg}}\right) = 1.16 \times 10^{-2} \text{ g}$$

or 11.6×10^{-3} **g**

$$\frac{1021 \text{ } \mu g}{1}\left(\frac{1 \times 10^{-6} \text{ g}}{1 \text{ } \mu g}\right)$$

$= 1.021 \times 10^{-3}$ **g**

$$\frac{0.000 \text{ } 006 \text{ kg}}{1}\left(\frac{10^{3} \text{ g}}{1 \text{ kg}}\right) = 6 \times 10^{-3} \text{ g}$$

$$\frac{0.31 \text{ mg}}{1}\left(\frac{1 \times 10^{-3} \text{ g}}{1 \text{ mg}}\right) = 3.1 \times 10^{-4} \text{ g}$$

or 0.31×10^{-3} **g**

0.31 mg, 1021 μg, 0.000 006 kg, 11.6 mg

Section 2.2

Level 1

34. State the number of significant digits in each of the following measurements.

a. 0.000 03 m

1

b. 64.01 fm

4

c. 80.001 m

5

d. 0.720 μg

3

35. State the number of significant digits in each of the following measurements.

a. 2.40×10^{6} kg

3

b. 6×10^{8} kg

1

c. 4.07×10^{16} m

3

36. Add or subtract as indicated.

a. 16.2 m + 5.008 m + 13.48 m

   16.2   **m**

    5.008 **m**

  13.48   **m**

  34.688 **m** = **34.7 m**

b. 5.006 m + 12.0077 m + 8.0084 m

    5.006 **m**

  12.0077 **m**

   8.0084 **m**

  25.0221 **m** = **25.022 m**

c. 78.05 cm^2 $- 32.046$ cm^2

   78.05   **cm^2**

 $-$**32.046** **cm^2**

  46.004 **cm^2** = **46.00 cm^2**

d. 15.07 kg $- 12.0$ kg

  15.07 **kg**

$-$**12.0** **kg**

   3.07 **kg** = **3.1 kg**

37. Multiply or divide as indicated.

a. $(6.2 \times 10^{18}$ m$)(4.7 \times 10^{-10}$ m$)$

$= 29.14 \times 10^{8}$ **m^2**

$= 2.9 \times 10^{9}$ **m^2**

b. $\dfrac{5.6 \times 10^{-7} \text{ m}}{2.8 \times 10^{-12} \text{ s}}$

$= 2.0 \times 10^{5}$ **m/s**

c. $(8.1 \times 10^{-4}$ km$)(1.6 \times 10^{-3}$ km$)$

$= 12.96 \times 10^{-7}$ **km^2**

$= 1.3 \times 10^{-6}$ **km^2**

Copyright © by Glencoe/McGraw-Hill

37. (continued)

d. $\dfrac{6.5 \times 10^5 \text{ kg}}{3.4 \times 10^3 \text{ m}^3}$

$= 1.91176 \ldots \times 10^2 \text{ kg/m}^3$

$= 1.9 \times 10^2 \text{ kg/m}^3$

38. Using a calculator, Chris obtained the following results. Give the answer to each operation using the correct number of significant digits.

a. 5.32 mm + 2.1 mm = 7.4200000 mm

7.4 mm

b. 13.597 m $\times$ 3.65 m = 49.62905 m^2

49.6 m^2

c. 83.2 kg $-$ 12.804 kg = 70.3960000 kg

70.4 kg

page 40

39. A rectangular floor has a length of 15.72 m and a width of 4.40 m. Calculate the area of the floor.

Area = *lw* = (15.72 m)(4.40 m)

$= 69.168 \text{ m}^2$

$= 69.2 \text{ m}^2$

40. A water tank has a mass of 3.64 kg when it is empty and a mass of 51.8 kg when it is filled to a certain level. What is the mass of the water in the tank?

<u>51.8 kg</u>

−3.64 kg

48.16 kg = 48.2 kg

Level 2

41. A lawn is 33.21 m long and 17.6 m wide.

a. What length of fence must be purchased to enclose the entire lawn?

Perimeter = 2*l* + 2*w*

$= 2(33.21 \text{ m}) + 2(17.6 \text{ m})$

$= 66.42 \text{ m} + 35.2 \text{ m}$

$= 101.62 \text{ m}$

$= 101.6 \text{ m}$

b. What area must be covered if the lawn is to be fertilized?

Area = *lw*

$= (33.21 \text{ m})(17.6 \text{ m})$

$= 584.496 \text{ m}^2 = 584 \text{ m}^2$

42. The length of a room is 16.40 m, its width is 4.5 m, and its height is 3.26 m. What volume does the room enclose?

V = lwh

$= (16.40 \text{ m})(4.5 \text{ m})(3.26 \text{ m})$

$= 240.588 \text{ m}^3 = 2.4 \times 10^2 \text{ m}^3$

43. The sides of a quadrangular plot of land are 132.68 m, 48.3 m, 132.736 m, and 48.37 m. What is the perimeter of the plot?

Perimeter

$= 132.68 \text{ m} + 48.3 \text{ m} + 132.736 \text{ m}$

$+ 48.37 \text{ m}$

$= 362.086 \text{ m}$

$= 362.1 \text{ m}$

Section 2.3

Level 1

44. Figure 2–14 shows the mass of the three substances for volumes between 0 and 60 cm^3.

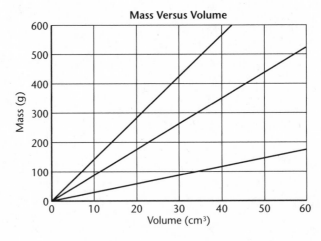

Copyright © by Glencoe/McGraw-Hill

44. (continued)

   a. What is the mass of 30 cm³ of each substance?

     (a) 80 g, (b) 260 g, (c) 400 g.

   b. If you had 100 g of each substance, what would their volumes be?

     (a) 34 cm³, (b) 11 cm³, (c) 7 cm³.

   c. In one or two sentences, describe the meaning of the steepness of the lines in this graph.

   The steepness represents the increased mass of each additional cubic centimeter of the substance.

Level 2

45. During an experiment, a student measured the mass of 10.0 cm³ of alcohol. The student then measured the mass of 20.0 cm³ of alcohol. In this way, the data in **Table 2–5** were collected.

TABLE 2-5	
Volume (cm³)	**Mass (g)**
10.0	7.9
20.0	15.8
30.0	23.7
40.0	31.6
50.0	39.6

   a. Plot the values given in the table and draw the curve that best fits all points.

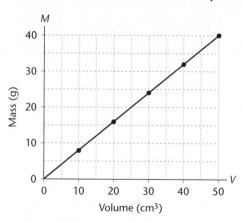

   b. Describe the resulting curve.

   a straight line

c. Use the graph to write an equation relating the volume to the mass of alcohol.

$$m = \frac{d}{V},\ \text{where } m \text{ is the slope}$$

d. Find the units of the slope of the graph. What is the name given to this quantity?

$$d = \frac{m}{V}$$

so the units of m are $\frac{g}{cm^3}$

   g/cm³; density

46. During a class demonstration, a physics instructor placed a 1.0-kg mass on a horizontal table that was nearly frictionless. The instructor then applied various horizontal forces to the mass and measured the rate at which it gained speed (was accelerated) for each force applied. The results of the experiment are shown in **Table 2–6.**

TABLE 2-6	
Force (N)	**Acceleration (m/s²)**
5.0	4.9
10.0	9.8
15.0	15.2
20.0	20.1
25.0	25.0
30.0	29.9

page 41

   a. Plot the values given in the table and draw the curve that best fits the results.

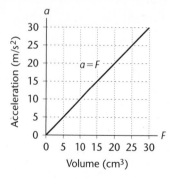

Copyright © by Glencoe/McGraw-Hill

46. (continued)

    b. Describe, in words, the relationship between force and acceleration according to the graph.

        The acceleration varies directly with the force.

    c. Write the equation relating the force and the acceleration that results from the graph.

        $F = ma$**, where** m **is the slope**

    d. Find the units of the slope of the graph.

$$m = \frac{a}{F} \text{ so the units of } m \text{ are } \frac{(m/s^2)}{N}$$

$$= \frac{m}{(s^2 \cdot N)}$$

47. The physics instructor who performed the experiment in problem 46 changed the procedure. The mass was varied while the force was kept constant. The acceleration of each mass was recorded. The results of the experiment are shown in **Table 2–7**.

TABLE 2-7	
Mass (kg)	**Acceleration (m/s²)**
1.0	12.0
2.0	5.9
3.0	4.1
4.0	3.0
5.0	2.5
6.0	2.0

    a. Plot the values given in the table and draw the curve that best fits all points.

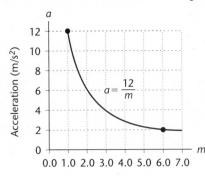

    b. Describe the resulting curve.

        hyperbola

    c. According to the graph, what is the relationship between mass and the acceleration produced by a constant force?

        Acceleration varies inversely with the mass.

    d. Write the equation relating acceleration to mass given by the data in the graph.

$$a = \frac{c}{m}$$

        c **= constant = 12**

        m **= mass**

    e. Find the units of the constant in the equation.

        $c = ma$

        so the units of c **are** (kg)(m/s²)

        = kg · m/s²

Critical Thinking Problems

48. Find the approximate time needed for a pitched baseball to reach home plate. Report your result to one significant digit. (Use a reference source to find the distance thrown and the speed of a fastball.)

    Answers will vary with the data available. Answer should be calculated from the equation: time = distance ÷ speed.

49. Have a student walk across the front of the classroom. Estimate his or her walking speed.

    Estimates will vary. Answers should be calculated from speed = distance ÷ time

50. How high can you throw a ball? Find a tall building whose height you can estimate and compare the height of your throw to that of the building.

    Estimates will vary.

Copyright © by Glencoe/McGraw-Hill

51. Use a graphing calculator or computer graphing program to graph reaction and braking distances versus original speed. Use the calculator or computer to find the slope of the reaction distance and the best quadratic fit to the braking distance.

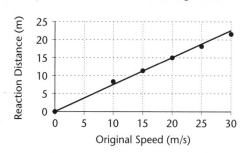

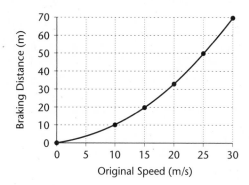

52. If the sun suddenly ceased to shine, how long would it take Earth to become dark? You will have to look up the speed of light in a vacuum and the distance from the sun to Earth. How long would it take to become dark on the surface of Jupiter?

Speed of light = 3.00×10^8 m/s

Mean distance from the sun to Earth = 1.50×10^{11} m

Mean distance from the sun to Jupiter = 7.78×10^{11} m

$$\text{time} = \frac{\text{distance}}{\text{speed}}$$

time for Earth to become dark:

$$\frac{1.50 \times 10^{11} \text{ m}}{3.00 \times 10^8 \text{ m/s}} = 5.00 \times 10^2 \text{ s}$$

time for the surface of Jupiter to become dark:

$$\frac{7.78 \times 10^{11} \text{ m}}{3.00 \times 10^8 \text{ m/s}} = 2.59 \times 10^3 \text{ s}$$

Copyright © by Glencoe/McGraw-Hill

3 Describing Motion

Practice Problems

3.1 Picturing Motion
pages 44–46

No practice problems.

3.2 Where and When?
pages 47–51

No practice problems.

3.3 Velocity and Acceleration
pages 53–59

No practice problems.

Chapter Review Problems

page 61

Create pictorial and physical models for the following problems.

Section 3.3

Level 1

17. A bike travels at a constant speed of 4.0 m/s for 5 s. How far does it go?

$$v_0 = 4.0 \text{ m/s} \qquad v_1 = 4.0 \text{ m/s}$$
$$d_0 = 0 \text{ m} \qquad d_1 = ?$$
$$t_0 = 0 \text{ s} \qquad t_1 = 5 \text{ s}$$

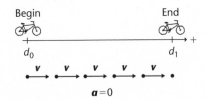

18. A bike accelerates from 0.0 m/s to 4.0 m/s in 4 s. What distance does it travel?

$$v_0 = 0 \text{ m/s} \qquad v_1 = 4.0 \text{ m/s}$$
$$d_0 = 0 \text{ m} \qquad d_1 = ?$$
$$t_0 = 0 \text{ s} \qquad t_1 = 4 \text{ s}$$

19. A student drops a ball from a window 3.5 m above the sidewalk. The ball accelerates at 9.80 m/s^2. How fast is it moving when it hits the sidewalk?

$$d_0 = 3.5 \text{ m} \qquad d_1 = 0$$
$$v_0 = 0 \qquad v_1 = ?$$
$$a = -9.80 \text{ m/s}^2$$

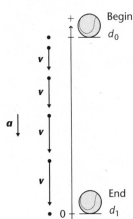

Level 2

20. A bike first accelerates from 0.0 m/s to 5.0 m/s in 4.5 s, then continues at this constant speed for another 4.5 s. What is the total distance traveled by the bike?

$$t_0 = 0 \qquad t_1 = 4.5 \text{ s} \qquad t_2 = 4.5 \text{ s} + 4.5 \text{ s}$$
$$= 9.0 \text{ s}$$
$$v_0 = 0.0 \quad v_1 = 5.0 \text{ m/s} \quad v_2 = 5.0 \text{ m/s}$$
$$d_0 = 0 \qquad\qquad\qquad d_2 = ?$$

Copyright © by Glencoe/McGraw-Hill

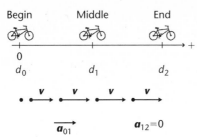

21. A car is traveling 20 m/s when the driver sees a child standing in the road. He takes 0.8 s to react, then steps on the brakes and slows at 7.0 m/s². How far does the car go before it stops?

$$a_{01} = 0 \qquad a_{12} = -7.0 \text{ m/s}^2$$
$$v_0 = 20 \text{ m/s} \quad v_1 = 20 \text{ m/s} \quad v_2 = 0$$
$$t_0 = 0 \qquad t_1 = 0.8 \text{ s} \qquad t_2 = ?$$
$$\qquad\qquad\qquad\qquad\qquad d_2 = ?$$

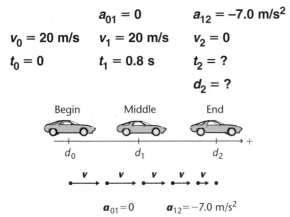

22. You throw a ball downward from a window at a speed of 2.0 m/s. The ball accelerates at 9.80 m/s². How fast is it moving when it hits the sidewalk 2.5 m below?

$$d_0 = 2.5 \text{ m} \qquad d_1 = 0 \text{ m}$$
$$v_0 = -2.0 \text{ m/s} \qquad v_1 = ?$$
$$\qquad\qquad a = -9.80 \text{ m/s}^2$$

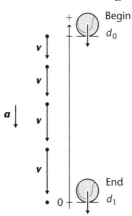

23. If you throw the ball in problem 22 up instead of down, how fast is it moving when it hits the sidewalk? **Hint:** Its acceleration is the same whether it is moving up or down.

$$d_0 = 2.5 \text{ m} \qquad d_1 = 0 \text{ m}$$
$$v_0 = 2.0 \text{ m/s} \qquad v_1 = ?$$
$$\qquad\qquad a = -9.80 \text{ m/s}^2$$

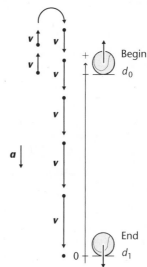

Critical Thinking Problems

Each of the following problems involves two objects. Draw the pictorial and physical models for each. Use different symbols to represent the position, velocity, and acceleration of each object. Do not solve the problem.

24. A truck is stopped at a stoplight. When the light turns green, it accelerates at 2.5 m/s². At the same instant, a car passes the truck going 15 m/s. Where and when does the truck catch up with the car?

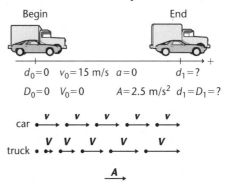

The lowercase symbols represent the car's position, velocity, and accleration. The uppercase symbols represent the truck's position, velocity, and acceleration.

Copyright © by Glencoe/McGraw-Hill

25. A truck is traveling at 18 m/s to the north. The driver of a car, 500 m to the north and traveling south at 24 m/s, puts on the brakes and slows at 3.5 m/s². Where do they meet?

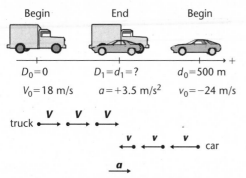

The lowercase symbols represent the car's position, velocity, and accleration. The uppercase symbols represent the truck's position, velocity, and acceleration.

Copyright © by Glencoe/McGraw-Hill

4 Vector Addition

Practice Problems

4.1 Properties of Vectors
pages 64–71

page 67

1. A car is driven 125 km due west, then 65 km due south. What is the magnitude of its displacement?

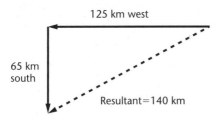

$$R^2 = A^2 + B^2$$
$$R^2 = (65\ km)^2 + (125\ km)^2$$
$$R^2 = 19\ 850\ km^2$$
$$R = 140\ km$$

2. A shopper walks from the door of the mall to her car 250 m down a lane of cars, then turns 90° to the right and walks an additional 60 m. What is the magnitude of the displacement of her car from the mall door?

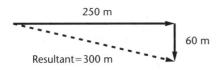

$$R^2 = (250\ m)^2 + (60\ m)^2$$
$$R^2 = 66\ 100\ m^2$$
$$R = 260\ m,\ or\ 300\ m\ to\ one$$
$$significant\ digit$$

3. A hiker walks 4.5 km in one direction, then makes a 45° turn to the right and walks another 6.4 km. What is the magnitude of her displacement?

$$R^2 = A^2 + B^2 - 2AB \cos \theta$$

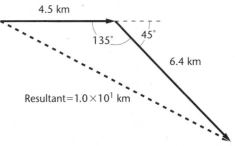

$$R = [(4.5\ km)^2 + (6.4\ km)^2$$
$$- (2)(4.5\ km)(6.4\ km)(\cos 135°)]^{1/2}$$
$$R = 1.0 \times 10^1\ km$$

4. What is the magnitude of your displacement when you follow directions that tell you to walk 225 m in one direction, make a 90° turn to the left and walk 350 m, then make a 30° turn to the right and walk 125 m?

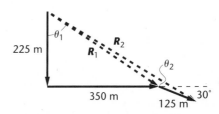

$$R_1 = [(225\ m)^2 + (350\ m)^2]^{1/2} = 416\ m$$
$$\theta_1 = \tan^{-1} \frac{350\ m}{225\ m} = 57.3°$$
$$\theta_2 = 180 - (60 - 57.3) = 177.3°$$
$$R_2 = [(416\ m)^2 + (125\ m)^2$$
$$- 2(416\ m)(125\ m)$$
$$(\cos 177.3°)]^{1/2}$$
$$R_2 = 540\ m$$

page 71

5. A car moving east at 45 km/h turns and travels west at 30 km/h. What are the magnitude and direction of the change in velocity?

5. (continued)

Magnitude of change in velocity

= 45 − (−30) = 75 km/h

direction of change is from east to west

6. You are riding in a bus moving slowly through heavy traffic at 2.0 m/s. You hurry to the front of the bus at 4.0 m/s relative to the bus. What is your speed relative to the street?

+2.0 m/s + 4.0 m/s

= 6.0 m/s relative to street

7. A motorboat heads due east at 11 m/s relative to the water across a river that flows due north at 5.0 m/s. What is the velocity of the motorboat with respect to the shore?

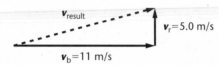

$v_{result} = [v_b^2 + v_r^2]^{1/2}$

$= [(11 \text{ m/s})^2 + (5.0 \text{ m/s})^2]^{1/2}$

= 12 m/s

$\theta = \tan^{-1} \dfrac{5.0 \text{ m/s}}{11 \text{ m/s}} = 24°$

v_{result} = 12 m/s, 66° east of north

8. A boat is rowed directly upriver at a speed of 2.5 m/s relative to the water. Viewers on the shore find that it is moving at only 0.5 m/s relative to the shore. What is the speed of the river? Is it moving with or against the boat?

2.5 m/s

⟶ boat

2.0 m/s   river

⟵

→

0.5 m/s   Resultant

2.5 m/s − 0.5 m/s

= 2.0 m/s against the boat

9. An airplane flies due north at 150 km/h with respect to the air. There is a wind blowing at 75 km/h to the east relative to the ground. What is the plane's speed with respect to the ground?

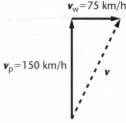

$v = [v_p^2 + v_w^2]^{1/2}$

$= [(150 \text{ km/h})^2 + (75 \text{ km/h})^2]^{1/2}$

= 170 km/h

10. An airplane flies due west at 185 km/h with respect to the air. There is a wind blowing at 85 km/h to the northeast relative to the ground. What is the plane's speed with respect to the ground?

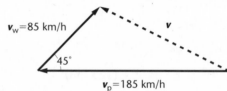

$v = [v_p^2 + v_w^2 - 2v_p v_w \cos \theta]^{1/2}$

$= [(185 \text{ km/h})^2 + (85 \text{ km/h})^2$

$- (2)(185 \text{ km/h})(85 \text{ km/h})(\cos 45°)]^{1/2}$

= 140 km/h

4.2   Components of Vectors
pages 72–76

page 74

11. What are the components of a vector of magnitude 1.5 m at an angle of 35° from the positive x-axis?

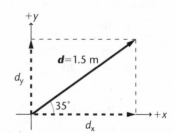

Copyright © by Glencoe/McGraw-Hill

11. (continued)

$$d_x = 1.5 \text{ m cos } 35° = 1.2 \text{ m}$$

$$d_y = 1.5 \text{ m sin } 35° = 0.86 \text{ m}$$

12. A hiker walks 14.7 km at an angle 35° south of east. Find the east and north components of this walk.

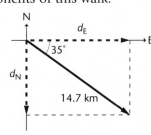

$$d_E = 14.7 \text{ km cos } 35° = 12.0 \text{ km}$$

$$d_N = -14.7 \text{ km sin } 35° = -8.43 \text{ km}$$

13. An airplane flies at 65 m/s in the direction 149° counterclockwise from east. What are the east and north components of the plane's velocity?

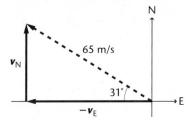

$$v_E = -65 \text{ m/s cos } 31° = -55.71 \text{ m/s}$$

$$= -56 \text{ m/s}$$

$$v_N = 65 \text{ m/s sin } 31° = 33.47 \text{ m/s}$$

$$= 33 \text{ m/s}$$

14. A golf ball, hit from the tee, travels 325 m in a direction 25° south of the east axis. What are the east and north components of its displacement?

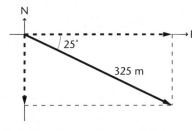

$$d_E = 325 \text{ m cos } 25° = 295 \text{ m}$$

$$d_N = -325 \text{ m sin } 25° = -137 \text{ m}$$

15. A powerboat heads due northwest at 13 m/s with respect to the water across a river that flows due north at 5.0 m/s. What is the velocity (both magnitude and direction) of the motorboat with respect to the shore?

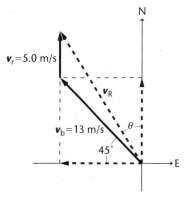

$$v_{bW} = (13 \text{ m/s}) \cos 45° = 9.2 \text{ m/s}$$

$$v_{bN} = (13 \text{ m/s}) \sin 45° = 9.2 \text{ m/s}$$

$$v_{RN} = 5.0 \text{ m/s}, \ v_{rW} = 0.0$$

$$v_{RW} = 9.2 \text{ m/s} + 0.0 = 9.2 \text{ m/s}$$

$$v_{RN} = 9.2 \text{ m/s} + 5.0 \text{ m/s} = 14.2 \text{ m/s}$$

$$v_R = [(9.2 \text{ m/s})^2 + (14.2 \text{ m/s})^2]^{1/2}$$

$$= 17 \text{ m/s}$$

$$\theta = \tan^{-1} \frac{9.2 \text{ m/s}}{14.2 \text{ m/s}} = \tan^{-1} 0.648$$

$$= 33°$$

$$v_R = 17 \text{ m/s, } 33° \text{ west of north}$$

16. An airplane flies due south at 175 km/h with respect to the air. There is a wind blowing at 85 km/h to the east relative to the ground. What are the plane's speed and direction with respect to the ground?

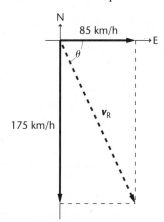

Copyright © by Glencoe/McGraw-Hill

16. (continued)

$$v_R = [(175 \text{ km/h})^2 + (85 \text{ km/h})^2]^{1/2}$$

$$= 190 \text{ km/h}$$

$$\theta = \tan^{-1} \frac{175 \text{ km/h}}{85 \text{ km/h}} = \tan^{-1} 2.06 = 64°$$

$$v_R = 190 \text{ km/h, } 64° \text{ south of east}$$

17. An airplane flies due north at 235 km/h with respect to the air. There is a wind blowing at 65 km/h to the northeast with respect to the ground. What are the plane's speed and direction with respect to the ground?

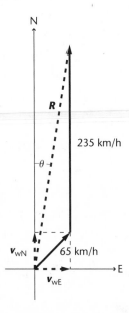

$$v_{wN} = 65 \text{ km/h sin } 45° = 46 \text{ km/h}$$

$$v_{wE} = 65 \text{ km/h cos } 45° = 46 \text{ km/h}$$

$$R_N = 46 \text{ km/h} + 235 \text{ km/h} = 281 \text{ km/h}$$

$$R_E = 46 \text{ km/h}$$

$$R = [(281 \text{ km/h})^2 + (46 \text{ km/h})^2]^{1/2}$$

$$= 280 \text{ km/h}$$

$$\theta = \tan^{-1} \frac{46 \text{ km/h}}{281 \text{ km/h}}$$

$$= 9.3° \text{ east of north}$$

18. An airplane has a speed of 285 km/h with respect to the air. There is a wind blowing at 95 km/h at 30° north of east with respect to Earth. In which direction should the plane head in order to land at an airport due north of its present location? What would be the plane's speed with respect to the ground?

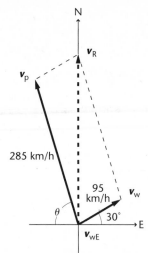

To travel north, the east components must be equal and opposite.

$$v_{pE} = v_{wE} = 95 \text{ km/h cos } 30°$$

$$= 82 \text{ km/h}$$

$$\theta = \cos^{-1} \frac{82 \text{ km/h}}{285 \text{ km/h}} = 73°$$

$$v_{pN} = 285 \text{ km/h sin } 73° = 273 \text{ km/h}$$

$$v_{wN} = 95 \text{ km/h sin } 30° = 47.5 \text{ km/h}$$

$$v_{RN} = 273 \text{ km/h} + 47.5 \text{ km/h}$$

$$= 320 \text{ km/h}$$

$$v_R = 320 \text{ km/h north}$$

Chapter Review Problems

pages 78–79

page 78

Section 4.1

Level 1

19. A car moves 65 km due east, then 45 km due west. What is its total displacement?

65 km ───────►
◄─── 45 km
Δd

$$65 \text{ km} - 45 \text{ km} = 20 \text{ km}$$

$$\Delta d = 2.0 \times 10^1 \text{ km, east}$$

Copyright © by Glencoe/McGraw-Hill

20. Graphically find the sum of the following pairs of vectors whose lengths and directions are shown in **Figure 4–12.**

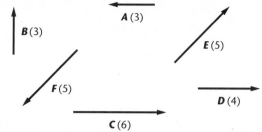

FIGURE 4-12

a. D and **A**

b. C and **D**

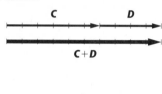

c. C and **A**

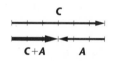

d. E and **F**

zero

21. An airplane flies at 200.0 km/h with respect to the air. What is the velocity of the plane relative to the ground if it flies with

a. a 50-km/h tailwind?

Tailwind is in the same direction as the airplane

200.0 km/h + 50 km/h = 250 km/h

b. a 50-km/h head wind?

Head wind is in the opposite direction of the airplane

200.0 km/h − 50 km/h = 150 km/h

22. Graphically add the following sets of vectors as shown in **Figure 4–12.**

a. A, C, and **D**

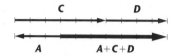

b. A, B, and **E**

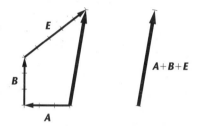

c. B, D, and **F**

zero

23. Path A is 8.0 km long heading 60.0° north of east. Path B is 7.0 km long in a direction due east. Path C is 4.0 km long heading 315° counterclockwise from east.

a. Graphically add the hiker's displacements in the order **A, B, C.**

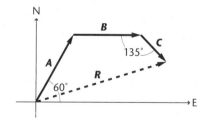

Copyright © by Glencoe/McGraw-Hill

23. (continued)

    b. Graphically add the hiker's displacements in the order **C, B, A.**

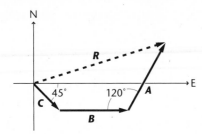

    c. What can you conclude about the resulting displacements?

    You can add vectors in any order. The result is always the same.

page 79

Level 2

24. A river flows toward the east. Because of your knowledge of physics, you head your boat 53° west of north and have a velocity of 6.0 m/s due north relative to the shore.

    a. What is the velocity of the current?

$$v_r = (6.0 \text{ m/s})(\tan 53°) = 8.0 \text{ m/s}$$

    b. What is your speed relative to the water?

$$v_b = \frac{6.0 \text{ m/s}}{\cos 53°} = 1.0 \times 10^1 \text{ m/s}$$

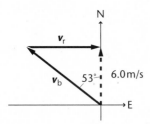

Section 4.2

Level 1

25. You walk 30 m south and 30 m east. Find the magnitude and direction of the resultant displacement both graphically and algebraically.

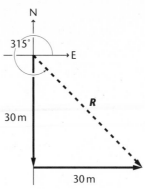

$$R^2 = A^2 + B^2$$
$$R = \sqrt{(30 \text{ m})^2 + (30 \text{ m})^2}$$
$$= \sqrt{1800 \text{ m}^2} = 40 \text{ m}$$
$$\tan \theta = \frac{30 \text{ m}}{30 \text{ m}} = 1$$
$$\theta = 45°$$
$$R = 40 \text{ m}, 315°$$

26. A ship leaves its home port expecting to travel to a port 500.0 km due south. Before it moves even 1 km, a severe storm blows it 100.0 km due east. How far is the ship from its destination? In what direction must it travel to reach its destination?

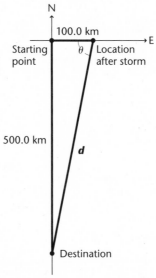

$$R^2 = A^2 + B^2$$
$$R = \sqrt{(100.0 \text{ km})^2 + (500.0 \text{ km})^2}$$
$$= \sqrt{260\ 000 \text{ km}^2}$$
$$= 509.9 \text{ km}$$
$$\tan \theta = \frac{500.0 \text{ km}}{100.0 \text{ km}} = 5.000$$
$$\theta = 78.69°$$
$$d = R = 509.9 \text{ km},$$
$$78.69° \text{ south of west}$$

Copyright © by Glencoe/McGraw-Hill

27. A descent vehicle landing on Mars has a vertical velocity toward the surface of Mars of 5.5 m/s. At the same time, it has a horizontal velocity of 3.5 m/s.

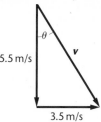

a. At what speed does the vehicle move along its descent path?

$$R^2 = A^2 + B^2$$

$$R = \sqrt{(5.5 \text{ m/s})^2 + (3.5 \text{ m/s})^2}$$

$$v = R = 6.5 \text{ m/s}$$

b. At what angle with the vertical is this path?

$$\tan \theta = \frac{3.5 \text{ m/s}}{5.5 \text{ m/s}} = 0.64$$

$$\theta = 32°$$

28. You are piloting a small plane, and you want to reach an airport 450 km due south in 3.0 hours. A wind is blowing from the west at 50.0 km/h. What heading and airspeed should you choose to reach your destination in time?

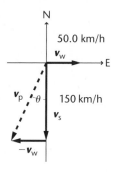

$$v_s = \frac{d_s}{t} = \frac{450 \text{ km}}{3.0 \text{ h}} = 150 \text{ km/h}$$

$$v_p = [(150 \text{ km/h})^2 + (50.0 \text{ km/h})^2]^{1/2}$$

$$= 160 \text{ km/h}$$

$$\theta = \tan^{-1} \frac{50.0 \text{ km/h}}{150 \text{ km/h}} = \tan^{-1} 0.33$$

$$= 18° \text{ west of south}$$

Level 2

29. A hiker leaves camp and, using a compass, walks 4 km E, then 6 km S, 3 km E, 5 km N, 10 km W, 8 km N, and finally 3 km S. At the end of three days, the hiker is lost. By drawing a diagram, compute how far the hiker is from camp and which direction should be taken to get back to camp.

Take north and east to be positive directions.

North: −6 km + 5 km + 8 km − 3 km

= 4 km

East: 4 km + 3 km − 10 km = −3 km

The hiker is 4 km north and 3 km west of camp. To return to camp, the hiker must go 3 km east and 4 km south.

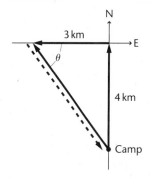

4 km E + 3 km E + 10 km W

= 3 km W

6 km S + 5 km N + 8 km N + 3 km S

= 4 km N

$$R^2 = A^2 + B^2$$

$$R = \sqrt{(3 \text{ km})^2 + (4 \text{ km})^2} = \sqrt{25 \text{ km}^2}$$

= 5 km

$$\tan \theta = \frac{4 \text{ km}}{3 \text{ km}} = 1.33$$

$$\theta = 53°$$

$$R = 5 \text{ km, } 53° \text{ south of east}$$

Copyright © by Glencoe/McGraw-Hill

30. You row a boat perpendicular to the shore of a river that flows at 3.0 m/s. The velocity of your boat is 4.0 m/s relative to the water.

    a. What is the velocity of your boat relative to the shore?

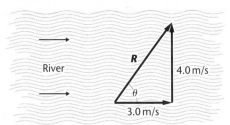

$$R = \sqrt{(3.0 \text{ m/s})^2 + (4.0 \text{ m/s})^2}$$

$$= 5.0 \text{ m/s}$$

$$\tan \theta = \frac{4.0}{3.0} = 1.33$$

$$\theta = 53° \text{ with the shore}$$

    b. What is the component of your velocity parallel to the shore?

3.0 m/s

Perpendicular to it?

4.0 m/s

31. A weather station releases a balloon that rises at a constant 15 m/s relative to the air, but there is a wind blowing at 6.5 m/s toward the west. What are the magnitude and direction of the velocity of the balloon?

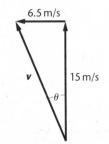

$$v = \sqrt{(6.5 \text{ m/s})^2 + (15 \text{ m/s})^2} = 16 \text{ m/s}$$

$$\tan \theta = \frac{6.5 \text{ m/s}}{15 \text{ m/s}} = 0.43$$

$$\theta = 23°$$

$$v = 16 \text{ m/s}, 113°$$

Critical Thinking Problems

32. An airplane, moving at 375 m/s relative to the ground, fires a missle at a speed of 782 m/s relative to the plane. What is the speed of the shell relative to the ground?

$$v_A + v_B = v_R$$

375 m/s + 782 m/s = 1157 m/s

33. A rocket in outer space that is moving at a speed of 1.25 km/s relative to an observer fires its motor. Hot gases are expelled out the rear at 2.75 km/s relative to the rocket. What is the speed of the gases relative to the observer?

$$v_A - v_B = v_R$$

1.25 km/s − 2.75 km/s = −1.50 km/s

Copyright © by Glencoe/McGraw-Hill

5 A Mathematical Model of Motion

Practice Problems

5.1 Graphing Motion in One Dimension
pages 82–89

page 85

1. Describe in words the motion of the four walkers shown by the four lines in **Figure 5–4.** Assume the positive direction is east and the origin is the corner of High Street.

   A starts at High St. and walks east at a constant velocity.

   B starts west of High St. and walks east at a slower constant velocity.

   C walks west from High St., at first fast, but slowing to a stop.

   D starts east of High St. and walks west at a constant velocity.

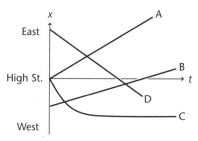

FIGURE 5-4

2. Describe the motion of the car shown in **Figure 5–5.**

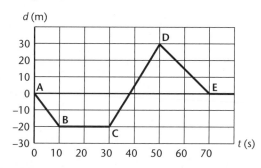

FIGURE 5-5

The car starts at the origin, moves backward (selected to be the negative direction) at a constant speed of 2 m/s for 10 s, then stops and stays at that location (–20 m) for 20 seconds. It then moves forward at 2.5 m/s for 20 seconds when it is at +30 m. It immediately goes backward at a speed of 1.5 m/s for 20 s, when it has returned to the origin.

3. Answer the following questions about the car whose motion is graphed in **Figure 5–5.**

   a. When was the car 20 m west of the origin?

   Between 10 and 30 s.

   b. Where was the car at 50 s?

   30 m east of the origin

   c. The car suddenly reversed direction. When and where did that occur?

   At point D, 30 m east of the origin at 50 s.

page 87

4. For each of the position-time graphs shown in **Figure 5–8,**

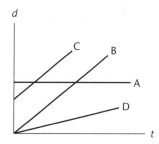

FIGURE 5-8

Copyright © by Glencoe/McGraw-Hill

4. (continued)

    a. write a description of the motion.

    A remains stationary. B starts at the origin and moves forward at a constant speed. C starts east (positive direction) of the origin and moves forward at the same speed as B. D starts at the origin and moves forward at a slower speed than B.

    b. draw a motion diagram.

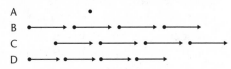

    c. rank the average velocities from largest to smallest.

    B = C > D > A

5. Draw a position-time graph for a person who starts on the positive side of the origin and walks with uniform motion toward the origin. Repeat for a person who starts on the negative side of the origin and walks toward the origin.

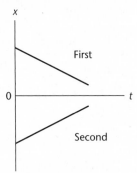

6. Chris claims that as long as average velocity is constant, you can write $v = d/t$. Use data from the graph of the airplane's motion in **Figure 5–6** to convince Chris that this is not true.

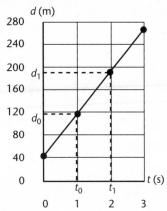

FIGURE 5-6

Average velocity is 75 m/s. At 1 second

$$\frac{d}{t} = \frac{115 \text{ m}}{1 \text{ s}} = 115 \text{ m/s},$$

while at 3 seconds, $\frac{d}{t} = 88$ m/s.

7. Use the factor-label method to convert the units of the following average velocities.

    a. speed of a sprinter: 10.0 m/s into mph and km/h

    Into mph:

    10.0 m/s × (3600 s/h) × (0.6214 mi/km)

                     × (0.001 km/m)

    = 22.4 mph

    Into km/h:

    10.0 m/s × (3600 s/h) × (0.001 km/m)

    = 36.0 km/h

    b. speed of a car: 65 mph into km/h and m/s

    Into km/h:

    65 mph × (5280 ft/mi) × $\left(\dfrac{0.3048 \text{ m/ft}}{1000 \text{ m/km}}\right)$

    = 1.0 × 10² km/h

Physics: Principles and Problems

Copyright © by Glencoe/McGraw-Hill

7. b. (continued)

   Into m/s:

   65 mph × (5280 ft/mi) × $\left(\dfrac{0.3048 \text{ m/ft}}{3600 \text{ s/h}}\right)$

   = 29 m/s

c. speed of a walker: 4 mph into km/h and m/s

   Into km/h:

   4 mph × (5280 ft/mi) × $\left(\dfrac{0.3048 \text{ m/ft}}{1000 \text{ m/km}}\right)$

   = 6 km/h

   Into m/s:

   4 mph × (5280 ft/mi) × $\left(\dfrac{0.3048 \text{ m/ft}}{3600 \text{ s/h}}\right)$

   = 2 m/s

8. Draw a position-time graph of a person who walks one block at a moderate speed, waits a short time for a traffic light, walks the next block slowly, and then walks the final block quickly. All blocks are of equal length.

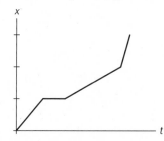

page 89

9. Consider the motion of bike rider A in **Figure 5–7.**

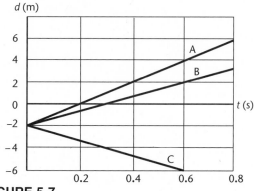

FIGURE 5-7

a. Write the equation that represents her motion.

$v = \dfrac{8.0 \text{ m}}{0.80 \text{ s}} = 1.0 \times 10^1 \text{ m/s}$

so $x = (-2.0 \text{ m})$

   $+ (1.0 \times 10^1 \text{ m/s})t$

b. Where will rider A be at 1.0 s?

   At +8.0 m.

10. Consider the motion of bike rider C in **Figure 5–7.**

a. Write the equation that represents her motion.

$v = \dfrac{-4.0 \text{ m}}{0.60 \text{ s}} = -6.7 \text{ m/s}$

so $x = (-2.0 \text{ m}) - (6.7 \text{ m/s})t$

b. When will rider C be at –10.0 m?

   At 1.2 s.

11. A car starts 2.0×10^2 m west of the town square and moves with a constant velocity of 15 m/s toward the east. Choose a coordinate system in which the x-axis points east and the origin is at the town square.

a. Write the equation that represents the motion of the car.

$x = -(2.0 \times 10^2 \text{ m}) + (15 \text{ m/s})t$

b. Where will the car be 10.0 min later?

x (at 6.00×10^2 s) = 8800 m

c. When will the car reach the town square?

The time at which $x = 0$ is given by

$t = \dfrac{2.0 \times 10^2 \text{ m}}{15 \text{ m/s}} = 13$ s.

12. At the same time the car in problem 11 left, a truck was 4.0×10^2 m east of the town square moving west at a constant velocity of 12 m/s. Use the same coordinate system as you did for problem 11.

a. Draw a graph showing the motion of both the car and the truck.

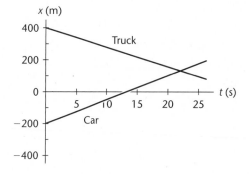

Copyright © by Glencoe/McGraw-Hill

12. (continued)

    b. Find the time and place where the car passed the truck using both the graph and your two equations.

      Equation for truck:

      $x_T = (4.0 \times 10^2 \text{ m}) - (12 \text{ m/s})t$. **They pass each other when**

$$-(2.0 \times 10^2 \text{ m}) + (15 \text{ m/s})t$$
$$= 4.0 \times 10^2 \text{ m} - (12 \text{ m/s})t$$

      or $-6.0 \times 10^2 \text{ m} = -(27 \text{ m/s}) \, t$

      That is, $t = 22.2 \text{ s} = 22 \text{ s}.$

      $x_T = 133.6 \text{ m} = 130 \text{ m}.$

5.2 Graphing Velocity in One Dimension
pages 90–93

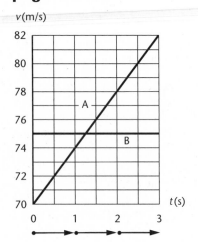

FIGURE 5-10

page 93

13. Use **Figure 5–10** to determine the velocity of the airplane that is speeding up at

    a. 1.0 s.

      At 1.0 s, $v = 74$ m/s.

    b. 2.0 s.

      At 2.0 s, $v = 78$ m/s.

    c. 2.5 s.

      At 2.5 s, $v = 80$ m/s.

14. Use the factor-label method to convert the speed of the airplane whose motion is graphed in **Figure 5–6** (75 m/s) to km/h.

$$\frac{(75 \text{ m/s}) \times (3600 \text{ s/h})}{1000 \text{ m/km}} = 270 \text{ km/h}$$

15. Sketch the velocity-time graphs for the three bike riders in **Figure 5–7**.

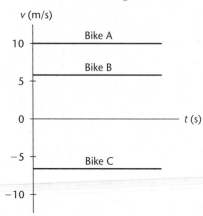

16. A car is driven at a constant velocity of 25 m/s for 10.0 min. The car runs out of gas, so the driver walks in the same direction at 1.5 m/s for 20.0 min to the nearest gas station. After spending 10.0 min filling a gasoline can, the driver walks back to the car at a slower speed of 1.2 m/s. The car is then driven home at 25 m/s (in the direction opposite that of the original trip).

    a. Draw a velocity-time graph for the driver, using seconds as your time unit. You will have to calculate the distance the driver walked to the gas station in order to find the time it took the driver to walk back to the car.

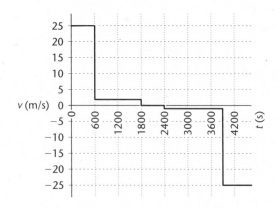

Copyright © by Glencoe/McGraw-Hill

16. (continued)

b. Draw a position-time graph for the problem using the areas under the curve of the velocity-time graph.

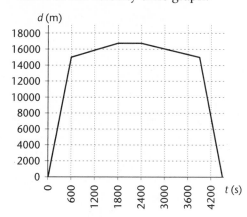

5.3 Acceleration
pages 94–103

page 97

17. An Indy 500 race car's velocity increases from +4.0 m/s to +36 m/s over a 4.0-s time interval. What is its average acceleration?

$$\bar{a} = \frac{\Delta v}{\Delta t} = \frac{36 \text{ m/s} - 4.0 \text{ m/s}}{4.0 \text{ s}}$$

$$= 8.0 \text{ m/s}^2$$

18. The race car in problem 17 slows from +36 m/s to +15 m/s over 3.0 s. What is its average acceleration?

$$\bar{a} = \frac{(v_2 - v_1)}{(t_2 - t_1)} = \frac{15 \text{ m/s} - 36 \text{ m/s}}{3.0 \text{ s}}$$

$$= -7.0 \text{ m/s}^2$$

19. A car is coasting downhill at a speed of 3.0 m/s when the driver gets the engine started. After 2.5 s, the car is moving uphill at a speed of 4.5 m/s. Assuming that uphill is the positive direction, what is the car's average acceleration?

$$\bar{a} = \frac{v_2 - v_1}{t_2 - t_1} = \frac{[4.5 \text{ m/s} - (-3.0 \text{ m/s})]}{2.5 \text{ s}}$$

$$= 3.0 \text{ m/s}^2$$

20. A bus is moving at 25 m/s when the driver steps on the brakes and brings the bus to a stop in 3.0 s.

a. What is the average acceleration of the bus while braking?

$$\bar{a} = \frac{v_2 - v_1}{t_2 - t_1} = \frac{0.0 \text{ m/s} - 25.0 \text{ m/s}}{3.0 \text{ s}}$$

$$= -8.3 \text{ m/s}^2$$

b. If the bus took twice as long to stop, how would the acceleration compare with what you found in part **a**?

Half as great (−4.2 m/s².).

21. Look at the v-t graph of the toy train in **Figure 5–14**.

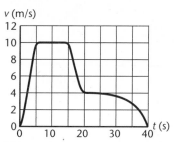

FIGURE 5-14

a. During which time interval or intervals is the speed constant?

5 to 15 s and 21 to 28 s

b. During which interval or intervals is the train's acceleration positive?

0 to 6 s

c. During which time interval is its acceleration most negative?

15 to 20 s, 28 to 40 s

22. Using **Figure 5–14**, find the average acceleration during the following time intervals.

a. 0 to 5 s

$$\bar{a} = \frac{v_2 - v_1}{t_2 - t_1} = \frac{10 \text{ m/s} - 0.0 \text{ m/s}}{5 \text{ s} - 0 \text{ s}}$$

$$= 2 \text{ m/s}^2$$

b. 15 to 20 s

$$\bar{a} = \frac{v_2 - v_1}{t_2 - t_1} = \frac{4 \text{ m/s} - 10 \text{ m/s}}{20 \text{ s} - 15 \text{ s}}$$

$$= -1.2 \text{ m/s}^2 = -1 \text{ m/s}^2$$

Copyright © by Glencoe/McGraw-Hill

22. (continued)

    c. 0 to 40 s

$$\bar{a} = \frac{v_2 - v_1}{t_2 - t_1} = \frac{0 \text{ m/s} - 0 \text{ m/s}}{40 \text{ s} - 0 \text{ s}} = 0 \text{ m/s}^2$$

page 98

23. A golf ball rolls up a hill toward a miniature-golf hole. Assign the direction toward the hole as being positive.

    a. If the ball starts with a speed of 2.0 m/s and slows at a constant rate of 0.50 m/s^2, what is its velocity after 2.0 s?

$$v = v_0 + at$$
$$= 2.0 \text{ m/s} + (-0.50 \text{ m/s}^2)(2.0 \text{ s})$$
$$= 1.0 \text{ m/s}$$

    b. If the constant acceleration continues for 6.0 s, what will be its velocity then?

$$v = v_0 + at$$
$$= 2.0 \text{ m/s} + (-0.50 \text{ m/s}^2)(6.0 \text{ s})$$
$$= -1.0 \text{ m/s}$$

    c. Describe in words and in a motion diagram the motion of the golf ball.

    1st case: $\overset{v}{\bullet\!\!\longrightarrow}\ \overset{v}{\bullet\!\!\longrightarrow}\ \overset{v}{\bullet\!\!\rightarrow}\ \overset{v}{\bullet\!\rightarrow}\ \bullet$

    2nd case:

The ball's velocity simply decreased in the first case. In the second case, the ball slowed to a stop and then began rolling back down the hill.

24. A bus, traveling at 30.0 km/h, speeds up at a constant rate of 3.5 m/s^2. What velocity does it reach 6.8 s later?

$$a = (3.5 \text{ m/s}^2)\left(\frac{1 \text{ km}}{1000 \text{ m}}\right)(3600 \text{ s/h})$$
$$= 12.6 \text{ (km/h)/s}$$
$$v = v_0 + at$$
$$= 30.0 \text{ km/h} + (12.6(\text{km/h})/\text{s})(6.8 \text{ s})$$
$$= 30.0 \text{ km/h} + 86 \text{ km/h}$$
$$= 116 \text{ km/h}$$

25. If a car accelerates from rest at a constant 5.5 m/s^2, how long will it need to reach a velocity of 28 m/s?

$$v = v_0 + at$$
$$\text{so } t = \frac{(v - v_0)}{a}$$
$$= \frac{28 \text{ m/s} - 0.0 \text{ m/s}}{5.5 \text{ m/s}^2}$$
$$= 5.1 \text{ s}$$

26. A car slows from 22 m/s to 3.0 m/s at a constant rate of 2.1 m/s^2. How many seconds are required before the car is traveling at 3.0 m/s?

$$v = v_0 + at$$
$$\text{so } t = \frac{(v - v_0)}{a}$$
$$= \frac{3.0 \text{ m/s} - 22 \text{ m/s}}{-2.1 \text{ m/s}^2}$$
$$= 9.0 \text{ s}$$

page 103

For all problems, sketch the situation, assign variables, create a motion diagram, and then develop a mathematical model.

27. A race car traveling at 44 m/s slows at a constant rate to a velocity of 22 m/s over 11 s. How far does it move during this time?

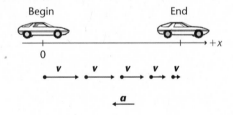

$$d = \frac{1}{2}(v + v_0)t$$
$$= \frac{1}{2}(22 \text{ m/s} + 44 \text{ m/s})(11 \text{ s})$$
$$= 3.6 \times 10^2 \text{ m}$$

Copyright © by Glencoe/McGraw-Hill

28. A car accelerates at a constant rate from 15 m/s to 25 m/s while it travels 125 m. How long does it take to achieve this speed?

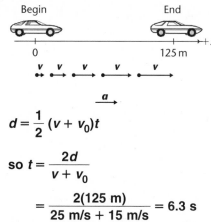

$$d = \frac{1}{2}(v + v_0)t$$

so $t = \dfrac{2d}{v + v_0}$

$$= \frac{2(125 \text{ m})}{25 \text{ m/s} + 15 \text{ m/s}} = 6.3 \text{ s}$$

29. A bike rider accelerates constantly to a velocity of 7.5 m/s during 4.5 s. The bike's displacement during the acceleration was 19 m. What was the initial velocity of the bike?

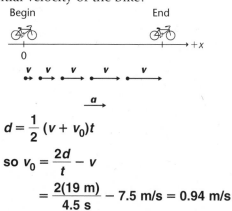

$$d = \frac{1}{2}(v + v_0)t$$

so $v_0 = \dfrac{2d}{t} - v$

$$= \frac{2(19 \text{ m})}{4.5 \text{ s}} - 7.5 \text{ m/s} = 0.94 \text{ m/s}$$

30. An airplane starts from rest and accelerates at a constant 3.00 m/s² for 30.0 s before leaving the ground.

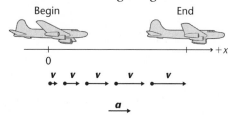

a. How far did it move?

$$d = v_0 t + \frac{1}{2}at^2$$

$$= (0 \text{ m/s})(30.0 \text{ s})$$

$$+ \frac{1}{2}(3.00 \text{ m/s}^2)(30.0 \text{ s})^2$$

$$= 0 \text{ m} + 1350 \text{ m} = 1.35 \times 10^3 \text{ m}$$

b. How fast was it going when it took off?

$$v = v_0 + at$$

$$= 0 \text{ m/s} + (3.00 \text{ m/s}^2)(30.0 \text{ s})$$

$$= 90.0 \text{ m/s}$$

5.4 Free Fall
pages 104–106

page 106

31. A brick is dropped from a high scaffold.

a. What is its velocity after 4.0 s?

$$v = v_0 + at, \ a = -g = -9.80 \text{ m/s}^2$$

$$= 0 \text{ m/s} + (-9.80 \text{ m/s}^2)(4.0 \text{ s})$$

$$v = -39 \text{ m/s (downward)}$$

b. How far does the brick fall during this time?

$$d = v_0 t + \frac{1}{2}at^2$$

$$= 0 + \frac{1}{2}(-9.80 \text{ m/s}^2)(4.0 \text{ s})^2$$

$$= \frac{1}{2}(-9.80 \text{ m/s}^2)(16 \text{ s}^2)$$

$$d = -78 \text{ m (downward)}$$

32. A tennis ball is thrown straight up with an initial speed of 22.5 m/s. It is caught at the same distance above ground.

a. How high does the ball rise?

Since $a = -g$, and, at the maximum height, $v = 0$, using $v^2 = v_0^2 + 2a(d - d_0)$, gives

$$v_0^2 = 2gd$$

or $d = \dfrac{v_0^2}{2g} = \dfrac{(22.5 \text{ m/s})^2}{2(9.80 \text{ m/s}^2)} = 25.8 \text{ m}$

Copyright © by Glencoe/McGraw-Hill

32. (continued)

b. How long does the ball remain in the air? (Hint: The time to rise equals the time to fall. Can you show this?)

Time to rise: use $v = v_0 + at$, giving

$$t = \frac{v_0}{g} = \frac{22.5 \text{ m/s}}{9.80 \text{ m/s}^2} = 2.30 \text{ s}$$

So, it is in the air for 4.6 s. To show that the time to rise equals the time to fall, when $d = d_0$

$$v^2 = v_0^2 + 2a(d - d_0)$$

gives $v^2 = v_0^2$ or $v = -v_0$. Now, using $v = v_0 + at$ where, for the fall, $v_0 = 0$ and $v = -v_0$, we get $t = \dfrac{v_0}{g}$.

33. A spaceship far from any star or planet accelerates uniformly from 65.0 m/s to 162.0 m/s in 10.0 s. How far does it move?

Given $v_0 = 65.0$ m/s, $v = 162.0$ m/s, and $t = 10.0$ s and needing d, we use

$$d = d_0 + \frac{1}{2}(v_0 + v)t$$

or $d = \dfrac{1}{2}$ (65.0 m/s + 162.0 m/s)(10.0 s)

$$= 1.14 \times 10^3 \text{ m}$$

Chapter Review Problems

pages 109–115

page 109

Section 5.1

Level 1

27. Light from the sun reaches Earth in 8.3 min. The velocity of light is 3.00×10^8 m/s. How far is Earth from the sun?

Time = 8.3 min = 498 s = 5.0×10^2 s

$$\bar{v} = \frac{\Delta d}{\Delta t}$$

so $\Delta d = \bar{v}\,\Delta t$

$$= (3.00 \times 10^8 \text{ m/s})(5.0 \times 10^2 \text{ s})$$

$$= 1.5 \times 10^{11} \text{ m}$$

28. You and a friend each drive 50.0 km. You travel at 90.0 km/h; your friend travels at 95.0 km/h. How long will your friend wait for you at the end of the trip?

It takes your friend

$$\frac{50.0 \text{ km}}{95.0 \text{ km/h}} = 0.526 \text{ h} = 31.6 \text{ minutes}$$

and it takes you

$$\frac{50.0 \text{ km}}{90.0 \text{ km/h}} = 0.555 \text{ h} = 33.3 \text{ minutes}$$

so your friend waits 1.7 minutes.

page 110

TABLE 5-3	
Distance versus Time	
Time (s)	**Distance (m)**
0.0	0.0
1.0	2.0
2.0	8.0
3.0	18.0
4.0	32.9
5.0	50.0

29. The total distance a steel ball rolls down an incline at various times is given in Table 5–3.

a. Draw a position-time graph of the motion of the ball. When setting up the axes, use five divisions for each 10 m of travel on the d-axis. Use five divisions for 1 s of time on t-axis.

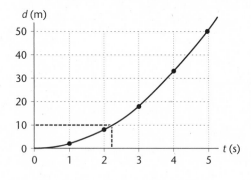

Copyright © by Glencoe/McGraw-Hill

29. (continued)

   b. What type of curve is the line of the graph?

     The curve is a parabola.

   c. What distance has the ball rolled at the end of 2.2 s?

     After 2.2 seconds the ball has rolled approximately 10 m.

30. A cyclist maintains a constant velocity of +5.0 m/s. At time $t = 0.0$, the cyclist is +250 m from point A.

   a. Plot a position-time graph of the cyclist's location from point A at 10.0-s intervals for 60.0 s.

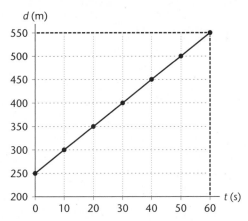

   b. What is the cyclist's position from point A at 60.0 s?

     550 m

   c. What is the displacement from the starting position at 60.0 s?

     550 m − 250 m = 3.0 × 10² m

31. From the position-time graph in **Figure 5–25,** construct a table showing the average velocity of the object during each 10-s interval over the entire 100 s.

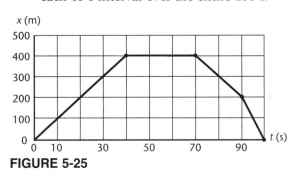

FIGURE 5-25

Time Interval (s)	Average Velocity (m/s)
0–10	10
10–20	10
20–30	10
30–40	10
40–50	0
50–60	0
60–70	0
70–80	−10
80–90	−10
90–100	−20

32. Plot the data in **Table 5–4** on a position-time graph. Find the average velocity in the time interval between 0.0 s and 5.0 s.

TABLE 5-4	
Position versus Time	
Clock Reading, t **(s)**	**Position,** d **(m)**
0.0	30
1.0	30
2.0	35
3.0	45
4.0	60
5.0	70

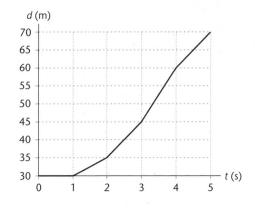

32. (continued)

or

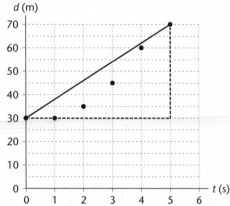

The average velocity is the

$$\text{slope} = \frac{\Delta d}{\Delta t} = \frac{70 \text{ m} - 30 \text{ m}}{5.0 \text{ s} - 0.0 \text{ s}} = 8 \text{ m/s}$$

Level 2

33. You drive a car for 2.0 h at 40 km/h, then for another 2.0 h at 60 km/h.

a. What is your average velocity?

Total distance:
80 km + 120 km = 200 km.
Total time is 4.0 hours, so,
$$\bar{v} = \frac{\Delta d}{\Delta t} = \frac{200 \text{ km}}{4.0 \text{ h}} = 50 \text{ km/h}$$

b. Do you get the same answer if you drive 1.0×10^2 km at each of the two speeds?

No. Total distance is 2.0×10^2 km;
$$\text{total time} = \frac{1.0 \times 10^2 \text{ km}}{40 \text{ km/h}}$$
$$+ \frac{1.0 \times 10^2 \text{ km}}{60 \text{ km/h}}$$
$$= 2.5 \text{ h} + 1.7 \text{ h} = 4.2 \text{ h}$$

So $\bar{v} = \dfrac{\Delta d}{\Delta t} = \dfrac{2.0 \times 10^2 \text{ km}}{4.2 \text{ h}} = 48 \text{ km/h}$

34. Use the position-time graph in **Figure 5–25** to find how far the object travels

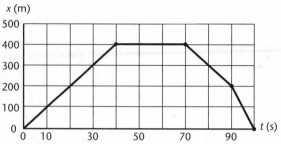

FIGURE 5-25

a. between $t = 0$ s and $t = 40$ s.

$$\Delta d = d_{40} - d_0 = 400 \text{ m} - 0 \text{ m} = 400 \text{ m}$$

b. between $t = 40$ s and $t = 70$ s.

$$\Delta d = d_{70} - d_{40} = 400 \text{ m} - 400 \text{ m} = 0$$

c. between $t = 90$ s and $t = 100$ s.

$$\Delta d = d_{100} - d_{90} = 0 - 200 \text{ m}$$
$$= -200 \text{ m}$$

35. Do this problem on a worksheet. Both car A and car B leave school when a clock reads zero. Car A travels at a constant 75 km/h, and car B travels at a constant 85 km/h.

a. Draw a position-time graph showing the motion of both cars.

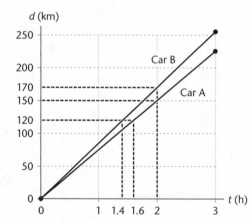

b. How far are the two cars from school when the clock reads 2.0 h? Calculate the distances using the equation for motion and show them on your graph.

$$d_A = v_A t = (75 \text{ km/h})(2.0 \text{ h}) = 150 \text{ km}$$
$$d_B = v_B t = (85 \text{ km/h})(2.0 \text{ h}) = 170 \text{ km}$$

Copyright © by Glencoe/McGraw-Hill

35. (continued)

    c. Both cars passed a gas station 120 km from the school. When did each car pass the gas station? Calculate the times and show them on your graph.

$$d = vt$$

$$\text{so } t = \frac{d}{v}$$

$$t_A = \frac{d}{v_A} = \frac{120 \text{ km}}{75 \text{ km/h}} = 1.6 \text{ h}$$

$$t_B = \frac{d}{v_B} = \frac{120 \text{ km}}{85 \text{ km/h}} = 1.4 \text{ h}$$

36. Draw a position-time graph for two cars driving to the beach, which is 50 km from school. At noon Car A leaves a store 10 km closer to the beach than the school is and drives at 40 km/h. Car B starts from school at 12:30 P.M. and drives at 100 km/h. When does each car get to the beach?

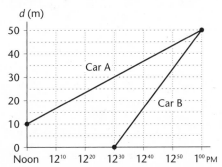

Both cars arrive at the beach at 1:00 P.M.

page 111

37. Two cars travel along a straight road. When a stopwatch reads $t = 0.00$ h, car A is at $d_A = 48.0$ km moving at a constant 36.0 km/h. Later, when the watch reads $t = 0.50$ h, car B is at $d_B = 0.00$ km moving at 48.0 km/h. Answer the following questions, first, graphically by creating a position-time graph, and second, algebraically by writing down equations for the positions d_A and d_B as a function of the stopwatch time, t.

    a. What will the watch read when car B passes car A?

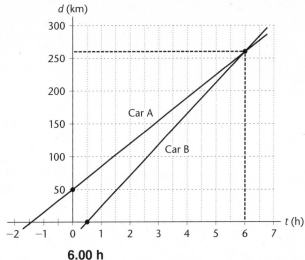

6.00 h

Cars pass when the distances are equal, $d_A = d_B$.

$$d_A = 48.0 \text{ km} + (36.0 \text{ km/h})t$$

$$\text{and } d_B = 0 + (48.0 \text{ km/h})(t - 0.50 \text{ h})$$

$$\text{so } 48.0 \text{ km} + (36.0 \text{ km/h})t$$

$$= (48.0 \text{ km/h})(t - 0.50 \text{ h})$$

$$48.0 \text{ km} + (36.0 \text{ km/h})t$$

$$= (48.0 \text{ km/h})t - 24 \text{ km}$$

$$72 \text{ km} = (12.0 \text{ km/h})t$$

$$t = 6.0 \text{ h}$$

b. At what position will car B pass car A?

$$d_A = 48.0 \text{ km} + (36.0 \text{ km/h})(6.0 \text{ h})$$

$$= 2.6 \times 10^2 \text{ km}$$

c. When the cars pass, how long will it have been since car A was at the reference point?

$$d = vt$$

$$\text{so } t = \frac{d}{v} = \frac{-48.0 \text{ km}}{36.0 \text{ km/h}} = -1.33 \text{ h}$$

Car A started 1.33 h before the clock started.

$$t = 6.0 \text{ h} + 1.33 \text{ h} = 7.3 \text{ h}$$

Copyright © by Glencoe/McGraw-Hill

38. A car is moving down a street at 55 km/h. A child suddenly runs into the street. If it takes the driver 0.75 s to react and apply the brakes, how many meters will the car have moved before it begins to slow down?

$$\bar{v} = \frac{\Delta d}{\Delta t}$$

so $\Delta d = \bar{v}\,\Delta t$

$$= \frac{(55 \text{ km/h})(0.75 \text{ s})(1000 \text{ m/km})}{(3600 \text{ s/h})}$$

$$= 11 \text{ m}$$

Section 5.2

Level 1

39. Refer to **Figure 5–23** to find the instantaneous speed for

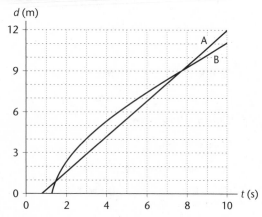

FIGURE 5-23

a. car B at 2.0 s.

$$\text{slope} = \frac{\Delta d}{\Delta t} = \frac{7.0 \text{ m} - 0.0 \text{ m}}{4.0 \text{ s} - 1.0 \text{ s}}$$

$$= 2.3 \text{ m/s}$$

b. car B at 9.0 s.

$$\text{slope} = \frac{\Delta d}{\Delta t} = \frac{11.0 \text{ m} - 7.0 \text{ m}}{10.0 \text{ s} - 4.0 \text{ s}}$$

$$= 0.67 \text{ m/s}$$

c. car A at 2.0 s.

$$\text{slope} = \frac{\Delta d}{\Delta t} = \frac{8.0 \text{ m} - 3.0 \text{ m}}{7.0 \text{ s} - 3.0 \text{ s}}$$

$$= 1.2 \text{ m/s}$$

Student answers will vary.

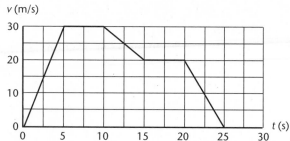

40. Refer to **Figure 5–26** to find the distance the moving object travels between

FIGURE 5-26

a. $t = 0$ s and $t = 5$ s.

$$\text{Area I} = \frac{1}{2}\,bh = \frac{1}{2}\,(5 \text{ s})(30 \text{ m/s})$$

$$= 75 \text{ m}$$

b. $t = 5$ s and $t = 10$ s.

$$\text{Area II} = bh = (10 \text{ s} - 5 \text{ s})(30 \text{ m/s})$$

$$= 150 \text{ m}$$

c. $t = 10$ s and $t = 15$ s.

$$\text{Area III} + \text{Area IV} = bh + \frac{1}{2}\,bh$$

$$= (15 \text{ s} - 10 \text{ s})(20 \text{ m/s})$$

$$+ \frac{1}{2}\,(15 \text{ s} - 10 \text{ s})(10 \text{ m/s})$$

$$= 100 \text{ m} + 25 \text{ m} = 125 \text{ m}$$

d. $t = 0$ s and $t = 25$ s.

$$75 \text{ m} + 150 \text{ m} + 125 \text{ m} + 100 \text{ m}$$

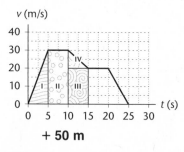

$$+ 50 \text{ m}$$

$$= 500 \text{ m}$$

41. Find the instantaneous speed of the car in **Figure 5–20** at 15 s.

Student answers will vary.

Approximately 23 m/s

Copyright © by Glencoe/McGraw-Hill

41. (continued)

v (m/s)

FIGURE 5-20

42. You ride your bike for 1.5 h at an average velocity of 10 km/h, then for 30 min at 15 km/h. What is your average velocity?

Average velocity is the total displacement divided by the total time.

$d_1 = (10 \text{ km/h})(1.5 \text{ h}) = 15 \text{ km}$

$d_2 = (15 \text{ km/h})(0.5 \text{ h}) = 7.5 \text{ km}$

So the average velocity

$$= \frac{15 \text{ km} + 7.5 \text{ km}}{1.5 \text{ h} + 0.5 \text{ h}}$$

$$= 10 \text{ km/h}$$

Level 2

43. Plot a velocity-time graph using the information in **Table 5–5,** then answer the questions.

TABLE 5-5			
Velocity versus Time			
Time (s)	**Velocity (m/s)**	**Time (s)**	**Velocity (m/s)**
0.0	4.0	7.0	12.0
1.0	8.0	8.0	8.0
2.0	12.0	9.0	4.0
3.0	14.0	10.0	0.0
4.0	16.0	11.0	-4.0
5.0	16.0	12.0	-8.0
6.0	14.0		

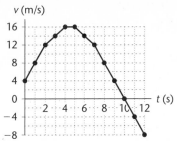

a. During what time interval is the object speeding up? Slowing down?

speeding up from 0.0 s to 4.0 s; slowing down from 5.0 s to 10.0 s

b. At what time does the object reverse direction?

at 10.0 s

c. How does the average acceleration of the object in the interval between 0 s and 2 s differ from the average acceleration in the interval between 7 s and 12 s?

$$\overline{a} = \frac{\Delta v}{\Delta t}$$

between 0 s and 2 s:

$$\overline{a} = \frac{12.0 \text{ m/s} - 4.0 \text{ m/s}}{2.0 \text{s} - 0.0 \text{ s}} = 4.0 \text{ m/s}^2$$

between 7 s and 12 s:

$$\overline{a} = \frac{-8.0 \text{ m/s} - 12.0 \text{ m/s}}{12.0 \text{s} - 7.0 \text{ s}} = -4.0 \text{ m/s}^2$$

Section 5.3

Level 1

44. Find the uniform acceleration that causes a car's velocity to change from 32 m/s to 96 m/s in an 8.0-s period.

$$\overline{a} = \frac{\Delta v}{\Delta t} = \frac{v_2 - v_1}{\Delta t}$$

$$= \frac{96 \text{ m/s} - 32 \text{ m/s}}{8.0 \text{ s}} = 8.0 \text{ m/s}^2$$

45. Use **Figure 5–26** to find the acceleration of the moving object

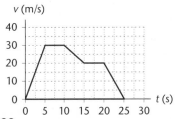

FIGURE 5-26

Copyright © by Glencoe/McGraw-Hill

45. (continued)

    a. during the first 5 s of travel.

$$a = \frac{\Delta v}{\Delta t} = \frac{30 \text{ m/s} - 0 \text{ m/s}}{5 \text{ s}} = 6 \text{ m/s}^2$$

    b. between the fifth and the tenth second of travel.

$$a = \frac{\Delta v}{\Delta t} = \frac{30 \text{ m/s} - 30 \text{ m/s}}{5 \text{ s}} = 0 \text{ m/s}^2$$

    c. between the tenth and the 15th second of travel.

$$a = \frac{\Delta v}{\Delta t} = \frac{20 \text{ m/s} - 30 \text{ m/s}}{5 \text{ s}} = -2 \text{ m/s}^2$$

    d. between the 20th and 25th second of travel.

$$a = \frac{\Delta v}{\Delta t} = \frac{0 - 20 \text{ m/s}}{5 \text{ s}} = -4 \text{ m/s}^2$$

46. A car with a velocity of 22 m/s is accelerated uniformly at the rate of 1.6 m/s² for 6.8 s. What is its final velocity?

$$v = v_0 + at$$
$$= 22 \text{ m/s} + (1.6 \text{ m/s}^2)(6.8 \text{ s})$$
$$= 33 \text{ m/s}$$

47. A supersonic jet flying at 145 m/s is accelerated uniformly at the rate of 23.1 m/s² for 20.0 s.

    a. What is its final velocity?

$$v = v_0 + at$$
$$= 145 \text{ m/s} + (23.1 \text{ m/s}^2)(20.0 \text{ s})$$
$$= 607 \text{ m/s}$$

    b. The speed of sound in air is 331 m/s. How many times the speed of sound is the plane's final speed?

$$N = \frac{607 \text{ m/s}}{331 \text{ m/s}}$$
$$= 1.83 \text{ times the speed of sound}$$

48. Determine the final velocity of a proton that has an initial velocity of 2.35×10^5 m/s, and then is accelerated uniformly in an electric field at the rate of -1.10×10^{12} m/s² for 1.50×10^{-7} s.

$$v = v_0 + at$$
$$= 2.35 \times 10^5 \text{ m/s}$$

$$+ (-1.10 \times 10^{12} \text{ m/s}^2)(1.50 \times 10^{-7} \text{ s})$$
$$= 2.35 \times 10^5 \text{ m/s} - 1.65 \times 10^5 \text{ m/s}$$
$$= 7.0 \times 10^4 \text{ m/s}$$

page 112

49. Determine the displacement of a plane that is uniformly accelerated from 66 m/s to 88 m/s in 12 s.

$$d = \frac{(v + v_0)t}{2}$$
$$= \frac{(88 \text{ m/s} + 66 \text{ m/s})(12 \text{ s})}{2}$$
$$= 9.2 \times 10^2 \text{ m}$$

50. How far does a plane fly in 15 s while its velocity is changing from 145 m/s to 75 m/s at a uniform rate of acceleration?

$$d = \frac{(v + v_0)t}{2}$$
$$= \frac{(75 \text{ m/s} + 145 \text{ m/s})(15 \text{ s})}{2}$$
$$= 1.7 \times 10^3 \text{ m}$$

51. A car moves at 12 m/s and coasts up a hill with a uniform acceleration of -1.6 m/s².

    a. How far has it traveled after 6.0 s?

$$d = v_0 t + \frac{1}{2} at^2$$
$$= (12 \text{ m/s})(6.0 \text{ s})$$
$$+ \frac{1}{2}(-1.6 \text{ m/s}^2)(6.0 \text{ s})^2$$
$$= 43 \text{ m}$$

    b. How far has it gone after 9.0 s?

$$d = v_0 t + \frac{1}{2} at^2$$
$$= (12 \text{ m/s})(9.0 \text{ s})$$
$$+ \frac{1}{2}(-1.6 \text{ m/s}^2)(9.0 \text{ s})^2$$
$$= 43 \text{ m}$$

The car is on the way back down the hill.

Copyright © by Glencoe/McGraw-Hill

52. A plane travels 5.0×10^2 m while being accelerated uniformly from rest at the rate of 5.0 m/s². What final velocity does it attain?

$v^2 = v_0^2 + 2a(d - d_0)$ and $d_0 = 0$, so

$v^2 = v_0^2 + 2ad$

$v = \sqrt{v_0^2 + 2ad}$

$= \sqrt{(0.0 \text{ m/s})^2 + 2(5.0 \text{ m/s}^2)(5.0 \times 10^2 \text{ m})}$

$= 71$ m/s

53. A race car can be slowed with a constant acceleration of –11 m/s².

a. If the car is going 55 m/s, how many meters will it take to stop?

$v^2 = v_0^2 + 2ad$

$d = \dfrac{v^2 - v_0^2}{2a}$

$= \dfrac{(0.0 \text{ m/s})^2 - (+55 \text{ m/s})^2}{(2)(-11 \text{ m/s}^2)}$

$= 1.4 \times 10^2$ m

b. How many meters will it take to stop a car going twice as fast?

$d = \dfrac{v^2 - v_0^2}{2a}$

$= \dfrac{(0.0 \text{ m/s})^2 - (110 \text{ m/s})^2}{(2)(-11 \text{ m/s}^2)}$

$= 5.5 \times 10^2$ m

54. An engineer must design a runway to accommodate airplanes that must reach a ground velocity of 61 m/s before they can take off. These planes are capable of being accelerated uniformly at the rate of 2.5 m/s².

a. How long will it take the planes to reach takeoff speed?

$v = v_0 + at$

so $t = \dfrac{v - v_0}{a} = \dfrac{61 \text{ m/s} - 0.0 \text{ m/s}}{2.5 \text{ m/s}^2}$

$= 24$ s

b. What must be the minimum length of the runway?

$v^2 = v_0^2 + 2ad$

so $d = \dfrac{v^2 - v_0^2}{2a}$

$= \dfrac{(61 \text{ m/s})^2 - (0.0 \text{ m/s})^2}{2(2.5 \text{ m/s}^2)}$

$= 7.4 \times 10^2$ m

55. Engineers are developing new types of guns that might someday be used to launch satellites as if they were bullets. One such gun can give a small object a velocity of 3.5 km/s, moving it through only 2.0 cm.

a. What acceleration does the gun give this object?

$v^2 = v_0^2 + 2ad$

or $v^2 = 2ad$

$a = \dfrac{v^2}{2d} = \dfrac{(3.5 \times 10^3 \text{ m/s})^2}{2(0.020 \text{ m})}$

$= 3.1 \times 10^8$ m/s²

b. Over what time interval does the acceleration take place?

$d = \dfrac{(v + v_0)t}{2}$

$t = \dfrac{2d}{v + v_0} = \dfrac{2(2.0 \times 10^{-2} \text{ m})}{3.5 \times 10^3 \text{ m/s} + 0.0 \text{ m/s}}$

$= 11 \times 10^{-6}$ s

$= 11$ microseconds

56. Highway safety engineers build soft barriers so that cars hitting them will slow down at a safe rate. A person wearing a seat belt can withstand an acceleration of -3.0×10^2 m/s². How thick should barriers be to safely stop a car that hits a barrier at 110 km/h?

$v_0 = \dfrac{(110 \text{ km/h})(1000 \text{ m/km})}{3600 \text{ s/h}} = 31$ m/s

$v^2 = v_0^2 + 2ad$

with $v = 0$ m/s, $v_0^2 = -2ad$, or

$d = \dfrac{-v_0^2}{2a} = \dfrac{-(31 \text{ m/s})^2}{2(-3.0 \times 10^2 \text{ m/s}^2)}$

$= 1.6$ m thick

Copyright © by Glencoe/McGraw-Hill

57. A baseball pitcher throws a fastball at a speed of 44 m/s. The acceleration occurs as the pitcher holds the ball in his hand and moves it through an almost straight-line distance of 3.5 m. Calculate the acceleration, assuming it is uniform. Compare this acceleration to the acceleration due to gravity, 9.80 m/s^2.

$$v^2 = v_0^2 + 2ad$$

$$a = \frac{v^2 - v_0^2}{2d}$$

$$= \frac{(44 \text{ m/s})^2 - 0}{2(3.5 \text{ m})} = 2.8 \times 10^2 \text{ m/s}^2$$

$$\frac{2.8 \times 10^2 \text{ m/s}^2}{9.80 \text{ m/s}^2} = 29, \text{ or 29 times } g$$

Level 2

58. Rocket-powered sleds are used to test the responses of humans to acceleration. Starting from rest, one sled can reach a speed of 444 m/s in 1.80 s and can be brought to a stop again in 2.15 s.

a. Calculate the acceleration of the sled when starting, and compare it to the magnitude of the acceleration due to gravity, 9.80 m/s^2.

$$a = \frac{\Delta v}{\Delta t} = \frac{v_2 - v_1}{\Delta t}$$

$$= \frac{444 \text{ m/s} - 0.00 \text{ m/s}}{1.80 \text{ s}}$$

$$= 247 \text{ m/s}^2$$

$$\frac{247 \text{ m/s}^2}{9.80 \text{ m/s}^2} = 25.2, \text{ or 25 times } g$$

b. Find the acceleration of the sled when braking and compare it to the magnitude of the acceleration due to gravity.

$$a = \frac{\Delta v}{\Delta t} = \frac{v_2 - v_1}{\Delta t}$$

$$= \frac{0.00 \text{ m/s} - 444 \text{ m/s}}{2.15 \text{ s}}$$

$$= -207 \text{ m/s}^2$$

$$\frac{207 \text{ m/s}^2}{9.80 \text{ m/s}^2} = 21.1, \text{ or 21 times } g$$

59. Draw a velocity-time graph for each of the graphs in **Figure 5–27**.

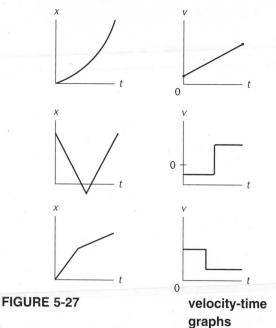

FIGURE 5-27   velocity-time graphs

60. The velocity of an automobile changes over an 8.0-s time period as shown in **Table 5–6**.

TABLE 5-6			
Velocity versus Time			
Time (s)	**Velocity (m/s)**	**Time (s)**	**Velocity (m/s)**
0.0	0.0	5.0	20.0
1.0	4.0	6.0	20.0
2.0	8.0	7.0	20.0
3.0	12.0	8.0	20.0
4.0	16.0		

a. Plot the velocity-time graph of the motion.

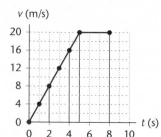

Copyright © by Glencoe/McGraw-Hill

60. (continued)

   b. Determine the displacement of the car during the first 2.0 s.

$$d = \frac{1}{2}\,bh = \frac{1}{2}\,(2.0\text{ s})(8.0\text{ m/s} - 0)$$
$$= 8.0\text{ m}$$

   c. What displacement does the car have during the first 4.0 s?

$$d = \frac{1}{2}\,bh = \frac{1}{2}\,(4.0\text{ s})(16.0\text{ m/s} - 0)$$
$$= 32\text{ m}$$

   d. What displacement does the car have during the entire 8.0 s?

$$d = \frac{1}{2}\,bh + bh$$
$$= \frac{1}{2}\,(5.0\text{ s})(20.0\text{ m/s} - 0)$$
$$\quad + (8.0\text{ s} - 5.0\text{ s})(20.0\text{ m/s})$$
$$= 110\text{ m}$$

   e. Find the slope of the line between $t = 0.0$ s and $t = 4.0$ s. What does this slope represent?

$$a = \frac{\Delta v}{\Delta t} = \frac{16.0\text{ m/s} - 0.0\text{ m/s}}{4.0\text{ s} - 0.0\text{ s}}$$
$$= 4.0\text{ m/s}^2\text{, acceleration}$$

   f. Find the slope of the line between $t = 5.0$ s and $t = 7.0$ s. What does this slope indicate?

$$a = \frac{\Delta v}{\Delta t} = \frac{20.0\text{ m/s} - 20.0\text{ m/s}}{7.0\text{ s} - 5.0\text{ s}}$$
$$= 0.0\text{ m/s}^2\text{, constant velocity}$$

page 113

61. Figure 5–28 shows the position-time and velocity-time graphs of a karate expert's fist as it breaks a wooden board.

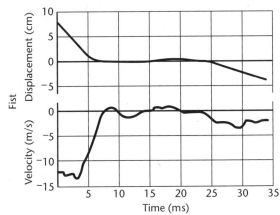

FIGURE 5-28

a. Use the velocity-time graph to describe the motion of the expert's fist during the first 10 ms.

The fist moves downward at about −13 m/s for about 4 ms. It then suddenly comes to a halt (accelerates).

b. Estimate the slope of the velocity-time graph to determine the acceleration of the fist when it suddenly stops.

$$a = \frac{\Delta v}{\Delta t} = \frac{0 - (-13\text{ m/s})}{7.5\text{ ms} - 4.0\text{ ms}}$$
$$= 3.7 \times 10^3\text{ m/s}^2$$

c. Express the acceleration as a multiple of the gravitational acceleration, $g = 9.80$ m/s^2.

$$\frac{3.7 \times 10^3\text{ m/s}^2}{9.80\text{ m/s}^2} = 3.8 \times 10^2$$

The acceleration is about 380 *g*.

d. Determine the area under the velocity-time curve to find the displacement of the fist in the first 6 ms. Compare this with the position-time graph.

The area is almost rectangular:

(−13 m/s)(0.006 s) = −8 cm

This is in agreement with the position-time graph where the hand moves from +8 cm to 0 cm, for a net displacement of −8 cm.

62. The driver of a car going 90.0 km/h suddenly sees the lights of a barrier 40.0 m ahead. It takes the driver 0.75 s to apply the brakes, and the average acceleration during braking is −10.0 m/s^2.

a. Determine whether the car hits the barrier.

$$v_0 = \frac{(90.0\text{ km/h})(1000\text{ m/km})}{(3600\text{ s/h})}$$
$$= 25.0\text{ m/s}$$
$$v = v_0 + at$$
$$t = \frac{v - v_0}{a} = \frac{0 - (25.0\text{ m/s})}{-10.0\text{ m/s}^2} = 2.50\text{ s}$$

Copyright © by Glencoe/McGraw-Hill

62. (continued)

The car will travel

$d = vt = (25.0 \text{ m/s})(0.75 \text{ s})$

$= 18.75 \text{ m} = 19 \text{ m}$

before the driver applies the brakes. The total distance car must travel to stop is

$d = 19 \text{ m} + v_0 t + \dfrac{1}{2} at^2$

$= 19 \text{ m} + (25.0 \text{ m/s})(2.50 \text{ s})$

$+ \dfrac{1}{2} (-10.0 \text{ m/s}^2)(2.50 \text{ s})^2$

$= 5.0 \times 10^1 \text{ m}$, yes it hits the barrier.

b. What is the maximum speed at which the car could be moving and not hit the barrier 40.0 m ahead? Assume that the acceleration rate doesn't change.

$d_{\text{total}} = d_{\text{constant } v} + d_{\text{decelerating}}$

$= 40.0 \text{ m}$

$d_c = vt = (0.75 \text{ s})v$

$d_d = \dfrac{-v^2}{2a} = \dfrac{-v^2}{2(-10.0 \text{ m/s}^2)}$

$= \dfrac{v^2}{20.0 \text{ m/s}^2}$

$40 \text{ m} = (0.75 \text{ s})v + \dfrac{v^2}{20.0 \text{ m/s}^2}$

$v^2 + 15v - 800 = 0$

Using the quadratic equation:

$v = 22 \text{ m/s}$ (The sense of the problem excludes the negative value.)

63. The data in **Table 5–7,** taken from a driver's handbook, show the distance a car travels when it brakes to a halt from a specific initial velocity.

TABLE 5-7	
Initial Velocity versus Braking Distance	
Initial Velocity (m/s)	**Braking Distance (m)**
11	10
15	20
20	34
25	50
29	70

a. Plot the braking distance versus the initial velocity. Describe the shape of the curve.

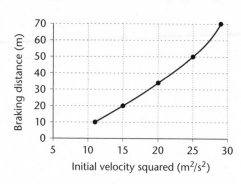

The curve is slightly parabolic in shape.

b. Plot the braking distance versus the square of the initial velocity. Describe the shape of the curve.

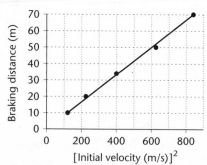

The curve is approximately a straight line.

c. Calculate the slope of your graph from part **b.** Find the value and units of the quantity 1/slope.

$\text{slope} = \dfrac{70 \text{ m} - 10 \text{ m}}{(29 \text{ m/s})^2 - (11 \text{ m/s})^2}$

$= 0.083 \text{ s}^2/\text{m}$

$\dfrac{1}{\text{slope}} = 12.3 \text{ m/s}^2$, or 10 m/s^2 to one significant digit

d. Does this curve agree with the equation $v_0^2 = -2ad$? What is the value of a?

yes, -6 m/s^2

Copyright © by Glencoe/McGraw-Hill

64. As a traffic light turns green, a waiting car starts with a constant acceleration of 6.0 m/s². At the instant the car begins to accelerate, a truck with a constant velocity of 21 m/s passes in the next lane.

a. How far will the car travel before it overtakes the truck?

$$d_{car} = v_0 t + \frac{1}{2}at^2 = 0 + \frac{1}{2}(6.0 \text{ m/s}^2)t^2$$

$$= (3.0 \text{ m/s}^2)t^2$$

$$d_{truck} = v_0 t + \frac{1}{2}at^2 = (21 \text{ m/s})t$$

$d_{car} = d_{truck}$, **when the car overtakes the truck**

$$(3.0 \text{ m/s}^2)t^2 = (21 \text{ m/s})t$$

$$t = 7.0 \text{ s}$$

$$d_{car} = (3.0 \text{ m/s}^2)(7.0 \text{ s})^2 = 1.5 \times 10^2 \text{ m}$$

b. How fast will the car be traveling when it overtakes the truck?

$$v = v_0 + at = 0 + (6.0 \text{ m/s}^2)(7.0 \text{ s})$$

$$= 42 \text{ m/s}$$

65. Use the information given in problem 64.

a. Draw velocity-time and position-time graphs for the car and truck.

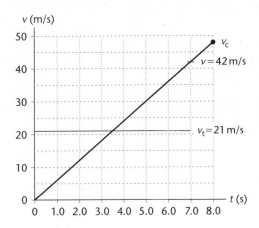

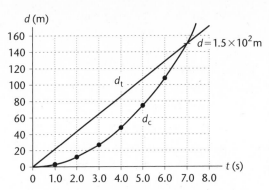

b. Do the graphs confirm the answer you calculated for problem 64?

Yes; The graphs confirm the calculated answer.

Section 5.4

Level 1

66. An astronaut drops a feather from 1.2 m above the surface of the moon. If the acceleration of gravity on the moon is 1.62 m/s² downward, how long does it take the feather to hit the moon's surface?

$$d = v_0 t + \frac{1}{2}at^2$$

$$t = \sqrt{\frac{2d}{a}} = \sqrt{\frac{(2)(-1.2 \text{ m})}{(1.62 \text{ m/s}^2)}} = 1.2 \text{ s}$$

67. A stone falls freely from rest for 8.0 s.

a. Calculate the stone's velocity after 8.0 s.

$$v = v_0 + at$$

$$= 0.0 \text{ m/s} + (-9.80 \text{ m/s}^2)(8.0 \text{ s})$$

$$= -78 \text{ m/s (downward)}$$

b. What is the stone's displacement during this time?

$$d = v_0 t + \frac{1}{2}at^2$$

$$= 0.0 \text{ m} + \frac{1}{2}(-9.80 \text{ m/s}^2)(8.0 \text{ s})^2$$

$$= -3.1 \times 10^2 \text{ m}$$

Copyright © by Glencoe/McGraw-Hill

68. A student drops a penny from the top of a tower and decides that she will establish a coordinate system in which the direction of the penny's motion is positive. What is the sign of the acceleration of the penny?

> **The direction of the velocity is positive, and velocity is increasing. Therefore, the acceleration is also positive.**

page 114

69. A bag is dropped from a hovering helicopter. When the bag has fallen 2.0 s,

a. what is the bag's velocity?

> $v = v_0 + at$
>
> $= 0.0 \text{ m/s} + (-9.80 \text{ m/s}^2)(2.0 \text{ s})$
>
> $= -2.0 \times 10^1 \text{ m/s}$

b. how far has the bag fallen?

> $d = v_0 t + \dfrac{1}{2} at^2$
>
> $= 0.0 \text{ m/s} + \dfrac{1}{2}(-9.80 \text{ m/s}^2)(2.0 \text{ s})^2$
>
> $= -2.0 \times 10^1 \text{ m}$
>
> **The bag has fallen 2.0×10^1 m.**

70. A weather balloon is floating at a constant height above Earth when it releases a pack of instruments.

a. If the pack hits the ground with a velocity of –73.5 m/s, how far did the pack fall?

> $v^2 = v_0^2 + 2ad$
>
> $d = \dfrac{v^2 - v_0^2}{2g}$
>
> $= \dfrac{(-73.5 \text{ m/s})^2 - (0.00 \text{ m/s})^2}{(2)(-9.80 \text{ m/s}^2)}$
>
> $= \dfrac{5402 \text{ m}^2/\text{s}^2}{-19.6 \text{ m/s}^2} = -276 \text{ m}$
>
> **The pack fell 276 m.**

b. How long did it take for the pack to fall?

> $v = v_0 + at$
>
> $t = \dfrac{v - v_0}{a}$
>
> $= \dfrac{-73.5 \text{ m/s} - 0.00 \text{ m/s}}{-9.80 \text{ m/s}^2}$
>
> $= 7.50 \text{ s}$

71. During a baseball game, a batter hits a high pop-up. If the ball remains in the air for 6.0 s, how high does it rise? **Hint:** Calculate the height using the second half of the trajectory.

> **The time to fall is 3.0 s**
>
> $d = vt + \dfrac{1}{2} at^2$
>
> $= 0.0 \text{ m} + \dfrac{1}{2}(-9.8 \text{ m/s}^2)(3.0 \text{ s})^2$
>
> $= -44 \text{ m}$
>
> **The ball rises 44 m, the same distance it falls.**

Level 2

72. **Table 5–8** gives the positions and velocities of a ball at the end of each second for the first 5.0 s of free fall from rest.

TABLE 5-8		
Position and Velocity in Free Fall		
Time (s)	**Position (m)**	**Velocity (m/s)**
0.0	0.0	0.0
1.0	–4.9	–9.8
2.0	–19.6	–19.6
3.0	–44.1	–29.4
4.0	–78.4	–39.2
5.0	–122.5	–49.0

a. Use the data to plot a velocity-time graph.

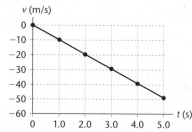

b. Use the data in the table to plot a position-time graph.

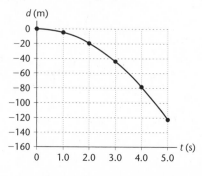

Copyright © by Glencoe/McGraw-Hill

72. (continued)

c. Find the slope of the curve at the end of 2.0 s and 4.0 s on the position-time graph. Do the values agree with the table of velocity?

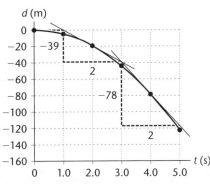

At $t = 2.0$ s,

$$\text{slope} = \frac{-40 \text{ m} - (-1 \text{ m})}{3.0 \text{ s} - 1.0 \text{ s}} = -20 \text{ m/s}$$

At $t = 4.0$ s,

$$\text{slope} = \frac{-118 \text{ m} - (-40 \text{ m})}{5.0 \text{ s} - 3.0 \text{ s}} = -39 \text{ m/s}$$

$$= -40 \text{ m/s}$$

Yes, the values agree.

d. Use the data in the table to plot a position-versus-time-squared graph. What type of curve is obtained?

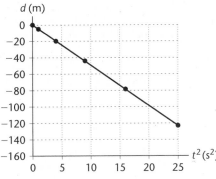

A straight line is obtained.

e. Find the slope of the line at any point. Explain the significance of the value.

$$\text{slope} = \frac{-122.5 \text{ m} - 0}{22 \text{ s}^2 - 0} = -4.9 \text{ m/s}^2$$

The slope is $\frac{1}{2}$ g.

f. Does this curve agree with the equation $d = 1/2 \, gt^2$?

Yes. Since it is a straight line $y = mx + b$ where y is d, m is $\frac{1}{2}$ g, x is t^2 and b is 0.

73. The same helicopter as in problem 69 is rising at 5.0 m/s when the bag is dropped. After 2.0 s

a. what is the bag's velocity?

$$v = v_0 + at$$
$$= 5.0 \text{ m/s} + (-9.80 \text{ m/s}^2)(2.0 \text{ s})$$
$$= -15 \text{ m/s}$$

b. how far has the bag fallen?

$$d = v_0 t + \frac{1}{2} \, at^2$$
$$= (5.0 \text{ m/s})(2.0 \text{ s})$$
$$\quad + \frac{1}{2}(-9.80 \text{ m/s}^2)(2.0 \text{ s})^2$$
$$= -1.0 \times 10^1 \text{ m}$$

The bag has fallen 1.0×10^1 m.

c. how far below the helicopter is the bag?

The helicopter has risen

$$d = v_0 t = (5.0 \text{ m/s})(2.0 \text{ s}) = 1.0 \times 10^1 \text{ m}$$

The bag is 1.0×10^1 m below the origin and 2.0×10^1 m below the helicopter.

74. The helicopter in problems 69 and 73 now descends at 5.0 m/s as the bag is released. After 2.0 s,

a. what is the bag's velocity?

$$v = v_0 + at$$
$$= -5.0 \text{ m/s} + (-9.80 \text{ m/s}^2)(2.0 \text{ s})$$
$$= -25 \text{ m/s}$$

b. how far has the bag fallen?

$$d = v_0 t + \frac{1}{2} \, at^2$$
$$= (-5.0 \text{ m/s})(2.0 \text{ s})$$
$$\quad + \frac{1}{2}(-9.80 \text{ m/s}^2)(2.0 \text{ s})^2$$
$$= -3.0 \times 10^1 \text{ m}$$

The bag has fallen 3.0×10^1 m.

Copyright © by Glencoe/McGraw-Hill

74. (continued)

c. how far below the helicopter is the bag?

$$d = vt = (-5.0 \text{ m/s})(2.0 \text{ s})$$

$$= -1.0 \times 10^1 \text{ m}$$

The helicopter has fallen 1.0×10^1 m and the bag is 2.0×10^1 m below the helicopter.

75. What is common to the answers to problems 69, 73, and 74?

The bag is 2.0×10^1 m below the helicopter after 2.0 s.

76. A tennis ball is dropped from 1.20 m above the ground. It rebounds to a height of 1.00 m.

a. With what velocity does it hit the ground?

Using $v^2 = v_0^2 + 2ad$,

$$v^2 = 2ad$$

$$= 2(-9.80 \text{ m/s}^2)(-1.20 \text{ m})$$

$$v = -4.85 \text{ m/s (downward)}$$

b. With what velocity does it leave the ground?

Using $v^2 = v_0^2 + 2ad$,

$$v_0^2 = -2ad$$

$$= -2(-9.80 \text{ m/s}^2)(1.00 \text{ m})$$

$$v_0 = 4.43 \text{ m/s}$$

c. If the tennis ball were in contact with the ground for 0.010 s, find its acceleration while touching the ground. Compare the acceleration to g.

$$a = \frac{v - v_0}{t} = \frac{4.43 \text{ m/s} - (-4.85 \text{ m/s})}{0.010 \text{ s}}$$

$$= 9.3 \times 10^2 \text{ m/s}^2 \text{, or about 95 times } g$$

Critical Thinking Problems

77. An express train, traveling at 36.0 m/s, is accidentally sidetracked onto a local train track. The express engineer spots a local train exactly 1.00×10^2 m ahead on the same track and traveling in the same direction. The local engineer is unaware of the situation. The express engineer jams on the brakes and slows the express at a constant rate of 3.00 m/s^2. If the speed of the local train is 11.0 m/s, will the express train be able to stop in time or will there be a collision? To solve this problem, take the position of the express train when it first sights the local train as a point of origin. Next, keeping in mind that the local train has exactly a 1.00×10^2 m lead, calculate how far each train is from the origin at the end of the 12.0 s it would take the express train to stop.

a. On the basis of your calculations, would you conclude that a collision will occur?

$$d_{\text{express}} = v_0 t + \frac{1}{2} at^2$$

$$= (36.0 \text{ m/s})(12.0 \text{ s})$$

$$+ \frac{1}{2}(-3.00 \text{ m/s}^2)(12.0 \text{ s})^2$$

$$= 432 \text{ m} - 216 \text{ m} = 216 \text{ m}$$

$$d_{\text{local}} = 100 \text{ m} + v_0 t + \frac{1}{2} at^2$$

$$= 100 \text{ m} + (11.0 \text{ m/s})(12.0 \text{ s}) + 0$$

$$= 100 \text{ m} + 132 \text{ m} = 232 \text{ m}$$

On this basis, no collision will occur.

Copyright © by Glencoe/McGraw-Hill

77. (continued)

b. The calculations you made do not allow for the possibility that a collision might take place before the end of the 12 s required for the express train to come to a halt. To check this, take the position of the express train when it first sights the local train as the point of origin and calculate the position of each train at the end of each second after sighting. Make a table showing the distance of each train from the origin at the end of each second. Plot these positions on the same graph and draw two lines. Use your graph to check your answer to part **a.**

t (s)	d (Local) (m)	d (Express) (m)
1	111	35
2	122	66
3	133	95
4	144	120
5	155	145
6	166	162
7	177	179
8	188	192
9	199	203
10	210	210
11	221	215
12	232	216

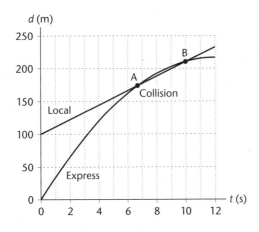

78. Which has the greater acceleration: a car that increases its speed from 50 to 60 km/h, or a bike that goes from 0 to 10 km/h in the same time? Explain.

$$a = \frac{v - v_0}{\Delta t}$$

For car, $a = \dfrac{60 \text{ km/h} - 50 \text{ km/h}}{\Delta t}$

$$= \frac{10 \text{ km/h}}{\Delta t}$$

For bike, $a = \dfrac{10 \text{ km/h} - 0 \text{ km/h}}{\Delta t}$

$$= \frac{10 \text{ km/h}}{\Delta t}$$

The accelerations are exactly the same because the change in velocity is the same and the change in time is the same.

79. You plan a car trip on which you want to average 90 km/h. You cover the first half of the distance at an average speed of only 48 km/h. What must your average speed be in the second half of the trip to meet your goal? Is this reasonable? Note that the velocities are based on half the distance, not half the time.

$$\bar{v} = \frac{\Delta d}{\Delta t}$$

so $\Delta t = \dfrac{\Delta d}{\bar{v}}$

Let $d = \dfrac{1}{2} d + \dfrac{1}{2} d$ and

$t_{total} = t_1 + t_2$, so

$$\frac{d}{v} = \frac{\frac{1}{2} d}{v_1} + \frac{\frac{1}{2} d}{v_2}$$

multiply by $\dfrac{2}{d}$

$$\frac{2}{v} = \frac{1}{v_1} + \frac{1}{v_2}$$

so $\dfrac{1}{v_2} = \dfrac{2}{v} - \dfrac{1}{v_1}$

$$= \frac{2}{90 \text{ km/h}} - \frac{1}{48 \text{ km/h}}$$

so $v_2 = 720$ km/h, or 700 km/h to one significant digit

No

Copyright © by Glencoe/McGraw-Hill

6 Forces

Practice Problems

6.1 Force and Motion
pages 118–125

page 119

1. Draw pictorial models for the following situations. Circle each system. Draw the forces exerted on the system. Name the agent for each force acting on each system.

    a. a book held in your hand

    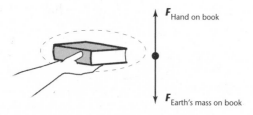

    b. a book pushed across the desk by your hand

    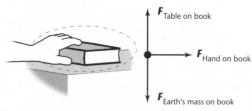

    c. a book pulled across the desk by a string

    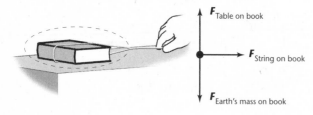

    d. a book on a desk when your hand is pushing down on it

    e. a ball just after the string that was holding it broke

    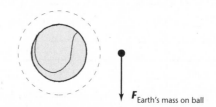

page 122

2. Two horizontal forces, 225 N and 165 N, are exerted in the same direction on a crate. Find the net horizontal force on the crate.

    Net force is

    225 N + 165 N = 3.90×10^2 N

    in the direction of the two forces.

3. If the same two forces are exerted in opposite directions, what is the net horizontal force on the crate? Be sure to indicate the direction of the net force.

    Net force is

    225 N − 165 N = 6.0×10^1 N

    in the direction of the larger force.

Copyright © by Glencoe/McGraw-Hill

4. The 225-N force is exerted on the crate toward the north and the 165-N force is exerted toward the east. Find the magnitude and direction of the net force.

Magnitude and direction

$$F = \sqrt{(225\ N)^2 + (165\ N)^2} = 279\ N$$

$$\tan \theta = \frac{225}{165} = 1.36$$

$$\theta = 53.7° \text{ N of E}$$

5. Your hand exerts a 6.5-N upward force on a pound of sugar. Considering the force of gravity on the sugar, what is the net force on the sugar? Give the magnitude and direction.

The downward force is one pound, or 4.5 N. The force is

6.5 N − 4.5 N = 2.0 N upward

6. Calculate the force you exert as you stand on the floor (1 lb = 0.454 kg). Is the force the same if you lie on the floor?

$$F = mg = (0.454\ kg/lb)(9.80\ m/s^2)$$

$$= 4.45\ N/lb$$

Same force if you lie on the floor.

page 124

For each problem, draw a motion diagram and a free-body diagram labeling all forces with their agents and indicating the direction of the acceleration and the net force. Draw arrows the appropriate lengths.

7. A skydiver falls downward through the air at constant velocity (air drag is important).

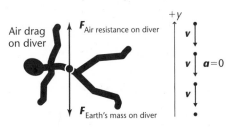

8. A cable pulls a crate at constant speed across a horizontal surface (there is friction).

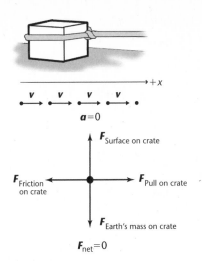

9. A rope lifts a bucket upward at constant speed (ignore air drag).

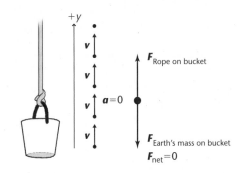

10. A rope lowers a bucket at constant speed (ignore air drag).

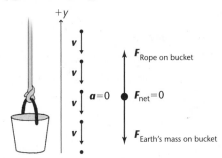

11. A rocket blasts off and its vertical velocity increases with time (ignore air drag).

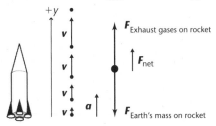

Copyright © by Glencoe/McGraw-Hill

6.2 Using Newton's Laws
pages 126–136

page 129

12. On Earth, a scale shows that you weigh 585 N.

    a. What is your mass?

    Scale reads 585 N. Since there is no acceleration your force equals the downward force of gravity. Mass

    $$m = \frac{F_g}{g} = 59.7 \text{ kg}$$

    b. What would the scale read on the moon ($g = 1.60$ m/s^2)?

    On the moon the scale would read 95.5 N.

13. Use the results from the first example problem to answer these questions about a scale in an elevator on Earth. What force would the scale exert when

    a. the elevator moves up at a constant speed?

    Mass = 75 kg

    b. it slows at 2.0 m/s^2 while moving upward?

    Slows while moving up or speeds up while moving down,

    $$F_{scale} = m(g + a)$$
    $$= (75 \text{ kg})(9.80 \text{ m/s}^2 - 2.0 \text{ m/s}^2)$$
    $$= 5.9 \times 10^2 \text{ N}$$

    c. it speeds up at 2.0 m/s^2 while moving downward?

    Slows while moving up or speeds up while moving down,

    $$F_{scale} = m(g + a)$$
    $$= (75 \text{ kg})(9.80 \text{ m/s}^2 - 2.0 \text{ m/s}^2)$$
    $$= 5.9 \times 10^2 \text{ N}$$

    d. it moves downward at a constant speed?

    $$F_{scale} = 7.4 \times 10^2 \text{ N}$$

    e. it slows to a stop at a constant magnitude of acceleration?

    Depends upon the magnitude of the acceleration.

page 133

14. A boy exerts a 36-N horizontal force as he pulls a 52-N sled across a cement sidewalk at constant speed. What is the coefficient of kinetic friction between the sidewalk and the metal sled runners? Ignore air resistance.

    $$F_N = mg = 52 \text{ N}$$

    Since the speed is constant, the friction force equals the force exerted by the boy, 36 N. But,

    $$F_f = \mu_k F_N$$

    so $\mu_k = \dfrac{F_f}{F_N} = \dfrac{36 \text{ N}}{52 \text{ N}} = 0.69$

15. Suppose the sled runs on packed snow. The coefficient of friction is now only 0.12. If a person weighing 650 N sits on the sled, what force is needed to pull the sled across the snow at constant speed?

    At constant speed, applied force equals friction force, so

    $$F_f = \mu F_N = (0.12)(52 \text{ N} + 650 \text{ N})$$
    $$= 84 \text{ N}$$

16. Consider the doubled force pushing the crate in the example problem *Unbalanced Friction Forces*. How long would it take for the velocity of the crate to double to 2.0 m/s?

    The initial velocity is 1.0 m/s, the final velocity 2.0 m/s, and the acceleration 2.0 m/s^2, so

    $$t = \frac{(v - v_0)}{a} = \frac{(1.0 \text{ m/s})}{(2.0 \text{ m/s}^2)} = 0.50 \text{ s}$$

page 136

17. What is the length of a pendulum with a period of 1.00 s?

    For a pendulum

    $$T = 2\pi \sqrt{\frac{l}{g}}$$

    so $l = g\left(\dfrac{T}{2\pi}\right)^2$

    $$= 9.80 \text{ m/s}^2 \left[\frac{1.00 \text{ s}}{(2)(3.14)}\right]^2$$
    $$= 0.248 \text{ m}$$

Copyright © by Glencoe/McGraw-Hill

18. Would it be practical to make a pendulum with a period of 10.0 s? Calculate the length and explain.

$$l = g\left(\frac{T}{2\pi}\right)^2$$

$$= (9.80 \text{ m/s}^2)\left(\frac{10.0 \text{ s}}{(2)(3.14)}\right)^2$$

$$= 24.8 \text{ m}$$

No. This is over 75 feet long!

19. On a planet with an unknown value of g, the period of a 0.65-m-long pendulum is 2.8 s. What is g for this planet?

$$g = l\left(\frac{2\pi}{T}\right)^2$$

$$= (0.65 \text{ m})\left(\frac{(2)(3.14)}{2.8 \text{ s}}\right)^2$$

$$= 3.3 \text{ m/s}^2$$

6.3 Interaction Forces
pages 138–143

page 141

20. You lift a bowling ball with your hand, accelerating it upward. What are the forces on the ball? What are the other parts of the action-reaction pairs? On what objects are they exerted?

The force of your hand on the ball, the gravitational force of Earth's mass on the ball. The force of the ball on your hand, the gravitational force of the ball's mass on Earth. The force of your feet on Earth, the force of Earth on your feet.

21. A car brakes to a halt. What forces act on the car? What are the other parts of the action-reaction pairs? On what objects are they exerted?

The backward (friction) and upward (normal) force of the road on the tires and the gravitational force of Earth's mass on the car. The forward (friction) and the downward force of the tires on the road and the gravitational force of the car's mass on Earth.

Chapter Review Problems
pages 145–147
Section 6.1

Level 1

20. A 873-kg (1930-lb) dragster, starting from rest, attains a speed of 26.3 m/s (58.9 mph) in 0.59 s.

   a. Find the average acceleration of the dragster during this time interval.

   $$a = \frac{\Delta v}{\Delta t} = \frac{(26.3 \text{ m/s} - 0)}{0.59 \text{ s}} = 45 \text{ m/s}^2$$

   b. What is the magnitude of the average net force on the dragster during this time?

   $$F = ma = (873 \text{ kg})(45 \text{ m/s}^2)$$

   $$= 3.9 \times 10^4 \text{ N}$$

page 146

   c. Assume that the driver has a mass of 68 kg. What horizontal force does the seat exert on the driver?

   $$F = ma = (68 \text{ kg})(45 \text{ m/s}^2)$$

   $$= 3.1 \times 10^3 \text{ N}$$

21. The dragster in problem 20 completed the 402.3 m (0.2500 mile) run in 4.936 s. If the car had a constant acceleration, what would be its acceleration and final velocity?

   $$d = \frac{1}{2} at^2$$

   so $$a = \frac{2d}{t^2} = \frac{2(402.3 \text{ m})}{(4.936 \text{ s})^2} = 33.02 \text{ m/s}^2$$

   $$d = \frac{1}{2} vt$$

   so $$v = \frac{2d}{t} = \frac{2(402.3 \text{ m})}{4.936 \text{ s}} = 163.0 \text{ m/s}$$

22. After a day of testing race cars, you decide to take your own 1550-kg car onto the test track. While moving down the track at 10.0 m/s, you uniformly accelerate to 30.0 m/s in 10.0 s. What is the average net force that the track has applied to the car during the 10.0-s interval?

   $$F = ma = \frac{m\,\Delta v}{t}$$

   $$= \frac{(1550 \text{ kg})(30.0 \text{ m/s} - 10.0 \text{ m/s})}{10.0 \text{ s}}$$

   $$= 3.10 \times 10^3 \text{ N}$$

Copyright © by Glencoe/McGraw-Hill

23. A 65-kg swimmer jumps off a 10.0-m tower.

a. Find the swimmer's velocity on hitting the water.

$$v^2 = v_0^2 + 2gd$$

$$v_0 = 0 \text{ m/s}$$

so $v = \sqrt{2gd}$

$$= \sqrt{2(9.80 \text{ m/s}^2)(10.0 \text{ m})}$$

$$= 14.0 \text{ m/s}$$

b. The swimmer comes to a stop 2.0 m below the surface. Find the net force exerted by the water.

$$v_f^2 = v_i^2 + 2ad$$

or $a = \dfrac{v_f^2 - v_i^2}{2d}$

$$= \dfrac{(0.0 \text{ m/s})^2 - (14.0 \text{ m/s})^2}{2(2.0 \text{ m})}$$

$$= -49 \text{ m/s}^2$$

and $F = ma = (65 \text{ kg})(-49 \text{ m/s}^2)$

$$= -3.2 \times 10^3 \text{ N}$$

Level 2

24. The dragster in problem 21 crossed the finish line going 126.6 m/s (283.1 mph). Does the assumption of constant acceleration hold true? What other piece of evidence could you use to see if the acceleration is constant?

126.6 m/s is slower than found in problem 21, so the acceleration cannot be constant. Further, the acceleration in the first half-second was 45 m/s², not 33.02 m/s².

25. A race car has a mass of 710 kg. It starts from rest and travels 40.0 m in 3.0 s. The car is uniformly accelerated during the entire time. What net force is exerted on it?

$F = ma$, where, since d and t are known, a can be found from

$$d = v_0 t + \left(\frac{1}{2}\right) at^2$$

Since $v_0 = 0$,

$$a = \frac{2d}{t^2}$$

and $F = ma$, so

$$F = \frac{2md}{t^2} = \frac{(2)(710 \text{ kg})(40.0 \text{ m})}{(3.0 \text{ s})^2}$$

$$= 6.3 \times 10^3 \text{ N}$$

Section 6.2

Level 1

26. What is your weight in newtons?

$$W = mg = (9.80 \text{ m/s}^2)(m)$$

Answers will vary.

27. Your new motorcycle weighs 2450 N. What is its mass in kg?

$$F_g = mg$$

so $m = \dfrac{W}{g} = \dfrac{-2450 \text{ N}}{-9.80 \text{ m/s}^2}$

$$= 2.50 \times 10^2 \text{ kg}$$

28. A pendulum has a length of 0.67 m.

a. Find its period.

$$T = 2\pi \sqrt{\frac{l}{g}} = 1.6 \text{ s}$$

b. How long would the pendulum have to be to double the period?

Because the period is proportional to the square root of the length, the pendulum would have to be four times as long, or 2.7 m.

29. You place a 7.50-kg television set on a spring scale. If the scale reads 78.4 N, what is the acceleration due to gravity at that location?

$$F_g = mg$$

so $g = \dfrac{F_g}{m} = \dfrac{78.4 \text{ N}}{7.50 \text{ kg}}$

$$= 10.5 \text{ m/s}^2, \text{ downward}$$

Copyright © by Glencoe/McGraw-Hill

30. If you use a horizontal force of 30.0 N to slide a 12.0 kg wooden crate across a floor at a constant velocity, what is the coefficient of kinetic friction between the crate and the floor?

$$\mu_K = \frac{F_f}{F_N}$$

$$= \frac{F_f}{F_g} = \frac{F_{horizontal}}{mg}$$

$$= \frac{30.0 \text{ N}}{(12.0 \text{ kg})(9.80 \text{ m/s}^2)} = 0.255$$

31. A 4500-kg helicopter accelerates upward at 2.0 m/s². What lift force is exerted by the air on the propellers?

$$ma = F_{net} = F_{appl} + F_g = F_{appl} + mg$$

so $F_{appl} = ma - mg = m(a - g)$

$$= (4500 \text{ kg})[(2.0 \text{ m/s}^2) - (-9.80 \text{ m/s}^2)]$$

$$= 5.3 \times 10^4 \text{ N}$$

32. The maximum force a grocery sack can withstand and not rip is 250 N. If 20.0 kg of groceries are lifted from the floor to the table with an acceleration of 5.0 m/s², will the sack hold?

$$ma = F_{net} = F_{appl} + F_g = F_{appl} + mg$$

so $F_{appl} = ma - mg = m(a - g)$

$$= (20.0 \text{ kg})[(5.0 \text{ m/s}^2) - (-9.80 \text{ m/s}^2)]$$

$$= 3.0 \times 10^2 \text{ N}$$

No, this force is greater than 250 N, hence the sack rips.

33. A force of 40.0 N accelerates a 5.0-kg block at 6.0 m/s² along a horizontal surface.

a. How large is the frictional force?

$$ma = F_{net} = F_{appl} - F_f$$

so $F_f = F_{appl} - ma$

$$= 40.0 \text{ N} - (5.0 \text{ kg})(6.0 \text{ m/s}^2)$$

$$= 1.0 \times 10^1 \text{ N}$$

b. What is the coefficient of friction?

$$F_f = \mu_K F_N = \mu mg$$

so $\mu_K = \dfrac{F_f}{mg} = \dfrac{10 \text{ N}}{(5.0 \text{ kg})(9.80 \text{ m/s}^2)}$

$$= 0.20$$

34. A 225-kg crate is pushed horizontally with a force of 710 N. If the coefficient of friction is 0.20, calculate the acceleration of the crate.

$$ma = F_{net} = F_{appl} - F_f$$

where $F_f = \mu F_N = \mu mg$

Therefore

$$a = \frac{F_{appl} - \mu mg}{m}$$

$$= \frac{710 \text{ N} - (0.20)(225 \text{ kg})(9.80 \text{ m/s}^2)}{225 \text{ kg}}$$

$$= 1.2 \text{ m/s}^2$$

Level 2

35. You are driving a 2500.0-kg car at a constant speed of 14.0 m/s along an icy, but straight, level road. As you approach an intersection, the traffic light turns red. You slam on the brakes. Your wheels lock, the tires begin skidding, and the car slides to a halt in a distance of 25.0 m. What is the coefficient of kinetic friction between your tires and the icy road?

$$F_f = \mu_K F_N = ma$$

$$-\mu_K mg = \frac{m(v^2 - v_0^2)}{2d} \text{ where } v = 0$$

(The minus sign indicates the force is acting opposite to the direction of motion.)

$$\mu_K = \frac{v_0^2}{2dg} = \frac{(14.0 \text{ m/s})^2}{2(25.0 \text{ m})(9.80 \text{ m/s}^2)}$$

$$= 0.400$$

36. A student stands on a bathroom scale in an elevator at rest on the 64th floor of a building. The scale reads 836 N.

a. As the elevator moves up, the scale reading increases to 936 N, then decreases back to 836 N. Find the acceleration of the elevator.

$$a = \frac{F_{appl} - F_g}{m} = \frac{936 \text{ N} - 836 \text{ N}}{(836 \text{ N})/(9.80 \text{ m/s}^2)}$$

$$= \frac{936 \text{ N} - 836 \text{ N}}{85.3 \text{ kg}}$$

$$= 1.17 \text{ m/s}^2$$

Copyright © by Glencoe/McGraw-Hill

36. (continued)

b. As the elevator approaches the 74th floor, the scale reading drops to 782 N. What is the acceleration of the elevator?

$$a = \frac{F_{appl} - F_g}{m}$$

$$= \frac{782 \text{ N} - 836 \text{ N}}{85.3 \text{ kg}}$$

$$= -0.633 \text{ m/s}^2$$

c. Using your results from parts **a** and **b**, explain which change in velocity, starting or stopping, would take the longer time.

Stopping, because the magnitude of the acceleration is less and

$$t = \frac{-v_0}{a}$$

d. What changes would you expect in the scale readings on the ride back down?

$$F_{appl} = F_g + ma = 836 \text{ N} + ma$$

As the elevator starts to descend *a* is negative and the scale reads less than 836 N. When constant downward velocity is reached, the scale reads 836 N because the acceleration is then zero. When the elevator is slowing at the bottom, the acceleration is positive and the scale reads more than 836 N.

37. A sled of mass 50.0 kg is pulled along flat, snow-covered ground. The static friction coefficient is 0.30, and the kinetic friction coefficient is 0.10.

a. What does the sled weigh?

$$W = mg = (50.0 \text{ kg})(9.80 \text{ m/s}^2)$$

$$= 4.90 \times 10^2 \text{ N}$$

b. What force will be needed to start the sled moving?

$$F_f = \mu_s F_N = \mu_s F_g = (0.30)(4.90 \times 10^2 \text{ N})$$

$$= 147 \text{ N, static friction}$$

c. What force is needed to keep the sled moving at a constant velocity?

$$F_f = \mu_K F_N = \mu_K F_g = (0.10)(4.90 \times 10^2 \text{ N})$$

$$= 49 \text{ N, kinetic friction}$$

d. Once moving, what total force must be applied to the sled to accelerate it at 3.0 m/s²?

$$ma = F_{net} = F_{appl} - F_f$$

$$\text{so } F_{appl} = ma + F_f$$

$$= (50.0 \text{ kg})(3.0 \text{ m/s}^2) + 49 \text{ N}$$

$$= 2.0 \times 10^2 \text{ N}$$

page 147

38. The instruments attached to a weather balloon have a mass of 5.0 kg. The balloon is released and exerts an upward force of 98 N on the instruments.

a. What is the acceleration of the balloon and instruments?

$$ma = F_{net} = F_{appl} + F_g$$

$$= 98 \text{ N} + (-49 \text{ N})$$

$$= +49 \text{ N (up)}$$

$$a = \frac{+49 \text{ N}}{5.0 \text{ kg}} = +9.8 \text{ m/s}^2 \text{ (up)}$$

b. After the balloon has accelerated for 10.0 s, the instruments are released. What is the velocity of the instruments at the moment of their release?

$$v = at = (+9.80 \text{ m/s}^2)(10.0 \text{ s})$$

$$= +98.0 \text{ m/s (up)}$$

c. What net force acts on the instruments after their release?

just the instrument weight, −49 N (down)

d. When does the direction of their velocity first become downward?

The velocity becomes negative after it passes through zero. Thus, use
$$v = v_0 + gt, \text{ where } v = 0, \text{ or}$$

$$t = \frac{v_0}{g} = \frac{-(+98.0 \text{ m/s})}{(-9.80 \text{ m/s}^2)}$$

$$= 10.0 \text{ s}$$

after release, or 20.0 s after launch.

Copyright © by Glencoe/McGraw-Hill

Section 6.3

Level 1

39. A 65-kg boy and a 45-kg girl use an elastic rope while engaged in a tug-of-war on an icy, frictionless surface. If the acceleration of the girl toward the boy is 3.0 m/s², find the magnitude of the acceleration of the boy toward the girl.

$$F_{1,2} = -F_{2,1} \text{ so } m_1 a_1 = -m_2 a_2$$

$$\text{and } a_1 = \frac{-(m_2 a_2)}{m_1}$$

$$= \frac{-(45 \text{ kg})(3.0 \text{ m/s}^2)}{(65 \text{ kg})}$$

$$= -2.0 \text{ m/s}^2$$

Magnitude of the acceleration: 2.0 m/s².

40. As a baseball is being caught, its speed goes from 30.0 m/s to 0.0 m/s in about 0.0050 s. The mass of the baseball is 0.145 kg.

a. What is the baseball's acceleration?

$$a = \frac{(0.0 \text{ m/s} - 30.0 \text{ m/s})}{0.0050 \text{ s}}$$

$$= -6.0 \times 10^3 \text{ m/s}^2$$

b. What are the magnitude and direction of the force acting on it?

$$F = ma$$

$$= (0.145 \text{ kg})(-6.0 \times 10^3 \text{ m/s}^2)$$

$$= -8.7 \times 10^2 \text{ N (opposite direction of the velocity of the ball)}$$

c. What are the magnitude and direction of the force acting on the player who caught it?

Same magnitude, opposite direction (in direction of velocity of ball).

Level 2

41. A 2.0-kg mass (m_A) and a 3.0-kg mass (m_B) are attached to a lightweight cord that passes over a frictionless pulley. The hanging masses are free to move. Choose coordinate systems for the two masses with the positive direction up for m_A and down for m_B.

a. Create a pictorial model.

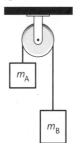

b. Create a physical model with motion and free-body diagrams.

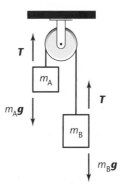

c. Find the acceleration of the smaller mass.

$ma = F_{net}$ **where m is the total mass being accelerated.**

For m_A, $m_A a = T - m_A g$

For m_B, $m_B a = -T + m_B g$

$$T = m_B g - m_B a = m_B(g - a)$$

$$= (3.0)(9.80 - 2.0) = 23 \text{ N}$$

Substituting into the equation for m_A gives

$$m_A a = m_B g - m_B a - m_A g$$

$$\text{or } (m_A + m_B)a = (m_B - m_A)g$$

Copyright © by Glencoe/McGraw-Hill

41. (continued)

Therefore $a = \left(\dfrac{m_B - m_A}{m_A + m_B}\right) g$

$= \left(\dfrac{3.0 - 2.0}{3.0 + 2.0}\right) 9.80$

$= \left(\dfrac{1.0}{5.0}\right) 9.80$

$= 2.0$ m/s², upward

42. Suppose the masses in problem 41 are now 1.00 kg and 4.00 kg. Find the acceleration of the larger mass.

Take the direction of the physical motion, smaller mass upward and larger mass downward, to be the positive direction of motion.

For m_A, $m_A a = T - mg$

For m_B, $m_B a = -T + m_B g$ or
$T = m_B g - m_B a$

Substitution into the equation for m_A gives

$m_A a = m_B g - m_B a - m_A g$

or $(m_A + m_B)a = (m_B - m_A)g$

Therefore,

$a = \left(\dfrac{m_B - m_A}{m_A + m_B}\right) g$

$= \left(\dfrac{4.00 - 1.00}{4.00 + 1.00}\right) 9.80$

$= \left(\dfrac{3.00}{5.00}\right) 9.80 = 5.88$ m/s², downward

Critical Thinking Problems

43. The force exerted on a 0.145-kg baseball by a bat changes from 0.0 N to 1.0×10^4 N over 0.0010 s, then drops back to zero in the same amount of time. The baseball was going toward the bat at 25 m/s.

a. Draw a graph of force versus time. What is the average force exerted on the ball by the bat?

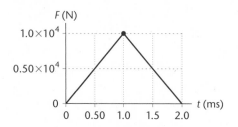

average $F = 5.0 \times 10^3$ N

b. What is the acceleration of the ball?

$a = \dfrac{F_{net}}{m} = \dfrac{5.0 \times 10^3 \text{ N}}{0145 \text{ kg}}$

$= 3.4 \times 10^4$ m/s²

c. What is the final velocity of the ball, assuming that it reverses direction?

$v = v_0 + at$

$= -25$ m/s $+ (3.4 \times 10^4$ m/s²$)$

$\times (0.0020$ s$)$

$= +43$ m/s

Copyright © by Glencoe/McGraw-Hill

7 Forces and Motion in Two Dimensions

Practice Problems

7.1 Forces in Two Dimensions
pages 150–154

page 151

1. The sign from the preceding example problem is now hung by ropes that each make an angle of 42° with the horizontal. What force does each rope exert?

$$F_A = F_B$$

$$F_A = \frac{F_g}{2 \sin \theta}$$

$$= \frac{168 \text{ N}}{2 \times \sin 42°}$$

$$= 126 \text{ N}$$

2. An 8.0-N weight has one horizontal rope exerting a force of 6.0 N on it.

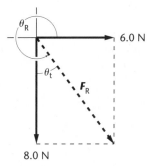

a. What are the magnitude and direction of the resultant force on the weight?

$$F_R = \sqrt{(6.0 \text{ N})^2 + (8.0 \text{ N})^2}$$

$$= 1.0 \times 10^1 \text{ N}$$

$$\theta_t = \tan^{-1}\left(\frac{6.0}{8.0}\right) = 37°$$

$$\theta_R = 270° + \theta_t = 307° = 310°$$

$$F_R = 1.0 \times 10^1 \text{ N at } 310°$$

b. What force (magnitude and direction) is needed to put the weight into equilibrium?

$$F_E = 1.0 \times 10^1 \text{ N at } 310° - 180°$$

$$= 130°$$

page 152

3. Two ropes pull on a ring. One exerts a 62-N force at 30.0°, the other a 62-N force at 60.0°.

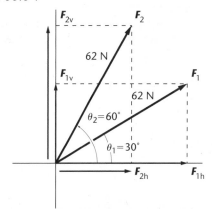

a. What is the net force on the ring?

Vector addition is most easily carried out by using the method of addition by components. The first step in this method is the resolution of the given vectors into their horizontal and vertical components.

$$F_{1h} = F_1 \cos \theta_1 = (62 \text{ N}) \cos 30°$$

$$= 54 \text{ N}$$

$$F_{1v} = F_1 \sin \theta_1 = (62 \text{ N}) \sin 30°$$

$$= 31 \text{ N}$$

$$F_{2h} = F_2 \cos \theta_2 = (62 \text{ N}) \cos 60°$$

$$= 31 \text{ N}$$

$$F_{2v} = F_2 \sin \theta_2 = (62 \text{ N}) \sin 60°$$

$$= 54 \text{ N}$$

Copyright © by Glencoe/McGraw-Hill

3. a. (continued)

At this point, the two original vectors have been replaced by four components, vectors that are much easier to add. The horizontal and vertical components of the resultant vector are found by simple addition.

$$F_{Rh} = F_{1h} + F_{2h} = 54 \text{ N} + 31 \text{ N} = 85 \text{ N}$$

$$F_{Rv} = F_{1v} + F_{2v} = 31 \text{ N} + 54 \text{ N} = 85 \text{ N}$$

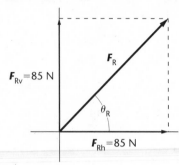

The magnitude and direction of the resultant vector are found by the usual method.

$$F_R = \sqrt{(F_{Rh})^2 + (F_{Rv})^2}$$

$$= \sqrt{(85 \text{ N})^2 + (85 \text{ N})^2}$$

$$= 120 \text{ N}$$

$$\tan \theta_R = \frac{F_{Rv}}{F_{Rh}} = \frac{85 \text{ N}}{85 \text{ N}} = 1.0$$

$$\theta_R = 45°$$

$$F_R = 120 \text{ N at } 45°$$

b. What are the magnitude and direction of the force that would cause the ring to be in equilibrium?

$$F_E = 120 \text{ N at } 45° + 180° = 225°$$

4. Two forces are exerted on an object. A 36-N force acts at 225° and a 48-N force acts at 315°. What are the magnitude and direction of the equilibrant?

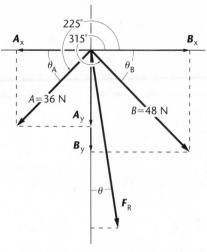

$$\theta_A = 225° - 180° = 45°$$

$$\theta_B = 360° - 315° = 45°$$

$$A_x = -A \cos \theta_A = -(36 \text{ N}) \cos 45°$$

$$= -25 \text{ N}$$

$$A_y = -A \sin \theta_A = (-36 \text{ N}) \sin 45°$$

$$= -25 \text{ N}$$

$$B_x = B \cos \theta_B = (48 \text{ N}) \cos 45°$$

$$= 34 \text{ N}$$

$$B_y = -B \sin \theta_B = -(48 \text{ N}) \sin 45°$$

$$= -34 \text{ N}$$

$$F_x = A_x + B_x = -25 \text{ N} + 34 \text{ N} = 9 \text{ N}$$

$$F_y = A_y + B_y = -25 \text{ N} - 34 \text{ N} = -59 \text{ N}$$

$$F_R = \sqrt{F_x^2 + F_y^2} = \sqrt{(+9 \text{ N})^2 + (-59 \text{ N})^2}$$

$$= 6.0 \times 10^1 \text{ N}$$

$$\tan \theta = \frac{9}{59} = 0.153; \quad \theta = 9°$$

$$\theta_R = 270° + 9° = 279°$$

$$F_R = 6.0 \times 10^1 \text{ N at } 279°$$

$$F_E = 6.0 \times 10^1 \text{ N}$$

$$\theta_E = 279° - 180° = 99°$$

Copyright © by Glencoe/McGraw-Hill

5. Consider the trunk on the incline in the Example Problem.

   a. Calculate the magnitude of the acceleration.

   $$a = \frac{F}{m} = \frac{+mg \sin \theta}{m}$$
   $$= +g \sin \theta$$
   $$= (+9.80 \text{ m/s}^2)(\sin 30.0°)$$
   $$= 4.90 \text{ m/s}^2$$

   b. After 4.00 s, how fast would the trunk be moving?

   $$v = v_0 + at = (4.90 \text{ m/s}^2)(4.00 \text{ s})$$
   $$= 19.6 \text{ m/s}$$

6. For the Example Problem *Skiing Downhill*, find the x- and y-components of the weight of the skier going downhill.

   $$F_{gx} = mg \sin \theta$$
   $$= (62 \text{ kg})(9.80 \text{ m/s}^2)(0.60)$$
   $$= 3.6 \times 10^2 \text{ N}$$
   $$F_{gy} = mg \cos \theta$$
   $$= (62 \text{ kg})(9.80 \text{ m/s}^2)(0.80)$$
   $$= 4.9 \times 10^2 \text{ N}$$

7. If the skier were on a 30° downhill slope, what would be the magnitude of the acceleration?

   Since $a = g(\sin \theta - \mu \cos \theta)$,

   $$a = 9.80 \text{ m/s}^2 [0.50 - (0.15)(0.866)]$$
   $$= 4.0 \text{ m/s}^2$$

8. After the skier on the 37° hill had been moving for 5.0 s, the friction of the snow suddenly increased making the net force on the skier zero. What is the new coefficient of friction? How fast would the skier now be going after skiing for 5.0 s?

   $$a = g(\sin \theta - \mu \cos \theta)$$
   $$a = g \sin \theta - g\mu \cos \theta$$
   If $a = 0$,
   $$0 = g \sin \theta - g\mu \cos \theta$$
   $$g\mu \cos \theta = g \sin \theta$$

$$\mu = \frac{g \sin \theta}{g \cos \theta} = \frac{\sin \theta}{\cos \theta}$$
$$\mu = \frac{\sin 37°}{\cos 37°} = 0.75$$

If $a = 0$, the velocity would be the same as before.

7.2 Projectile Motion
pages 155–161

page 158

9. A stone is thrown horizontally at a speed of 5.0 m/s from the top of a cliff 78.4 m high.

   a. How long does it take the stone to reach the bottom of the cliff?

   Since $v_y = 0$, $y - v_y t = -\frac{1}{2} gt^2$ becomes

   $$y = -\frac{1}{2} gt^2$$
   or $t^2 = -\frac{2y}{g} = \frac{-2(-78.4 \text{ m})}{9.80 \text{ m/s}^2} = 16 \text{ s}^2$
   $$t = \sqrt{16 \text{ s}^2} = 4.0 \text{ s}$$

   b. How far from the base of the cliff does the stone hit the ground?

   $$x = v_x t = (5.0 \text{ m/s})(4.0 \text{ s})$$
   $$= 2.0 \times 10^1 \text{ m}$$

   c. What are the horizontal and vertical components of the stone's velocity just before it hits the ground?

   $v_x = 5.0$ m/s. This is the same as the initial horizontal speed because the acceleration of gravity influences only the vertical motion. For the vertical component, use $v = v_0 + gt$ with $v = v_y$ and v_0, the initial vertical component of velocity, zero.

   At $t = 4.0$ s
   $$v_y = gt = (9.80 \text{ m/s}^2)(4.0 \text{ s})$$
   $$= 39 \text{ m/s}$$

Copyright © by Glencoe/McGraw-Hill

10. How would the three answers to problem 9 change if

a. the stone were thrown with twice the horizontal speed?

(a) no change; 4.0 s

(b) twice the previous distance; 4.0×10^1 m

(c) v_x doubles; 1.0×10^1 m/s no change in v_y; 39 m/s

b. the stone were thrown with the same speed, but the cliff were twice as high?

(a) increases by $\sqrt{2}$, because $t = \sqrt{\dfrac{-2y}{g}}$ and y doubles; 5.7 s

(b) increases by $\sqrt{2}$, because t increases by $\sqrt{2}$; 28 m

(c) no change in v_x; 5.0 m/s v_y increases by $\sqrt{2}$, because t increases by $\sqrt{2}$; 55 m/s

11. A steel ball rolls with constant velocity across a tabletop 0.950 m high. It rolls off and hits the ground 0.352 m from the edge of the table. How fast was the ball rolling?

Since $v_y = 0$, $y = -\dfrac{1}{2} gt^2$ and the time to reach the ground is

$$t = \sqrt{\dfrac{-2y}{g}} = \sqrt{\dfrac{-2(-0.950 \text{ m})}{9.80 \text{ m/s}^2}}$$

$$= 0.440 \text{ s}$$

From $x = v_x t$,

$$v_x = \dfrac{x}{t} = \dfrac{0.352 \text{ m}}{0.440 \text{ s}}$$

$$= 0.800 \text{ m/s}$$

page 160

12. A player kicks a football from ground level with an initial velocity of 27.0 m/s, 30.0° above the horizontal as shown in **Figure 7–8**. Find the ball's hang time, range, and maximum height. Assume air resistance is negligible.

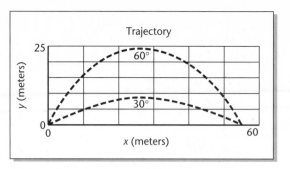

FIGURE 7-8

$$v_x = v_0 \cos \theta = (27.0 \text{ m/s}) \cos 30.0°$$

$$= 23.4 \text{ m/s}$$

$$v_y = v_0 \sin \theta = (27.0 \text{ m/s}) \sin 30.0°$$

$$= 13.5 \text{ m/s}$$

When it lands, $y = v_y t - \dfrac{1}{2} gt^2 = 0$.

Therefore,

$$t = \dfrac{2v_y}{g} = \dfrac{2(13.5 \text{ m/s})}{9.80 \text{ m/s}^2} = 2.76 \text{ s}$$

Distance:

$$x = v_x t = (23.4 \text{ m/s})(2.76 \text{ s}) = 64.6 \text{ m}$$

Maximum height occurs at half the "hang time," or 1.38 s. Thus,

$$y = v_y t - \dfrac{1}{2} gt^2$$

$$= (13.5 \text{ m/s})(1.38 \text{ s})$$

$$- \dfrac{1}{2} (+9.80 \text{ m/s}^2)(1.38 \text{ s})^2$$

$$= 18.6 \text{ m} - 9.33 \text{ m} = 9.27 \text{ m}$$

13. The player then kicks the ball with the same speed, but at 60.0° from the horizontal. What are the ball's hang time, range, and maximum height?

Following the method of Practice Problem 5,

$$v_x = v_0 \cos \theta = (27.0 \text{ m/s}) \cos 60.0°$$

$$= 13.5 \text{ m/s}$$

$$v_y = v_0 \sin \theta = (27.0 \text{ m/s}) \sin 60.0°$$

$$= 23.4 \text{ m/s}$$

$$t = \dfrac{2v_y}{g} = \dfrac{2(23.4 \text{ m/s})}{9.80 \text{ m/s}^2} = 4.78 \text{ s}$$

Copyright © by Glencoe/McGraw-Hill

13. (continued)

Distance:

$x = v_x t = (13.5 \text{ m/s})(4.78 \text{ s}) = 64.5 \text{ m}$

Maximum height:

at $t = \dfrac{1}{2}(4.78 \text{ s}) = 2.39 \text{ s}$

$y = v_y t - \dfrac{1}{2}gt^2$

$= (23.4 \text{ m/s})(2.39 \text{ s})$

$\qquad - \dfrac{1}{2}(+9.80 \text{ m/s}^2)(2.39 \text{ s})^2$

$= 27.9 \text{ m}$

7.3 Circular Motion
pages 163–168

page 166

14. Consider the following changes to the Example Problem.

    a. The mass is doubled, but all other quantities remain the same. What would be the effect on the velocity, acceleration, and force?

    Since r and T remain the same,

    $v = \dfrac{2\pi r}{T}$ and $a = \dfrac{v^2}{r}$

    remain the same. The new value of the mass is $m_2 = 2m_1$. The new force is $F_2 = m_2 a = 2m_1 a = 2F_1$, double the original force.

    b. The radius is doubled, but all other quantities remain the same. What would be the effect on the velocity, acceleration, and force?

    The new radius is $r_2 = 2r_1$, so the new velocity is

    $v_2 = \dfrac{2\pi r_2}{T} = \dfrac{2\pi(2r_1)}{T} = 2v_1$

    twice the original velocity. The new acceleration is

    $a_2 = \dfrac{(v_2)^2}{r_2} = \dfrac{(2v_1)^2}{2r_1} = 2a_1$

    twice the original. The new force is

    $F_2 = ma_2 = m(2a_1) = 2F_1$

    twice the original.

    c. The period of revolution is half as large, but all other quantities remain the same. What would be the effect on the velocity, acceleration, and force?

    new velocity,

    $v_2 = \dfrac{2\pi r}{T_2} = \dfrac{2\pi r}{\left(\dfrac{1}{2}T\right)} = 2v_1$

    twice the original; new acceleration

    $a_2 = \dfrac{(v_2)^2}{r} = \dfrac{(2v_1)^2}{r} = 4a_1$

    four times original; new force,

    $F_2 = ma_2 = m(4a_1) = 4F_1$

    four times original

15. A runner moving at a speed of 8.8 m/s rounds a bend with a radius of 25 m.

    a. What is the centripetal acceleration of the runner?

    $a_c = \dfrac{v^2}{r} = \dfrac{(8.8 \text{ m/s})^2}{25 \text{ m}} = 3.1 \text{ m/s}^2$

    b. What agent exerts the force on the runner?

    The frictional force of the track acting on the runner's shoes exerts the force on the runner.

16. Racing on a flat track, a car going 32 m/s rounds a curve 56 m in radius.

    a. What is the car's centripetal acceleration?

    $a_c = \dfrac{v^2}{r} = \dfrac{(32 \text{ m/s})^2}{56 \text{ m}} = 18 \text{ m/s}^2$

    b. What minimum coefficient of static friction between the tires and road would be needed for the car to round the curve without slipping?

    Recall $F_f = \mu F_N$. The friction force must supply the centripetal force so $F_f = ma_c$. The normal force is $F_N = -mg$. The coefficient of friction must be at least

    $\mu = \dfrac{F_f}{F_N} = \dfrac{ma_c}{mg} = \dfrac{a_c}{g} = \dfrac{18 \text{ m/s}^2}{9.80 \text{ m/s}^2}$

    $= 1.8$

Copyright © by Glencoe/McGraw-Hill

Chapter Review Problems

pages 171–173

page 171

Section 7.1

Level 1

30. An object in equilibrium has three forces exerted on it. A 33-N force acts at 90° from the *x*-axis and a 44-N force acts at 60°. What are the magnitude and direction of the third force?

$F_1 = 33$ N, 90°

$F_2 = 44$ N, 60°

$F_3 = ?$

$F_{1h} = (33$ N$) \cos 90° = 0$

$F_{2h} = (44$ N$) \cos 60° = 22$ N

$F_{3h} = x$

$F_{1v} = (33$ N$) \sin 90° = 33$ N

$F_{2v} = (44$ N$) \sin 60° = 38$ N

$F_{3v} = y$

For equilibrium, the sum of the components must equal zero, so

$0 + 22$ N $+ x = 0$ and $x = -22$ N

33 N $+ 38$ N $+ y = 0$ and $y = -71$ N

$R = \sqrt{(-22 \text{ N})^2 + (-71 \text{ N})^2} = 74$ N

$\tan \theta = \dfrac{-71 \text{ N}}{-22 \text{ N}} = 3.23$

so $\theta = 73°$

$F_3 = 74$ N, 253°

31. A street lamp weighs 150 N. It is supported by two wires that form an angle of 120° with each other. The tensions in the wires are equal.

   a. What is the tension in each wire?

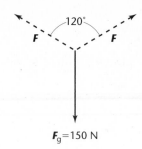

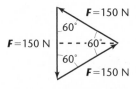

Horizontal: $T_{1h} + T_{2h} = 0$

so $T_{1h} = T_{1v}$ and

$\qquad T_1 \cos 30° = T_2 \cos 30°$

so $T_1 = T_2$

Vertical: $T_{1v} + T_{2v} - 150$ N $= 0$

so $T_1 \sin 30° + T_2 \sin 30° = 150$ N

$T_1 = T_2 = \dfrac{150 \text{ N}}{2 \sin 30°} = 150$ N

b. If the angle between the wires is reduced to 90.0°, what is the tension in each wire?

$T_1 = T_2 = \dfrac{150 \text{ N}}{2 \sin 45°} = 106$ N ≈ 110 N

32. A 215-N box is placed on an inclined plane that makes a 35.0° angle with the horizontal. Find the component of the weight force parallel to the plane's surface.

$F_{||} = F_g \sin \theta$

$\quad = (215$ N$) \sin 35.0°$

$\quad = 123$ N

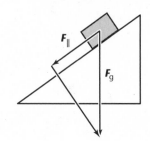

Copyright © by Glencoe/McGraw-Hill

Level 2

33. Five forces act on an object: (1) 60.0 N at 90°, (2) 40.0 N at 0°, (3) 80.0 N at 270°, (4) 40.0 N at 180°, and (5) 50.0 N at 60°. What is the magnitude and direction of a sixth force that would produce equilibrium?

Solutions by components

$F_1 = 60.0$ N, 90°

$F_2 = 40.0$ N, 0°

$F_3 = 80.0$ N, 270°

$F_4 = 40.0$ N, 180°

$F_5 = 50.0$ N, 60°

$F_6 = ?$

$F_{1h} = (60.0$ N$) \cos 90° = 0.00$

$F_{2h} = (40.0$ N$) \cos 0° = 40.0$ N

$F_{3h} = (80.0$ N$) \cos 270° = 0.00$

$F_{4h} = (40.0$ N$) \cos 180° = -40.0$ N

$F_{5h} = (50.0$ N$) \cos 60° = 25.0$ N

$F_{6h} = x$

$F_{1v} = (60.0$ N$) \sin 90° = 60.0$ N

$F_{2v} = (40.0$ N$) \sin 0° = 0.00$

$F_{3v} = (80.0$ N$) \sin 270° = -80.0$ N

$F_{4v} = (40.0$ N$) \sin 180° = 0.00$

$F_{5v} = (50.0$ N$) \sin 60° = 43.0$ N

$F_{6v} = y$

$0.00 + 40.0$ N $+ 0.00 + (-40.0$ N$) + 25.0$ N $+ x = 0.00$

so $x = -25.0$ N

60.0 N $+ 0.00 + (-80.0$ N$) + 0.00 + 43.0$ N $+ y = 0.00$

so $y = -23.0$ N

$R = \sqrt{(-25.0 \text{ N})^2 + (-23.0 \text{ N})^2} = 34.0$ N

$\tan \theta = \dfrac{-23.0 \text{ N}}{-25 \text{ N}} = 0.920$

so $\theta = 42.6°$ in quadrant III for equilibrant

$\theta = 42.6° + 180° = 222.6°$

$F_6 = 34.0$ N, 222.6°

34. Joe wishes to hang a sign weighing 7.50×10^2 N so that cable A attached to the store makes a 30.0° angle, as shown in **Figure 7–16**. Cable B is horizontal and attached to an adjoining building. What is the tension in cable B?

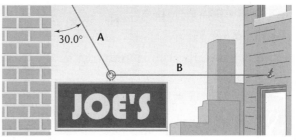

FIGURE 7-16

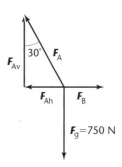

Solution by components.

The sum of the components must equal zero, so

$F_{Av} - F_g = 0$ and

$F_{Av} = F_A \sin 60.0° = 7.50 \times 10^2$ N

$F_A = \dfrac{7.50 \times 10^2 \text{ N}}{\sin 60°} = 8.70 \times 10^2$ N

Also, $F_B - F_{Ah} = 0$, so

$F_B = F_{Ah} = (8.70 \times 10^2$ N$) \cos 60.0°$

$= 435$ N, right

35. You pull your 18-kg suitcase at constant speed on a horizontal floor by exerting a 43-N force on the handle, which makes an angle θ with the horizontal. The force of friction on the suitcase is 27 N.

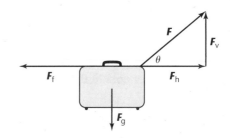

Copyright © by Glencoe/McGraw-Hill

35. (continued)

a. What angle does the handle make with the horizontal?

$$F_h - F_f = 0$$

so $F_h = F_f = 27$ N

and $\cos \theta = \dfrac{F_h}{F} = \dfrac{27 \text{ N}}{43 \text{ N}}$

so $\theta = 51°$

b. What is the normal force on the suitcase?

$$F_N + F_v - F_g = 0$$

so $F_N = F_g - F_v = mg - F \sin \theta$

$= (18 \text{ kg})(9.80 \text{ m/s}^2) - 43 \text{ N} \sin 51°$

$= 1.4 \times 10^2$ N, upward
or 140 N, upward

c. What is the coefficient of friction?

$$\mu = \dfrac{F_f}{F_N} = \dfrac{27 \text{ N}}{140 \text{ N}} = 0.19$$

36. You push a 325-N trunk up a 20.0° inclined plane at a constant velocity by exerting a 211-N force parallel to the plane's surface.

a. What is the component of the trunk's weight parallel to the plane?

$$F_{||} = F_g \sin \theta = (325 \text{ N}) \sin 20.0°$$
$$= 111 \text{ N}$$

b. What is the sum of all forces parallel to the plane's surface?

zero, because the velocity is constant

c. What are the magnitude and direction of the friction force?

Let up plane be positive, then

$$F - F_{||} + F_f = 0$$

$$211 \text{ N} - 111 \text{ N} + F_f = 0$$

so $F_f = -1.00 \times 10^2$ N, downward along the plane

d. What is the coefficient of friction?

$$\mu = \dfrac{F_f}{F_N} = \dfrac{1.00 \times 10^2 \text{ N}}{325 \text{ N} \cos 20.0°}$$

$$= 0.327$$

page 172

37. What force must be exerted on the trunk in problem 36 so that it would slide down the plane with a constant velocity? In which direction should the force be exerted?

$$F - F_{||} + F_f = 0$$

so $F = F_{||} - F_f$

$= F_g \sin \theta - \mu F_g \cos \theta$

$= (325 \text{ N}) \sin 20.0°$

$\quad - (0.327)(325) \cos 20.0°$

$= 11.3$ N, up plane

38. A 2.5-kg block slides down a 25° inclined plane with constant acceleration. The block starts from rest at the top. At the bottom, its velocity is 0.65 m/s. The incline is 1.6 m long.

a. What is the acceleration of the block?

$$v^2 = v_0^2 + 2ad$$

but $v_0 = 0$

so $a = \dfrac{v^2}{2d} = \dfrac{(0.65 \text{ m/s})^2}{2(1.6 \text{ m})} = 0.13 \text{ m/s}^2$

b. What is the coefficient of friction?

Let up plane be positive. Then,

$$F_f - F_{||} = -(ma)$$

so $F_f = F_{||} - ma$

$$\mu = \dfrac{F_f}{F_N} = \dfrac{F_{||} - ma}{F_N}$$

$$= \dfrac{F_g \sin \theta - ma}{F_g \cos \theta}$$

$$= \dfrac{mg \sin \theta - ma}{mg \cos \theta} = \dfrac{m(g \sin \theta - a)}{mg \cos \theta}$$

$$= \dfrac{(9.80 \text{ m/s}^2) \sin 25° - 0.13 \text{ m/s}^2}{(9.80 \text{ m/s}^2) \cos 25°}$$

$$= \dfrac{4.0 \text{ m/s}^2}{8.9 \text{ m/s}^2}$$

$$= 0.45$$

c. Does the result of either **a** or **b** depend on the mass of the block?

No. In part b, the mass divides out.

Copyright © by Glencoe/McGraw-Hill

Section 7.2

Level 1

39. You accidentally throw your car keys horizontally at 8.0 m/s from a cliff 64 m high. How far from the base of the cliff should you look for the keys?

$$y = v_y t - \frac{1}{2} gt^2$$

Since initial vertical velocity is zero,

$$t = \sqrt{\frac{-2y}{g}} = \sqrt{\frac{(-2)(-64 \text{ m})}{9.80 \text{ m/s}^2}} = 3.6 \text{ s}$$

$$x = v_x t = (8.0 \text{ m/s})(3.6 \text{ s}) = 28.8 \text{ m}$$
$$= 29 \text{ m}$$

40. A toy car runs off the edge of a table that is 1.225 m high. If the car lands 0.400 m from the base of the table,

a. how long did it take the car to fall?

$$y = v_{y0} t - \frac{1}{2} gt^2$$

and since initial velocity is zero,

$$t = \sqrt{\frac{-2y}{g}} = \sqrt{\frac{(-2)(-1.225 \text{ m})}{9.80 \text{ m/s}^2}}$$
$$= 0.500 \text{ s}$$

b. how fast was the car going on the table?

$$v_x = \frac{x}{t} = \frac{0.400 \text{ m}}{0.500 \text{ s}} = 0.800 \text{ m/s}$$

41. You take a running leap off a high-diving platform. You were running at 2.8 m/s and hit the water 2.6 s later. How high was the platform, and how far from the edge of the platform did you hit the water? Neglect air resistance.

$$y = v_{y0} t - \frac{1}{2} gt^2$$
$$= 0(2.6 \text{ s}) - \frac{1}{2} (9.8 \text{ m/s}^2)(2.6 \text{ s})^2$$
$$= -33 \text{ m, so the platform is 33 m high}$$

$$x = v_x t = (2.8 \text{ m/s})(2.6 \text{ s}) = 7.3 \text{ m}$$

42. An arrow is shot at 30.0° above the horizontal. Its velocity is 49 m/s and it hits the target.

a. What is the maximum height the arrow will attain?

$$v_y^2 = v_{y0}^2 - 2gd$$

At the high point $v_y = 0$, so

$$d = \frac{(v_{y0})^2}{2g} = \frac{(24.5 \text{ m/s})^2}{2(9.80 \text{ m/s}^2)} = 31 \text{ m}$$

b. The target is at the height from which the arrow was shot. How far away is it?

$$y = v_{y0} t - \frac{1}{2} gt^2$$

but the arrow lands at the same height, so

$$y = 0 \text{ and } 0 = v_{y0} - \frac{1}{2} gt$$

so $t = 0$ **or**

$$t = \frac{v_{y0}}{\frac{1}{2}(g)} = \frac{-24.5 \text{ m/s}}{\frac{1}{2}(9.80 \text{ m/s}^2)} = 5.0 \text{ s}$$

and $x = v_x t = (49 \text{ m/s} \cos 30°)(5.0 \text{ s})$
$$= 2.1 \times 10^2 \text{ m}$$

43. A pitched ball is hit by a batter at a 45° angle and just clears the outfield fence, 98 m away. Assume that the fence is at the same height as the pitch and find the velocity of the ball when it left the bat. Neglect air resistance.

The components of the initial velocity are

$$v_x = v_0 \cos \theta_0 \text{ and } v_{y0} = v_0 \sin \theta_0$$

Now $x = v_x t = (v_0 \cos \theta_0)t$, **so**

$$t = \frac{x}{v_0 \cos \theta_0}$$

And $y = v_{y0} t - \frac{1}{2} gt^2$, **but** $y = 0$, **so**

$$0 = \left[v_{y0} - \frac{1}{2} gt \right] t$$

so $t = 0$ **or** $v_{y0} - \frac{1}{2} gt = 0$

From above

$$v_0 \sin \theta_0 - \frac{1}{2} g \left[\frac{x}{v_0 \cos \theta_0} \right] = 0$$

Multiplying by $v_0 \cos \theta_0$ **gives**

$$v_0^2 \sin \theta_0 \cos \theta_0 - \frac{1}{2} gx = 0$$

so $v_0^2 = \frac{gx}{2 \sin \theta_0 \cos \theta_0}$

$$= \frac{(9.80 \text{ m/s}^2)(98 \text{ m})}{2(\sin 45°)(\cos 45°)}$$

$$= 9.6 \times 10^2 \text{ m}^2/\text{s}^2$$

$$v_0 = 31 \text{ m/s at } 45°$$

Copyright © by Glencoe/McGraw-Hill

Level 2

44. The two baseballs in **Figure 7–17** were hit with the same speed, 25 m/s. Draw separate graphs of y versus t and x versus t for each ball.

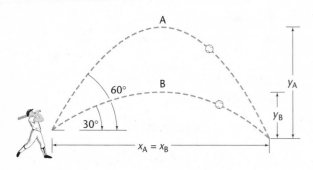

FIGURE 7-17

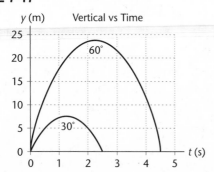

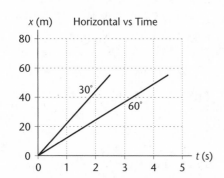

45. An airplane traveling 1001 m above the ocean at 125 km/h is to drop a box of supplies to shipwrecked victims below.

   a. How many seconds before being directly overhead should the box be dropped?

$$y = v_{y0}t - \frac{1}{2} gt^2$$

$$-1001 \text{ m} = 0(t) - \frac{1}{2} (9.80 \text{ m/s}^2)t^2$$

$$t = 14.3 \text{ s}$$

b. What is the horizontal distance between the plane and the victims when the box is dropped?

$$v_x = 125 \text{ km/h} \left(\frac{1 \text{ h}}{3600 \text{ s}} \right) \left(\frac{1000 \text{ m}}{1 \text{ km}} \right)$$

$$= 34.7 \text{ m/s}$$

$$x = v_x t = (34.7 \text{ m/s})(14.3 \text{ s}) = 496 \text{ m}$$

46. Divers in Acapulco dive from a cliff that is 61 m high. If the rocks below the cliff extend outward for 23 m, what is the minimum horizontal velocity a diver must have to clear the rocks?

$$y = v_{y0}t - \frac{1}{2} gt^2$$

   and since initial velocity is zero,

$$t = \sqrt{\frac{-2y}{g}} = \sqrt{\frac{(-2)(-61 \text{ m})}{9.80 \text{ m/s}^2}}$$

$$= \sqrt{12.4 \text{ s}^2} = 3.53 \text{ s}$$

$$v_x = \frac{x}{t} = \frac{23 \text{ m}}{3.53 \text{ s}} = 6.5 \text{ m/s}$$

47. A dart player throws a dart horizontally at a speed of 12.4 m/s. The dart hits the board 0.32 m below the height from which it was thrown. How far away is the player from the board?

$$y = v_{y0}t - \frac{1}{2} gt^2$$

   and since $v_{y0} = 0$

$$t = \sqrt{\frac{-2y}{g}} = \sqrt{\frac{-2(-0.32 \text{ m})}{9.80 \text{ m/s}^2}}$$

$$= 0.26 \text{ s}$$

   Now $x = v_x t = (12.4 \text{ m/s})(0.26 \text{ s})$

$$= 3.2 \text{ m}$$

48. A basketball player tries to make a half-court jump shot, releasing the ball at the height of the basket. Assuming that the ball is launched at 51.0°, 14.0 m from the basket, what speed must the player give the ball?

   The components of the initial velocity are

$$v_{x0} = v_0 \cos \theta_0 \text{ and } v_{y0} = v_0 \sin \theta_0$$

Copyright © by Glencoe/McGraw-Hill

48. (continued)

Now $x = v_{x0}t = (v_0 \cos \theta_0)t$, so

$$t = \frac{x}{v_0 \cos \theta_0}$$

And $y = v_{y0}t - \frac{1}{2}gt^2$, but $y = 0$, so

$$0 = \left[v_{y0} - \frac{1}{2}gt\right]t$$

Therefore, $t = 0$ or $v_{y0} - \frac{1}{2}gt = 0$, or, from above,

$$v_0 \sin \theta_0 - \frac{1}{2}g\left[\frac{x}{v_0 \cos \theta_0}\right] = 0$$

Multiplying by $v_0 \cos \theta_0$ gives

$$v_0^2 \sin \theta_0 \cos \theta_0 - \frac{1}{2}gx = 0$$

so $v_0 = \sqrt{\dfrac{gx}{2 \sin \theta \cos \theta}}$

$$= \sqrt{\frac{(9.80 \text{ m/s}^2)(14.0 \text{ m})}{2(\sin 51.0°)(\cos 51.0°)}}$$

$v_0 = 11.8$ m/s

Section 7.3

Level 1

49. A 615-kg racing car completes one lap in 14.3 s around a circular track with a radius of 50.0 m. The car moves at constant speed.

a. What is the acceleration of the car?

$$v = \frac{2\pi r}{T} = \frac{2\pi (50.0 \text{ m})}{14.3 \text{ s}}$$

$$= 22.0 \text{ m/s}$$

$$a_c = \frac{v^2}{r}$$

$$= \frac{(22.0 \text{ m/s})^2}{50.0 \text{ m}} = 9.68 \text{ m/s}^2$$

b. What force must the track exert on the tires to produce this acceleration?

$$F_c = ma_c = (615 \text{ kg})(9.68 \text{ m/s}^2)$$

$$= 5.95 \times 10^3 \text{ N}$$

50. An athlete whirls a 7.00-kg hammer tied to the end of a 1.3-m chain in a horizontal circle. The hammer makes one revolution in 1.0 s.

a. What is the centripetal acceleration of the hammer?

$$a_c = \frac{4\pi^2 r}{T^2} = \frac{(4\pi^2)(1.3 \text{ m})}{(1.0 \text{ s})^2} = 51 \text{ m/s}^2$$

b. What is the tension in the chain?

$$F_c = ma_c = (7.00 \text{ kg})(51 \text{ m/s}^2)$$

$$= 3.6 \times 10^2 \text{ N}$$

51. A coin is placed on a vinyl stereo record making 33 1/3 revolutions per minute.

a. In what direction is the acceleration of the coin?

The acceleration is toward the center of the record.

b. Find the magnitude of the acceleration when the coin is placed 5.0, 10.0, and 15.0 cm from the center of the record.

$$T = \frac{1}{f} = \frac{1}{33\frac{1}{3} \text{ /min}}$$

$$= (0.0300 \text{ min})\left(\frac{60 \text{ s}}{1 \text{ min}}\right) = 1.80 \text{ s}$$

$r = 5.0$ cm: $a_c = \dfrac{4\pi^2 r}{T^2} = \dfrac{4\pi^2(0.05 \text{ m})}{(1.80 \text{ s})^2}$

$$= 0.61 \text{ m/s}^2$$

$r = 10.0$ cm: $a_c = \dfrac{4\pi^2 r}{T^2} = \dfrac{4\pi^2(0.100 \text{ m})}{(1.80 \text{ s})}$

$$= 1.22 \text{ m/s}^2$$

$r = 15.0$ cm: $a_c = \dfrac{4\pi^2 r}{T^2} = \dfrac{4\pi^2(0.150 \text{ m})}{(1.80 \text{ s})^2}$

$$= 1.83 \text{ m/s}^2$$

c. What force accelerates the coin?

frictional force between coin and record

d. In which of the three radii listed in **b** would the coin be most likely to fly off? Why?

15 cm

The largest radius because force needed to hold it is the greatest.

Copyright © by Glencoe/McGraw-Hill

52. According to the *Guinness Book of World Records* (1990) the highest rotary speed ever attained was 2010 m/s (4500 mph). The rotating rod was 15.3 cm (6 in.) long. Assume that the speed quoted is that of the end of the rod.

a. What is the centripetal acceleration of the end of the rod?

$$a_c = \frac{v^2}{r} = \frac{(2010 \text{ m/s})^2}{0.153 \text{ m}}$$

$$= 2.64 \times 10^7 \text{ m/s}^2$$

b. If you were to attach a 1.0-g object to the end of the rod, what force would be needed to hold it on the rod?

$$F_c = ma_c$$

$$= (0.0010 \text{ kg})(2.64 \times 10^7 \text{ m/s}^2)$$

$$= 2.6 \times 10^4 \text{ N}$$

53. Early skeptics of the idea of a rotating Earth said that the fast spin of Earth would throw people at the equator into space. The radius of Earth is about 6.38×10^3 km. Show why this objection is wrong by calculating

a. the speed of a 97-kg person at the equator.

$$v = \frac{\Delta d}{\Delta t} = \frac{2\pi r}{T} = \frac{2\pi(6.38 \times 10^6 \text{ m})}{\left(\frac{24 \text{ h}}{1}\right)\left(\frac{3600 \text{ s}}{1 \text{ h}}\right)}$$

$$= 464 \text{ m/s}$$

b. the force needed to accelerate the person in the circle.

$$F_c = ma_c = \frac{mv^2}{r} = \frac{(97 \text{ kg})(464 \text{ m/s})^2}{6.38 \times 10^6 \text{ m}}$$

$$= 3.3 \text{ N}$$

c. the weight of the person.

$$F_g = mg = (97 \text{ kg})(9.80 \text{ m/s}^2) = 950 \text{ N}$$

$$= 9.5 \times 10^2 \text{ N}$$

d. the normal force of Earth on the person, that is, the person's apparent weight.

$$F_N = 9.5 \times 10^2 \text{ N} - 3.3 \text{ N}$$

$$= 9.5 \times 10^2 \text{ N}$$

Level 2

54. The carnival ride shown in **Figure 7–18** has a 2.0-m radius and rotates once each 0.90 s.

a. Find the speed of a rider.

$$v = \frac{\Delta d}{\Delta t} = \frac{2\pi r}{T} = \frac{2\pi(2.0 \text{ m})}{0.90 \text{ s}} = 14 \text{ m/s}$$

b. Find the centripetal acceleration of a rider.

$$a_c = \frac{v^2}{r} = \frac{(14 \text{ m/s})^2}{2.0 \text{ m}} = 98 \text{ m/s}^2$$

c. What produces this acceleration?

force of the drum walls

d. When the floor drops down, riders are held up by friction. Draw motion and free-body diagrams of the situation.

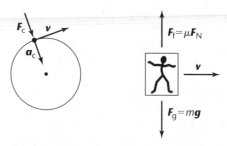

e. What coefficient of static friction is needed to keep the riders from slipping?

Downward force of gravity $F_g = mg$.

Frictional force $F_f = \mu F_N$.

F_N is the force of the drum, ma_c.

To balance, $mg = \mu ma_c$, or $g = \mu a_c$, so we need

$$\mu = \frac{g}{a_c} = \frac{9.80 \text{ m/s}^2}{98 \text{ m/s}^2} = 0.10$$

Copyright © by Glencoe/McGraw-Hill

55. Friction provides the force needed for a car to travel around a flat, circular race track. What is the maximum speed at which a car can safely travel if the radius of the track is 80.0 m and the coefficient of friction is 0.40?

$$F_c = F_f = \mu F_N = \mu mg$$

But $F_c = \dfrac{mv^2}{r}$, thus $\dfrac{mv^2}{r} = \mu mg$.

The mass of the car divides out to

give $v^2 = \mu gr$, so

$v = \sqrt{\mu gr}$
$= \sqrt{(0.40)(9.80 \text{ m/s}^2)(80.0 \text{ m})}$
$= 18 \text{ m/s}$

Critical Thinking Problems

56. A ball on a light string moves in a vertical circle. Analyze and describe the motion of this system. Be sure to consider the effects of gravity and tension. Is this system in uniform circular motion? Explain your answer.

It is not uniform circular motion. Gravity increases the speed of the ball when it moves downward and reduces the speed when it is moving upward. Therefore, the centripetal acceleration needed to keep it moving in a circle will be larger at the bottom and smaller at the top of the circle. At the top, tension and gravity are in the same direction, so the tension needed will be even smaller. At the bottom, gravity is outward while the tension is inward. Thus, the tension exerted by the string must be even larger.

57. Consider a roller coaster loop. Are the cars traveling through the loop in uniform circular motion? Explain. What about the ride in **Figure 7–18?**

The vertical gravitational force changes the speed of the cars, so the motion is not uniform circular motion. The ride in 7-18 is in uniform circular motion as long as the motor keeps its speed constant. When the ride is level, the outer rim of the ride provides the centripetal force on the rider. When it is tilted, the gravitational force is inward at the top of the ride and outward at the bottom. Therefore, the force of the rim (or fence) on the rider varies.

58. A 3-point jump shot is released 2.2 m above the ground, 6.02 m from the basket, which is 3.05 m high. For launch angles of 30° and 60°, find the speed needed to make the basket.

Let h be the height of the basket above the release point (0.85 m) and R the horizontal distance to the basket (6.02 m). Then the speed

$$v = \frac{R}{\cos\theta}\left(\frac{g}{R\tan\theta - h}\right)^{1/2}$$

At 30 degrees the speed is 13.4 m/s. At 60 degrees it is 12.2 m/s.

59. For which angle in problem 58 is it more important that the player get the speed right? To explore this question, vary the speed at each angle by 5% and find the change in the range of the throw.

Varying the speed by 5% at 30 degrees changes R by 0.90 m in either direction. At 60 degrees it changes R by only 0.65 m. Thus the high launch angle is less sensitive to speed variations.

Copyright © by Glencoe/McGraw-Hill

8 Universal Gravitation

Practice Problems

8.1 Motion in the Heavens and on Earth
pages 176–184

page 180

1. An asteroid revolves around the sun with a mean (average) orbital radius twice that of Earth's. Predict the period of the asteroid in Earth years.

$$\left(\frac{T_a}{T_E}\right)^2 = \left(\frac{r_a}{r_E}\right)^3 \text{ with } r_a = 2r_E$$

Thus, $T_a = \left[\left(\frac{r_a}{r_E}\right)^3 T_E^2\right]^{1/2}$

$$= \left[\left(\frac{2r_E}{r_E}\right)^3 (1.0 \text{ yr})^2\right]^{1/2} = 2.8 \text{ yr}$$

page 181

2. From **Table 8–1,** you can calculate that, on the average, Mars is 1.52 times as far from the sun as Earth is. Predict the time required for Mars to circle the sun in Earth days.

$$\left(\frac{T_M}{T_E}\right)^2 = \left(\frac{r_M}{r_E}\right)^3 \text{ with } r_M = 1.52r_E$$

Thus, $T_M^2 = \left(\frac{r_M}{r_E}\right)^3 T_E^2 = \left(\frac{1.52r_E}{r_E}\right)^3 (365 \text{ days})^2$

$$= 4.68 \times 10^5 \text{ days}^2$$

$T_M = 684 \text{ days}$

3. The moon has a period of 27.3 days and has a mean distance of 3.90×10^5 km from the center of Earth. Find the period of an artificial satellite that is in orbit 6.70×10^3 km from the center of Earth.

$$\left(\frac{T_s}{T_m}\right)^2 = \left(\frac{r_s}{r_m}\right)^3$$

so $T_s^2 = \left(\frac{r_s}{r_m}\right)^3 T_m^2$

$$= \left(\frac{6.70 \times 10^3 \text{ km}}{3.90 \times 10^5 \text{ km}}\right)^3 (27.3 \text{ days})^2$$

$$= 3.78 \times 10^{-3} \text{ days}^2$$

$T_s = 6.15 \times 10^{-2} \text{ days} = 88.6 \text{ min}$

Copyright © by Glencoe/McGraw-Hill

Physics: Principles and Problems

4. Using the data on the period and radius of revolution of the moon in problem 3, predict what the mean distance from Earth's center would be for an artificial satellite that has a period of 1.00 day.

$$\left(\frac{T_s}{T_m}\right)^2 = \left(\frac{r_s}{r_m}\right)^3$$

so $r_s^3 = r_m^3 \left(\frac{T_s}{T_m}\right)^2 = (3.90 \times 10^5 \text{ km})^3 \left(\frac{1.00}{27.3}\right)^2$

$\quad = 7.96 \times 10^{13} \text{ km}^3$

So $r_s = 4.30 \times 10^4 \text{ km}$

8.2 Using the Law of Universal Gravitation
pages 185–192

page 188

Assume a circular orbit for all calculations.

5. Use Newton's thought experiment on the motion of satellites to solve the following.

   a. Calculate the speed that a satellite shot from the cannon must have in order to orbit Earth 150 km above its surface.

   $$v = \sqrt{\frac{Gm_E}{r}} = \sqrt{\frac{(6.67 \times 10^{-11} \text{ N} \cdot \text{m}^2/\text{kg}^2)(5.97 \times 10^{24} \text{ kg})}{6.52 \times 10^6 \text{ m}}}$$

   $\quad = 7.81 \times 10^3 \text{ m/s}$

   b. How long, in seconds and minutes, would it take for the satellite to complete one orbit and return to the cannon?

   $$T = 2\pi \sqrt{\frac{r^3}{Gm_E}} = 2\pi \sqrt{\frac{(6.52 \times 10^6 \text{ m})^3}{(6.67 \times 10^{-11} \text{ N} \cdot \text{m}^2/\text{kg}^2)(5.97 \times 10^{24} \text{ kg})}}$$

   $\quad = 5.24 \times 10^3 \text{ s} = 87.3 \text{ min}$

6. Use the data for Mercury in **Table 8–1** to find

   a. the speed of a satellite in orbit 265 km above Mercury's surface.

   $$v = \sqrt{\frac{Gm_M}{r}} \text{ with } r = r_M + 265 \text{ km}$$
   $$r = 2.44 \times 10^6 \text{ m} + 0.265 \times 10^6 \text{ m}$$
   $$\quad = 2.71 \times 10^6 \text{ m}$$

   $$v = \sqrt{\frac{(6.67 \times 10^{-11} \text{ N} \cdot \text{m}^2/\text{kg}^2)(3.30 \times 10^{23} \text{ kg})}{2.71 \times 10^6 \text{ m}}}$$

   $\quad = 2.85 \times 10^3 \text{ m/s}$

   b. the period of the satellite.

   $$T = 2\pi \sqrt{\frac{r^3}{Gm_M}} = 2\pi \sqrt{\frac{(2.71 \times 10^6 \text{ m})^3}{(6.67 \times 10^{-11} \text{ N} \cdot \text{m}^2/\text{kg}^2)(3.30 \times 10^{23} \text{ kg})}}$$

   $\quad = 5.97 \times 10^3 \text{ s} = 1.66 \text{ h}$

Copyright © by Glencoe/McGraw-Hill

7. Find the speeds with which Mercury and Saturn move around the sun. Does it make sense that Mercury is named after a speedy messenger of the gods, whereas Saturn is named after the father of Jupiter?

$$v = \sqrt{\frac{Gm}{r}}\text{ , where here } m \text{ is the mass of the sun.}$$

$$v_M = \sqrt{\frac{(6.67 \times 10^{-11}\text{ N} \cdot \text{m}^2/\text{kg}^2)(1.99 \times 10^{30}\text{ kg})}{5.79 \times 10^{10}\text{ m}}}$$

$$= 4.79 \times 10^4\text{ m/s}$$

$$v_S = \sqrt{\frac{(6.67 \times 10^{-11}\text{ N} \cdot \text{m}^2/\text{kg}^2)(1.99 \times 10^{30}\text{ kg})}{1.43 \times 10^{12}\text{ m}}}$$

$$= 9.63 \times 10^3\text{ m/s, about 1/5 as fast as Mercury}$$

Mercury is the smallest of the planets and revolves about the sun with a period of about 88 days. Following in order of distance from the sun are Venus, Earth, Mars, Jupiter, Saturn, Uranus, Neptune, and Pluto. Jupiter is the largest of the planets, but Saturn is nearly one-third the mass of Jupiter. Saturn is the last planet to be visible to the naked eye. At one time, it was assumed to *be* the last planet.

8. The sun is considered to be a satellite of our galaxy, the Milky Way. The sun revolves around the center of the galaxy with a radius of 2.2×10^{20} m. The period of one revolution is 2.5×10^8 years.

a. Find the mass of the galaxy.

$$\text{Use } T = 2\pi\sqrt{\frac{r^3}{Gm}}\text{ , with}$$

$$T = 2.5 \times 10^8\text{ y} = 7.9 \times 10^{15}\text{ s}$$

$$m = \frac{4\pi^2 r^3}{GT^2} = \frac{4\pi^2(2.2 \times 10^{20}\text{ m})^3}{(6.67 \times 10^{-11}\text{ N} \cdot \text{m}^2/\text{kg}^2)(7.9 \times 10^{15}\text{ s})^2}$$

$$= 1.0 \times 10^{41}\text{ kg}$$

b. Assuming that the average star in the galaxy has the same mass as the sun, find the number of stars.

$$\text{number of stars} = \frac{\text{total galaxy mass}}{\text{mass per star}}$$

$$= \frac{1.0 \times 10^{41}\text{ kg}}{2.0 \times 10^{30}\text{ kg}} = 5.0 \times 10^{10}$$

c. Find the speed with which the sun moves around the center of the galaxy.

$$v = \sqrt{\frac{Gm}{r}} = \sqrt{\frac{(6.67 \times 10^{-11}\text{ N} \cdot \text{m}^2/\text{kg}^2)(1.0 \times 10^{41}\text{ kg})}{2.2 \times 10^{20}\text{ m}}}$$

$$= 1.7 \times 10^5\text{ m/s} = 6.1 \times 10^5\text{ km/h}$$

Copyright © by Glencoe/McGraw-Hill

Physics: Principles and Problems

Chapter Review Problems

pages 195–197

page 195

Section 8.1

Level 1

Use $G = 6.67 \times 10^{-11}$ N $\cdot$ m^2/kg^2.

31. Jupiter is 5.2 times farther from the sun than Earth is. Find Jupiter's orbital period in Earth years.

$$\left(\frac{T_J}{T_E}\right)^2 = \left(\frac{r_J}{r_E}\right)^3$$

So $T_J^2 = \left(\frac{r_J}{r_E}\right)^3 T_E^2 = \left(\frac{5.2}{1.0}\right)^3 (1.0 \text{ yr})^2 = 141 \text{ yr}^2$

So $T_J = 12$ yr

32. An apparatus like the one Cavendish used to find G has a large lead ball that is 5.9 kg in mass and a small one that is 0.047 kg. Their centers are separated by 0.055 m. Find the force of attraction between them.

$$F = \frac{Gm_1m_2}{d^2} = \frac{(6.67 \times 10^{-11} \text{ N} \cdot \text{m}^2/\text{kg}^2)(5.9 \text{ kg})(4.7 \times 10^{-2} \text{ kg})}{(5.5 \times 10^{-2} \text{ m})^2} = 6.1 \times 10^{-9} \text{ N}$$

33. Use the data in **Table 8–1** to compute the gravitational force that the sun exerts on Jupiter.

$$F = \frac{Gm_Sm_J}{d^2} = \frac{(6.67 \times 10^{-11} \text{ N} \cdot \text{m}^2/\text{kg}^2)(1.99 \times 10^{30} \text{ kg})(1.90 \times 10^{27} \text{ kg})}{(7.78 \times 10^{11} \text{ m})^2}$$

$$= 4.17 \times 10^{23} \text{ N}$$

34. Tom has a mass of 70.0 kg and Sally has a mass of 50.0 kg. Tom and Sally are standing 20.0 m apart on the dance floor. Sally looks up and sees Tom. She feels an attraction. If the attraction is gravitational, find its size. Assume that both Tom and Sally can be replaced by spherical masses.

$$F = \frac{Gm_Tm_S}{d^2} = \frac{(6.67 \times 10^{-11} \text{ N} \cdot \text{m}^2/\text{kg}^2)(70.0 \text{ kg})(50.0 \text{ kg})}{(20.0 \text{ m})^2} = 5.84 \times 10^{-10} \text{ N}$$

35. Two balls have their centers 2.0 m apart. One ball has a mass of 8.0 kg. The other has a mass of 6.0 kg. What is the gravitational force between them?

$$F = \frac{Gm_1m_2}{r^2} = \frac{(6.67 \times 10^{-11} \text{ N} \cdot \text{m}^2/\text{kg}^2)(8.0 \text{ kg})(6.0 \text{ kg})}{(2.0 \text{ m})^2} = 8.0 \times 10^{-10} \text{ N}$$

36. Two bowling balls each have a mass of 6.8 kg. They are located next to each other with their centers 21.8 cm apart. What gravitational force do they exert on each other?

$$F = \frac{Gm_1m_2}{r^2} = \frac{(6.67 \times 10^{-11} \text{ N} \cdot \text{m}^2/\text{kg}^2)(6.8 \text{ kg})(6.8 \text{ kg})}{(0.218 \text{ m})^2} = 6.5 \times 10^{-8} \text{ N}$$

37. Assume that you have a mass of 50.0 kg and Earth has a mass of 5.97×10^{24} kg. The radius of Earth is 6.38×10^6 m.

a. What is the force of gravitational attraction between you and Earth?

$$F = \frac{Gm_Sm_E}{d^2} = \frac{(6.67 \times 10^{-11} \text{ N} \cdot \text{m}^2/\text{kg}^2)(50.0 \text{ kg})(5.97 \times 10^{24} \text{ kg})}{(6.38 \times 10^6 \text{ m})^2} = 489 \text{ N}$$

Copyright © by Glencoe/McGraw-Hill

Physics: Principles and Problems

37. (continued)

    b. What is your weight?

$$F_g = mg = (50.0 \text{ kg})(9.80 \text{ m/s}^2) = 4.90 \times 10^2 \text{ N}$$

38. The gravitational force between two electrons 1.00 m apart is 5.42×10^{-71} N. Find the mass of an electron.

$$F = \frac{Gm_1 m_2}{d^2} \text{ but } m_1 = m_2 = m_E$$

So $m_E^2 = \dfrac{Fd^2}{G} = \dfrac{(5.42 \times 10^{-71} \text{ N})(1.00 \text{ m})^2}{6.67 \times 10^{-11} \text{ N} \cdot \text{m}^2/\text{kg}^2} = 8.13 \times 10^{-61} \text{ kg}^2$

So $m_E = 9.01 \times 10^{-31}$ kg

39. A 1.0-kg mass weighs 9.8 N on Earth's surface, and the radius of Earth is roughly 6.4×10^6 m.

    a. Calculate the mass of Earth.

$$F = \frac{G\, m_1 m_2}{r^2}$$

$$m_E = \frac{Fr^2}{Gm} = \frac{(9.8 \text{ N})(6.4 \times 10^6 \text{ m})^2}{(6.67 \times 10^{-11} \text{ N} \cdot \text{m}^2/\text{kg}^2)(1.0 \text{ kg})} = 6.0 \times 10^{24} \text{ kg}$$

    b. Calculate the average density of Earth.

$$V = \frac{4}{3}\pi r^3 = \frac{(4\pi)(6.4 \times 10^6 \text{ m})^3}{3} = 1.1 \times 10^{21} \text{ m}^3$$

$$D = \frac{m}{V} = \frac{6.0 \times 10^{24} \text{kg}}{1.1 \times 10^{21}} \text{ m}^3 = 5.5 \times 10^3 \text{ kg/m}^3$$

40. Use the information for Earth in **Table 8–1** to calculate the mass of the sun, using Newton's version of Kepler's third law.

$$T^2 = \left(\frac{4\pi^2}{Gm}\right)r^3 \text{ so } mT^2 = \left(\frac{4\pi^2}{G}\right)r^3$$

and $m = \left(\dfrac{4\pi^2}{G}\right)\dfrac{r^3}{T^2} = \left(\dfrac{4\pi^2}{6.67 \times 10^{-11} \text{ N} \cdot \text{m}^2/\text{kg}^2}\right)\dfrac{(1.50 \times 10^{11} \text{ m})^3}{(3.156 \times 10^7 \text{ s})^2} = 2.01 \times 10^{30} \text{ kg}$

Level 2

41. Uranus requires 84 years to circle the sun. Find Uranus's orbital radius as a multiple of Earth's orbital radius.

$$\left(\frac{T_U}{T_E}\right)^2 = \left(\frac{r_U}{r_E}\right)^3$$

So $r_U^3 = \left(\dfrac{T_U}{T_E}\right)^2 r_E^3 = \left(\dfrac{84 \text{ yr}}{1.0 \text{ yr}}\right)^2 (1.0 r_E)^3 = 7.1 \times 10^3 \, r_E^3$

So $r_U = 19 r_E$

42. Venus has a period of revolution of 225 Earth days. Find the distance between the sun and Venus as a multiple of Earth's orbital radius.

$$\left(\frac{T_V}{T_E}\right)^2 = \left(\frac{r_V}{r_E}\right)^3$$

So $r_V^3 = \left(\dfrac{T_V}{T_E}\right)^2 r_E^3 = \left(\dfrac{225}{365}\right)^2 r_E^3 = 0.380 \, r_E^3$

So $r_V = 0.724 \, r_E$

Copyright © by Glencoe/McGraw-Hill

43. If a small planet were located 8.0 times as far from the sun as Earth is, how many years would it take the planet to orbit the sun?

$$\left(\frac{T_x}{T_E}\right)^2 = \left(\frac{r_x}{r_E}\right)^3$$

So $T_x^2 = \left(\frac{r_x}{r_E}\right)^3 T_E^2 = \left(\frac{8.0}{1.0}\right)^2 (1.0 \text{ yr})^2 = 512 \text{ yr}^2$

So $T_x = 23 \text{ yr}$

44. A satellite is placed in an orbit with a radius that is half the radius of the moon's orbit. Find its period in units of the period of the moon.

$$\left(\frac{T_s}{T_m}\right)^2 = \left(\frac{r_s}{r_m}\right)^3$$

So $T_s^2 = \left(\frac{r_s}{r_m}\right)^3 T_m^2 = \left(\frac{0.50 r_m}{r_m}\right)^3 T_m^2 = 0.125 \, T_m^2$

So $T_s = 0.35 T_m$

45. Two spherical balls are placed so that their centers are 2.6 m apart. The force between the two balls is 2.75×10^{-12} N. What is the mass of each ball if one ball is twice the mass of the other ball?

$$F = \frac{G m_1 m_2}{d^2}, \text{ but } m_2 = 2m_1$$

So $F = \frac{G(m_1)(2m_1)}{d^2}$

and $m_1 = \sqrt{\frac{Fd^2}{2G}} = \sqrt{\frac{(2.75 \times 10^{-12} \text{ N})(2.6 \text{ m})^2}{2(6.67 \times 10^{-11} \text{ N} \cdot \text{m}^2/\text{kg}^2)}}$

$m_1 = 0.37 \text{ kg}$

$m_2 = 2m_1 = 0.75 \text{ kg}$

46. The moon is 3.9×10^5 km from Earth's center and 1.5×10^8 km from the sun's center. If the masses of the moon, Earth, and the sun are 7.3×10^{22} kg, 6.0×10^{24} kg, and 2.0×10^{30} kg, respectively, find the ratio of the gravitational forces exerted by Earth and the sun on the moon.

$$F = \frac{G m_1 m_2}{d^2}$$

Earth on moon: $F_E = \frac{G(6.0 \times 10^{24} \text{ kg})(7.3 \times 10^{22} \text{ kg})}{(3.9 \times 10^8 \text{ m})^2} = 1.9 \times 10^{20} \text{ N}$

Sun on moon: $F_S = \frac{G(2.0 \times 10^{30} \text{ kg})(7.3 \times 10^{22} \text{ kg})}{(1.5 \times 10^{11} \text{ m})^2} = 4.3 \times 10^{20} \text{ N}$

Ratio is $\frac{F_E}{F_S} = \frac{1.9 \times 10^{20} \text{ N}}{4.3 \times 10^{20} \text{ N}} = \frac{1.0}{2.3}$

The sun pulls more than twice as hard on the moon as does Earth.

47. A force of 40.0 N is required to pull a 10.0-kg wooden block at a constant velocity across a smooth glass surface on Earth. What force would be required to pull the same wooden block across the same glass surface on the planet Jupiter?

$$\mu = \frac{F_f}{F_N} = \frac{F_f}{m_b g} \text{ where } m_b \text{ is the mass of the block.}$$

Copyright © by Glencoe/McGraw-Hill

47. (continued)

On Jupiter the normal force is equal to the gravitational attraction between the block and Jupiter, or

$$F_N = \frac{Gm_b m_J}{r_J^2}$$

Now $\mu = \dfrac{F_f}{F_N}$, so $F_{fJ} = \mu F_N = \mu \dfrac{Gm_b m_J}{r_J^2}$

But $\mu = \dfrac{F_f}{m_b g}$ so

$$F_{fJ} = \frac{F_f Gm_b m_J}{m_b g r_J^2} = \frac{(40.0 \text{ N})(6.67 \times 10^{-11} \text{ N} \cdot \text{m}^2/\text{kg}^2)(1.90 \times 10^{27} \text{ kg})}{(9.80 \text{ m/s}^2)(7.15 \times 10^7 \text{ m})^2} = 101 \text{ N}$$

Note, the mass of the block divided out.

48. Mimas, one of Saturn's moons, has an orbital radius of 1.87×10^8 m and an orbital period of about 23 h. Use Newton's version of Kepler's third law and these data to find Saturn's mass.

$$T^2 = \left(\frac{4\pi^2}{Gm}\right) r^3$$

so $m = \dfrac{4\pi^2 r^3}{GT^2} = \dfrac{4\pi^2 (1.87 \times 10^8 \text{ m})^3}{(6.67 \times 10^{-11} \text{ N} \cdot \text{m}^2/\text{kg}^2)(82\,800 \text{ s})^2} = 5.6 \times 10^{26} \text{ kg}$

page 196

49. Use Newton's version of Kepler's third law to find the mass of Earth. The moon is 3.9×10^8 m away from Earth, and the moon has a period of 27.33 days. Compare this mass to the mass found in problem 39.

$$T^2 = \left(\frac{4\pi^2}{Gm}\right) r^3$$

so $m = \left(\dfrac{4\pi^2}{G}\right) \dfrac{r^3}{T^2} = \left[\dfrac{4\pi^2}{6.67 \times 10^{-11} \text{ N} \cdot \text{m}^2/\text{kg}^2}\right] \dfrac{(3.9 \times 10^8 \text{ m})^3}{(2.361 \times 10^6 \text{ s})^2} = 6.3 \times 10^{24} \text{ kg}$

very close

Section 8.2

Level 1

50. A geosynchronous satellite is one that appears to remain over one spot on Earth. Assume that a geosynchronous satellite has an orbital radius of 4.23×10^7 m.

   a. Calculate its speed in orbit.

   $$v = \sqrt{\frac{Gm_E}{r}} = \sqrt{\frac{(6.67 \times 10^{-11} \text{ N} \cdot \text{m}^2/\text{kg}^2)(5.97 \times 10^{24} \text{ kg})}{(4.23 \times 10^7 \text{ m})}} = 9.43 \times 10^6 \text{ m}^2/\text{s}^2$$

   $= 3.07 \times 10^3$ m/s or 3.07 km/s

   b. Calculate its period.

   $$T = 2\pi \sqrt{\frac{r^3}{Gm_E}} = 2\pi \sqrt{\frac{(4.23 \times 10^7 \text{ m})^3}{(6.67 \times 10^{-11} \text{ N} \cdot \text{m}^2/\text{kg}^2)(5.97 \times 10^{24} \text{ kg})}} = 2\pi \sqrt{1.90 \times 10^8 \text{ s}^2}$$

   $= 8.66 \times 10^4$ s or 24.1 h

Copyright © by Glencoe/McGraw-Hill

51. The asteroid Ceres has a mass of 7×10^{20} kg and a radius of 500 km.

a. What is g on the surface?

$$g = \frac{Gm}{d^2} = \frac{(6.67 \times 10^{-11} \text{ N} \cdot \text{m}^2/\text{kg}^2)(7 \times 10^{20} \text{ kg})}{(500 \times 10^3 \text{ m})^2} = 0.2 \text{ m/s}^2$$

b. How much would an 85-kg astronaut weigh on Ceres?

$$F_g = mg = (85 \text{ kg})(0.2 \text{ m/s}^2) = 2 \times 10^1 \text{ N}$$

52. A 1.25-kg book in space has a weight of 8.35 N. What is the value of the gravitational field at that location?

$$g = \frac{F}{m} = \frac{8.35 \text{ N}}{1.25 \text{ kg}} = 6.68 \text{ N/kg}$$

53. The moon's mass is 7.34×10^{22} kg, and it is 3.8×10^8 m away from Earth. Earth's mass can be found in **Table 8–1**.

a. Calculate the gravitational force of attraction between Earth and the moon.

$$F = \frac{Gm_E m_m}{d^2} = \frac{(6.67 \times 10^{-11} \text{ N} \cdot \text{m}^2/\text{kg}^2)(5.97 \times 10^{24} \text{ kg})(7.34 \times 10^{22} \text{ kg})}{(3.8 \times 10^8 \text{ m})^2}$$

$$= 2.0 \times 10^{20} \text{ N}$$

b. Find Earth's gravitational field at the moon.

$$g = \frac{F}{m} = \frac{2.0 \times 10^{20} \text{ N}}{7.34 \times 10^{22} \text{ kg}} = 0.0028 \text{ N/kg}$$

54. Earth's gravitational field is 7.83 N/kg at the altitude of the space shuttle. What is the size of the force of attraction between a student with a mass of 45.0 kg and Earth?

$$g = \frac{F}{m}$$

So $F = mg = (45.0 \text{ kg})(7.83 \text{ N/kg}) = 352 \text{ N}$

Level 2

55. On July 19, 1969, *Apollo 11*'s orbit around the moon was adjusted to an average orbit of 111 km. The radius of the moon is 1785 km, and the mass of the moon is 7.3×10^{22} kg.

a. How many minutes did *Apollo 11* take to orbit the moon once?

$$T = 2\pi \sqrt{\frac{r^3}{Gm}} = 2\pi \sqrt{\frac{(1896 \times 10^3 \text{ m})^3}{(6.67 \times 10^{-11} \text{ N} \cdot \text{m}^2/\text{kg}^2)(7.3 \times 10^{22} \text{ kg})}} = 2\pi \sqrt{1.4 \times 10^6 \text{ s}^2}$$

$$= 7.4 \times 10^3 \text{ s} = 1.2 \times 10^2 \text{ min}$$

b. At what velocity did it orbit the moon?

$$v = \sqrt{\frac{Gm}{r}} = \sqrt{\frac{(6.67 \times 10^{-11} \text{ N} \cdot \text{m}^2/\text{kg}^2)(7.3 \times 10^{22} \text{ kg})}{1896 \times 10^3 \text{ m}}} = \sqrt{2.6 \times 10^6 \text{ m}^2/\text{s}^2}$$

$$= 1.6 \times 10^3 \text{ m/s}$$

56. The radius of Earth is about 6.38×10^3 km. A 7.20×10^3-N spacecraft travels away from Earth. What is the weight of the spacecraft at the following distances from Earth's surface?

a. 6.38×10^3 km

$$d = r_E + r_E = 2r_E$$

Therefore, $F_g = \frac{1}{4}$ original weight $= \frac{1}{4}(7.20 \times 10^3 \text{ N}) = 1.80 \times 10^3 \text{ N}$

Copyright © by Glencoe/McGraw-Hill

56. (continued)

    b. 1.28×10^4 km

$$d = r_E + 2r_E = 3r_E$$

$$F_g = \frac{1}{9}(7.20 \times 10^3 \text{ N}) = 8.00 \times 10^2 \text{ N}$$

57. How high does a rocket have to go above Earth's surface before its weight is half what it would be on Earth?

    Now $F_g \propto \dfrac{1}{d^2}$

    so $d \propto \sqrt{\dfrac{1}{F_g}}$

    If the weight is $\dfrac{1}{2}$, the distance is $\sqrt{2}(r_E)$ or

$$d = \sqrt{2}\,(6.38 \times 10^6 \text{ m}) = 9.02 \times 10^6 \text{ m}$$

$$9.02 \times 10^6 \text{ m} - 6.38 \times 10^6 \text{ m} = 2.64 \times 10^6 \text{ m} = 2.64 \times 10^3 \text{ km}$$

58. The following formula represents the period of a pendulum, T.

$$T = 2\pi \sqrt{\frac{l}{g}}$$

    a. What would be the period of a 2.0-m-long pendulum on the moon's surface? The moon's mass is 7.34×10^{22} kg, and its radius is 1.74×10^6 m.

$$g_m = \frac{Gm_m}{d_m^2} = \frac{(6.67 \times 10^{-11} \text{ Nm}^2/\text{kg}^2)(7.34 \times 10^{22} \text{ kg})}{(1.74 \times 10^6 \text{ m})^2} = 1.62 \text{ m/s}^2$$

$$T = 2\pi \sqrt{\frac{l}{g}} = 2\pi \sqrt{\frac{2.0 \text{ m}}{1.62 \text{ m/s}^2}} = 7.0 \text{ s}$$

    b. What is the period of this pendulum on Earth?

$$T = 2\pi \sqrt{\frac{l}{g}} = 2\pi \sqrt{\frac{2.0 \text{ m}}{9.80 \text{ m/s}^2}} = 2.8 \text{ s}$$

Critical Thinking Problems

59. Some people say that the tides on Earth are caused by the pull of the moon. Is this statement true?

    a. Determine the forces that the moon and the sun exert on a mass, m, of water on Earth. Your answer will be in terms of m with units of N.

$$F_{s,m} = 6.67 \times 10^{-11} \frac{\text{N} \cdot \text{m}^2}{\text{kg}^2} \left(\frac{(1.99 \times 10^{30} \text{ kg})(m)}{(1.50 \times 10^{11} \text{ m})^2} \right) = (5.90 \times 10^{-3} \text{ N})\, m$$

$$F_{m,m} = 6.67 \times 10^{-11} \frac{\text{N} \cdot \text{m}^2}{\text{kg}^2} \left(\frac{(7.36 \times 10^{22} \text{ kg})(m)}{(3.80 \times 10^8 \text{ m})^2} \right) = (3.40 \times 10^{-5} \text{ N})\, m$$

    b. Which celestial body, the sun or the moon, has a greater pull on the waters of Earth?

    The sun pulls approximately 100 times stronger on the waters of Earth.

Copyright © by Glencoe/McGraw-Hill

59. (continued)

   c. Determine the difference in force exerted by the moon on the water at the near surface and the water at the far surface (on the opposite side of Earth), as illustrated in **Figure 8–13**. Again, your answer will be in terms of m with units of N.

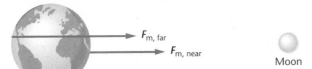

Earth   Moon

FIGURE 8-13

$F_{m,mA} - F_{m,mB}$

$$= \left(6.67 \times 10^{-11} \frac{N \cdot m^2}{kg^2}\right)(7.36 \times 10^{22} \text{ kg})(m)$$

$$\times \left[\frac{1}{(3.80 \times 10^8 \text{ m} - 6.37 \times 10^6 \text{ m})^2} - \frac{1}{(3.80 \times 10^8 \text{ m} + 6.37 \times 10^6 \text{ m})^2}\right]$$

$$= (2.28 \times 10^{-6} \text{ N}) \, m$$

   d. Determine the difference in force exerted by the sun on water at the near surface and water at the far surface (on the opposite side of Earth.)

$F_{s,mA} - F_{s,mB}$

$$= \left(6.67 \times 10^{-11} \frac{N \cdot m^2}{kg^2}\right)(1.99 \times 10^{30} \text{ kg})(m)$$

$$\times \left[\frac{1}{(1.50 \times 10^{11} \text{ m} - 6.37 \times 10^6 \text{ m})^2} - \frac{1}{(1.50 \times 10^{11} \text{ m} + 6.37 \times 10^6 \text{ m})^2}\right]$$

$$= (1.00 \times 10^{-6} \text{ N}) \, m$$

page 197

   e. Which celestial body has a greater difference in pull from one side of Earth to the other?

   the moon

   f. Why is the statement that the tides are due to the pull of the moon misleading? Make a correct statement to explain how the moon causes tides on Earth.

   The tides are due to the difference between the pull of the moon on Earth's near side and Earth's far side.

60. Graphing Calculator Use Newton's law of universal gravitation to find an equation where x is equal to an object's distance from Earth's center, and y is its acceleration due to gravity. Use a graphing calculator to graph this equation, using 6400–6600 km as the range for x and 9–10 m/s² as the range for y. The equation should be of the form $y = c(1/x^2)$. Trace along this graph and find y

   a. at sea level, 6400 km.

      9.77 m/s²

   b. on top of Mt. Everest, 6410 km.

      9.74 m/s²

   c. in a typical satellite orbit, 6500 km.

      9.47 m/s²

   d. in a much higher orbit, 6600 km.

      9.18 m/s²

Copyright © by Glencoe/McGraw-Hill

9 Momentum and Its Conservation

Practice Problems

9.1 Impulse and Momentum
pages 200–206

page 204

1. A compact car, mass 725 kg, is moving at 1.00×10^2 km/h toward the east. Sketch the moving car.

1.00×10² km/h

2.01×10⁴ kg·m/s east

   a. Find the magnitude and direction of its momentum. Draw an arrow on your picture showing the momentum.

   1.00×10^2 km/h = 27.8 m/s

   $p = mv = (725 \text{ kg})(27.8 \text{ m/s})$

   $= 2.01 \times 10^4$ kg · m/s eastward

   b. A second car, mass 2175 kg, has the same momentum. What is its velocity?

   $v = \dfrac{p}{m} = \dfrac{(2.01 \times 10^4 \text{ kg} \cdot \text{m/s})}{(2175 \text{ kg})}$

   $= 9.24 \text{ m/s} = 33.3$ km/h eastward

2. The driver of the compact car suddenly applies the brakes hard for 2.0 s. As a result, an average force of 5.0×10^3 N is exerted on the car to slow it. Sketch the situation.

   $\Delta t = 2.0$ s

   $F = -5.0 \times 10^3$ N

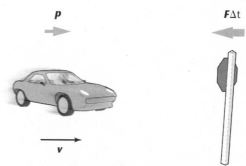

p   FΔt

v

   a. What is the change in momentum, that is the magnitude and direction of the impulse, on the car?

   Impulse $= F \Delta t = (-5.0 \times 10^3$ N)(2.0 s)

   $= -1.0 \times 10^4$ kg · m/s westward

   The impulse is directed westward and has a magnitude of 1.0×10^4 kg · m/s.

   b. Complete the "before" and "after" diagrams, and determine the new momentum of the car.

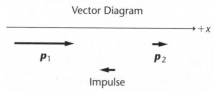

Before (State 1)   After (State 2)

v_1 v_2

Vector Diagram

+x

p_1 p_2

Impulse

   $p_1 = mv_1 = (725 \text{ kg})(27.8 \text{ m/s})$

   $= 2.01 \times 10^4$ kg · m/s eastward

   $F \Delta t = \Delta p = p_2 - p_1$

   $p_2 = F \Delta t + p_1$

   $= -1.0 \times 10^4$ kg · m/s

   $+ 2.01 \times 10^4$ kg · m/s

   $p_2 = 1.0 \times 10^4$ kg · m/s eastward

Copyright © by Glencoe/McGraw-Hill

2. (continued)

    c. What is the velocity of the car now?

$$p_2 = mv_2$$

$$v_2 = \frac{p_2}{m} = \frac{1.0 \times 10^4 \text{ kg} \cdot \text{m/s}}{725 \text{ kg}}$$

$$= 14 \text{ m/s} = 50 \text{ km/h eastward}$$

3. A 7.0-kg bowling ball is rolling down the alley with a velocity of 2.0 m/s. For each impulse, **a** and **b,** as shown in **Figure 9–3,** find the resulting speed and direction of motion of the bowling ball.

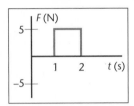
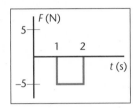

FIGURE 9-3

    a. impulse = $F \, \Delta t$

$$p_1 = mv_1 = (7.0 \text{ kg})(2.0 \text{ m/s})$$

$$= 14 \text{ kg} \cdot \text{m/s}$$

$$\text{impulse}_A = (5.0 \text{ N})(2.0 \text{ s} - 1.0 \text{ s})$$

$$= 5.0 \text{ N} \cdot \text{s} = 5.0 \text{ kg} \cdot \text{m/s}$$

$$F \, \Delta t = \Delta p = p_2 - p_1$$

$$p_2 = F \, \Delta t + p_1$$

$$p_2 = 5.0 \text{ kg} \cdot \text{m/s} + 14 \text{ kg} \cdot \text{m/s}$$

$$= 19 \text{ kg} \cdot \text{m/s}$$

$$p_2 = mv_2$$

$$v_2 = \frac{p_2}{m} = \frac{19 \text{ kg} \cdot \text{m/s}}{7.0 \text{ kg}}$$

$$= 2.7 \text{ m/s in the same direction}$$

    b. impulse = $F \, \Delta t$

$$\text{impulse}_B = (-5.0 \text{ N})(2.0 \text{ s} - 1.0 \text{ s})$$

$$= -5.0 \text{ N} \cdot \text{s} = -5.0 \text{ kg} \cdot \text{m/s}$$

$$F \, \Delta t = \Delta p = p_2 - p_1$$

$$p_2 = F \, \Delta t + p_1$$

$$p_2 = -5.0 \text{ kg} \cdot \text{m/s} + 14 \text{ kg} \cdot \text{m/s}$$

$$= 9.0 \text{ kg} \cdot \text{m/s}$$

$$p_2 = mv_2$$

$$v_2 = \frac{p_2}{m} = \frac{9.0 \text{ kg} \cdot \text{m/s}}{7.0 \text{ kg}}$$

$$= 1.3 \text{ m/s in the same direction}$$

page 205

4. The driver accelerates a 240.0 kg snowmobile, which results in a force being exerted that speeds the snowmobile up from 6.00 m/s to 28.0 m/s over a time interval of 60.0 s.

    a. Sketch the event, showing the initial and final situations.

    b. What is the snowmobile's change in momentum? What is the impulse on the snowmobile?

$$\Delta p = F \, \Delta t$$

$$= m(v_2 - v_1)$$

$$= 240.0 \text{ kg}(28.0 \text{ m/s} - 6.00 \text{ m/s})$$

$$= 5.28 \times 10^3 \text{ kg} \cdot \text{m/s}$$

    c. What is the magnitude of the average force that is exerted on the snowmobile?

$$F = \frac{\Delta p}{\Delta t} = \frac{5.28 \times 10^3 \text{ kg} \cdot \text{m/s}}{60.0 \text{ s}}$$

$$= 88.0 \text{ N}$$

Copyright © by Glencoe/McGraw-Hill

5. A 0.144-kg baseball is pitched horizontally at 38.0 m/s. After it is hit by the bat, it moves at the same speed, but in the opposite direction.

a. Draw arrows showing the ball's momentum before and after it hits the bat.

$m\mathbf{v}_1$ (ball)

$\mathbf{F}_{\text{Bat on ball}}t$

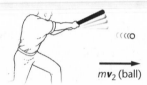

$m\mathbf{v}_2$ (ball)

Given: $m = 0.144$ kg
initial velocity, $v_1 = +38.0$ m/s
final velocity, $v_2 = -38.0$ m/s

Unknown: impulse

Basic equation: $F\Delta t = \Delta p$

b. What was the change in momentum of the ball?

Take the positive direction to be the direction of the ball after it leaves the bat.

$\Delta p = mv_2 - mv_1 = m(v_2 - v_1)$

$= (0.144 \text{ kg})(+38.0 \text{ m/s} - (-38.0 \text{ m/s}))$

$= (0.144 \text{ kg})(76.0 \text{ m/s})$

$= 10.9 \text{ kg} \cdot \text{m/s}$

c. What was the impulse delivered by the bat?

$F\Delta t = \Delta p = 10.9 \text{ kg} \cdot \text{m/s}$

d. If the bat and ball were in contact for 0.80 ms, what was the average force the bat exerted on the ball?

$F\Delta t = \Delta p$

So $F = \dfrac{\Delta p}{\Delta t} = \dfrac{10.9 \text{ kg} \cdot \text{m/s}}{8.0 \times 10^{-4} \text{ s}}$

$= 1.4 \times 10^4 \text{ N}$

6. A 60-kg person was in the car that hit the concrete wall in the example problem. The velocity of the person equals that of the car both before and after the crash, and the velocity changes in 0.20 s. Sketch the problem.

Before

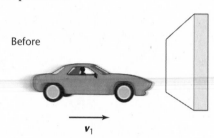

v_1

2200-kg car   60-kg person
94 km/h   94 km/h

During

v_2

2200-kg car   60-kg person
0 km/h   94 km/h

During

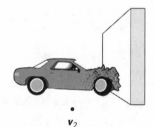

v_2

2200-kg car   60-kg person
0 km/h   0 km/h

Copyright © by Glencoe/McGraw-Hill

6. (continued)

a. What is the average force exerted on the person?

$F \Delta t = \Delta p = p_2 - p_1$

$p_2 = 0 \quad p_1 = mv_1$

$\left(\dfrac{94 \text{ km}}{1 \text{ h}}\right)\left(\dfrac{1000 \text{ m}}{1 \text{ km}}\right)\left(\dfrac{1 \text{ h}}{3600 \text{ s}}\right) = 26 \text{ m/s}$

$F = \dfrac{0 - mv_1}{\Delta t}$

$F = \dfrac{0 - (60 \text{ kg})(26 \text{ m/s})}{0.20 \text{ s}}$

$= 8 \times 10^3 \text{ N}$ opposite to the direction of motion

b. Some people think that they can stop themselves rushing forward by putting their hands on the dashboard. Find the mass of the object that has a weight equal to the force you just calculated. Could you lift such a mass? Are you strong enough to stop yourself with your arms?

$F_g = mg$

$m = \dfrac{F_g}{g} = \dfrac{8 \times 10^3 \text{ N}}{9.80 \text{ m/s}^2} = 800 \text{ kg}$

Such a mass is too heavy to lift. You cannot safely stop yourself with your arms.

9.2 The Conservation of Momentum
pages 207–216

page 210

7. Two freight cars, each with a mass of 3.0×10^5 kg, collide. One was initially moving at 2.2 m/s; the other was at rest. They stick together. What is their final speed?

$p_1 = p_2$

$(3.0 \times 10^5 \text{ kg})(2.2 \text{ m/s})$

$= (2)(3.0 \times 10^5 \text{ kg})(v)$

$v = 1.1 \text{ m/s}$

8. A 0.105-kg hockey puck moving at 24 m/s is caught and held by a 75-kg goalie at rest. With what speed does the goalie slide on the ice?

$p_{h1} + p_{g1} = p_{h2} + p_{g2}$

$m_h v_{h1} + m_g v_{g1} = m_h v_{h2} + m_g v_{g2}$

Since $v_{g1} = 0$, $m_h v_{h1} = (m_h + m_g)v_2$

where $v_2 = v_{h2} = v_{g2}$ is the common final speed of goalie and puck.

$v_2 = \dfrac{m_h v_{h1}}{(m_h + m_g)}$

$= \dfrac{(0.105 \text{ kg})(24 \text{ m/s})}{(0.105 \text{ kg} + 75 \text{ kg})} = 0.034 \text{ m/s}$

9. A 35.0-g bullet strikes a 5.0-kg stationary wooden block and embeds itself in the block. The block and bullet fly off together at 8.6 m/s. What was the original speed of the bullet?

$m_b v_{b1} + m_w v_{w1} = (m_b + m_w)v_2$

where v_2 is the common final velocity of bullet and wooden block.

Since $v_{w1} = 0$,

$v_{b1} = \dfrac{(m_b + m_w)v_2}{m_b}$

$= \dfrac{(0.0350 + 5.0 \text{ kg})(8.6 \text{ m/s})}{0.0350 \text{ kg}}$

$= 1.2 \times 10^3 \text{ m/s}$

10. A 35.0-g bullet moving at 475 m/s strikes a 2.5-kg wooden block that is at rest. The bullet passes through the block, leaving at 275 m/s. How fast is the block moving when the bullet leaves?

$m_b v_{b1} + m_w v_{w1}$

$= m_b v_{b2} + m_w v_{w2}$ with $v_{w1} = 0$

$v_{w2} = \dfrac{(m_b v_{b1} - m_b v_{b2})}{m_w}$

$= \dfrac{m_b(v_{b1} - v_{b2})}{m_w}$

$= \dfrac{(0.0350 \text{ kg})(475 \text{ m/s} - 275 \text{ m/s})}{2.5 \text{ kg}}$

$= 2.8 \text{ m/s}$

Copyright © by Glencoe/McGraw-Hill

11. Glider A, with a mass of 0.355 kg, moves along a frictionless air track with a velocity of 0.095 m/s, as in **Figure 9–7.** It collides with glider B, with a mass of 0.710 kg and a speed of 0.045 m/s in the same direction. After the collision, glider A continues in the same direction at 0.035 m/s. What is the speed of glider B?

$$p_{A1} + p_{B1} = p_{A2} + p_{B2}$$

so $p_{B2} = p_{B1} + p_{A1} - p_{A2}$

$$m_B v_{B2} = m_B v_{B1} + m_A v_{A1} - m_A v_{A2}$$

or $v_{B2} = \dfrac{m_B v_{B1} + m_A v_{A1} - m_A v_{A2}}{m_B}$

$$= \dfrac{(0.710 \text{ kg})(+0.045 \text{ m/s})}{0.710 \text{ kg}}$$

$$+ \dfrac{(0.355 \text{ kg})(+0.095 \text{ m/s})}{0.710 \text{ kg}}$$

$$- \dfrac{(0.355 \text{ kg})(+0.035 \text{ m/s})}{0.710 \text{ kg}}$$

$$= 0.075 \text{ m/s in the initial}$$
direction

12. A 0.50-kg ball traveling at 6.0 m/s collides head-on with a 1.00-kg ball moving in the opposite direction at a speed of 12.0 m/s. The 0.50-kg ball bounces backward at 14 m/s after the collision. Find the speed of the second ball after the collision.

$$m_A v_{A1} + m_B v_{B1} = m_A v_{A2} + m_B v_{B2}$$

so v_{B2}

$$= \dfrac{m_A v_{A1} + m_B v_{B1} - m_A v_{A2}}{m_B}$$

$$= \dfrac{(0.50 \text{ kg})(6.0 \text{ m/s})}{1.00 \text{ kg}}$$

$$+ \dfrac{(1.00 \text{ kg})(-12.0 \text{ m/s})}{1.00 \text{ kg}}$$

$$- \dfrac{(0.50 \text{ kg})(-14 \text{ m/s})}{1.00 \text{ kg}}$$

$$= 2.0 \text{ m/s in the opposite direction}$$

page 214

13. A 4.00-kg model rocket is launched, shooting 50.0 g of burned fuel from its exhaust at a speed of 625 m/s. What is the velocity of the rocket after the fuel has burned? **Hint:** Ignore external forces of gravity and air resistance.

$$p_{r1} + p_{f1} = p_{r2} + p_{f2}$$

where $p_{r1} + p_{f1} = 0$

If the initial mass of the rocket (including fuel) is $m_r = 4.00$ kg, then the final mass of the rocket is

$$m_{r2} = 4.00 \text{ kg} - 0.0500 \text{ kg} = 3.95 \text{ kg}$$

$$0 = m_{r2} v_{r2} + m_f v_{f2}$$

$$v_{r2} = \dfrac{-m_f v_{f2}}{m_{r2}}$$

$$= \dfrac{-(0.0500 \text{ kg})(-625 \text{ m/s})}{3.95 \text{ kg}}$$

$$= 7.91 \text{ m/s}$$

14. A thread holds two carts together, as shown in **Figure 9-9.** After the thread is burned, a compressed spring pushes the carts apart, giving the 1.5-kg cart a speed of 27 cm/s to the left. What is the velocity of the 4.5-kg cart?

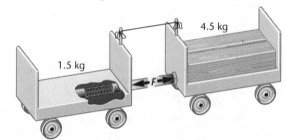

FIGURE 9-9

$$p_{A1} + p_{B1} = p_{A2} + p_{B2}$$

with $p_{A1} = p_{B1} = 0$

$$m_B v_{B2} = -m_A v_{A2}$$

So $v_{B2} = \dfrac{-m_A v_{A2}}{m_B}$

$$= \dfrac{-(1.5 \text{ kg})(-27 \text{ cm/s})}{4.5 \text{ kg}}$$

$$= 9.0 \text{ cm/s to the right}$$

Physics: Principles and Problems

Copyright © by Glencoe/McGraw-Hill

15. Two campers dock a canoe. One camper has a mass of 80.0 kg and moves forward at 4.0 m/s as she leaves the boat to step onto the dock. With what speed and direction do the canoe and the other camper move if their combined mass is 115 kg?

$$p_{A1} + p_{B1} = p_{A2} + p_{B2}$$

with $p_{A1} = p_{B1} = 0$

$$m_A v_{A2} = -m_B v_{B2}$$

So $v_{B2} = \dfrac{-m_A v_{A2}}{m_B}$

$$= \dfrac{-(80.0 \text{ kg})(4.0 \text{ m/s})}{115 \text{ kg}}$$

= 2.8 m/s in the opposite direction

16. A colonial gunner sets up his 225-kg cannon at the edge of the flat top of a high tower. It shoots a 4.5-kg cannonball horizontally. The ball hits the ground 215 m from the base of the tower. The cannon also moves on frictionless wheels, and falls off the back of the tower, landing on the ground.

a. What is the horizontal distance of the cannon's landing, measured from the base of the back of the tower?

Both the cannon and the ball fall to the ground in the same time from the same height. In that fall time, the ball moves 215 m, the cannon an unknown distance we will call x. Now

$$t = \dfrac{d}{v}$$

so $\dfrac{215 \text{ m}}{v_{\text{ball}}} = \dfrac{x}{v_{\text{cannon}}}$

so $x = 215 \text{ m} \left(\dfrac{v_{\text{cannon}}}{v_{\text{ball}}} \right)$ **related by**

conservation of momentum;

$$(4.5 \text{ kg}) v_{\text{ball}} = -(225 \text{ kg}) v_{\text{cannon}}$$

so $\left(\dfrac{-v_{\text{cannon}}}{v_{\text{ball}}} \right) = \dfrac{4.5 \text{ kg}}{225 \text{ kg}}$

Thus $x = -\left[\dfrac{4.5}{225} (215 \text{ m}) \right] = -4.3 \text{ m}$

b. Why don't you need to know the width of the tower?

While on top, the cannon moves with no friction, and its velocity doesn't change, so it can take any amount of time to reach the back edge.

page 216

17. A 1325-kg car moving north at 27.0 m/s collides with a 2165-kg car moving east at 17.0 m/s. They stick together. In what direction and with what speed do they move after the collision?

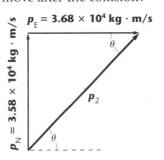

$$p_N + p_E = p_2 \text{ (vector sum)}$$

$$p_N = m_N v_N = (1325 \text{ kg})(27.0 \text{ m/s})$$

$$= 3.58 \times 10^4 \text{ kg} \cdot \text{m/s}$$

$$p_E = m_E v_E = (2165 \text{ kg})(17.0 \text{ m/s})$$

$$= 3.68 \times 10^4 \text{ kg} \cdot \text{m/s}$$

$$\tan \theta = \dfrac{p_N}{p_E} = \dfrac{3.58 \times 10^4 \text{ kg} \cdot \text{m/s}}{3.68 \times 10^4 \text{ kg} \cdot \text{m/s}}$$

$$= 0.973$$

$$\theta = 44.2° \text{ north of east}$$

$$(p_2)^2 = (p_N)^2 + (p_E)^2$$

$$= (3.58 \times 10^4 \text{ kg} \cdot \text{m/s})^2$$

$$\qquad + (3.68 \times 10^4 \text{ kg} \cdot \text{m/s})^2$$

$$= 2.64 \times 10^9 \text{ kg}^2 \text{ m}^2/\text{s}^2$$

$$p_2 = 5.13 \times 10^4 \text{ kg} \cdot \text{m/s}$$

$$p_2 = m_2 v_2 = (m_N + m_E) v_2$$

$$v_2 = \dfrac{p_2}{m_N + m_E}$$

$$= \dfrac{5.13 \times 10^4 \text{ kg} \cdot \text{m/s}}{1325 \text{ kg} + 2165 \text{ kg}} = 14.7 \text{ m/s}$$

Copyright © by Glencoe/McGraw-Hill

18. A stationary billiard ball, mass 0.17 kg, is struck by an identical ball moving at 4.0 m/s. After the collision, the second ball moves off at 60° to the left of its original direction. The stationary ball moves off 30° to the right of the moving ball's original direction. What is the velocity of each ball after the collision?

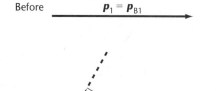

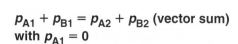

$p_{A1} + p_{B1} = p_{A2} + p_{B2}$ (vector sum) with $p_{A1} = 0$

$m_1 = m_2 = m = 0.17$ kg

$p_{B1} = m_{B1}v_{B1} = (0.17$ kg$)(4.0$ m/s$)$

$\quad = 0.68$ kg · m/s

$p_{A2} = p_{B1} \sin 60.0°$

$mv_{A2} = mv_{B1} \sin 60.0°$

$v_{A2} = v_{B1} \sin 60.0°$

$\quad = (4.0$ m/s$) \sin 60.0°$

$\quad = 3.5$ m/s, 30.0° to right

$p_{B2} = p_{B1} \cos 60.0°$

$mv_{B2} = mv_{B1} \cos 60.0°$

$v_{B2} = v_{B1} \cos 60.0°$

$\quad = (4.0$ m/s$) \cos 60.0°$

$\quad = 2.0$ m/s, 60.0° to left

Chapter Review Problems

page 218–221

page 218

Section 9.1

Level 1

22. Your brother's mass is 35.6 kg, and he has a 1.3-kg skateboard. What is the combined momentum of your brother and his skateboard if they are going 9.50 m/s?

Total mass is 35.6 kg + 1.3 kg

= 36.9 kg

$mv = (36.9$ kg$)(9.50$ m/s$)$

= 351 kg · m/s

23. A hockey player makes a slap shot, exerting a constant force of 30.0 N on the hockey puck for 0.16 s. What is the magnitude of the impulse given to the puck?

$F \Delta t = (30.0$ N$)(0.16$ s$) = 4.8$ kg · m/s

24. A hockey puck has a mass of 0.115 kg and is at rest. A hockey player makes a shot, exerting a constant force of 30.0 N on the puck for 0.16 s. With what speed does it head toward the goal?

$F \Delta t = m \Delta v$

so $\Delta v = \dfrac{F \Delta t}{m} = \dfrac{4.8 \text{ kg} \cdot \text{m/s}}{0.115 \text{ kg}} = 42$ m/s

25. Before a collision, a 25-kg object is moving at +12 m/s. Find the impulse that acted on the object if, after the collision, it moves at:

a. +8.0 m/s

$F \Delta t = m \Delta v$

$\quad = (25$ kg$)(8.0$ m/s $- 12$ m/s$)$

$\quad = -1.0 \times 10^2$ kg · m/s

b. −8.0 m/s

$F \Delta t = m \Delta v$

$\quad = (25$ kg$)(-8.0$ m/s $- 12$ m/s$)$

$\quad = -5.0 \times 10^2$ kg · m/s

Copyright © by Glencoe/McGraw-Hill

26. A constant force of 6.00 N acts on a 3.00-kg object for 10.0 s. What are the changes in the object's momentum and velocity?

$$m \, \Delta v = F \, \Delta t = (6.00 \text{ N})(10.0 \text{ s})$$

$$= 60.0 \text{ N} \cdot \text{s}$$

$$\text{So } \Delta v = \frac{F \, \Delta t}{m} = \frac{60.0 \text{ N} \cdot \text{s}}{3.00 \text{ kg}}$$

$$= 20.0 \text{ m/s}$$

27. The velocity of a 625-kg auto is changed from 10.0 m/s to 44.0 m/s in 68.0 s by an external, constant force.

a. What is the resulting change in momentum of the car?

$$\Delta p = m \, \Delta v$$

$$= (625 \text{ kg})(44.0 \text{ m/s} - 10.0 \text{ m/s})$$

$$= 2.13 \times 10^4 \text{ kg} \cdot \text{m/s}$$

b. What is the magnitude of the force?

$$F \, \Delta t = m \, \Delta v$$

$$\text{so } F = \frac{m \, \Delta v}{\Delta t} = \frac{2.13 \times 10^4 \text{ kg} \cdot \text{m/s}}{68.0 \text{ s}}$$

$$= 313 \text{ N}$$

28. An 845-kg dragster accelerates from rest to 100 km/h in 0.90 seconds.

a. What is the change in momentum of the car?

$$m \, \Delta v = (845 \text{ kg})$$

$$\times \left[\left(100 \, \frac{\text{km}}{\text{h}} \right) \left(\frac{1000 \text{ m}}{1 \text{ km}} \right) \left(\frac{1 \text{ h}}{3600 \text{ s}} \right) - 0 \right]$$

$$= 2 \times 10^4 \text{ kg} \cdot \text{m/s}$$

b. What is the average force exerted on the car?

$$F \, \Delta t = m \, \Delta v$$

$$\text{so } F = \frac{m \, \Delta v}{\Delta t} = \frac{2 \times 10^4 \text{ kg} \cdot \text{m/s}}{0.90 \text{ s}}$$

$$= 2 \times 10^4 \text{ N}$$

c. What exerts that force?

The force is exerted by the track through friction.

Level 2

29. A 0.150-kg ball, moving in the positive direction at 12 m/s, is acted on by the impulse shown in the graph in **Figure 9-12.** What is the ball's speed at 4.0 s?

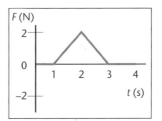

FIGURE 9-12

$$F \, \Delta t = m \, \Delta v$$

$$\text{Area of graph} = m \, \Delta v$$

$$\frac{1}{2} (2.0 \text{ N} \times 2.0 \text{ s}) = m(v - v_0)$$

$$2.0 \text{ N} \cdot \text{s} = (0.150 \text{ kg})(v - 12 \text{ m/s})$$

$$v = \frac{2.0 \text{ kg} \cdot \text{m/s}}{0.150 \text{ kg}} + 12 \text{ m/s}$$

$$v = 25 \text{ m/s}$$

30. Small rockets are used to make tiny adjustments in the speed of satellites. One such rocket has a thrust of 35 N. If it is fired to change the velocity of a 72 000-kg spacecraft by 63 cm/s, how long should it be fired?

$$F \, \Delta t = m \, \Delta v$$

$$\text{so } \Delta t = \frac{m \, \Delta v}{F} = \frac{(72 \text{ 000 kg})(0.63 \text{ m/s})}{35 \text{ N}}$$

$$= 1.3 \times 10^3 \text{ s or 22 min}$$

31. A car moving at 10 m/s crashes into a barrier and stops in 0.050 s. There is a 20-kg child in the car. Assume that the child's velocity is changed by the same amount as the car's in the same time period.

a. What is the impulse needed to stop the child?

$$F \, \Delta t = m \, \Delta v = (20 \text{ kg})(-10 \text{ m/s})$$

$$= -2 \times 10^2 \text{ kg} \cdot \text{m/s}$$

Copyright © by Glencoe/McGraw-Hill

31. (continued)

b. What is the average force on the child?

$$F \Delta t = m \Delta v$$

$$\text{so } F = \frac{m \Delta v}{\Delta t} = \frac{-2 \times 10^2 \text{ kg} \cdot \text{m/s}}{5.0 \times 10^{-2} \text{ s}}$$

$$= -4 \times 10^3 \text{ N}$$

c. What is the approximate mass of an object whose weight equals the force in part **b**?

$$F_g = mg$$

$$\text{so } m = \frac{F_g}{g} = \frac{4 \times 10^3 \text{ N}}{9.80 \text{ m/s}^2}$$

$$= 4 \times 10^2 \text{ kg}$$

d. Could you lift such a weight with your arm?

No

e. Why is it advisable to use a proper infant restraint rather than hold a child on your lap?

You would not be able to protect a child on your lap in the event of a collision.

32.

An animal-rescue plane flying due east at 36.0 m/s drops a bale of hay from an altitude of 60.0 m. If the bale of hay weighs 175 N, what is the momentum of the bale the moment before it strikes the ground? Give both magnitude and direction.

First use projectile motion to find the velocity of the bale.

$$v_x = 36.0 \text{ m/s}$$

$$v_y^2 = v_{0y}^2 + 2dg$$

$$\text{so } v_y = \sqrt{2dg}$$

$$= \sqrt{2(-60.0 \text{ m})(-9.80 \text{ m/s}^2)}$$

$$= \sqrt{1.18 \times 10^3 \text{ m}^2/\text{s}^2} = 34.3 \text{ m/s}$$

$$v = \sqrt{v_x^2 + v_y^2}$$

$$= \sqrt{(36.0 \text{ m/s})^2 + (34.3 \text{ m/s})^2}$$

$$= 49.7 \text{ m/s}$$

Now find the mass from $F = mg$, so

$$m = \frac{F_g}{g}$$

$$\text{and } mv = \frac{F_g v}{g}$$

$$= \frac{(175 \text{ N})(49.7 \text{ m/s})}{9.80 \text{ m/s}^2} = 888 \text{ kg} \cdot \text{m/s}$$

Now to find the angle from the two velocities.

$$\tan \theta = \frac{v_y}{v_x} = \frac{34.3 \text{ m/s}}{36.0 \text{ m/s}}$$

$$\text{so } \theta = 43.6°$$

The momentum is 888 kg · m/s at 43.6° below horizontal.

33.

A 60.0-kg dancer leaps 0.32 m high.

a. With what momentum does the dancer reach the ground?

$$v^2 = v_0^2 + 2gd$$

$$\text{so } v = \sqrt{2gd}$$

$$p = mv = m\sqrt{2gd}$$

$$p = (60.0 \text{ kg})$$

$$\times \sqrt{2(9.80 \text{ m/s}^2)(0.32 \text{ m})}$$

$$= 1.5 \times 10^2 \text{ kg} \cdot \text{m/s down}$$

b. What impulse is needed to stop the dancer?

$$F \Delta t = m \Delta v = 1.5 \times 10^2 \text{ N} \cdot \text{s up}$$

c. As the dancer lands, his knees bend, lengthening the stopping time to 0.050 s. Find the average force exerted on the dancer's body.

$$F \Delta t = m \Delta v = m\sqrt{2gd}$$

$$\text{so } F = \frac{m\sqrt{2gd}}{\Delta t}$$

$$= \frac{(60.0 \text{ kg})[2(9.80 \text{ m/s}^2)(0.32 \text{ m})]^{1/2}}{0.050 \text{ s}}$$

$$= 3.0 \times 10^3 \text{ N}$$

d. Compare the stopping force to the dancer's weight.

$$F_g = mg = (60.0 \text{ kg})(9.80 \text{ m/s}^2)$$

$$= 5.98 \times 10^2 \text{ N}$$

or the force is about 5 times the weight.

Copyright © by Glencoe/McGraw-Hill

Section 9.2

Level 1

34. A 95-kg fullback, running at 8.2 m/s, collides in midair with 128-kg defensive tackle moving in the opposite direction. Both players end up with zero speed.

a. Identify "before" and "after" and make a diagram of the situations.

Before   After

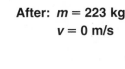

Before: m_f = 95 kg   After: m = 223 kg
     v_f = 8.2 m/s v = 0 m/s
     m_t = 128 kg
     v_t = ?

b. What was the fullback's momentum before the collision?

$m_f v_f$ = (95 kg)(8.2 m/s)

    = 7.8×10^2 kg · m/s

c. What was the change in the fullback's momentum?

$mv - m_f v_f = 0 - 7.8 \times 10^2$ kg · m/s

    = -7.8×10^2 kg · m/s

d. What was the change in the tackle's momentum?

-7.8×10^2 kg · m/s, using the tackle's original direction as positive

e. What was the tackle's original momentum?

7.8×10^2 kg · m/s

f. How fast was the tackle moving originally?

$m_t v_t = 7.8 \times 10^2$ kg · m/s

so $v = \dfrac{7.8 \times 10^2 \text{ kg · m/s}}{128 \text{ kg}}$ = 6.1 m/s

35. Marble A, mass 5.0 g, moves at a speed of 20.0 cm/s. It collides with a second marble, B, mass 10.0 g, moving at 10.0 cm/s in the same direction. After the collision, marble A continues with a speed of 8.0 cm/s in the same direction.

a. Sketch the situation, identify the system, define "before" and "after," and assign a coordinate axis.

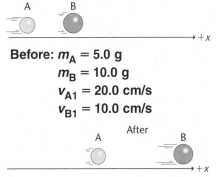

Before

Before: m_A = 5.0 g
        m_B = 10.0 g
        v_{A1} = 20.0 cm/s
        v_{B1} = 10.0 cm/s

After: m_A = 5.0 g m_B = 10.0 g
        v_{A2} = 8.0 cm/s v_{B2} = ?

b. Calculate the marbles' momenta before the collision.

$m_A v_{A1}$ = (5.0×10^{-3} kg)(0.200 m/s)

    = 1.0×10^{-3} kg · m/s

$m_B v_{B1}$ = (1.00×10^{-2} kg)(0.100 m/s)

    = 1.00×10^{-3} kg · m/s

c. Calculate the momentum of marble A after the collision.

$m_A v_{A2}$ = (5.0×10^{-3} kg)(0.080 m/s)

    = 4.0×10^{-4} kg · m/s

d. Calculate the momentum of marble B after the collision.

$p_{A1} + p_{B1} = p_{A2} + p_{B2}$

1.0×10^{-3} kg · m/s

     + 1.00×10^{-3} kg · m/s

= 4.0×10^{-4} kg · m/s + p_{B2}

p_{B2} = 2.0×10^{-3} kg · m/s

     − 4.0×10^{-4} kg · m/s

= 1.6×10^{-3} kg · m/s

e. What is the speed of marble B after the collision?

$p_{B2} = m_B v_{B2}$

so $v_{B2} = \dfrac{p_{B2}}{m_B} = \dfrac{1.6 \times 10^{-3} \text{ kg · m/s}}{1.00 \times 10^{-2} \text{ kg}}$

    = 1.6×10^{-1} m/s = 0.16 m/s

    = 16 cm/s

Copyright © by Glencoe/McGraw-Hill

36. A 2575-kg van runs into the back of an 825-kg compact car at rest. They move off together at 8.5 m/s. Assuming the friction with the road can be negligible, find the initial speed of the van.

$$p_{A1} + p_{B1} = p_{A2} + p_{B2}$$

$$m_A v_{A1} = (m_A + m_B)v_2$$

so $v_{A1} = \dfrac{m_A + m_B}{m_A}$

$$v_2 = \frac{(2575 \text{ kg} + 825 \text{ kg})(8.5 \text{ m/s})}{2575 \text{ kg}}$$

$$= 11 \text{ m/s}$$

page 220

37. A 0.115-kg hockey puck, moving at 35.0 m/s, strikes 0.265-kg octopus thrown onto the ice by a hockey fan. The puck and octopus slide off together. Find their velocity.

$$m_p v_{p1} + m_o v_{o1} = (m_p + m_o)v_2$$

so $v_2 = \dfrac{m_p v_{p1}}{m_p + m_o}$

$$= \frac{(0.115 \text{ kg})(35.0 \text{ m/s})}{0.115 \text{ kg} + 0.265 \text{ kg}}$$

$$= 10.6 \text{ m/s}$$

38. A 50-kg woman, riding on a 10-kg cart, is moving east at 5.0 m/s. The woman jumps off the front of the cart and hits the ground at 7.0 m/s eastward, relative to the ground.

a. Sketch the situation, identifying "before" and "after," and assigning a coordinate axis.

Before: $m_w = 50$ kg   **After:** $m_w = 50$ kg
     $m_c = 10$ kg $m_c = 10$ kg
     $v = 5.0$ m/s $v_{w2} = 7.0$ m/s
                           $v_{c2} = ?$

b. Find the velocity of the cart after the woman jumps off.

$$(m_w + m_c)v = m_w v_{w2} + m_c v_{c2}$$

so $v_{c2} = \dfrac{(m_w + m_c)v - m_w v_{w2}}{m_c}$

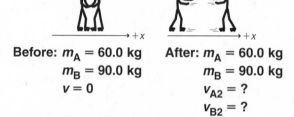

$$= -5 \text{ m/s} \quad \text{or} \quad 5 \text{ m/s, west}$$

39. Two students on roller skates stand face-to-face, then push each other away. One student has a mass of 90.0 kg; the other has a mass of 60.0 kg.

a. Sketch the situation, identifying "before" and "after," and assigning a coordinate axis.

Before   After

Before: $m_A = 60.0$ kg   **After:** $m_A = 60.0$ kg
        $m_B = 90.0$ kg $m_B = 90.0$ kg
        $v = 0$ $v_{A2} = ?$
                                $v_{B2} = ?$

b. Find the ratio of the students' velocities just after their hands lose contact.

$$p_{A1} + p_{B1} = 0 = p_{A2} + p_{B2}$$

so $m_A v_{A2} + m_B v_{B2} = 0$

and $m_A v_{A2} = -m_B v_{B2}$

$$\frac{v_{A2}}{v_{B2}} = -\frac{m_B}{m_A} = -\frac{90.0}{60.0} = -1.50$$

The negative sign shows that the velocities are in opposite directions.

c. Which student has the greater speed?

The student with the smaller mass has the greater speed.

d. Which student pushed harder?

The forces were equal and opposite.

Copyright © by Glencoe/McGraw-Hill

40. A 0.200-kg plastic ball moves with a velocity of 0.30 m/s. It collides with a second plastic ball of mass 0.100 kg, which is moving along the same line at a speed of 0.10 m/s. After the collision, both balls continue moving in the same, original direction, and the speed of the 0.100-kg ball is 0.26 m/s. What is the new velocity of the first ball?

$$m_A v_{A1} + m_B v_{B1} = m_A v_{A2} + m_B v_{B2}$$

$$\text{so } v_{A2} = \frac{m_A v_{A1} + m_B v_{B1} - m_B v_{B2}}{m_A}$$

$$= \frac{(0.200 \text{ kg})(0.30 \text{ m/s})}{0.200 \text{ kg}}$$

$$+ \frac{(0.100 \text{ kg})(0.10 \text{ m/s})}{0.200 \text{ kg}}$$

$$- \frac{(0.100 \text{ kg})(0.26 \text{ m/s})}{0.200 \text{ kg}}$$

$$= 0.22 \text{ m/s in the original direction.}$$

Level 2

41. A 92-kg fullback, running at 5.0 m/s, attempts to dive directly across the goal line for a touchdown. Just as he reaches the line, he is met head-on in midair by two 75-kg linebackers, both moving in the direction opposite the fullback. One is moving at 2.0 m/s, the other at 4.0 m/s. They all become entangled as one mass.

a. Sketch the situation, identifying "before" and "after."

Before

→ +x

Before: $m_A = 92$ kg
$m_B = 75$ kg
$m_C = 75$ kg
$v_{A1} = 5.0$ m/s
$v_{B1} = -2.0$ m/s
$v_{C1} = -4.0$ m/s

After

→ +x

After: $m_A = 92$ kg
$m_B = 75$ kg
$m_C = 75$ kg
$v_2 = ?$

b. What is their velocity after the collision?

$$p_{A1} + p_{B1} + p_{C1} = p_{A2} + p_{B2} + p_{C2}$$

$$m_A v_{A1} + m_B v_{B1} + m_C v_{C1}$$
$$= m_A v_{A2} + m_B v_{B2} + m_C v_{C2}$$
$$= (m_A + m_B + m_C)v_2$$

$$v_2 = \frac{m_A v_{A1} + m_B v_{B1} + m_C v_{C1}}{m_A + m_B + m_C}$$

$$= \frac{(92 \text{ kg})(5.0 \text{ m/s})}{92 \text{ kg} + 75 \text{ kg} + 75 \text{ kg}}$$

$$+ \frac{(75 \text{ kg})(-2.0 \text{ m/s})}{92 \text{ kg} + 75 \text{ kg} + 75 \text{ kg}}$$

$$+ \frac{(75 \text{ kg})(-4.0 \text{ m/s})}{92 \text{ kg} + 75 \text{ kg} + 75 \text{ kg}}$$

$$= 0.041 \text{ m/s}$$

c. Does the fullback score?

Yes. The velocity is positive so the football crosses the goal line for a touchdown.

42. A 5.00-g bullet is fired with a velocity of 100.0 m/s toward a 10.00-kg stationary solid block resting on a frictionless surface.

a. What is the change in momentum of the bullet if it is embedded in the block?

$$m_b v_{b1} = m_b v_2 + m_w v_2 = (m_b + m_w)v_2$$

$$\text{so } v_2 = \frac{m_b v_{b1}}{m_b + m_w}$$

$$= \frac{(5.00 \times 10^{-3} \text{ kg})(100.0 \text{ m/s})}{5.00 \times 10^{-3} \text{ kg} + 10.00 \text{ kg}}$$

$$= 5.00 \times 10^{-2} \text{ m/s}$$

Copyright © by Glencoe/McGraw-Hill

42. (continued)

$$\Delta mv = m_b(v_2 - v_1)$$
$$= (5.00 \times 10^{-3} \text{ kg})$$
$$\times (5.00 \times 10^{-2} \text{ m/s} - 100.0 \text{ m/s})$$
$$= -0.500 \text{ kg} \cdot \text{m/s}$$

b. What is the change in momentum of the bullet if it ricochets in the opposite direction with a speed of 99 m/s?

$$\Delta mv = m_b(v_2 - v_1)$$
$$= (5.00 \times 10^{-3} \text{ kg})$$
$$\times (-99 \text{ m/s} - 100.0 \text{ m/s})$$
$$= -0.995 \text{ kg} \cdot \text{m/s}$$

c. In which case does the block end up with a greater speed?

When the bullet ricochets, its change in momentum is larger in magnitude, and so is the block's change in momentum, so the block ends up with a greater speed.

43. The diagrams in **Figure 9–13** show a brick weighing 24.5 N being released from rest on a 1.00-m frictionless plane, inclined at an angle of 30.0°. The brick slides down the incline and strikes a second brick weighing 36.8 N.

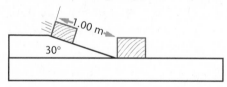
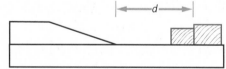

FIGURE 9-13

a. Calculate the speed of the first brick at the bottom of the incline.

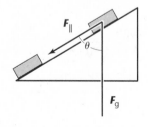

$$F_{\parallel} = F_g \sin \theta$$

$$a = \frac{F_{\parallel}}{m} \quad \text{and} \quad m = \frac{F_g}{g}$$

$$\text{so } a = \frac{F_g \sin \theta}{F_g/g} = g \sin \theta$$

$$v^2 = 2ad$$

$$\text{so } v = \sqrt{2ad} = \sqrt{(2)(g \sin \theta)(d)}$$

$$v = [(2)(9.80 \text{ m/s}^2)(\sin 30.0°)$$
$$\times (1.00 \text{ m})]^{1/2}$$

$$= 3.13 \text{ m/s}$$

b. If the two bricks stick together, with what initial speed will they move along?

$$m_A v_{A1} = (m_A + m_B)v_2$$

$$\text{so } v_2 = \frac{m_A v_{A1}}{m_A + m_B}$$

$$= \frac{(2.50 \text{ kg})(3.13 \text{ m/s})}{2.50 \text{ kg} + 3.76 \text{ kg}}$$

$$= 1.25 \text{ m/s}$$

c. If the force of friction acting on the two bricks is 5.0 N, how much time will elapse before the bricks come to rest?

$$F \Delta t = m \Delta v, \text{ so}$$

$$\Delta t = \frac{(2.50 \text{ kg} + 3.76 \text{ kg})(1.25 \text{ m/s})}{5.0 \text{ N}}$$

$$= 1.6 \text{ s}$$

d. How far will the two bricks slide before coming to rest?

$$d = \frac{1}{2}(v_2 + v)t$$

$$= \frac{1}{2}(1.25 \text{ m/s} + 0)(1.57 \text{ s})$$

$$= 0.98 \text{ m}$$

Physics: Principles and Problems

Copyright © by Glencoe/McGraw-Hill

44. Ball A, rolling west at 3.0 m/s, has a mass of 1.0 kg. Ball B has a mass of 2.0 kg and is stationary. After colliding with ball B, ball A moves south at 2.0 m/s.

a. Sketch the system, showing the velocities and momenta before and after the collision.

Westward and southward are positive.

Before

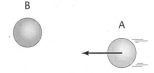

Before: $p_{B1} = 0$ $v_{A1} = 3.0$ m/s west
                               $p_{A1} = 3.0$ kg · m/s west

After

After: $v_{B2} = ?$
           $p_{B2} = ?$
           $v_{A2} = 2.0$ m/s south
           $p_{A2} = 2.0$ kg · m/s south

b. Calculate the momentum and velocity of ball B after the collision.

Horizontal: $m_A v_{A1} = m_B v_{B2}$

So $m_B v_{B2} = (1.0$ kg$)(3.0$ m/s$)$

            $= 3.0$ kg · m/s

Vertical: $0 = m_A v_{A2} + m_B v_{B2}$

So $m_B v_{B2} = -(1.0$ kg$)(2.0$ m/s$)$

            $= -2.0$ kg · m/s

The vector sum is:

$mv = \sqrt{(3.0 \text{ kg} \cdot \text{m/s})^2 + (-2.0 \text{ kg} \cdot \text{m/s})^2}$

     $= 3.6$ kg · m/s

and $\tan \theta = \dfrac{2.0 \text{ kg} \cdot \text{m/s}}{3.0 \text{ kg} \cdot \text{m/s}}$

so $\theta = 34°$

Therefore, $m_B v_{B2} = 3.6$ kg · m/s at 34° N of W

$$v_{B2} = \frac{3.6 \text{ kg} \cdot \text{m/s}}{2.0 \text{ kg}}$$

     $= 1.8$ m/s at 34° N of W

45. A space probe with a mass of 7.600×10^3 kg is traveling through space at 125 m/s. Mission control decides that a course correction of 30.0° is needed and instructs the probe to fire rockets perpendicular to its present direction of motion. If the gas expelled by the rockets has a speed of 3.200 km/s, what mass of gas should be released?

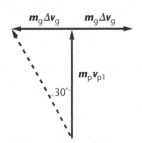

$$\tan 30.0° = \frac{m_g \Delta v_g}{m_p v_{p1}}$$

$$m_g = \frac{m_p v_{p1}(\tan 30.0°)}{\Delta v_g}$$

$$= \frac{(7.600 \times 10^3 \text{ kg})(125 \text{ ms})(\tan 30.0°)}{3.200 \times 10^3 \text{ m/s}}$$

     $= 171$ kg

Page 221

46. The diagram in **Figure 9–14,** which is drawn to scale, shows two balls during a collision. The balls enter from the left, collide, and then bounce away. The heavier ball at the bottom of the diagram has a mass of 0.600 kg; the other has a mass of 0.400 kg. Using a vector diagram, determine whether momentum is conserved in this collision. What could explain any difference in the momentum of the system before and after the collision?

Copyright © by Glencoe/McGraw-Hill

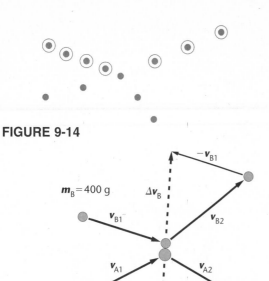

FIGURE 9-14

$m_B = 400$ g $\Delta \mathbf{v}_B$ $-\mathbf{v}_{B1}$

$\mathbf{v}_{B1}$ $\mathbf{v}_{B2}$

$\mathbf{v}_{A1}$ $\mathbf{v}_{A2}$

$\Delta \mathbf{v}_A$

$m_A = 600$ g $-\mathbf{v}_{A1}$

Dotted lines show that the changes of momentum for each ball are equal and opposite: $\Delta(m_A \mathbf{v}_A) = \Delta(m_B \mathbf{v}_B)$. Since the masses are in a 3:2 ratio, a 2:3 ratio of velocity changes will compensate.

Critical Thinking Problems

47. A compact car, mass 875 kg, moving south at 15 m/s, is struck by a full-sized car, mass 1584 kg, moving east at 12 m/s. The two cars stick together, and momentum is conserved in the collision.

   a. Sketch the situation, assigning coordinate axes and identifying "before" and "after."

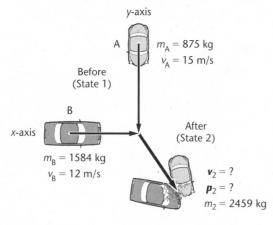

y-axis

A $m_A = 875$ kg
      $v_A = 15$ m/s

Before
(State 1)

B

x-axis

$m_B = 1584$ kg
$v_B = 12$ m/s

After
(State 2)

$v_2 = ?$
$p_2 = ?$
$m_2 = 2459$ kg

b. Find the direction and speed of the wreck immediately after the collision, remembering that momentum is a vector quantity.

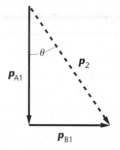

θ $\mathbf{p}_2$

$\mathbf{p}_{A1}$

$\mathbf{p}_{B1}$

$p_{A1} = m_A v_A = (875 \text{ kg})(15 \text{ m/s})$
$\quad = 1.31 \times 10^4 \text{ kg} \cdot \text{m/s south}$

$p_{B1} = m_B v_B = (1584 \text{ kg})(12 \text{ m/s})$
$\quad = 1.90 \times 10^4 \text{ kg} \cdot \text{m/s east}$

$p_2 = \sqrt{p_{A1}^2 + p_{B1}^2}$

p_2
$= \sqrt{(1.31 \times 10^4 \text{ kg} \cdot \text{m/s})^2 + (1.90 \times 10^4 \text{ kg} \cdot \text{m/s})^2}$
$= 2.3 \times 10^4 \text{ kg} \cdot \text{m/s}$

$\tan \theta = \dfrac{1.90 \times 10^4}{1.31 \times 10^4}$

$\theta = 55°$ **east of south**

$v_2 = \dfrac{p_2}{m_2} = \dfrac{2.3 \times 10^4 \text{ kg} \cdot \text{m/s}}{2459 \text{ kg}}$

$v_2 = 9.4$ m/s

c. The wreck skids along the ground and comes to a stop. The coefficient of kinetic friction while the wreck is skidding is 0.55. Assume that the acceleration is constant. How far does the wreck skid?

$\mu_k = 0.55$

$F = \mu_k F_N = \mu_k F_g = \mu_k (mg)$

$\quad = (0.55)(2459 \text{ kg})(9.8 \text{ m/s}^2)$

$F = 1.33 \times 10^4$ N

$F \Delta t = \Delta mv = 2.3 \times 10^4 \text{ kg} \cdot \text{m/s}$

$\Delta t = \dfrac{2.3 \times 10^4 \text{ kg} \cdot \text{m/s}}{1.33 \times 10^4 \text{ kg} \cdot \text{m/s}^2} = 1.73 \text{ s}$

$a = \dfrac{\Delta v}{\Delta t} = \dfrac{-9.4 \text{ m/s}}{1.73 \text{ s}} = -5.4 \text{ m/s}^2$

Copyright © by Glencoe/McGraw-Hill

47. c. (continued)

$$d = v_0 t + \frac{1}{2} at^2$$

$$= (9.4 \text{ m/s})(1.73 \text{ s})$$

$$+ \left(\frac{1}{2}\right)(-5.4 \text{ m/s}^2)(1.73 \text{ s})^2$$

$$d = 8.2 \text{ m}$$

48. Your friend has been in a car accident and wants your help. She was driving her 1265-kg car north on Oak Street when she was hit by a 925-kg compact car going west on Maple Street. The cars stuck together and slid 23.1 m at 42° north of west. The speed limit on both streets is 50 mph (22 m/s). Your friend claims that she wasn't speeding, but that the other car was. Can you support her case in court? Assume that momentum was conserved during the collision and that acceleration was constant during the skid. The coefficient of kinetic friction between the tires and the pavement is 0.65.

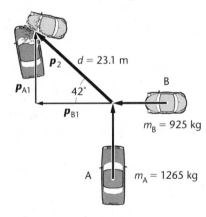

$$m_2 = 925 \text{ kg} + 1265 \text{ kg}$$

$$m_2 = 2190 \text{ kg}$$

$$F = \mu_k F_N = \mu_k F_g = \mu_k (mg)$$

$$F = (0.65)(2190 \text{ kg})(9.8 \text{ m/s}^2)$$

$$F = 1.39 \times 10^4 \text{ N}$$

$$a = \frac{F}{m} = \frac{1.39 \times 10^4 \text{ N}}{2190 \text{ kg}} = 6.35 \text{ m/s}^2$$

$$d = \frac{1}{2} at^2$$

$$t = \sqrt{\frac{2}{ad}} = \sqrt{\frac{(2)(23.1\text{m})}{6.35 \text{ m/s}^2}} = 2.70 \text{ s}$$

$$v_2 = at = (6.35 \text{ m/s}^2)(2.70 \text{ s})$$

$$= 17.1 \text{ m/s}$$

$$p_2 = m_2 v_2 = (2190 \text{ kg})(17.1 \text{ m/s})$$

$$= 3.74 \times 10^4 \text{ kg} \cdot \text{m/s}$$

$$p_{A1} = p_2 \sin 42°$$

$$= (3.74 \times 10^4 \text{ kg} \cdot \text{m/s})(\sin 42°)$$

$$= 2.5 \times 10^4 \text{ kg} \cdot \text{m/s}$$

$$v_{A1} = \frac{p_{A1}}{m_A} = \frac{2.5 \times 10^4 \text{ kg} \cdot \text{m/s}}{1265 \text{ kg}}$$

$$= 2.0 \times 10^1 \text{ m/s}$$

Car A, the friend's car, was going 2.0×10^1 m/s before the crash.

Yes. She was not speeding.

$$p_{B1} = p_2 \cos 42°$$

$$= (3.74 \times 10^4 \text{ kg} \cdot \text{m/s})(\cos 42°)$$

$$= 2.78 \times 10^4 \text{ kg} \cdot \text{m/s}$$

$$v_{B1} = \frac{p_{B1}}{m_B} = \frac{2.78 \times 10^4 \text{ kg} \cdot \text{m/s}}{925 \text{ kg}}$$

$$= 30.1 \text{ m/s}$$

Car B was speeding, since it was going 30.1 m/s before the crash.

10 Energy, Work, and Simple Machines

Practice Problems

10.1 Energy and Work
pages 224–231

page 227

1. A student lifts a box of books that weighs 185 N. The box is lifted 0.800 m. How much work does the student do on the box?

    $W = Fd = (185 \text{ N})(0.800 \text{ m}) = 148 \text{ J}$

2. Two students together exert a force of 825 N in pushing a car 35 m.

    a. How much work do they do on the car?

    $W = Fd = (825 \text{ N})(35 \text{ m})$

    $= 2.9 \times 10^4 \text{ J}$

    b. If the force were doubled, how much work would they do pushing the car the same distance?

    $W = Fd$

    $= (2)(825 \text{ N})(35 \text{ m})$

    $= 5.8 \times 10^4 \text{ J}$

    The amount of work doubles.

3. A 0.180-kg ball falls 2.5 m. How much work does the force of gravity do on the ball?

    $F_g = mg = (0.180 \text{ kg})(9.80 \text{ m/s}^2)$

    $= 1.76 \text{ N}$

    $W = Fd = (1.76 \text{ N})(2.5 \text{ m}) = 4.4 \text{ J}$

4. A forklift raises a box 1.2 m doing 7.0 kJ of work on it. What is the mass of the box?

    $W = Fd = mgd$

    so $m = \dfrac{W}{gd} = \dfrac{7.0 \times 10^3 \text{ J}}{(9.80 \text{ m/s}^2)(1.2 \text{ m})}$

    $= 6.0 \times 10^2 \text{ kg}$

5. You and a friend each carry identical boxes to a room one floor above you and down the hall. You choose to carry it first up the stairs, then down the hall. Your friend carries it down the hall, then up another stairwell. Who does more work?

    Both do the same amount of work. Only the height lifted and the vertical force exerted count.

page 229

6. How much work does the force of gravity do when a 25-N object falls a distance of 3.5 m?

    Both the force and displacement are in the same direction, so

    $W = Fd = (25 \text{ N})(3.5 \text{ m}) = 88 \text{ J}$

7. An airplane passenger carries a 215-N suitcase up the stairs, a displacement of 4.20 m vertically and 4.60 m horizontally.

    a. How much work does the passenger do?

    Since gravity acts vertically, only the vertical displacement needs to be considered.

    $W = Fd = (215 \text{ N})(4.20 \text{ m}) = 903 \text{ J}$

    b. The same passenger carries the same suitcase back down the same stairs. How much work does the passenger do now?

    Force is upward, but vertical displacement is downward, so

    $W = Fd \cos \theta = Fd \cos 180°$

    $= (215 \text{ N})(4.20 \text{ m})(\cos 180°) = -903 \text{ J}$

Copyright © by Glencoe/McGraw-Hill

8. A rope is used to pull a metal box 15.0 m across the floor. The rope is held at an angle of 46.0° with the floor and a force of 628 N is used. How much work does the force on the rope do?

$$W = Fd \cos \theta$$
$$= (628 \text{ N})(15.0 \text{ m})(\cos 46.0°)$$
$$= 6.54 \times 10^3 \text{ J}$$

page 231

9. A box that weighs 575 N is lifted a distance of 20.0 m straight up by a cable attached to a motor. The job is done in 10.0 s. What power is developed by the motor in watts and kilowatts?

$$P = \frac{W}{t} = \frac{Fd}{t} = \frac{(575 \text{ N})(20.0 \text{ m})}{10.0 \text{ s}}$$
$$= 1.15 \times 10^3 \text{ W} = 1.15 \text{ kW}$$

10. A rock climber wears a 7.5-kg knapsack while scaling a cliff. After 30 min, the climber is 8.2 m above the starting point.

a. How much work does the climber do on the knapsack?

$$W = mgd = (7.5 \text{ kg})(9.80 \text{ m/s}^2)(8.2 \text{ m})$$
$$= 6.0 \times 10^2 \text{ J}$$

b. If the climber weighs 645 N, how much work does she do lifting herself and the knapsack?

$$W = Fd + 6.0 \times 10^2 \text{ J}$$
$$= (645 \text{ N})(8.2 \text{ m}) + 6.0 \times 10^2 \text{ J}$$
$$= 5.9 \times 10^3 \text{ J}$$

c. What is the average power developed by the climber?

$$P = \frac{W}{t} = \frac{5.9 \times 10^3 \text{ J}}{(30 \text{ min})(60 \text{ s/min})}$$
$$= 3 \text{ W}$$

11. An electric motor develops 65 kW of power as it lifts a loaded elevator 17.5 m in 35 s. How much force does the motor exert?

$$P = \frac{W}{t} \text{ and } W = Fd$$
$$\text{So } F = \frac{Pt}{d} = \frac{(65 \times 10^3 \text{ W})(35 \text{ s})}{17.5 \text{ m}}$$
$$= 1.3 \times 10^5 \text{ N}$$

12. Your car has stalled and you need to push it. You notice as the car gets going that you need less and less force to keep it going. Suppose that for the first 15 m your force decreased at a constant rate from 210 N to 40 N. How much work did you do on the car? Draw a force-displacement graph to represent the work done during this period.

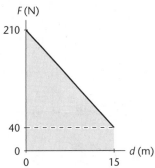

The work done is the area of the trapezoid under the solid line:

$$W = \frac{1}{2} d (F_1 + F_2)$$
$$= \frac{1}{2} (15 \text{ m})(210 \text{ N} + 40 \text{ N})$$
$$= 1.9 \times 10^3 \text{ J}$$

10.2 Machines
pages 233–239

page 238

13. A sledgehammer is used to drive a wedge into a log to split it. When the wedge is driven 0.20 m into the log, the log is separated a distance of 5.0 cm. A force of 1.9×10^4 N is needed to split the log, and the sledgehammer exerts a force of 9.8×10^3 N.

a. What is the *IMA* of the wedge?

$$IMA = \frac{d_e}{d_r} = \frac{2.0 \times 10^1 \text{ cm}}{5.0 \text{ cm}} = 4.0$$

b. Find the *MA* of the wedge.

$$MA = \frac{F_r}{F_e} = \frac{1.9 \times 10^4 \text{ N}}{9.8 \times 10^3 \text{ N}} = 1.9$$

c. Calculate the efficiency of the wedge as a machine.

$$\text{efficiency} = \left(\frac{MA}{IMA} \right) \times 100$$
$$= \left(\frac{1.9}{4.0} \right) \times 100 = 48\%$$

Copyright © by Glencoe/McGraw-Hill

14. A worker uses a pulley system to raise a 24.0-kg carton 16.5 m. A force of 129 N is exerted and the rope is pulled 33.0 m.

a. What is the mechanical advantage of the pulley system?

$$F_r = mg = (24.0 \text{ kg})(9.80 \text{ m/s}^2)$$
$$= 235 \text{ N}$$

$$MA = \frac{F_r}{F_e} = \frac{235 \text{ N}}{129 \text{ N}} = 1.82$$

b. What is the efficiency of the system?

$$\text{efficiency} = \left(\frac{MA}{IMA}\right) \times 100 \text{ where}$$

$$IMA = \frac{d_e}{d_r} = \frac{33.0 \text{ m}}{16.5 \text{ m}} = 2.00$$

$$\text{so efficiency} = \frac{1.82}{2.00} \times 100 = 91.0\%$$

15. A boy exerts a force of 225 N on a lever to raise a 1.25×10^3-N rock a distance of 13 cm. If the efficiency of the lever is 88.7%, how far did the boy move his end of the lever?

$$\text{efficiency} = \frac{W_o}{W_i} \times 100$$

$$= \frac{F_r d_r}{F_e d_e} \times 100$$

$$\text{So } d_e = \frac{F_r d_r (100)}{F_e (\text{efficiency})}$$

$$= \frac{(1.25 \times 10^3 \text{ N})(0.13 \text{ m})(100)}{(225 \text{ N})(88.7\%)}$$

$$= 0.81 \text{ m}$$

16. If the gear radius in the bicycle in the Example Problem is doubled, while the force exerted on the chain and the distance the wheel rim moves remain the same, what quantities change, and by how much?

$$IMA = \frac{8.00 \text{ cm}}{35.6 \text{ cm}} = 0.225$$

$$MA = \frac{(95.0\%)\, 0.225}{100} = 0.214$$

$$F_r = (MA)(F_e) = (0.214)(155 \text{ N})$$
$$= 33.2 \text{ N}$$

$$d_e = (IMA)(d_r) = (0.225)(14.0 \text{ cm})$$
$$= 3.15 \text{ cm}$$

All of the above quantities are doubled.

Chapter Review Problems

pages 242–245

page 242

Section 10.1

Level 1

19. Lee pushes a 20-kg mass 10 m across a floor with a horizontal force of 80 N. Calculate the amount of work Lee does.

$$W = Fd = (80 \text{ N})(10 \text{ m}) = 800 \text{ J}$$

The mass is not important to this problem.

20. The third floor of a house is 8 m above street level. How much work is needed to move a 150-kg refrigerator to the third floor?

$$F = mg$$

$$\text{so } W = Fd = mgd$$

$$= (150 \text{ kg})(9.80 \text{ m/s}^2)(8 \text{ m})$$

$$= 1 \times 10^4 \text{ J}$$

21. Stan does 176 J of work lifting himself 0.300 m. What is Stan's mass?

$$F = mg, \text{ so } W = Fd = mgd; \text{ therefore,}$$

$$m = \frac{W}{gd} = \frac{176 \text{ J}}{(9.80 \text{ m/s}^2)(0.300 \text{ m})}$$

$$= 59.9 \text{ kg}$$

22. Mike pulls a 4.5-kg sled across level snow with a force of 225 N along a rope that is 35.0° above the horizontal. If the sled moves a distance of 65.3 m, how much work does Mike do?

$$W = Fd \cos \theta$$

$$= (225 \text{ N})(65.3 \text{ m}) \cos 35.0°$$

$$= 1.20 \times 10^4 \text{ J}$$

Copyright © by Glencoe/McGraw-Hill

23. Sau-Lan has a mass of 52 kg. She rides the up escalator at Ocean Park in Hong Kong. This is the world's longest escalator, with a length of 227 m and an average inclination of 31°. How much work does the escalator do on Sau-Lan?

$$W = Fd \sin \theta = mgd \sin \theta$$
$$= (52 \text{ kg})(9.80 \text{ m/s}^2)(227 \text{ m})(\sin 31°)$$
$$= 6.0 \times 10^4 \text{ J}$$

24. Chris carries a carton of milk, weight 10 N, along a level hall to the kitchen, a distance of 3.5 m. How much work does Chris do?

No work, because the force and the displacement are perpendicular.

25. A student librarian picks up a 2.2-kg book from the floor to a height of 1.25 m. He carries the book 8.0 m to the stacks and places the book on a shelf that is 0.35 m above the floor. How much work does he do on the book?

Only the net vertical displacement counts.

$$W = Fd = mgd$$
$$= (2.2 \text{ kg})(9.80 \text{ m/s}^2)(0.35 \text{ m})$$
$$= 7.5 \text{ J}$$

26. Brutus, a champion weightlifter, raises 240 kg of weights a distance of 2.35 m.

a. How much work is done by Brutus lifting the weights?

$$W = Fd = mgd$$
$$= (240 \text{ kg})(9.80 \text{ m/s}^2)(2.35 \text{ m})$$
$$= 5.5 \times 10^3 \text{ J}$$

b. How much work is done by Brutus holding the weights above his head?

$d = 0$, so no work

c. How much work is done by Brutus lowering them back to the ground?

d is opposite of motion in part a, so W is also the opposite, -5.5×10^3 J.

d. Does Brutus do work if he lets go of the weights and they fall back to the ground?

No. He exerts no force, so he does no work, positive or negative.

e. If Brutus completes the lift in 2.5 s, how much power is developed?

$$P = \frac{W}{t} = \frac{5.5 \times 103 \text{ J}}{2.5 \text{ s}} = 2.2 \text{ kW}$$

27. A force of 300.0 N is used to push a 145-kg mass 30.0 m horizontally in 3.00 s.

a. Calculate the work done on the mass.

$$W = Fd = (300.0 \text{ N})(30.0 \text{ m})$$
$$= 9.00 \times 10^3 \text{ J}$$
$$= 9.00 \text{ kJ}$$

b. Calculate the power developed.

$$P = \frac{W}{t} = \frac{9.00 \times 10^3 \text{ J}}{3.00 \text{ s}}$$
$$= 3.00 \times 10^3 \text{ W}$$
$$= 3.00 \text{ kW}$$

28. Robin pushes a wheelbarrow by exerting a 145-N force horizontally. Robin moves it 60.0 m at a constant speed for 25.0 s.

a. What power does Robin develop?

$$P = \frac{W}{t} = \frac{Fd}{t} = \frac{(145 \text{ N})(60.0 \text{ m})}{25.0 \text{ s}}$$
$$= 348 \text{ W}$$

b. If Robin moves the wheelbarrow twice as fast, how much power is developed?

Either d is doubled or t is halved, so P is doubled to 696 W.

29. A horizontal force of 805 N is needed to drag a crate across a horizontal floor with a constant speed. You drag the crate using a rope held at an angle of 32°.

a. What force do you exert on the rope?

$$F_x = F \cos \theta$$
$$\text{so } F = \frac{F_x}{\cos \theta} = \frac{805 \text{ N}}{\cos 32°}$$
$$= 9.50 \times 10^2 \text{ N}$$

b. How much work do you do on the crate when moving it 22 m?

$$W = F_x d = (805 \text{ N})(22 \text{ m})$$
$$= 1.8 \times 10^4 \text{ J}$$

Copyright © by Glencoe/McGraw-Hill

29. (continued)

    c. If you complete the job in 8.0 s, what power is developed?

$$P = \frac{W}{t} = \frac{1.8 \times 104 \text{ J}}{8.0 \text{ s}} = 2.3 \text{ kW}$$

page 243

30. Wayne pulls a 305-N sled along a snowy path using a rope that makes a 45.0° angle with the ground. Wayne pulls with a force of 42.3 N. The sled moves 16 m in 3.0 s. What power does Wayne produce?

$$P = \frac{W}{t} = \frac{F_{||}d}{t} = \frac{Fd \cos \theta}{t}$$

$$= \frac{(42.3 \text{ N})(16 \text{ m})(\cos 45.0°)}{3.0 \text{ s}}$$

$$= 1.6 \times 10^2 \text{ W}$$

31. A lawn roller is pushed across a lawn by a force of 115 N along the direction of the handle, which is 22.5° above the horizontal. If you develop 64.6 W of power for 90.0 s, what distance is the roller pushed?

$$P = \frac{W}{t} = \frac{Fd \cos \theta}{t}$$

$$d = \frac{Pt}{F \cos \theta} = \frac{(64.6 \text{ W})(90.0 \text{ s})}{(115 \text{ N})(\cos 22.5°)}$$

$$= 54.7 \text{ m}$$

Level 2

32. A crane lifts a 3.50×10^3-N bucket containing 1.15 m³ of soil (density = 2.00×10^3 kg/m³) to a height of 7.50 m. Calculate the work the crane performs. Disregard the weight of the cable.

    W = Fd, where F is the weight of bucket plus soil. The soil mass is

$$(1.15 \text{ m}^3)(2.00 \times 10^3 \text{ kg/m}^3)$$

$$= 2.30 \times 10^3 \text{ kg}$$

The soil's weight is

$$(2.30 \times 10^3 \text{ kg})(9.80 \text{ m/s}^2)$$

$$= 2.25 \times 10^4 \text{ N}$$

The bucket's weight is 3.50×10^3 N, so the total weight is 2.60×10^4 N. Thus,

$$W = Fd = (2.60 \times 10^4 \text{ N})(7.50 \text{ m})$$

$$= 1.95 \times 10^5 \text{ J}$$

33. In **Figure 10–13,** the magnitude of the force necessary to stretch a spring is plotted against the distance the spring is stretched.

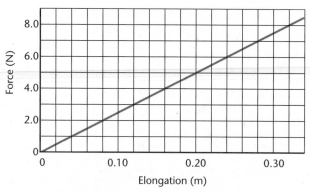

FIGURE 10-13

    a. Calculate the slope of the graph and show that $F = kd$, where $k = 25$ N/m.

$$m = \frac{\Delta y}{\Delta x} = \frac{5.0 \text{ N} - 0.0 \text{ N}}{0.20 \text{ m} - 0.00 \text{ m}}$$

$$= \frac{5.0 \text{ N}}{0.20 \text{ m}} = 25 \text{ N/m}$$

$$F = kd = (25 \text{ N/m})(0.16 \text{ m}) = 4.0 \text{ N}$$

    b. Find the amount of work done in stretching the spring from 0.00 m to 0.20 m by calculating the area under the curve from 0.00 m to 0.20 m.

$$A = \frac{1}{2} \text{(base)(height)}$$

$$= \left(\frac{1}{2}\right) (5.0 \text{ N})(0.20 \text{ m})$$

$$= 0.50 \text{ J}$$

Copyright © by Glencoe/McGraw-Hill

33. (continued)

    c. Show that the answer to part **b** can be calculated using the formula, $W = \frac{1}{2} kd^2$, where W is the work, $k = 25$ N/m (the slope of the graph), and d is the distance the spring is stretched (0.20 m).

$$W = \frac{1}{2} kd^2 = \left(\frac{1}{2}\right)(25 \text{ N/m})(0.20 \text{ m})^2$$

$$= 0.50 \text{ J}$$

34. The graph in **Figure 10–13** shows the force needed to stretch a spring. Find the work needed to stretch it from 0.12 m to 0.28 m.

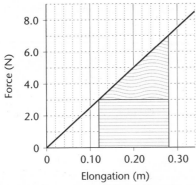

Elongation (m)

Add the areas of the triangle and rectangle. The area of the triangle is

$$\frac{\text{(base)(height)}}{2} = \frac{(0.16 \text{ m})(4.0 \text{ N})}{2}$$

$$= 0.32 \text{ J}$$

The area of the rectangle is

$$\text{(base)(height)} = (0.16 \text{ m})(3.0 \text{ N})$$

$$= 0.48 \text{ J}$$

Total work is 0.32 J + 0.48 J = 0.80 J

35. John pushes a crate across the floor of a factory with a horizontal force. The roughness of the floor changes, and John must exert a force of 20 N for 5 m, then 35 N for 12 m, and then 10 N for 8 m.

    a. Draw a graph of force as a function of distance.

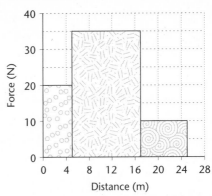

Distance (m)

    b. Find the work John does pushing the crate.

Add the areas under the rectangles

(5 m)(20 N) + (12 m)(35 N)

$$+ \text{ (8 m)(10 N)}$$

= 100 J + 420 J + 80 J = 600 J

36. Sally expends 11 400 J of energy to drag a wooden crate 25.0 m across a floor with a constant speed. The rope makes an angle of 48.0° with the horizontal.

    a. How much force does the the rope exert on the crate?

$$W = Fd \cos \theta$$

$$\text{so } F = \frac{W}{d \cos \theta} = \frac{11400 \text{ J}}{(25.0 \text{ m})(\cos 48.0°)}$$

$$= 681 \text{ N}$$

    b. What is the force of friction acting on the crate to impede its motion?

The crate moves with constant speed, so the force of friction equals the horizontal component of the force of the rope.

$$F_f = F_x = F \cos \theta = (681 \text{ N})(\cos 48.0°)$$

= 456 N, opposite to the direction of motion

Copyright © by Glencoe/McGraw-Hill

36. (continued)

c. What work is done by the floor through the force of friction between the floor and the crate?

Force and displacement are in opposite directions, so

$$W = -(456 \text{ N})(25.0 \text{ m}) = -1.14 \times 10^4 \text{ J}$$

(Because no net forces act on the crate, the work done on the crate must be equal in magnitude but opposite in sign to the energy Sally expends: -1.14×10^4 J.)

37. An 845-N sled is pulled a distance of 185 m. The task requires 1.20×10^4 J of work and is done by pulling on a rope with a force of 125 N. At what angle is the rope held?

$$W = Fd \cos \theta, \text{ so}$$

$$\cos \theta = \frac{W}{Fd} = \frac{1.20 \times 10^4 \text{ J}}{(125 \text{ N})(185 \text{ m})} = 0.519$$

Therefore, $\theta = 58.7°$.

38. You slide a crate up a ramp at an angle of 30.0° by exerting a 225-N force parallel to the ramp. The crate moves at constant speed. The coefficient of friction is 0.28. How much work have you done on the crate when it is raised a vertical distance of 1.15 m?

To find the distance, d, along the plane from h, the vertical distance

$$d = \frac{h}{\sin 30.0°} = \frac{1.15 \text{ m}}{0.500} = 2.30 \text{ m}$$

F and d are parallel so

$$W = Fd = (225 \text{ N})(2.30 \text{ m}) = 518 \text{ J}$$

39. A 4.2-kN piano is to be slid up a 3.5-m frictionless plank at a constant speed. The plank makes an angle of 30.0° with the horizontal. Calculate the work done by the person sliding the piano up the plank.

The force parallel to the plane is given by

$$F_{||} = F \sin \theta$$

so $W = F_{||} d = Fd \sin \theta$

$$W = (4200 \text{ N})(3.5 \text{ m})(\sin 30.0°)$$

$$= 7.4 \times 10^3 \text{ J}$$

40. Rico slides a 60-kg crate up an inclined ramp 2.0-m long onto a platform 1.0 m above floor level. A 400-N force, parallel to the ramp, is needed to slide the crate up the ramp at a constant speed.

a. How much work does Rico do in sliding the crate up the ramp?

$$W = Fd = (400 \text{ N})(2.0 \text{ m}) = 800 \text{ J}$$

b. How much work would be done if Rico simply lifted the crate straight up from the floor to the platform?

$$W = Fd = mgd$$

$$= (60 \text{ kg})(9.80 \text{ m/s}^2)(1.0 \text{ m})$$

$$= 600 \text{ J}$$

41. A worker pushes a crate weighing 93 N up an inclined plane. The worker pushes the crate horizontally, parallel to the ground, as illustrated in **Figure 10–14.**

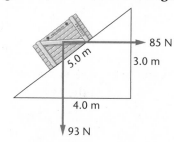

FIGURE 10-14

a. The worker exerts a force of 85 N. How much work does he do?

Displacement in direction of force is 4.0 m, so $W = (85 \text{ N})(4.0 \text{ m}) = 340$ J.

b. How much work is done by gravity? (Be careful with the signs you use.)

Displacement in direction of force is -3.0 m, so $W = (93 \text{ N})(-3.0 \text{ m}) = -280$ J (work done against gravity).

Copyright © by Glencoe/McGraw-Hill

41. (continued)

    c. The coefficient of friction is $\mu = 0.20$. How much work is done by friction? (Be careful with the signs you use.)

$$W = \mu F_N d = \mu (F_{you,\perp} + F_{g,\perp})d$$

$$= 0.20(85 \text{ N} \cdot \sin \theta$$

$$+ 93 \text{ N} \cdot \cos \theta)(-5.0 \text{ m})$$

$$= 0.20 \left(85 \text{ N} \cdot \frac{3}{5} + 93 \text{ N} \cdot \frac{4}{5} \right)(-5.0 \text{ m})$$

$$= -1.3 \times 10^2 \text{ J (work done against friction)}$$

page 244

42. The graph in **Figure 10–15** shows the force and displacement of an object being pulled.

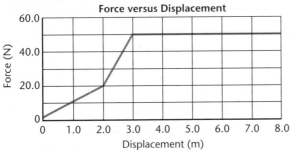

Force versus Displacement

FIGURE 10-15

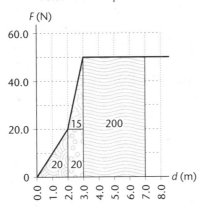

Force versus Displacement

    a. Calculate the work done to pull the object 7.0 m.

    Find the area under the curve (see graph):

    0 to 2 m:

$$\frac{1}{2} (20.0 \text{ N})(2.0 \text{ m}) = 2.0 \times 10^1 \text{ J}$$

2 m to 3 m:

$$\frac{1}{2} (30.0 \text{ N})(1.0 \text{ m}) + (20 \text{ N})(1.0 \text{ m})$$

$$= 15 \text{ J} + 20 \text{ J} = 35 \text{ J}$$

3 m to 7 m:

$$(50.0 \text{ N})(4.0 \text{ m}) = 2.0 \times 10^2 \text{ J}$$

Total work:

$$20 \text{ J} + 35 \text{ J} + 2.0 \times 10^2 \text{ J}$$

$$= 2.6 \times 10^2 \text{ J}$$

    b. Calculate the power developed if the work were done in 2.0 s.

$$P = \frac{W}{t} = \frac{2.6 \times 10^2 \text{ J}}{2.0 \text{ s}} = 1.3 \times 10^2 \text{ W}$$

43. In 35.0 s, a pump delivers 0.550 m^3 of oil into barrels on a platform 25.0 m above the pump intake pipe. The density of the oil is 0.820 g/cm^3.

    a. Calculate the work done by the pump.

    Mass lifted $= (0.550 \text{ m}^3)$

$$\times (1.00 \times 10^6 \text{ cm}^3/\text{m}^3)(0.820 \text{ g/cm}^3)$$

$$= 4.51 \times 10^5 \text{ g} = 451 \text{ kg}$$

    The work done is

$$W = F_g d = mg(h)$$

$$= (451 \text{ kg})(9.80 \text{ m/s}^2)(25.0 \text{ m})$$

$$= 1.10 \times 10^5 \text{ J} = 1.10 \times 10^2 \text{ kJ}$$

    b. Calculate the power produced by the pump.

$$P = \frac{W}{t} = \frac{1.10 \times 10^2 \text{ kJ}}{35.0 \text{ s}} = 3.14 \text{ kW}$$

44. A 12.0-m long conveyor belt, inclined at 30.0°, is used to transport bundles of newspapers from the mailroom up to the cargo bay to be loaded on to delivery trucks. Each newspaper has a mass of 1.0 kg, and there are 25 newspapers per bundle. Determine the power of the conveyor if it delivers 15 bundles per minute.

$$P = \frac{W}{t} = \frac{Fd}{t} = \frac{mgd}{t}$$

$$= \frac{(25)(15)(1.0 \text{ kg})(9.80 \text{ m/s}^2)(12.0 \text{ m})(\sin 30.0°)}{60.0 \text{ s}}$$

$$= 3.7 \times 10^2 \text{ W}$$

Copyright © by Glencoe/McGraw-Hill

45. An engine moves a boat through the water at a constant speed of 15 m/s. The engine must exert a force of 6.0×10^3 N to balance the force that water exerts against the hull. What power does the engine develop?

$$P = \frac{W}{t} = \frac{Fd}{t} = Fv$$

$$= (6.0 \times 10^3 \text{ N})(15 \text{ m/s})$$

$$= 9.0 \times 10^4 \text{ W} = 9.0 \times 10^1 \text{ kW}$$

46. A 188-W motor will lift a load at the rate (speed) of 6.50 cm/s. How great a load can the motor lift at this rate?

$$v = 6.50 \text{ cm/s} = 0.0650 \text{ m/s}$$

$$P = \frac{W}{t} = \frac{Fd}{t} = F\left(\frac{d}{t}\right) = Fv$$

$$P = F_g v$$

$$F_g = \frac{P}{v} = \frac{188 \text{ W}}{0.0650 \text{ m/s}} = 2.89 \times 10^3 \text{ N}$$

47. A car is driven at a constant speed of 76 km/h down a road. The car's engine delivers 48 kW of power. Calculate the average force that is resisting the motion of the car.

$$P = \frac{W}{t} = \frac{Fd}{t} = Fv$$

$$\text{so } F = \frac{P}{v}$$

$$= \frac{48\ 000 \text{ W}}{\left(76\ \frac{\text{km}}{\text{h}}\right)\left(\frac{1000 \text{ m}}{1 \text{ km}}\right)\left(\frac{1 \text{ h}}{3600 \text{ s}}\right)}$$

$$= 2.3 \times 10^3 \text{ N}$$

Section 10.2

Level 1

48. Stan raises a 1200-N piano a distance of 5.00 m using a set of pulleys. Stan pulls in 20.0 m of rope.

a. How much effort force would Stan apply if this were an ideal machine?

$$F_e d_e = F_r d_r$$

$$\text{so } F_e = \frac{F_r d_r}{d_e} = \frac{(1200 \text{ N})(5.00 \text{ m})}{20.0 \text{ m}}$$

$$= 3.0 \times 10^2 \text{ N}$$

b. What force is used to balance the friction force if the actual effort is 340 N?

$$F_e = F_f + F_{e,\text{ ideal}}$$

$$F_f = F_e - F_{e,\text{ ideal}} = 340 \text{ N} - 3.0 \times 10^2 \text{ N}$$

$$= 40 \text{ N}$$

c. What is the work output?

$$W_o = F_r d_r = (1200 \text{ N})(5.00 \text{ m})$$

$$= 6.0 \times 10^3 \text{ J}$$

d. What is the input work?

$$W_i = F_e d_e = (340 \text{ N})(20.0 \text{ m})$$

$$= 6.8 \times 10^3 \text{ J}$$

e. What is the mechanical advantage?

$$MA = \frac{F_r}{F_e} = \frac{1200 \text{N}}{340 \text{N}} = 3.5$$

49. A mover's dolly is used to transport a refrigerator up a ramp into a house. The refrigerator has a mass of 115 kg. The ramp is 2.10 m long and rises 0.850 m. The mover pulls the dolly with a force of 496 N up the ramp. The dolly and ramp constitute a machine.

a. What work does the mover do?

$$W_i = Fd = (496 \text{ N})(2.10 \text{ m})$$

$$= 1.04 \times 10^3 \text{ J}$$

b. What is the work done on the refrigerator by the machine?

$$d = \text{height raised} = 0.850 \text{ m}$$

$$W_o = mgd$$

$$= (115 \text{ kg})(9.80 \text{ m/s}^2)(0.850 \text{ m})$$

$$= 958 \text{ J}$$

c. What is the efficiency of the machine?

$$\text{efficiency} = \frac{W_o}{W_i} \times 100$$

$$= \frac{958 \text{ J}}{1.04 \times 10^3 \text{ J}} \times 100$$

$$= 92.1\%$$

Copyright © by Glencoe/McGraw-Hill

50. A pulley system lifts a 1345-N weight a distance of 0.975 m. Paul pulls the rope a distance of 3.90 m, exerting a force of 375 N.

a. What is the ideal mechanical advantage of the system?

$$IMA = \frac{d_e}{d_r} = \frac{3.90m}{0.975m} = 4.00$$

b. What is the mechanical advantage?

$$MA = \frac{F_r}{F_e} = \frac{1345N}{375N} = 3.59$$

c. How efficient is the system?

$$\text{efficiency} = \frac{MA}{IMA} \times 100$$

$$= \frac{3.59}{4.00} \times 100$$

$$= 89.8\%$$

51. Because there is very little friction, the lever is an extremely efficient simple machine. Using a 90.0% efficient lever, what input work is required to lift an 18.0-kg mass through a distance of 0.50 m?

$$\text{efficiency} = \frac{W_o}{W_i} \times 100$$

$$W_i = \frac{(W_o)(100)}{\text{efficiency}} = \frac{(mgd)(100)}{(90.0\%)}$$

$$= \frac{(18.0 \text{ kg})(9.80 \text{ m/s}^2)(0.50 \text{ m})(100)}{90.0\%}$$

$$= 98 \text{ J}$$

52. What work is required to lift a 215-kg mass a distance of 5.65 m using a machine that is 72.5% efficient?

$$W_o = F_r d_r$$

$$= (215 \text{ kg})(9.80 \text{ m/s}^2)(5.65 \text{ m})$$

$$= 1.19 \times 10^4 \text{ J}$$

$$\frac{W_o}{W_i} \times 100 = 72.5\%; \quad \frac{W_o}{W_i} = 0.725$$

$$W_i = \frac{W_o}{0.725} = \frac{1.19 \times 104 \text{ J}}{0.725}$$

$$= 1.64 \times 10^4 \text{ J}$$

Level 2

53. The ramp in **Figure 10-16** is 18 m long and 4.5 m high.

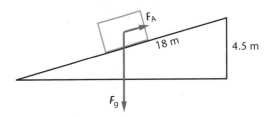

FIGURE 10-16

a. What force parallel to the ramp (F_A) is required to slide a 25-kg box at constant speed to the top of the ramp if friction is disregarded?

$$W = F_g h = (25 \text{ kg})(9.8 \text{ m/s}^2)(4.5 \text{ m})$$

$$= 1.1 \times 10^3 \text{ J}$$

$$W = F_A d$$

$$F_A = \frac{W}{d} = \frac{1.1 \times 10^3 \text{ J}}{18 \text{ m}} = 61 \text{ N}$$

b. What is the *IMA* of the ramp?

$$IMA = \frac{d_e}{d_f} = \frac{18 \text{ m}}{4.5 \text{ m}} = 4.0$$

page 245

c. What are the real *MA* and the efficiency of the ramp if a parallel force of 75 N is actually required?

$$MA = \frac{F_r}{F_e} = \frac{(25 \text{ kg})(9.8 \text{ m/s}^2)}{75 \text{ N}} = 3.3$$

$$\text{efficiency} = \frac{MA}{IMA} \times 100$$

$$= \frac{3.3}{4.0} \times 100 = 82\%$$

Copyright © by Glencoe/McGraw-Hill

54. A motor having an efficiency of 88% operates a crane having an efficiency of 42%. With what constant speed does the crane lift a 410-kg crate of machine parts if the power supplied to the motor is 5.5 kW?

Total efficiency = 88% × 42% = 37%

Useful power = 5.5 kW × 37%

$$= 2.0 \text{ kW}$$

$$= 2.0 \times 10^3 \text{ W}$$

$$P = \frac{W}{t} = \frac{Fd}{t} = F\left(\frac{d}{t}\right) = Fv$$

$$v = \frac{P}{F_g} = \frac{2.0 \times 10^3 \text{ W}}{(410 \text{ kg})(9.8 \text{ m/s}^2)}$$

$$= 0.50 \text{ m/s}$$

55. A compound machine is constructed by attaching a lever to a pulley system. Consider an ideal compound machine consisting of a lever with an *IMA* of 3.0 and a pulley system with an *IMA* of 2.0.

a. Show that the *IMA* of this compound machine is 6.0.

$$W_{i1} = W_{o1} = W_{i2} = W_{o2}$$

$$W_{i1} = W_{o2}$$

$$F_{e1}d_{e1} = F_{r2}d_{r2}$$

For the compound machine

$$IMA_c = \frac{d_{e1}}{d_{r2}}$$

$$\frac{d_{e1}}{d_{r1}} = IMA_1 \text{ and } \frac{d_{e2}}{d_{r2}} = IMA_2$$

$$d_{r1} = d_{e2}$$

$$\frac{d_{e1}}{IMA_1} = d_{r1} = d_{e2} = (IMA_2)(d_{r2})$$

$$d_{e1} = (IMA_1)(IMA_2)(d_{r2})$$

$$\frac{d_{e1}}{d_{r2}} = IMA_c = (IMA_1)(IMA_2)$$

$$= (3.0)(2.0) = 6.0$$

b. If the compound machine is 60.0% efficient, how much effort must be applied to the lever to lift a 540-N box?

$$\frac{F_{r2}}{F_{e1}} = MA_c = \frac{(IMA_c) \times (\text{eff})}{100}$$

$$\frac{F_{r2}}{F_{e1}} = \frac{(6.0)(60.0\%)}{100} = 3.6$$

$$F_{e1} = \frac{F_{r2}}{3.6} = \frac{540 \text{ N}}{3.6} = 150 \text{ N}$$

c. If you move the effort side of the lever 12.0 cm, how far is the box lifted?

$$\frac{d_{e1}}{d_{r2}} = IMA_c$$

$$d_{r2} = \frac{d_{e1}}{IMA_c} = \frac{12.0 \text{ cm}}{6.0} = 2.0 \text{ cm}$$

Critical Thinking Problems

56. A sprinter, mass 75 kg, runs the 50-meter dash in 8.50 s. Assume that the sprinter's acceleration is constant throughout the race.

a. What is the average power of the sprinter over the 50.0 m?

Assume constant acceleration, therefore constant force

$$x = \frac{1}{2} at^2$$

$$\text{so } a = \frac{2x}{t^2} = \frac{(2)(50.0 \text{ m})}{(8.50 \text{ s})^2}$$

$$a = 1.38 \text{ m/s}^2$$

$$P = \frac{W}{t} = \frac{Fd}{t} = \frac{mad}{t}$$

$$P_{ave} = \frac{(75 \text{ kg})(1.38 \text{ m/s}^2)(50.0 \text{ m})}{8.50 \text{ s}}$$

$$= 6.1 \times 10^2 \text{ W}$$

b. What is the maximum power generated by the sprinter?

Power increaes linearly from zero, since the velocity increases linearly. Therefore

$$P_{max} = 2P_{ave} = 1.2 \times 10^3 \text{ W}$$

Copyright © by Glencoe/McGraw-Hill

56. (continued)

   c. Make a quantitative graph of power versus time for the entire race.

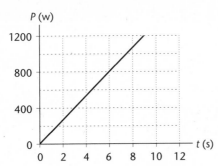

57. A sprinter in problem 56 runs the 50-meter dash in the same time, 8.50 s. However, this time the sprinter accelerates at a constant rate in the first second and runs the rest of the race at a constant velocity.

   a. Calculate the average power produced for that first second.

   Distance 1st second + Distance rest of race = 50.0 m

   $$\frac{1}{2} a (1.00 \text{ s})^2 + v_1(7.50 \text{ s}) = 50.0 \text{ m}$$

   Final velocity:

   $$v_1 = at = a(1.00 \text{ s})$$

   $$\frac{1}{2} a (1.00 \text{ s})^2 + (a)(1.00 \text{ s})(7.50 \text{ s})$$

   $$= 50.0 \text{ m}$$

So, using SI units:

$$(0.50a + 7.50a)\text{s}^2 = 50.0 \text{ m}$$

$$a = 6.25 \text{ m/s}^2$$

For the 1st second:

$$d = \frac{1}{2} at^2 = \left(\frac{1}{2}\right)(6.25 \text{ m/s}^2)(1.00 \text{ s})^2$$

$$= 3.13 \text{ m}$$

From Problem 56,

$$P = \frac{mad}{t}$$

$$P_{ave} = \frac{(75 \text{ kg})(6.25 \text{ m/s}^2)(3.13 \text{ m})}{1.00 \text{ s}}$$

$$P_{ave} = 1.5 \times 10^3 \text{ W}$$

b. What is the maximum power the sprinter now generates?

$$P_{max} = 2P_{ave} = 2.9 \times 10^3 \text{ W}$$

Copyright © by Glencoe/McGraw-Hill

11 Energy

Practice Problems

11.1 The Many Forms of Energy
pages 248–256

page 251

1. Consider the compact car in the Example Problem.

   a. Write 22.0 m/s and 44.0 m/s in km/h.

   $$\frac{22.0 \text{ m}}{\text{s}} \times \frac{3600 \text{ s}}{1 \text{ h}} \times \frac{1 \text{ km}}{1000 \text{ m}}$$

   $$= 79.2 \text{ km/h}$$

   $$\frac{44.0 \text{ m}}{\text{s}} \times \frac{3600 \text{ s}}{1 \text{ h}} \times \frac{1 \text{ km}}{1000 \text{ m}}$$

   $$= 158 \text{ km/h}$$

   b. How much work is done in slowing the car to 22.0 m/s?

   $$W = \Delta K = K_f - K_i$$

   $$= 2.12 \times 10^5 \text{ J} - 8.47 \times 10^5 \text{ J}$$

   $$= -6.35 \times 10^5 \text{ J}$$

   c. How much work is done in bringing it to rest?

   $$W = \Delta K = 0 - 8.47 \times 10^5 \text{ J}$$

   $$= -8.47 \times 10^5 \text{ J}$$

   d. Assume that the force that does the work slowing the car is constant. Find the ratio of the distance needed to slow the car from 44.0 m/s to 22.0 m/s to the distance needed to slow it from 22.0 m/s to rest.

   $W = Fd$, so distance is proportional to work. The ratio is

   $$\frac{-6.35 \times 10^5 \text{ J}}{-2.12 \times 10^5 \text{ J}} = 3.00$$

   It takes three times the distance to slow the car to half its speed than it does to slow it to a complete stop.

2. A rifle can shoot a 4.20-g bullet at a speed of 965 m/s.

   a. Draw work-energy bar graphs and free-body diagrams for all parts of this problem.

   Work-Energy Bar Graph

   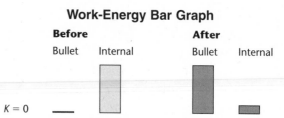

   b. Find the kinetic energy of the bullet as it leaves the rifle.

   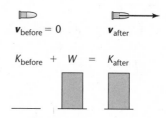

   $$K = \frac{1}{2}mv^2$$

   $$= \frac{1}{2}(0.00420 \text{ kg})(965 \text{ m/s})^2$$

   $$= 1.96 \times 10^3 \text{ J}$$

   c. What work is done on the bullet if it starts from rest?

   $$W = \Delta K = 1.96 \times 10^3 \text{ J}$$

Copyright © by Glencoe/McGraw-Hill

d. If the work is done over a distance of 0.75 m, what is the average force on the bullet?

$$W = Fd$$

$$\text{so } F = \frac{W}{d} = \frac{1.96 \times 10^3 \text{ J}}{0.75 \text{m}}$$

$$= 2.6 \times 10^3 \text{ N}$$

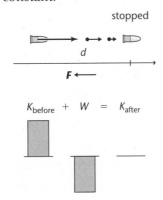

e. If the bullet comes to rest by penetrating 1.5 cm into metal, what is the magnitude and direction of the force the metal exerts? Again, assume that the force is constant.

$$F = \frac{W}{d} = \frac{\Delta K}{d} = \frac{1.96 \times 10^3 \text{ J}}{0.015 \text{ m}}$$

$$= 1.3 \times 10^5 \text{ N, forward}$$

3. A comet with a mass of 7.85×10^{11} kg strikes Earth at a speed of 25.0 km/s.

a. Find the kinetic energy of the comet in joules.

$$K = \frac{1}{2} mv^2$$

$$= \frac{1}{2} (7.85 \times 10^{11} \text{ kg})(2.50 \times 10^4 \text{ m/s})^2$$

$$= 2.45 \times 10^{20} \text{ J}$$

b. Compare the work that is done by Earth in stopping the comet to the 4.2×10^{15} J of energy that were released by the largest nuclear weapon ever built. Such a comet collision has been suggested as having caused the extinction of the dinosaurs.

$$\frac{K_{comet}}{K_{bomb}} = \frac{2.45 \times 10^{20} \text{ J}}{4.2 \times 10^{15} \text{ J}}$$

$$= 5.8 \times 10^4 \text{ bombs would be required.}$$

4. **Table 11–1** shows that 2.2×10^6 J of work are needed to accelerate a 5700-kg trailer truck to 1.0×10^2 km/h.

a. What would be the truck's speed if half as much work were done on it?

Since $W_A = \Delta K = \frac{1}{2} mv_A^2$, then

$$v_A = \sqrt{\frac{2W_A}{m}}.$$

If $W_B = \frac{1}{2} W_A$,

$$v_B = \sqrt{\frac{2W_B}{m}}$$

$$= \sqrt{\frac{2 (1/2) W_A}{m}} = \sqrt{\frac{1}{2}} v_A$$

$$= (0.707)(1.0 \times 10^2 \text{ km/h}) = 71 \text{ km/h}$$

b. What would be the truck's speed if twice as much work were done on it?

If $W_C = 2W_A$,

$$v_C = \sqrt{2} (1.0 \times 10^2 \text{ km/h}) = 140 \text{ km/h}$$

page 254

5. For the preceding Example Problem, select the shelf as the reference level. The system is the book plus Earth.

a. What is the gravitational potential energy of the book at the top of your head?

$$U_g = mgh$$

$$U_g = (2.00 \text{ kg})(9.80 \text{ m/s}^2)$$

$$\times (0.00 \text{ m} - 2.10 \text{ m} + 1.65 \text{ m})$$

$$U_g = -8.82 \text{ J}$$

Copyright © by Glencoe/McGraw-Hill

5. (continued)

b. What is the gravitational potential energy of the book at the floor?

$U_g = mgh$

$U_g = (2.00 \text{ kg})(9.80 \text{ m/s}^2)$
$\times (0.00 \text{ m} - 2.10 \text{ m})$

$U_g = -41.2 \text{ J}$

page 255

6. A 90-kg rock climber first climbs 45 m up to the top of a quarry, then descends 85 m from the top to the bottom of the quarry. If the initial height is the reference level, find the potential energy of the system (the climber plus Earth) at the top and the bottom. Draw bar graphs for both situations.

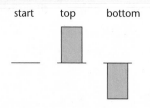

$U_g = mgh$

At the edge,

$U_g = (90 \text{ kg})(9.80 \text{ m/s}^2)(+45 \text{ m})$
$= 4 \times 10^4 \text{ J}$

At the bottom,

$U_g = (90 \text{ kg})(9.80 \text{ m/s}^2)(+45 \text{ m} - 85 \text{ m})$
$= -4 \times 10^4 \text{ J}$

7. A 50.0-kg shell is shot from a cannon at Earth's surface to a height of 425 m. The system is the shell plus Earth, and the reference level is Earth's surface.

a. What is the gravitational potential energy of the system when the shell is at this height?

$U_g = mgh$
$= (50.0 \text{ kg})(9.80 \text{ m/s}^2)(425 \text{ m})$
$= 2.08 \times 10^5 \text{ J}$

b. What is the change in the potential energy when the shell falls to a height of 225 m?

$\Delta U_g = mgh_f - mgh_i = mg(h_f - h_i)$
$= (50.0 \text{ kg})(9.80 \text{ m/s}^2)$
$\times (225 \text{ m} - 425 \text{ m})$
$= -9.80 \times 10^4 \text{ J}$

8. A 7.26-kg bowling ball hangs from the end of a 2.5-m rope. The ball is pulled back until the rope makes a 45° angle with the vertical.

a. What is the gravitational potential energy of the system?

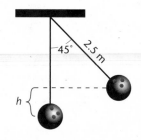

$h = (2.5 \text{ m})(1 - \cos \theta) = 0.73 \text{ m}$

$U_g = mgh$
$= (7.26 \text{ kg})(9.80 \text{ m/s}^2)(0.73 \text{ m})$
$= 52 \text{ J}$

b. What system and what reference level did you use in your calculation?

the height of the ball when the rope was vertical

11.2 Conservation of Energy
pages 258–265

page 261

9. A bike rider approaches a hill at a speed of 8.5 m/s. The mass of the bike and rider together is 85 kg.

a. Identify a suitable system.

The system is the bike + rider + Earth. No external forces, so total energy is conserved.

Copyright © by Glencoe/McGraw-Hill

9. (continued)

page 262

b. Find the initial kinetic energy of the system.

$$K = \frac{1}{2}mv^2$$

$$= \frac{1}{2}(85 \text{ kg})(8.5 \text{ m/s})^2 = 3.1 \times 10^3 \text{ J}$$

c. The rider coasts up the hill. Assuming that there is no friction, at what height will the bike come to rest?

$$K_{before} + U_{g \text{ before}} = K_{after} + U_{g \text{ after}}$$

$$\frac{1}{2}mv^2 + 0 = 0 + mgh,$$

$$h = \frac{v^2}{2g} = \frac{(8.5 \text{ m/s})^2}{(2)(9.80 \text{ m/s}^2)} = 3.7 \text{ m}$$

d. Does your answer to **c** depend on the mass of the system? Explain.

No. It cancels because both K and U_g are proportional to m.

10. Tarzan, mass 85 kg, swings down on the end of a 20-m vine from a tree limb 4.0 m above the ground. Sketch the situation.

a. How fast is Tarzan moving when he reaches the ground?

$$K_{before} + U_{g \text{ before}} = K_{after} + U_{g \text{ after}}$$

$$0 + mgh = \frac{1}{2}mv^2 + 0$$

$$v^2 = 2gh = 2(9.80 \text{ m/s}^2)(4.0 \text{ m})$$

$$= 78.4 \text{ m}^2/\text{s}^2$$

$$v = 8.9 \text{ m/s}$$

b. Does your answer to **a** depend on Tarzan's mass?

No

c. Does your answer to **a** depend on the length of the vine?

No

11. A skier starts from rest at the top of a 45-m hill, skis down a 30° incline into a valley, and continues up a 40-m-high hill. Both hill heights are measured from the valley floor. Assume that you can neglect friction and the effect of ski poles.

a. How fast is the skier moving at the bottom of the valley?

$$K_{before} + U_{g \text{ before}} = K_{after} + U_{g \text{ after}}$$

$$0 + mgh = \frac{1}{2}mv^2 + 0$$

$$v^2 = 2gh = 2(9.80 \text{ m/s}^2)(45 \text{ m})$$

$$= 880 \text{ m}^2/\text{s}^2$$

$$v = 3.0 \times 10^1 \text{ m/s}$$

b. What is the skier's speed at the top of the next hill?

$$K_{before} + U_{g \text{ before}} = K_{after} + U_{g \text{ after}}$$

$$0 + mgh_i = \frac{1}{2}mv^2 + mgh_f$$

$$v^2 = 2g(h_i - h_f)$$

$$= 2(9.80 \text{ m/s}^2)(45 \text{ m} - 40 \text{ m})$$

$$= 98 \text{ m}^2/\text{s}^2$$

$$v = 10 \text{ m/s}$$

c. Does your answer to **a** or **b** depend on the angles of the hills?

No

12. Suppose, in the case of problem 9, that the bike rider pedaled up the hill and never came to a stop.

a. In what system is energy conserved?

The system of Earth, bike, and rider remains the same, but now the energy involved is not mechanical energy alone. The rider must be considered as having stored energy, some of which is converted to mechanical energy.

b. From what form of energy did the bike gain mechanical energy?

Energy came from the chemical potential energy stored in the rider's body.

Copyright © by Glencoe/McGraw-Hill

13. A 2.00-g bullet, moving at 538 m/s, strikes a 0.250-kg piece of wood at rest on a frictionless table. The bullet sticks in the wood, and the combined mass moves slowly down the table.

a. Draw energy bar graphs and momentum vectors for the collision.

$$K_{bullet} + K_{wood} = K_{b+w}$$

b. Find the speed of the system after the collision.

From the conservation of momentum,

$$mv = (m + M)V$$

so $V = \dfrac{mv}{m + M}$

$$= \dfrac{(0.00200 \text{ kg})(538 \text{ m/s})}{0.00200 \text{ kg} + 0.250 \text{ kg}}$$

$$= 4.27 \text{ m/s}$$

c. Find the kinetic energy of the system before the collision.

$$K = \dfrac{1}{2} mv^2$$

$$= \dfrac{1}{2}(0.00200 \text{ kg})(538 \text{ m/s})^2$$

$$= 289 \text{ J}$$

d. Find the kinetic energy of the system after the collision.

$$K_f = \dfrac{1}{2}(m + M)V^2$$

$$= \dfrac{1}{2}(0.00200 \text{ kg} + 0.250 \text{ kg})$$

$$\times (4.27 \text{ m/s})^2$$

$$= 2.30 \text{ J}$$

e. What percentage of the system's original kinetic energy was lost?

$$\% K \text{ lost} = \left(\dfrac{\Delta K}{K_i}\right) \times 100$$

$$= \left(\dfrac{287 \text{ J}}{289 \text{ J}}\right) \times 100$$

$$= 99.3\%$$

14. An 8.00-g bullet is fired horizontally into a 9.00-kg block of wood on an air table and is embedded in it. After the collision, the block and bullet slide along the frictionless surface together with a speed of 10.0 cm/s. What was the initial speed of the bullet?

Conservation of momentum

$$mv = (m + M)V, \text{ or}$$

$$v = \dfrac{(m + M)V}{m}$$

$$= \dfrac{(0.00800 \text{ kg} + 9.00 \text{ kg})(0.10 \text{ m/s})}{0.00800 \text{ kg}}$$

$$= 112.6 \text{ m/s} = 110 \text{ m/s}$$

15. Bullets can't penetrate Superman's chest. Suppose that Superman, with mass 104 kg, while not moving, is struck by a 4.20-g bullet moving with a speed of 835 m/s. The bullet drops straight down with no horizontal velocity. How fast was Superman moving after the collision if his superfeet are frictionless?

This is a conservation of momentum question.

$$mv_i + MV_i = mv_f + MV_f$$

where m, v_i, v_f **refer to the bullet and** M, V_i, V_f **to Superman. The final momentum is the same as the initial momentum because the frictionless superfeet mean there are no external forces. The final momentum is that of Superman alone because the horizontal velocity of the bullet is zero.**

$V_i = 0$ m/s and $v_f = 0$ m/s which gives $mv_i = MV_f$

$$V_f = \dfrac{mv_i}{M} = \dfrac{(0.0042 \text{ kg})(835 \text{ m/s})}{104 \text{ kg}}$$

$$= 0.034 \text{ m/s}$$

Copyright © by Glencoe/McGraw-Hill

16. A 0.73-kg magnetic target is suspended on a string. A 0.025-kg magnetic dart, shot horizontally, strikes it head-on. The dart and the target together, acting like a pendulum, swing up 12 cm above the initial level before instantaneously coming to rest.

a. Sketch the situation and decide on the system.

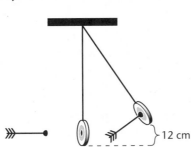

b. This is a two-part problem. Decide what is conserved in each part and explain your decision.

Only momentum is conserved in the inelastic dart-target collision, so

$$mv_i + MV_i = (m + M)V_f$$

where $V_i = 0$ since the target is initially at rest and V_f is the common velocity just after impact. As the dart-target combination swings upward, energy is conserved, so $\Delta U_g = \Delta K$ or, at the top of the swing,

$$(m + M)gh = \frac{1}{2}(m + M)V_f^2$$

c. What was the initial velocity of the dart?

Solving this for V_f and inserting into the momentum equation gives

$$v_i = (m + M)\frac{\sqrt{2gh_f}}{m}$$

$$= \frac{(0.025 \text{ kg} + 0.73 \text{ kg})\sqrt{2(9.8 \text{ m/s}^2)(0.12 \text{ m})}}{0.025 \text{ kg}}$$

$$= 46 \text{ m/s}$$

Chapter Review Problems

pages 269–271

page 269

Unless otherwise directed, assume that air resistance is negligible. Draw energy bar graphs to solve the problems.

Section 11.1

Level 1

38. A 1600-kg car travels at a speed of 12.5 m/s. What is its kinetic energy?

$$K = \frac{1}{2}mv^2 = \left(\frac{1}{2}\right)(1600 \text{ kg})(12.5 \text{ m/s})^2$$

$$= 1.3 \times 10^5 \text{ J}$$

39. A racing car has a mass of 1525 kg. What is its kinetic energy if it has a speed of 108 km/h?

$$v = \frac{(108 \text{ km/h})(1000 \text{ m/km})}{3600 \text{ s/h}}$$

$$= 30.0 \text{ m/s}$$

$$K = \frac{1}{2}mv^2 = \left(\frac{1}{2}\right)(1525 \text{ kg})(30.0 \text{ m/s})^2$$

$$= 6.86 \times 10^5 \text{ J}$$

40. Toni has a mass of 45 kg and is moving with a speed of 10.0 m/s.

a. Find Toni's kinetic energy.

$$K = \frac{1}{2}mv^2 = \left(\frac{1}{2}\right)(45 \text{ kg})(10.0 \text{ m/s})^2$$

$$= 2.3 \times 10^3 \text{ J}$$

b. Toni's speed changes to 5.0 m/s. Now what is her kinetic energy?

$$K = \frac{1}{2}mv^2 = \left(\frac{1}{2}\right)(45 \text{ kg})(5.0 \text{ m/s})^2$$

$$= 5.6 \times 10^2 \text{ J}$$

Copyright © by Glencoe/McGraw-Hill

40. (continued)

    c. What is the ratio of the kinetic energies in **a** and **b?** Explain the ratio.

$$\frac{1/2\ (mv_1^2)}{1/2\ (mv_2^2)} = \frac{v_1^2}{v_2^2} = \frac{(10.0)^2}{(5.0)^2} = \frac{4}{1}$$

    Twice the velocity gives four times the kinetic energy.

41. Shawn and his bike have a total mass of 45.0 kg. Shawn rides his bike 1.80 km in 10.0 min at a constant velocity. What is Shawn's kinetic energy?

$$v = \frac{d}{t} = \frac{(1.80\ \text{km})(1000\ \text{m/km})}{(10.0\ \text{min})(60\ \text{s/min})}$$

$$= 3.00\ \text{m/s}$$

$$K = \frac{1}{2}\ mv^2 = \left(\frac{1}{2}\right)(45.0\ \text{kg})(3.00\ \text{m/s})^2$$

$$= 203\ \text{J}$$

42. Ellen and Angela each has a mass of 45 kg, and they are moving together with a speed of 10.0 m/s.

    a. What is their combined kinetic energy?

$$K_c = \frac{1}{2}\ mv^2 = \frac{1}{2}\ (m_E + m_A)(v^2)$$

$$= \frac{1}{2}\ (45\ \text{kg} + 45\ \text{kg})(10.0\ \text{m/s})^2$$

$$= 4.5 \times 10^3\ \text{J}$$

    b. What is the ratio of their combined mass to Ellen's mass?

$$\frac{m_E + m_A}{m_E} = \frac{45\ \text{kg} + 45\ \text{kg}}{45\ \text{kg}} = \frac{90\ \text{kg}}{45\ \text{kg}}$$

$$= \frac{2}{1}$$

    c. What is the ratio of their combined kinetic energy to Ellen's kinetic energy? Explain.

$$K_E = \frac{1}{2}\ m_E v^2 = \frac{1}{2}\ (45\ \text{kg})(10.0\ \text{m/s})^2$$
$$= 2.3 \times 10^3\ \text{J}$$

$$\frac{K_c}{K_E} = \frac{4.5 \times 10^3\ \text{J}}{2.3 \times 10^3\ \text{J}} = \frac{2}{1}$$

    The ratio of the kinetic energies is the same as the ratio of their masses.

43. In the 1950s, an experimental train that had a mass of 2.50×10^4 kg was powered across a level track by a jet engine that produced a thrust of 5.00×10^5 N for a distance of 509 m.

    a. Find the work done on the train.

$$W = F \cdot d = (5.00 \times 10^5\ \text{N})(509\ \text{m})$$

$$= 2.55 \times 10^8\ \text{J}$$

    b. Find the change in kinetic energy.

$$\Delta K = W = 2.55 \times 10^8\ \text{J}$$

    c. Find the final kinetic energy of the train if it started from rest.

$$\Delta K = K_f - K_i$$

$$\text{so } K_f = \Delta K + K_i$$

$$= 2.55 \times 10^8\ \text{J} + 0.00$$

$$= 2.55 \times 10^8\ \text{J}$$

    d. Find the final speed of the train if there were no friction.

$$K_f = \frac{1}{2}\ mv^2$$

$$\text{So } v^2 = \frac{K_f}{(1/2)\ m}$$

$$= \frac{2.55 \times 10^8\ \text{J}}{(1/2)(2.50 \times 10^4\ \text{kg})}$$

$$\text{So } v = \sqrt{2.04 \times 10^4\ \text{m}^2/\text{s}^2} = 143\ \text{m/s}$$

44. A 14 700-N car is traveling at 25 m/s. The brakes are applied suddenly, and the car slides to a stop. The average braking force between the tires and the road is 7100 N. How far will the car slide once the brakes are applied?

$$W = F \cdot d = \frac{1}{2}\ mv^2$$

$$\text{Now } m = \frac{F_g}{g} = \frac{14\ 700\ \text{N}}{9.80\ \text{m/s}^2}$$

$$= 1.50 \times 10^3\ \text{kg}$$

$$\text{So } d = \frac{\frac{1}{2}\ mv^2}{F}$$

$$= \frac{\frac{1}{2}\ (1.50 \times 10^3\ \text{kg})(25\ \text{m/s})^2}{7100\ \text{N}}$$

$$= 66\ \text{m}$$

Copyright © by Glencoe/McGraw-Hill

45. A 15.0-kg cart is moving with a velocity of 7.50 m/s down a level hallway. A constant force of –10.0 N acts on the cart, and its velocity becomes 3.20 m/s.

a. What is the change in kinetic energy of the cart?

$$\Delta K = K_f - K_i = \frac{1}{2}\, m(v_f^2 - v_i^2)$$

$$= \frac{1}{2}\,(15.0\text{ kg})[(3.20\text{ m/s})^2$$
$$- (7.50\text{ m/s})^2]$$

$$= -345\text{ J}$$

b. How much work was done on the cart?

$$W = \Delta K = -345\text{ J}$$

c. How far did the cart move while the force acted?

$$W = Fd$$

$$\text{so } d = \frac{W}{F} = \frac{-345\text{ J}}{-10.0\text{ N}} = 34.5\text{ m}$$

46. How much potential energy does Tim, with mass 60.0 kg, gain when he climbs a gymnasium rope a distance of 3.5 m?

$$U_g = mgh$$

$$= (60.0\text{ kg})(9.80\text{ m/s}^2)(3.5\text{ m})$$

$$= 2.1 \times 10^3\text{ J}$$

page 270

47. A 6.4-kg bowling ball is lifted 2.1 m into a storage rack. Calculate the increase in the ball's potential energy.

$$U_g = mgh = (6.4\text{ kg})(9.80\text{ m/s}^2)(2.1\text{ m})$$

$$= 1.3 \times 10^2\text{ J}$$

48. Mary weighs 505 N. She walks down a flight of stairs to a level 5.50 m below her starting point. What is the change in Mary's potential energy?

$$U_g = mg\,\Delta h = W\,\Delta h$$

$$= (505\text{ N})(-5.50\text{ m})$$

$$= -2.78 \times 10^3\text{ J}$$

49. A weight lifter raises a 180-kg barbell to a height of 1.95 m. What is the increase in the potential energy of the barbell?

$$U_g = mgh$$

$$= (180\text{ kg})(9.80\text{ m/s}^2)(1.95\text{ m})$$

$$= 3.4 \times 10^3\text{ J}$$

50. A 10.0-kg test rocket is fired vertically from Cape Canaveral. Its fuel gives it a kinetic energy of 1960 J by the time the rocket engine burns all of the fuel. What additional height will the rocket rise?

$$U_g = mgh = K$$

$$h = \frac{K}{mg} = \frac{1960\text{ J}}{(10.0\text{ kg})(9.80\text{ m/s}^2)}$$

$$= 20.0\text{ m}$$

51. Antwan raised a 12.0-N physics book from a table 75 cm above the floor to a shelf 2.15 m above the floor. What was the change in the potential energy of the system?

$$U_g = mg\,\Delta h = F_g\Delta h = F_g(h_f - h_i)$$

$$= (12.0\text{ N})(2.15\text{ m} - 0.75\text{ m})$$

$$= 16.8\text{ J}$$

52. A hallway display of energy is constructed in which several people pull on a rope that lifts a block 1.00 m. The display indicates that 1.00 J of work is done. What is the mass of the block?

$$W = U_g = mgh$$

$$\text{so } m = \frac{W}{gh} = \frac{1.00\text{ J}}{(9.80\text{ m/s}^2)(1.00\text{ m})}$$

$$= 0.102\text{ kg}$$

Copyright © by Glencoe/McGraw-Hill

Level 2

53. It is not uncommon during the service of a professional tennis player for the racket to exert an average force of 150.0 N on the ball. If the ball has a mass of 0.060 kg and is in contact with the strings of the racket for 0.030 s, what is the kinetic energy of the ball as it leaves the racket? Assume that the ball starts from rest.

$$Ft = m \, \Delta v = mv_f - mv_i \text{ and } v_i = 0$$

$$\text{so } v_f = \frac{Ft}{m} = \frac{(150.0 \text{ N})(3.0 \times 10^{-2} \text{ s})}{6.0 \times 10^{-2} \text{ kg}}$$

$$= 75 \text{ m/s}$$

$$K = \frac{1}{2} mv^2$$

$$= \frac{1}{2} (6.0 \times 10^{-2} \text{ kg})(75 \text{ m/s})^2$$

$$= 1.7 \times 10^2 \text{ J}$$

54. Pam, wearing a rocket pack, stands on frictionless ice. She has a mass of 45 kg. The rocket supplies a constant force for 22.0 m, and Pam acquires a speed of 62.0 m/s.

a. What is the magnitude of the force?

$$F = ma \text{ and } v_f^2 = v_i^2 + 2ad$$

$$\text{so } a = \frac{v_f^2 - v_i^2}{2d}$$

but $v_i = 0$, so

$$a = \frac{v_f^2}{2d}$$

$$= \frac{(62.0 \text{ m/s})^2}{2(22.0)} = 87.4 \text{ m/s}^2$$

Therefore,

$$F = ma = (45 \text{ kg})(87.4 \text{ m/s}^2)$$

$$= 3.9 \times 10^3 \text{ N}$$

b. What is Pam's final kinetic energy?

$$K = \frac{1}{2} mv^2 = \frac{1}{2} (45 \text{ kg})(62.0 \text{ m/s})^2$$

$$= 8.6 \times 10^4 \text{ J}$$

55. A 2.00×10^3-kg car has a speed of 12.0 m/s. The car then hits a tree. The tree doesn't move, and the car comes to rest.

a. Find the change in kinetic energy of the car.

$$\Delta K = K_f - K_i = \frac{1}{2} m(v_f^2 - v_i^2)$$

$$= \frac{1}{2} (2.00 \times 10^3 \text{ kg})$$

$$\times [(0.0 \text{ m/s})^2 - (12.0 \text{ m/s})^2]$$

$$= -1.44 \times 10^5 \text{ J}$$

b. Find the amount of work done in pushing in the front of the car.

$$W = \Delta K = -1.44 \times 10^5 \text{ J}$$

c. Find the size of the force that pushed in the front of the car by 50.0 cm.

$$W = F \cdot d$$

$$\text{so } F = \frac{W}{d} = \frac{-1.44 \times 10^5 \text{ J}}{0.500 \text{ m}}$$

$$= -2.88 \times 10^5 \text{ N}$$

The negative sign implies a retarding force.

56. A constant net force of 410 N is applied upward to a stone that weighs 32 N. The upward force is applied through a distance of 2.0 m, and the stone is then released. To what height, from the point of release, will the stone rise?

$$W = Fd = (410 \text{ N})(2.0 \text{ m}) = 8.2 \times 10^2 \text{ J}$$

But $W = \Delta U_g = mg\Delta h$, so

$$\Delta h = \frac{W}{mg} = \frac{8.2 \times 10^2 \text{ J}}{32 \text{ N}} = 26 \text{ m}$$

Copyright © by Glencoe/McGraw-Hill

Section 11.2

Level 1

57. A 98-N sack of grain is hoisted to a storage room 50 m above the ground floor of a grain elevator.

    a. How much work is required?

    $W = Fd = (98 \text{ N})(50 \text{ m}) = 5 \times 10^3 \text{ J}$

    b. What is the increase in potential energy of the sack of grain at this height?

    $\Delta U_g = W = 5 \times 10^3 \text{ J}$

    c. The rope being used to lift the sack of grain breaks just as the sack reaches the storage room. What kinetic energy does the sack have just before it strikes the ground floor?

    $K = \Delta U_g = 5 \times 10^3 \text{ J}$

58. A 20-kg rock is on the edge of a 100-m cliff.

    a. What potential energy does the rock possess relative to the base of the cliff?

    $U_g = mgh = (20 \text{ kg})(9.80 \text{ m/s}^2)(100 \text{ m})$
    $= 2 \times 10^4 \text{ J}$

    b. The rock falls from the cliff. What is its kinetic energy just before it strikes the ground?

    $K = \Delta U_g = 2 \times 10^4 \text{ J}$

    c. What speed does the rock have as it strikes the ground?

    $K = \frac{1}{2} mv^2$

    $v = \sqrt{\frac{2K}{m}} = \sqrt{\frac{(2)(2 \times 10^4 \text{ J})}{20 \text{ kg}}}$

    $= 40 \text{ m/s}$

59. An archer puts a 0.30-kg arrow to the bowstring. An average force of 201 N is exerted to draw the string back 1.3 m.

    a. Assuming that all the energy goes into the arrow, with what speed does the arrow leave the bow?

    $W = K$

    $Fd = \frac{1}{2} mv^2$

    $v^2 = \frac{2Fd}{m}$

    $v = \sqrt{\frac{2Fd}{m}} = \sqrt{\frac{(2)(201 \text{ N})(1.3 \text{ m})}{0.30 \text{ kg}}}$

    $= 42 \text{ m/s}$

    b. If the arrow is shot straight up, how high does it rise?

    $U_g = \Delta K$

    $mgh = \frac{1}{2} mv^2$

    $h = \frac{v^2}{2g} = \frac{(42 \text{ m/s})^2}{(2)(9.80 \text{ m/s}^2)} = 9.0 \times 10^1 \text{ m}$

60. A 2.0-kg rock initially at rest loses 407 J of potential energy while falling to the ground.

    a. Calculate the kinetic energy that the rock gains while falling.

    $U_{g_i} + K_i = U_{g_f} + K_f$
    $K_f = U_{g_i} = 407 \text{ J}$

    b. What is the rock's speed just before it strikes the ground?

    $K = \frac{1}{2} mv^2$

    so $v^2 = (2) \dfrac{K}{m} = \dfrac{(2)(407 \text{ J})}{2.0 \text{ kg}}$

    $= 407 \text{ m}^2/\text{s}^2$

    so $v = 2.0 \times 10^1 \text{ m/s}$

Copyright © by Glencoe/McGraw-Hill

61. A physics book of unknown mass is dropped 4.50 m. What speed does the book have just before it hits the ground?

$$K = U_g$$

$$\frac{1}{2} mv^2 = mgh$$

The mass of the book divides out, so

$$\frac{1}{2} v^2 = gh$$

$$\text{or } v = \sqrt{2gh} = \sqrt{2(9.80 \text{ m/s}^2)(4.50 \text{ m})}$$

$$= 9.39 \text{ m/s}$$

62. A 30.0-kg gun is resting on a frictionless surface. The gun fires a 50.0-g bullet with a muzzle velocity of 310.0 m/s.

a. Calculate the momenta of the bullet and the gun after the gun is fired.

$$p_g = -p_b \text{ and}$$

$$p_b = m_b v_b$$

$$= (0.0500 \text{ kg})(310.0 \text{ m/s})$$

$$= 15.5 \text{ kg} \cdot \text{m/s}$$

$$p_g = -p_b = -15.5 \text{ kg} \cdot \text{m/s}$$

b. Calculate the kinetic energy of both the bullet and the gun just after firing.

$$K_b = \frac{1}{2} m_b v_b^2$$

$$= \frac{1}{2} (0.0500 \text{ kg})(310.0 \text{ m/s})^2$$

$$= 2.40 \times 10^3 \text{ J}$$

$$p_g = m_g v_g$$

$$\text{so } v_g = \frac{p_g}{m_g} = \frac{-15.5 \text{ kg} \cdot \text{m/s}}{30.0 \text{ kg}}$$

$$= -0.517 \text{ m/s}$$

$$K_g = \frac{1}{2} m_g v_g^2$$

$$= \frac{1}{2} (30.0 \text{ kg})(-0.517 \text{ m/s})^2$$

$$= 4.00 \text{ J}$$

63. A railroad car with a mass of 5.0×10^5 kg collides with a stationary railroad car of equal mass. After the collision, the two cars lock together and move off at 4.0 m/s.

page 271

a. Before the collision, the first railroad car was moving at 8.0 m/s. What was its momentum?

$$mv = (5.0 \times 10^5 \text{ kg})(8.0 \text{ m/s})$$

$$= 4.0 \times 10^6 \text{ kg} \cdot \text{m/s}$$

b. What was the total momentum of the two cars after the collision?

Since momentum is conserved, it must be

$$4.0 \times 10^6 \text{ kg} \cdot \text{m/s}$$

c. What were the kinetic energies of the two cars before and after the collision?

Before the collision:

$$K_1 = \frac{1}{2} mv^2$$

$$= \left(\frac{1}{2}\right)(5.0 \times 10^5 \text{ kg})(8.0 \text{ m/s})^2$$

$$= 1.6 \times 10^7 \text{ J}$$

$$K_2 = 0.0 \text{ J since it is at rest.}$$

After the collision:

$$K = \frac{1}{2} mv^2$$

$$= \left(\frac{1}{2}\right)(5.0 \times 10^5 \text{ kg} + 5.0 \times 10^5 \text{ kg})$$

$$\times (4.0 \text{ m/s})^2$$

$$= 8.0 \times 10^6 \text{ J}$$

d. Account for the loss of kinetic energy.

While momentum was conserved during the collision, kinetic energy was not. The amount not conserved was turned into heat and sound.

Copyright © by Glencoe/McGraw-Hill

64. From what height would a compact car have to be dropped to have the same kinetic energy that it has when being driven at 1.00×10^2 km/h?

$$v = \left(1.00 \times 10^2 \, \frac{km}{h}\right)\left(\frac{1000 \, m}{1 \, km}\right)\left(\frac{1 \, h}{3600 \, s}\right)$$

$$= 27.8 \, m/s$$

$$K = U_g$$

$\frac{1}{2} mv^2 = mgh$; the mass of the car divides out, so

$$\frac{1}{2} v^2 = gh$$

so $h = \dfrac{v^2}{2g} = \dfrac{(27.8 m/s)^2}{2(9.80 m/s^2)} = 40 \, m$

65. A steel ball has a mass of 4.0 kg and rolls along a smooth, level surface at 62 m/s.

a. Find its kinetic energy.

$$K = \frac{1}{2} mv^2 = \left(\frac{1}{2}\right)(4.0 \, kg)(62 \, m/s)^2$$

$$= 7.7 \times 10^3 \, J$$

b. At first, the ball was at rest on the surface. A constant force acted on it through a distance of 22 m to give it the speed of 62 m/s. What was the magnitude of the force?

$$W = Fd$$

$$F = \frac{W}{d} = \frac{7.7 \times 10^3 \, J}{22 \, m} = 3.5 \times 10^2 \, N$$

Level 2

66. Kelli weighs 420 N, and she is sitting on a playground swing seat that hangs 0.40 m above the ground. Tom pulls the swing back and releases it when the seat is 1.00 m above the ground.

a. How fast is Kelli moving when the swing passes through its lowest position?

$$U_g = Fd = (420 \, N)(0.40 \, m - 1.00 \, m)$$

$$= -250 \, J$$

$$K = -\Delta U_g = \frac{1}{2} mv^2$$

$$v = \sqrt{\frac{2K}{m}} = \sqrt{\frac{(2)(250 \, J)}{(420 \, N/9.80 \, m/s^2)}}$$

$$= 3.4 \, m/s$$

b. If Kelli moves through the lowest point at 2.0 m/s, how much work was done on the swing by friction?

$$W = U_g - K = 250 \, J - \frac{1}{2} mv^2$$

$$= 250 \, J - \left(\frac{1}{2}\right)\left(\frac{420 \, N}{9.80 \, m/s^2}\right)$$

$$\times (2.0 \, m/s)^2$$

$$= 250 \, J - 86 \, J = 160 \, J$$

$$= 1.6 \times 10^2 \, J$$

67. Justin throws a 10.0-g ball straight down from a height of 2.0 m. The ball strikes the floor at a speed of 7.5 m/s. What was the initial speed of the ball?

$$K_f = K_i + U_{g_i}$$

$$\frac{1}{2} mv_2^2 = \frac{1}{2} mv_1^2 + mgh$$

the mass of the ball divides out, so
$$v_1^2 = v_2^2 - 2gh,$$

$$v_1 = \sqrt{v_2^2 - 2gh}$$

$$= \sqrt{(7.5 \, m/s)^2 - (2)(9.80 \, m/s^2)(2.0 \, m)}$$

$$= 4.1 \, m/s$$

Copyright © by Glencoe/McGraw-Hill

68. Megan's mass is 28 kg. She climbs the 4.8-m ladder of a slide and reaches a velocity of 3.2 m/s at the bottom of the slide. How much work was done by friction on Megan?

At the top,

$$U_g = mgh = (28 \text{ kg})(9.80 \text{ m/s}^2)(4.8 \text{ m})$$

$$= 1.3 \times 10^3 \text{ J}$$

At the bottom,

$$K = \frac{1}{2}mv^2 = \left(\frac{1}{2}\right)(28 \text{ kg})(3.2 \text{ m/s})^2$$

$$= 1.4 \times 10^2 \text{ J}$$

$$W = U_g - K = 1.2 \times 10^3 \text{ J}$$

69. A person weighing 635 N climbs up a ladder to a height of 5.0 m. Use the person and Earth as the system.

a. Draw energy bar graphs of the system before the person starts to climb the ladder and after the person stops at the top. Has the mechanical energy changed? If so, by how much?

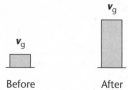

v_g	v_g
Before	After

Yes. The mechanical energy has changed, increase in potential energy of (635 N)(5.0 m) = 3200 J.

b. Where did this energy come from?

From the internal energy of the person.

Critical Thinking Problems

70. A golf ball with mass 0.046 kg rests on a tee. It is struck by a golf club with an effective mass of 0.220 kg and a speed of 44 m/s. Assuming that the collision is elastic, find the speed of the ball when it leaves the tee.

From the conservation of momentum,

$$m_c v_{c1} = m_c v_{c2} + m_b v_{b2}$$

Solve for v_{c2}, $v_{c2} = v_{c1} - \dfrac{m_b v_{b2}}{m_c}$

From conservation of energy,

$$\frac{1}{2}m_c v_{c1}^2 = \frac{1}{2}m_c(v_{c2})^2 + \frac{1}{2}m_b(v_{b2})^2$$

Multiply by two and substitute to get:

$$m_c v_{c1}^2 = m_c\left(v_{c1} - \frac{m_b v_{b2}}{m_c}\right)^2 + m_b(v_{b2})^2$$

or $m_c v_{c1}^2 = m_c v_{c1}^2 - 2m_b v_{b2}\,v_{c1}$

$$+ \frac{m_b^2(v_{b2})^2}{m_c} + m_b(v_{b2})^2$$

Simplify and factor:

$$0 = (m_b v_{b2})\left(-2v_{c1} + \frac{m_b(v_{b2})}{m_c} + v_{b2}\right)$$

$m_b v_{b2} = 0$ **or**

$$-2v_{c1} + \left(\frac{m_b}{m_c} + 1\right)v_{b2} = 0$$

so $v_{b2} = \dfrac{2v_{c1}}{\left(\dfrac{m_b}{m_c} + 1\right)}$

$$= \frac{2(44 \text{ m/s})}{\left(\dfrac{0.046 \text{ kg}}{0.220 \text{ kg}} + 1\right)} = 73 \text{ m/s}$$

Copyright © by Glencoe/McGraw-Hill

71. In a perfectly elastic collision, both momentum and mechanical energy are conserved. Two balls with masses m_A and m_B are moving toward each other with speeds v_A and v_B, respectively. Solve the appropriate equations to find the speeds of the two balls after the collision.

Conservation of momentum

$(1)\ m_A v_{A1} + m_B v_{B1} = m_A v_{A2} + m_B v_{B2}$

$m_A v_{A1} - m_A v_{A2} = -m_B v_{B1} + m_B v_{B2}$

$(2)\ m_A(v_{A1} - v_{A2}) = -m_B(v_{B1} - v_{B2})$

Conservation of energy

$\frac{1}{2} m_A v_{A1}^2 + \frac{1}{2} m_B v_{B1}^2 = \frac{1}{2} m_A v_{A2}^2 + \frac{1}{2} m_B v_{B2}^2$

$m_A v_{A1}^2 - m_A v_{A2}^2 = -m_B v_{B1}^2 + m_B v_{B2}^2$

$m_A(v_{A1}^2 - v_{A2}^2) = -m_B(v_{B1}^2 - v_{B2}^2)$

$(3)\ m_A(v_{A1} + v_{A2})(v_{A1} - v_{A2})$
$$= -m_B(v_{B1} + v_{B2})(v_{B1} - v_{B2})$$

Divide equation (3) by (2) to obtain $(4)\ v_{A1} + v_{A2} = v_{B1} + v_{B2}$

Solve equation (1) for v_{A2} and v_{B2}

$v_{A2} = v_{A1} + \dfrac{m_B}{m_A}(v_{B1} - v_{B2})$

$v_{B2} = v_{B1} + \dfrac{m_A}{m_B}(v_{A1} - v_{A2})$

Substitute into (4) and solve for v_{B2} and v_{A2}

$v_{A1} + v_{A1} + \dfrac{m_B}{m_A}(v_{B1} - v_{B2}) = v_{B1} + v_{B2}$

$2m_A v_{A1} + m_B v_{B1} - m_B v_{B2}$
$= m_A v_{B1} + m_A v_{B2}$

$v_{B2} = \dfrac{2m_A}{m_A + m_B} v_{A1} + \dfrac{m_B - m_A}{m_A + m_B} v_{B1}$

$v_{A1} + v_{A2} = v_{B1} + v_{B1} + \dfrac{m_A}{m_B}(v_{A1} - v_{A2})$

$m_B v_{A1} + m_B v_{A2}$
$= 2m_B v_{B1} + m_A v_{A1} - m_A v_{A2}$

$v_{A2} = \dfrac{m_A - m_B}{m_A + m_B} v_{A1} + \dfrac{2m_B}{m_A + m_B} v_{B1}$

72. A 25-g ball is fired with an initial speed v_1 toward a 125-g ball that is hanging motionless from a 1.25-m string. The balls have a perfectly elastic collision. As a result, the 125-g ball swings out until the string makes an angle of 37° with the vertical. What was v_1?

Object 1 is the incoming ball. Object 2 is the one attached to the string. In the collision momentum is conserved:

$P_1 = P_1 + P_2$ or
$m_1 v_1 = m_1 V_1 + m_2 V_2$

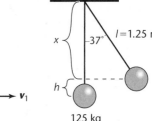

In the collision kinetic energy is conserved:

$\frac{1}{2} m_1 v_1^2 = \frac{1}{2} m_1 V_1^2 + \frac{1}{2} m_2 V_2^2$

$m_1 v_1^2 = m_1 V_1^2 + m_2 V_2^2$

$m_1 v_1^2 \times \dfrac{m_1}{m_1} = m_1 V_1^2 \times \dfrac{m_1}{m_1} + m_2 V_2^2 \times \dfrac{m_2}{m_2}$

$\dfrac{m_1^2 v_1^2}{m_1} = \dfrac{m_1^2 V_1^2}{m_1} + \dfrac{m_2^2 V_2^2}{m_2}$

$\dfrac{p_1^2}{m_1} = \dfrac{P_1^2}{m_1} + \dfrac{P_2^2}{m_2}$

Copyright © by Glencoe/McGraw-Hill

72. (continued)

$$p_1^2 = P_1^2 + \frac{m_1}{m_2}P_2^2$$

We don't care about V_1, so get rid of P_1 using $P_1 = p_1 - P_2$

$$p_1^2 = (p_1 - P_2)^2 + \frac{m_1}{m_2}P_2^2$$

$$p_1^2 = p_1^2 - 2p_1P_2 + P_2^2 + \frac{m_1}{m_2}P_2^2$$

$$2p_1P_2 = \left(1 + \frac{m_1}{m_2}\right)P_2^2$$

$$p_1 = \frac{1}{2}\left(1 + \frac{m_1}{m_2}\right)P_2$$

$$m_1v_1 = \frac{1}{2}(m_2 + m_1)V_2$$

$$v_1 = \frac{1}{2}\left(\frac{m_2}{m_1} + 1\right)V_2$$

Now consider the pendulum:

$$\frac{1}{2}m_2V_2^2 = m_2gh$$

or $V_2 = \sqrt{2gh}$

$h = L(1 - \cos\theta)$

$\quad = L(1 - \cos 37°)$

Thus, $V_2 = \sqrt{2gL(1 - \cos 37°)}$

$$V_2 = \sqrt{2(9.80 \text{ m/s}^2)(1.25 \text{ m})(1 - \cos 37°)}$$

$V_2 = 2.2$ m/s

$$v_1 = \frac{1}{2}\left(\frac{125 \text{ g}}{25 \text{ g}} + 1\right)2.2 \text{ m/s}$$

$v_1 = 6.6$ m/s

Copyright © by Glencoe/McGraw-Hill

12 Thermal Energy

Practice Problems

12.1 Temperature and Thermal Energy
pages 274-284

page 278

1. Make the following conversions.

   a. 0°C to kelvins

   $T_K = T_C + 273 = 0 + 273 = 273$ K

   b. 0 K to degrees Celsius

   $T_C = T_K - 273 = 0 - 273 = -273°C$

   c. 273°C to kelvins

   $T_K = T_C + 273 = 273 + 273 = 546$ K

   d. 273 K to degrees Celsius

   $T_C = T_K - 273 = 273 - 273 = 0°C$

2. Convert the following Celsius temperatures to Kelvin temperatures.

   a. 27°C

   $T_K = T_C + 273 = 27 + 273$
   $= 3.00 \times 10^2$ K

   b. 150°C

   $T_K = T_C + 273 = 150 + 273 = 423$ K
   $= 4.23 \times 10^2$ K

   c. 560°C

   $T_K = T_C + 273 = 560 + 273 = 833$ K
   $= 8.33 \times 10^2$ K

   d. -50°C

   $T_K = T_C + 273 = -50 + 273 = 223$ K
   $= 2.23 \times 10^2$ K

   e. -184°C

   $T_K = T_C + 273 = -184 + 273 = 89$ K

   f. -300°C

   $T_K = T_C + 273 = -300 + 273 = -27$ K

   impossible temperature—below absolute zero

3. Convert the following Kelvin temperatures to Celsius temperatures.

   a. 110 K

   $T_C = T_K - 273 = 110 - 273$
   $= -163°C$

   b. 70 K

   $T_C = T_K - 273 = 70 - 273$
   $= -203°C$

   c. 22 K

   $T_C = T_K - 273 = 22 - 273 = -251°C$

   d. 402 K

   $T_C = T_K - 273 = 402 - 273 = 129°C$

   e. 323 K

   $T_C = T_K - 273 = 323 - 273 = 50°C$
   $= 5.0 \times 10^{1}°C$

   f. 212 K

   $T_C = T_K - 273 = 212 - 273 = -61°C$

4. Find the Celsius and Kelvin temperatures for the following.

   a. room temperature

   about 72°F is about 22°C, 295 K

   b. refrigerator temperature

   about 40°F is about 4°C, 277 K

   c. typical hot summer day

   about 86°F is about 30°C, 303 K

   d. typical winter night

   about 0°F is about -18°C, 255 K

Copyright © by Glencoe/McGraw-Hill

5. How much heat is absorbed by 60.0 g of copper when its temperature is raised from 20.0°C to 80.0°C?

$$Q = mC\Delta T = (0.0600 \text{ kg})(385 \text{ J/kg} \cdot °C)(80.0°C - 20.0°C) = 1.39 \times 10^3 \text{ J}$$

6. The cooling system of a car engine contains 20.0 L of water (1 L of water has a mass of 1 kg).

   a. What is the change in the temperature of the water if the engine operates until 836.0 kJ of heat are added?

   $$Q = mC\Delta T$$

   $$\Delta T = \frac{Q}{mC} = \frac{836.0 \times 10^3 \text{ J}}{(20.0 \text{ kg})(4180 \text{ J/kg} \cdot °C)} = 10.0°C$$

   b. Suppose it is winter and the system is filled with methanol. The density of methanol is 0.80 g/cm^3. What would be the increase in temperature of the methanol if it absorbed 836.0 kJ of heat?

   Using 1 L = 1000 cm^3, the mass of methanol required is

   $$m = \rho V = (0.80 \text{ g/cm}^3)(20.0 \text{ L})(1000 \text{ cm}^3/\text{L}) = 16\ 000 \text{ g or 16 kg}$$

   $$\Delta T = \frac{Q}{mC} = \frac{836.0 \times 10^3 \text{ J}}{(16 \text{ kg})(2450 \text{ J/kg} \cdot °C)} = 21°C$$

   c. Which is the better coolant, water or methanol? Explain.

   Water is the better coolant because its temperature increase is less than half that of methanol when absorbing the same amount of heat.

7. A 2.00×10^2-g sample of water at 80.0°C is mixed with 2.00×10^2 g of water at 10.0°C. Assume no heat loss to the surroundings. What is the final temperature of the mixture?

   $$m_A C_A(T_f - T_{Ai}) + m_B C_B(T_f - T_{Bi}) = 0$$

   Since $m_A = m_B$ and $C_A = C_B$,
   there is cancellation in this particular case so that

   $$T_f = \frac{(T_{Ai} + T_{Bi})}{2} = \frac{(80.0°C + 10.0°C)}{2} = 45.0°C$$

8. A 4.00×10^2-g sample of methanol at 16.0°C is mixed with 4.00×10^2 g of water at 85.0°C. Assume that there is no heat loss to the surroundings. What is the final temperature of the mixture?

   $$m_A C_A(T_f - T_{Ai}) + m_W C_W(T_f - T_{Wi}) = 0$$

   Since, in this particular case, $m_A = m_W$, the masses cancel and

   $$T_f = \frac{C_A T_{Ai} + C_W T_{Wi}}{C_A + C_W}$$

   $$= \frac{(2450 \text{ J/kg} \cdot \text{K})(16.0°C) + (4180 \text{ J/kg} \cdot \text{K})(85.0°C)}{2450 \text{ J/kg} \cdot \text{K} + 4180 \text{ J/kg} \cdot \text{K}} = 59.5° \text{C}$$

Copyright © by Glencoe/McGraw-Hill

Physics: Principles and Problems

9. A 1.00×10^2-g brass block at 90.0°C is placed in a plastic foam cup containing 2.00×10^2 g of water at 20.0°C. No heat is lost to the cup or the surroundings. Find the final temperature of the mixture.

$$m_B C_B(T_f - T_{Bi}) + m_W C_W(T_f - T_{Wi}) = 0$$

$$T_f = \frac{m_B C_B T_{Bi} + m_W C_W T_{Wi}}{m_B C_B + m_W C_W}$$

$$= \frac{(0.100 \text{ kg})(376 \text{ J/kg} \cdot \text{K})(90.0°C) + (0.200 \text{ kg})(4180 \text{ J/kg} \cdot \text{K})(20.0°C)}{(0.100 \text{ kg})(376 \text{ J/kg} \cdot \text{K}) + (0.200 \text{ kg})(4180 \text{ J/kg} \cdot \text{K})}$$

$$= 23.0°C$$

10. A 1.00×10^2-g aluminum block at 100.0°C is placed in 1.00×10^2 g of water at 10.0°C. The final temperature of the mixture is 25.0°C. What is the specific heat of the aluminum?

$$m_A C_A(T_f - T_{Ai}) + m_W C_W(T_f - T_{Wi}) = 0$$

Since $m_A = m_W$, the masses cancel and

$$C_A = \frac{-C_W(T_f - T_{Wi})}{(T_f - T_{Ai})} = \frac{-(4180 \text{ J/kg} \cdot \text{K})(25.0°C - 10.0°C)}{(25.0°C - 100.0°C)} = 836 \text{ J/kg} \cdot \text{K}$$

12.2 Change of State and Laws of Thermodynamics
pages 285–294

page 289

11. How much heat is absorbed by 1.00×10^2 g of ice at –20.0°C to become water at 0.0°C?

To warm the ice to 0.0°C:

$$Q_W = mC\Delta T = (0.100 \text{ kg})(2060 \text{ J/kg} \cdot °C)[0.0°C - (-20.0°C)] = 4120 \text{ J} = 0.41 \times 10^4 \text{ J}$$

To melt the ice:

$$Q_M = mH_f = (0.100 \text{ kg})(3.34 \times 10^5 \text{ J/kg}) = 3.34 \times 10^4 \text{ J}$$

Total heat required: $Q = Q_W + Q_M = 0.41 \times 10^4 \text{ J} + 3.34 \times 10^4 \text{ J} = 3.75 \times 10^4 \text{ J}$

12. A 2.00×10^2-g sample of water at 60.0°C is heated to steam at 140.0°C. How much heat is absorbed?

To heat the water from 60.0°C to 100.0°C:

$$Q_1 = mC\Delta T = (0.200 \text{ kg})(4180 \text{ J/kg} \cdot °C)(40.0°C) = 0.334 \times 10^5 \text{ J}$$

To change the water to steam:

$$Q_2 = mH_v = (0.200 \text{ kg})(2.26 \times 10^6 \text{ J/kg}) = 4.52 \times 10^5 \text{ J}$$

To heat the steam from 100.0°C to 140.0°C:

$$Q_3 = mC\Delta T = (0.200 \text{ kg})(2020 \text{ J/kg} \cdot °C)(40.0°C) = 0.162 \times 10^5 \text{ J}$$

$$Q_{total} = Q_1 + Q_2 + Q_3 = 5.02 \times 10^5 \text{ J}$$

13. How much heat is needed to change 3.00×10^2 g of ice at –30.0°C to steam at 130.0°C?

Warm ice from –30.0°C to 0.0°C:

$$Q_1 = mC\Delta T = (0.300 \text{ kg})(2060 \text{ J/kg} \cdot °C)(30.0°C) = 0.185 \times 10^5 \text{ J}$$

Melt ice:

$$Q_2 = mH_f = (0.300 \text{ kg})(3.34 \times 10^5 \text{ J/kg}) = 1.00 \times 10^5 \text{ J}$$

Heat water 0.0°C to 100.0°C:

$$Q_3 = mC\Delta T = (0.300 \text{ kg})(4180 \text{ J/kg} \cdot °C)(100.0°C) = 1.25 \times 10^5 \text{ J}$$

Copyright © by Glencoe/McGraw-Hill

13. (continued)

Vaporize water:

$Q_4 = mH_v = (0.300 \text{ kg})(2.26 \times 10^6 \text{ J/kg}) = 6.78 \times 10^5 \text{ J}$

Heat steam 100.0°C to 130.0°C:

$Q_5 = mC\Delta T = (0.300 \text{ kg})(2020 \text{ J/kg} \cdot °C)(30.0°C) = 0.182 \times 10^5 \text{ J}$

$Q_{total} = Q_1 + Q_2 + Q_3 + Q_4 + Q_5 = 9.40 \times 10^5 \text{ J}$

14. A 175-g lump of molten lead at its melting point, 327°C, is dropped into 55 g of water at 20.0°C.

a. What is the temperature of the water when the lead becomes solid?

To freeze, lead must absorb

$Q = -mH_f = -(0.175 \text{ kg})(2.04 \times 10^4 \text{ J/kg}) = -3.57 \times 10^3 \text{ J}$

This will heat the water

$\Delta T = \dfrac{Q}{mC} = \dfrac{3.57 \times 10^3 \text{ J}}{(0.055 \text{ kg})(4180 \text{ J/kg} \cdot °C)} = 16°C$

$T = T_i + \Delta T = 20.0°C + 16°C = 36°C$

b. When the lead and water are in thermal equilibrium, what is the temperature?

Now, $T_f = \dfrac{m_A C_A T_{Ai} + m_B C_B T_{Bi}}{m_A C_A + m_B C_B}$

$= \dfrac{(0.175 \text{ kg})(130 \text{ J/kg} \cdot K)(327°C) + (0.055 \text{ kg})(4180 \text{ J/kg} \cdot K)(36.0°C)}{(0.175 \text{ kg})(130 \text{ J/kg} \cdot K) + (0.055 \text{ kg})(4180 \text{ J/kg} \cdot K)}$

$= 62°C$

Chapter Review Problems

pages 296–297

page 296

Section 12.1

Level 1

21. Liquid nitrogen boils at 77 K. Find this temperature in degrees Celsius.

$T_C = T_K - 273 = 77 - 273 = -196°C$

22. The melting point of hydrogen is –259.14°C. Find this temperature in kelvins.

$T_K = T_C + 273.15 = -259.14 + 273.15$

$= 14.01 \text{ K}$

23. How much heat is needed to raise the temperature of 50.0 g of water from 4.5°C to 83.0°C?

$Q = mC\Delta T = (0.0500 \text{ kg})(4180 \text{ J/kg} \cdot °C)(83.0°C - 4.5°C) = 1.64 \times 10^4 \text{ J}$

24. A 5.00×10^2-g block of metal absorbs 5016 J of heat when its temperature changes from 20.0°C to 30.0°C. Calculate the specific heat of the metal.

$Q = mC\Delta T$

so $C = \dfrac{Q}{m\Delta T} = \dfrac{5016 \text{ J}}{(5.00 \times 10^{-1} \text{ kg})(30.0°C - 20.0°C)} = 1.00 \times 10^3 \text{ J/kg} \cdot °C$

$= 1.00 \times 10^3 \text{ J/kg·K}$

Copyright © by Glencoe/McGraw-Hill

25. A 4.00×10^2-g glass coffee cup is at room temperature, 20.0°C. It is then plunged into hot dishwater, 80.0°C. If the temperature of the cup reaches that of the dishwater, how much heat does the cup absorb? Assume the mass of the dishwater is large enough so its temperature doesn't change appreciably.

$$Q = mC\Delta T = (4.00 \times 10^{-1} \text{ kg})(664 \text{ J/kg} \cdot \text{°C})(80.0\text{°C} - 20.0\text{°C}) = 1.59 \times 10^4 \text{ J}$$

26. A 1.00×10^2-g mass of tungsten at 100.0°C is placed in 2.00×10^2 g of water at 20.0°C. The mixture reaches equilibrium at 21.6°C. Calculate the specific heat of tungsten.

$$\Delta Q_T + \Delta Q_W = 0$$

or $m_T C_T \Delta T_T = -m_W C_W \Delta T_W$

so $C_T = \dfrac{-m_W C_W \Delta T_W}{m_T \Delta T_T} = \dfrac{-(0.200 \text{ kg})(4180 \text{ J/kg} \cdot \text{K})(21.6\text{°C} - 20.0\text{°C})}{(0.100 \text{ kg})(21.6\text{°C} - 100.0\text{°C})} = 171 \text{ J/kg} \cdot \text{K}$

27. A 6.0×10^2-g sample of water at 90.0°C is mixed with 4.00×10^2 g of water at 22.0°C. Assume no heat loss to the surroundings. What is the final temperature of the mixture?

$$T_f = \frac{m_A C_A T_{Ai} + m_B C_B T_{Bi}}{m_A C_A + m_B C_B}$$

but $C_A = C_B$ because both liquids are water, and the C's will divide out.

$$T_f = \frac{m_A T_{Ai} + m_B T_{Bi}}{m_A + m_B} = \frac{(6.0 \times 10^2 \text{ g})(90.0\text{°C}) + (4.00 \times 10^2 \text{ g})(22.0\text{°C})}{6.0 \times 10^2 \text{ g} + 4.00 \times 10^2 \text{ g}} = 63\text{°C}$$

28. A 10.0-kg piece of zinc at 71.0°C is placed in a container of water. The water has a mass of 20.0 kg and has a temperature of 10.0°C before the zinc is added. What is the final temperature of the water and zinc?

$$T_f = \frac{m_{Zn} C_{Zn} T_{Zni} + m_W C_W T_{Wi}}{m_{Zn} C_{Zn} + m_W C_W}$$

$$= \frac{(10.0 \text{ kg})(388 \text{ J/kg} \cdot \text{K})(71.0\text{°C}) + (20.0 \text{ kg})(4180 \text{ J/kg} \cdot \text{K})(10.0\text{°C})}{(10.0 \text{ kg})(388 \text{ J/kg} \cdot \text{K}) + (20.0 \text{ kg})(4180 \text{ J/kg} \cdot \text{K})}$$

$$= 12.7\text{°C}$$

page 297

Level 2

29. To get a feeling for the amount of energy needed to heat water, recall from **Table 11–1** that the kinetic energy of a compact car moving at 100 km/h is 2.9×10^5 J. What volume of water (in liters) would 2.9×10^5 J of energy warm from room temperature (20°C) to boiling (100°C)?

$$Q = mC\Delta T = \rho V C \, \Delta T \text{ where } \rho \text{ is the density of the material}$$

so $V = \dfrac{Q}{\rho C \Delta T} = \dfrac{2.9 \times 10^5 \text{ J}}{(1 \text{ kg/L})(4180 \text{ J/kg} \cdot \text{°C})(100\text{°C} - 20\text{°C})} = 0.87$ L, or 0.9 L to one significant digit

Copyright © by Glencoe/McGraw-Hill

30. A 3.00×10^2-W electric immersion heater is used to heat a cup of water. The cup is made of glass and its mass is 3.00×10^2 g. It contains 250 g of water at 15°C. How much time is needed to bring the water to the boiling point? Assume that the temperature of the cup is the same as the temperature of the water at all times and that no heat is lost to the air.

$$Q = m_G C_G \Delta T_G + m_W C_W \Delta T_W$$

but $\Delta T_G = \Delta T_W$, so

$$Q = [m_G C_G + m_W C_W] \Delta T$$

$$= [(0.300 \text{ kg})(664 \text{ J/kg} \cdot °C) + (0.250 \text{ kg})(4180 \text{ J/kg} \cdot °C)](100.0°C - 15°C)$$

$$= 1.1 \times 10^5 \text{ J}$$

Now $P = \dfrac{E}{t} = \dfrac{Q}{t}$, so

$$t = \frac{Q}{P} = \frac{1.1 \times 10^5 \text{ J}}{3.00 \times 10^2 \text{ W}} = 3.7 \times 10^2 \text{ s}$$

31. A 2.50×10^2-kg cast-iron car engine contains water as a coolant. Suppose the engine's temperature is 35.0°C when it is shut off. The air temperature is 10.0°C. The heat given off by the engine and water in it as they cool to air temperature is 4.4×10^6 J. What mass of water is used to cool the engine?

$$Q = m_W C_W \Delta T + m_i C_i \Delta T$$

$$m_W = \frac{Q - m_i C_i \Delta T}{C_W \Delta T} = \frac{(4.4 \times 10^6 \text{ J}) - [(2.50 \times 10^2 \text{ kg})(450 \text{ J/kg} \cdot °C)(35.0°C - 10.0°C)]}{(4180 \text{ J/kg} \cdot °C)(35.0°C - 10.0°C)}$$

$$= 15 \text{ kg}$$

Section 12.2

Level 1

32. Years ago, a block of ice with a mass of about 20.0 kg was used daily in a home icebox. The temperature of the ice was 0.0°C when delivered. As it melted, how much heat did a block of ice that size absorb?

$$Q = m H_f = (20.0 \text{ kg})(3.34 \times 10^5 \text{ J/kg}) = 6.68 \times 10^6 \text{ J}$$

33. A 40.0-g sample of chloroform is condensed from a vapor at 61.6°C to a liquid at 61.6°C. It liberates 9870 J of heat. What is the heat of vaporization of chloroform?

$$Q = m H_v$$

$$H_v = \frac{Q}{m} = \frac{9870 \text{ J}}{0.0400 \text{ kg}} = 2.47 \times 10^5 \text{ J/kg}$$

34. A 750-kg car moving at 23 m/s brakes to a stop. The brakes contain about 15 kg of iron, which absorbs the energy. What is the increase in temperature of the brakes?

During braking, the kinetic energy of the car is converted into heat energy. So
$\Delta KE_C + Q_B = 0$, and $\Delta KE_C + m_B C_B \Delta T = 0$ so

$$\Delta T = \frac{-\Delta KE_C}{m_B C_B} = -\frac{\frac{1}{2} m_C (v_f^2 - v_i^2)}{m_B C_B} = -\frac{\frac{1}{2}(750 \text{ kg})[0^2 - (23 \text{ m/s})^2]}{(15 \text{ kg})(450 \text{ J/kg} \cdot °C)} = 29°C$$

Copyright © by Glencoe/McGraw-Hill

Level 2

35. How much heat is added to 10.0 g of ice at –20.0°C to convert it to steam at 120.0°C?

Amount of heat needed to heat ice to 0.0°C:

$Q = m_c \Delta T = (0.0100 \text{ kg})(2060 \text{ J/kg} \cdot °\text{C})[0.0°\text{C} - (-20.0°\text{C})] = 412 \text{ J}$

Amount of heat to melt ice:

$Q = mH_f = (0.0100 \text{ kg})(3.34 \times 10^5 \text{ J/kg}) = 3.34 \times 10^3 \text{ J}$

Amount of heat to heat water to 100.0°C:

$Q = mC\Delta T = (0.0100 \text{ kg})(4180 \text{ J/kg} \cdot °\text{C})(100.0°\text{C} - 0.0°\text{C}) = 4.18 \times 10^3 \text{ J}$

Amount of heat to boil water:

$Q = mH_v = (0.0100 \text{ kg})(2.26 \times 10^6 \text{ J/kg}) = 2.26 \times 10^4 \text{ J}$

Amount of heat to heat steam to 120.0°C:

$Q = mC\Delta T = (0.0100)(2020 \text{ J/kg} \cdot °\text{C})(120.0°\text{C} - 100.0°\text{C}) = 404 \text{ J}$

The total heat is

$412 \text{ J} + 3.34 \times 10^3 \text{ J} + 4.18 \times 10^3 \text{ J} + 2.26 \times 10^4 \text{ J} + 404 \text{ J} = 3.09 \times 10^4 \text{ J}$

36. A 4.2-g lead bullet moving at 275 m/s strikes a steel plate and stops. If all its kinetic energy is converted to thermal energy and none leaves the bullet, what is its temperature change?

Because the kinetic energy is converted to thermal energy, $\Delta KE + Q = 0$. So $\Delta KE = -m_B C_B \Delta T$ and

$$\Delta T = -\frac{\Delta KE}{m_B C_B} = -\frac{\frac{1}{2} m_B (v_f^2 - v_i^2)}{m_B C_B}$$

and the mass of the bullet divides out so

$$\Delta T = -\frac{\frac{1}{2}(v_f^2 - v_i^2)}{C_B} = -\frac{\frac{1}{2}[(0.0 \text{ m/s})^2 - (275 \text{ m/s})^2]}{130 \text{ J/kg} \cdot °\text{C}} = 290°\text{C}$$

37. A soft drink from Australia is labeled "Low Joule Cola." The label says "100 mL yields 1.7 kJ." The can contains 375 mL. Sally drinks the cola and then wants to offset this input of food energy by climbing stairs. How high would Sally have to climb if she has a mass of 65.0 kg?

Sally gained $(3.75)(1.7 \text{ kJ}) = 6.4 \times 10^3 \text{ J}$ of energy from the drink.

To conserve energy, $E + \Delta PE = 0$, or $6.4 \times 10^3 \text{ J} = -mg\Delta h$ so,

$$\Delta h = \frac{6.4 \times 10^3 \text{ J}}{-mg} = \frac{6.4 \times 10^3 \text{ J}}{-(65.0 \text{ kg})(-9.80 \text{ m/s}^2)} = 1.0 \times 10^1 \text{ m,}$$

or about three flights of stairs

Critical Thinking Problems

38. Your mother demands that you clean your room. You know that reducing the disorder of your room will reduce its entropy, but the entropy of the universe cannot be decreased. Evaluate how you increase entropy as you clean.

Process 1
To increase the order of your room, you must expend energy. This results in heat (your perspiration) which is given off to the universe. This increases the entropy of the universe.

Process 2
Any item moved to a new location to create an order also creates a disorder from its previous arrangement. This also increases the entropy of the universe.

Copyright © by Glencoe/McGraw-Hill

13 States of Matter

Practice Problems

13.1 The Fluid States
pages 300–313

page 303

1. The atmospheric pressure at sea level is about 1.0×10^5 Pa. What is the force at sea level that air exerts on the top of a typical office desk, 152 cm long and 76 cm wide?

$$P = \frac{F}{A}$$
$$\text{so } F = PA$$
$$= (1.0 \times 10^5 \text{ Pa})(1.52 \text{ m})(0.76 \text{ m})$$
$$= 1.2 \times 10^5 \text{ N}$$

2. A car tire makes contact with the ground on a rectangular area of 12 cm by 18 cm. The car's mass is 925 kg. What pressure does the car exert on the ground?

$$F = mg$$
$$A = 4(l \times w)$$
$$P = \frac{F}{A} = \frac{(925 \text{ kg})(9.80 \text{ m/s}^2)}{(4)(0.12 \text{ m})(0.18 \text{ m})}$$
$$= 1.0 \times 10^5 \text{ N/m}^2 = 1.0 \times 10^5 \text{ Pa}$$

3. A lead brick, $5.0 \times 10.0 \times 20.0$ cm, rests on the ground on its smallest face. What pressure does it exert on the ground? (Lead has a density of 11.8 g/cm^3.)

$$F_g = (11.8 \text{ g/cm}^3)(10^{-3} \text{ kg/g})$$
$$\times (5.0 \text{ cm})(10.0 \text{ cm})$$
$$\times (20.0 \text{ cm})(9.80 \text{ m/s}^2)$$
$$= 116 \text{ N}$$
$$A = (0.050 \text{ m})(0.100 \text{ m}) = 0.0050 \text{ m}^2$$
$$P = \frac{F}{A} = \frac{116 \text{ N}}{0.0050 \text{ m}^2} = 23 \text{ kPa}$$

4. In a tornado, the pressure can be 15% below normal atmospheric pressure. Sometimes a tornado can move so quickly that this pressure drop can occur in one second. Suppose a tornado suddenly occurred outside your front door, which is 182 cm high and 91 cm wide. What net force would be exerted on the door? In what direction would the force be exerted?

$$F_{net} = F_{outside} - F_{inside}$$
$$= (P_{outside} - P_{inside})A$$
$$= (0.85 \times 10^5 \text{ Pa} - 1.00 \times 10^5 \text{ Pa})$$
$$\times (1.82 \text{ m})(0.91 \text{ m})$$
$$= -2.5 \times 10^4 \text{ N (toward the outside)}$$

page 304

5. Dentists' chairs are examples of hydraulic-lift systems. If a chair weighs 1600 N and rests on a piston with a cross-sectional area of 1440 cm^2, what force must be applied to the smaller piston with a cross-sectional area of 72 cm^2 to lift the chair?

$$\frac{F_1}{A_1} = \frac{F_2}{A_2}$$
$$F_1 = \frac{F_2 A_1}{A_2} = \frac{(1600 \text{ N})(72 \text{ cm}^2)}{1440 \text{ cm}^2}$$
$$= 8.0 \times 10^1 \text{ N}$$

Copyright © by Glencoe/McGraw-Hill

6. A girl is floating in a freshwater lake with her head just above the water. If she weighs 600 N, what is the volume of the submerged part of her body?

$$F_g = F_{buoyant} = \rho_{water} \, Vg$$

$$V = \frac{F_g}{\rho_{water} \, g}$$

$$= \frac{600 \text{ N}}{(1000 \text{ kg/m}^3)(9.80 \text{ m/s}^2)}$$

$$= 0.06 \text{ m}^3$$

This volume does not include that portion of her head that is above the water.

7. What is the tension in a wire supporting a 1250-N camera submerged in water? The volume of the camera is 8.3×10^{-2} m^3.

$F_T + F_{buoyant} = F_g$ where F_g is the air weight of the camera.

$$F_T = F_g - F_{buoyant} = F_g - \rho_{water} \, Vg$$

$$= 1250 \text{ N}$$

$$- (1000 \text{ kg/m}^3)(0.083 \text{ m}^3)(9.80 \text{ m/s}^2)$$

$$= 4.4 \times 10^2 \text{ N}$$

13.2 The Solid State
pages 314–321

page 319

8. A piece of aluminum house siding is 3.66 m long on a cold winter day of –28°C. How much longer is it on a very hot summer day at 39°C?

$$\Delta L = \alpha L_i \Delta T$$

$$= [25 \times 10^{-6}(°C)^{-1}](3.66 \text{ m})(67°C)$$

$$= 6.1 \times 10^{-3} \text{ m, or 6.1 mm}$$

9. A piece of steel is 11.5 m long at 22°C. It is heated to 1221°C, close to its melting temperature. How long is it?

$$L_2 = L_1 + \alpha L_1(T_2 - T_1)$$

$$= (11.5 \text{ m}) + [12 \times 10^{-6}(°C)^{-1}]$$

$$\times (11.5 \text{ m})(1221°C - 22°C)$$

$$= 12 \text{ m}$$

10. An aluminum soft drink can, with a capacity of 354 mL, is filled to the brim with water and put in a refrigerator set at 4.4°C. The can of water is later taken from the refrigerator and allowed to reach the temperature outside, which is 34.5°C.

a. What will be the volume of the liquid?

For water $\beta = 210 \times 10^{-6}(°C)^{-1}$, so

$$\Delta V = \beta V \Delta T$$

$$= [210 \times 10^{-6}(°C)^{-1}](354 \text{ mL})(30.1°C)$$

$$= 2.2 \text{ mL}$$

$$V = 354 \text{ mL} + 2.2 \text{ mL} = 356 \text{ mL}$$

b. What will be the volume of the can?
Hint: The can will expand as much as a block of metal the same size.

For Al $\beta = 75 \times 10^{-6}(°C)^{-1}$, so

$$\Delta V = \beta V \Delta T$$

$$= [75 \times 10^{-6}(°C)^{-1}](354 \text{ mL})(30.1°C)$$

$$= 0.80 \text{ mL}$$

$$V = 354 \text{ mL} + 0.80 \text{ mL} = 355 \text{ mL}$$

c. How much liquid will spill?

The difference will spill,

2.2 mL − 0.80 mL = 1.4 mL

11. A tank truck takes on a load of 45 725 liters of gasoline in Houston at 32.0°C. The coefficient of volume expansion, β, for gasoline is $950 \times 10^{-6}(°C)^{-1}$. The truck delivers its load in Omaha, where the temperature is –18.0°C.

a. How many liters of gasoline does the truck deliver?

$$V_2 = V_1 + \beta V_1(T_2 - T_1)$$

$$= 45\ 725 \text{ L} + [950 \times 10^{-6}(°C)^{-1}]$$

$$\times (45\ 725 \text{ L})(-18.0°C - 32.0°C)$$

$$= 43\ 553 \text{ L} = 43\ 600 \text{ L}$$

b. What happened to the gasoline?

Its volume has decreased because of a temperature decrease.

Copyright © by Glencoe/McGraw-Hill

Chapter Review Problems

page 324

Section 13.1

Level 1

30. A 0.75-kg physics book with dimensions of 24.0 cm by 20.0 cm is on a table.

a. What force does the book apply to the table?

$$F_g = mg = (0.75 \text{ kg})(9.80 \text{ m/s}^2)$$
$$= 7.4 \text{ N}$$

b. What pressure does the book apply?

$$P = \frac{F_g}{A} = \frac{F_g}{lw}$$
$$= \frac{7.4 \text{ N}}{(0.240 \text{ m})(0.200 \text{ m})} = 150 \text{ Pa}$$

31. A reservoir behind a dam is 15 m deep. What is the pressure of the water in the following situations?

a. at the base of the dam

$$P = \rho h g$$
$$\rho_{H_2O} = 1.0 \text{ g/cm}^3 = 1.0 \times 10^3 \text{ kg/m}^3$$
$$P = (1.0 \times 10^3 \text{ kg/m}^3)(15 \text{ m})(9.80 \text{ m/s}^2)$$
$$= 1.5 \times 10^5 \text{ Pa} = 1.5 \times 10^2 \text{ kPa}$$

b. 5.0 m from the top of the dam

$$P = (1.0 \times 10^3 \text{ kg/m}^3)(5.0 \text{ m})(9.80 \text{ m/s}^2)$$
$$= 49 \text{ kPa}$$

32. A 75-kg solid cylinder, 2.5 m long and with an end radius of 5.0 cm, stands on one end. How much pressure does it exert?

$$P = \frac{F_g}{A} = \frac{mg}{\pi r^2} = \frac{(75 \text{ kg})(9.80 \text{ m/s}^2)}{\pi (0.050 \text{ m})^2}$$
$$= 94 \text{ kPa}$$

33. A test tube standing vertically in a test-tube rack contains 2.5 cm of oil ($\rho = 0.81$ g/cm^3) and 6.5 cm of water. What is the pressure on the bottom of the test tube?

$$P = P_{oil} + P_{water}$$
$$= \rho_{oil} h_{oil} g + \rho_{water} h_{water} g$$
$$= (810 \text{ kg/m}^3)(0.025 \text{ m})(9.80 \text{ m/s}^2)$$
$$\quad + (1000 \text{ kg/m}^3)(0.065 \text{ m})(9.80 \text{ m/s}^2)$$
$$= 198 \text{ Pa} + 637 \text{ Pa} = 8.4 \times 10^2 \text{ Pa}$$

34. A metal object is suspended from a spring scale. The scale reads 920 N when the object is suspended in air, and 750 N when the object is completely submerged in water.

a. Find the volume of the object.

$$F_{buoyant} = V\rho_{water}\, g$$
$$V = \frac{F_{buoyant}}{\rho_{water}\, g}$$
$$= \frac{920 \text{ N} - 750 \text{ N}}{(1.00 \times 10^3 \text{ kg/m}^3)(9.80 \text{ m/s}^2)}$$
$$= 1.7 \times 10^{-2} \text{ m}^3$$

b. Find the density of the metal.

$$\rho_{object} = \frac{m}{V} = \frac{F_g}{Vg}$$
$$= \frac{920 \text{ N}}{(1.73 \times 10^{-2} \text{ m}^3)(9.80 \text{ m/s}^2)}$$
$$= 5.4 \times 10^3 \text{ kg/m}^3$$

35. During an ecology experiment, an aquarium half filled with water is placed on a scale. The scale reads 195 N.

a. A rock weighing 8 N is added to the aquarium. If the rock sinks to the bottom of the aquarium, what will the scale read?

$$F_g = 195 \text{ N} + 8 \text{ N} = 203 \text{ N}$$

Copyright © by Glencoe/McGraw-Hill

35. (continued)

b. The rock is removed from the aquarium, and the amount of water is adjusted until the scale again reads 195 N. A fish weighing 2 N is added to the aquarium. What is the scale reading with the fish in the aquarium?

$F_g = 195 \text{ N} + 2 \text{ N} = 197 \text{ N}$

In each case the buoyant force is equal to the weight of the water displaced. That is

$F_{g_{total}}$

$= F_{g_{aquarium}}$
$\quad + [(F_{g_{rock(fish)}} - F_{buoyant})$
$\quad + F_{g_{water displaced}}]$
$= F_{g_{aquarium}} + F_{g_{rock(fish)}}$

(or: By Pascal's principle, the weight of the rock (fish) is transferred throughout the water, and thus to the scale.)

36. What is the size of the buoyant force that acts on a floating ball that normally weighs 5.0 N?

$F_B = F_g = 5.0 \text{ N}$

37. What is the apparent weight of a rock submerged in water if the rock weighs 54 N in air and has a volume of $2.3 \times 10^{-3} \text{ m}^3$?

$W_{net} = F_g - V\rho g$

$\quad = 54 \text{ N} - (2.3 \times 10^{-3} \text{ m}^3)$
$\quad\quad \times (1.00 \times 10^3 \text{ kg/m}^3)(9.80 \text{ m/s}^2)$
$\quad = 54 \text{ N} - 23 \text{ N} = 31 \text{ N}$

38. If a rock weighing 54 N is submerged in a liquid with a density exactly twice that of water, what will be its new apparent weight reading in the liquid?

The buoyant force will be twice as great as in water, or $2.00 \times 10^3 \text{ kg/m}^3$

$W_{net} = 54 \text{ N} - (2.3 \times 10^{-3} \text{ m}^3)$
$\quad\quad \times (2.00 \times 10^3 \text{ kg/m}^3)(9.80 \text{ m/s}^2)$
$\quad = 8.9 \text{ N}$

39. A 1.0-L container completely filled with mercury has a weight of 133.3 N. If the container is submerged in water, what is the buoyant force acting on it? Explain.

$F_B = V\rho g = (0.0010 \text{ m}^3)(1000 \text{ kg/m}^3)$
$\quad\quad\quad\quad\quad \times (9.80 \text{ m/s}^2)$
$\quad = 9.8 \text{ N}$

The buoyant force depends only on the volume of the water displaced.

40. What is the maximum weight that a balloon filled with 1.00 m^3 of helium can lift in air? Assume that the density of air is 1.20 kg/m^3 and that of helium is 0.177 kg/m^3. Neglect the mass of the balloon.

$F_{net} = F_g - F_{buoyant} = V\rho_{He}g - V\rho_{air}g$
$\quad = (1.00 \text{ m}^3)(0.177 \text{ kg/m}^3)(9.80 \text{ m/s}^2)$
$\quad\quad - (1.00 \text{ m}^3)(1.20 \text{ kg/m}^3)(9.80 \text{ m/s}^2)$
$\quad = -10.0 \text{ N (Net buoyant force is}$
$\quad\quad\quad\quad\quad 10.0 \text{ N upward.)}$

$F_{max} = 10.0 \text{ N}$

Level 2

41. A hydraulic jack used to lift cars is called a three-ton jack. The large piston is 22 mm in diameter, the small one 6.3 mm. Assume that a force of 3 tons is $3.0 \times 10^4 \text{ N}$.

a. What force must be exerted on the small piston to lift the 3-ton weight?

$\dfrac{F_1}{A_1} = \dfrac{F_2}{A_2}$

so $F_2 = F_1 \dfrac{A_2}{A_1} = \dfrac{F_1 \pi (r_2)^2}{\pi (r_1)^2}$

$\quad = F_1 \left(\dfrac{r_2}{r_1}\right)^2$

$F_2 = (3.0 \times 10^4 \text{ N}) \left(\dfrac{6.3 \text{ mm/2}}{22 \text{ mm/2}}\right)^2$

$\quad = 2.5 \times 10^3 \text{ N}$

Copyright © by Glencoe/McGraw-Hill

41. (continued)

b. Most jacks use a lever to reduce the force needed on the small piston. If the resistance arm is 3.0 cm, how long is the effort arm of an ideal lever to reduce the force to 100.0 N?

$$MA = \frac{F_r}{F_e} = \frac{2.5 \times 10^3 \text{ N}}{100.0 \text{ N}} = 25$$

and $IMA = \frac{L_e}{L_r}$ with $MA = IMA$

$$L_e = (MA)L_r = 25(3.0 \text{ cm}) = 75 \text{ cm}$$

42. In a machine shop, a hydraulic lift is used to raise heavy equipment for repairs. The system has a small piston with a cross-sectional area of 7.0×10^{-2} m^2 and a large piston with a cross-sectional area of 2.1×10^{-1} m^2. An engine weighing 2.7×10^3 N rests on the large piston.

a. What force must be applied to the small piston in order to lift the engine?

$$\frac{F_1}{A_1} = \frac{F_2}{A_2}$$

$$F_1 = \frac{F_2 A_1}{A_2}$$

$$= \frac{(2.7 \times 10^3 \text{ N})(7.0 \times 10^{-2} \text{ m}^2)}{2.1 \times 10^{-1} \text{ m}^2}$$

$$= 9.0 \times 10^2 \text{ N}$$

b. If the engine rises 0.20 m, how far does the smaller piston move?

$$V_1 = V_2 \quad \text{and} \quad A_1 h_1 = A_2 h_2$$

$$h_1 = \frac{A_2 h_2}{A_1}$$

$$= \frac{(2.1 \times 10^{-1} \text{ m}^2)(0.20 \text{ m})}{7.0 \times 10^{-2} \text{ m}^2}$$

$$= 0.60 \text{ m}$$

43. What is the acceleration of a small metal sphere as it falls through water? The sphere weighs 2.8×10^{-1} N in air and has a volume of 13 cm^3.

$$F_{net} = F_g - V\rho g$$

$$= 2.8 \times 10^{-1} \text{ N}$$

$$- (13 \text{ cm}^3)(10^{-6} \text{ m}^3/\text{cm}^3)$$

$$\times (1.00 \times 10^3 \text{ kg/m}^3)(9.80 \text{ m/s}^2)$$

$$= (2.8 \times 10^{-1} \text{ N}) - (1.3 \times 10^{-1} \text{ N})$$

$$= 1.5 \times 10^{-1} \text{ N}$$

$$a = \frac{F_{net}}{m} = \frac{1.5 \times 10^{-1} \text{ N}}{2.8 \times 10^{-1} \text{ N}/9.80 \text{ m/s}^2}$$

$$= 5.3 \text{ m/s}^2$$

Section 13.2

Level 1

44. What is the change in length of a 2.00-m copper pipe if its temperature is raised from 23°C to 978°C?

$$\Delta L = L_1 \alpha \Delta T$$

$$= (2.00 \text{ m})[1.6 \times 10^{-5}(°C)^{-1}]$$

$$\times (978°C - 23°C)$$

$$= 3.1 \times 10^{-2} \text{ m}$$

45. Bridge builders often use rivets that are larger than the rivet hole to make the joint tighter. The rivet is cooled before it is put into the hole. A builder drills a hole 1.2230 cm in diameter for a steel rivet 1.2250 cm in diameter. To what temperature must the rivet be cooled if it is to fit into the rivet hole that is at 20°C?

$$L_2 = L_1 + \alpha L_1(T_2 - T_1)$$

$$T_2 = T_1 + \frac{(L_2 - L_1)}{\alpha L_1}$$

$$= 20°C + \frac{1.2230 \text{ cm} - 1.2250 \text{ cm}}{(12 \times 10^{-6}/°C)(1.2250 \text{ cm})}$$

$$= 20°C - 140°C = -120°C$$

Copyright © by Glencoe/McGraw-Hill

46. A steel tank is built to hold methanol. The tank is 2.000 m in diameter and 5.000 m high. It is completely filled with methanol at 10.0°C. If the temperature rises to 40.0°C, how much methanol (in liters) will flow out of the tank, given that both the tank and the methanol will expand?

$$\Delta V = \beta V_1 \, \Delta T$$
$$= (\beta_{methanol} - \beta_{steel}) V_1 \, \Delta T$$
$$= (1100 \times 10^{-6}/°C - 35 \times 10^{-6}/°C)(\pi)$$
$$\times (1.000 \text{ m})^2 (5.000 \text{ m})(30.0°C)$$
$$= 5.0 \times 10^{-1} \text{ m}^3 = 5.0 \times 10^2 \text{ L}$$

47. An aluminum sphere is heated from 11°C to 580°C. If the volume of the sphere is 1.78 cm³ at 11°C, what is the increase in volume of the sphere at 580°C?

$$\Delta V = \beta V_1 \, \Delta T$$
$$= (75 \times 10^{-6}/°C)(1.78 \text{ cm}^3)$$
$$\times (580°C - 11°C)$$
$$= 7.6 \times 10^{-2} \text{ cm}^3$$

48. The volume of a copper sphere is 2.56 cm³ after being heated from 12°C to 984°C. What was the volume of the copper sphere at 12°C?

$$V_2 = V_1 + V_1 \, \beta \Delta T = V_1 (1 + \beta \Delta T)$$
$$V_1 = \frac{V_2}{1 + \beta \Delta T}$$
$$= \frac{2.56 \text{ cm}^3}{[1 + (48 \times 10^{-6}/°C)(984°C - 12°C)]}$$
$$V_2 = 2.45 \text{ cm}^3$$

Critical Thinking Problems

49. Persons confined to bed are less likely to develop bedsores if they use a water bed rather than an ordinary mattress. Explain.

> **The surface of the water bed conforms more than the surface of a mattress to the contours of your body. One "sinks" more easily into a waterbed because $\rho_{H_2O} < \rho_{mattress}$, the buoyant force from a waterbed is less.**

50. Hot air balloons contain a fixed volume of gas. When the gas is heated, it expands, and pushes some gas out at the lower open end. As a result, the mass of the gas in the balloon is reduced. Why would the air in a balloon have to be hotter to lift the same number of people above Vail, Colorado, which has an altitude of 2400 m, than above the tidewater flats of Virginia, at an altitude of 6 m?

> **Atmospheric pressure is lower at higher altitudes. Therefore the mass of the volume of fluid displaced by a balloon of the same volume is less at higher altitudes. To obtain the same buoyant force, at higher altitudes a balloon must expel more gas, requiring higher temperatures.**

Copyright © by Glencoe/McGraw-Hill

14 Waves and Energy Transfer

Practice Problems

14.1 Wave Properties
pages 328–335

page 335

1. A sound wave produced by a clock chime is heard 515 m away 1.50 s later.

   a. What is the speed of sound of the clock's chime in air?

   $$v = \frac{d}{t} = \frac{515 \text{ m}}{1.50 \text{ s}} = 343 \text{ m/s}$$

   b. The sound wave has a frequency of 436 Hz. What is its period?

   $$T = \frac{1}{f} = \frac{1}{436 \text{ Hz}} = 2.29 \text{ ms}$$

   c. What is its wavelength?

   $$\lambda = \frac{v}{f} = \frac{d}{ft}$$

   $$\lambda = \frac{515 \text{ m}}{(436 \text{ Hz})(1.50 \text{ s})} = 0.787 \text{ m}$$

2. A hiker shouts toward a vertical cliff 685 m away. The echo is heard 4.00 s later.

   a. What is the speed of sound of the hiker's voice in air?

   $$v = \frac{d}{t} = \frac{685 \text{ m}}{2.00 \text{ s}} = 343 \text{ m/s}$$

   b. The wavelength of the sound is 0.750 m. What is its frequency?

   $$v = \lambda f$$

   $$f = \frac{v}{\lambda} = \frac{343 \text{ m/s}}{0.750 \text{ m}} = 457 \text{ Hz}$$

   c. What is the period of the wave?

   $$T = \frac{1}{f} = \frac{1}{457 \text{ Hz}} =$$

   $$= \frac{1}{457 \text{ s}^{-1}} = 2.19 \times 10^{-3} \text{ s, or}$$

   $$2.19 \text{ ms}$$

3. If you want to increase the wavelength of waves in a rope, should you shake it at a higher or lower frequency?

   at a lower frequency, because wavelength varies inversely with frequency

4. What is the speed of a periodic wave disturbance that has a frequency of 2.50 Hz and a wavelength of 0.600 m?

   $$v = \lambda f = (0.600 \text{ m})(2.50 \text{ Hz}) = 1.50 \text{ m/s}$$

5. The speed of a transverse wave in a string is 15.0 m/s. If a source produces a disturbance that has a frequency of 5.00 Hz, what is its wavelength?

   $$\lambda = \frac{v}{f} = \frac{15.0 \text{ m/s}}{5.00 \text{ Hz}} = 3.00 \text{ m}$$

6. Five pulses are generated every 0.100 s in a tank of water. What is the speed of propagation of the wave if the wavelength of the surface wave is 1.20 cm?

   $$\frac{0.100 \text{ s}}{5 \text{ pulses}} = 0.0200 \text{ s/pulse, so}$$

   $$T = 0.0200 \text{ s}$$

   $$v = \frac{\lambda}{T} = \frac{1.20 \text{ cm}}{0.0200 \text{ s}} = 60.0 \text{ cm/s}$$

   $$= 0.600 \text{ m/s}$$

7. A periodic longitudinal wave that has a frequency of 20.0 Hz travels along a coil spring. If the distance between successive compressions is 0.400 m, what is the speed of the wave?

   $$v = \lambda f = (0.400 \text{ m})(20.0 \text{ Hz}) = 8.00 \text{ m/s}$$

Copyright © by Glencoe/McGraw-Hill

14.2 Wave Behavior
pages 336–343

page 337

8. A pulse is sent along a spring. The spring is attached to a lightweight thread that is tied to a wall, as shown in **Figure 14–9.**

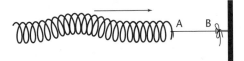

FIGURE 14-9

a. What happens when the pulse reaches point A?

The pulse is partially reflected, partially transmitted.

b. Is the pulse reflected from point A erect or inverted?

erect, because reflection is from a less dense medium

c. What happens when the transmitted pulse reaches point B?

It is almost totally reflected from the wall.

d. Is the pulse reflected from point B erect or inverted?

inverted, because reflection is from a more dense medium

9. A long spring runs across the floor of a room and out the door. A pulse is sent along the spring. After a few seconds, an inverted pulse returns. Is the spring attached to the wall in the next room or is it lying loose on the floor?

Pulse inversion means rigid boundary; spring is attached to wall.

10. A pulse is sent along a thin rope that is attached to a thick rope, which is tied to a wall, as shown in **Figure 14–10.**

FIGURE 14-10

a. What happens when the pulse reaches point A? Point B?

The pulse is partially reflected, partially transmitted; it is almost totally reflected from the wall.

b. Is the pulse reflected from A displaced in the same direction as the incident pulse, or is it inverted? What about the pulse reflected from point B?

inverted, because reflection is from a more dense medium; inverted, because reflection is from a more dense medium

Chapter Review Problems
pages 346–347
page 346
Section 14.1

Level 1

32. The Sears Building in Chicago sways back and forth in the wind with a frequency of about 0.10 Hz. What is its period of vibration?

$$T = \frac{1}{f} = \frac{1}{0.10 \text{ Hz}} = 1.0 \times 10^1 \text{ s}$$

33. An ocean wave has a length of 10.0 m. A wave passes a fixed location every 2.0 s. What is the speed of the wave?

$$v = \lambda f = (10.0 \text{ m}) \frac{1}{2.0 \text{ s}} = 5.0 \text{ m/s}$$

34. Water waves in a shallow dish are 6.0 cm long. At one point, the water oscillates up and down at a rate of 4.8 oscillations per second.

a. What is the speed of the water waves?

$$v = \lambda f = (0.060 \text{ m})(4.8 \text{ Hz}) = 0.29 \text{ m/s}$$

b. What is the period of the water waves?

$$T = \frac{1}{f} = \frac{1}{4.8 \text{ Hz}} = 0.21 \text{ s}$$

Copyright © by Glencoe/McGraw-Hill

35. Water waves in a lake travel 4.4 m in 1.8 s. The period of oscillation is 1.2 s.

a. What is the speed of the water waves?

$$v = \frac{d}{t} = \frac{4.4 \text{ m}}{1.8 \text{ s}} = 2.4 \text{ m/s}$$

b. What is their wavelength?

$$\lambda = \frac{v}{f} = vT = (2.4 \text{ m/s})(1.2 \text{ s})$$

$$= 2.9 \text{ m}$$

36. The frequency of yellow light is 5.0×10^{14} Hz. Find the wavelength of yellow light. The speed of light is 300 000 km/s.

$$\lambda = \frac{c}{f} = \frac{3.00 \times 10^8 \text{ m/s}}{5.0 \times 10^{14} \text{ Hz}}$$

$$= 6.0 \times 10^{-7} \text{ m}$$

37. AM-radio signals are broadcast at frequencies between 550 kHz and 1600 kHz (kilohertz) and travel 3.0×10^8 m/s.

a. What is the range of wavelengths for these signals?

$$v = \lambda f$$

$$\lambda_1 = \frac{v}{f_1} = \frac{3.0 \times 10^8 \text{ m/s}}{5.5 \times 10^5 \text{ Hz}}$$

$$= 550 \text{ m}$$

$$\lambda_2 = \frac{v}{f_2} = \frac{3.0 \times 10^8 \text{ m/s}}{1.6 \times 10^6 \text{ Hz}}$$

$$= 190 \text{ m}$$

Range is 190 m to 550 m.

b. FM frequencies range between 88 MHz and 108 MHz (megahertz) and travel at the same speed. What is the range of FM wavelengths?

$$\lambda = \frac{v}{f} = \frac{3.0 \times 10^8 \text{ m/s}}{8.8 \times 10^7 \text{ Hz}}$$

$$= 3.4 \text{ m}$$

$$\lambda = \frac{v}{f} = \frac{3.0 \times 10^8 \text{ m/s}}{1.08 \times 10^8 \text{ Hz}}$$

$$= 2.8 \text{ m}$$

Range is 2.8 m to 3.4 m.

38. A sonar signal of frequency 1.00×10^6 Hz has a wavelength of 1.50 mm in water.

a. What is the speed of the signal in water?

$$v = \lambda f = (1.50 \times 10^{-3} \text{ m})(1.00 \times 10^6 \text{ Hz})$$

$$= 1.50 \times 10^3 \text{ m/s}$$

b. What is its period in water?

$$T = \frac{1}{f} = \frac{1}{1.00 \times 10^6 \text{ Hz}}$$

$$= 1.00 \times 10^{-6} \text{ s}$$

c. What is its period in air?

$$1.00 \times 10^{-6} \text{ s}$$

The period and frequency remain unchanged.

39. A sound wave of wavelength 0.70 m and velocity 330 m/s is produced for 0.50 s.

a. What is the frequency of the wave?

$$v = \lambda f$$

$$\text{so } f = \frac{v}{\lambda} = \frac{330 \text{ m/s}}{0.70 \text{ m}}$$

$$= 470 \text{ Hz}$$

b. How many complete waves are emitted in this time interval?

$$ft = (470 \text{ Hz})(0.50 \text{ s})$$

$$= 240 \text{ complete waves}$$

c. After 0.50 s, how far is the front of the wave from the source of the sound?

$$d = vt$$

$$= (330 \text{ m/s})(0.50 \text{ s})$$

$$= 170 \text{ m}$$

Copyright © by Glencoe/McGraw-Hill

40. The speed of sound in water is 1498 m/s. A sonar signal is sent straight down from a ship at a point just below the water surface, and 1.80 s later the reflected signal is detected. How deep is the ocean beneath the ship?

> **The time for the wave to travel down and back up is 1.80 s. The time one way is half 1.80 s or 0.900 s.**
>
> $d = vt = (1498\text{ m/s})(0.900\text{ s}) = 1350\text{ m}$

41. The time needed for a water wave to change from the equilibrium level to the crest is 0.18 s.

a. What fraction of a wavelength is this?

> $\frac{1}{4}$ **wavelength**

b. What is the period of the wave?

> $T = 4(0.18\text{ s}) = 0.72\text{ s}$

c. What is the frequency of the wave?

> $f = \dfrac{1}{T} = \dfrac{1}{0.72\text{ s}} = 1.4\text{ Hz}$

Level 2

42. Pepe and Alfredo are resting on an offshore raft after a swim. They estimate that 3.0 m separates a trough and an adjacent crest of surface waves on the lake. They count 14 crests that pass by the raft in 20.0 s. Calculate how fast the waves are moving.

> $\lambda = 2(3.0\text{ m}) = 6.0\text{ m}$
>
> $f = \dfrac{14\text{ waves}}{20.0\text{ s}}$
>
> $= 0.70\text{ Hz}$
>
> $v = \lambda f = (6.0\text{ m})(0.70\text{ Hz})$
>
> $= 4.2\text{ m/s}$

43. The velocity of the transverse waves produced by an earthquake is 8.9 km/s, and that of the longitudinal waves is 5.1 km/s. A seismograph records the arrival of the transverse waves 73 s before the arrival of the longitudinal waves. How far away was the earthquake?

> $d = vt$**. We don't know** t**, only the difference in time** Δt**. The transverse distance,** $d_T = v_T t$**, is the same as the longitudinal distance,** $d_L = v_L (t + \Delta t)$**. Use** $v_T t = v_L(t + \Delta t)$**, and solve for** t**:**
>
> $t = \dfrac{v_L\, \Delta t}{v_T - v_L}$
>
> $t = \dfrac{(5.1\text{ km/s})(73\text{ sec})}{(8.9\text{ km/s} - 5.1\text{ km/s})} = 98\text{ s}$
>
> **Then putting** t **back into**
>
> $d = v_T t = (8.9\text{ km/s})(98\text{ s})$
>
> $= 8.7 \times 10^2\text{ km}$
>
> **or 870 000 m**

44. The velocity of a wave on a string depends on how hard the string is stretched, and on the mass per unit length of the string. If F_T is the tension in the string, and μ is the mass/unit length, then the velocity, v, can be determined.

$$v = \sqrt{\dfrac{F_T}{\mu}}$$

A piece of string 5.30 m long has a mass of 15.0 g. What must the tension in the string be to make the wavelength of a 125-Hz wave 120.0 cm?

> $v = \lambda f = (1.200\text{ m})(125\text{ Hz})$
>
> $= 1.50 \times 10^2\text{ m/s}$
>
> **and** $\mu = \dfrac{m}{L} = \dfrac{1.50 \times 10^{-2}\text{ kg}}{5.30\text{ m}}$
>
> $= 2.83 \times 10^{-3}\text{ kg/m}$
>
> **Now** $v = \sqrt{\dfrac{F_T}{\mu}}$**, so**
>
> $F_T = v^2\mu = (1.50 \times 10^2\text{ m/s})^2$
>
> $\qquad\qquad \times (2.83 \times 10^{-3}\text{ kg/m})$
>
> $= 63.7\text{ N}$

Copyright © by Glencoe/McGraw-Hill

Section 14.2

Level 1

45. Sketch the result for each of the three cases shown in **Figure 14-21,** when centers of the two wave pulses lie on the dashed line so that the pulses exactly overlap.

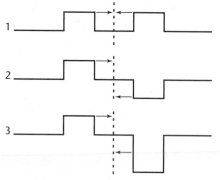

   FIGURE 14-21

1. **The amplitude is doubled.**

2. **The amplitudes cancel each other.**

   _____

3. **If the amplitude of the first pulse is $\frac{1}{2}$ of the second, the resultant pulse is $\frac{1}{2}$ the amplitude of the second.**

46. If you slosh the water back and forth in a bathtub at the correct frequency, the water rises first at one end and then at the other. Suppose you can make a standing wave in a 150-cm-long tub with a frequency of 0.30 Hz. What is the velocity of the water wave?

   $d = 3.0$ m

   $v = \dfrac{d}{t} = df = (3.0 \text{ m})(0.30 \text{ Hz})$

   $= 0.90$ m/s

Level 2

47. The wave speed in a guitar string is 265 m/s. The length of the string is 63 cm. You pluck the center of the string by pulling it up and letting go. Pulses move in both directions and are reflected off the ends of the string.

   a. How long does it take for the pulse to move to the string end and return to the center?

   $d = 2(63 \text{ cm})/2 = 63$ cm

   so $t = \dfrac{d}{v} = \dfrac{0.63 \text{ m}}{265 \text{ m/s}} = 2.4 \times 10^{-3}$ s

   b. When the pulses return, is the string above or below its resting location?

   Pulses are inverted when reflected from a more dense medium, so returning pulse is down (below).

   c. If you plucked the string 15 cm from one end of the string, where would the two pulses meet?

   15 cm from the other end, where the distances traveled are the same

Critical Thinking Problems

48. Gravel roads often develop regularly spaced ridges that are perpendicular to the road. This effect, called washboarding, occurs because most cars travel at about the same speed and the springs that connect the wheels to the cars oscillate at about the same frequency. If the ridges are 1.5 m apart and cars travel at about 5 m/s, what is the frequency of the springs' oscillation?

   $v = \lambda f$

   $f = \dfrac{v}{\lambda} = \dfrac{5 \text{ m/s}}{1.5 \text{ m}} = 3$ Hz

Copyright © by Glencoe/McGraw-Hill

15 Sound

Practice Problems

15.1 Properties of Sound
pages 350–355

page 352

1. Find the frequency of a sound wave moving in air at room temperature with a wavelength of 0.667 m.

   $$v = \lambda f$$

   So $f = \dfrac{v}{\lambda} = \dfrac{343 \text{ m/s}}{0.667 \text{ m}} = 514 \text{ Hz}$

2. The human ear can detect sounds with frequencies between 20 Hz and 16 kHz. Find the largest and smallest wavelengths the ear can detect, assuming that the sound travels through air with a speed of 343 m/s at 20°C.

   From $v = \lambda f$ the largest wavelength is

   $\lambda = \dfrac{v}{f} = \dfrac{343 \text{ m/s}}{20 \text{ Hz}} = 17 \text{ m} = 20 \text{ m}$

   the smallest is

   $\lambda = \dfrac{v}{f} = \dfrac{343 \text{ m/s}}{16000 \text{ Hz}} = 0.021 \text{ m}$

3. If you clap your hands and hear the echo from a distant wall 0.20 s later, how far away is the wall?

   Assume that $v = 343$ m/s

   $2d = vt = (343 \text{ m/s})(0.20 \text{ s}) = 68.6 \text{ m}$

   $d = \dfrac{68.6 \text{ m}}{2} = 34 \text{ m}$

4. What is the frequency of sound in air at 20°C having a wavelength equal to the diameter of a 15 in. (38 cm) woofer loudspeaker? Of a 3.0 in. (7.6 cm) tweeter?

   Woofer diameter 38 cm:

   $f = \dfrac{v}{\lambda} = \dfrac{343 \text{ m/s}}{0.38 \text{ m}} = 0.90 \text{ kHz}$

   Tweeter diameter 7.6 cm:

   $f = \dfrac{v}{\lambda} = \dfrac{343 \text{ m/s}}{0.076 \text{ m}} = 4.5 \text{ kHz}$

15.2 The Physics of Music
pages 357–367

page 363

5. A 440-Hz tuning fork is held above a closed pipe. Find the spacings between the resonances when the air temperature is 20°C.

   Resonance spacing is $\dfrac{\lambda}{2}$ so using $v = \lambda f$ the resonance spacing is

   $\dfrac{\lambda}{2} = \dfrac{v}{2f} = \dfrac{343 \text{ m/s}}{2(440 \text{ Hz})} = 0.39 \text{ m}$

6. The 440-Hz tuning fork is used with a resonating column to determine the velocity of sound in helium gas. If the spacings between resonances are 110 cm, what is the velocity of sound in He?

   Resonance spacing $= \dfrac{\lambda}{2} = 1.10$ m so

   $\lambda = 2.20 \text{ m}$

   and $v = f\lambda = (440 \text{ Hz})(2.20 \text{ m})$

   $= 970 \text{ m/s}$

7. The frequency of a tuning fork is unknown. A student uses an air column at 27°C and finds resonances spaced by 20.2 cm. What is the frequency of the tuning fork?

   From the previous Example Problem $v = 347$ m/s at 27°C and the resonance spacing gives

   $\dfrac{\lambda}{2} = 0.202 \text{ m}$

   or $\lambda = 0.404$ m

   Using $v = \lambda f$,

   $f = \dfrac{v}{\lambda} = \dfrac{347 \text{ m/s}}{0.404 \text{ m}} = 859 \text{ Hz}$

Copyright © by Glencoe/McGraw-Hill

8. A bugle can be thought of as an open pipe. If a bugle were straightened out, it would be 2.65 m long.

   a. If the speed of sound is 343 m/s, find the lowest frequency that is resonant in a bugle (ignoring end corrections).

   $$\lambda_1 = 2L = 2(2.65 \text{ m}) = 5.30 \text{ m}$$

   so that the lowest frequency is

   $$f_1 = \frac{v}{\lambda_1} = \frac{343 \text{ m/s}}{5.30 \text{ m}} = 64.7 \text{ Hz}$$

   b. Find the next two higher resonant frequencies in the bugle.

   $$f_2 = \frac{v}{\lambda_2} = \frac{v}{L} = \frac{343 \text{ m/s}}{2.65 \text{ m}} = 129 \text{ Hz}$$

   $$f_3 = \frac{v}{\lambda_3} = \frac{3v}{2L} = \frac{3(343 \text{ m/s})}{2(2.65 \text{ m})} = 194 \text{ Hz}$$

9. A soprano saxophone is an open pipe. If all keys are closed, it is approximately 65 cm long. Using 343 m/s as the speed of sound, find the lowest frequency that can be played on this instrument (ignoring end corrections).

   The lowest resonant frequency corresponds to the wavelength given by $\frac{\lambda}{2} = L$, **the length of the pipe.**

   $$\lambda = 2L = 2(0.65 \text{ m}) = 1.3 \text{ m}$$

   so $f = \dfrac{v}{\lambda} = \dfrac{343 \text{ m/s}}{1.3 \text{ m}} = 260 \text{ Hz}$

page 367

10. A 330.0-Hz and a 333.0-Hz tuning fork are struck simultaneously. What will the beat frequency be?

   Beat frequency $= |f_2 - f_1|$

   $$= |333.0 \text{ Hz} - 330.0 \text{ Hz}|$$

   $$= 3.0 \text{ Hz}$$

Chapter Review Problems

pages 369–371

page 369

Section 15.1

Level 1

24. You hear the sound of the firing of a distant cannon 6.0 s after seeing the flash. How far are you from the cannon?

   $$d = v_s t = (343 \text{ m/s})(6.0 \text{ s}) = 2.1 \text{ km}$$

25. If you shout across a canyon and hear an echo 4.0 s later, how wide is the canyon?

   $$d = vt = (343 \text{ m/s})(4.0 \text{ s}) = 1400 \text{ m}$$

   is the total distance traveled. The distance to the wall is

   $$\frac{1}{2}(1400) = 7.0 \times 10^2 \text{ m}$$

26. A sound wave has a frequency of 9800 Hz and travels along a steel rod. If the distance between compressions, or regions of high pressure, is 0.580 m, what is the speed of the wave?

   $$v = \lambda f = (0.580 \text{ m})(9800 \text{ Hz})$$

   $$= 5700 \text{ m/s}$$

27. A rifle is fired in a valley with parallel vertical walls. The echo from one wall is heard 2.0 s after the rifle was fired. The echo from the other wall is heard 2.0 s after the first echo. How wide is the valley?

   The time it takes sound to go to wall 1 and back is 2.0 s. The time it takes to go to the wall is half the total time, or 1.0 s,

   $$d_1 = v_s t_1 = (343 \text{ m/s})(1.0 \text{ s})$$

   $$= 3.4 \times 10^2 \text{ m}$$

   The total time for the sound to go to wall 2 is half of 4.0 s or 2.0 s.

   $$d_2 = v_s t_2 = (343 \text{ m/s})(2.0 \text{ s})$$

   $$= 6.8 \times 10^2 \text{ m}$$

   The total distance is

   $$d_1 + d_2 = 1.02 \times 10^3 \text{ m} = 1.0 \text{ km}$$

Copyright © by Glencoe/McGraw-Hill

28. A certain instant camera determines the distance to the subject by sending out a sound wave and measuring the time needed for the echo to return to the camera. How long would it take the sound wave to return to the camera if the subject were 3.00 m away?

The total distance the sound must travel is 6.00 m.

$$v = \frac{d}{t}$$

so $t = \dfrac{d}{v} = \dfrac{6.00 \text{ m}}{343 \text{ m/s}} = 0.0175 \text{ s}$

page 370

29. Sound with a frequency of 261.6 Hz travels through water at a speed of 1435 m/s. Find the sound's wavelength in water. Don't confuse sound waves moving through water with surface waves moving through water.

$$v = \lambda f$$

so $\lambda = \dfrac{v}{f} = \dfrac{1435 \text{ m/s}}{261.6 \text{ Hz}} = 5.485 \text{ m}$

30. If the wavelength of a 4.40×10^2 Hz sound in freshwater is 3.30 m, what is the speed of sound in water?

$$v = \lambda f = (3.30 \text{ m})(4.40 \times 10^2 \text{ Hz})$$

$$= 1.45 \times 10^3 \text{ m/s}$$

31. Sound with a frequency of 442 Hz travels through steel. A wavelength of 11.66 m is measured. Find the speed of the sound in steel.

$$v = \lambda f = (11.66 \text{ m})(442 \text{ Hz})$$

$$= 5.15 \times 10^3 \text{ m/s}$$

32. The sound emitted by bats has a wavelength of 3.5 mm. What is the sound's frequency in air?

$$f = \frac{v}{\lambda} = \frac{343 \text{ m/s}}{0.0035 \text{ m}} = 9.8 \times 10^4 \text{ Hz}$$

33. Ultrasound with a frequency of 4.25 MHz can be used to produce images of the human body. If the speed of sound in the body is the same as in salt water, 1.50 km/s, what is the wavelength of the pressure wave in the body?

$$v = \lambda f$$

so $\lambda = \dfrac{v}{f} = \dfrac{1.50 \times 10^3 \text{ m/s}}{4.25 \times 10^6 \text{ Hz}}$

$$= 3.53 \times 10^{-4} \text{ m}$$

34. The equation for the Doppler shift of a sound wave of speed v reaching a moving detector is

$$f_d = f_s \left(\frac{v + v_d}{v - v_s} \right)$$

where v_d is the speed of the detector, v_s is the speed of the source, f_s is the frequency of the source, f_d is the frequency of the detector. If the detector moves toward the source, v_d is positive; if the source moves toward the detector, v_s is positive. A train moving toward a detector at 31 m/s blows a 305-Hz horn. What frequency is detected by

a. a stationary train?

$$f_d = f_s \left(\frac{v + v_d}{v - v_s} \right)$$

$$= \frac{(305 \text{ Hz})(343 \text{ m/s} + 0)}{343 \text{ m/s} - 31 \text{ m/s}}$$

$$= 335 \text{ Hz}$$

b. a train moving toward the first train at 21 m/s?

$$f_d = f_s \left(\frac{v + v_d}{v - v_s} \right)$$

$$= \frac{(305 \text{ Hz})(343 \text{ m/s} + 21 \text{ m/s})}{343 \text{ m/s} - 31 \text{ m/s}}$$

$$= 356 \text{ Hz}$$

35. The train in problem 34 is moving away from the detector. Now what frequency is detected by

a. a stationary train?

$$f_d = f_s \left(\frac{v + v_d}{v - v_s} \right)$$

$$= (305 \text{ Hz}) \left[\frac{343 \text{ m/s} + 0}{343 \text{ m/s} - (-31 \text{ m/s})} \right]$$

$$= 2.80 \times 10^2 \text{ Hz}$$

Copyright © by Glencoe/McGraw-Hill

35. (continued)

    b. a train moving away from the first train at a speed of 21 m/s?

$$f_d = f_s \left(\frac{v + v_d}{v - v_s} \right)$$

$$= (305 \text{ Hz}) \left[\frac{343 \text{ m/s} + (-21 \text{ m/s})}{343 \text{ m/s} - (-31 \text{ m/s})} \right]$$

$$= 2.60 \times 10^2 \text{ Hz}$$

36. Adam, an airport employee, is working near a jet plane taking off. He experiences a sound level of 150 dB.

    a. If Adam wears ear protectors that reduce the sound level to that of a chain saw (110 dB), what decrease in dB will be required?

    Chain saw is 110 dB, so 40 dB reduction is needed.

    b. If Adam now hears something that sounds like a whisper, what will a person not wearing the protectors hear?

    A soft whisper is 10 dB, so the actual level would be 50 dB, or that of an average classroom.

37. A rock band plays at an 80-dB sound level. How many times greater is the sound pressure from another rock band playing at

    a. 100 dB?

    Each 20 dB increases pressure by a factor of 10, so 10 times greater pressure.

    b. 120 dB?

    10 × 10 = 100 times greater pressure

Level 2

38. If your drop a stone into a mine shaft 122.5 m deep, how soon after you drop the stone do you hear it hit the bottom of the shaft?

    First find the time it takes the stone to fall down the shaft by $d = \frac{1}{2} gt^2$, so

$$t = \sqrt{\frac{d}{\frac{1}{2} g}} = \sqrt{\frac{-122.5 \text{ m}}{\frac{1}{2}(-9.80 \text{ m/s}^2)}} = 5.00 \text{ s}$$

The time it takes the sound to come back up is found with $d = v_s t$, so

$$t = \frac{d}{v_s} = \frac{122.5 \text{ m}}{343 \text{ m/s}} = 0.357 \text{ s}$$

The total time is 5.00 s + 0.357 s = 5.36 s.

Section 15.2

Level 1

39. A slide whistle has a length of 27 cm. If you want to play a note one octave higher, the whistle should be how long?

$$\lambda = \frac{4L}{3} = \frac{4(27 \text{ cm})}{3} = 36 \text{ cm}$$

A note one octave higher is the first overtone of the fundamental. Resonances are spaced by 1/2 wavelength. Since the original whistle length of 27 cm = 3/4 the wavelength of the first overtone (octave), then the shortest whistle length for the first overtone equals

$$\frac{3\lambda}{4} - \frac{\lambda}{2} = \frac{\lambda}{4} = \frac{36 \text{ cm}}{4} = 9.0 \text{ cm}$$

40. An open vertical tube is filled with water, and a tuning fork vibrates over its mouth. As the water level is lowered in the tube, resonance is heard when the water level has dropped 17 cm, and again after 49 cm of distance exists from the water to the top of the tube. What is the frequency of the tuning fork?

    49 cm − 17 cm = 32 cm

    or 0.32 m

    Since the tube is closed at one end, 1/2 λ exists between points of resonance.

$$\frac{1}{2} \lambda = 0.32 \text{ m}$$

    So λ = 0.64 m

$$f = \frac{v}{\lambda} = \frac{343 \text{ m/s}}{0.64 \text{ m}} = 540 \text{ Hz}$$

Copyright © by Glencoe/McGraw-Hill

41. The auditory canal, leading to the eardrum, is a closed pipe 3.0 cm long. Find the approximate value (ignoring end correction) of the lowest resonance frequency.

$$L = \frac{\lambda}{4}$$

$$v = \lambda f$$

So $f = \dfrac{v}{4L} = \dfrac{343 \text{ m/s}}{4 \times 0.030 \text{ m}} = 2.9 \text{ kHz}$

42. If you hold a 1.0-m aluminum rod in the center and hit one end with a hammer, it will oscillate like an open pipe. Antinodes of air pressure correspond to nodes of molecular motion, so there is a pressure antinode in the center of the bar. The speed of sound in aluminum is 5150 m/s. What would be the lowest frequency of oscillation?

The rod length is $\frac{1}{2}\lambda$, so $\lambda = 2.0$ m

$$f = \frac{v}{\lambda} = \frac{5150 \text{ m/s}}{2.0 \text{ m}} = 2.6 \text{ kHz}$$

43. The lowest note on an organ is 16.4 Hz.

a. What is the shortest open organ pipe that will resonate at this frequency?

$$\lambda = \frac{v}{f} = \frac{343 \text{ m/s}}{16.4 \text{ Hz}} = 20.9 \text{ m}$$

$$L = \frac{\lambda}{2} = \frac{20.9 \text{ m}}{2} = 10.5 \text{ m}$$

b. What would be the pitch if the same organ pipe were closed?

Since a closed pipe produces a fundamental with wavelength twice as long as that of an open pipe, of the same length, the pitch would be $\frac{1}{2}$ (16.4 Hz) = 8.20 Hz

44. One tuning fork has a 445-Hz pitch. When a second fork is struck, beat notes occur with a frequency of 3 Hz. What are the two possible frequencies of the second fork?

445 Hz − 3 Hz = 442 Hz

and 445 Hz + 3 Hz = 448 Hz

45. A flute acts as an open pipe and sounds a note with a 370-Hz pitch. What are the frequencies of the second, third, and fourth harmonics of this pitch?

$f_2 = 2f_1 = (2)(370 \text{ Hz}) = 740 \text{ Hz}$

$f_3 = 3f_1 = (3)(370 \text{ Hz}) = 1110 \text{ Hz}$
$$= 1100 \text{ Hz}$$

$f_4 = 4f_1 = (4)(370 \text{ Hz})$
$$= 1480 \text{ Hz} = 1500 \text{ Hz}$$

46. A clarinet sounds the same note, with a pitch of 370 Hz, as in problem 45. The clarinet, however, produces harmonics that are only odd multiples of the fundamental frequency. What are the frequencies of the lowest three harmonics produced by this instrument?

$3f = (3)(370 \text{ Hz}) = 1110 \text{ Hz} = 1100 \text{ Hz}$

$5f = (5)(370 \text{ Hz}) = 1850 \text{ Hz} = 1900 \text{ Hz}$

$7f = (7)(370 \text{ Hz}) = 2590 \text{ Hz} = 2600 \text{ Hz}$

page 371

Level 2

47. During normal conversation, the amplitude of a pressure wave is 0.020 Pa.

a. If the area of the eardrum is 0.52 cm², what is the force on the eardrum?

$F = PA = (0.020 \text{ N/m}^2)(0.52 \times 10^{-4} \text{ m}^2)$
$$= 1.0 \times 10^{-6} \text{ N}$$

b. The mechanical advantage of the bones in the inner ear is 1.5. What force is exerted on the oval window?

$$MA = \frac{F_r}{F_e}$$

so $F_r = (MA)(F_r)$

$F_r = (1.5)(1.0 \times 10^{-6} \text{ N}) = 1.5 \times 10^{-6} \text{ N}$

c. The area of the oval window is 0.026 cm². What is the pressure increase transmitted to the liquid in the cochlea?

$$P = \frac{F}{A} = \frac{1.5 \times 10^{-6} \text{ N}}{0.026 \times 10^{-4} \text{ m}^2} = 0.58 \text{ Pa}$$

48. One closed organ pipe has a length of 2.40 m.

a. What is the frequency of the note played by this pipe?

$\lambda = 4\lambda = (4)(2.40 \text{ m}) = 9.60 \text{ m}$

$v = \lambda f$

$f = \dfrac{v}{\lambda} = \dfrac{343 \text{ m/s}}{9.60 \text{ m}} = 35.7 \text{ Hz}$

Copyright © by Glencoe/McGraw-Hill

48. (continued)

b. When a second pipe is played at the same time, a 1.40-Hz beat note is heard. By how much is the second pipe too long?

$f = 35.7\text{ Hz} - 1.40\text{ Hz} = 34.3\text{ Hz}$

$v = \lambda f$

$\lambda = \dfrac{v}{f} = \dfrac{343\text{ m/s}}{34.3\text{ Hz}} = 10.0\text{ m}$

$\lambda = 4L$

$L = \dfrac{\lambda}{4} = \dfrac{10.0\text{ m}}{4} = 2.50\text{ m}$

The difference in lengths is
2.50 m − 2.40 m = 0.10 m.

49. One open organ pipe has a length of 836 mm. A second open pipe should have a pitch one major third higher. The pipe should be how long?

$L = \dfrac{\lambda}{2}$ $\quad$ so $\lambda = 2L$

and $v = \lambda f$

So $f = \dfrac{v}{2L} = \dfrac{343\text{ m/s}}{(2)(0.836\text{ m})} = 205\text{ Hz}$

The ratio of a frequency one major third higher is 5:4, so

$(205\text{ Hz})\left(\dfrac{5}{4}\right) = 256\text{ Hz}$

The length of the second pipe is

$L = \dfrac{v}{2f} = \dfrac{343\text{ m/s}}{(2)(256\text{ Hz})} = 6.70 \times 10^2\text{ mm}$

50. In 1845, French scientist B. Ballot first tested the Doppler shift. He had a trumpet player sound an A, 440 Hz, while riding on a flatcar pulled by a locomotive. At the same time, a stationary trumpeter played the same note. Ballot heard 3.0 beats per second. How fast was the train moving toward him? (Refer to problem 34 for the Doppler shift equation.)

$fd = 440\text{ Hz} + 3.0\text{ Hz} = 443\text{ Hz}$

$f_d = f_s\left(\dfrac{v + v_d}{v - v_s}\right)$

so $(v - v_s)f_d = (v + v_d)f_s$

and $v_s = v - \dfrac{(v + v_d)f_s}{f_d}$

$= 343\text{ m/s} - \dfrac{(343\text{ m/s} + 0)(440\text{ Hz})}{443\text{ Hz}}$

$= 2.3\text{ m/s}$

51. You try to repeat Ballot's experiment. You plan to have a trumpet played in a rapidly moving car. Rather than listening for beat notes, however, you want to have the car move fast enough so that the moving trumpet sounds a major third above a stationary trumpet. (Refer to problem 34 for the Doppler shift equation.)

a. How fast would the car have to move?

major third ratio $= \dfrac{5}{4}$

$f_d = f_s\left(\dfrac{v + v_d}{v - v_s}\right)$

so $(v - v_s)f_d = (v + v_d)f_s$

and $v_s = v - \dfrac{(v + v_d)f_s}{f_d}$

$= v - (v + v_d)\dfrac{f_s}{f_d}$

$= 343\text{ m/s} - (343\text{ m/s} + 0)\left(\dfrac{4}{5}\right)$

$= 68.6\text{ m/s}$

b. Should you try the experiment?

$v = (68.6\text{ m/s})\left(\dfrac{3600\text{ s}}{\text{hr}}\right)\left(\dfrac{1\text{ mi}}{1609\text{ m}}\right)$

$= 153$ mph, so the car would be moving dangerously fast

No, do not try the experiment.

Critical Thinking Problems

52. Suppose that the frequency of a car horn (when not moving) is 300 Hz. What would the graph of the frequency versus time look like as the car approached and then moved past you? Complete a rough sketch.

The graph should show a fairly steady frequency above 300 Hz as it approaches and a fairly steady frequency below 300 Hz as it moves away.

Copyright © by Glencoe/McGraw-Hill

52. (continued)

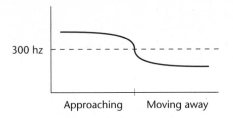

Approaching   Moving away

53. Describe how you could use a stopwatch to estimate the speed of sound if you were near the green on a 200-m golf hole as another group of golfers were hitting their tee shots. Would your estimate of their velocities be too large or too small?

You could start the watch when you saw the hit and stop the watch when the sound reached you. The speed would be calculated by dividing the distance, 200 m, by the time. The time estimate would be too large because you could anticipate the impact by sight, but you could not anticipate the sound. The calculated velocity would be too small.

54. A light wave coming from a point on the left edge of the sun is found by astronomers to have a slightly higher frequency than light from the right side. What do these measurements tell you about the sun's motion?

The sun must be rotating on its axis in the same manner as Earth. The Doppler shift indicates that the left side of the sun is coming toward us, while the right side is moving away.

Copyright © by Glencoe/McGraw-Hill

16 Light

Practice Problems

16.1 Light Fundamentals
pages 374–381

page 376

1. What is the frequency of yellow light, $\lambda = 556$ nm?

   $c = \lambda f$

   So $f = \dfrac{c}{\lambda} = \dfrac{(3.00 \times 10^8 \text{ m/s})}{(556 \times 10^{-9} \text{ m})}$

   $= 5.40 \times 10^{14}$ Hz

2. One nanosecond (ns) is 10^{-9} s. Laboratory workers often estimate the distance light travels in a certain time by remembering the approximation "light goes one foot in one nanosecond." How far, in feet, does light actually travel in exactly 1 ns?

   $d = ct$

   $= (3.00 \times 10^8 \text{ m/s})(1.00 \times 10^{-9} \text{ s})$

   $\times (3.28 \text{ ft/1 m})$

   $= 0.984$ ft

3. Modern lasers can create a pulse of light that lasts only a few femtoseconds.

   a. What is the length of a pulse of violet light that lasts 6.0 fs?

   $d = ct$

   $= (3.00 \times 10^8 \text{ m/s})(6.0 \times 10^{-15} \text{ s})$

   $= 1.8 \times 10^{-6}$ m

   b. How many wavelengths of violet light ($\lambda = 400$ nm) are included in such a pulse?

   Number of wavelengths
   $= \dfrac{\text{pulse length}}{\lambda_{\text{violet}}}$

   $= \dfrac{1.8 \times 10^{-6} \text{ m}}{4.0 \times 10^{-7} \text{ m}}$

   $= 4.5$

4. The distance to the moon can be found with the help of mirrors left on the moon by astronauts. A pulse of light is sent to the moon and returns to Earth in 2.562 s. Using the defined speed of light, calculate the distance from Earth to the moon.

   $d = ct$

   $= (299\ 792\ 458 \text{ m/s})\left(\dfrac{1}{2}\right)(2.562 \text{ s})$

   $= 3.840 \times 10^8$ m

5. Use the correct time taken for light to cross Earth's orbit, 16 minutes, and the diameter of the orbit, 3.0×10^{11} m, to calculate the speed of light using Roemer's method.

   $v = \dfrac{d}{t} = \dfrac{(3.0 \times 10^{11} \text{ m})}{(16 \text{ min})(60 \text{ s/min})}$

   $= 3.1 \times 10^8$ m/s

page 381

6. A lamp is moved from 30 cm to 90 cm above the pages of a book. Compare the illumination on the book before and after the lamp is moved.

   $\dfrac{E_{\text{after}}}{E_{\text{before}}} = \dfrac{P/4\pi d^2_{\text{after}}}{P/4\pi d^2_{\text{before}}} = \dfrac{d^2_{\text{before}}}{d^2_{\text{after}}}$

   $= \dfrac{(30 \text{ cm})^2}{(90 \text{ cm})^2} = \dfrac{1}{9}$

7. What is the illumination on a surface 3.0 m below a 150-watt incandescent lamp that emits a luminous flux of 2275 lm?

   $E = \dfrac{P}{4\pi d^2} = \dfrac{2275 \text{ lm}}{4\pi(3.0 \text{ m})^2}$

   $= 2.0 \times 10^1$ lx

Copyright © by Glencoe/McGraw-Hill

8. Draw a graph of the illuminance from a 150-watt incandescent lamp between 0.50 m and 5.0 m.

Illuminance of a 150-watt bulb

$P = 2275$, $d = 0.5, 0.75, \ldots, 5$

$$E(d) = \frac{P}{4\pi d^2}$$

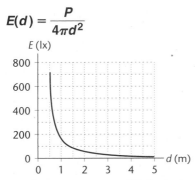

9. A 64-cd point source of light is 3.0 m above the surface of a desk. What is the illumination on the desk's surface in lux?

$P = 4\pi I = 4\pi (64 \text{ cd}) = 256\pi \text{ lm}$

so $E = \dfrac{P}{4\pi d^2} = \dfrac{256\pi \text{ lm}}{4\pi(3.0 \text{ m})^2} = 7.1$ lx

10. The illumination on a tabletop is 2.0×10^1 lx. The lamp providing the illumination is 4.0 m above the table. What is the intensity of the lamp?

From $E = \dfrac{P}{4\pi d^2}$

$P = 4\pi d^2 E = 4\pi (4.0 \text{ m})^2(2.0 \times 10^1 \text{ lx})$

$= 1280\pi$ lm

So $I = \dfrac{P}{4\pi d^2} = \dfrac{1280\pi \text{ lm}}{4\pi}$

$= 3.2 \times 10^2$ cd $= 320$ cd

11. A public school law requires a minimum illumination of 160 lx on the surface of each student's desk. An architect's specifications call for classroom lights to be located 2.0 m above the desks. What is the minimum luminous flux the lights must deliver?

$E = \dfrac{P}{4\pi d^2}$

$P = 4\pi E d^2 = 4\pi(160 \text{ lm/m}^2)(2.0 \text{ m})^2$

$= 8.0 \times 10^3$ lm

16.2 Light and Matter
pages 382–388

No practice problems.

Chapter Review Problems

pages 390–391

page 390

Section 16.1

Level 1

31. Convert 700 nm, the wavelength of red light, to meters.

$$\frac{700 \text{ nm}}{1} \left(\frac{1 \times 10^{-9} \text{ m}}{1 \text{ nm}}\right) = 7 \times 10^{-7} \text{ m}$$

32. Light takes 1.28 s to travel from the moon to Earth. What is the distance between them?

$d = vt = (3.00 \times 10^8 \text{ m/s})(1.28 \text{ s})$

$= 3.84 \times 10^8$ m

33. The sun is 1.5×10^8 km from Earth. How long does it take for the sun's light to reach us?

$d = vt$

So $t = \dfrac{d}{v} = \dfrac{(1.5 \times 10^8 \text{ km})(10^3 \text{ m/km})}{(3.00 \times 10^8 \text{ m/s})}$

$= 5.0 \times 10^2$ s

34. Radio stations are usually identified by their frequency. One radio station in the middle of the FM band has a frequency of 99.0 MHz. What is its wavelength?

$c = \lambda f$

so $\lambda = \dfrac{c}{f} = \dfrac{3.00 \times 10^8 \text{ m/s}}{99.0 \text{ MHz}}$

$= \dfrac{3.00 \times 10^8 \text{ m/s}}{99.0 \times 10^6 /\text{s}}$

$= 3.03$ m

Copyright © by Glencoe/McGraw-Hill

35. What is the frequency of a microwave that has a wavelength of 3.0 cm?

$$c = \lambda f$$

$$\text{so } f = \frac{c}{\lambda} = \frac{3.00 \times 10^8 \text{ m/s}}{0.030 \text{ m}}$$

$$= 1.0 \times 10^{10} \text{ Hz}$$

36. Find the illumination 4.0 m below a 405-lm lamp.

$$E = \frac{P}{4\pi d^2} = \frac{405 \text{ lm}}{4\pi (4.0 \text{ m})^2} = 2.0 \text{ lx}$$

37. A screen is placed between two lamps so that they illuminate the screen equally. The first lamp emits a luminous flux of 1445 lm and is 2.5 m from the screen. What is the distance of the second lamp from the screen if the luminous flux is 2375 lm?

Since the illumination is equal,

$$E_1 = E_2$$

$$\text{So } \frac{P_1}{d_1^2} = \frac{P_2}{d_2^2}$$

$$\text{or } d_2 = d_1 \sqrt{(P_2/P_1)}$$

$$= (2.5 \text{ m}) \sqrt{(2375/1445)} = 3.2 \text{ m}$$

page 391

38. A three-way bulb uses 50, 100, or 150 W of electrical power to deliver 665, 1620, or 2285 lm in its three settings. The bulb is placed 80 cm above a sheet of paper. If an illumination of at least 175 lx is needed on the paper, what is the minimum setting that should be used?

$$E = \frac{P}{4\pi d^2}$$

$$P = 4\pi E d^2 = 4\pi [175 \text{ lx} \times (0.80 \text{ m})^2]$$

$$= 1.4 \times 10^3 \text{ lm}$$

Thus, the 100 W (1620 lm) setting is needed.

39. Two lamps illuminate a screen equally. The first lamp has an intensity of 101 cd and is 5.0 m from the screen. The second lamp is 3.0 m from the screen. What is the intensity of the second lamp?

$$E = \frac{I}{d^2}$$

Since the illumination is equal,

$$E_1 = E_2$$

$$\text{So } \frac{I_1}{d_1^2} = \frac{I_2}{d_2^2}$$

$$\text{or } I_2 = \frac{(I_1)(d_2^2)}{(d_1^2)}$$

$$I_2 = \frac{(101 \text{ cd})(3.0 \text{ m})^2}{(5.0 \text{ m})^2} = 36 \text{ cd}$$

Level 2

40. Ole Roemer found that the maximum increased delay in the disappearance of Io from one orbit to the next is 14 s.

a. How far does light travel in 14 s?

$$d = vt = (3.00 \times 10^8 \text{ m/s})(14 \text{ s})$$

$$= 4.2 \times 10^9 \text{ m}$$

b. Each orbit of Io takes 42.5 h. Earth travels in the distance calculated in **a** in 42.5 h. Find the speed of Earth in km/s.

$$v = \frac{d}{t} = \frac{4.2 \times 10^9 \text{ m}}{42.5 \text{ h}}$$

$$\times \left(\frac{1 \text{ km}}{10^3 \text{ m}}\right)\left(\frac{1 \text{ h}}{3600 \text{ s}}\right)$$

$$= 27 \text{ km/s}$$

c. See if your answer for **b** is reasonable. Calculate Earth's speed in orbit using the orbital radius, 1.5×10^8 km, and the period, one year.

$$v = \frac{d}{t}$$

$$= \frac{2\pi(1.5 \times 10^8 \text{ km})}{365 \text{ d}}\left(\frac{1 \text{ d}}{24 \text{ h}}\right)\left(\frac{1 \text{ h}}{3600 \text{ s}}\right)$$

$$= 3.0 \times 10^1 \text{ km/s}$$

so fairly accurate

Physics: Principles and Problems

Copyright © by Glencoe/McGraw-Hill

41. Suppose you wanted to measure the speed of light by putting a mirror on a distant mountain, setting off a camera flash, and measuring the time it takes the flash to reflect off the mirror and return to you. Without instruments, a person can detect a time interval of about 0.1 s. How many kilometers away would the mirror have to be? Compare this distance with that of some known objects.

$$d = vt = (3.00 \times 10^8 \text{ m/s})(0.1 \text{ s})$$
$$= 3 \times 10^4 \text{ km}$$

The mirror would be half this distance, or 15 000 km away. Earth is 40 000 km in circumference, so this is 3/8 of the way around Earth!

42. A streetlight contains two identical bulbs 3.3 m above the ground. If the community wants to save electrical energy by removing one bulb, how far from the ground should the streetlight be positioned to have the same illumination on the ground under the lamp?

$$E = \frac{P}{4\pi d^2}$$

If P is reduced by a factor of 2, so must d^2.

Thus, d is reduced by a factor of $\sqrt{2}$, becoming

$$\frac{(3.3 \text{ m})}{\sqrt{2}} = 2.3 \text{ m}$$

43. A student wants to compare the luminous flux from a bulb with that of a 1750-lm lamp. The two bulbs illuminate a sheet of paper equally. The 1750-lm lamp is 1.25 m away; the unknown bulb is 1.08 m away. What is its luminous flux?

$$E = \frac{P}{4\pi d^2}$$

Since the illumination is equal,

$$E_1 = E_2$$

$$\text{So } \frac{P_1}{d_1^2} = \frac{P_2}{d_2^2}$$

$$\text{or } P_2 = \frac{(P_1)(d_2)^2}{(d_1)^2}$$
$$= \frac{(1750 \text{ lm})(1.08 \text{ m})^2}{(1.25 \text{ m})^2}$$
$$= 1.31 \times 10^3 \text{ lm}$$

44. A 10.0-cd point source lamp and a 60.0-cd point source lamp cast equal intensities on a wall. If the 10.0-cd lamp is 6.0 m from the wall, how far is the 60.0-cd lamp?

$$E = \frac{I}{d^2} \text{ and since the intensities on}$$
the wall are equal, the wall is equally illuminated and

$$E_1 = E_2$$

$$\text{So } \frac{I_1}{d_1^2} = \frac{I_2}{d_2^2}$$

$$\text{or } d_2 = d_1 \sqrt{\frac{I_2}{I_1}} = (6.0 \text{ m}) \sqrt{\frac{60 \text{ cd}}{10 \text{ cd}}}$$

$$= 15 \text{ m}$$

Critical Thinking Problems

45. Suppose you illuminated a thin soap film with red light from a laser. What would you see?

You would see bands of red light. The bands would form whenever the thickness of the film was an odd multiple of quarter wavelengths: $\frac{\lambda}{4}, \frac{3\lambda}{4}, \frac{5\lambda}{4}$, and so on.

46. If you were to drive at sunset in a city filled with buildings that have glass-covered walls, you might be temporarily blinded by the setting sun reflected off the buildings' walls. Would polarizing glasses solve this problem?

Yes. Light reflected off glass is partially polarized, so polarizing sunglasses will reduce much of the glare, if the sunglasses are aligned correctly.

Copyright © by Glencoe/McGraw-Hill

17 Reflection and Refraction

Practice Problems

17.1 How Light Behaves at a Boundary
pages 394–402

page 400

1. Light in air is incident upon a piece of crown glass at an angle of 45.0°. What is the angle of refraction?

   The light is incident from air. From
   $n_i \sin \theta_i = n_r \sin \theta_r$,

   $$\sin \theta_r = \frac{n_i \sin \theta_i}{n_r} = \frac{(1.00) \sin 45.0°}{1.52}$$

   $$= 0.465, \text{ or } \theta_r = 27.7°$$

2. A ray of light passes from air into water at an angle of 30.0°. Find the angle of refraction.

   $$n_i \sin \theta_i = n_r \sin \theta_r$$

   so $\sin \theta_r = \dfrac{n_i \sin \theta_i}{n_r} = \dfrac{(1.00) \sin 30.0°}{1.33}$

   $$= 0.376$$

   or $\theta_r = 22.1°$

3. A ray of light is incident upon a diamond at 45.0°.

   a. What is the angle of refraction?

   Assume the light is incident from air.

   $n_i \sin \theta_i = n_r \sin \theta_r$ **gives**

   $\sin \theta_r = \dfrac{n_i \sin \theta_i}{n_r} = \dfrac{(1.00) \sin 45.0°}{2.42}$

   $$= 0.292$$

   or $\theta_r = 17.0°$

   b. Compare your answer for **3a** to your answer for problem 1. Does glass or diamond bend light more?

   Diamond bends the light more.

4. A block of unknown material is submerged in water. Light in the water is incident on the block at an angle of 31°. The angle of refraction in the block is 27°. What is the index of refraction of the unknown material?

   $$n_1 \sin \theta_1 = n_2 \sin \theta_2$$

   so $n_2 = \dfrac{n_1 \sin \theta_1}{\sin \theta_2} = \dfrac{(1.33)(\sin 31°)}{\sin 27°}$

   $$= 1.51$$

page 402

TABLE 17-1	
Indices of Refraction	
Medium	**n**
vacuum	1.00
air	1.0003
water	1.33
ethanol	1.36
crown glass	1.52
quartz	1.54
flint glass	1.61
diamond	2.42

5. Use **Table 17–1** to find the speed of light in the following.

   a. ethanol

   $$v_{ethanol} = \frac{c}{n_{ethanol}} = \frac{3.00 \times 10^8 \text{ m/s}}{1.36}$$

   $$= 2.21 \times 10^8 \text{ m/s}$$

   b. quartz

   $$v_{quartz} = \frac{c}{n_{quartz}} = \frac{3.00 \times 10^8 \text{ m/s}}{1.54}$$

   $$= 1.95 \times 10^8 \text{ m/s}$$

   c. flint glass

   $$v_{flint\ glass} = \frac{c}{n_{flint\ glass}}$$

   $$= \frac{3.00 \times 10^8 \text{ m/s}}{1.61}$$

   $$= 1.86 \times 10^8 \text{ m/s}$$

Copyright © by Glencoe/McGraw-Hill

6. The speed of light in one type of plastic is 2.00×10^8 m/s. What is the index of refraction of the plastic?

$$n = c/v = \frac{3.00 \times 10^8 \text{ m/s}}{2.00 \times 10^8 \text{ m/s}} = 1.50$$

7. What is the speed of light for the unknown material in problem 4?

$n = 1.51$

So $v = \dfrac{c}{n} = \dfrac{3.00 \times 10^8 \text{ m/s}}{1.51}$

$\qquad = 1.99 \times 10^8$ m/s

8. Suppose two pulses of light were "racing" each other, one in air, the other in a vacuum. You could tell the winner if the time difference were 10 ns (10×10^{-9} s). How long would the race have to be to determine the winner?

$$t = \frac{d}{v} = \frac{dn}{c}$$

$$\Delta t = \frac{d\,(n_{\text{air}} - n_{\text{vacuum}})}{c}$$

$$\quad = \frac{d\,(1.0003 - 1.0000)}{3.00 \times 10^8 \text{ m/s}}$$

$$\quad = d\,(1.00 \times 10^{-12} \text{ s/m})$$

Thus, $d = \dfrac{\Delta t}{1.00 \times 10^{-12} \text{ s/m}}$

$$\quad = \frac{1. \times 10^{-8} \text{ s}}{1.00 \times 10^{-12} \text{ s/m}}$$

$$\quad = 10^4 \text{ m} = 10 \text{ km}$$

Chapter Review Problems

pages 411–413

page 411

Section 17.1

Level 1

31. A ray of light strikes a mirror at an angle of 53° to the normal.

   a. What is the angle of reflection?

     The angle of reflection is 53°.

   b. What is the angle between the incident ray and the reflected ray?

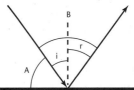

     The angle between the incident ray and the reflected ray, angle B, in the diagram is

     53° + 53° = 106°

32. A ray of light incident upon a mirror makes an angle of 36.0° with the mirror. What is the angle between the incident ray and the reflected way?

     Angle A in the diagram is 36.0° so the angle of incidence is
     90.0 − 36.0 = 54.0° and angle B is

     54.0° + 54.0° = 108.0°

33. A ray of light has an angle of incidence of 30.0° on a block of quartz and an angle of refraction of 20.0°. What is the index of refraction for this block of quartz?

$$n = \frac{\sin \theta_i}{\sin \theta_r} = \frac{\sin 30.0°}{\sin 20.0°} = 1.46$$

page 412

34. A ray of light travels from air into a liquid. The ray is incident upon the liquid at an angle of 30.0°. The angle of refraction is 22.0°.

   a. What is the index of refraction of the liquid?

$$n = \frac{\sin \theta_i}{\sin \theta_r} = \frac{\sin 30.0°}{\sin 22.0°} = 1.33$$

Copyright © by Glencoe/McGraw-Hill

34. (continued)

    b. Refer to **Table 17–1**. What might the liquid be?

TABLE 17-1	
Indices of Refraction	
Medium	***n***
vacuum	1.00
air	1.0003
water	1.33
ethanol	1.36
crown glass	1.52
quartz	1.54
flint glass	1.61
diamond	2.42

    water

35. A ray of light is incident at an angle of 60.0° upon the surface of a piece of crown glass. What is the angle of refraction?

$$n = \frac{\sin \theta_i}{\sin \theta_r}$$

So $\sin \theta_r = \dfrac{\sin \theta_i}{\sin n} = \dfrac{\sin 60.0°}{1.52} = 0.570$

$\theta_r = 34.7°$

36. A light ray strikes the surface of a pond at an angle of incidence of 36.0°. At what angle is the ray refracted?

$$n = \frac{\sin \theta_i}{\sin \theta_r}$$

So $\sin \theta_r = \dfrac{\sin \theta_i}{n} = \dfrac{\sin 36.0°}{1.33} = 0.442$

$\theta_r = 26.2°$

37. Light is incident at an angle of 60.0° on the surface of a diamond. Find the angle of refraction.

$$n = \frac{\sin \theta_i}{\sin \theta_r}$$

So $\sin \theta_r = \dfrac{\sin\theta_i}{n} = \dfrac{\sin 60.0°}{2.42} = 0.358$

$\theta_r = 21.0°$

38. A ray of light has an angle of incidence of 33.0° on the surface of crown glass. What is the angle of refraction into the air?

$$n_A \sin \theta_A = n_g \sin \theta_g$$

So $\sin \theta_A = \dfrac{n_g}{n_A} \sin \theta_g$

$\qquad = \dfrac{1.52 \sin 33.0°}{1.00 \sin 33.0°} = 0.828$

$\theta_A = 55.9°$

39. A ray of light passes from water into crown glass at an angle of 23.2°. Find the angle of refraction.

$$n_w \sin \theta_w = n_g \sin \theta_g$$

So $\sin \theta_g = \dfrac{n_w \sin \theta_w}{n_g}$

$\qquad = \dfrac{1.33 \sin 23.2°}{1.52} = 0.345.$

$\theta_r = 20.2°$

40. Light goes from flint glass into ethanol. The angle of refraction in the ethanol is 25.0°. What is the angle of incidence in the glass?

$$n_g \sin \theta_g = n_e \sin \theta_e$$

So $\sin \theta_g = \dfrac{n_e \sin \theta_e}{n_g}$

$\qquad = \dfrac{1.36 \sin 25.0°}{1.61} = 0.357$

$\theta_i = 20.9°$

41. A beam of light strikes the flat, glass side of a water-filled aquarium at an angle of 40.0° to the normal. For glass, $n = 1.50$. At what angle does the beam

    a. enter the glass?

$$n_A \sin \theta_A = n_g \sin \theta_g$$

So $\sin \theta_g = \dfrac{n_A \sin \theta_A}{n_g}$

$\qquad = \dfrac{1.00 \sin 40.0°}{1.50} = 0.429$

$\theta_g = 25.4°$

    b. enter the water?

$$n_g \sin \theta_g = n_w \sin \theta_w$$

So $\sin \theta_w = \dfrac{n_g \sin \theta_g}{n_w}$

$\qquad = \dfrac{1.50 \sin 25.4°}{1.33} = 0.484$

$\theta_w = 28.9°$

Copyright © by Glencoe/McGraw-Hill

42. What is the speed of light in diamond?

$$n_d = \frac{c}{v_d}$$

So $v_d = \dfrac{c}{n_d} = \dfrac{3.00 \times 10^8 \text{ m/s}}{2.42}$

$$= 1.24 \times 10^8 \text{ m/s}$$

43. The speed of light in chloroform is 1.99×10^8 m/s. What is its index of refraction?

$$n_c = \frac{c}{v_c} = \frac{3.00 \times 10^8 \text{ m/s}}{1.99 \times 10^8 \text{ m/s}} = 1.51$$

Level 2

44. A thick sheet of plastic, $n = 1.500$, is used as the side of an aquarium tank. Light reflected from a fish in the water has an angle of incidence of 35.0°. At what angle does the light enter the air?

$$n_w \sin \theta_w = n_p \sin \theta_p$$

So $\sin \theta_p = \dfrac{n_w \sin \theta_w}{n_p}$

$$= \frac{1.33 \sin 35.0°}{1.500}$$

$$= 0.509$$

The angle of refraction from the water into the plastic is equal to the angle of incidence from the plastic into the air.

$$n_A \sin \theta_A = n_p \sin \theta_p$$

So $\sin \theta_A = \dfrac{n_p \sin \theta_p}{n_A}$

$$= \frac{(1.500)(0.509)}{1.00} = 0.764$$

$$\theta_r = 49.8°$$

45. A light source, S, is located 2.0 m below the surface of a swimming pool and 1.5 m from one edge of the pool. The pool is filled to the top with water.

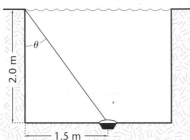

a. At what angle does the light reaching the edge of the pool leave the water?

$$\tan \theta_i = \frac{1.5 \text{ m}}{2.0 \text{ m}} = 0.75$$

$$\theta_i = 37°$$

Then find the angle in air

$$n_A \sin \theta_A = n_w \sin \theta_w$$

So $\sin \theta_A = \dfrac{n_w \sin \theta_w}{n_A}$

$$= \frac{1.33 \sin 37°}{1.00} = 0.80$$

$$\theta_r = 53°$$

b. Does this cause the light source viewed from this angle to appear deeper or shallower than it actually is?

$$\tan 53° = \frac{\text{side opposite}}{\text{side adjacent}}$$

$$\text{side adjacent} = \frac{\text{side opposite}}{\tan 53°}$$

$$= \frac{1.5 \text{ m}}{\tan 53°}$$

$$= 1.1 \text{ m, shallower}$$

46. A ray light is incident upon a 60°–60°–60° glass prism, $n = 1.5$, **Figure 17–17.**

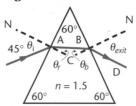

FIGURE 17-17

a. Using Snell's law, determine the angle θ_r to the nearest degree.

$$n_A \sin \theta_A = n_g \sin \theta_r$$

So $\sin \theta_r = \dfrac{n_A \sin \theta_A}{n_g}$

$$= \frac{1.00 \sin 45°}{1.5} = 0.47$$

$$\theta_r = 28°$$

b. Using elementary geometry, determine the values of angles A, B, and C.

$$A = 90° - 28° = 62°$$

$$B = 180° - (62° + 60°) = 58°$$

$$\theta_b = 90° - 58° = 320°$$

$$C = 180° - (28° + 32°) = 120°$$

Copyright © by Glencoe/McGraw-Hill

6. (continued)

   c. Determine the angle, θ_{exit}.

$$n_A \sin \theta_{exit} = n_g \sin C$$

$$\text{So } \sin \theta_{exit} = \frac{n_g \sin C}{n_A} = \frac{1.5 \sin 32°}{1.0}$$

$$= 0.795$$

$$\theta_{exit} = 53°$$

47. A sheet of plastic, $n = 1.5$, 25 mm thick is used in a bank teller's window. A ray of light strikes the sheet at an angle of 45°. The ray leaves the sheet at 45° but at a different location. Use a ray diagram to find the distance between the ray that leaves and the one that would have left if the plastic were not there.

8 mm

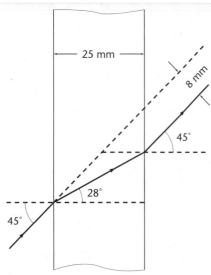

48. The speed of light in a clear plastic is 1.90×10^8 m/s. A ray of light strikes the plastic at an angle of 22.0°. At what angle is the ray refracted?

$$n_A \sin \theta_A = n_p \sin \theta_p \text{ and } n_p = \frac{c}{v_p}, \text{ so}$$

$$n_A \sin \theta_A = \frac{c}{v_p} \sin \theta_p$$

$$\text{so } \sin \theta_p = \frac{v_p n_A \sin \theta_A}{c}$$

$$= \frac{(1.90 \times 10^8 \text{ m/s})(1.00) \sin 22.0°}{3.00 \times 10^8 \text{ m/s}}$$

$$= 0.237$$

$$\theta_p = 13.7°$$

49. How many more minutes would it take light from the sun to reach Earth if the space between them were filled with water rather than a vacuum? The sun is 1.5×10^8 km from Earth.

Time through vacuum

$$t = \frac{d}{v} = \frac{(1.5 \times 10^8 \text{ km})(10^3 \text{ m/km})}{3.00 \times 10^8 \text{ m/s}}$$

$$= 5.0 \times 10^2 \text{ s}$$

Speed through water

$$v = \frac{c}{n} = \frac{3.00 \times 10^8 \text{ m/s}}{1.33}$$

$$= 2.26 \times 10^8 \text{ m/s}$$

Time through water

$$t = \frac{d}{v} = \frac{(1.5 \times 10^8 \text{ km})(10^3 \text{ m/km})}{2.26 \times 10^8 \text{ m/s}}$$

$$= 660 \text{ s}$$

$$\Delta t = 660 \text{ s} - 500 \text{ s} = 160 \text{ s}$$

$$= (160 \text{ s})(1 \text{ min}/60 \text{ s}) = 2.7 \text{ min}$$

Section 17.2

Level 1

50. Find the critical angle for diamond.

$$\sin \theta_c = \frac{1}{n} = \frac{1}{2.42} = 0.413$$

$$\theta_c = 24.4°$$

51. A block of glass has a critical angle of 45.0°. What is its index of refraction?

$$\sin \theta_c = \frac{1}{n}$$

$$\text{so } n = \frac{1}{\sin \theta_c} = \frac{1}{\sin 45.0°} = 1.41$$

52. A ray of light in a tank of water has an angle of incidence of 55.0°. What is the angle of refraction in air?

$$n_w \sin \theta_w = n_A \sin \theta_A$$

$$\text{so } \sin \theta_A = \frac{n_w \sin \theta_w}{n_A}$$

$$= \frac{1.33 \sin 55.0°}{1.00} = 1.1$$

There is no angle for which $\sin \theta_r = 1.1$, therefore total internal reflection occurs.

Copyright © by Glencoe/McGraw-Hill

53. The critical angle for a special glass in air is 41.0°. What is the critical angle if the glass is immersed in water?

$$n_g \sin \theta_g = n_w \sin \theta_w = n_w \sin 90°$$
$$= n_w(1.00)$$

and $\sin \theta_c = \dfrac{1}{n_g}$, so $n_g = \dfrac{1}{\sin \theta_c}$

Therefore $\left(\dfrac{1}{\sin \theta_c}\right) \sin \theta_g = n_w$, so

$$\sin \theta_g = n_w \sin \theta_c = 1.33 \sin 41.0°$$

$$= 0.873$$

$$\theta_g = 60.8°$$

54. A diamond's index of refraction for red light, 656 nm, is 2.410, while that for blue light, 434 nm, is 2.450. Suppose white light is incident on the diamond at 30.0°. Find the angles of refraction for these two colors.

$$n_A \sin \theta_A = n_d \sin \theta_d$$

So $\sin \theta_d = \dfrac{1.00 \sin \theta_A}{n_d}$

For red light

$$\sin \theta_r = \dfrac{\sin 30.0°}{2.410} = 0.207$$

$$\theta_r = 12.0°$$

For blue light

$$\sin \theta_r = \dfrac{\sin 30.0°}{2.450} = 0.204$$

$$\theta_r = 11.8°$$

55. The index of refraction of crown glass is 1.53 for violet light, and it is 1.51 for red light.

page 413

a. What is the speed of violet light in crown glass?

$$v = \dfrac{c}{n} = \dfrac{3.00 \times 10^8 \text{ m/s}}{1.53}$$

$$= 1.96 \times 10^8 \text{ m/s}$$

b. What is the speed of red light in crown glass?

$$v = \dfrac{c}{n} = \dfrac{3.00 \times 10^8 \text{ m/s}}{1.51}$$

$$= 1.99 \times 10^8 \text{ m/s}$$

56. Just before sunset, you see a rainbow in the water being sprayed from a lawn sprinkler. Carefully draw your location and the locations of the sun and the water coming from the sprinkler.

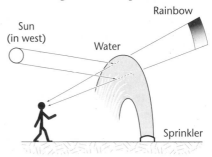

Level 2

57. A light ray enters a rectangle of crown glass, as illustrated in **Figure 17–18**. Use a ray diagram to trace the path of the ray until it leaves the glass.

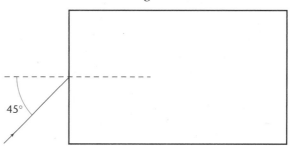

FIGURE 17-18

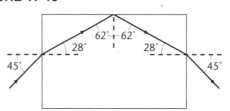

Copyright © by Glencoe/McGraw-Hill

57. (continued)

$n_A \sin \theta_A = n_g \sin \theta_g$

So $\sin \theta_g = \dfrac{n_A \sin \theta_A}{n_g}$

$= \dfrac{1.00 \sin 45°}{1.52} = 0.465$

$\theta_g = 28°$

Find the critical angle for crown glass:

$\sin \theta_c = \dfrac{1}{n} = \dfrac{1}{1.52} = 0.658$

$\theta_c = 41°$, so when the light ray in the glass strikes the surface at a 62° angle, total internal reflection occurs.

58. Crown glass's index of refraction for red light is 1.514, while that for blue light is 1.528. White light is incident on the glass at 30.0°.

a. Find the angles of refraction for these two colors.

$n_A \sin \theta_A = n_g \sin \theta_g$

So $\sin \theta_g = \dfrac{n_A \sin \theta_A}{n_g} = \dfrac{1.00 \sin \theta_A}{n_g}$

For red light

$\sin \theta_r = \dfrac{\sin 30.0°}{1.514} = 0.330$

$\theta_r = 19.3°$

For blue light

$\sin \theta_r = \dfrac{\sin 30.0°}{1.528} = 0.327$

$\theta_r = 19.1°$

b. Compare the difference between the angles of reflection and refraction for the crown glass and diamond. Angles for diamond were calculated in problem 54.

	Diamond		Crown Glass	
	Red	**Blue**	**Red**	**Blue**
Angle of Incidence	30.0°	30.0°	30.0°	30.0°
Angle of Refraction	12.0°	11.8°	19.3°	19.1°
Difference	18.0°	18.2°	10.7°	10.9°

c. Use the results to explain why diamonds are said to have "fire."

There is a much larger difference between the angles of incidence and refraction for diamond than for crown glass. This means that diamond has a much smaller critical angle. As a result, less light incident upon a diamond will pass completely through. Instead, more light will be reflected internally until it comes back out of the top of the diamond. Blue light has a smaller critical angle than red light. This means that more red light will emerge from a diamond than blue light. Hence, a diamond appears to have "fire."

Critical Thinking Problems

59. How much dispersion is there when light goes through a slab of glass? For dense flint glass, $n = 1.7708$ for blue light ($\lambda = 435.8$ nm) and $n = 1.7273$ for red light ($\lambda = 643.8$ nm). White light in air ($n = 1.0003$) is incident at exactly 45°. Find the angles of refraction for the two colors, then find the difference in those angles in degrees. You should use five significant digits in all calculations.

Use Snell's law, $n_i \sin \theta_i = n_r \sin \theta_r$.

Thus $\sin \theta_r = \left(\dfrac{n_i}{n_r}\right) \sin \theta_i$.

For red light

$\sin \theta_r = \left(\dfrac{1.0003}{1.7273}\right) \sin 45°$

$= 0.40949$

$\theta_r = 24.173°$

For blue light

$\sin \theta_r = \left(\dfrac{1.0003}{1.7708}\right) \sin 45°$

$= 0.39943$

$\theta_r = 23.543°$

Difference

$24.173° - 23.543° = 0.630°$

Copyright © by Glencoe/McGraw-Hill

60. Suppose the glass slab in problem 59 were rectangular. At what angles would the two colors leave the glass?

They would both leave the slab at 45°. They would be separate, but parallel rays.

61. Find the critical angle for ice ($n = 1.31$). In a very cold world, would fiber-optic cables made of ice be better or worse than those made of glass? Explain.

$$\sin \theta_c = \frac{1}{n} = \frac{1}{1.31} = 0.763$$

$$\theta_c = 49.8°$$

In comparison the critical angle for glass, $n = 1.54$, is 40.5°. The larger critical angle means that fewer rays would be totally internally reflected in an ice core than in a glass core. Thus they would not be able to transmit as much light.

Copyright © by Glencoe/McGraw-Hill

18 Mirrors and Lenses

Practice Problems

18.1 Mirrors
pages 416–428

page 425

Calculating a real image formed by a concave mirror.

1. Use a ray diagram drawn to scale to solve the Example Problem.

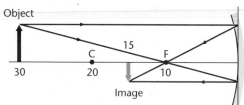

2. An object 3.0 mm high is 10.0 cm in front of a concave mirror having a 6.0-cm focal length. Find the image and its height by means of

   a. a ray diagram drawn to scale.

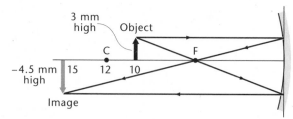

   b. the lens/mirror and magnification equations.

$$\frac{1}{f} = \frac{1}{d_i} + \frac{1}{d_o}$$

So $d_i = \dfrac{fd_o}{d_o - f}$

$$= \frac{(6.0 \text{ cm})(10.0 \text{ cm})}{10.0 \text{ cm} - 6.0 \text{ cm}}$$

$$= 15 \text{ cm}$$

$$m = \frac{-d_i}{d_o} = \frac{-15 \text{ cm}}{10.0 \text{ cm}} = -1.5$$

$$m = \frac{h_i}{h_o}$$

So $h_i = mh_o = (-1.5)(3.0 \text{ mm})$

$$= -4.5 \text{ mm}$$

3. An object is 4.0 cm in front of a concave mirror having a 12.0-cm radius. Locate the image using the lens/mirror equation and a scale ray diagram.

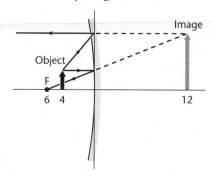

$$f = \frac{r}{2} = \frac{12.0 \text{ cm}}{2} = 6.00 \text{ cm}$$

$$\frac{1}{d_o} + \frac{1}{d_i} = \frac{1}{f}$$

So $d_i = \dfrac{fd_o}{d_o - f}$

$$= \frac{(6.00 \text{ cm})(4.0 \text{ cm})}{4.0 \text{ cm} - 6.00 \text{ cm}} = -12 \text{ cm}$$

4. A 4.0-cm high candle is placed 10.0 cm from a concave mirror having a focal length of 16.0 cm. Find the location and height of the image.

$$\frac{1}{d_o} + \frac{1}{d_i} = \frac{1}{f}$$

So $d_i = \dfrac{fd_o}{d_o - f}$

$$= \frac{(16.0 \text{ cm})(10.0 \text{ cm})}{10.0 \text{ cm} - 16.0 \text{ cm}}$$

$$= -26.7 \text{ cm}$$

Copyright © by Glencoe/McGraw-Hill

4. (continued)

$$m = \frac{h_i}{h_o} = \frac{-d_i}{d_o}$$

$$= \frac{-(-26.7 \text{ cm})}{(10.0 \text{ cm})}$$

$$= +2.67$$

So $h_i = mh_o = (2.67)(4.0 \text{ cm}) = 11 \text{ cm}$

5. What is the radius of curvature of a concave mirror that magnifies by a factor of +3.0 an object placed 25 cm from the mirror?

$$m = \frac{-d_i}{d_o} = 3.0$$

So $d_i = -md_o = -3.0(25 \text{ cm}) = -75 \text{ cm}$

$$\frac{1}{f} = \frac{1}{d_o} + \frac{1}{d_i}$$

So $f = \dfrac{d_o d_i}{d_o + d_i}$

$$= \frac{(25 \text{ cm})(-75 \text{ cm})}{25 \text{ cm} + (-75 \text{ cm})}$$

$$= 37.5 \text{ cm, and } r = 2f = 75 \text{ cm}$$

page 427

6. An object is 20.0 cm in front of a convex mirror with a −15.0-cm focal length. Find the location of the image using

a. a scale ray diagram.

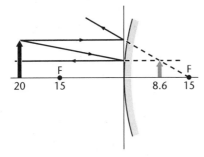

b. the lens/mirror equation.

$$\frac{1}{d_o} + \frac{1}{d_i} = \frac{1}{f}$$

So $d_i = \dfrac{fd_o}{d_o - f}$

$$= \frac{(-15.0 \text{ cm})(20.0 \text{ cm})}{20.0 \text{ cm} - (-15.0 \text{ cm})}$$

$$= -8.57 \text{ cm}$$

7. A convex mirror has a focal length of −12 cm. A lightbulb with a diameter of 6.0 cm is placed 60.0 cm in front of the mirror. Locate the image of the lightbulb. What is its diameter?

$$\frac{1}{d_o} + \frac{1}{d_i} = \frac{1}{f}$$

So $d_i = \dfrac{fd_o}{d_o - f}$

$$= \frac{(-12 \text{ cm})(60.0 \text{ cm})}{60.0 \text{ cm} - (-12 \text{ cm})}$$

$$= -1.0 \times 10^1 \text{ cm}$$

$$m = \frac{h_i}{h_o} = -\frac{d_i}{d_o}$$

$$= \frac{-(-1.0 \times 10^1 \text{ cm})}{60.0 \text{ cm}} = 0.17$$

So $h_i = mh_o = (0.17)(6.0 \text{ cm}) = 1.0 \text{ cm}$

8. A convex mirror is needed to produce an image three-fourths the size of the object and located 24 cm behind the mirror. What focal length should be specified?

$$\frac{1}{f} = \frac{1}{d_o} + \frac{1}{d_i}$$

So $f = \dfrac{d_o d_i}{d_o + d_i}$

and $m = -\dfrac{d_i}{d_o}$ so $d_o = -\dfrac{d_i}{m}$

Since $d_i = -24 \text{ cm}$ and $m = 0.75$,

$$d_o = \frac{-(-24 \text{ cm})}{0.75} = 32 \text{ cm}$$

and $f = \dfrac{(32 \text{ cm})(-24 \text{ cm})}{32 \text{ cm} + (-24 \text{ cm})} = -96 \text{ cm}$

18.2 Lenses
pages 429–438

page 432

9. Use a ray diagram to find the image position of an object 30 cm to the left of a convex lens with a 10-cm focal length. (Let 1 cm on the drawing represent 20 cm.)

Copyright © by Glencoe/McGraw-Hill

9. (continued)

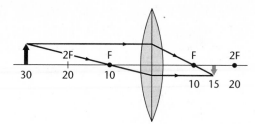

10. An object, 2.25 mm high, is 8.5 cm to the left of a convex lens of 5.5-cm focal length. Find the image location and height.

$$\frac{1}{d_o} + \frac{1}{d_i} = \frac{1}{f}$$

So $d_i = \dfrac{fd_o}{d_o - f}$

$$= \frac{(5.5 \text{ cm})(8.5 \text{ cm})}{8.5 \text{ cm} - 5.5 \text{ cm}}$$

$$= 16 \text{ cm}$$

$$h_i = \frac{-d_i h_o}{d_o}$$

$$= \frac{-(16 \text{ cm})(2.25 \text{ mm})}{8.5 \text{ cm}} = -4.2 \text{ mm}$$

11. An object is placed to the left of a 25-mm focal length convex lens so that its image is the same size as the object. What are the image and object locations?

$$\frac{1}{d_o} + \frac{1}{d_i} = \frac{1}{f}$$

with $d_o = d_i$ because

$$m = \frac{-d_i}{d_o} \quad \text{and} \quad m = -1$$

Therefore,

$$\frac{2}{d_i} = \frac{1}{f} \quad \text{and} \quad \frac{2}{d_o} = \frac{1}{f}$$

$$d_i = 2f = 2(25 \text{ mm}) = 50 \text{ mm}$$

$$= 5.0 \times 10^1 \text{ mm}$$

$$d_o = 2f = 2(25 \text{ mm}) = 5.0 \times 10^1 \text{ mm}$$

page 435

12. A newspaper is held 6.0 cm from a convex lens of 20.0-cm focal length. Find the image distance of the newsprint image.

$$\frac{1}{d_o} + \frac{1}{d_1} = \frac{1}{f}$$

So $d_i = \dfrac{fd_o}{d_o - f}$

$$= \frac{(20.0 \text{ cm})(6.0 \text{ cm})}{6.0 \text{ cm} - 20.0 \text{ cm}}$$

$$= -8.6 \text{ cm}$$

13. A magnifying glass has a focal length of 12.0 cm. A coin, 2.0 cm in diameter, is placed 3.4 cm from the lens. Locate the image of the coin. What is the diameter of the image?

$$\frac{1}{d_o} + \frac{1}{d_i} = \frac{1}{f}$$

So $d_i = \dfrac{fd_o}{d_o - f}$

$$= \frac{(12.0 \text{ cm})(3.4 \text{ cm})}{3.4 \text{ cm} - 12.0 \text{ cm}}$$

$$= -4.7 \text{ cm}$$

$$h_i = \frac{-h_o d_i}{d_o} = \frac{-(2.0 \text{ cm})(-4.7 \text{ cm})}{3.4 \text{ cm}}$$

$$= 2.8 \text{ cm}$$

14. A stamp collector wants to magnify an image by 4.0 when the stamp is 3.5 cm from the lens. What focal length is needed for the lens?

$$m = \frac{-d_i}{d_o}$$

So $d_i = -md_o = -(4.0)(3.5 \text{ cm})$

$$= -14 \text{ cm}$$

$$\frac{1}{f} = \frac{1}{d_o} + \frac{1}{d_i}$$

so $f = \dfrac{d_o d_i}{d_o + d_i} = \dfrac{(3.5 \text{ cm})(-14 \text{ cm})}{3.5 \text{ cm} + (-14 \text{ cm})}$

$$= 4.7 \text{ cm}$$

Physics: Principles and Problems

Copyright © by Glencoe/McGraw-Hill

Chapter Review Problems

pages 440–441

page 440

Section 18.1

Level 1

25. Penny wishes to take a picture of her image in a plane mirror. If the camera is 1.2 m in front of the mirror, at what distance should the camera lens be focused?

> **The image is 1.2 m behind the mirror, so the camera lens should be set to 2.4 m.**

26. A concave mirror has a focal length of 10.0 cm. What is its radius of curvature?

> $r = 2f = 2(10.0 \text{ cm}) = 20.0 \text{ cm}$

27. Light from a star is collected by a concave mirror. How far from the mirror is the image of the star if the radius of curvature is 150 cm?

> **Stars are far enough away that the light coming into the mirror can be considered to be parallel and parallel light will converge at the focal point. Since $r = 2f$,**
>
> $$f = \frac{r}{2} = \frac{150 \text{ cm}}{2} = 75 \text{ cm}$$

28. An object is 30.0 cm from a concave mirror of 15-cm focal length. The object is 1.8 cm high. Use the lens/mirror equation to find the image. How high is the image?

> $$\frac{1}{d_o} + \frac{1}{d_i} = \frac{1}{f}$$
>
> so $d_i = \dfrac{d_o f}{d_o - f}$
>
> $$= \frac{(30.0 \text{ cm})(15 \text{ cm})}{30.0 \text{ cm} - 15 \text{ cm}}$$
>
> $$= 3.0 \times 10^1 \text{ cm}$$

$$h_i = \frac{-h_o d_i}{d_o}$$

$$= \frac{-(3.0 \times 10^1 \text{ cm})(1.8 \text{ cm})}{30.0 \text{ cm}}$$

$$= -1.8 \text{ cm}$$

29. A jeweler inspects a watch with a diameter of 3.0 cm by placing it 8.0 cm in front of a concave mirror of 12.0-cm focal length.

a. Where will the image of the watch appear?

> $$\frac{1}{d_o} + \frac{1}{d_i} = \frac{1}{f}$$
>
> so $d_i = \dfrac{d_o f}{d_o - f}$
>
> $$= \frac{(8.0 \text{ cm})(12.0 \text{ cm})}{8.0 \text{ cm} - 12.0 \text{ cm}} = -24 \text{ cm}$$

b. What will be the diameter of the image?

> $$\frac{h_i}{h_o} = \frac{-d_i}{d_o}$$
>
> so $h_i = \dfrac{-d_i h_o}{d_o}$
>
> $$= \frac{-(-24 \text{ cm})(3.0 \text{ cm})}{8.0 \text{ cm}} = 9.0 \text{ cm}$$

30. A dentist uses a small mirror of radius 40 mm to locate a cavity in a patient's tooth. If the mirror is concave and is held 16 mm from the tooth, what is the magnification of the image?

> $$f = \frac{r}{2} = \frac{40 \text{ mm}}{2} = 20 \text{ mm}$$
>
> $$\frac{1}{d_o} + \frac{1}{d_i} = \frac{1}{f}$$
>
> $$d_i = \frac{d_o f}{d_o - f}$$
>
> $$= \frac{(16 \text{ mm})(20 \text{ mm})}{16 \text{ mm} - 20 \text{ mm}} = -80 \text{ mm}$$
>
> $$m = \frac{-d_i}{d_o} = \frac{-(-80 \text{ mm})}{16 \text{ mm}} = 5$$

Copyright © by Glencoe/McGraw-Hill

Level 2

31. Draw a ray diagram of a plane mirror to show that if you want to see yourself from your feet to the top of your head, the mirror must be at least half your height.

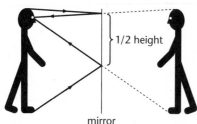

mirror

The ray from top of head hits mirror halfway between eyes and top of head. Ray from feet hits mirror halfway between eyes and feet. Distance between the point the two rays hit the mirror is half the total height.

32. The sun falls on a concave mirror and forms an image 3.0 cm from the mirror. If an object 24 mm high is placed 12.0 cm from the mirror, where will its image be formed?

a. Use a ray diagram.

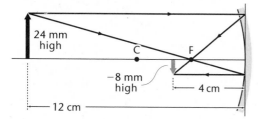

b. Use the lens/mirror equation.
$$\frac{1}{d_o} + \frac{1}{d_i} = \frac{1}{f}$$
$$d_i = \frac{fd_o}{d_o - f}$$
$$= \frac{(3.0 \text{ cm})(12.0 \text{ cm})}{12.0 \text{ cm} - 3.0 \text{ cm}}$$
$$= 4.0 \text{ cm}$$

c. How high is the image?
$$m = \frac{-d_i}{d_o} = \frac{-4.0 \text{ cm}}{12.0 \text{ cm}} = -0.33$$
$$h_i = mh_o = (-0.33)(24 \text{ mm}) = -8.0 \text{ mm}$$

33. A production line inspector wants a mirror that produces an upright image with magnification of 7.5 when it is located 14.0 mm from a machine part.

a. What kind of mirror would do this job?

An enlarged, upright image results only from a concave mirror, with object inside the focal length.

b. What is its radius of curvature?
$$m = -\frac{d_i}{d_o}$$
So $d_i = -md_o$
$$= -(7.5)(14.0 \text{ mm}) = -105 \text{ mm}$$
$$\frac{1}{d_o} + \frac{1}{d_i} = \frac{1}{f}$$
So $f = \dfrac{d_o d_i}{d_i + d_o}$
$$= \frac{(14.0 \text{ mm})(-105 \text{ mm})}{14.0 \text{ mm} + (-105 \text{ mm})}$$
$$= 16 \text{ mm}$$

radius of curvature = 2f
$$= (2)(16 \text{ mm}) = 32 \text{ mm}$$

page 441

34. Shiny lawn spheres placed on pedestals are convex mirrors. One such sphere has a diameter of 40.0 cm. A 12-cm robin sits in a tree 1.5 m from the sphere. Where is the image of the robin and how long is the image?
$$r = 20.0 \text{ cm}, f = -10.0 \text{ cm}$$
$$\frac{1}{d_o} + \frac{1}{d_i} = \frac{1}{f}$$
so $d_i = \dfrac{fd_o}{d_o - f}$
$$= \frac{(-10.0 \text{ cm})(150 \text{ cm})}{150 \text{ cm} - (-10.0 \text{ cm})}$$
$$= -9.4 \text{ cm}$$
$$m = \frac{h_i}{h_o} = \frac{-d_i}{d_o} = \frac{-(-9.4 \text{ cm})}{150 \text{ cm}} = +0.063$$
$$h_i = mh_o = (0.063)(12 \text{ cm}) = 0.75 \text{ cm}$$

Copyright © by Glencoe/McGraw-Hill

Section 18.2

Level 1

35. The focal length of a convex lens is 17 cm. A candle is placed 34 cm in front of the lens. Make a ray diagram to locate the image.

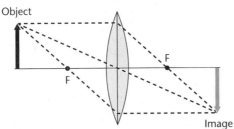

36. The convex lens of a copy machine has a focal length of 25.0 cm. A letter to be copied is placed 40.0 cm from the lens.

    a. How far from the lens is the copy paper?

    $$\frac{1}{d_o} + \frac{1}{d_i} = \frac{1}{f}$$

    so $d_i = \dfrac{d_o f}{d_o - f}$

    $$= \frac{(40.0 \text{ cm})(25.0 \text{ cm})}{40.0 \text{ cm} - 25.0 \text{ cm}} = 66.7 \text{ cm}$$

    b. The machine was adjusted to give an enlarged copy of the letter. How much larger will the copy be?

    $$\frac{h_i}{h_o} = \frac{d_i}{d_o}$$

    $$h_i = \frac{d_i h_o}{d_o} = \frac{(66.7 \text{ cm})(h_o)}{40.0 \text{ cm}} = 1.67 \, h_o$$

    The copy is enlarged and inverted.

37. Camera lenses are described in terms of their focal length. A 50.0-mm lens has a focal length of 50.0 mm.

    a. A camera with a 50.0-mm lens is focused on an object 3.0 m away. Locate the image.

    $$\frac{1}{d_o} + \frac{1}{d_i} = \frac{1}{f}$$

    So $d_i = \dfrac{d_o f}{d_o - f}$

    $$= \frac{(3.0 \times 10^3 \text{ mm})(50.0 \text{ mm})}{3.0 \times 10^3 \text{ mm} - 50.0 \text{ mm}}$$

    $$= 51 \text{ mm}$$

    b. A 1000.0-mm lens is focused on an object 125 m away. Locate the image.

    $$\frac{1}{d_o} + \frac{1}{d_i} = \frac{1}{f}$$

    So $d_i = \dfrac{d_o f}{d_o - f}$

    $$= \frac{(125 \text{ m})(1000.0 \text{ m})}{125 \text{ m} - 1.00 \text{ m}}$$

    $$= 1.01 \text{ m} = 1.01 \times 10^3 \text{ mm}$$

38. A convex lens is needed to produce an image that is 0.75 the size of the object and located 24 cm behind the lens. What focal length should be specified?

    The image is real and inverted, so $m = -0.75$.

    $$d_i = -md_o$$

    So $d_o = \dfrac{d_i}{0.75} = \dfrac{24 \text{ cm}}{0.75} = 32 \text{ cm}$

    $$\frac{1}{f} = \frac{1}{d_i} + \frac{1}{d_o}$$

    So $f = \dfrac{d_o d_i}{d_o + d_i} = \dfrac{(32 \text{ cm})(24 \text{ cm})}{32 \text{ cm} + 24 \text{ cm}}$

    $$= 14 \text{ cm}$$

39. In order to clearly read a book 25 cm away, a farsighted person needs an image distance of –45 cm from the eye. What focal length is needed for the lens?

    $$\frac{1}{f} = \frac{1}{d_o} + \frac{1}{d_i}$$

    so $f = \dfrac{d_o d_i}{d_o + d_i} = \dfrac{(25 \text{ cm})(-45 \text{ cm})}{25 \text{ cm} + (-45 \text{ cm})}$

    $$= 56 \text{ cm}$$

Level 2

40. A slide of an onion cell is placed 12 mm from the objective lens of a microscope. The focal length of the objective lens is 10.0 mm.

    a. How far from the lens is the image formed?

    $$\frac{1}{d_o} + \frac{1}{d_i} = \frac{1}{f}$$

    $$d_i = \frac{d_o f}{d_o - f}$$

40. (continued)

Copyright © by Glencoe/McGraw-Hill

$$= \frac{(12 \text{ mm})(10.9 \text{ mm})}{12 \text{ mm} - 10.0 \text{ mm}}$$

$$= 6.0 \times 10^1 \text{ mm}$$

b. What is the magnification of this image?

$$m_o = \frac{-d_i}{d_o} = \frac{-6.0 \times 10^1 \text{ mm}}{12.0 \text{ mm}} = -5.0$$

c. The real image formed is located 10.0 mm beneath the eyepiece lens. If the focal length of the eyepiece is 20.0 mm, where does the final image appear?

$$\frac{1}{d_o} + \frac{1}{d_i} = \frac{1}{f}$$

$$d_i = \frac{d_o f}{d_o - f}$$

$$= \frac{(10.0 \text{ mm})(20.0 \text{ mm})}{10.0 \text{ mm} - 20.0 \text{ mm}}$$

$$= -20.0 \text{ mm}$$

d. What is the final magnification of this compound system?

$$m_e = -\frac{d_i}{d_o} = \frac{-(-20.0 \text{ mm})}{10.0 \text{ mm}} = 2.00$$

$$m_{total} = (m_o)(m_e) = (-5.0)(2.00)$$

$$= -10.0$$

Critical Thinking Problems

41. Your lab partner used a convex lens to produce an image with $d_i = 25$ cm and $h_i = 4.0$ cm. You are examining a concave lens with a focal length of –15 cm. You place the concave lens between convex lens and the original image, 10 cm from the image. To your surprise, you see a real, enlarged image on the wall. You are told that the image from the convex lens is now the object for the concave lens, and because it is on the opposite side of the concave lens, it is a virtual object. Use these hints to find the location and size of the new image and to predict whether the concave lens changed the orientation of the original image.

The new $d_o = -10$ cm. Thus

$$d_i = \frac{f d_o}{d_o - f} = \frac{(-15 \text{ cm})(-10 \text{ cm})}{-10 \text{ cm} - (-15 \text{ cm})}$$

$$= +30 \text{ cm}$$

$$m = \frac{-d_i}{d_o} = \frac{-30 \text{ cm}}{-10 \text{ cm}} = +3$$

$$h_i = mh_o = (3)(4.0 \text{ cm}) = 10 \text{ cm}$$

The image orientation is not changed.

42. What is responsible for the rainbow-colored fringe commonly seen at the edges of a spot of white light from a slide or overhead projector?

The light that passes through a lens near the edges of the lens is slightly dispersed, because the edges of a lens resemble a prism and refract different wavelengths of light at slightly different angles. The result is that white light is dispersed into its spectrum. The effect is called chromatic aberration.

43. A lens is used to project the image of an object onto a screen. Suppose you cover the right half of the lens. What will happen to the image?

It will get dimmer, because fewer light rays will converge.

Copyright © by Glencoe/McGraw-Hill

19 Diffraction and Interference of Light

Practice Problems

19.1 When Light Waves Interferfere
pages 444–451

page 448

1. Violet light falls on two slits separated by 1.90×10^{-5} m. A first-order line appears 13.2 mm from the central bright line on a screen 0.600 m from the slits. What is the wavelength of the violet light?

$$\lambda = \frac{xd}{L}$$

$$= \frac{(13.2 \times 10^{-3} \text{ m})(1.90 \times 10^{-5} \text{ m})}{0.600 \text{ m}}$$

$$= 418 \text{ nm}$$

2. Yellow-orange light from a sodium lamp of wavelength 596 nm is aimed at two slits separated by 1.90×10^{-5} m. What is the distance from the central line to the first-order yellow line if the screen is 0.600 m from the slits?

$$x = \frac{\lambda L}{d}$$

$$= \frac{(5.96 \times 10^{-7} \text{ m})(0.600 \text{ m})}{1.90 \times 10^{-5} \text{ m}}$$

$$= 1.88 \times 10^{-2} \text{ m} = 18.8 \text{ mm}$$

3. In a double-slit experiment, physics students use a laser with a known wavelength of 632.8 nm. The slit separation is unknown. A student places the screen 1.000 m from the slits and finds the first-order line 65.5 mm from the central line. What is the slit separation?

$$d = \frac{\lambda L}{x}$$

$$= \frac{(6.328 \times 10^{-7} \text{ m})(1.000 \text{ m})}{65.5 \times 10^{-3} \text{ m}}$$

$$= 9.66 \times 10^{-6} \text{ m} = 9.66 \ \mu\text{m}$$

page 451

4. A double-slit apparatus, $d = 15 \ \mu$m, is used to determine the wavelength of an unknown green light. The first-order line is 55.8 mm from the central line on a screen that is 1.6 m from the slits. What is the wavelength of the light?

$$\lambda = \frac{xd}{L}$$

$$= \frac{(55.8 \times 10^{-3} \text{ m})(15 \times 10^{-6} \text{ m})}{1.6 \text{ m}}$$

$$= 520 \text{ nm}$$

5. Monochromatic green light of wavelength 546 nm falls on a single slit with width 0.095 mm. The slit is located 75 cm from a screen. How far from the center of the central band is the first dark band?

$$x = \frac{\lambda L}{w}$$

$$= \frac{(5.46 \times 10^{-7} \text{ m})(0.75 \text{ m})}{9.5 \times 10^{-5} \text{ m}} = 4.3 \text{ mm}$$

Copyright © by Glencoe/McGraw-Hill

6. Light from a He-Ne laser ($\lambda = 632.8$ nm) falls on a slit of unknown width. A pattern is formed on a screen 1.15 m away on which the first dark band is 7.5 mm from the center of the central bright band. How wide is the slit?

$$w = \frac{\lambda L}{x}$$

$$= \frac{(6.328 \times 10^{-7} \text{ m})(1.15 \text{ m})}{7.5 \times 10^{-3} \text{ m}}$$

$$= 97 \; \mu m$$

7. Yellow light falls on a single slit 0.0295 mm wide. On a screen 60.0 cm away, there is a dark band 12.0 mm from the center of the bright central band. What is the wavelength of the light?

$$\lambda = \frac{wx}{L}$$

$$= \frac{(2.95 \times 10^{-5} \text{ m})(1.20 \times 10^{-2} \text{ m})}{6.00 \times 10^{-1} \text{ m}}$$

$$= 5.90 \times 10^2 \text{ nm}$$

8. White light falls on a single slit 0.050 mm wide. A screen is placed 1.00 m away. A student first puts a blue-violet filter ($\lambda = 441$ nm) over the slit, then a red filter ($\lambda = 622$ nm). The student measures the width of the central peak, that is, the distance between the two dark bands.

a. Which filter produces the wider band?

Red, because central peak width is proportional to wavelength.

b. Calculate the width of the central bright band for each of the two filters.

Width $= 2x = \dfrac{2\lambda L}{w}$

For blue,

$$2x = \frac{2(4.41 \times 10^{-7} \text{ m})(1.00 \text{ m})}{5.0 \times 10^{-5} \text{ m}}$$

$$= 18 \text{ mm}$$

For red,

$$2x = \frac{2(6.22 \times 10^{-7} \text{ m})(1.00 \text{ m})}{5.0 \times 10^{-5} \text{ m}}$$

$$= 25 \text{ mm}$$

Chapter Review Problems

pages 458–459

page 458

Section 19.1

Level 1

16. Light falls on a pair of slits 19.0 μm apart and 80.0 cm from the screen. The first-order bright line is 1.90 cm from the central bright line. What is the wavelength of the light?

$$\lambda = \frac{xd}{L} = \frac{(1.90 \text{ cm})(1.90 \times 10^{-3} \text{ cm})}{80.0 \text{ cm}}$$

$$= 4.51 \times 10^{-5} \text{ cm} = 451 \text{ nm}$$

17. Light of wavelength 542 nm falls on a double slit. First-order bright bands appear 4.00 cm from the central bright line. The screen is 1.20 m from the slits. How far apart are the slits?

$$\lambda = \frac{xd}{L}$$

So $d = \dfrac{\lambda L}{x} = \dfrac{(5.42 \times 10^{-7} \text{ m})(1.20 \text{ m})}{4.00 \times 10^{-2} \text{ m}}$

$$= 16.3 \; \mu m$$

18. Monochromatic light passes through a single slit with a width of 0.010 cm and falls on a screen 100 cm away. If the distance from the center of the pattern to the first band is 0.60 cm, what is the wavelength of the light?

$$x = \frac{\lambda L}{w}$$

So $\lambda = \dfrac{xw}{L} = \dfrac{(0.60 \text{ cm})(0.010 \text{ cm})}{100 \text{ cm}}$

$$= 600 \text{ nm}$$

Copyright © by Glencoe/McGraw-Hill

19. Light with a wavelength of 4.5×10^{-5} cm passes through a single slit and falls on a screen 100 cm away. If the slit is 0.015 cm wide, what is the distance from the center of the pattern to the first dark band?

$$x = \frac{\lambda L}{w} = \frac{(4.5 \times 10^{-5} \text{ cm})(100 \text{ cm})}{0.015 \text{ cm}}$$

$$= 0.3 \text{ cm}$$

20. Monochromatic light with a wavelength of 400 nm passes through a single slit and falls on a screen 90 cm away. If the distance of the first-order dark band is 0.30 cm from the center of the pattern, what is the width of the slit?

$$x = \frac{\lambda L}{w}$$

So $w = \dfrac{\lambda L}{x} = \dfrac{(4.00 \times 10^{-5} \text{ cm})(90 \text{ cm})}{0.30 \text{ cm}}$

$$= 1 \times 10^{-2} \text{ cm}$$

Level 2

21. Using a compass and ruler, construct a scale diagram of the interference pattern that results when waves 1 cm in length fall on two slits 2 cm apart. The slits may be represented by two dots spaced 2 cm apart and kept to one side of the paper. Draw a line through all points of reinforcement. Draw dotted lines through all nodal lines.

See Figure 19-21 at top right.

Section 19.2

Level 1

22. A good diffraction grating has 2.5×10^3 lines per cm. What is the distance between two lines in the grating?

$$d = \frac{1}{2.5 \times 10^3 \text{ lines/cm}}$$

$$= 4.0 \times 10^{-4} \text{ cm}$$

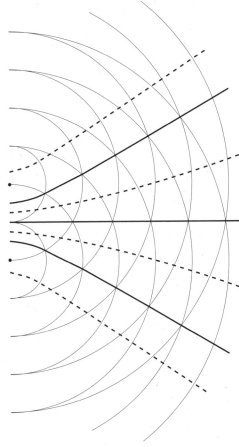

FIGURE 19-21

23. A spectrometer uses a grating with 12 000 lines/cm. Find the angles at which red light, 632 nm, and blue light, 421 nm, have first-order bright bands.

$$d = \frac{1}{12\ 000 \text{ lines/cm}} = 8.33 \times 10^{-5} \text{ cm}$$

$$\lambda = d \sin \theta$$

So $\sin \theta = \dfrac{\lambda}{d}$

For red light,

$$\sin \theta = \frac{6.32 \times 10^{-5} \text{ cm}}{8.33 \times 10^{-5} \text{ cm}} = 0.758$$

so $\theta = 49°$

For blue light,

$$\sin \theta = \frac{4.21 \times 10^{-5} \text{ cm}}{8.33 \times 10^{-5} \text{ cm}} = 0.505$$

so $\theta = 30°$

Copyright © by Glencoe/McGraw-Hill

24. A camera with a 50-mm lens set at f/8 aperture has an opening 6.25 mm in diameter.

a. Suppose this lens acts like a slit 6.25 mm wide. For light with $\lambda = 550$ nm, what is the resolution of the lens—the distance from the middle of the central bright band to the first-order dark band? The film is 50.0 mm from the lens.

$$x = \frac{\lambda L}{w} = \frac{(5.5 \times 10^{-4} \text{ mm})(50.0 \text{ mm})}{6.25 \text{ mm}}$$

$$= 4.4 \times 10^{-3} \text{ mm}$$

b. The owner of a camera needs to decide which film to buy for it. The expensive one, called fine-grained film, has 200 grains/mm. The less costly, coarse-grained film has only 50 grains/mm. If the owner wants a grain to be no smaller than the width of the central bright band calculated above, which film should be purchased?

Central bright band width

$$w_c = 2x = 8.8 \times 10^{-3} \text{ mm}$$

the 200 grains/mm film has $\dfrac{1}{200 \text{ mm}}$ between grains

$= 5 \times 10^{-3}$ mm (so this film will work)

the 50 grains/mm film has $\dfrac{1}{50 \text{ mm}}$ between grains

$= 20 \times 10^{-3}$ mm (so this film won't work)

25. Suppose the Hubble Space Telescope, 2.4 m in diameter, is in orbit 100 km above Earth and is turned to look at Earth, as in **Figure 19–11.** If you ignore the effect of the atmosphere, what is the resolution of this telescope? Use $\lambda = 500$ nm.

$$x = \frac{\lambda L}{w} = \frac{(5 \times 10^{-7} \text{ m})(1 \times 10^5 \text{ m})}{2.4 \text{ m}}$$

$$= 2 \times 10^{-2} \text{ m}$$

$$= 2 \text{ cm}$$

26. After passing through a grating with a spacing of 4.00×10^{-4} cm, a red line appears 16.5 cm from the central line on a screen. The screen is 1.00 m from the grating. What is the wavelength of the red light?

$$\lambda = \frac{xd}{L} = \frac{(16.5 \text{ cm})(4.00 \times 10^{-4} \text{ cm})}{1.00 \times 10^2 \text{ cm}}$$

$$= 6.60 \times 10^{-5} \text{ cm} = 6.60 \times 10^2 \text{ nm}$$

Level 2

27. Marie uses an old 33-1/3 rpm record as a diffraction grating. She shines a laser, $\lambda = 632.8$ nm, on the record. On a screen 4.0 m from the record, a series of red dots 21 mm apart are visible.

a. How many ridges are there in a centimeter along the radius of the record?

$$\lambda = \frac{xd}{L}$$

so $d = \dfrac{\lambda L}{x} = \dfrac{(6.328 \times 10^{-7} \text{ m})(4.0 \text{ m})}{0.021 \text{ m}}$

$$= 1.2 \times 10^{-4} \text{ m} = 1.2 \times 10^{-2} \text{ cm}$$

$$\frac{1}{d} = \frac{1}{1.2 \times 10^{-2} \text{ cm}} = 83 \text{ ridges/cm}$$

b. Marie checks her results by noting that the ridges came from a song that lasted 4.01 minutes and took up 16 mm on the record. How many ridges should there be in a centimeter?

Number of ridges is

$(4.01 \text{ min})(33.3 \text{ rev/min}) = 134 \text{ ridges}$

$\dfrac{(134 \text{ ridges})}{1.6 \text{ cm}} = 84 \text{ ridges/cm}$

Copyright © by Glencoe/McGraw-Hill

Critical Thinking Problems

28. Yellow light falls on a diffraction grating. On a screen behind the grating you see three spots, one at zero degrees, where there is no diffraction, and one each at +30° and –30°. You now add a blue light of equal intensity that is in the same direction as the yellow light. What pattern of spots will you now see on the screen?

> **A green spot at 0°, yellow spots at +30° and –30°, and two blue spots slightly closer in.**

29. Blue light of wavelength λ passes through a single slit of width w. A diffraction pattern appears on a screen. If you now replace the blue light with a green light of wavelength 1.5λ, to what width should you change the slit in order to get the original pattern back?

> **The angle of diffraction depends on the ratio of slit width to wavelength. Thus you would increase the width to $1.5w$.**

30. At night, the pupil of a human eye can be considered to be a slit with a diameter of 8.0 mm. The diameter would be smaller in daylight. An automobile's headlights are separated by 1.8 m. How far away can the human eye distinguish the two headlights at night? **Hint:** Assume a wavelength of 500 nm and recall that Rayleigh's criterion stated that the peak of one image should be at the first minimum of the other.

> **The first minimum is at $x = \dfrac{\lambda L}{w}$**
>
> **Thus $L = \dfrac{xw}{\lambda}$, $x = 1.80$ m,**
>
> **$w = 8.0$ mm, and $\lambda = 500$ nm**
>
> **$L = \dfrac{(1.80 \text{ m})(8.0 \times 10^{-3} \text{ m})}{5.00 \times 10^{-7} \text{ m}}$**
>
> **$= 2.9 \times 10^4$ m $= 29$ km**

Copyright © by Glencoe/McGraw-Hill

20 Static Electricity

Practice Problems

20.2 Electrical Force
pages 468–476

page 476

1. A negative charge of -2.0×10^{-4} C and a positive charge of 8.0×10^{-4} C are separated by 0.30 m. What is the force between the two charges?

$$F = \frac{Kq_A q_B}{d_{AB}^2} = \frac{(9.0 \times 10^9 \text{ N} \cdot \text{m}^2/\text{C}^2)(2.0 \times 10^{-4} \text{ C})(8.0 \times 10^{-4} \text{ C})}{(0.30 \text{ m})^2} = 1.6 \times 10^4 \text{ N}$$

2. A negative charge of -6.0×10^{-6} C exerts an attractive force of 65 N on a second charge 0.050 m away. What is the magnitude of the second charge?

$$F = \frac{Kq_A q_B}{d_{AB}^2}$$

$$q_B = \frac{Fd_{AB}^2}{Kq_A} = \frac{(65 \text{ N})(0.050 \text{ m})^2}{(9.0 \times 10^9 \text{ N} \cdot \text{m}^2/\text{C}^2)(6.0 \times 10^{-6} \text{ C})} = 3.0 \times 10^{-6} \text{ C}$$

3. Two positive charges of 6.0 µC are separated by 0.50 m. What force exists between the charges?

$$F = \frac{Kq_A q_B}{d_{AB}^2} = \frac{(9.0 \times 10^9 \text{ N} \cdot \text{m}^2/\text{C}^2)(6.0 \times 10^{-6} \text{ C})(6.0 \times 10^{-6} \text{ C})}{(0.50 \text{ m})^2} = 1.3 \text{ N}$$

4. An object with charge $+7.5 \times 10^{-7}$ C is placed at the origin. The position of a second object, charge $+1.5 \times 10^{-7}$ C, is varied from 1.0 cm to 5.0 cm. Draw a graph of the force on the object at the origin.

At $d = 1.0$ cm,

$$F = \frac{Kq_A q_B}{d_{AB}^2} = \frac{(9.0 \times 10^9 \text{ N} \cdot \text{m}^2/\text{C}^2)(7.5 \times 10^{-7} \text{ C})(1.5 \times 10^{-7} \text{ C})}{(1.0 \times 10^{-2} \text{ m})^2} = 1.0 \times 10^1 \text{ N}$$

Because force varies as distance squared, the force at $d = 5.0$ cm is $\frac{1}{25}$ the force at

$d = 1.0$ cm, or 4.1×10^{-2} N. The force varies as $\frac{1}{d^2}$, so the graph looks like

Copyright © by Glencoe/McGraw-Hill

Physics: Principles and Problems

4. (continued)

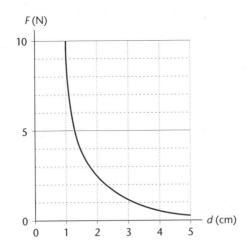

5. The charge on B in the second Example Problem is replaced by +3.00 μC. Use graphical methods to find the net force on A.

Magnitudes of all forces remain the same. The direction changes to 42° above the $-x$ axis, or 138°.

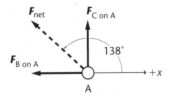

Chapter Review Problems

pages 478–479

page 478

Section 20.2

Level 1

20. Two charges, q_A and q_B, are separated by a distance, d, and exert a force, F, on each other. Analyze Coulomb's law and identify what new force will exist if

    a. q_A is doubled.

        $2q_A$, then new force $= 2F$

    b. q_A and q_B are cut in half.

        $\frac{1}{2} q_A$ and $\frac{1}{2} q_B$, then new force $= \left(\frac{1}{2}\right)\left(\frac{1}{2}\right) F = \frac{1}{4} F$

    c. d is tripled.

        $3d$, then new force $= \dfrac{F}{(3)^2} = \dfrac{1}{9} F$

Copyright © by Glencoe/McGraw-Hill

20. (continued)

d. *d* is cut in half.

$\frac{1}{2}$ *d*, then new force $= \dfrac{F}{\left(\frac{1}{2}\right)^2} = \left(\dfrac{2}{1}\right)^2 F = 4F$

e. q_A is tripled and d is doubled.

$3q_A$ and 2*d*, then new force $= \dfrac{(3)F}{(2)^2} = \dfrac{3}{4} F$

21. How many excess electrons are on a ball with a charge of -4.00×10^{-17} C?

$\dfrac{(-4.00 \times 10^{-17} \text{ C})}{1} \left(\dfrac{1 \text{ electron}}{-1.60 \times 10^{-19} \text{ C}} \right) = 2.50 \times 10^2$ electrons

22. How many coulombs of charge are on the electrons in a nickel? Use the following method to find the answer.

a. Find the number of atoms in a nickel. A nickel has a mass of about 5 g. Each mole $(6.02 \times 10^{23}$ atoms) has a mass of about 58 g.

A coin is $\dfrac{5 \text{ g}}{58 \text{ g}} = 0.09$ mole. Thus it has $(0.09)(6.02 \times 10^{23}) = 5 \times 10^{22}$ atoms

b. Find the number of electrons in the coin. A nickel is 75% Cu and 25% Ni, so each atom on average has 28.75 electrons.

$(5 \times 10^{22}$ atoms$)(28.75$ electrons/atom$) = 1 \times 10^{24}$ electrons

c. Find how many coulombs of charge are on the electrons.

$(1.6 \times 10^{-19}$ coulombs/electron$)(1 \times 10^{24}$ electrons$) = 2 \times 10^5$ coulombs

23. A strong lightning bolt transfers about 25 C to Earth.

a. How many electrons are transferred?

$\dfrac{-25 \text{ C}}{1} \left(\dfrac{1 \text{ electron}}{-1.60 \times 10^{-19} \text{ C}} \right) = 1.6 \times 10^{20}$ electrons

b. If each water molecule donates one electron, what mass of water lost an electron to the lightning? One mole of water has a mass of 18 g.

$\dfrac{1.6 \times 10^{20} \text{ electrons}}{1} \left(\dfrac{1 \text{ molecule}}{1 \text{ electron}} \right) \left(\dfrac{1 \text{ mole}}{6.02 \times 10^{23} \text{ molecule}} \right) \left(\dfrac{18 \text{ g}}{\text{mole}} \right) = 4.8 \times 10^{-3}$ g

24. Two electrons in an atom are separated by 1.5×10^{-10} m, the typical size of an atom. What is the electrical force between them?

$F = \dfrac{Kq_A q_B}{d^2} = \dfrac{(9.0 \times 10^9 \text{ N} \cdot \text{m}^2/\text{C}^2)(1.6 \times 10^{-19} \text{ C})(1.6 \times 10^{-19} \text{ C})}{(1.5 \times 10^{-10} \text{ m})^2} = 1.0 \times 10^{-8}$ N, away

from each other

25. A positive and a negative charge, each of magnitude 1.5×10^{-5} C, are separated by a distance of 15 cm. Find the force on each of the particles.

$F = \dfrac{Kq_A q_B}{d^2} = \dfrac{(9.0 \times 10^9 \text{ N} \cdot \text{m}^2/\text{C}^2)(1.5 \times 10^{-5} \text{ C})(1.5 \times 10^{-5} \text{ C})}{(1.5 \times 10^{-1} \text{ m})^2} = 9.0 \times 10^1$ N, toward

the other charge

Copyright © by Glencoe/McGraw-Hill

26. Two negatively charged bodies each with charge -5.0×10^{-5} C are 0.20 m from each other. What force acts on each particle?

$$F = \frac{Kq_A q_B}{d^2} = \frac{(9.0 \times 10^9 \text{ N} \cdot \text{m}^2/\text{C}^2)(5.0 \times 10^{-5} \text{ C})^2}{(0.20 \text{ m})^2} = 5.6 \times 10^2 \text{ N}$$

27. How far apart are two electrons if they exert a force of repulsion of 1.0 N on each other?

$$F = \frac{Kq_A q_B}{d^2}$$

$$\text{So } d = \sqrt{\frac{Kq_A q_B}{F}} = \sqrt{\frac{(9.0 \times 10^9 \text{ N} \cdot \text{m}^2/\text{C}^2)(1.60 \times 10^{-19} \text{ C})^2}{1.0 \text{ N}}} = 1.5 \times 10^{-14} \text{ m}$$

28. A force of -4.4×10^3 N exists between a positive charge of 8.0×10^{-4} C and a negative charge of -3.0×10^{-4} C. What distance separates the charges?

$$F = \frac{Kq_A q_B}{d^2}$$

$$\text{So } d = \sqrt{\frac{Kq_A q_B}{F}} = \sqrt{\frac{(9.0 \times 10^9 \text{ N} \cdot \text{m}^2/\text{C}^2)(8.0 \times 10^{-4} \text{ C})(3.0 \times 10^{-4} \text{ C})}{4.4 \times 10^3 \text{ N}}} = 0.70 \text{ m}$$

29. Two identical positive charges exert a repulsive force of 6.4×10^{-9} N when separated by a distance of 3.8×10^{-10} m. Calculate the charge of each.

$$F = \frac{Kq_A q_B}{d^2} = \frac{Kq^2}{d^2}$$

$$\text{So } q = \sqrt{\frac{Fd^2}{K}} = \sqrt{\frac{(6.4 \times 10^{-9} \text{ N})(3.8 \times 10^{-10} \text{ m})^2}{9.0 \times 10^9 \text{ N} \cdot \text{m}^2/\text{C}^2}} = 3.2 \times 10^{-19} \text{ C}$$

Level 2

30. A positive charge of 3.0 μC is pulled on by two negative charges. One, -2.0 μC, is 0.050 m to the north and the other, -4.0 μC, is 0.030 m to the south. What total force is exerted on the positive charge?

$$F_1 = \frac{(9.0 \times 10^9 \text{ N} \cdot \text{m}^2/\text{C}^2)(3.0 \times 10^{-6} \text{ C})(2.0 \times 10^{-6} \text{ C})}{(0.050 \text{ m})^2} = 2.2 \times 10^1 \text{ N, north}$$

$$F_2 = \frac{(9.0 \times 10^9 \text{ N} \cdot \text{m}^2/\text{C}^2)(3.0 \times 10^{-6} \text{ C})(4.0 \times 10^{-6} \text{ C})}{(0.030 \text{ m})^2} = 1.2 \times 10^2 \text{ N, south}$$

$$F = F_2 + F_1 = (1.2 \times 10^2 \text{ N}) - (2.2 \times 10^1 \text{ N}) = 98 \text{ N, south}$$

31. Three particles are placed in a line. The left particle has a charge of -67 μC, the middle, $+45$ μC, and the right, -83 μC. The middle particle is 72 cm from each of the others, as shown in **Figure 20–13**.

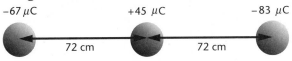

-67μC $+45 \mu$C -83μC

72 cm   72 cm

FIGURE 20-13

Copyright © by Glencoe/McGraw-Hill

31. (continued)

    a. Find the net force on the middle particle.

$$F_{net} = F_l + (-F_r) = \frac{Kq_mq_l}{d^2} - \frac{Kq_mq_r}{d^2}$$

$$= \frac{(9.0 \times 10^9 \text{ N} \cdot \text{m}^2/\text{C}^2)(45 \times 10^{-6} \text{ C})(67 \times 10^{-6} \text{ C})}{(0.72 \text{ m})^2}$$

$$- \frac{(9.0 \times 10^9 \text{ N} \cdot \text{m}^2/\text{C}^2)(45 \times 10^{-6} \text{ C})(83 \times 10^{-6} \text{ C})}{(0.72 \text{ m})^2}$$

    = **13 N, right**

    b. Find the net force on the right particle.

$$F_{net} = (-F_l) + (F_m) = -\frac{Kq_lq_r}{(2d)^2} + \frac{Kq_mq_r}{d^2}$$

$$= -\frac{(9.0 \times 10^9 \text{ N} \cdot \text{m}^2/\text{C}^2)(67 \times 10^{-6} \text{ C})(83 \times 10^{-6} \text{ C})}{[2(0.72 \text{ m})]^2}$$

$$+ \frac{(9.0 \times 10^9 \text{ N} \cdot \text{m}^2/\text{C}^2)(45 \times 10^{-6} \text{ C})(83 \times 10^{-6} \text{ C})}{(0.72 \text{ m})^2}$$

    = **41 N, left**

Critical Thinking Problems

32. Three charged spheres are located at the positions shown in **Figure 20–14.** Find the total force on sphere B.

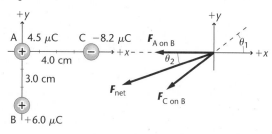

FIGURE 20-14

$$F_1 = F_{A \text{ on } B} = \frac{Kq_Aq_B}{d^2} = \frac{(9.0 \times 10^9 \text{ N} \cdot \text{m}^2/\text{C}^2)(4.5 \times 10^{-6} \text{ C})(-8.2 \times 10^{-6} \text{ C})}{(0.040 \text{ m})^2}$$

    = **−208 N = 208 N, to left**

The distance between the other two charges is

$$\sqrt{(0.040 \text{ m})^2 + (0.030 \text{ m})^2} = 0.050 \text{ m}$$

and $\tan \theta_1 = \dfrac{0.030 \text{ m}}{0.040 \text{ m}}$

So $\theta_1 = 37°$ **with the x-axis**

$$F_2 = F_{C \text{ on } B} = \frac{Kq_Bq_C}{d^2} = \frac{(9.0 \times 10^9 \text{ N} \cdot \text{m}^2/\text{C}^2)(-8.2 \times 10^{-6} \text{ C})(6.0 \times 10^{-6} \text{ C})}{(0.050 \text{ m})^2}$$

    = **−177 N = 177 N at 37° with the x-axis toward C**

Copyright © by Glencoe/McGraw-Hill

32. (continued)

The components of F_2 are:

$F_{2x} = F_2 \cos \theta = 177 \cos 37° = 142$ N, to left

$F_{2y} = F_2 \sin \theta = 177 \sin 37° = 106$ N, down

The components of the net (resultant) force are

$F_{net, x} = -208$ N $- 142$ N $= -350$ N $= 360$ N, to left

$F_{net, y} = 106$ N, down

$F_{net} = \sqrt{(350 \text{ N})^2 + (106 \text{ N})^2} = 366$ N $= 3.7 \times 10^2$ N

and $\tan \theta_2 = \dfrac{106 \text{ N}}{350 \text{ N}}$

So $\theta_2 = 19°$

$F = 3.7 \times 10^2$ N at 19° to left and down from horizontal

33. Two charges, q_A and q_B, are at rest near a positive test charge, q_T, of 7.2 μC. The first charge, q_A, is a positive charge of 3.6 μC, located 2.5 cm away from q_T at 35°; q_B is a negative charge of –6.6 μC, located 6.8 cm away at 125°.

a. Determine the magnitude of each of the forces acting on q_T.

$F_A = \dfrac{Kq_T q_A}{d^2} = \dfrac{(9.0 \times 10^9 \text{ N} \cdot \text{m}^2/\text{C}^2)(7.2 \times 10^{-6} \text{ C})(3.6 \times 10^{-6} \text{ C})}{(0.025 \text{ m})^2}$

$= 3.7 \times 10^2$ N, away (toward q_T)

$F_B = \dfrac{Kq_T q_A}{d^2} = \dfrac{(9.0 \times 10^9 \text{ N} \cdot \text{m}^2/\text{C}^2)(7.2 \times 10^{-6} \text{ C})(6.6 \times 10^{-6} \text{ C})}{(0.068 \text{ m})^2}$

$= 92$ N, toward (away from q_T)

b. Sketch a force diagram.

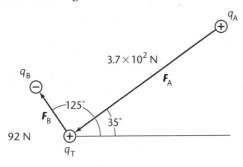

c. Graphically determine the resultant force acting on q_T.

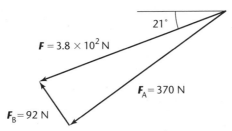

Copyright © by Glencoe/McGraw-Hill

34. The two pith balls shown in **Figure 20–15** have masses of 1.0 g each and equal charge. One pith ball is suspended by an insulating thread. The other is brought to 3.0 cm from the suspended ball. The suspended ball is now hanging with the thread forming an angle of 30.0° with the vertical. The ball is in equilibrium with F_E, F_g, and F_T. Calculate each of the following.

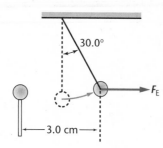

30.0°

F_E

3.0 cm

FIGURE 20-15

a. F_g

$$F_g = mg = (1.0 \times 10^{-3} \text{ kg})(9.80 \text{ m/s}^2) = 9.8 \times 10^{-3} \text{ N}$$

b. F_E

$$\tan 30.0° = \frac{F_E}{F_g}$$

$$F_E = mg \tan 30.0° = (1.0 \times 10^{-3} \text{ kg})(9.80 \text{ m/s}^2)(\tan 30.0°) = 5.7 \times 10^{-3} \text{ N}$$

c. the charge on the balls

$$F = \frac{Kq_A q_B}{d^2}$$

$$F = \frac{Kq^2}{d^2}$$

$$q = \sqrt{\frac{Fd^2}{K}} = \sqrt{\frac{(5.7 \times 10^{-3} \text{ N})(3.0 \times 10^{-2} \text{ m})^2}{(9.0 \times 10^9 \text{ N} \cdot \text{m}^2/\text{C}^2)}} = 2.4 \times 10^{-8} \text{ C}$$

Physics: Principles and Problems

Copyright © by Glencoe/McGraw-Hill

21 Electric Fields

Practice Problems

21.1 Creating and Measuring Electric Fields
pages 482–486

page 484

1. A negative charge of 2.0×10^{-8} C experiences a force of 0.060 N to the right in an electric field. What are the field magnitude and direction?

$$E = \frac{F}{q} = \frac{0.060 \text{ N}}{2.0 \times 10^{-8} \text{ C}}$$

$$= 3.0 \times 10^6 \text{ N/C directed to the left}$$

2. A positive test charge of 5.0×10^{-4} C is in an electric field that exerts a force of 2.5×10^{-4} N on it. What is the magnitude of the electric field at the location of the test charge?

$$E = \frac{F}{q} = \frac{2.5 \times 10^{-4} \text{ N}}{5.0 \times 10^{-4} \text{ C}} = 0.50 \text{ N/C}$$

3. Suppose the electric field in problem 2 was caused by a point charge. The test charge is moved to a distance twice as far from the charge. What is the magnitude of the force that the field exerts on the test charge now?

$$\frac{F_2}{F_1} = \frac{Kq_A q_B / d_2^2}{Kq_A q_B / d_1^2}$$

$$= \left(\frac{d_1}{d_2}\right)^2 \text{ with } d_2 = 2d_1$$

$$F_2 = \left(\frac{d_1}{d_2}\right)^2 F_1 = \left(\frac{d_1}{2d_1}\right)^2 (2.5 \times 10^{-4} \text{ N})$$

$$= 6.3 \times 10^{-5} \text{ N}$$

4. You are probing the field of a charge of unknown magnitude and sign. You first map the field with a 1.0×10^{-6} C test charge, then repeat your work with a 2.0×10^{-6} C test charge.

a. Would you measure the same forces with the two test charges? Explain.

No. The force on the 2.0 μC charge would be twice that on the 1.0 μC charge.

b. Would you find the same fields? Explain.

Yes. You would divide the force by the strength of the test charge, so the results would be the same.

21.2 Applications of Electric Fields
pages 488–501

page 493

5. The electric field intensity between two large, charged, parallel metal plates is 8000 N/C. The plates are 0.05 m apart. What is the electric potential difference between them?

$$\Delta V = Ed = (8000 \text{ N/C})(0.05 \text{ m})$$

$$= 400 \text{ J/C}$$

$$= 4 \times 10^2 \text{ V}$$

6. A voltmeter reads 500 V across two charged, parallel plates that are 0.020 m apart. What is the electric field between them?

$$\Delta V = Ed$$

$$E = \frac{\Delta V}{d} = \frac{500 \text{ V}}{0.020 \text{ m}} = 3 \times 10^4 \text{ N/C}$$

7. What electric potential difference is applied to two metal plates 0.500 m apart if the electric field between them is 2.50×10^3 N/C?

$$\Delta V = Ed = (2.50 \times 10^3 \text{ N/C})(0.500 \text{ m})$$

$$= 1.25 \times 10^3 \text{ V}$$

Copyright © by Glencoe/McGraw-Hill

Physics: Principles and Problems

8. What work is done when 5.0 C is moved through an electric potential difference of 1.5 V?

$$W = q\,\Delta V = (5.0\ \text{C})(1.5\ \text{V}) = 7.5\ \text{J}$$

page 495

9. A drop is falling in a Millikan oil-drop apparatus when the electric field is off.

a. What are the forces acting on the oil drop, regardless of its acceleration?

Gravitational force (weight) downward, frictional force of air upward.

b. If the drop is falling at constant velocity, what can be said about the forces acting on it?

The two are equal in magnitude.

10. An oil drop weighs 1.9×10^{-15} N. It is suspended in an electric field of 6.0×10^3 N/C.

a. What is the charge on the drop?

$$F = Eq$$

$$q = \frac{F}{E} = \frac{1.9 \times 10^{-15}\ \text{N}}{6.0 \times 10^3\ \text{N/C}}$$

$$= 3.2 \times 10^{-19}\ \text{C}$$

b. How many excess electrons does it carry?

 # electrons

$$= \frac{q}{q_e} = \frac{3.2 \times 10^{-19}\ \text{C}}{1.6 \times 10^{-19}\ \text{C/electron}}$$

$$= 2.0\ \text{electrons}$$

11. A positively charged oil drop weighs 6.4×10^{-13} N. An electric field of 4.0×10^6 N/C suspends the drop.

a. What is the charge on the drop?

$$F = Eq$$

$$q = \frac{F}{E} = \frac{6.4 \times 10^{-13}\ \text{N}}{4.0 \times 10^6\ \text{N/C}}$$

$$= 1.6 \times 10^{-19}\ \text{C}$$

b. How many electrons is the drop missing?

 # electrons

$$= \frac{q}{1.6 \times 10^{-19}\ \text{C/electron}}$$

$$= 1\ \text{electron}$$

12. If three more electrons were removed from the drop in problem 11, what field would be needed to balance the drop?

$$E = \frac{F}{q} = \frac{6.4 \times 10^{-13}\ \text{N}}{(4)(1.6 \times 10^{-19}\ \text{C})}$$

$$= 1.0 \times 10^6\ \text{N/C}$$

page 501

13. A 27-μF capacitor has an electric potential difference of 25 V across it. What is the charge on the capacitor?

$$q = C\Delta V = (27\ \mu\text{F})(25\ \text{V})$$

$$= 6.8 \times 10^{-4}\ \text{C}$$

14. Both a 3.3-μF and a 6.8-μF capacitor are connected across a 15-V electric potential difference. Which capacitor has a greater charge? What is it?

$$q = C\Delta V,\ \text{so the larger capacitor has a greater charge.}$$

$$q = (6.8 \times 10^{-6}\ \text{F})(15\ \text{V}) = 1.0 \times 10^{-4}\ \text{C}$$

15. The same two capacitors are each charged to 2.5×10^{-4} C. Which has the larger electric potential difference? What is it?

$$\Delta V = q/C,\ \text{so the smaller capacitor has the larger potential difference.}$$

$$\Delta V = \frac{(2.5 \times 10^{-4}\ \text{C})}{(3.3 \times 10^{-6}\ \text{F})}$$

$$= 76\ \text{V}$$

16. A 2.2-μF capacitor is first charged so that the electric potential difference is 6.0 V. How much additional charge is needed to increase the electric potential difference to 15.0 V?

$$q = C\Delta V \quad \text{so } \Delta q = C(\Delta V_2 - \Delta V_1)$$

$$\Delta q = (2.2\ \mu\text{F})(15.0\ \text{V} - 6.0\ \text{V})$$

$$= 2.0 \times 10^{-5}\ \text{C}$$

Copyright © by Glencoe/McGraw-Hill

Chapter Review Problems

pages 503–505

Section 21.1

page 503

Level 1

The charge of an electron is -1.60×10^{-19} C.

23. A positive charge of 1.0×10^{-5} C experiences a force of 0.20 N when located at a certain point. What is the electric field intensity at that point?

$$E = \frac{F}{q} = \frac{0.20 \text{ N}}{1.0 \times 10^{-5} \text{ C}} = 2.0 \times 10^4 \text{ N/C}$$

24. What charge exists on a test charge that experiences a force of 1.4×10^{-8} N at a point where the electric field intensity is 2.0×10^{-4} N/C?

$$E = \frac{F}{q}$$

$$\text{so } q = \frac{F}{E} = \frac{1.4 \times 10^{-8} \text{ N}}{2.0 \times 10^{-4} \text{ N/C}}$$

$$= 7.0 \times 10^{-5} \text{ C}$$

25. A test charge experiences a force of 0.20 N on it when it is placed in an electric field intensity of 4.5×10^5 N/C. What is the magnitude of the charge?

$$E = \frac{F}{q}$$

$$\text{So } q = \frac{F}{E} = \frac{0.20 \text{ N}}{4.5 \times 10^5 \text{ N/C}}$$

$$= 4.4 \times 10^{-7} \text{ C}$$

26. The electric field in the atmosphere is about 150 N/C, downward.

a. What is the direction of the force on a charged particle?

downward

b. Find the electric force on a proton with charge $+1.6 \times 10^{-19}$ C.

$$E = \frac{F}{q}$$

$$\text{So } F = qE = (1.6 \times 10^{-19} \text{ C})(150 \text{ N/C})$$

$$= 2.4 \times 10^{-17} \text{ N}$$

c. Compare the force in **b** with the force of gravity on the same proton (mass = 1.7×10^{-27} kg).

$$F = mg = (1.7 \times 10^{-27} \text{ kg})(9.80 \text{ m/s}^2)$$

$$= 1.7 \times 10^{-26} \text{ N (downward), more than one billion times smaller}$$

27. Carefully sketch

a. the electric field produced by a $+1.0\text{-}\mu$C charge.

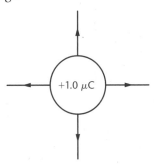

b. the electric field resulting from a $+2.0\text{-}\mu$C charge. Make the number of field lines proportional to the change in charge.

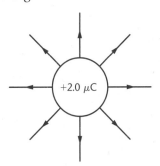

page 504

28. Charges X, Y, and Z are all equidistant from each other. X has a $+1.0\text{-}\mu$C charge, Y has a $+2.0\text{-}\mu$C charge, and Z has a small negative charge.

a. Draw an arrow showing the force on charge Z.

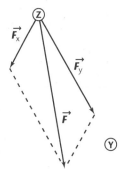

Copyright © by Glencoe/McGraw-Hill

28. (continued)

b. Charge Z now has a small positive charge on it. Draw an arrow showing the force on it.

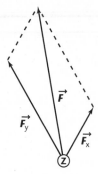

Ⓧ   Ⓨ

29. A positive test charge of 8.0×10^{-5} C is placed in an electric field of 50.0-N/C intensity. What is the strength of the force exerted on the test charge?

$$E = \frac{F}{q}$$

so $F = Eq = (8.0 \times 10^{-5}$ C$)(50.0$ N/C$)$

$$= 4.0 \times 10^{-3} \text{ N}$$

Level 2

TABLE 21–1	
Approximate Values of Typical Electric Fields	
Field	**Value (N/C)**
Nearby a charged hard rubber rod	1×10^3
In a television picture tube	1×10^5
Needed to create a spark in air	3×10^6
At an electron orbit in hydrogen atom	5×10^{11}

30. Electrons are accelerated by the electric field in a television picture tube, whose value is given in **Table 21-1.**

a. Find the force on an electron.

$$E = \frac{F}{q}$$

So $F = qE$

$$= (-1.6 \times 10^{-19} \text{ C})(1 \times 10^5 \text{ N/C})$$

$$= -2 \times 10^{-14} \text{ N opposite the field}$$

b. If the field is constant, find the acceleration of the electron (mass = 9.11×10^{-31} kg).

$$F = ma$$

So $a = \dfrac{F}{m} = \dfrac{-2 \times 10^{-14} \text{ N}}{9.11 \times 10^{-31} \text{ kg}}$

$$= -2 \times 10^{16} \text{ m/s}^2$$

31. A lead nucleus has the charge of 82 protons.

a. What are the direction and magnitude of the electric field at 1.0×10^{-10} m from the nucleus?

$Q = (82$ protons$)(1.6 \times 10^{-19}$ C/proton$)$

$$= 1.3 \times 10^{-17} \text{ C}$$

$$E = \frac{F}{q}$$

So $F = Eq$ and $F = \dfrac{KqQ}{d^2}$

So $E = \dfrac{KQ}{d^2}$

$$= \frac{(9.0 \times 10^9 \text{ N} \cdot \text{m}^2/\text{C}^2)(1.3 \times 10^{-17} \text{ C})}{(1.0 \times 10^{-10} \text{ m})^2}$$

$$= 1.2 \times 10^{13} \text{ N/C, outward}$$

b. What are the direction and magnitude of the force exerted on an electron located at this distance?

$$F = Eq$$

$$= (1.2 \times 10^{13} \text{ N/C})(-1.6 \times 10^{-19} \text{ C})$$

$$= -1.9 \times 10^{-6} \text{ N, toward the nucleus}$$

Section 21.2

Level 1

32. If 120 J of work are performed to move one coulomb of charge from a positive plate to a negative plate, what potential difference exists between the plates?

$$\Delta V = \frac{W}{q} = \frac{120 \text{ J}}{1.0 \text{ C}} = 120 \text{ V}$$

Copyright © by Glencoe/McGraw-Hill

33. How much work is done to transfer 0.15 C of charge through an electric potential difference of 9.0 V?

$$\Delta V = \frac{W}{q}$$

So $W = q\,\Delta V = (0.15\ \text{C})(9.0\ \text{V}) = 1.4\ \text{J}$

34. An electron is moved through an electric potential difference of 500 V. How much work is done on the electron?

$$\Delta V = \frac{W}{q}$$

So $W = q\,\Delta V$

$$= (-1.60 \times 10^{-19}\ \text{C})(500\ \text{V})$$

$$= -8 \times 10^{-17}\ \text{J}$$

35. A 12-V battery does 1200 J of work transferring charge. How much charge is transferred?

$$\Delta V = \frac{W}{q}$$

So $q = \dfrac{W}{\Delta V} = \dfrac{1200\ \text{J}}{12\ \text{V}} = 1.0 \times 10^2\ \text{C}$

36. The electric field intensity between two charged plates is 1.5×10^3 N/C. The plates are 0.080 m apart. What is the electric potential difference, in volts, between the plates?

$$\Delta V = Ed = (1.5 \times 10^3\ \text{N/C})(0.080\ \text{m})$$

$$= 1.2 \times 10^2\ \text{V}$$

37. A voltmeter indicates that the electric potential difference between two plates is 50.0 V. The plates are 0.020 m apart. What electric field intensity exists between them?

$$\Delta V = Ed$$

So $E = \dfrac{\Delta V}{d} = \dfrac{50.0\ \text{V}}{0.020\ \text{m}} = 2500\ \text{V/m}$

38. An oil drop is negatively charged and weighs 8.5×10^{-15} N. The drop is suspended in an electric field intensity of 5.3×10^3 N/C.

a. What is the charge on the drop?

$$E = \frac{F}{q}$$

So $q = \dfrac{F}{E} = \dfrac{8.5 \times 10^{-15}\ \text{N}}{5.3 \times 10^3\ \text{N/C}}$

$$= 1.6 \times 10^{-18}\ \text{C}$$

b. How many electrons does it carry?

$$\frac{1.6 \times 10^{-18}\ \text{C}}{1}\left(\frac{\text{electron}}{1.6 \times 10^{-19}\ \text{C}}\right)$$

$$= 10\ \text{electrons}$$

39. A capacitor that is connected to a 45.0-V source contains 90.0 μC of charge. What is the capacitor's capacitance?

$$C = \frac{q}{\Delta V} = \frac{90.0 \times 10^{-6}\ \text{C}}{45.0\ \text{V}} = 2.00\ \mu\text{F}$$

40. What electric potential difference exists across a 5.4-μF capacitor that has a charge of 2.7×10^{-3} C?

$$C = \frac{q}{\Delta V}$$

so $\Delta V = \dfrac{q}{C} = \dfrac{2.7 \times 10^{-3}\ \text{C}}{5.4 \times 10^{-6}\ \text{F}}$

$$= 5.0 \times 10^2\ \text{V}$$

41. What is the charge in a 15.0-pF capacitor when it is connected across a 75.0-V source?

$$C = \frac{q}{\Delta V}$$

so $q = C\Delta V = (15.0 \times 10^{-12}\ \text{F})(75.0\ \text{V})$

$$= 1.13 \times 10^{-9}\ \text{C}$$

Level 2

42. A force of 0.053 N is required to move a charge of 37 μC a distance of 25 cm in an electric field. What is the size of the electric potential difference between the two points?

$$W = F \cdot d$$

and $\Delta V = \dfrac{W}{q} = \dfrac{F \cdot d}{q}$

$$= \frac{(0.053\ \text{N})(0.25\ \text{m})}{37 \times 10^{-6}\ \text{C}}$$

$$= 3.6 \times 10^2\ \text{V}$$

Copyright © by Glencoe/McGraw-Hill

43. In an early set of experiments in 1911, Millikan observed that the following measured charges, among others, appeared at different times on a single oil drop. What value of elementary charge can be deduced from these data?

a. 6.563×10^{-19} C

b. 8.204×10^{-19} C

c. 11.50×10^{-19} C

d. 13.13×10^{-19} C

e. 16.48×10^{-19} C

f. 18.08×10^{-19} C

g. 19.71×10^{-19} C

h. 22.89×10^{-19} C

i. 26.13×10^{-19} C

1.63 × 10⁻¹⁹ C. Subtracting adjacent values, *b* − *a*, *c* − *b*, *d* − *c*, etc. yields 1.641 × 10⁻¹⁹ C, 3.30 × 10⁻¹⁹ C, 1.63 × 10⁻¹⁹ C, 3.35 × 10⁻¹⁹ C, 1.60 × 10⁻¹⁹ C, 1.63 × 10⁻¹⁹ C, 3.18 × 10⁻¹⁹ C, 3.24 × 10⁻¹⁹ C.

There are two numbers, approximately 1.63 × 10⁻¹⁹ C and 3.2 × 10⁻¹⁹ C, that are common. Averaging each similar group produces one charge of 1.63 × 10⁻¹⁹ C and one charge of 3.27 × 10⁻¹⁹ C (which is two times 1.63 × 10⁻¹⁹ C).

Dividing 1.63 × 10⁻¹⁹ C into each piece of data yields nearly whole number quotients, indicating it is the value of an elementary charge.

44. The energy stored in a capacitor with capacitance C, having an electric potential difference ΔV, is represented by $W = (1/2) C (\Delta V)^2$. One application of this is in the electronic photoflash of a strobe light. In such a unit, a capacitor of 10.0 μF is charged to 300 V. Find the energy stored.

$$W = \frac{1}{2} C (\Delta V)^2$$

$$= \frac{1}{2} (10.0 \times 10^{-6} \text{ F})(3.00 \times 10^2 \text{ V})^2$$

$$= 0.450 \text{ J}$$

45. Suppose it took 30 s to charge the capacitor in problem 44.

a. Find the power required to charge it in this time.

$$P = \frac{W}{t} = \frac{0.450 \text{ J}}{30 \text{ s}} = 2 \times 10^{-2} \text{ W}$$

b. When this capacitor is discharged through the strobe lamp, it transfers all its energy in 1.0×10^{-4} s. Find the power delivered to the lamp.

$$P = \frac{W}{t} = \frac{0.450 \text{ J}}{1.0 \times 10^{-4} \text{ s}} = 4.5 \times 10^3 \text{ W}$$

c. How is such a large amount of power possible?

Power is inversely proportional to the time. The shorter the time for a given amount of energy to be expended, the greater the power.

page 505

46. Lasers are used to try to produce controlled fusion reactions that might supply large amounts of electrical energy. The lasers require brief pulses of energy that are stored in large rooms filled with capacitors. One such room has a capacitance of 61×10^{-3} F charged to a potential difference of 10.0 kV.

a. Find the energy stored in the capacitors, given that $W = \frac{1}{2} C(\Delta V)^2$.

$$W = \frac{1}{2} C (\Delta V)^2$$

$$= \left(\frac{1}{2}\right)(61 \times 10^{-3} \text{ F})(1.00 \times 10^4 \text{ V})^2$$

$$= 3.1 \times 10^6 \text{ J}$$

b. The capacitors are discharged in 10 ns (1.0×10^{-8} s). What power is produced?

$$P = \frac{W}{t} = \frac{3.1 \times 10^6 \text{ J}}{1.0 \times 10^{-8} \text{ s}}$$

$$= 3.1 \times 10^{14} \text{ W}$$

c. If the capacitors are charged by a generator with a power capacity of 1.0 kW, how many seconds will be required to charge the capacitors?

$$t = \frac{W}{P} = \frac{3.1 \times 10^6 \text{ J}}{1.0 \times 10^3 \text{ W}} = 3.1 \times 10^3 \text{ s}$$

Copyright © by Glencoe/McGraw-Hill

47. Two point charges, one at $+3.00 \times 10^{-5}$ C and the other at -5.00×10^{-5} C, are placed at adjacent corners of a square 0.800 m on a side. A third charge of $+6.00 \times 10^{-5}$ C is placed at the corner diagonally opposite to the negative charge. Calculate the magnitudes and direction of the force acting on the third charge. For the direction, determine the angle the force makes with the edge of the square parallel to the line joining the first two charges.

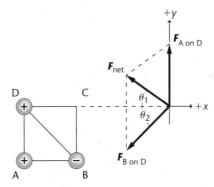

$q_A = +3.00 \times 10^{-5}$ C

$q_B = -5.00 \times 10^{-5}$ C

$q_D = +6.00 \times 10^{-5}$ C

$d = 0.800$ m

$$F_{A \text{ on } D} = \frac{Kq_A q_D}{d^2} = \frac{9.0 \times 10^9 \text{ N} \cdot \text{m}^2/\text{C}^2 \, (+3.00 \times 10^{-5} \text{ C})(+6.00 \times 10^{-5} \text{ C})}{(0.800 \text{ m})^2}$$

$$= +25.3 \text{ N} = 25.3 \text{ N, up}$$

$d_1 = \sqrt{d^2 + d^2} = d\sqrt{2} = 1.13$ m, $d_1^2 = 2d^2 = 1.28$ m^2

$$\tan \theta_1 = \frac{0.800 \text{ m}}{0.800 \text{ m}} = 1.00, \; \theta_1 = 45.0°$$

$$F_{B \text{ on } D} = \frac{Kq_B q_D}{d_1^2} = \frac{9.0 \times 10^9 \text{ N} \cdot \text{m}^2/\text{C}^2 \, (-5.00 \times 10^{-5} \text{ C})(+6.00 \times 10^{-5} \text{ C})}{1.28 \text{ m}^2}$$

$$= -21.1 \text{ N} = 21.1 \text{ N at } 45.0° \text{ with the } x\text{-axis, toward D}$$

The components of $F_{B \text{ on } D}$ are

$F_{B \text{ on } D, x} = F_{B \text{ on } D} \cos 45.0° = -14.9$ N $= 14.9$ N, to left

$F_{B \text{ on } D, y} = F_{B \text{ on } D} \sin 45.0° = -14.9$ N $= 14.9$ W, down

The components of the net (resultant) force are

$F_{net, x} = -14.9$ N $= 14.9$ N, left

$F_{net, y} = -25.3$ N $- 14.9$ N $= 10.4$ N, up

$F_{net} = \sqrt{(14.9 \text{ N})^2 + (10.4 \text{ N})^2} = 18.2$ N

and $\tan \theta_2 = \dfrac{10.4 \text{ N}}{14.9 \text{ N}}$

so $\theta_2 = 34.9°$

$F = 18.2$ N at $34.9°$ to left and down from horizontal

Copyright © by Glencoe/McGraw-Hill

Critical Thinking Problems

48. In an ink-jet printer, drops of ink are given a certain amount of charge before they move between two large parallel plates. The purpose of the plates is to deflect the charges so that they are stopped by a gutter and do not reach the paper. This is shown in **Figure 21-16**. The plates are 1.5 cm long and have an electric field of $E = 1.2 \times 10^6$ N/C between them. Drops with a mass $m = 0.10$ ng and a charge $q = 1.0 \times 10^{-16}$ C are moving horizontally at a speed of $v = 15$ m/s parallel to the plates. What is the vertical displacement of the drops when they leave the plates? To answer this question, go through the following steps.

a. What is the vertical force on the drops?

$$F = qE$$
$$= (1.0 \times 10^{-16} \text{ C})(1.2 \times 10^6 \text{ N/C})$$
$$= 1.2 \times 10^{-10} \text{ N}$$

b. What is their vertical acceleration?

$$a = \frac{F}{m} = \frac{(1.2 \times 10^{-10} \text{ N})}{(1.0 \times 10^{-13} \text{ kg})}$$
$$= 1.2 \times 10^3 \text{ m/s}^2$$

c. How long are they between the plates?

$$t = \frac{L}{v} = \frac{(1.5 \times 10^{-2} \text{ m})}{(15 \text{ m/s})} = 1.0 \times 10^{-3} \text{ s}$$

d. Given that acceleration and time, how far are they displaced?

$$y = \frac{1}{2} at^2$$
$$= \frac{1}{2} (1.2 \times 10^3 \text{ m/s}^2)(1.0 \times 10^{-3} \text{ s})^2$$
$$= 6.0 \times 10^{-4} \text{ m} = 0.60 \text{ mm}$$

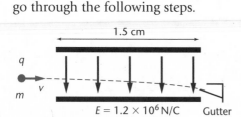

1.5 cm

q

v

m

$E = 1.2 \times 10^6$ N/C   Gutter

FIGURE 21-16

49. Suppose the moon had a net negative charge equal to $-q$ and Earth had a net positive charge equal to $+10q$. What value of q would yield the same magnitude force that you now attribute to gravity?

Equate the expressions for gravitational force and Coulombic force between Earth and the moon:

$$F = \frac{Gm_E m_m}{d^2} = \frac{Kq_E q_m}{d^2}$$

where $-q$ is the net negative charge of the moon and q_E, the net positive charge of Earth, is $+10q$.

$$\frac{(6.67 \times 10^{-11} \text{ N} \cdot \text{m}^2/\text{kg}^2)(6.00 \times 10^{24} \text{ kg})(7.31 \times 10^{22} \text{ kg})}{d^2}$$
$$= \frac{(9.0 \times 10^9 \text{ N} \cdot \text{m}^2/\text{C}^2)(q_E q_m)}{d^2}$$

(Note that the minus sign is disregarded; the forces are considered to be positive.)

Cancel d^2, and measure q in coulombs. Multiply terms to get

$$2.95 \times 10^{37} \text{ NC}^2 = 9.0 \times 10^{10} \text{ N}q^2$$
$$q^2 = 3.28 \times 10^{26} \text{ C}^2$$
$$q = 1.8 \times 10^{13} \text{ C}$$

Copyright © by Glencoe/McGraw-Hill

22 Current Electricity

Practice Problems

22.1 Current and Circuits
pages 508–519

page 511

1. The current through a lightbulb connected across the terminals of a 120-V outlet is 0.50 A. At what rate does the bulb convert electric energy to light?

$$P = VI = (120 \text{ V})(0.5 \text{ A}) = 60 \text{ J/s}$$
$$= 60 \text{ W}$$

2. A car battery causes a current of 2.0 A through a lamp while 12 V is across it. What is the power used by the lamp?

$$P = VI = (12 \text{ V})(2.0 \text{ A}) = 24 \text{ W}$$

3. What is the current through a 75-W lightbulb connected to a 120-V outlet?

$$P = VI$$
$$I = \frac{P}{V} = \frac{75 \text{ W}}{120 \text{ V}} = 0.63 \text{ A}$$

4. The current through the starter motor of a car is 210 A. If the battery keeps 12 V across the motor, what electric energy is delivered to the starter in 10.0 s?

$$P = VI = (12 \text{ V})(210 \text{ A}) = 2500 \text{ W}$$
In 10 s,
$$E = Pt = (2500 \text{ J/s})(10 \text{ s})$$
$$= 25\ 000 \text{ J} = 2.5 \times 10^4 \text{ J}$$

page 515

For all problems, you should assume that the battery voltage is constant, no matter what current is present.

5. An automobile headlight with a resistance of 30 Ω is placed across a 12-V battery. What is the current through the circuit?

$$I = \frac{V}{R} = \frac{12 \text{ V}}{30 \text{ Ω}} = 0.4 \text{ A}$$

6. A motor with an operating resistance of 32 Ω is connected to a voltage source. The current in the circuit is 3.8 A. What is the voltage of the source?

$$V = IR = (3.8 \text{ A})(32 \text{ Ω}) = 1.2 \times 10^2 \text{ V}$$

7. A transistor radio uses 2.0×10^{-4} A of current when it is operated by a 3.0-V battery. What is the resistance of the radio circuit?

$$R = \frac{V}{I} = \frac{3.0 \text{ V}}{2.0 \times 10^{-4} \text{ A}} = 1.5 \times 10^4 \text{ Ω}$$

8. A lamp draws a current of 0.50 A when it is connected to a 120-V source.

   a. What is the resistance of the lamp?

   $$R = \frac{V}{I} = \frac{120 \text{ V}}{0.50 \text{ A}} = 2.4 \times 10^2 \text{ Ω}$$

   b. What is the power consumption of the lamp?

   $$P = VI = (120 \text{ V})(0.50 \text{ A}) = 6.0 \times 10^1 \text{ W}$$

9. A 75-W lamp is connected to 120 V.

   a. What is the current through the lamp?

   $$I = \frac{P}{V} = \frac{75 \text{ W}}{120 \text{ V}} = 0.63 \text{ A}$$

   b. What is the resistance of the lamp?

   $$R = \frac{V}{I} = \frac{120 \text{ V}}{0.63 \text{ A}} = 190 \text{ Ω}$$

Copyright © by Glencoe/McGraw-Hill

10. A resistor is added in series with the lamp in problem 9 to reduce the current to half its original value.

   a. What is the potential difference across the lamp? Assume that the lamp resistance is constant.

     The new value of the current is

$$\frac{0.63\ A}{2} = 0.315\ A$$

     So $V = IR = (0.315\ A)(190\ \Omega)$

$$= 6.0 \times 10^1\ V$$

   b. How much resistance was added to the circuit?

     The total resistance of the circuit is now

$$R_{total} = \frac{V}{I} = \frac{120\ V}{0.315\ A} = 380\ \Omega$$

     Therefore,

$$R_{res} = R_{total} - R_{lamp}$$
$$= 380\ \Omega - 190\ \Omega = 190\ \Omega$$

   c. How much power is now dissipated in the lamp?

$$P = VI = (6.0 \times 10^1\ V)(0.315\ A) = 19\ W$$

page 517

11. Draw a circuit diagram to include a 60.0-V battery, an ammeter, and a resistance of 12.5 Ω in series. Indicate the ammeter reading and the direction of current.

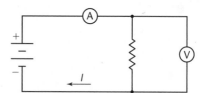

$$I = \frac{V}{R} = \frac{60.0\ V}{12.5\ \Omega} = 4.80\ A$$

12. Draw a series-circuit diagram showing a 4.5-V battery, a resistor, and an ammeter reading 90 mA. Label the size of the resistor. Choose a direction for the conventional current and indicate the positive terminal of the battery.

$$R = \frac{V}{I} = \frac{4.5\ V}{0.09\ A} = 50\ \Omega$$

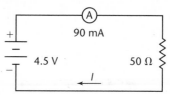

13. Add a voltmeter that measures the potential difference across the resistors in problems 11 and 12 and repeat the problems.

     Both circuits will take the form

     Because the ammeter resistance is assumed zero, the voltmeter readings will be

     6.0×10^1 **V for Practice Problem 11**

     4.5 V for Practice Problem 12.

22.2 Using Electric Energy
pages 520–525

page 522

14. A 15-Ω electric heater operates on a 120-V outlet.

   a. What is the current through the heater?

$$I = \frac{V}{R} = \frac{120\ V}{15\ \Omega} = 8.0\ A$$

   b. How much energy is used by the heater in 30.0 s?

$$E = I^2Rt = (8.0\ A)^2(15\ \Omega)(30.0\ s)$$
$$= 2.9 \times 10^4\ J$$

   c. How much thermal energy is liberated by the heater in this time?

     2.9×10^4 **J, because all electrical energy is converted to thermal energy.**

Copyright © by Glencoe/McGraw-Hill

15. A 30-Ω resistor is connected across a 60-V battery.

    a. What is the current in the circuit?

$$I = \frac{V}{R} = \frac{60 \text{ V}}{30 \text{ } \Omega} = 2 \text{ A}$$

    b. How much energy is used by the resistor in 5.0 min?

$$E = I^2Rt$$
$$= (2 \text{ A})^2(30 \text{ } \Omega)(5 \text{ min})(60 \text{ s/min})$$
$$= 4 \times 10^4 \text{ J}$$

16. A 100.0-W lightbulb is 20.0 percent efficient. This means that 20.0 percent of the electric energy is converted to light energy.

    a. How many joules does the lightbulb convert into light each minute it is in operation?

$$E = (0.200)(100.0 \text{ J/s})(60.0 \text{ s})$$
$$= 1.20 \times 10^3 \text{ J}$$

    b. How many joules of thermal energy does the lightbulb produce each minute?

$$E = (0.800)(100.0 \text{ J/s})(60.0 \text{ s})$$
$$= 4.80 \times 10^3 \text{ J}$$

17. The resistance of an electric stove element at operating temperature is 11 Ω.

    a. If 220 V are applied across it, what is the current through the stove element?

$$I = \frac{V}{R} = \frac{220 \text{ V}}{11 \text{ } \Omega} = 2.0 \times 10^1 \text{ A}$$

    b. How much energy does the element convert to thermal energy in 30.0 s?

$$E = I^2Rt = (2.0 \times 10^1 \text{ A})^2(11 \text{ } \Omega)(30.0 \text{ s})$$
$$= 1.3 \times 10^5 \text{ J}$$

    c. The element is being used to heat a kettle containing 1.20 kg of water. Assume that 70 percent of the heat is absorbed by the water. What is its increase in temperature during the 30.0 s?

$$Q = mC\Delta T \quad \text{with } Q = 0.70E$$

$$\Delta T = \frac{0.70E}{mC}$$
$$= \frac{(0.70)(1.3 \times 10^5 \text{ J})}{(1.20 \text{ kg})(4180 \text{ J/kg} \cdot \text{C}°)}$$
$$= 18°\text{C}$$

page 525

18. An electric space heater draws 15.0 A from a 120-V source. It is operated, on the average, for 5.0 h each day.

    a. How much power does the heater use?

$$P = IV = (15.0 \text{ A})(120 \text{ V})$$
$$= 1800 \text{ W} = 1.8 \text{ kW}$$

    b. How much energy in kWh does it consume in 30 days?

$$E = Pt = (1.8 \text{ kW})(5.0 \text{ h/day})(30 \text{ days})$$
$$= 270 \text{ kWh}$$

    c. At 11¢ per kWh, how much does it cost to operate the heater for 30 days?

$$\text{Cost} = (0.11 \text{ \$/kWh})(270 \text{ kWh}) = \$30$$

19. A digital clock has resistance of 12 000 Ω and is plugged into a 115-V outlet.

    a. How much current does it draw?

$$I = \frac{V}{R} = \frac{115 \text{ V}}{12 \text{ }000 \text{ } \Omega} = 9.6 \times 10^{-3} \text{ A}$$

    b. How much power does it use?

$$P = VI = (115 \text{ V})(9.6 \times 10^{-3} \text{ A}) = 1.1 \text{ W}$$

    c. If the owner of the clock pays 9¢ per kWh, how much does it cost to operate the clock for 30 days?

$$\text{Cost}$$
$$= (1.1 \times 10^{-3} \text{ kW})(\$0.09/\text{kWh})$$
$$\times (30 \text{ days})(24 \text{ h/day})$$
$$= \$0.07$$

20. A four-slice toaster is rated at 1200 W and designed for use with 120-V circuits.

    a. What is the resistance of the toaster?

$$I = \frac{P}{V} = \frac{1200 \text{ W}}{120 \text{ V}} = 1.0 \times 10^1 \text{ A}$$
$$R = \frac{V}{I} = \frac{120 \text{ V}}{1.0 \times 10^1 \text{ A}} = 12 \text{ } \Omega$$

Copyright © by Glencoe/McGraw-Hill

20. (continued)

b. How much current will flow when the toaster is turned on?

1.0×10^1 A

c. At what rate is heat generated in the toaster?

$P = IV = (1.0 \times 10^1 \text{ A})(120 \text{ V})$

$= 1200 \text{ W} = 1.2 \times 10^3 \text{ J/s}$

d. If all the heat generated were concentrated into 500 g of water at room temperature, at what rate would the temperature be rising?

$Q = mC\Delta T$

In one s,

$\Delta T = \dfrac{Q}{mC}$

$= \dfrac{1.2 \times 10^3 \text{ J/s}}{(0.500 \text{ kg})(4180 \text{ J/kg} \cdot \text{K})}$

$= 0.57°\text{C/s}$

e. The nichrome heating wires in the toaster total 2.00 m long if pulled straight. What is the electric field in the wire during operation if all the energy is converted in the nichrome wire?

$\dfrac{120 \text{ V}}{2.00 \text{ m}} = 6.0 \times 10^1 \text{ V/m}$

f. If it takes 3 minutes to properly make toast and the cost per kilowatt-hour is 10 cents, how much does it cost to make one slice of toast?

$P = 1.2 \times 10^3 \text{ W} = 1.2 \text{ kW}$

Cost/3 min

$= (1.2 \text{ kW})(\$0.10) \times \left(\dfrac{3 \text{ min}}{6.0 \text{ min/h}}\right)$

$= \$0.0060 \text{ or } 0.60 \text{ cents}$

If only one slice is made, 0.60 cents; if four slices are made, 0.15 cents per slice.

Chapter Review Problems

pages 527–529

page 527

Section 22.1

Level 1

21. The current through a toaster connected to a 120-V source is 8.0 A. What power is dissipated by the toaster?

$P = VI = (120 \text{ V})(8.0 \text{ A}) = 9.6 \times 10^2 \text{ W}$

22. A current of 1.2 A is measured through a lightbulb when it is connected across a 120-V source. What power is dissipated by the bulb?

$P = VI = (120 \text{ V})(1.2 \text{ A}) = 1.4 \times 10^2 \text{ W}$

23. A lamp draws 0.50 A from a 120-V generator.

a. How much power is delivered?

$P = VI = (120 \text{ V})(0.50 \text{ A}) = 6.0 \times 10^1 \text{ W}$

b. How much energy does the lamp convert in 5.0 min?

The definition of power is $P = \dfrac{E}{t}$, **so**

$E = Pt$

$= 6.0 \times 10^1 \text{ W} \left(\dfrac{5.0 \text{ min}}{1}\right)\left(\dfrac{60 \text{ s}}{\text{min}}\right)$

$= 18\ 000 \text{ J} = 1.8 \times 10^4 \text{ J}$

24. A 12-V automobile battery is connected to an electric starter motor. The current through the motor is 210 A.

a. How many joules of energy does the battery deliver to the motor each second?

$P = IV = (210 \text{ A})(12 \text{ V}) = 2500 \text{ J/s}$,

or 2.5×10^3 J/s

b. What power, in watts, does the motor use?

$P = 2.5 \times 10^3$ W

Copyright © by Glencoe/McGraw-Hill

25. A 4000-W clothes dryer is connected to a 220-V circuit. How much current does the dryer draw?

$P = VI$

So $I = \dfrac{P}{V} = \dfrac{4000\ W}{220\ V} = 20\ A$

26. A flashlight bulb is connected across a 3.0-V potential difference. The current through the lamp is 1.5 A.

a. What is the power rating of the lamp?

$P = VI = (3.0\ V)(1.5\ A) = 4.5\ W$

b. How much electric energy does the lamp convert in 11 min?

The definition for power is $P = \dfrac{E}{t}$, so

$E = Pt$

$= (4.5\ W)\left(\dfrac{11\ min}{1}\right)\left(\dfrac{60\ s}{min}\right)$

$= 3.0 \times 10^3\ J$

27. A resistance of 60.0 Ω has a current of 0.40 A through it when it is connected to the terminals of a battery. What is the voltage of the battery?

$V = IR = (0.40\ A)(60.0\ \Omega) = 24\ V$

28. What voltage is applied to a 4.0-Ω resistor if the current is 1.5 A?

$V = IR = (1.5\ A)(4.0\ \Omega) = 6.0\ V$

29. What voltage is placed across a motor of 15-Ω operating resistance if there is 8.0 A of current?

$V = IR = (8.0\ A)(15\ \Omega) = 1.2 \times 10^2\ V$

30. A voltage of 75 V is placed across a 15-Ω resistor. What is the current through the resistor?

$V = IR$

So $I = \dfrac{V}{R} = \dfrac{75\ V}{15\ W} = 5.0\ A$

31. A 20.0-Ω resistor is connected to a 30.0-V battery. What is the current through the resistor?

$V = IR$

So $I = \dfrac{V}{R} = \dfrac{30.0\ V}{20.0\ \Omega} = 1.50\ A$

32. A 12-V battery is connected to a device and 24 mA of current is measured. If the device obeys Ohm's law, how much current is present when a 24-V battery is used?

_I_ is proportional to _V_, so doubling _V_ doubles _I_ to 48 mA.

33. A person with dry skin has a resistance from one arm to the other of about $1 \times 10^5\ \Omega$. When skin is wet, resistance drops to about $1.5 \times 10^3\ \Omega$. (Refer to **Table 22–1.**)

TABLE 22-1	
The Damage Caused by Electric Shock	
Current	**Possible Effects**
1 mA	mild shock can be felt
5 mA	shock is painful
15 mA	muscle control is lost
100 mA	death can occur

page 528

a. What is the minimum voltage placed across the arms that would produce a current that could be felt by a person with dry skin?

$V = IR$

$= (1 \times 10^{-3}\ A)(1 \times 10^5\ \Omega)$

$= 1 \times 10^2\ V$

b. What effect would the same voltage have if the person had wet skin?

$V = IR$

So $I = \dfrac{V}{R}$

$= \dfrac{1 \times 10^2\ V}{1.5 \times 10^3\ \Omega} = 7 \times 10^{-2}\ A$

$= 70\ mA$, **near level where death may occur**

c. What would be the minimum voltage that would produce a current that could be felt when the skin is wet?

$V = IR$

$= (1 \times 10^{-3}\ A)(1.5 \times 10^3\ \Omega)$

$= 1.5\ V$, **or between 1 and 2 V**

Copyright © by Glencoe/McGraw-Hill

34. A lamp draws a 66-mA current when connected to a 6.0-V battery. When a 9.0-V battery is used, the lamp draws 75 mA.

a. Does the lamp obey Ohm's law?

No. The voltage is increased by a factor of $\dfrac{9.0}{6.0} = 1.5$, but the current is increased by a factor of $\dfrac{75}{66} = 1.1$

b. How much power does the lamp dissipate at 6.0 V?

$P = IV = (66 \times 10^{-3} \text{ A})(6.0 \text{ V}) = 0.40 \text{ W}$

c. How much power does it dissipate at 9.0 V?

$P = IV = (75 \times 10^{-3} \text{ A})(9.0 \text{ V}) = 0.68 \text{ W}$

TABLE 22-2		
Voltage V (volts)	**Current** I (amps)	**Resistance** $R = V/I$ (ohms)
2.00	0.014	143 Ω
4.00	0.027	148 Ω
6.00	0.040	150 Ω
8.00	0.052	154 Ω
10.00	0.065	154 Ω
−2.00	−0.014	143 Ω
−4.00	−0.028	143 Ω
−6.00	−0.039	154 Ω
−8.00	−0.051	157 Ω
−10.00	−0.064	156 Ω

Level 2

35. How much energy does a 60.0-W lightbulb use in half an hour? If the lightbulb is 12 percent efficient, how much thermal energy does it generate during the half hour?

$P = \dfrac{E}{t}$

so $E = Pt = (60.0 \text{ W})(1800 \text{ s})$

$= 1.08 \times 10^5 \text{ J}$

If the bulb is 12% efficient, 88% of the energy is lost to heat, so

$Q = 0.88(1.08 \times 10^5 \text{ J}) = 9.5 \times 10^4 \text{ J}$

36. Some students connected a length of nichrome wire to a variable power supply that could produce from 0.00 V to 10.00 V across the wire. They then measured the current through the wire for several voltages. They recorded the data showing the voltages used and currents measured. These are presented in **Table 22–2.**

a. For each measurement, calculate the resistance.

$R = 143 \text{ Ω}, 148 \text{ Ω}, 150 \text{ Ω}, 154 \text{ Ω},$
$154 \text{ Ω}, 143 \text{ Ω}, 143 \text{ Ω}, 154 \text{ Ω},$
$157 \text{ Ω}, 156 \text{ Ω}$

b. Graph I versus V.

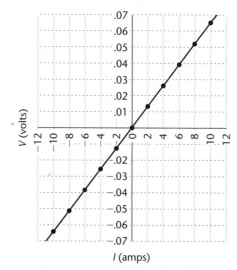

c. Does the nichrome wire obey Ohm's law? If not, for all the voltages, specify the voltage range for which Ohm's law holds.

Ohm's law is obeyed when the resistance of a device is constant and independent of the potential difference. The resistance of the nichrome wire increases somewhat

Copyright © by Glencoe/McGraw-Hill

as the magnitude of the voltage increases, so the wire does not quite obey Ohm's law.

37. The current through a lamp connected across 120 V is 0.40 A when the lamp is on.

    a. What is the lamp's resistance when it is on?

    $V = IR$

    so $R = \dfrac{V}{I} = \dfrac{120\,V}{0.40A} = 3.0 \times 10^2\,\Omega$

    b. When the lamp is cold, its resistance is one fifth as large as it is when the lamp is hot. What is its cold resistance?

    $\dfrac{1}{5}\,(3.0 \times 10^2\,\Omega) = 6.0 \times 10^1\,\Omega$

    c. What is the current through the lamp as it is turned on if it is connected to a potential difference of 120 V?

    $V = IR$

    so $I = \dfrac{V}{R} = \dfrac{120\,V}{6.0 \times 10^1\,\Omega} = 2.0\,A$

38. The graph in **Figure 22–14** shows the current through a device called a silicon diode.

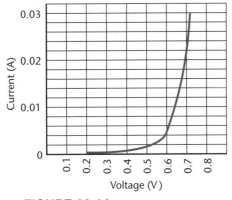

FIGURE 22-14

    a. A potential difference of +0.70 V is placed across the diode. What resistance would be calculated?

    From the graph, I = 22 mA, and $V = IR$, so

    $R = \dfrac{V}{I} = \dfrac{0.70\,V}{2.2 \times 10^{-2}\,A} = 32\,\Omega$

    b. What resistance would be calculated

if a +0.60-V potential difference were used?

From the graph, I = 5.2 mA and

$R = \dfrac{V}{I} = \dfrac{0.60\,V}{5.2 \times 10^{-3}\,A} = 1.2 \times 10^2\,\Omega$

    c. Does the diode obey Ohm's law?

    No. Resistance depends on voltage.

39. Draw a schematic diagram to show a circuit that includes a 90-V battery, an ammeter, and a resistance of 45 Ω connected in series. What is the ammeter reading? Draw arrows showing the direction of conventional current.

    $V = IR$

    so $I = \dfrac{V}{R} = \dfrac{90\,V}{45\,\Omega} = 2\,A$

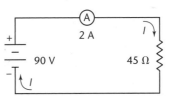

40. Draw a series circuit diagram to include a 16-Ω resistor, a battery, and an ammeter that reads 1.75 A. Conventional current is measured through the meter from left to right. Indicate the positive terminal and the voltage of the battery.

    $V = IR = (1.75\,A)(16\,\Omega) = 28\,V$

Section 22.2

Level 1

41. What is the maximum current that should be allowed in a 5.0-W, 220-Ω resistor?

    $P = I^2R$

    so $I = \sqrt{\dfrac{P}{R}} = \sqrt{\dfrac{5.0\,W}{220\,\Omega}} = 0.15\,A$

Copyright © by Glencoe/McGraw-Hill

42. The wire in a house circuit is rated at 15.0 A and has a resistance of 0.15 Ω.

a. What is its power rating?

$P = I^2R = (15.0 \text{ A})^2(0.15 \ \Omega) = 34 \text{ W}$

b. How much heat does the wire give off in 10.0 min?

$Q = E = I^2Rt$

$= (15.0 \text{ A})^2(0.15 \ \Omega)(10.0 \text{ min}) \left(\dfrac{60 \text{ s}}{\text{min}}\right)$

$= 2.0 \times 10^4 \text{ J}$

43. A current of 1.2 A is measured through a 50.0-Ω resistor for 5.0 min. How much heat is generated by the resistor?

$Q = E = I^2Rt$

$= (1.2 \text{ A})^2(50.0 \ \Omega)(5.0 \text{ min})\left(\dfrac{60 \text{ s}}{\text{min}}\right)$

$= 2.2 \times 10^4 \text{ J}$

44. A 6.0-Ω resistor is connected to a 15-V battery.

a. What is the current in the circuit?

$V = IR$

so $I = \dfrac{V}{R} = \dfrac{15 \text{ V}}{6.0 \ \Omega} = 2.5 \text{ A}$

b. How much thermal energy is produced in 10.0 min?

$Q = E = I^2Rt$

$= (2.5 \text{ A})^2(6.0 \ \Omega)(10.0 \text{ min}) \left(\dfrac{60 \text{ s}}{\text{min}}\right)$

$= 2.3 \times 10^4 \text{ J}$

45. A 110-V electric iron draws 3.0 A of current. How much thermal energy is developed each hour?

$V = IR$

so $R = \dfrac{V}{I} = \dfrac{110 \text{ V}}{3.0 \text{ A}} = 37 \ \Omega$

and $Q = E = I^2Rt$

$= (3.0 \text{ A})^2(37 \ \Omega)(1 \text{ h}) \left(\dfrac{3600 \text{ s}}{\text{h}}\right)$

$= 1.2 \times 10^6 \text{ J}$

Level 2

46. An electric motor operates a pump that irrigates a farmer's crop by pumping 10 000 L of water a vertical distance of 8.0 m into a field each hour. The motor has an operating resistance of 22.0 Ω and is connected across a 110-V source.

a. What current does it draw?

$V = IR$

so $I = \dfrac{V}{R} = \dfrac{110 \text{ V}}{22.0 \ \Omega} = 5.0 \text{ A}$

b. How efficient is the motor?

$E_W = mgd$

$= (1.0 \times 10^4 \text{ kg})(9.80 \text{ m/s}^2)(8.0 \text{ m})$

$= 7.8 \times 10^5 \text{ J}$

$E_m = IVt = (5.0 \text{ A})(110 \text{ V})(3600 \text{ s})$

$= 2.0 \times 10^6 \text{ J}$

$\text{Eff} = \dfrac{E_W}{E_m} \times 100$

$= \dfrac{7.8 \times 10^5 \text{ J}}{2.0 \times 10^6 \text{ J}} \times 100 = 39\%$

47. A transistor radio operates by means of a 9.0-V battery that supplies it with a 50-mA current.

a. If the cost of the battery is $0.90 and its lasts for 300 h, what is the cost per kWh to operate the radio in this manner?

$P = IV = (0.050 \text{ A})(9.0 \text{ V}) = 0.45 \text{ W}$

$= 4.5 \times 10^{-4} \text{ kW}$

$\text{Cost} = \dfrac{\$0.90}{(4.5 \times 10^{-4} \text{ kW})(300 \text{ h})}$

$= \$7.00/\text{kWh}$

b. The same radio, by means of a converter, is plugged into a household circuit by a homeowner who pays 8¢ per kWh. What does it now cost to operate the radio for 300 h?

$\text{Cost} = \dfrac{\$0.08}{\text{kWh}} (4.5 \times 10^{-4} \text{ kW})(300 \text{ h})$

$= 1 \text{ cent}$

Copyright © by Glencoe/McGraw-Hill

Critical Thinking Problems

48. A heating coil has a resistance of 4.0 Ω and operates on 120 V.

a. What is the current in the coil while it is operating?

$$V = IR$$

so $I = \dfrac{V}{R} = \dfrac{120 \text{ V}}{4.0 \text{ }\Omega} = 3.0 \times 10^1 \text{ A}$

b. What energy is supplied to the coil in 5.0 min?

$$E = I^2Rt$$
$$= (3.0 \times 10^1 \text{ A})^2(4.0 \text{ }\Omega)(5.0 \text{ min})\left(\dfrac{60 \text{ s}}{\text{min}}\right)$$
$$= 1.1 \times 10^6 \text{ J}$$

c. If the coil is immersed in an insulated container holding 20.0 kg of water, what will be the increase in the temperature of the water? Assume that 100 percent of the heat is absorbed by the water.

$$Q = mC \,\Delta T$$
so $\Delta T = \dfrac{Q}{mC}$

$$= \dfrac{1.1 \times 10^6 \text{ J}}{(20.0 \text{ kg})(4180 \text{ J/kg} \cdot \text{C}°)}$$
$$= 13°\text{C}$$

d. At 8¢ per kWh, how much does it cost to operate the heating coil 30 min per day for 30 days?

$$\text{Cost} = \left(\dfrac{1.1 \times 10^6 \text{ J}}{5 \text{ min}}\right)\left(\dfrac{30 \text{ min}}{\text{day}}\right)$$
$$\times (30 \text{ days})\left(\dfrac{1 \text{ kWh}}{3.6 \times 10^6 \text{ J}}\right)\left(\dfrac{\$0.08}{\text{kWh}}\right)$$
$$= \$4.40$$

49. An electric heater is rated at 500 W.

a. How much energy is delivered to the heater in half an hour?

$$E = Pt = (5 \times 10^2 \text{ W})(1800 \text{ s})$$
$$= 9 \times 10^5 \text{ J}$$

b. The heater is being used to heat a room containing 50 kg of air. If the specific heat of air is 1.10 kJ/kg · °C, and 50 percent of the thermal energy heats the air in the room, what is the change in air temperature in half an hour?

$$Q = mC \,\Delta T$$
so $\Delta T = \dfrac{Q}{mC}$

$$= \dfrac{(0.5)(9 \times 10^5 \text{ J})}{(50.0 \text{ kg})(1100 \text{ J/kg} \cdot \text{C}°)}$$
$$= 8°\text{C}$$

c. At 8¢ per kWh, how much does it cost to run the heater 6.0 h per day for 30 days?

$$\text{Cost} = \left(\dfrac{500 \text{ J}}{\text{s}}\right)\left(\dfrac{6.0 \text{ h}}{\text{day}}\right)\left(\dfrac{3600 \text{ s}}{\text{h}}\right)$$
$$\times (30 \text{ days})\left(\dfrac{1 \text{ kWh}}{3.6 \times 10^6 \text{ J}}\right)\left(\dfrac{\$0.08}{\text{kWh}}\right)$$
$$= \$7.20$$

Copyright © by Glencoe/McGraw-Hill

23 Series and Parallel Circuits

Practice Problems

23.1 Simple Circuits
pages 532–541

page 534

1. Three 20-Ω resistors are connected in series across a 120-V generator. What is the equivalent resistance of the circuit? What is the current in the circuit?

$$R = R_1 + R_2 + R_3$$
$$= 20\ \Omega + 20\ \Omega + 20\ \Omega$$
$$= 60\ \Omega$$

$$I = \frac{V}{R} = \frac{120\ \text{V}}{60\ \Omega} = 2\ \text{A}$$

2. A 10-Ω resistor, a 15-Ω resistor, and a 5-Ω resistor are connected in series across a 90-V battery. What is the equivalent resistance of the circuit? What is the current in the circuit?

$$R = 10\ \Omega + 15\ \Omega + 5\ \Omega = 30\ \Omega$$

$$I = \frac{V}{R} = \frac{90\ \text{V}}{30\ \Omega} = 3\ \text{A}$$

3. Consider a 9-V battery in a circuit with three resistors connected in series.

   a. If the resistance of one of the resistors increases, how will the series resistance change?

   It will increase.

   b. What will happen to the current?

   $I = \dfrac{V}{R}$, **so it will decrease.**

   c. Will there be any change in the battery voltage?

   No. It does not depend on the resistance.

4. A string of holiday lights has ten bulbs with equal resistances connected in series. When the string of lights is connected to a 120-V outlet, the current through the bulbs is 0.06 A.

   a. What is the equivalent resistance of the circuit?

   $$R = \frac{V}{I} = \frac{120\ \text{V}}{0.06\ \text{A}} = 2000\ \Omega$$

   b. What is the resistance of each bulb?

   $$\frac{2000\ \Omega}{10} = 200\ \Omega$$

5. Calculate the voltage drops across the three resistors in problem 2, and check to see that their sum equals the voltage of the battery.

$$V = IR = 3\ \text{A}(10\ \Omega + 15\ \Omega + 5\ \Omega)$$
$$= 30\ \text{V} + 45\ \text{V} + 15\ \text{V} = 90\ \text{V}$$
$$= \textbf{voltage of battery}$$

page 537

6. A 20.0-Ω resistor and a 30.0-Ω resistor are connected in series and placed across a 120-V potential difference.

   a. What is the equivalent resistance of the circuit?

   $$R = 20.0\ \Omega + 30.0\ \Omega = 50.0\ \Omega$$

   b. What is the current in the circuit?

   $$I = \frac{V}{R} = \frac{120\ \text{V}}{50.0\ \Omega} = 2.4\ \text{A}$$

   c. What is the voltage drop across each resistor?

   $$V = IR$$

   Across 20.0-Ω resistor,

   $$V = (2.4\ \text{A})(20.0\ \Omega) = 48\ \text{V}$$

   Across 30.0-Ω resistor,

   $$V = (2.4\ \text{A})(30.0\ \Omega) = 72\ \text{V}$$

Copyright © by Glencoe/McGraw-Hill

6. (continued)

    d. What is the voltage drop across the two resistors together?

$$V = 48\ V + 72\ V = 1.20 \times 10^2\ V$$

7. Three resistors of 3.0 kΩ, 5.0 kΩ, and 4.0 kΩ are connected in series across a 12-V battery.

    a. What is the equivalent resistance?

$$R = 3.0\ k\Omega + 5.0\ k\Omega + 4.0\ k\Omega$$
$$= 12.0\ k\Omega$$

    b. What is the current through the resistors?

$$I = \frac{V}{R} = \frac{12\ V}{12.0\ k\Omega}$$
$$= 1.0\ mA = 1.0 \times 10^{-3}\ A$$

    c. What is the voltage drop across each resistor?

$$V = IR$$

    so $V = 3.0\ V,\ 5.0\ V,\ and\ 4.0\ V$

    d. Find the total voltage drop across the three resistors.

$$V = 3.0\ V + 5.0\ V + 4.0\ V = 12.0\ V$$

page 538

8. A photoresistor is used in a voltage divider as R_B. $V = 9.0\ V$ and $R_A = 500\ \Omega$.

    a. What is the output voltage, V_B, across R_B, when a bright light strikes the photoresistor and $R_B = 475\ \Omega$?

$$V_B = \frac{VR_B}{R_A + R_B} = \frac{(9.0\ V)(475\ \Omega)}{500\ \Omega + 475\ \Omega} = 4\ V$$

    b. When the light is dim, $R_B = 4.0\ k\Omega$. What is V_B?

$$V_B = \frac{VR_B}{R_A + R_B} = \frac{(9.0\ V)(4.0\ k\Omega)}{0.5\ k\Omega + 4.0\ k\Omega}$$
$$= 8\ V$$

    c. When the photoresistor is in total darkness, $R_B = 0.40\ M\Omega\ (0.40 \times 10^6\ \Omega)$. What is V_B?

$$V_B = \frac{VR_B}{R_A + R_B}$$
$$= \frac{(9.0\ V)(4.0 \times 10^5\ \Omega)}{0.005 \times 10^5\ \Omega + 4.0 \times 10^5\ \Omega}$$
$$= 9\ V$$

9. A student makes a voltage divider from a 45-V battery, a 475-kΩ ($475 \times 10^3\ \Omega$) resistor, and a 235-kΩ resistor. The output is measured across the smaller resistor. What is the voltage?

$$V_2 = \frac{VR_2}{R_1 + R_2} = \frac{(45\ V)(235\ k\Omega)}{475\ k\Omega + 235\ k\Omega}$$
$$= 15\ V$$

page 540

10. Three 15-Ω resistors are connected in parallel and placed across a 30-V battery.

    a. What is the equivalent resistance of the parallel circuit?

$$\frac{1}{R} = \frac{1}{R_1} + \frac{1}{R_2} + \frac{1}{R_3} = \frac{3}{15\ \Omega}$$
$$R = 5.0\ \Omega$$

    b. What is the current through the entire circuit?

$$I = \frac{V}{R} = \frac{30\ V}{5.0\ \Omega} = 6\ A$$

    c. What is the current through each branch of the circuit?

$$I = \frac{V}{R} = \frac{30\ V}{15.0\ \Omega} = 2\ A$$

11. A 120.0-Ω resistor, a 60.0-Ω resistor, and a 40.0-Ω resistor are connected in parallel and placed across a 12.0-V battery.

    a. What is the equivalent resistance of the parallel circuit?

$$\frac{1}{R} = \frac{1}{120.0\ \Omega} + \frac{1}{60.0\ \Omega} + \frac{1}{40.0\ \Omega}$$
$$R = 20.0\ \Omega$$

    b. What is the current through the entire circuit?

$$I = \frac{V}{R} = \frac{12.0\ V}{20.0\ \Omega} = 0.600\ A$$

Copyright © by Glencoe/McGraw-Hill

11. (continued)

c. What is the current through each branch of the circuit?

$$I_1 = \frac{V}{R_1} = \frac{12.0\ V}{120.0\ \Omega} = 0.100\ A$$

$$I_2 = \frac{V}{R_2} = \frac{12.0\ V}{60.0\ \Omega} = 0.200\ A$$

$$I_3 = \frac{V}{R_3} = \frac{12.0\ V}{40.0\ \Omega} = 0.300\ A$$

12. Suppose one of the 15.0-Ω resistors in problem 10 is replaced by a 10.0-Ω resistor.

a. Does the equivalent resistance change? If so, how?

Yes, smaller

page 541

b. Does the amount of current through the entire circuit change? In what way?

Yes, gets larger

c. Does the amount of current through the other 15.0-Ω resistors change? In what way?

No, it remains the same. Currents are independent.

23.2 Applications of Circuits
pages 542–548

page 547

13. Two 60-Ω resistors are connected in parallel. This parallel arrangement is connected in series with a 30-Ω resistor. The combination is then placed across a 120-V battery.

a. Draw a diagram of the circuit.

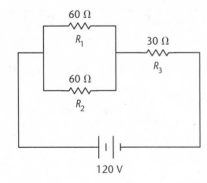

b. What is the equivalent resistance of the parallel portion of the circuit?

$$\frac{1}{R} = \frac{1}{60\ \Omega} + \frac{1}{60\ \Omega} = \frac{2}{60\ \Omega}$$

$$R = \frac{60\ \Omega}{2} = 30\ \Omega$$

c. What single resistance could replace the three original resistors?

$$R_E = 30\ \Omega + 30\ \Omega = 60\ \Omega$$

d. What is the current in the circuit?

$$I = \frac{V}{R} = \frac{120\ V}{60\ \Omega} = 2\ A$$

e. What is the voltage drop across the 30-Ω resistor?

$$V_3 = IR_3 = (2\ A)(30\ \Omega) = 60\ V$$

f. What is the voltage drop across the parallel portion of the circuit?

$$V = IR = (2\ A)(30\ \Omega) = 60\ V$$

g. What is the current in each branch of the parallel portion of the circuit?

$$I = \frac{V}{R_1} = \frac{V}{R_2} = \frac{60V}{60\ \Omega} = 1\ A$$

Chapter Review Problems
pages 551–553
page 551
Section 23.1

Level 1

21. A 20.0-Ω lamp and a 5.0-Ω lamp are connected in series and placed across a potential difference of 50.0 V. What is

a. the equivalent resistance of the circuit?

$$20.0\ \Omega + 5.0\ \Omega = 25.0\ \Omega$$

b. the current in the circuit?

$$I = \frac{V}{R} = \frac{50.0\ V}{25.0\ \Omega} = 2.00\ A$$

c. the voltage drop across each lamp?

$$V = IR = (2.00\ A)(20.0\ \Omega)$$
$$= 4.00 \times 10^1\ V$$

$$V = IR = (2.00\ A)(5.0\ \Omega) = 1.0 \times 10^1\ V$$

Copyright © by Glencoe/McGraw-Hill

21. (continued)

d. the power dissipated in each lamp?

$$P = IV = (2.00 \text{ A})(4.00 \times 10^1 \text{ V})$$
$$= 8.00 \times 10^1 \text{ W}$$
$$P = IV = (2.00 \text{ A})(1.0 \times 10^1 \text{ V})$$
$$= 2.0 \times 10^1 \text{ W}$$

22. The load across a battery consists of two resistors, with values of 15 Ω and 45 Ω, connected in series.

a. What is the total resistance of the load?

$$R = R_1 + R_2 = 15 \text{ Ω} + 45 \text{ Ω}$$
$$= 6.0 \times 10^1 \text{ Ω}$$

b. What is the voltage of the battery if the current in the circuit is 0.10 A?

$$V = IR = (6.0 \times 10^1 \text{ Ω})(0.10 \text{ A}) = 6.0 \text{ V}$$

23. A lamp having resistance of 10.0 Ω is connected across a 15-V battery.

a. What is the current through the lamp?

$$V = IR$$

So $$I = \frac{V}{R} = \frac{15 \text{ V}}{10.0 \text{ Ω}} = 1.5 \text{ A}$$

b. What resistance must be connected in series with the lamp to reduce the current to 0.50 A?

$$V = IR$$

So the total resistance is given by

$$R = \frac{V}{I} = \frac{15 \text{ V}}{0.50 \text{ A}} = 3.0 \times 10^1 \text{ Ω}$$

And $R = R_1 + R_2$

So $R_2 = R - R_1 = 3.0 \times 10^1 - 1.00 \times 10^1 \text{ Ω} = 2.0 \times 10^1 \text{ Ω}$

page 552

24. A string of 18 identical holiday tree lights is connected in series to a 120-V source. The string dissipates 64.0 W.

a. What is the equivalent resistance of the light string?

$$P = IV, \text{ so}$$

$$I = \frac{P}{V} = \frac{64 \text{ W}}{120 \text{ V}} = 0.53 \text{ A}$$

and $V = IR$, so

$$R = \frac{V}{I} = \frac{120 \text{ V}}{0.53 \text{ A}} = 2.3 \times 10^2 \text{ Ω}$$

b. What is the resistance of a single light?

R is sum of resistances of 18 lamps, so each resistance is

$$\frac{2.3 \times 10^2 \text{ Ω}}{18} = 13 \text{ Ω}$$

c. What power is dissipated by each lamp?

$$\frac{64 \text{ W}}{18} = 3.6 \text{ W}$$

25. One of the bulbs in problem 24 burns out. The lamp has a wire that shorts out the lamp filament when it burns out. This drops the resistance of the lamp to zero.

a. What is the resistance of the light string now?

There are now 17 lamps in series instead of 18 lamps. The resistance is

$$\frac{17}{18}(2.3 \times 10^2 \text{ Ω}) = 2.2 \times 10^2 \text{ Ω}$$

b. Find the power dissipated by the string.

$$I = \frac{V}{R} = \frac{120 \text{ V}}{2.2 \times 10^2 \text{ Ω}} = 0.55 \text{ A}$$

and $P = IV = (0.55 \text{ A})(120 \text{ V}) = 66 \text{ W}$

c. Did the power go up or down when a bulb burned out?

It increased!

26. A 75.0-W bulb is connected to a 120-V source.

a. What is the current through the bulb?

$$P = IV$$

so $I = \frac{P}{V} = \frac{75.0 \text{ W}}{120 \text{ V}} = 0.63 \text{ A}$

b. What is the resistance of the bulb?

$$V = IR$$

so $R = \frac{V}{I} = \frac{120 \text{ V}}{0.625 \text{ A}} = 190 \text{ Ω}$

c. A lamp dimmer puts a resistance in series with the bulb. What resistance would be needed to reduce the current to 0.300 A?

$$V = IR$$

so $R = \frac{V}{I} = \frac{120 \text{ V}}{0.300 \text{ A}} = 4.0 \times 10^2 \text{ Ω}$

and $R = R_1 + R_2$, so

$$R_2 = R - R_1 = 4.0 \times 10^2 \text{ Ω} - 1.9 \times 10^2 \text{ Ω} = 2.1 \times 10^2 \text{ Ω} \text{ or } 210 \text{ Ω}$$

Copyright © by Glencoe/McGraw-Hill

27. In problem 26, you found the resistance of a lamp and a dimmer resistor.

    a. Assuming that the resistances are constant, find the voltage drops across the lamp and the resistor.

$$\Delta V = IR = (0.300 \text{ A})(190 \ \Omega) = 57 \text{ V}$$

$$\Delta V = IR = (0.300 \text{ A})(210 \ \Omega) = 63 \text{ V}$$

    b. Find the power dissipated by the lamp.

$$P = IV = (0.300 \text{ A})(57 \text{ V}) = 17 \text{ W}$$

    c. Find the power dissipated by the dimmer resistor.

$$P = IV = (0.300 \text{ A})(63 \text{ V}) = 19 \text{ W}$$

28. A 16.0-Ω and a 20.0-Ω resistor are connected in parallel. A difference in potential of 40.0 V is applied to the combination.

    a. Compute the equivalent resistance of the parallel circuit.

$$\frac{1}{R} = \frac{1}{R_1} + \frac{1}{R_2} = \frac{1}{16.0 \ \Omega} + \frac{1}{20.0 \ \Omega}$$

$$R = \frac{1}{0.1125 \ \Omega} = 8.89 \ \Omega$$

    b. What is the current in the circuit?

$$I = \frac{V}{R} = \frac{40.0 \text{ V}}{8.89 \ \Omega} = 4.50 \text{ A}$$

    c. How large is the current through the 16.0-Ω resistor?

$$I_1 = \frac{V}{R_1} = \frac{40.0 \text{ V}}{16.0 \ \Omega} = 2.50 \text{ A}$$

Level 2

29. Amy needs 5.0 V for some integrated circuit experiments. She uses a 6.0-V battery and two resistors to make a voltage divider. One resistor is 330 Ω. She decides to make the other resistor smaller. What value should it have?

$$V_2 = \frac{VR_2}{R_1 + R_2}$$

$$R_1 = \frac{VR_2}{V_2} - R_2$$

$$= \frac{(6.0 \text{ V})(330 \ \Omega)}{5.0 \text{ V}} - 330 \ \Omega = 66 \ \Omega$$

30. Pete is designing a voltage divider using a 12.0-V battery and a 100.0-Ω resistor as R_B. What resistor should be used as R_A if the output voltage across R_B is to be 4.00 V?

$$V_B = \frac{VR_B}{R_A + R_B}$$

$$\text{or } R_A + R_B = \frac{VR_B}{V_B}$$

$$\text{so } R_A = \frac{VR_B}{V_B} - R_B$$

$$= \frac{(12.0 \text{ V})(100.0 \ \Omega)}{400 \text{ V}} - 100.0 \ \Omega$$

$$= 2.00 \times 10^2 \ \Omega$$

31. A typical television dissipates 275 W when it is plugged into a 120-V outlet.

    a. Find the resistance of the television.

$$P = IV \text{ and } I = \frac{V}{R}, \text{ so } P = \frac{V^2}{R}, \text{ or}$$

$$R = \frac{V^2}{P} = \frac{(120 \text{ V})^2}{275 \text{ W}} = 52 \ \Omega$$

    b. The television and 2.5-Ω wires connecting the outlet to the fuse form a series circuit that works like a voltage divider. Find the voltage drop across the television.

$$V_1 = \frac{VR_1}{R_1 + R_2} = \frac{(120 \text{ V})(52 \ \Omega)}{52 \ \Omega + 2.5 \ \Omega} = 110 \text{ V}$$

    c. A 12-Ω hair dryer is plugged into the same outlet. Find the equivalent resistance of the two appliances.

$$\frac{1}{R} = \frac{1}{R_1} + \frac{1}{R_2} = \frac{1}{52 \ \Omega} + \frac{1}{12 \ \Omega}$$

$$R = 9.8 \ \Omega$$

    d. Find the voltage drop across the television and hair dryer. The lower voltage explains why the television picture sometimes shrinks when another appliance is turned on.

$$V_1 = \frac{VR_1}{R_1 + R_2} = \frac{(120 \text{ V})(9.8 \ \Omega)}{9.8 \ \Omega + 2.5 \ \Omega} = 96 \text{ V}$$

Copyright © by Glencoe/McGraw-Hill

Section 23.2

Level 1

32. A circuit contains six 240-Ω lamps (60-W bulbs) and a 10.0-Ω heater connected in parallel. The voltage across the circuit is 120 V. What is the current in the circuit

a. when four lamps are turned on?

$$\frac{1}{R} = \frac{1}{R_1} + \frac{1}{R_2} + \frac{1}{R_3} + \frac{1}{R_4}$$

$$= \frac{1}{240\ \Omega} + \frac{1}{240\ \Omega} + \frac{1}{240\ \Omega} + \frac{1}{240\ \Omega}$$

$$= \frac{4}{240\ \Omega}$$

so $R = \dfrac{240\ \Omega}{4} = 60\ \Omega$

$I = \dfrac{V}{R} = \dfrac{120\ \text{V}}{60\ \Omega} = 2.0\ \text{A}$

b. when all lamps are on?

$$\frac{1}{R} = \frac{6}{240\ \Omega}$$

$$R = \frac{240\ \Omega}{6} = 4.0 \times 10^1\ \Omega$$

$$I = \frac{V}{R} = \frac{120\ \text{V}}{4.0 \times 10^1\ \Omega} = 3.0\ \text{A}$$

c. when six lamps and the heater are operating?

$$\frac{1}{R} = \frac{1}{4.0 \times 10^1\ \Omega} + \frac{1}{10.0\ \Omega}$$

$$= \frac{5}{4.0 \times 10^1\ \Omega}$$

$$R = \frac{4.0 \times 10^1\ \Omega}{5} = 8.0\ \Omega$$

$$I = \frac{V}{R} = \frac{120\ \text{V}}{8.0\ \Omega} = 15\ \text{A}$$

33. If the circuit in problem 32 has a fuse rated at 12 A, will it melt if everything is on?

Yes. The 15-A current will melt the 12-A fuse.

34. Determine the reading of each ammeter and each voltmeter in **Figure 23-15.**

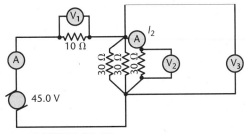

FIGURE 23-15

Physics: Principles and Problems

The three resistors in parallel have a total resistance of

$$\frac{1}{R_E} = \frac{1}{R_2} + \frac{1}{R_3} + \frac{1}{R_4}$$

$$= \frac{1}{30.0\ \Omega} + \frac{1}{30.0\ \Omega} + \frac{1}{30.0\ \Omega}$$

so $R_E = 10.0\ \Omega$

The total resistance of the circuit is

$R_T = R_1 + R_E = 10.0\ \Omega + 10.0\ \Omega$

$\quad = 20.0\ \Omega$

$I_1 = \dfrac{V}{R_T} = \dfrac{45.0\ \text{V}}{20.0\ \Omega} = 2.25\ \text{A}$

$V_1 = IR_1 = (2.25\ \text{A})(10.0\ \Omega) = 22.5\ \text{V}$

Because the ammeter has an internal resistance of almost zero,

$V_2 = V_3 = 45.0\ \text{V} - V_1$

$\quad = 45.0\ \text{V} - 22.5\ \text{V} = 22.5\ \text{V}$

$I_2 = \dfrac{V_2}{R_2} = \dfrac{22.5\ \text{V}}{30.0\ \Omega} = 0.750\ \text{A}$

35. Determine the power used by each resistance shown in **Figure 23-15.**

Some information is from the previous problem. See figure from Problem 34.

In the 10.0 Ω resistor,

$P_1 = I_1 V_1 = (2.25\ \text{A})(22.5\ \text{V}) = 50.6\ \text{W}$

In each of the 30-Ω resistors the power will be equal to

$P = IV = (0.750\ \text{A})(22.5\ \text{V}) = 16.9\ \text{W}$

Level 2

36. During a laboratory exercise, you are supplied with a battery of potential difference V, two heating elements of low resistance that can be placed in water, an ammeter of very small resistance, a voltmeter of extremely high resistance, wires of negligible resistance, a beaker that is well insulated and has negligible heat capacity, and 100.0 g of water at 25°C.

Copyright © by Glencoe/McGraw-Hill

36. (continued)

a. By means of a diagram and standard symbols, show how these components should be connected to heat the water as rapidly as possible.

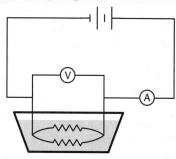

page 553

b. If the voltmeter reading holds steady at 50.0 V and the ammeter reading holds steady at 5.0 A, estimate the time in seconds required to completely vaporize the water in the beaker. Use 4200 J/kg · °C as the specific heat of water and 2.3 × 10⁶ J/kg as the heat of vaporization of water.

$\Delta Q = mC\,\Delta T$

$\quad = (100.0\text{ g})(4.2\text{ J/g} \cdot {}°\text{C})(75°\text{C})$

$\quad = 31\ 500\text{ J}$

$\Delta Q = mH_v = (100.0\text{ g})(2300\text{ J/g})$

$\quad = 230\ 000\text{ J}$

$\Delta Q_{total} = 31\ 500\text{ J} + 230\ 000\text{ J}$

$\quad\quad = 261\ 500\text{ J}$

Energy is provided at the rate of

$P = IV = (5.0\text{ A})(50.0\text{ V}) = 250\text{ J/s}$

The time required is

$t = \dfrac{261\ 500\text{ J}}{250\text{ J/s}} = 1.0 \times 10^3\text{ s}$

37. A typical home circuit is diagrammed in **Figure 23-16.** The lead lines to the kitchen lamp each has a very low resistance of 0.25 Ω. The lamp has a resistance of 240.0 Ω. Although the circuit is a parallel circuit, the lead lines are in series with each of the components of the circuit.

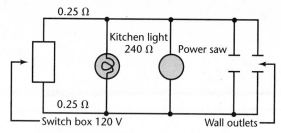

FIGURE 23-16

a. Compute the equivalent resistance of the circuit consisting of just the light and the lead lines to and from the light.

$R = 0.25\ \Omega + 0.25\ \Omega + 240\ \Omega = 240\ \Omega$

b. Find the current to the bulb.

$I = \dfrac{V}{R} = \dfrac{120\text{ V}}{240\ \Omega} = 0.50\text{ A}$

c. Find the power dissipated in the bulb.

$P = IV = (0.50\text{ A})(120\text{ V}) = 6.0 \times 10^1\text{ W}$

38. A power saw is operated by an electric motor. When electric motors are first turned on, they have a very low resistance. Suppose that a kitchen light in problem 37 is on and a power saw is turned on. The saw and lead lines have an initial total resistance of 6.0 Ω.

a. Compute the equivalent resistance of the light-saw parallel circuit.

$\dfrac{1}{R} = \dfrac{1}{240.5\ \Omega} + \dfrac{1}{6.0\ \Omega}$

$R = 5.9\ \Omega$

b. What is the total current flowing in the circuit?

$I = \dfrac{V}{R} = \dfrac{120\text{ V}}{5.9\ \Omega} = 21\text{ A}$

c. What is the total voltage drop across the two leads to the light?

$V = IR = (21\text{ A})(0.50\ \Omega) = 11\text{ V}$

d. What voltage remains to operate the light? Will this cause the light to dim temporarily?

$V = 120\text{ V} - 11\text{ V} = 110\text{ V}$

Yes, this will cause a momentary dimming.

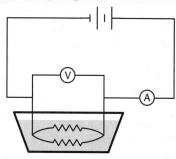

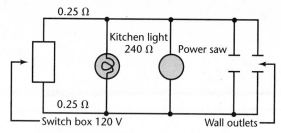

Physics: Principles and Problems

Copyright © by Glencoe/McGraw-Hill

Critical Thinking Problems

39. A 50-200-250-W three-way bulb has three terminals on its base. Sketch how these terminals could be connected inside the bulb to provide the three brightnesses. Explain how to connect 120 V across two terminals at a time to obtain a low, medium, and high level of brightness.

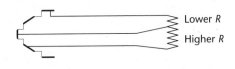

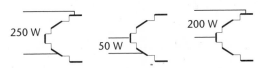

40. Batteries consist of an ideal source of potential difference in series with a small resistance. The electrical energy of the battery is produced by chemical reactions that occur in the battery. However, these reactions also result in a small resistance that, unfortunately, cannot be completely eliminated. A flashlight contains two batteries in series. Each has a potential difference of 1.50 V and an internal resistance of 0.200 Ω. The bulb has a resistance of 22.0 Ω.

a. What is the current through the bulb?

Circuit has two 1.50-V batteries in series with three resistors: 0.20 Ω, 0.20 Ω, and 22.0 Ω. The equivalent resistance is 22.4 Ω. The current is

$$I = \frac{V}{R} = \frac{2(1.50)\ V}{[2(0.20) + 22.0]\ \Omega}$$

$$= \frac{3.00\ V}{22.4\ \Omega} = 0.134\ A$$

b. How much power does the bulb dissipate?

The power dissipated is

$$P = I^2 R$$

$$= (0.134\ A)^2 (22.0\ \Omega)$$

$$= 0.395\ W$$

c. How much greater would the power be if the batteries had no internal resistance?

Without the internal resistance of the batteries,

$$P = IV = \frac{V^2}{R} = \frac{(3.00\ V)^2}{22.0\ \Omega} = 0.409\ W$$

Copyright © by Glencoe/McGraw-Hill

24 Magnetic Fields

Practice Problems

24.1 Magnets: Permanent and Temporary
pages 556–566

page 560

1. If you hold a bar magnet in each hand and bring your hands close together, will the force be attractive or repulsive if the magnets are held so that

   a. the two north poles are brought close together?

   repulsive

   b. a north pole and a south pole are brought together?

   attractive

2. **Figure 24–7** shows five disk magnets floating above each other. The north pole of the top-most disk faces up. Which poles are on the top side of the other magnets?

   south, north, south, north

3. A magnet attracts a nail, which, in turn, attracts many small tacks, as shown in **Figure 24–3.** If the N-pole of the permanent magnet is the top face, which end of the nail is the N-pole?

   the bottom (the point)

page 563

4. A long, straight, current-carrying wire runs from north to south.

   a. A compass needle placed above the wire points with its N-pole toward the east. In what direction is the current flowing?

   from south to north

   b. If a compass is put underneath the wire, in which direction will the compass needle point?

   west

5. How does the strength of the magnetic field 1 cm from a current-carrying wire compare with

   a. the strength of the field 2 cm from the wire?

   Because magnetic field strength varies inversely with the distance from the wire, it will be half as strong.

   b. the strength of the field 3 cm from the wire?

   It is one-third as strong.

6. A student makes a magnet by winding wire around a nail and connecting it to a battery, as shown in **Figure 24–13.** Which end of the nail, the pointed end or the head, will be the north pole?

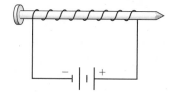

   FIGURE 24–13

   the pointed end

24.2 Forces Caused by Magnetic Fields
pages 567–574

page 569

7. A wire 0.50 m long carrying a current of 8.0 A is at right angles to a 0.40-T magnetic field. How strong a force acts on the wire?

$$F = BIL = (0.40 \text{ N/A} \cdot \text{m})(8.0 \text{ A})(0.50 \text{ m})$$
$$= 1.6 \text{ N}$$

Copyright © by Glencoe/McGraw-Hill

8. A wire 75 cm long carrying a current of 6.0 A is at right angles to a uniform magnetic field. The magnitude of the force acting on the wire is 0.60 N. What is the strength of the magnetic field?

$$B = \frac{F}{IL} = \frac{0.60 \text{ N}}{(6.0 \text{ A})(0.75 \text{ m})} = 0.13 \text{ T}$$

9. A copper wire 40 cm long carries a current of 6.0 A and weighs 0.35 N. A certain magnetic field is strong enough to balance the force of gravity on the wire. What is the strength of the magnetic field?

F = BIL, F = weight of wire.

$$B = \frac{F}{IL} = \frac{0.35 \text{ N}}{(6.0 \text{ A})(0.4 \text{ m})} = 0.1 \text{ T}$$

page 574

10. An electron passes through a magnetic field at right angles to the field at a velocity of 4.0×10^6 m/s. The strength of the magnetic field is 0.50 T. What is the magnitude of the force acting on the electron?

F = Bqv

$$= (0.50 \text{ T})(1.6 \times 10^{-19} \text{ C})(4.0 \times 10^6 \text{ m/s})$$

$$= 3.2 \times 10^{-13} \text{ N}$$

11. A stream of doubly ionized particles (missing two electrons and thus carrying a net charge of two elementary charges) moves at a velocity of 3.0×10^4 m/s perpendicular to a magnetic field of 9.0×10^{-2} T. What is the magnitude of the force acting on each ion?

F = Bqv

$$= (9.0 \times 10^{-2} \text{ T})(2)(1.60 \times 10^{-19} \text{ C})$$

$$\times (3.0 \times 10^4 \text{ m/s})$$

$$= 8.6 \times 10^{-16} \text{ N}$$

12. Triply ionized particles in a beam carry a net positive charge of three elementary charge units. The beam enters a magnetic field of 4.0×10^{-2} T. The particles have a speed of 9.0×10^6 m/s. What is the magnitude of the force acting on each particle?

F = Bqv

$$= (4.0 \times 10^{-2} \text{ T})(3)(1.60 \times 10^{-19} \text{ C})$$

$$\times (9.0 \times 10^6 \text{ m/s})$$

$$= 1.7 \times 10^{-13} \text{ N}$$

13. Doubly ionized helium atoms (alpha particles) are traveling at right angles to a magnetic field at a speed of 4.0×10^{-2} m/s. The field strength is 5.0×10^{-2} T. What force acts on each particle?

F = Bqv

$$= (5.0 \times 10^{-2} \text{ T})(2)(1.60 \times 10^{-19} \text{ C})$$

$$\times (4.0 \times 10^{-2} \text{ m/s})$$

$$= 6.4 \times 10^{-22} \text{ N}$$

Chapter Review Problems

pages 576–579

page 576

Section 24.1

Level 1

27. A wire 1.50 m long carrying a current of 10.0 A is at right angles to a uniform magnetic field. The force acting on the wire is 0.60 N. What is the strength of the magnetic field?

F = BIL, so

$$B = \frac{F}{IL} = \frac{0.60 \text{ N}}{10.0 \text{ A} \times 1.50 \text{ m}}$$

$$= 0.040 \text{ N/A} \cdot \text{m}$$

$$= 0.040 \text{ T}$$

28. A conventional current is in a wire as shown in **Figure 24–24**. Copy the wire segment and sketch the magnetic field that the current generates.

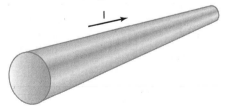

FIGURE 24–24

28. (continued)

page 577

29. The current is coming straight out of the page in **Figure 24–25.** Copy the figure and sketch the magnetic field that the current generates.

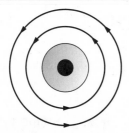

FIGURE 24–25

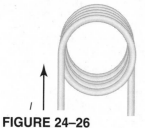

30. Figure 24–26 shows the end view of an electromagnet with the current as shown.

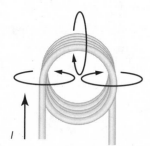

FIGURE 24–26

a. What is the direction of the magnetic field inside the loop?

down

b. What is the direction of the magnetic field outside the loop?

up (out of the page)

Level 2

31. The repulsive force between two ceramic magnets was measured and found to depend on distance, as given in **Table 24–2.**

TABLE 24-2	
Separation, d (mm)	Force, F (N)
10	3.93
12	0.40
14	0.13
16	0.057
18	0.030
20	0.018
22	0.011
24	0.0076
26	0.0053
28	0.0038
30	0.0028

a. Plot the force as a function of distance.

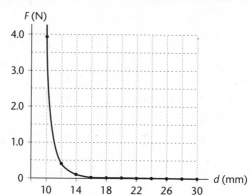

b. Does this force follow an inverse square law?

No.

Copyright © by Glencoe/McGraw-Hill

Section 24.2

Level 1

32. A current-carrying wire is placed between the poles of a magnet, as shown in **Figure 24–27**. What is the direction of the force on the wire?

FIGURE 24–27

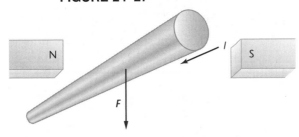

33. A wire 0.50 m long carrying a current of 8.0 A is at right angles to a uniform magnetic field. The force on the wire is 0.40 N. What is the strength of the magnetic field?

$F = BIL$, so

$$B = \frac{F}{IL} = \frac{0.40 \text{ N}}{8.0 \text{ A} \times 0.50 \text{ m}}$$

$$= 0.10 \text{ N/A} \cdot \text{m} = 0.10 \text{ T}$$

34. The current through a wire 0.80 m long is 5.0 A. The wire is perpendicular to a 0.60-T magnetic field. What is the magnitude of the force on the wire?

$F = BIL$

$$= (0.60 \text{ N/A} \cdot \text{m})(5.0 \text{ A})(0.80 \text{ m})$$

$$= 2.4 \text{ N}$$

35. A wire 25 cm long is at right angles to a 0.30-T uniform magnetic field. The current through the wire is 6.0 A. What is the magnitude of the force on the wire?

$F = BIL$

$$= (0.30 \text{ N/A} \cdot \text{m})(6.0 \text{ A})(0.25 \text{ m})$$

$$= 0.45 \text{ N}$$

36. A wire 35 cm long is parallel to a 0.53-T uniform magnetic field. The current through the wire is 4.5 A. What force acts on the wire?

If the wire is parallel to the field, no cutting is taking place, so no force is produced.

37. A wire 625 m long is in a 0.40-T magnetic field. A 1.8-N force acts on the wire. What current is in the wire?

$F = BIL$, so

$$I = \frac{F}{BL} = \frac{1.8 \text{ N}}{(0.40 \text{ T})(625 \text{ m})} = 0.0072 \text{ A}$$

$$= 7.2 \text{ mA}$$

38. The force on a 0.80-m wire that is perpendicular to Earth's magnetic field is 0.12 N. What is the current in the wire?

$F = BIL$, so

$$I = \frac{F}{BL} = \frac{0.12 \text{ N}}{(5.0 \times 10^{-5} \text{ T})(0.80 \text{ m})}$$

$$= 3.0 \times 10^3 \text{ A} = 3.0 \text{ kA}$$

39. The force acting on a wire at right angles to a 0.80-T magnetic field is 3.6 N. The current in the wire is 7.5 A. How long is the wire?

$F = BIL$, so

$$L = \frac{F}{BI} = \frac{3.6 \text{ N}}{(0.80 \text{ T})(7.5 \text{ A})} = 0.60 \text{ m}$$

40. A power line carries a 225-A current from east to west parallel to the surface of Earth.

a. What is the magnitude of the force resulting from Earth's magnetic field acting on each meter of the wire?

$F = BIL$, so

$$\frac{F}{L} = IB = (225 \text{ A})(5.0 \times 10^{-5} \text{ T})$$

$$= 0.011 \text{ N/m}$$

b. What is the direction of the force?

The force would be south.

Copyright © by Glencoe/McGraw-Hill

40. (continued)

c. In your judgment, would this force be important in designing towers to hold these power lines?

No; the force is much smaller than the weight of the wires.

page 578

41. A galvanometer deflects full-scale for a 50.0-μA current.

a. What must be the total resistance of the series resistor and the galvanometer to make a voltmeter with 10.0-V full-scale deflection?

$V = IR$, so

$$R = \frac{V}{I} = \frac{10.0 \text{ V}}{50.0 \times 10^{-6} \text{ A}}$$

$$= 2.00 \times 10^5 \, \Omega = 2.00 \times 10^2 \text{ k}\Omega$$

b. If the galvanometer has a resistance of 1.0 kΩ, what should be the resistance of the series (multiplier) resistor?

Total resistance = 2.00×10^2 kΩ, so series resistor is

$$2.00 \times 10^2 \text{ k}\Omega - 1.0 \text{ k}\Omega = 199 \text{ k}\Omega$$

42. The galvanometer in problem 41 is used to make an ammeter that deflects full-scale for 10 mA.

a. What is the potential difference across the galvanometer (1.0 kΩ resistance) when a current of 50 μA passes through it?

$$V = IR = (50 \times 10^{-6} \text{ A})(1.0 \times 10^3 \, \Omega)$$

$$= 0.05 \text{ V}$$

b. What is the equivalent resistance of parallel resistors that have the potential difference calculated in **a** for a circuit with a total current of 10 mA?

$V = IR$, so

$$R = \frac{V}{I} = \frac{5 \times 10^{-2} \text{ V}}{1 \times 10^{-2} \text{ A}} = 5 \, \Omega$$

c. What resistor should be placed in parallel with the galvanometer to make the resistance calculated in **b**?

$$\frac{1}{R} = \frac{1}{R_1} + \frac{1}{R_2}$$

so $$\frac{1}{R_1} = \frac{1}{R} - \frac{1}{R_2}$$

$$= \frac{1}{5 \, \Omega} - \frac{1}{1.0 \times 10^3 \, \Omega}$$

so $R_1 = 5 \, \Omega$

43. A beam of electrons moves at right angles to a magnetic field 6.0×10^{-2} T. The electrons have a velocity of 2.5×10^6 m/s. What is the magnitude of the force on each electron?

$F = Bqv$

$$= (6.0 \times 10^{-2} \text{ T})(1.6 \times 10^{-19} \text{ C})$$

$$\times (2.5 \times 10^6 \text{ m/s})$$

$$= 2.4 \times 10^{-14} \text{ N}$$

44. A beta particle (high-speed electron) is traveling at right angles to a 0.60-T magnetic field. It has a speed of 2.5×10^7 m/s. What size force acts on the particle?

$F = Bqv$

$$= (0.60 \text{ T})(1.6 \times 10^{-19} \text{ C})$$

$$\times (2.5 \times 10^7 \text{ m/s})$$

$$= 2.4 \times 10^{-12} \text{ N}$$

45. The mass of an electron is 9.11×10^{-31} kg. What is the acceleration of the beta particle described in problem 44?

$F = ma$, so

$$a = \frac{F}{m} = \frac{2.4 \times 10^{-12} \text{ N}}{9.11 \times 10^{-31} \text{ kg}}$$

$$= 2.6 \times 10^{18} \text{ m/s}^2$$

46. A magnetic field of 16 T acts in a direction due west. An electron is traveling due south at 8.1×10^5 m/s. What are the magnitude and direction of the force acting on the electron?

$F = Bqv$

$$= (16 \text{ T})(1.6 \times 10^{-19} \text{ C})$$

$$\times (8.1 \times 10^5 \text{ m/s})$$

$$= 2.1 \times 10^{-12} \text{ N, upward (right-hand rule—remembering that electron flow is opposite to current flow)}$$

Copyright © by Glencoe/McGraw-Hill

47. A muon (a particle with the same charge as an electron) is traveling at 4.21×10^7 m/s at right angles to a magnetic field. The muon experiences a force of 5.00×10^{-12} N. How strong is the field?

$F = Bqv$, so

$$B = \frac{F}{qv}$$

$$= \frac{5.00 \times 10^{-12} \text{ N}}{(4.21 \times 10^7 \text{ m/s})(1.60 \times 10^{-19} \text{ C})}$$

$$= 0.742 \text{ T}$$

48. The mass of a muon is 1.88×10^{-28} kg. What acceleration does the muon described in problem 47 experience?

$F = ma$, so

$$a = \frac{F}{m} = \frac{5.00 \times 10^{-12} \text{ N}}{1.88 \times 10^{-28} \text{ kg}}$$

$$= 2.66 \times 10^{16} \text{ m/s}^2$$

49. A singly ionized particle experiences a force of 4.1×10^{-13} N when it travels at right angles through a 0.61-T magnetic field. What is the velocity of the particle?

$F = Bqv$, so

$$v = \frac{F}{Bq} = \frac{4.1 \times 10^{-13} \text{ N}}{(0.61 \text{ T})(1.6 \times 10^{-19} \text{ C})}$$

$$= 4.2 \times 10^6 \text{ m/s}$$

Level 2

50. A room contains a strong, uniform magnetic field. A loop of fine wire in the room has current flowing through it. Assuming you rotate the loop until there is no tendency for it to rotate as a result of the field, what is the direction of the magnetic field relative to the plane of the coil?

The magnetic field is perpendicular to the plane of the coil. The right-hand rule would be used to find the direction of the field produced by the coil. The field in the room is in the same direction.

51. The magnetic field in a loudspeaker is 0.15 T. The wire consists of 250 turns wound on a 2.5-cm diameter cylindrical form. The resistance of the wire is 8.0 Ω. Find the force exerted on the wire when 15 V is placed across the wire.

$$I = \frac{V}{R}$$

L = (# of turns)(circumference) = $n\pi d$

$F = BIL$

$$F = \frac{BVn\pi d}{R}$$

$$= \frac{(0.15 \text{ T})(15 \text{ V})(250)(\pi)(0.025 \text{ m})}{8.0 \text{ }\Omega}$$

$$= 5.5 \text{ N}$$

52. A wire carrying 15 A of current has a length of 25 cm in a magnetic field of 0.85 T. The force on a current-carrying wire in a uniform magnetic field can be found using the equation $F = BIL \sin \theta$. Find the force on the wire if it makes an angle with the magnetic field lines of

a. 90°.

$F = BIL \sin \theta$

$= (0.85 \text{ T})(15 \text{ A})(0.25 \text{ m})(\sin 90°)$

$= 3.2 \text{ N}$

b. 45°.

$F = BIL \sin \theta$

$= (0.85 \text{ T})(15 \text{ A})(0.25 \text{ m})(\sin 45°)$

$= 2.3 \text{ N}$

c. 0°.

$\sin 0° = 0$

so $F = 0 \text{ N}$

53. An electron is accelerated from rest through a potential difference of 20 000 V, which exists between plates P_1 and P_2, shown in **Figure 24–28**. The electron then passes through a small opening into a magnetic field of uniform field strength, B. As indicated, the magnetic field is directed into the page.

Copyright © by Glencoe/McGraw-Hill

53. (continued)

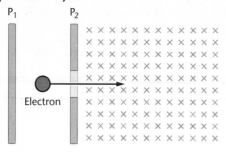

FIGURE 24-28

a. State the direction of the electric field between the plates as either P_1 to P_2 or P_2 to P_1.

from P_2 to P_1

b. In terms of the information given, calculate the electron's speed at plate P_2.

$E = (20\ 000\ \text{J/C})(1.6 \times 10^{-19}\ \text{C})$

$= 3.2 \times 10^{-15}\ \text{J}$

$E = \dfrac{1}{2}\, mv^2$

so $v = \sqrt{\dfrac{2E}{m}} = \sqrt{\dfrac{(2)(3.2 \times 10^{-15}\ \text{J})}{9.11 \times 10^{-31}\ \text{kg}}}$

$= 8 \times 10^7\ \text{m/s}$

c. Describe the motion of the electron through the magnetic field.

clockwise

54. A force of 5.78×10^{-16} N acts on an unknown particle traveling at a 90° angle through a magnetic field. If the velocity of the particle is 5.65×10^4 m/s and the field is 3.20×10^{-2} T, how many elementary charges does the particle carry?

$F = Bqv$, so

$q = \dfrac{F}{Bv}$

$= \dfrac{5.78 \times 10^{-16}\ \text{N}}{(3.20 \times 10^{-2}\ \text{T})(5.65 \times 10^4\ \text{m/s})}$

$= 3.20 \times 10^{-19}\ \text{C}$

$(3.20 \times 10^{-19}\ \text{C})\left(\dfrac{e}{1.60 \times 10^{-19}\ \text{C}}\right)$

$= \textbf{2 charges}$

page 579

Critical Thinking Problems

55. A current is sent through a vertical spring as shown in **Figure 24-29**. The end of the spring is in a cup filled with mercury. What will happen? Why?

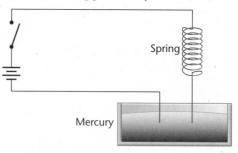

FIGURE 24-29

When the current passes through the coil, the magnetic field increases and the spring compresses. The wire comes out of the mercury, the circuit opens, the magnetic field decreases, and the spring drops down. The spring will oscillate up and down.

56. The magnetic field produced by a long, current-carrying wire is represented by $B = 2 \times 10^{-7}\ (\text{T} \cdot \text{m/A})\ I/d$, where B is the field strength in teslas, I is the current in amps, and d is the distance from the wire in meters. Use this equation to estimate some magnetic fields that you encounter in everyday life.

a. The wiring in your home seldom carries more than 10 A. How does the field 0.5 m from such a wire compare to Earth's magnetic field?

$I = 10\ \text{A},\ d = 0.5\ \text{m}$, so

$B = \dfrac{(2 \times 10^{-7}\ \text{T} \cdot \text{m/A})\ I}{d}$

$= \dfrac{(2 \times 10^{-7}\ \text{T} \cdot \text{m/A})(10\ \text{A})}{0.5\ \text{m}}$

$= 4 \times 10^{-6}\ \text{T}$

Earth's field is 5×10^{-5} T, so Earth's field is 12.5 times stronger than that of the wire.

Copyright © by Glencoe/McGraw-Hill

56. (continued)

    b. High-voltage power transmission lines often carry 200 A at voltages as high as 765 kV. Estimate the magnetic field on the ground under such a line, assuming that it is about 20 m high. How does this field compare with that in your home?

$I = 200$ A, $d = 20$ m, so

$$B = \frac{(2 \times 10^{-7} \text{ T} \cdot \text{m/A}) I}{d}$$

$$= \frac{(2 \times 10^{-7} \text{ T} \cdot \text{m/A})(200 \text{ A})}{20 \text{ m}}$$

$$= 2 \times 10^{-6} \text{ T}$$

This is half as strong as the fields in part a.

    c. Some consumer groups have recommended that pregnant women not use electric blankets in case the magnetic fields cause health problems. Blankets typically carry currents of about 1 A. Estimate the distance a fetus might be from such a wire, clearly stating your assumptions, and find the magnetic field at the location of the fetus. Compare this with Earth's magnetic field.

At an early stage, the fetus might be 5 cm from the blanket. At later stages, the center of the fetus may be 10 cm away. $I = 1$ A, $d = 0.05$ m, so

$$B = \frac{(2 \times 10^{-7} \text{ T} \cdot \text{m/A}) I}{d}$$

$$= \frac{(2 \times 10^{-7} \text{ T} \cdot \text{m/A})(1 \text{ A})}{0.05 \text{ m}}$$

$$= 4 \times 10^{-6} \text{ T}$$

Earth's field is 5×10^{-5} T, so Earth's field is 12.5 times stronger. In the later case the field might be half as strong, so Earth's field is 25 times stronger.

Copyright © by Glencoe/McGraw-Hill

25 Electromagnetic Induction

Practice Problems

25.1 Creating Electric Current from Changing Magnetic Fields
pages 582–589

page 585

1. A straight wire, 0.5 m long, is moved straight up at a speed of 20 m/s through a 0.4-T magnetic field pointed in the horizontal direction.

   a. What *EMF* is induced in the wire?

   $EMF = BLv$

   $\quad = (0.4 \text{ N/A} \cdot \text{m})(0.5 \text{ m})(20 \text{ m/s})$

   $\quad = 4 \text{ V}$

   b. The wire is part of a circuit of total resistance of 6.0 Ω. What is the current in the circuit?

   $I = \dfrac{V}{R} = \dfrac{4 \text{ V}}{6.0 \, \Omega} = 0.7 \text{ A}$

2. A straight wire, 25 m long, is mounted on an airplane flying at 125 m/s. The wire moves in a perpendicular direction through Earth's magnetic field ($B = 5.0 \times 10^{-5}$ T). What *EMF* is induced in the wire?

   $EMF = BLv$

   $\quad = (5.0 \times 10^{-5} \text{ T})(25 \text{ m})(125 \text{ m/s})$

   $\quad = 0.16 \text{ V}$

3. A straight wire, 30.0 m long, moves at 2.0 m/s in a perpendicular direction through a 1.0-T magnetic field.

   a. What EMF is induced in the wire?

   $EMF = BLv = (1.0 \text{ T})(30.0 \text{ m})(2.0 \text{ m/s})$

   $\quad = 6.0 \times 10^1 \text{ V}$

b. The total resistance of the circuit of which the wire is a part is 15.0 Ω. What is the current?

$I = \dfrac{V}{R} = \dfrac{BLv}{R}$

$I = \dfrac{(1.0 \text{ T})(30.0 \text{ m})(2.0 \text{ m/s})}{15.0 \, \Omega} = 4.0 \text{ A}$

4. A permanent horseshoe magnet is mounted so that the magnetic field lines are vertical. If a student passes a straight wire between the poles and pulls it toward herself, the current flow through the wire is from right to left. Which is the N-pole of the magnet?

   Using the right-hand rule, the north pole is at the bottom.

page 589

5. A generator develops a maximum voltage of 170 V.

   a. What is the effective voltage?

   $V_{eff} = (0.707)V_{max} = (0.707)(170 \text{ V})$

   $\quad = 120 \text{ V}$

   b. A 60-W lightbulb is placed across the generator with an I_{max} of 0.70 A. What is the effective current through the bulb?

   $I_{eff} = (0.707)I_{max} = (0.707)(0.70 \text{ A})$

   $\quad = 0.49 \text{ A}$

   c. What is the resistance of the lightbulb when it is working?

   $R = \dfrac{V_{eff}}{I_{eff}} = \dfrac{120 \text{ V}}{0.49 \text{ A}} = 240 \, \Omega$

6. The effective voltage of an AC household outlet is 117 V.

   a. What is the maximum voltage across a lamp connected to the outlet?

   $V_{max} = \dfrac{V_{eff}}{0.707} = \dfrac{117 \text{ V}}{0.707} = 165 \text{ V}$

Copyright © by Glencoe/McGraw-Hill

6. (continued)

   b. The effective current through the lamp is 5.5 A. What is the maximum current in the lamp?

   $$I_{max} = \frac{I_{eff}}{0.707} = \frac{5.5\text{ A}}{0.707} = 7.8\text{ A}$$

7. An AC generator delivers a peak voltage of 425 V.

   a. What is the V_{eff} in a circuit placed across the generator?

   $$V_{eff} = (0.707)(425\text{ V}) = 3.00 \times 10^2\text{ V}$$

   b. The resistance of the circuit is $5.0 \times 10^2\ \Omega$. What is the effective current?

   $$I_{eff} = \frac{V_{eff}}{R} = \frac{3.00 \times 10^2\text{ V}}{5.0 \times 10^2\ \Omega} = 0.60\text{ A}$$

8. If the average power dissipated by an electric light is 100 W, what is the peak power?

   $$P = V_{eff}I_{eff}$$
   $$= (0.707\ V_{max})(0.707\ I_{max})$$
   $$= \frac{1}{2}\ P_{max}$$

   So $P_{max} = 2P = 2(100\text{ W}) = 200\text{ W}$

25.2 Changing Magnetic Fields Induce *EMF*
pages 590–597

page 596

For all problems, effective currents and voltages are indicated.

9. A step-down transformer has 7500 turns on its primary coil and 125 turns on its secondary coil. The voltage across the primary circuit is 7.2 kV.

page 597

   a. What voltage is across the secondary circuit?

   $$\frac{V_S}{V_P} = \frac{N_S}{N_P}$$
   $$V_S = \frac{V_P N_S}{N_P} = \frac{(7200\text{ V})(125)}{7500} = 120\text{ V}$$

   b. The current in the secondary circuit is 36 A. What is the current in the primary circuit?

   $$V_P I_P = V_S I_S$$
   $$I_P = \frac{V_S I_S}{V_P} = \frac{(120\text{ V})(36\text{ A})}{7200\text{ V}} = 0.60\text{ A}$$

10. A step-up transformer's primary coil has 500 turns. Its secondary coil has 15 000 turns. The primary circuit is connected to an AC generator having an *EMF* of 120 V.

   a. Calculate the *EMF* of the secondary circuit.

   $$\frac{V_P}{V_S} = \frac{N_P}{N_S}$$
   $$V_S = \frac{V_P N_S}{N_P} = \frac{(120\text{ V})(15\ 000)}{500}$$
   $$= 3.6 \times 10^3\text{ V}$$

   b. Find the current in the primary circuit if the current in the secondary circuit is 3.0 A.

   $$V_P I_P = V_S I_S$$
   $$I_P = \frac{V_S I_S}{V_P} = \frac{(3600\text{ V})(3.0\text{ A})}{120\text{ V}}$$
   $$= 9.0 \times 10^1\text{ A}$$

   c. What power is drawn by the primary circuit? What power is supplied by the secondary circuit?

   $$V_P I_P = (120\text{ V})(9.0 \times 10^1\text{ A})$$
   $$= 1.1 \times 10^4\text{ W}$$
   $$V_S I_S = (3600\text{ V})(3.0\text{ A}) = 1.1 \times 10^4\text{ W}$$

11. A step-up transformer has 300 turns on its primary coil and 90 000 turns on its secondary coil. The *EMF* of the generator to which the primary circuit is attached is 60.0 V.

   a. What is the *EMF* in the secondary circuit?

   $$V_S = \frac{V_P N_S}{N_P} = \frac{(60.0\text{ V})(90\ 000)}{300}$$
   $$= 1.80 \times 10^4\text{ V}$$

Copyright © by Glencoe/McGraw-Hill

11. (continued)

b. The current in the secondary circuit is 0.50 A. What current is in the primary circuit?

$$I_P = \frac{V_S I_S}{V_P} = \frac{(1.80 \times 10^4 \text{ V})(0.50 \text{ A})}{60.0 \text{ V}}$$

$$= 1.5 \times 10^2 \text{ A}$$

Chapter Review Problems

pages 600–601

page 600

Section 25.1

Level 1

28. A wire, 20.0 m long, moves at 4.0 m/s perpendicularly through a magnetic field. An *EMF* of 40 V is induced in the wire. What is the strength of the magnetic field?

$$EMF = BLv$$

so $B = \dfrac{EMF}{Lv}$

$$B = \frac{EMF}{Lv} = \frac{40 \text{ V}}{(20.0 \text{ m})(4.0 \text{ m/s})}$$

$$= 0.5 \text{ T}$$

29. An airplane traveling at 9.50×10^2 km/h passes over a region where Earth's magnetic field is 4.5×10^{-5} T and is nearly vertical. What voltage is induced between the plane's wing tips, which are 75 m apart?

$$EMF = BLv$$

$$= (4.5 \times 10^{-5} \text{ T})(75 \text{ m})(264 \text{ m/s})$$

$$= 0.89 \text{ V}$$

30. A straight wire, 0.75 m long, moves upward through a horizontal 0.30-T magnetic field at a speed of 16 m/s.

a. What *EMF* is induced in the wire?

$$EMF = BLv$$

$$= (0.30 \text{ T})(0.75 \text{ m})(16 \text{ m/s})$$

$$= 3.6 \text{ V}$$

b. The wire is part of a circuit with a total resistance of 11 Ω. What is the current?

$$V = IR$$

So $I = \dfrac{V}{R} = \dfrac{3.6 \text{ V}}{11 \text{ Ω}} = 0.33 \text{ A}$

31. At what speed would a 0.20-m length of wire have to move across a 2.5-T magnetic field to induce an *EMF* of 10 V?

$$EMF = BLv$$

So $v = \dfrac{EMF}{BL} = \dfrac{10 \text{ V}}{(2.5 \text{ T})(0.20 \text{ m})}$

$$= 20 \text{ m/s}$$

32. An AC generator develops a maximum *EMF* of 565 V. What effective *EMF* does the generator deliver to an external circuit?

$$V_{eff} = 0.707(V_{max}) = 0.707(565 \text{ V})$$

$$= 399 \text{ V}$$

33. An AC generator develops a maximum voltage of 150 V. It delivers a maximum current of 30.0 A to an external circuit.

a. What is the effective voltage of the generator?

$$V_{eff} = 0.707(V_{max}) = 0.707(150 \text{ V})$$

$$= 106 \text{ V} = 110 \text{ V}$$

b. What effective current does it deliver to the external circuit?

$$I_{eff} = 0.707(I_{max}) = 0.707(30.0 \text{ A})$$

$$= 21.2 \text{ A}$$

c. What is the effective power dissipated in the circuit?

$$P_{eff} = I_{eff} V_{eff} = (21.2 \text{ A})(106 \text{ A})$$

$$= 2.25 \times 10^3 \text{ W}$$

$$= 2.25 \text{ kW}$$

34. An electric stove is connected to an AC source with an effective voltage of 240 V.

a. Find the maximum voltage across one of the stove's elements when it is operating.

$$V_{eff} = (0.707)V_{max}$$

so $V_{max} = \dfrac{V_{eff}}{0.707} = \dfrac{240 \text{ V}}{0.707} = 340 \text{ V}$

Copyright © by Glencoe/McGraw-Hill

34. (continued)

b. The resistance of the operating element is 11 Ω. What is the effective current?

$V = IR$

so $I = \dfrac{V}{R} = \dfrac{240\text{ V}}{11\text{ }\Omega} = 22$ A

35. You wish to generate an *EMF* of 4.5 V by moving a wire at 4.0 m/s through a 0.050 T magnetic field. How long must the wire be, and what should be the angle between the field and direction of motion to use the shortest wire?

$EMF = BLv$

$L = \dfrac{EMF}{Bv}$

$L = \dfrac{4.5\text{ V}}{(0.050\text{ T})(4.0\text{ m/s})}$

$L = 23$ m

When the wire is perpendicular to the magnetic field 23 m can be used to generate an *EMF* of 4.5 V.

Level 2

36. A 40.0-cm wire is moved perpendicularly through a magnetic field of 0.32 T with a velocity of 1.3 m/s. If this wire is connected into a circuit of 10-Ω resistance, what is the current?

$EMF = BLv$

$= (0.32\text{ T})(0.400\text{ m})(1.3\text{ m/s})$

$= 0.17$ V

$I = \dfrac{V}{R} = \dfrac{0.17\text{ V}}{10\text{ }\Omega} = 17$ mA

37. You connect both ends of a copper wire, total resistance 0.10 Ω, to the terminals of a galvanometer. The galvanometer has a resistance of 875 Ω. You then move a 10.0-cm segment of the wire upward at 1.0 m/s through a 2.0×10^{-2}-T magnetic field. What current will the galvanometer indicate?

$EMF = BLv$

$= (2.0 \times 10^{-2}\text{ T})(0.100\text{ m})(1.0\text{ m/s})$

$= 2.0 \times 10^{-3}$ V

$I = \dfrac{V}{R} = \dfrac{2.0 \times 10^{-3}\text{ V}}{875\text{ }\Omega} = 2.3$ μA

38. The direction of a 0.045-T magnetic field is 60° above the horizontal. A wire, 2.5 m long, moves horizontally at 2.4 m/s.

a. What is the vertical component of the magnetic field?

The vertical component of magnetic field is

$B \sin 60° = (0.045\text{ T})(\sin 60°)$

$= 0.039$ T

b. What *EMF* is induced in the wire?

$EMF = BLv$

$= (0.039\text{ T})(2.5\text{ m})(2.4\text{ m/s})$

$= 0.23$ V

39. A generator at a dam can supply 375 MW (375×10^6 W) of electrical power. Assume that the turbine and generator are 85% efficient.

a. Find the rate at which falling water must supply energy to the turbine.

$\text{eff} = \dfrac{P_{out}}{P_{in}} \times 100$

So $P_{in} = P_{out} \times \dfrac{100}{\text{eff}}$

$= 375\text{ MW} \left(\dfrac{100}{85\%} \right)$

$= 440$ MW input

b. The energy of the water comes from a change in potential energy, $U = mgh$. What is the change in U needed each second?

440 MW = 440 MJ/s

$= 4.4 \times 10^8$ J each second

c. If the water falls 22 m, what is the mass of the water that must pass through the turbine each second to supply this power?

$PE = mgh$

so $m = \dfrac{PE}{gh} = \dfrac{4.4 \times 10^8\text{ J}}{(9.80\text{ m/s}^2)(22\text{ m})}$

$= 2.0 \times 10^6$ kg each second

Copyright © by Glencoe/McGraw-Hill

Section 25.2

Level 1

40. The primary coil of a transformer has 150 turns. It is connected to a 120-V source. Calculate the number of turns on the secondary coil needed to supply these voltages.

   a. 625 V

   $$\frac{V_s}{V_p} = \frac{N_s}{N_p}$$

   so $N_s = \left(\dfrac{V_s}{V_p}\right) N_p = \left(\dfrac{625 \text{ V}}{120 \text{ V}}\right)(150)$

   $$= 781 \text{ turns rounded to } 780$$

   b. 35 V

   $$N_s = \left(\frac{V_s}{V_p}\right) N_p = \left(\frac{35 \text{ V}}{120 \text{ V}}\right)(150)$$

   $$= 44 \text{ turns}$$

   c. 6.0 V

   $$N_s = \left(\frac{V_s}{V_p}\right) N_p = \left(\frac{6.0 \text{ V}}{120 \text{ V}}\right)(150)$$

   $$= 7.5 \text{ turns}$$

41. A step-up transformer has 80 turns on its primary coil. It has 1200 turns on its secondary coil. The primary circuit is supplied with an alternating current at 120 V.

   a. What voltage is across the secondary circuit?

   $$\frac{V_p}{V_s} = \frac{N_p}{N_s}$$

   so $V_s = \dfrac{V_p N_s}{N_p} = \dfrac{(120 \text{ V})(1200)}{80}$

   $$= 1.8 \text{ kV}$$

   b. The current in the secondary circuit is 2.0 A. What current is in the primary circuit?

   $$V_p I_p = V_s I_s$$

   $I_p = \dfrac{V_s I_s}{V_p} = \dfrac{(1.8 \times 10^3 \text{ V})(2.0 \text{ A})}{120 \text{ V})}$

   $$= 3.0 \times 10^1 \text{ A}$$

   c. What are the power input and output of the transformer?

   $$V_p I_p = (120 \text{ V})(30.0 \text{ A}) = 3.6 \text{ kW}$$
   $$V_s I_s = (1800 \text{ V})(2.0 \text{ A}) = 3.6 \text{ kW}$$

42. A laptop computer requires an effective voltage of 9.0 volts from the 120-V line.

   a. If the primary coil has 475 turns, how many does the secondary coil have?

   $$\frac{V_s}{V_p} = \frac{N_s}{N_p}$$

   so $N_s = \dfrac{V_s N_p}{V_p} = \dfrac{(9.0 \text{ V})(475)}{120 \text{ V}}$

   $$= 36 \text{ turns}$$

   b. A 125-mA current is in the computer. What current is in the primary circuit?

   $$V_p I_p = V_s I_s$$

   $I_p = \dfrac{V_s I_s}{V_p} = \dfrac{(9.0 \text{ V})(125 \text{ mA})}{120 \text{ V}} = 9.4 \text{ mA}$

43. A hair dryer uses 10 A at 120 V. It is used with a transformer in England, where the line voltage is 240 V.

   a. What should be the ratio of the turns of the transformer?

   $$\frac{V_p}{V_s} = \frac{N_p}{N_s} = \frac{240 \text{ V}}{120 \text{ V}} = \frac{2.0}{1.0}$$

   or 2 to 1

   b. What current will the hair dryer now draw?

   $$V_p I_p = V_s I_s$$

   so $I_p = \dfrac{V_s I_s}{V_p} = \dfrac{(120 \text{ V})(10 \text{ A})}{240 \text{ V}} = 5 \text{ A}$

Level 2

44. A 150-W transformer has an input voltage of 9.0 V and an output current of 5.0 A.

   a. Is this a step-up or step-down transformer?

   a step-up transformer

Copyright © by Glencoe/McGraw-Hill

44. (continued)

b. What is the ratio of V_{output} to V_{input}?

$$P = V_s I_s$$

so $V_s = \dfrac{P}{I_s} = \dfrac{150 \text{ W}}{5.0 \text{ A}} = 30 \text{ V}$

$$\frac{30 \text{ V}}{9 \text{ V}} = \frac{10}{3}$$

or 10 to 3

45. Scott connects a transformer to a 24-V source and measures 8.0 V at the secondary circuit. If the primary and secondary circuit were reversed, what would the new output voltage be?

The turns ratio is

$$\frac{N_s}{N_p} = \frac{V_s}{V_p} = \frac{8.0 \text{ V}}{24 \text{ V}} = \frac{1.0}{3.0}$$

Reversed, it would be $\dfrac{3}{1}$.

Thus, the voltage would now be found by

$$\frac{N_s}{N_p} = \frac{V_s}{V_p}$$

so $V_s = \left(\dfrac{N_s}{N_p}\right) V_p = 3(24 \text{ V}) = 72 \text{ V}$

Critical Thinking Problems

46. Suppose an "anti-Lenz's law" existed that meant a force was exerted to increase the change in magnetic field. Thus, when more energy was demanded, the force needed to turn the generator would be reduced. What conservation law would be violated by this new "law"? Explain.

It would violate the law of conservation of energy. More energy would come out than went in. A generator would create energy, not just change it from one form to another.

47. Real transformers are not 100% efficient. That is, the efficiency, in percent, is represented by $e = \dfrac{(100)P_s}{P_p}$. A step-down transformer that has an efficiency of 92.5% is used to obtain 28.0 V from the 125-V household voltage. The current in the secondary circuit is 25.0 A. What is the current in the primary circuit?

Secondary power:

$$P_s = V_s I_s = (28.0 \text{ V})(25.0 \text{ A})$$
$$= 7.00 \times 10^2 \text{ W}$$

Primary power:

$$P_p = \frac{(100)P_s}{\text{eff}} = \frac{100 \times 700 \text{ W}}{92.5\%} = 757 \text{ W}$$

Primary current:

$$I_p = \frac{P_p}{V_p} = \frac{757 \text{ W}}{125 \text{ V}} = 6.05 \text{ A}$$

48. A transformer that supplies eight homes has an efficiency of 95%. All eight homes have electric ovens running that draw 35 A from 240 V lines. How much power is supplied to the ovens in eight homes? How much power is dissipated as heat in the transformer?

Secondary power:

$$P_s = (\text{\# of homes}) V_s I_s$$
$$= 8(240 \text{ V})(35 \text{ A}) = 67 \text{ kW}$$

Primary power:

$$P_p = \frac{(100)P_s}{\text{eff}} = \frac{100 \times 67 \text{ kW}}{95\%}$$
$$= 71 \text{ kW}$$

The difference between these two is the power dissipated as heat, 4 kW.

Copyright © by Glencoe/McGraw-Hill

26 Electromagnetism

Practice Problems

26.1 Interaction Between Electric and Magnetic Fields and Matter
pages 604–611

page 607

Assume that the direction of all moving charged particles is perpendicular to the uniform magnetic field.

1. Protons passing without deflection through a magnetic field of 0.60 T are balanced by a 4.5×10^3-N/C electric field. What is the speed of the moving protons?

   $$Bqv = Eq$$

   $$v = \frac{E}{B} = \frac{4.5 \times 10^3 \text{ N/C}}{0.60 \text{ T}}$$

   $$= 7.5 \times 10^3 \text{ m/s}$$

2. A proton moves at a speed of 7.5×10^3 m/s as it passes through a 0.60-T magnetic field. Find the radius of the circular path. The charge carried by the proton is equal to that of the electron, but it is positive.

   $$Bqv = \frac{mv^2}{r}$$

   $$r = \frac{mv}{Bq}$$

   $$= \frac{(1.67 \times 10^{-27} \text{ kg})(7.5 \times 10^3 \text{ m/s})}{(0.60 \text{ T})(1.60 \times 10^{-19} \text{ C})}$$

   $$= 1.3 \times 10^{-4} \text{ m}$$

3. Electrons move through a 6.0×10^{-2}-T magnetic field balanced by a 3.0×10^3-N/C electric field. What is the speed of the electrons?

   $$Bqv = Eq$$

   $$v = \frac{E}{B} = \frac{3.0 \times 10^3 \text{ N/C}}{6.0 \times 10^{-2} \text{ T}}$$

   $$= 5.0 \times 10^4 \text{ m/s}$$

4. Calculate the radius of the circular path that the electrons in Practice Problem 3 follow in the absence of the electric field.

   $$Bqv = \frac{mv^2}{r}$$

   $$r = \frac{mv}{Bq}$$

   $$= \frac{(9.11 \times 10^{-31} \text{ kg})(5.0 \times 10^4 \text{ m/s})}{(6.0 \times 10^{-2} \text{ T})(1.60 \times 10^{-19} \text{ C})}$$

   $$= 4.7 \times 10^{-6} \text{ m}$$

page 610

5. A stream of singly ionized lithium atoms is not deflected as it passes through a 1.5×10^{-3}-T magnetic field perpendicular to a 6.0×10^2-V/m electric field.

page 611

   a. What is the speed of the lithium atoms as they pass through the crossed fields?

   $$Bqv = Eq$$

   $$v = \frac{E}{B} = \frac{6.0 \times 10^2 \text{ N/C}}{1.5 \times 10^{-3} \text{ T}}$$

   $$= 4.0 \times 10^5 \text{ m/s}$$

   b. The lithium atoms move into a magnetic field of 0.18 T. They follow a circular path of radius 0.165 m. What is the mass of a lithium atom?

   $$Bqv = \frac{mv^2}{r}$$

   $$m = \frac{Bqr}{v}$$

   $$= \frac{(0.18 \text{ T})(1.60 \times 10^{-19} \text{ C})(0.165 \text{ m})}{4.0 \times 10^5 \text{ m/s}}$$

   $$= 1.2 \times 10^{-26} \text{ kg}$$

Copyright © by Glencoe/McGraw-Hill

6. A mass spectrometer analyzes and gives data for a beam of doubly ionized argon atoms. The values are $q = 2(1.60 \times 10^{-19} \text{ C})$, $B = 5.0 \times 10^{-2}$ T, $r = 0.106$ m, and $V = 66.0$ V. Find the mass of an argon atom.

$$m = \frac{B^2 r^2 q}{2V} = \frac{(5.0 \times 10^{-2} \text{ T})^2 (0.106 \text{ m})^2 (2)(1.60 \times 10^{-19} \text{ C})}{2(66.0 \text{ V})} = 6.8 \times 10^{-26} \text{ kg}$$

7. A beam of singly ionized oxygen atoms is sent through a mass spectrometer. The values are $B = 7.2 \times 10^{-2}$ T, $q = 1.60 \times 10^{-19}$ C, $r = 0.085$ m, and $V = 110$ V. Find the mass of an oxygen atom.

$$m = \frac{B^2 r^2 q}{2V} = \frac{(7.2 \times 10^{-2} \text{ T})^2 (0.085 \text{ m})^2 (1.60 \times 10^{-19} \text{ C})}{2(110 \text{ V})} = 2.7 \times 10^{-26} \text{ kg}$$

8. You found the mass of a neon isotope in the last Example Problem. Another neon isotope has a mass of 22 proton masses. How far from the first isotope would these ions land on the photographic film?

Use $r = \frac{1}{B} \sqrt{\frac{2Vm}{q}}$ to find the ratio of radii of the two isotopes. If M represents the

number of proton masses, then $\dfrac{r_{22}}{r_{20}} = \sqrt{\dfrac{M_{22}}{M_{20}}}$, so

$$r_{22} = r_{20} \left(\frac{22}{20}\right)^{1/2} = 0.056 \text{ m}$$

Separation then is

$2(0.056 \text{ m} - 0.053 \text{ m}) = 6$ mm

Chapter Review Problems

pages 622–623

page 622

Section 26.1

Level 1

19. A beam of ions passes undeflected through a pair of crossed electric and magnetic fields. E is 6.0×10^5 N/C and B is 3.0×10^{-3} T. What is the ions' speed?

$$v = \frac{E}{B} = \frac{6.0 \times 10^5 \text{ N/C}}{3.0 \times 10^{-3} \text{ T}} = 2.0 \times 10^8 \text{ m/s}$$

20. Electrons moving at 3.6×10^4 m/s pass through an electric field with an intensity of 5.8×10^3 N/C. How large a magnetic field must the electrons also experience for their path to be undeflected?

$$v = \frac{E}{B} \text{, so}$$

$$B = \frac{E}{v} = \frac{5.8 \times 10^3 \text{ N/C}}{3.6 \times 10^4 \text{ m/s}} = 0.16 \text{ T}$$

Copyright © by Glencoe/McGraw-Hill

21. The electrons in a beam move at 2.8×10^8 m/s in an electric field of 1.4×10^4 N/C. What value must the magnetic field have if the electrons pass through the crossed fields undeflected?

$$v = \frac{E}{B}, \text{ so}$$

$$B = \frac{E}{v} = \frac{1.4 \times 10^4 \text{ N/C}}{2.8 \times 10^8 \text{ m/s}} = 5.0 \times 10^{-5} \text{ T} = 5.0 \times 10^1 \ \mu\text{T}$$

22. A proton moves across a 0.36-T magnetic field in a circular path of radius 0.20 m. What is the speed of the proton?

$$\frac{q}{m} = \frac{v}{Br}, \text{ so}$$

$$v = \frac{Brq}{m} = \frac{(0.36 \text{ T})(0.20 \text{ m})(1.60 \times 10^{-19} \text{ C})}{1.67 \times 10^{-27} \text{ kg}} = 6.9 \times 10^6 \text{ m/s}$$

23. Electrons move across a 4.0-mT magnetic field. They follow a circular path with radius 2.0 cm.

   a. What is their speed?

$$\frac{q}{m} = \frac{v}{Br}$$

$$\text{so } v = \frac{Brq}{m} = \frac{(4.0 \times 10^{-3} \text{ T})(2.0 \times 10^{-2} \text{ m})(1.60 \times 10^{-19} \text{ C})}{9.11 \times 10^{-31} \text{ kg}} = 1.4 \times 10^7 \text{ m/s}$$

   b. An electric field is applied perpendicularly to the magnetic field. The electrons then follow a straight-line path. Find the magnitude of the electric field.

$$v = \frac{E}{B}$$

$$\text{so } E = Bv = (4.0 \times 10^{-3} \text{ T})(1.4 \times 10^7 \text{ m/s}) = 5.6 \times 10^4 \text{ N/C}$$

24. A proton enters a 6.0×10^{-2}-T magnetic field with a speed of 5.4×10^4 m/s. What is the radius of the circular path it follows?

$$r = \frac{mv}{qB} = \frac{(1.67 \times 10^{-27} \text{ kg})(5.4 \times 10^4 \text{ m/s})}{(1.60 \times 10^{-19} \text{ C})(6.0 \times 10^{-2} \text{ T})} = 9.4 \times 10^{-3} \text{ m}$$

25. A proton enters a magnetic field of 6.4×10^{-2} T with a speed of 4.5×10^4 m/s. What is the circumference of its circular path?

$$r = \frac{mv}{Bq} = \frac{(1.67 \times 10^{-27} \text{ kg})(4.5 \times 10^4 \text{ m/s})}{(6.4 \times 10^{-2} \text{ T})(1.6 \times 10^{-19} \text{ C})} = 7.3 \times 10^{-3} \text{ m}$$

$$C = 2\pi r = 2\pi (7.3 \times 10^{-3} \text{ m}) = 4.6 \times 10^{-2} \text{ m}$$

26. A 3.0×10^{-2}-T magnetic field in a mass spectrometer causes an isotope of sodium to move in a circular path with a radius of 0.081 m. If the ions have a single positive charge and are moving with a speed of 1.0×10^4 m/s, what is the isotope's mass?

$$r = \frac{mv}{qB}$$

$$\text{so } m = \frac{Brq}{v} = \frac{(3.0 \times 10^{-2} \text{ T})(0.081 \text{ m})(1.60 \times 10^{-19} \text{ C})}{1.0 \times 10^4 \text{ m/s}} = 3.9 \times 10^{-26} \text{ kg}$$

Copyright © by Glencoe/McGraw-Hill

27. An alpha particle, a doubly ionized helium atom, has a mass of 6.7×10^{-27} kg and is accelerated by a voltage of 1.0 kV. If a uniform magnetic field of 6.5×10^{-2} T is maintained on the alpha particle, what will be the particle's radius of curvature?

$$r = \frac{1}{B}\sqrt{\frac{2Vm}{q}} = \frac{1}{(6.5 \times 10^{-2}\,\text{T})}\sqrt{\frac{(2)(1.0 \times 10^3\,\text{V})(6.7 \times 10^{-27}\,\text{kg})}{(2)(1.60 \times 10^{-19}\,\text{C})}} = 0.10\,\text{m}$$

28. An electron is accelerated by a 4.5-kV potential difference. How strong a magnetic field must be experienced by the electron if its path is a circle of radius 5.0 cm?

$$r = \frac{1}{B}\sqrt{\frac{2Vm}{q}}$$

$$\text{so } B = \frac{1}{r}\sqrt{\frac{2Vm}{q}} = \frac{1}{(0.050\,\text{m})}\sqrt{\frac{(2)(4.5 \times 10^3\,\text{V})(9.11 \times 10^{-31}\,\text{kg})}{1.60 \times 10^{-19}\,\text{C}}} = 4.5 \times 10^{-3}\,\text{T}$$

29. A mass spectrometer yields the following data for a beam of doubly ionized sodium atoms: $B = 8.0 \times 10^{-2}$ T, $q = 2(1.60 \times 10^{-19}$ C), $r = 0.077$ m, and $V = 156$ V. Calculate the mass of a sodium atom.

$$\frac{q}{m} = \frac{2V}{B^2 r^2}$$

$$\text{so } m = \frac{qB^2 r^2}{2V} = \frac{(2)(1.60 \times 10^{-19}\,\text{C})(8.0 \times 10^{-2}\,\text{T})^2(0.077\,\text{m})^2}{(2)(156\,\text{V})} = 3.9 \times 10^{-26}\,\text{kg}$$

Level 2

30. An alpha particle has a mass of approximately 6.6×10^{-27} kg and bears a double elementary positive charge. Such a particle is observed to move through a 2.0-T magnetic field along a path of radius 0.15 m.

page 623

a. What speed does the particle have?

$$r = \frac{mv}{qB}$$

$$\text{so } v = \frac{Bqr}{m} = \frac{(2.0\,\text{T})(2)(1.60 \times 10^{-19}\,\text{C})(0.15\,\text{m})}{6.6 \times 10^{-27}\,\text{kg}} = 1.5 \times 10^7\,\text{m/s}$$

b. What is its kinetic energy?

$$KE = \frac{1}{2}mv^2 = \frac{(6.6 \times 10^{-27}\,\text{kg})(1.5 \times 10^7\,\text{m/s})^2}{2} = 7.4 \times 10^{-13}\,\text{J}$$

c. What potential difference would be required to give it this kinetic energy?

$$KE = qV$$

$$\text{so } V = \frac{KE}{q} = \frac{7.4 \times 10^{-13}\,\text{J}}{2(1.60 \times 10^{-19}\,\text{C})} = 2.3\,\text{MV}$$

Copyright © by Glencoe/McGraw-Hill

31. In a mass spectrometer, ionized silicon atoms have curvatures with radii of 16.23 cm and 17.97 cm. If the smaller radius corresponds to a mass of 28 proton masses, what is the mass of the other silicon isotope?

$$\frac{q}{m} = \frac{2V}{B^2 r^2}$$

so m is proportional to r^2.

$$\frac{m_2}{m_1} = \frac{r_2^2}{r_1^2}$$

so $m_2 = m_1 \left(\frac{r_2}{r_1}\right)^2$

$$= (28\ m_p)\left(\frac{17.97\ \text{cm}}{16.23\ \text{cm}}\right)^2 = 34\ m_p$$

$$m_2 = 34 m_p = (34)(1.67 \times 10^{-27}\ \text{kg})$$
$$= 5.7 \times 10^{-26}\ \text{kg}$$

32. A mass spectrometer analyzes carbon-containing molecules with a mass of 175×10^3 proton masses. What percent differentiation is needed to produce a sample of molecules in which only carbon isotopes of mass 12, and none of mass 13, are present?

One proton mass out of 175×10^3 is 1/1750 of one percent, or about one two-thousandth of one percent differentiation ability.

Section 26.2

Level 1

33. The radio waves reflected by a parabolic dish are 2.0 cm long. How long should the antenna be that detects the waves?

The antenna is $\frac{\lambda}{2}$, or 1.0 cm long.

Level 2

34. The difference in potential between the cathode and anode of a spark plug is 1.0×10^4 V.

a. What energy does an electron give up as it passes between the electrodes?

$$E = qV$$
$$= (1.60 \times 10^{-19}\ \text{C})(1.0 \times 10^4\ \text{J/C})$$
$$= 1.6 \times 10^{-15}\ \text{J}$$

b. One-fourth of the energy given up by the electron is converted to electromagnetic radiation. The frequency of the wave is related to the energy by the equation $E = hf$, where h is Planck's constant, 6.6×10^{-34} J/Hz. What is the frequency of the waves?

$$E = hf$$

so $f = \dfrac{E}{h} = \dfrac{1.60 \times 10^{-15}\ \text{J}}{(4)(6.6 \times 10^{-34}\ \text{J/Hz})}$

$$= 6.1 \times 10^{17}\ \text{Hz}$$

Critical Thinking Problems

35. H.G. Wells wrote a science fiction book called *The Invisible Man*, in which a man drinks a potion and becomes invisible, although he retains all of his other faculties. Explain why it wouldn't be possible for an invisible person to be able to see.

To see, you must detect the light, which means the light will be absorbed or scattered. The lack of light going through the invisible person's eye would make him visible.

Copyright © by Glencoe/McGraw-Hill

36. You are designing a mass spectrometer using the principles discussed in this chapter, but with an electronic detector replacing the photographic film. You want to distinguish singly ionized molecules of 175 proton masses from those with 176 proton masses, but the spacing between adjacent cells in your detector is 0.1 mm. The molecules must have been accelerated by a potential difference of at least 500 volts to be detected. What are some of the values of V, B, and r that your apparatus should have?

The spacing between cells is twice the difference between the radii of the circular paths of the two molecules, so

$$r_2 - r_1 = \Delta r = \frac{0.1 \text{ mm}}{2} = 0.05 \text{ mm}$$

$$= 5 \times 10^{-5} \text{ m}$$

$$r = \frac{1}{B}\sqrt{\frac{2Vm}{q}}$$

$$\Delta r = r_2 - r_1$$

$$= \frac{1}{B}\sqrt{\frac{2Vm_2}{q}} - \frac{1}{B}\sqrt{\frac{2Vm_1}{q}}$$

$$= \frac{1}{B}\sqrt{\frac{2V}{q}}(\sqrt{m_2} - \sqrt{m_1})$$

or $B = \frac{1}{\Delta r}\sqrt{\frac{2V}{q}}(\sqrt{m_2} - \sqrt{m_1})$

Substituting the values

$\Delta r = 5 \times 10^{-5}$ m

$V = 500$ V

$q = 1.6 \times 10^{-19}$ C

$m_2 = 176(1.67 \times 10^{-27} \text{ kg})$

$m_1 = 175(1.67 \times 10^{-27} \text{ kg})$

gives $B = 2.44$ T

$$r_2 = \frac{1}{B}\sqrt{\frac{2Vm_2}{q}} = 0.01757 \text{ m}$$

$$= 17.57 \text{ mm}$$

$$r_1 = \frac{1}{B}\sqrt{\frac{2Vm_1}{q}} = 0.01752 \text{ m}$$

$$= 17.52 \text{ mm}$$

Raising the voltage will produce other values for B, but r_1 and r_2 will remain unchanged.

Copyright © by Glencoe/McGraw-Hill

27 Quantum Theory

Practice Problems

27.1 Waves Behave Like Particles
pages 626–636

page 633

1. The stopping potential required to prevent current through a photocell is 3.2 V. Calculate the kinetic energy in joules of the photoelectrons as they are emitted.

$$K = -qV_0$$
$$= -(-1.60 \times 10^{-19} \text{ C})(3.2 \text{ J/C}) = 5.1 \times 10^{-19} \text{ J}$$

2. The stopping potential for a photoelectric cell is 5.7 V. Calculate the kinetic energy of the emitted photoelectrons in eV.

$$K = -qV_0$$
$$= \frac{-(-1.60 \times 10^{-19} \text{ C})(5.7 \text{ J/C})}{1.60 \times 10^{-19} \text{ J/eV}} = 5.7 \text{ eV}$$

3. The threshold wavelength of zinc is 310 nm.

   a. Find the threshold frequency of zinc.

   $$c = f_0 \lambda_0$$
   $$f_0 = \frac{c}{\lambda_0} = \frac{3.00 \times 10^8 \text{ m/s}}{310 \times 10^{-9} \text{ m}} = 9.7 \times 10^{14} \text{ Hz}$$

   b. What is the work function in eV of zinc?
   $$W = hf_0 = (6.63 \times 10^{-34} \text{ J/Hz})(9.7 \times 10^{14} \text{ Hz}) \left(\frac{\text{eV}}{1.60 \times 10^{-19} \text{ J}} \right) = 4.0 \text{ eV}$$

   c. Zinc in a photocell is irradiated by ultraviolet light of 240 nm wavelength. What is the kinetic energy of the photoelectrons in eV?

   $$K_{max} = \frac{hc}{\lambda} - hf_0 = \frac{\left[(6.63 \times 10^{-34} \text{ J/Hz})(3.00 \times 10^8 \text{ m/s}) \left(\frac{\text{eV}}{1.60 \times 10^{-19} \text{ J}} \right) \right]}{240 \times 10^{-9} \text{ m}} - 4.0 \text{ eV}$$

   $$= 5.2 \text{ eV} - 4.0 \text{ eV} = 1.2 \text{ eV}$$

4. The work function for cesium is 1.96 eV.

   a. Find the threshold wavelength for cesium.
   $$W = \text{work function} = hf_0 = \frac{1240 \text{ eV} \cdot \text{nm}}{\lambda_0}$$

   where λ_0 has units of nm and W has units of eV.

   $$\lambda_0 = \frac{1240 \text{ eV} \cdot \text{nm}}{W} = \frac{1240 \text{ eV} \cdot \text{nm}}{1.96 \text{ eV}} = 633 \text{ nm}$$

Copyright © by Glencoe/McGraw-Hill

4. (continued)

b. What is the kinetic energy in eV of photoelectrons ejected when 425-nm violet light falls on the cesium?

$$K_{max} = hf - hf_0 = E_{photon} - hf_0$$

$$= \frac{1240 \text{ eV} \cdot \text{nm}}{\lambda} - hf_0$$

$$= \frac{1240 \text{ eV} \cdot \text{nm}}{425 \text{ nm}} - 1.96 \text{ eV}$$

$$= 2.92 \text{ eV} - 1.96 \text{ eV} = 0.96 \text{ eV}$$

27.2 Particles Behave Like Waves
pages 637–640

page 638

5. An electron is accelerated by a potential difference of 250 V.

a. What is the speed of the electron?

$$\frac{1}{2}mv^2 = qV_0$$

$$v^2 = \frac{2qV}{m}$$

$$= \frac{2(1.60 \times 10^{-19} \text{ C})(250 \text{ J/C})}{9.11 \times 10^{-31} \text{ kg}}$$

$$= 8.8 \times 10^{13} \text{ m}^2/\text{s}^2$$

$$v = 9.4 \times 10^6 \text{ m/s}$$

b. What is the de Broglie wavelength of this electron?

$$\lambda = \frac{h}{mv}$$

$$= \frac{6.63 \times 10^{-34} \text{ J} \cdot \text{s}}{(9.11 \times 10^{-31} \text{ kg})(9.4 \times 10^6 \text{ m/s})}$$

$$= 7.7 \times 10^{-11} \text{ m}$$

6. A 7.0-kg bowling ball rolls with a velocity of 8.5 m/s.

a. What is the de Broglie wavelength of the bowling ball?

$$\lambda = \frac{h}{mv} = \frac{6.63 \times 10^{-34} \text{ J} \cdot \text{s}}{(7.0 \text{ kg})(8.5 \text{ m/s})}$$

$$= 1.1 \times 10^{-35} \text{ m}$$

b. Why does the bowling ball exhibit no observable wave behavior?

The wavelength is too small to show observable effects.

7. An X ray with a wavelength 5.0×10^{-12} m is traveling in a vacuum.

a. Calculate the momentum associated with this X ray.

$$p = \frac{h}{\lambda} = \frac{6.63 \times 10^{-34} \text{ J} \cdot \text{s}}{5.0 \times 10^{-12} \text{ m}}$$

$$= 1.3 \times 10^{-22} \text{ kg} \cdot \text{m/s}$$

b. Why does the X ray exhibit little particle behavior?

Its momentum is too small to affect objects of ordinary size.

Chapter Review Problems
pages 642–643
page 642
Section 27.1

Level 1

16. The stopping potential of a certain metal is 5.0 V. What is the maximum kinetic energy of the photoelectrons in

a. electron volts?

$$K = -qV_0 = -(-1 \text{ elem charge})(5.0 \text{ V})$$

$$= 5.0 \text{ eV}$$

b. joules?

$$\frac{5.0 \text{ eV}}{1}\left(\frac{1.60 \times 10^{-19} \text{ J}}{1 \text{ eV}}\right)$$

$$= 8.0 \times 10^{-19} \text{ J}$$

17. What potential difference is needed to stop electrons having a maximum kinetic energy of 4.8×10^{-19} J?

$$K = -qV_0$$

$$\text{so } V_0 = \frac{K}{-q} = \frac{4.8 \times 10^{-19} \text{ C}}{-(-1.60 \times 10^{-19} \text{ C})}$$

$$= 3.0 \text{ V}$$

Copyright © by Glencoe/McGraw-Hill

18. The threshold frequency of sodium is 4.4×10^{14} Hz. How much work must be done to free an electron from the surface of sodium?

$\text{Work} = hf_0$

$= (6.626 \times 10^{-34} \text{ J/Hz})(4.4 \times 10^{14} \text{ Hz})$

$= 2.9 \times 10^{-19} \text{ J}$

19. If light with a frequency of 1.00×10^{15} Hz falls on the sodium in the previous problem, what is the maximum kinetic energy of the photoelectrons?

$K = hf - hf_0$

$= (6.63 \times 10^{-34} \text{ J/Hz})(1.00 \times 10^{15} \text{ Hz})$

$\qquad\qquad - 2.9 \times 10^{-19} \text{ J}$

$= 3.7 \times 10^{-19} \text{ J}$

20. Barium has a work function of 2.48 eV. What is the longest wavelength of light that will cause electrons to be emitted from barium?

$\text{Work function} = 2.48 \text{ eV} = hf_0 = \dfrac{hc}{\lambda_0}$,

so

$\lambda_0 = \dfrac{hc}{2.48 \text{ eV}}$

$= \dfrac{(6.63 \times 10^{-34} \text{ J} \cdot \text{s})(3.00 \times 10^8 \text{ m/s})}{(2.48 \text{ eV}) \left(\dfrac{1.60 \times 10^{-19} \text{ J}}{\text{eV}} \right)}$

$= 5.01 \times 10^{-7} \text{ m}$

$= 501 \text{ nm}$

21. A photocell is used by a photographer to measure the light falling on the subject to be photographed. What should be the work function of the cathode if the photocell is to be sensitive to red light ($\lambda = 680$ nm) as well as the other colors?

$W = \dfrac{1240 \text{ eV} \cdot \text{nm}}{\lambda_0} = \dfrac{1240 \text{ eV} \cdot \text{nm}}{680 \text{ nm}}$

$= 1.8 \text{ eV}$

22. The threshold frequency of tin is 1.2×10^{15} Hz.

a. What is the threshold wavelength?

$c = \lambda f$, so

$\lambda = \dfrac{c}{f} = \dfrac{3.0 \times 10^8 \text{ m/s}}{1.2 \times 10^{15} \text{ Hz}} = 2.5 \times 10^{-7} \text{ m}$

b. What is the work function of tin?

$W = hf_0$

$= (6.63 \times 10^{-34} \text{ J/Hz})(1.2 \times 10^{15} \text{ Hz})$

$= 8.0 \times 10^{-19} \text{ J}$

c. Electromagnetic radiation with a wavelength of 167 nm falls on tin. What is the kinetic energy of the ejected electrons in eV?

$KE_{\text{max}} = \dfrac{hc}{\lambda} - hf_0$

$= \dfrac{(6.63 \times 10^{-34} \text{ J/Hz})(3.0 \times 10^8 \text{ m/s})}{167 \times 10^{-9} \text{ m}}$

$\qquad\qquad\qquad\qquad - 8.0 \times 10^{-19} \text{ J}$

$= 3.9 \times 10^{-19} \text{ J}$

$(3.9 \times 10^{-19} \text{ J}) \left(\dfrac{\text{eV}}{1.60 \times 10^{-19} \text{ J}} \right)$

$= 2.4 \text{ eV}$

23. What is the momentum of a photon of yellow light whose wavelength is 600 nm?

$p = \dfrac{h}{\lambda} = \dfrac{6.626 \times 10^{-34} \text{ J} \cdot \text{s}}{6 \times 10^{-7} \text{ m}}$

$= 1 \times 10^{-27} \text{ kg} \cdot \text{m/s}$

Level 2

24. A home uses about 4×10^{11} J of energy each year. In many parts of the United States, there are about 3000 h of sunlight each year.

a. How much energy from the sun falls on one square meter each year?

Earth receives about 1000 J per square meter each second, so

$E = \left(1000 \dfrac{\text{J}}{\text{m}^2 \cdot \text{s}} \right) \left(\dfrac{3600 \text{ s}}{\text{h}} \right) \left(\dfrac{3000 \text{ h}}{\text{yr}} \right)$

$= 1 \times 10^{10} \text{ J/m}^2 \text{ per year}$

Copyright © by Glencoe/McGraw-Hill

24. (continued)

b. If this solar energy can be converted to useful energy with an efficiency of 20 percent, how large an area of converters would produce the energy needed by the home?

$$\text{Area} = \frac{4 \times 10^{11}\ \text{J}}{(0.2)(1 \times 10^{10}\ \text{J/m}^2)}$$

$$= 2 \times 10^2\ \text{m}^2$$

25. The work function of iron is 4.7 eV.

a. What is the threshold wavelength of iron?

$$W = \frac{hc}{\lambda_0} = \frac{1240}{\lambda}$$

$$\text{so } \lambda = \frac{1240\ \text{eV} \cdot \text{nm}}{W} = \frac{1240\ \text{eV} \cdot \text{nm}}{4.7\ \text{eV}}$$

$$= 2.6 \times 10^2\ \text{nm}$$

b. Iron is exposed to radiation of wavelength 150 nm. What is the maximum kinetic energy of the ejected electrons in eV?

$$K = \frac{hc}{\lambda} - \frac{hc}{\lambda_0} = \frac{1240\ \text{eV} \cdot \text{nm}}{150\ \text{nm}} - 4.7\ \text{eV}$$

$$= 3.6\ \text{eV}$$

26. Suppose a 5.0-g object, such as a nickel, vibrates while connected to a spring. Its maximum velocity is 1.0 cm/s.

a. Find the maximum kinetic energy of the vibrating object.

$$K = \frac{1}{2}\,mv^2$$

$$= \left(\frac{1}{2}\right)(5.0 \times 10^{-3}\ \text{kg})(1.0 \times 10^{-2}\ \text{m/s})^2$$

$$= 2.5 \times 10^{-7}\ \text{J}$$

page 643

b. The object emits energy in the form of light of frequency 5.0×10^{14} Hz and its energy is reduced by one step. Find the energy lost by the object.

$$E = hf$$

$$= (6.63 \times 10^{-34}\ \text{J/Hz})(5.0 \times 10^{14}\ \text{Hz})$$

$$= 3.3 \times 10^{-19}\ \text{J}$$

c. How many step reductions would this object have to make to lose all its energy?

$$\frac{2.5 \times 10^{-7}\ \text{J}}{3.3 \times 10^{-19}\ \text{J/step}} = 7.6 \times 10^{11}\ \text{steps}$$

Section 27.2

Level 1

27. Find the de Broglie wavelength of a deuteron of mass 3.3×10^{-27} kg that moves with a speed of 2.5×10^4 m/s.

$$\lambda = \frac{h}{mv}$$

$$= \frac{6.63 \times 10^{-34}\ \text{J/Hz}}{(3.3 \times 10^{-27}\ \text{kg})(2.5 \times 10^4\ \text{m/s})}$$

$$= 8.0 \times 10^{-12}\ \text{m}$$

28. An electron is accelerated across a potential difference of 54 V.

a. Find the maximum velocity of the electron.

$$K_{\text{max}} = \frac{1}{2}\,mv^2 = qV$$

$$\text{so } v = \sqrt{\frac{2qV}{m}}$$

$$= \sqrt{\frac{(2)(1.60 \times 10^{-19}\ \text{C})(54\ \text{V})}{9.1 \times 10^{-31}\ \text{kg}}}$$

$$= 4.4 \times 10^6\ \text{m/s}$$

b. Calculate the de Broglie wavelength of the electron.

$$\lambda = \frac{h}{mv}$$

$$= \frac{6.63 \times 10^{-34}\ \text{J/Hz}}{(9.11 \times 10^{-31}\ \text{kg})(4.4 \times 10^6\ \text{m/s})}$$

$$= 1.7 \times 10^{-10}\ \text{m} = 0.17\ \text{nm}$$

29. A neutron is held in a trap with a kinetic energy of only 0.025 eV.

a. What is the velocity of the neutron?

$$K = \frac{1}{2}\,mv^2$$

$$= 0.025\ \text{eV} \left(\frac{1.60 \times 10^{-19}\ \text{J}}{\text{eV}}\right)$$

$$= 4.0 \times 10^{-21}\ \text{J}$$

Copyright © by Glencoe/McGraw-Hill

29. (continued)

$$v = \sqrt{\frac{2K}{m}} = \sqrt{\frac{(2)(4.0 \times 10^{-21} \text{ J})}{1.67 \times 10^{-27} \text{ kg}}}$$

$$= 2.2 \times 10^3 \text{ m/s}$$

b. Find the de Broglie wavelength of the neutron.

$$\lambda = \frac{h}{mv}$$

$$= \frac{6.63 \times 10^{-34} \text{ J/Hz}}{(1.67 \times 10^{-27} \text{ kg})(2.2 \times 10^3 \text{ m/s})}$$

$$= 1.8 \times 10^{-10} \text{ m}$$

30. The kinetic energy of the hydrogen atom electron is 13.65 eV.

a. Find the velocity of the electron.

$$K = \frac{1}{2} mv^2$$

$$\text{so } v = \sqrt{\frac{2K}{m}}$$

$$= \sqrt{\frac{(2)(13.65 \text{ eV})(1.60 \times 10^{-19} \text{ J/eV})}{9.11 \times 10^{-31} \text{ kg}}}$$

$$= 2.19 \times 10^6 \text{ m/s}$$

b. Calculate its de Broglie wavelength.

$$\lambda = \frac{h}{mv}$$

$$= \frac{6.63 \times 10^{-34} \text{ J/Hz}}{(9.11 \times 10^{-31} \text{ kg})(2.19 \times 10^6 \text{ m/s})}$$

$$= 3.32 \times 10^{-10} \text{ m}$$

c. Compare your answer with the radius of the hydrogen atom, 5.19 nm.

$$5.19 \text{ nm} = 51.9 \times 10^{-10} \text{ m}$$

$$\frac{3.32 \times 10^{-10}}{51.9 \times 10^{-10}}$$

$$= \frac{1}{16} \text{ the radius of the atom}$$

Level 2

31. An electron has a de Broglie wavelength of 400.0 nm, the shortest wavelength of visible light.

a. Find the velocity of the electron.

$$\lambda = \frac{h}{mv}$$

$$\text{so } v = \frac{h}{m\lambda}$$

$$= \frac{6.63 \times 10^{-34} \text{ J/Hz}}{(9.11 \times 10^{-31} \text{ kg})(400.0 \times 10^{-9} \text{ m})}$$

$$= 1.82 \times 10^3 \text{ m/s}$$

b. Calculate the energy of the electron in eV.

$$K = \frac{1}{2} mv^2$$

$$= \frac{1}{2} (9.11 \times 10^{-31} \text{ kg})$$

$$\times (1.82 \times 10^3 \text{ m/s})^2$$

$$= 1.51 \times 10^{-24} \text{ J}$$

$$(1.51 \times 10^{-24} \text{ J}) \left(\frac{\text{eV}}{1.60 \times 10^{-19} \text{ J}} \right)$$

$$= 1 \times 10^{-5} \text{ eV}$$

32. An electron microscope is useful because the de Broglie wavelength of electrons can be made smaller than the wavelength of visible light. What energy in eV has to be given to an electron for it to have a de Broglie wavelength of 20.0 nm?

$$\lambda = \frac{h}{mv}$$

$$\text{so } v = \frac{h}{m\lambda}$$

$$= \frac{6.63 \times 10^{-34} \text{ J/Hz}}{(9.11 \times 10^{-31} \text{ kg})(20.0 \times 10^{-9} \text{ m})}$$

$$= 3.64 \times 10^4 \text{ m/s}$$

$$K = \frac{1}{2} mv^2$$

$$= \frac{(9.11 \times 10^{-31} \text{ kg})(3.64 \times 10^4 \text{ m/s})^2}{2(1.60 \times 10^{-19} \text{ J/eV})}$$

$$= 3.77 \times 10^{-3} \text{ eV}$$

33. An electron has a de Broglie wavelength of 0.18 nm.

a. How large a potential difference did it experience if it started from rest?

$$v = \frac{h}{m\lambda}$$

$$= \frac{6.63 \times 10^{-34} \text{ J} \cdot \text{s}}{(9.11 \times 10^{-31} \text{ kg})(1.8 \times 10^{-10} \text{ m})}$$

$$= 4.04 \times 10^6 \text{ m/s}$$

Copyright © by Glencoe/McGraw-Hill

Physics: Principles and Problems

33. (continued)

$$K = \frac{1}{2} mv^2$$

$$= \frac{1}{2}(9.1 \times 10^{-31} \text{ kg})(4.04 \times 10^6 \text{ m/s})^2$$

$$= 7.43 \times 10^{-18} \text{ J}$$

$$K = qV$$

$$V = \frac{K}{q} = \frac{7.43 \times 10^{-18} \text{ J}}{1.60 \times 10^{-19} \text{ C}} = 46 \text{ V}$$

b. If a proton has a de Broglie wavelength of 0.18 nm, how large is the potential difference it experienced if it started from rest?

$$v = \frac{h}{m\lambda}$$

$$= \frac{6.63 \times 10^{-34} \text{ J} \cdot \text{s}}{(1.7 \times 10^{-27} \text{ kg})(1.8 \times 10^{-10} \text{ m})}$$

$$= 2.17 \times 10^3 \text{ m/s}$$

$$K = \frac{1}{2} mv^2$$

$$= \frac{1}{2}(1.67 \times 10^{-27} \text{ kg})(2.17 \times 10^3 \text{ m/s})^2$$

$$= 3.93 \times 10^{-21} \text{ J}$$

$$V = \frac{K}{q} = \frac{3.93 \times 10^{-21} \text{ J}}{1.60 \times 10^{-19} \text{ C}}$$

$$= 2.5 \times 10^{-2} \text{ V}$$

Critical Thinking Problems

34. A HeNe laser emits photons with a wavelength of 632.8 nm.

a. Find the energy, in joules, of each photon.

Each photon has energy

$$E = \frac{hc}{\lambda}$$

$$= \frac{(6.63 \times 10^{-34} \text{ J} \cdot \text{s})(3.00 \times 10^8 \text{ m/s})}{632.8 \times 10^{-9} \text{ m}}$$

$$= 3.14 \times 10^{-19} \text{ J}$$

b. A typical small laser has a power of 0.5 mW = 5×10^{-4} J/s. How many photons are emitted each second by the laser?

$$n = \frac{P}{E} = \frac{5 \times 10^{-4} \text{ J/s}}{3 \times 10^{-19} \text{ J/photon}}$$

$$= 2 \times 10^{15} \text{ photons/s}$$

35. The intensity of a light that is just barely visible is 1.5×10^{-11} W/m^2.

a. If this light shines into your eye, passing through the pupil with a diameter of 7.0 mm, what is the power, in watts, that enters your eye?

Power = intensity × area

$$= (1.5 \times 10^{-11} \text{ W/m}^2)[\pi (3.5 \times 10^{-3} \text{ m})^2]$$

$$= 5.8 \times 10^{-16} \text{ W}$$

b. If the light has a wavelength of 550 nm, how many photons per second enter your eye?

Energy per photon

$$E = \frac{hc}{\lambda}$$

$$= \frac{(6.63 \times 10^{-34} \text{ J} \cdot \text{s})(3.00 \times 10^8 \text{ m/s})}{550 \times 10^{-9} \text{ m}}$$

$$= 3.62 \times 10^{-19} \text{ J}$$

$$n = \frac{P}{E} = \frac{5.8 \times 10^{-16} \text{ J/s}}{3.62 \times 10^{-19} \text{ J/photon}}$$

$$= 1600 \text{ photons/s}$$

Copyright © by Glencoe/McGraw-Hill

28 The Atom

Practice Problems

28.1 The Bohr Model of the Atom
pages 646–657

page 657

1. According to the Bohr model, how many times larger is the orbit of a hydrogen electron in the second level than in the first?

   Four times as large because orbit radius is proportional to n^2, where n is the integer labeling the level.

2. You learned how to calculate the radius of the innermost orbit of the hydrogen atom. Note that all factors in the equation are constants with the exception of n^2. Use the solution to the Example Problem "Orbital Energy of Electrons in the Hydrogen Atom" to find the radius of the orbit of the second, third, and fourth allowable energy levels in the hydrogen atom.

$r_n = n^2k$, where $k = 5.30 \times 10^{-11}$ m

$r_2 = (2)^2(5.30 \times 10^{-11}$ m$)$

$\quad = 2.12 \times 10^{-10}$ m

$r_3 = (3)^2(5.30 \times 10^{-11}$ m$)$

$\quad = 4.77 \times 10^{-10}$ m

$r_4 = (4)^2(5.30 \times 10^{-11}$ m$)$

$\quad = 8.48 \times 10^{-10}$ m

3. Calculate the energies of the second, third, and fourth energy levels in the hydrogen atom.

$E_n = \dfrac{-13.6 \text{ eV}}{n^2}$

$E_2 = \dfrac{-13.6 \text{ eV}}{(2)^2} = -3.40 \text{ eV}$

$E_3 = \dfrac{-13.6 \text{ eV}}{(3)^2} = -1.51 \text{ eV}$

$E_4 = \dfrac{-13.6 \text{ eV}}{(4)^2} = -0.850 \text{ eV}$

4. Calculate the energy difference between E_3 and E_2 in the hydrogen atom. Find the wavelength of the light emitted. Which line in **Figure 28–8** is the result of this transmission?

FIGURE 28–8

Using the results of Practice Problem 3,

$E_3 - E_2 = (-1.51 \text{ eV}) - (-3.40 \text{ eV})$

$\quad = 1.89 \text{ eV}$

$\lambda = \dfrac{hc}{\Delta E} = \dfrac{(6.63 \times 10^{-34} \text{ J} \cdot \text{s})(3.00 \times 10^8 \text{ m/s})}{(1.89 \text{ eV})(1.61 \times 10^{-19} \text{ J/eV})}$

$\quad = 6.54 \times 10^{-7}$ m = 654 nm

Copyright © by Glencoe/McGraw-Hill

5. The diameter of the hydrogen nucleus is 2.5×10^{-15} m and the distance between the nucleus and the first electron is about 5×10^{-9} m. If you use a baseball with diameter of 7.5 cm to represent the nucleus, how far away would the electron be?

$$\frac{x}{0.075 \text{ m}} = \frac{5 \times 10^{-9} \text{ m}}{2.5 \times 10^{-15} \text{ m}}$$

$$x = 200\ 000 \text{ m, or } 200 \text{ km}$$

6. A mercury atom drops from 8.82 eV to 6.67 eV.

a. What is the energy of the photon emitted by the mercury atom?

$$\Delta E = 8.82 \text{ eV} - 6.67 \text{ eV} = 2.15 \text{ eV}$$

b. What is the frequency of the photon emitted by the mercury atom?

$$\Delta E = hf = 2.15 \text{ eV} \left[\frac{1.60 \times 10^{-19} \text{ J}}{\text{eV}} \right]$$

$$= 3.44 \times 10^{-19} \text{ J}$$

$$\text{So } f = \frac{\Delta E}{h} = \frac{3.44 \times 10^{-19} \text{ J}}{6.63 \times 10^{-34} \text{ J} \cdot \text{s}}$$

$$= 5.19 \times 10^{14} \text{ Hz}$$

c. What is the wavelength of the photon emitted by the mercury atom?

$$c = \lambda f, \text{ so}$$

$$\lambda = \frac{c}{f} = \frac{3.00 \times 10^8 \text{ m/s}}{5.19 \times 10^{14}/\text{s}}$$

$$= 5.78 \times 10^{-7} \text{ m, or } 578 \text{ nm}$$

Chapter Review Problems

pages 666–667

page 666

Section 28.1

Level 1

See **Figure 28–21** *for Problems 21, 22, and 23.*

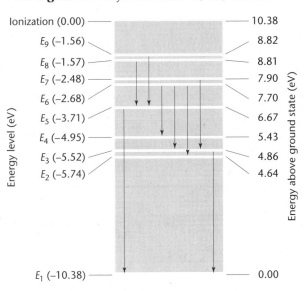

FIGURE 28–21

21. A mercury atom is in an excited state when its energy level is 6.67 eV above the ground state. A photon of energy 2.15 eV strikes the mercury atom and is absorbed by it. To what energy level is the mercury atom raised?

$$E = 6.67 \text{ eV} + 2.15 \text{ eV}$$

$$= 8.82 \text{ eV, which is } E_9$$

22. A mercury atom is in an excited state at the E_6 energy level.

a. How much energy would be needed to ionize the atom?

$$E_6 = 7.70 \text{ eV}$$

$$10.38 \text{ eV} - 7.70 \text{ eV} = 2.68 \text{ eV}$$

Copyright © by Glencoe/McGraw-Hill

22. (continued)

b. How much energy would be released if the electron dropped down to the E_2 energy level instead?

$E_2 = 4.64$ eV

7.70 eV $- 4.64$ eV $= 3.06$ eV

23. A mercury atom in an excited state has an energy of -4.95 eV. It absorbs a photon that raises it to the next higher energy level.

a. What is the energy of the photon?

$E_5 - E_4 = -3.71$ eV $- (-4.95$ eV$)$

$= 1.24$ eV

b. What is the photon's frequency?

$E = hf$

so $f = \dfrac{E}{h} = \dfrac{1.24 \text{ eV} \left(\dfrac{1.60 \times 10^{-19} \text{ J}}{\text{eV}} \right)}{6.63 \times 10^{-34} \text{ J} \cdot \text{s}}$

$= 2.99 \times 10^{14}$ Hz

24. A photon with an energy of 14.0 eV enters a hydrogen atom in the ground state and ionizes it. With what kinetic energy will the electron be ejected from the atom?

It takes 13.6 eV to ionize the atom, so 14.0 eV $-$ 13.6 eV $=$ 0.4 eV kinetic energy.

---

page 667

25. Calculate the radius of the orbital associated with the energy levels E_5 and E_6 of the hydrogen atom.

$r_5 = \dfrac{h^2 n^2}{4\pi^2 Kmq^2} = \dfrac{(6.63 \times 10^{-34} \text{ J} \cdot \text{s})^2 (5)^2}{4\pi^2 [9.00 \times 10^9 \text{ N} \cdot \text{m}^2/\text{C}^2] (9.11 \times 10^{-31} \text{ kg})(1.60 \times 10^{-19} \text{ C})^2}$

$= 1.33 \times 10^{-9}$ m

$r_6 = \dfrac{(6.63 \times 10^{-34} \text{ J} \cdot \text{s})^2 (6)^2}{4\pi^2 (9.00 \times 10^9 \text{ N} \cdot \text{m}^2/\text{C}^2)(9.11 \times 10^{-31} \text{ kg})(1.60 \times 10^{-19} \text{ C})^2} = 1.91 \times 10^{-9}$ m

---

26. What energies are associated with a hydrogen atom's energy levels E_2, E_3, E_4, E_5, and E_6?

$E_2 = \dfrac{-13.6 \text{ eV}}{n^2} = \dfrac{-13.6 \text{ eV}}{(2)^2} = -3.40$ eV

$E_3 = \dfrac{-13.6 \text{ eV}}{(3)^2} = -1.51$ eV

$E_4 = \dfrac{-13.6 \text{ eV}}{(4)^2} = -0.850$ eV

$E_5 = \dfrac{-13.6 \text{ eV}}{(5)^2} = -0.544$ eV

$E_6 = \dfrac{-13.6 \text{ eV}}{(6)^2} = -0.378$ eV

27. Using the values that are calculated in problem 26, calculate the following energy differences for a hydrogen atom.

a. $E_6 - E_5$

$(-0.378$ eV$) - (-0.544$ eV$) = 0.166$ eV

b. $E_6 - E_3$

$(-0.378$ eV$) - (-1.51$ eV$) = 1.13$ eV

c. $E_4 - E_2$

$(-0.850$ eV$) - (-3.40$ eV$) = 2.55$ eV

d. $E_5 - E_2$

$(-0.544$ eV$) - (-3.40$ eV$) = 2.86$ eV

e. $E_5 - E_3$

$(-0.544$ eV$) - (-1.51$ eV$) = 0.97$ eV

28. Use the values from problem 27 to determine the frequencies of the photons emitted when an electron in a hydrogen atom makes the level changes listed.

a. $E = hf$, so $f = \dfrac{E}{h}$

$hf = E_6 - E_5 = 0.166$ eV

$f = \dfrac{(0.166 \text{ eV})(1.60 \times 10^{-19} \text{ J/eV})}{6.63 \times 10^{-34} \text{ J/Hz}}$

$= 4.01 \times 10^{13}$ Hz

b. $hf = E_6 - E_3 = 1.13$ eV

$f = \dfrac{(1.13 \text{ eV})(1.60 \times 10^{-19} \text{ J/eV})}{6.63 \times 10^{-34} \text{ J/Hz}}$

$= 2.73 \times 10^{14}$ Hz

Copyright © by Glencoe/McGraw-Hill

28. (continued)

c. $hf = E_4 - E_2 = 2.55$ eV

$$f = \frac{(2.55 \text{ eV})(1.60 \times 10^{-19} \text{ J/eV})}{6.63 \times 10^{-34} \text{ J/Hz}}$$

$$= 6.15 \times 10^{14} \text{ Hz}$$

d. $hf = E_5 - E_2 = 2.86$ eV

$$f = \frac{(2.86 \text{ eV})(1.60 \times 10^{-19} \text{ J/eV})}{6.63 \times 10^{-34} \text{ J/Hz}}$$

$$= 6.90 \times 10^{14} \text{ Hz}$$

e. $hf = E_5 - E_3 = 0.97$ eV

$$f = \frac{(0.97 \text{ eV})(1.60 \times 10^{-19} \text{ J/eV})}{6.6 \times 10^{-34} \text{ J/Hz}}$$

$$= 2.4 \times 10^{14} \text{ Hz}$$

29. Determine the wavelengths of the photons of the frequencies that you calculated in problem 28.

a. $c = \lambda f$, so

$$\lambda = \frac{c}{f} = \frac{3.00 \times 10^8 \text{ m/s}}{4.01 \times 10^{13} \text{ Hz}}$$

$$= 7.48 \times 10^{-6} \text{ m} = 7480 \text{ nm}$$

b. $\lambda = \frac{c}{f} = \frac{3.00 \times 10^8 \text{ m/s}}{2.73 \times 10^{14} \text{ Hz}}$

$$= 1.10 \times 10^{-6} \text{ m} = 1.10 \times 10^3 \text{ nm}$$

c. $\lambda = \frac{c}{f} = \frac{3.00 \times 10^8 \text{ m/s}}{6.15 \times 10^{14} \text{ Hz}}$

$$= 4.87 \times 10^{-7} \text{ m} = 487 \text{ nm}$$

d. $\lambda = \frac{c}{f} = \frac{3.00 \times 10^8 \text{ m/s}}{6.90 \times 10^{14} \text{ Hz}}$

$$= 4.34 \times 10^{-7} \text{ m} = 434 \text{ nm}$$

e. $\lambda = \frac{c}{f} = \frac{3.00 \times 10^8 \text{ m/s}}{2.3 \times 10^{14} \text{ Hz}}$

$$= 1.3 \times 10^{-6} \text{ m} = 1.3 \times 10^3 \text{ nm}$$

30. Determine the frequency and wavelength of the photon emitted when an electron drops

a. from E_3 to E_2 in an excited hydrogen atom.

$$E_3 - E_2 = -1.51 \text{ eV} - (-3.40 \text{ eV})$$

$$= 1.89 \text{ eV}$$

$$1.89 \text{ eV} \left(\frac{1.60 \times 10^{-19} \text{ J}}{\text{eV}} \right)$$

$$= 3.02 \times 10^{-19} \text{ J}$$

$E = hf$, so

$$f = \frac{E}{h} = \frac{3.02 \times 10^{-19} \text{ J}}{6.63 \times 10^{-34} \text{ J} \cdot \text{s}}$$

$$= 4.56 \times 10^{14} \text{ Hz}$$

$c = \lambda f$, so

$$\lambda = \frac{c}{f} = \frac{3.00 \times 10^8 \text{ m/s}}{4.56 \times 10^{14} \text{ Hz}}$$

$$= 6.58 \times 10^{-7} \text{ m} = 658 \text{ nm}$$

b. from E_4 to E_3 in an excited hydrogen atom.

$$E_4 - E_3 = -0.850 \text{ eV} - (-1.51 \text{ eV})$$

$$= 0.66 \text{ eV}$$

$$0.66 \text{ eV} \left(\frac{1.60 \times 10^{-19} \text{ J}}{\text{eV}} \right)$$

$$= 1.1 \times 10^{-19} \text{ J}$$

$E = hf$, so

$$f = \frac{E}{h} = \frac{1.1 \times 10^{-19} \text{ J}}{6.63 \times 10^{-34} \text{ J} \cdot \text{s}}$$

$$= 1.6 \times 10^{14} \text{ Hz}$$

$c = \lambda f$, so

$$\lambda = \frac{c}{f} = \frac{3.00 \times 10^8 \text{ m/s}}{1.6 \times 10^{14} \text{ Hz}} = 1900 \text{ nm}$$

31. What is the difference between the energies of the E_4 and E_1 energy levels of the hydrogen atom?

$$E_4 - E_1 = (-0.85 \text{ eV}) - (-13.6 \text{ eV})$$

$$= 12.8 \text{ eV}$$

Copyright © by Glencoe/McGraw-Hill

Level 2

32. From what energy level did an electron fall if it emits a photon of 94.3 nm wavelength when it reaches ground state within a hydrogen atom?

$c = \lambda f$, so

$$f = \frac{c}{\lambda} = \frac{3.00 \times 10^8 \text{ m/s}}{9.43 \times 10^{-8} \text{ m}}$$

$$= 3.18 \times 10^{15} \text{ Hz}$$

$E_N - E_1$

$$= (6.626 \times 10^{-34} \text{ J/Hz})(3.18 \times 10^{15} \text{ Hz})$$

$$= 2.11 \times 10^{-18} \text{ J}$$

$E_N = (-2.17 \times 10^{-18} \text{ J})$

$$+ 2.11 \times 10^{-18} \text{ J}$$

$E_N = -6 \times 10^{-20} \text{ J}$

$$\frac{-2.17 \times 10^{-18} \text{ J}}{N^2} = -6 \times 10^{-20} \text{ J}$$

$N^2 = 36$

$N = 6$

33. For a hydrogen atom in the $n = 3$ Bohr orbital, find

a. the radius of the orbital.

$$r = \frac{h^2 n^2}{4\pi^2 K m q^2}$$

$h = 6.63 \times 10^{-34} \text{ J} \cdot \text{s}$

$k = 9.00 \times 10^9 \text{ N} \cdot \text{m}^2/\text{C}^2$

$m = 9.11 \times 10^{-31} \text{ kg}$

$q = 1.60 \times 10^{-19} \text{ C}$

Thus,

$n = 1$, $r = 5.30 \times 10^{-11} \text{ m}$

when $n = 3$, $r = 4.77 \times 10^{-10} \text{ m}$

b. the electric force acting between the proton and the electron.

$$F = \frac{Kq^2}{r^2}$$

$$= \frac{(9.00 \times 10^9 \text{ N} \cdot \text{m}^2/\text{C}^2)(1.60 \times 10^{-19} \text{ C})^2}{(4.77 \times 10^{-10} \text{ m})^2}$$

$$= 1.01 \times 10^{-9} \text{ N}$$

c. the centripetal acceleration of the electron.

$F = ma$, so

$$a = \frac{F}{m} = \frac{1.01 \times 10^{-9} \text{ N}}{9.11 \times 10^{-31} \text{ kg}}$$

$$= 1.11 \times 10^{21} \text{ m/s}^2$$

d. the orbital speed of the electron. Compare this speed with the speed of light.

$$a = \frac{v^2}{r}, \text{ so}$$

$$v = \sqrt{ar}$$

$$= \sqrt{(1.11 \times 10^{21} \text{ m/s}^2)(4.77 \times 10^{-10} \text{ m})}$$

$$= 7.28 \times 10^5 \text{ m/s, or 0.2\% of } c$$

34. A hydrogen atom has its electron in the $n = 2$ level.

a. If a photon with a wavelength of 332 nm strikes the atom, show that the atom will be ionized.

$$E_2 = \frac{13.6 \text{ eV}}{n^2} = \frac{13.6 \text{ eV}}{4} = 3.40 \text{ eV}$$

$$E = hf = \frac{hc}{\lambda}$$

$$= \frac{(6.63 \times 10^{-34} \text{ J/Hz})(3.00 \times 10^8 \text{ m/s})}{332 \times 10^{-9} \text{ m}}$$

$$= 5.99 \times 10^{-19} \text{ J}$$

$$= 3.74 \text{ eV}$$

Yes, the atom is ionized.

b. When the atom is ionized, assume that the electron receives the excess energy from the ionization. What will be the kinetic energy of the electron in joules?

$3.74 \text{ eV} - 3.40 \text{ eV} = 0.340 \text{ eV}$

$$= 5.4 \times 10^{-20} \text{ J}$$

Copyright © by Glencoe/McGraw-Hill

Section 28.2

Level 2

35. Gallium arsenide lasers are used in CD players. If such a laser emits at 840 nm, what is the difference in eV between the two lasing energy levels?

$c = \lambda f$, so

$$f = \frac{c}{\lambda} = \frac{3.00 \times 10^8 \text{ m/s}}{840 \times 10^{-9} \text{ m}}$$

$$= 3.57 \times 10^{14} \text{ Hz}$$

$E = hf$

$$= \frac{(6.64 \times 10^{-34} \text{ J/Hz})(3.57 \times 10^{14} \text{ Hz})}{1.60 \times 10^{-19} \text{ J/eV}}$$

$$= 1.5 \text{ eV}$$

36. A carbon dioxide laser emits very high-power infrared radiation. What is the energy difference in eV between the two lasing energy levels?

$c = \lambda f$, so

$$f = \frac{c}{\lambda} = \frac{3.00 \times 10^8 \text{ m/s}}{10\,600 \times 10^{-19} \text{ m}}$$

$$= 2.83 \times 10^{13} \text{ Hz}$$

$E = hf$

$$= \frac{(6.63 \times 10^{-34} \text{ J/Hz})(2.83 \times 10^{13} \text{ Hz})}{1.60 \times 10^{-19} \text{ J/eV}}$$

$$= 0.117 \text{ eV}$$

Critical Thinking Problems

37. The four brightest lines in the mercury spectrum have wavelengths of 405 nm, 436 nm, 546 nm, and 578 nm. What are the differences in energy levels for each of these lines?

405 nm (3.06 eV) from E_6 to E_2

436 nm (2.84 eV) from E_6 to E_3

546 nm (2.27 eV) from E_6 to E_4

578 nm (2.15 eV) from E_8 to E_5

38. After the emission of these visible photons, the mercury atom continues to emit photons until it reaches the ground state. From inspection of **Figure 28–21**, determine whether or not any of these photons would be visible. Explain.

No. The three highest energy lines leave the atom in states at least 4.64 eV above the ground state. A photon with this energy has a wavelength of 227 nm, in the ultraviolet. The change from E_4 to E_2 involves an energy change of only 0.79 eV, resulting in light with a wavelength of 1570 nm, in the infrared.

Copyright © by Glencoe/McGraw-Hill

29 Solid State Electronics

Practice Problems

29.1 Conduction in Solids
pages 670–678

page 672

1. Zinc, density 7.13 g/cm^3, atomic mass 65.37 g/mole, has two free electrons per atom. How many free electrons are there in each cubic centimeter of zinc?

$$\frac{\text{free e}^-}{\text{cm}^3} = \frac{(2 \text{ e}^-/\text{atom})(6.02 \times 10^{23} \text{ atoms/mol})(7.13 \text{ g/cm}^3)}{(65.37 \text{ g/mol})}$$

$$= 1.31 \times 10^{23} \text{ free e}^-/\text{cm}^3$$

page 675

2. In pure germanium, density 5.23 g/cm^3, atomic mass 72.6 g/mole, there are 2×10^{16} free electrons/cm^3 at room temperature. How many free electrons are there per atom?

atoms/cm^3

$$= \frac{(6.02 \times 10^{23} \text{ atoms/mol})(5.23 \text{ g/cm}^3)}{72.6 \text{ g/mol}}$$

$$= 4.34 \times 10^{22} \text{ atoms/cm}^3$$

$$\text{free e}^-/\text{atom} = \frac{(2 \times 10^{16} \text{ free e}^-/\text{cm}^3)}{(4.34 \times 10^{22} \text{ atoms/cm}^3)}$$

$$= 5 \times 10^{-7}$$

page 677

3. If you wanted to have 5×10^3 as many electrons from As doping as thermally free electrons in the germanium semiconductor described in Practice Problem 2, how many As atoms should there be per Ge atom?

   There were 5×10^{-7} free e$^-$/Ge atom, so we need 5×10^3 as many As dopant atoms, or 3×10^{-3} As atom/Ge atom.

29.2 Electronic Devices
pages 679–686

page 681

4. What battery voltage would be needed to produce a current of 2.5 mA in the diode in the preceding Example Problem?

   At $I = 2.5$ mA, $V_d = 0.7$ V, so

   $$V = V_d + IR$$
   $$= 0.7 \text{ V} + (2.5 \times 10^{-3} \text{ A})(470 \text{ } \Omega)$$
   $$= 1.9 \text{ V}$$

5. A Ge diode has a voltage drop of 0.4 V when 12 mA flow through it. If the same 470-Ω resistor is used, what battery voltage is needed?

   $$V = V_d + IR$$
   $$= 0.4 \text{ V} + (1.2 \times 10^{-2} \text{ A})(470 \text{ } \Omega)$$
   $$= 6.0 \text{ V}$$

Copyright © by Glencoe/McGraw-Hill

Chapter Review Problems

pages 688–689

page 688

Section 29.1

Level 1

17. The forbidden gap in silicon is 1.1 eV. Electromagnetic waves striking the silicon cause electrons to move from the valence band to the conduction band. What is the longest wavelength of radiation that could excite an electron in this way? Recall that

$$E = \frac{1240 \text{ eV} \cdot \text{nm}}{\lambda}$$

$E = \dfrac{1240 \text{ eV} \cdot \text{nm}}{\lambda}$, where the energy must be in eV and the wavelength must be in nm.

So $\lambda = \dfrac{1240 \text{ eV} \cdot \text{nm}}{1.1 \text{ eV}} = 1.1 \times 10^3$ nm

$= 1.1 \ \mu m$ (infrared)

18. A light-emitting diode (LED) produces green light with a wavelength of 550 nm when an electron moves from the conduction band to the valence band. Find the width of the forbidden gap in eV in this diode.

$E = \dfrac{1240 \text{ eV} \cdot \text{nm}}{\lambda} = \dfrac{1240 \text{ eV} \cdot \text{nm}}{550 \text{ nm}}$

$= 2.3$ eV

19. How many free electrons exist in a cubic centimeter of sodium? Its density is 0.971 g/cm³, its atomic mass is 22.99 g/mole, and there is one free electron per atom.

$\dfrac{\text{free } e^-}{\text{cm}^3}$

$= \left(\dfrac{1 \ e^-}{\text{atom}}\right)\left(\dfrac{6.02 \times 10^{23} \text{ atoms}}{\text{mole}}\right)$

$\times \left(\dfrac{\text{mole}}{22.99 \text{ g}}\right)\left(\dfrac{0.971 \text{ g}}{\text{cm}^3}\right)$

$= 2.54 \times 10^{22} \ \dfrac{\text{free } e^-}{\text{cm}^3}$

Level 2

20. At a temperature of 0°C, thermal energy frees 1.1×10^{12} e⁻/cm³ in pure silicon. The density of silicon is 2.33 g/cm³, and the atomic mass of silicon is 28.09 g/mole. What is the fraction of atoms that have free electrons?

$$\frac{\text{free } e^-}{\text{atom}} = \frac{\left(\dfrac{\text{free } e^-}{\text{cm}^3}\right)}{\left(\dfrac{\text{atom}}{\text{cm}^3}\right)}$$

$$= \frac{1.1 \times 10^{12} \ e^-/\text{cm}^3}{\left(6.02 \times 10^{23} \dfrac{\text{atom}}{\text{mole}}\right)\left(\dfrac{\text{mole}}{28.09 \text{ g}}\right)\left(\dfrac{2.33 \text{ g}}{\text{cm}^3}\right)}$$

$$= \frac{1.1 \times 10^{12} \ \dfrac{e^-}{\text{cm}^3}}{4.99 \times 10^{22} \ \dfrac{\text{atom}}{\text{cm}^3}} = 2.2 \times 10^{-11} \ \frac{e^-}{\text{atom}}$$

21. Use the periodic table to determine which of the following elements could be added to germanium to make a *p*-type semiconductor: B, C, N, P, Si, Al, Ge, Ga, As, In, Sn, and Sb.

B, Al, Ba, In (Group 3)

22. Which of the elements listed in problem 21 would produce an *n*-type semiconductor?

N, P, As, Sb (Group 5)

Section 29.2

Level 1

23. The potential drop across a glowing LED is about 1.2 V. In **Figure 29–16,** the potential drop across the resistor is the difference between the battery voltage and the LED's potential drop, 6.0 V − 1.2 V = 4.8 V. What is the current through

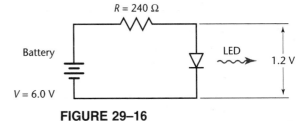

FIGURE 29–16

a. the LED?

$I = \dfrac{V}{R} = \dfrac{4.8 \text{ V}}{240 \ \Omega} = 0.020$ A $=$

2.0×10^1 mA

Copyright © by Glencoe/McGraw-Hill

23. (continued)

    b. the resistor?

    2.0×10^1 mA. The current is the same through both.

24. Jon wanted to raise the current through the LED in problem 23 up to 30 mA so that it would glow brighter. Assume that the potential drop across the LED is still 1.2 V. What resistor should be used?

    $V = IR$, so

    $$R = \frac{V}{I} = \frac{4.8\ V}{0.030\ A} = 160\ \Omega$$

25. **Figure 29–17** shows a battery, diode, and bulb connected in series so that the bulb lights. Note that the diode is forward-biased. State whether the bulb in each of the pictured circuits, 1, 2, and 3, is lighted.

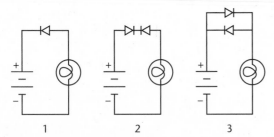

FIGURE 29–17

    Circuit 1 No (diode reverse-biased).

    Circuit 2 No (no current through second reverse-biased diode).

    Circuit 3 Yes (current through forward-biased diode).

26. In the circuit shown in **Figure 29–18,** tell whether lamp L_1, lamp L_2, both, or neither is lighted.

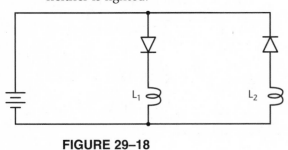

FIGURE 29–18

    a. L_1 is on, L_2 is off.

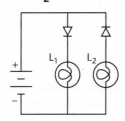

27. A silicon diode whose I/V characteristics are shown in **Figure 29–11** is connected to a battery through a 270-Ω resistor. The battery forward-biases the diode, and its voltage is adjusted until the diode current is 15 mA. What is the battery voltage?

    The diode voltage drop is 0.7 V. The voltage drop across the resistor is

    $(270\ \Omega)(1.5 \times 10^{-2}\ A) = 4.1$ V

    Thus the battery voltage is 4.8 V.

page 689

28. What bulbs are lighted in the circuit shown in **Figure 29–19** when

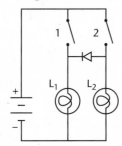

FIGURE 29–19

    a. switch 1 is closed and switch 2 is open?

    Light 1 only.

    b. switch 2 is closed and switch 1 is open?

    Both lights 1 and 2.

Level 2

29. Which element or elements could be used as the second dopant used to make a diode, if the first dopant were boron?

    N, P, As, or Sb (all Group 5, n-types)

Copyright © by Glencoe/McGraw-Hill

Critical Thinking Problems

30. The *I/V* characteristics of two LEDs that glow with different colors are shown in **Figure 29–20.** Each is to be connected through a resistor to a 9.0-V battery. If each is to be run at a current of 0.040 A, what resistors should be chosen for each?

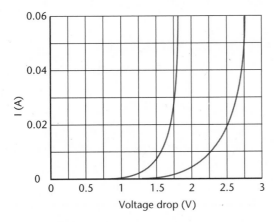

FIGURE 29–20

For the lower-voltage one, at 0.040 A, the voltage drop is 1.8 V. So, the potential drop across the resistor is

9.0 V − 1.8 V = 7.2 V

The resistor is then

$$R = \frac{\Delta V}{I} = \frac{7.2 \text{ V}}{0.040 \text{ A}} = 180 \ \Omega$$

The higher-voltage LED would require

$$R = \frac{9.0 - 2.7}{0.040 \text{ A}} = 160 \ \Omega$$

31. Suppose that the two LEDs in problem 30 are now connected in series. If the same battery is to be used and a current of 0.035 A is desired, what resistor should be used?

In series, the voltage drop across the two diodes at 0.035 A is

1.7 + 2.6 = 4.3 V

Therefore, the resistance is

$$\frac{9.0 \text{ V} - 4.3 \text{ V}}{0.035 \text{ A}} = 134 \ \Omega = 130 \ \Omega$$

Copyright © by Glencoe/McGraw-Hill

30 The Nucleus

Practice Problems

30.1 Radioactivity
pages 692–699

page 694

1. Three isotopes of uranium have mass numbers of 234, 235, and 238. The atomic number of uranium is 92. How many neutrons are in the nuclei of each of these isotopes?

   $A - Z = $ *neutrons*

   $234 - 92 = 142$ neutrons

   $235 - 92 = 143$ neutrons

   $238 - 92 = 146$ neutrons

2. An isotope of oxygen has a mass number of 15. How many neutrons are in the nuclei of this isotope?

   $A - Z = 15 - 8 = 7$ neutrons

3. How many neutrons are in the mercury isotope $^{200}_{80}$Hg?

   $A - Z = 200 - 80 = 120$ neutrons

4. Write the symbols for the three isotopes of hydrogen which have zero, one, and two neutrons in the nucleus.

   $^{1}_{1}$H, $^{2}_{1}$H, $^{3}_{1}$H

page 697

5. Write the nuclear equation for the transmutation of a radioactive uranium isotope, $^{234}_{92}$U, into a thorium isotope, $^{230}_{90}$Th, by the emission of an α particle.

   $^{234}_{92}$U → $^{230}_{90}$Th + $^{4}_{2}$He

6. Write the nuclear equation for the transmutation of a radioactive thorium isotope, $^{230}_{90}$Th, into a radioactive radium isotope, $^{226}_{88}$Ra, by the emission of an α particle.

   $^{230}_{90}$Th → $^{226}_{88}$Ra + $^{4}_{2}$He

page 698

7. Write the nuclear equation for the transmutation of a radioactive radium isotope, $^{266}_{88}$Ra, into a radon isotope, $^{222}_{86}$Rn, by α decay.

   $^{226}_{88}$Ra → $^{222}_{86}$Rn + $^{4}_{2}$He

8. A radioactive lead isotope, $^{214}_{82}$Pb, can change to a radioactive bismuth isotope, $^{214}_{83}$Bi, by the emission of a β particle and an antineutrino. Write the nuclear equation.

   $^{214}_{82}$Pb → $^{214}_{83}$Bi + $^{0}_{-1}$e + $^{0}_{0}$$\bar{v}$

page 699

Refer to **Figure 30–5** *and* **Table 30–1** *to solve the following problems.*

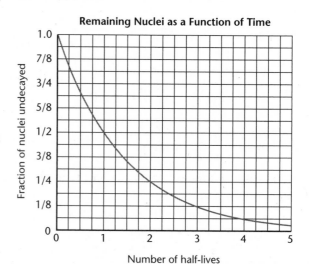

FIGURE 30–5

Copyright © by Glencoe/McGraw-Hill

TABLE 30–1			
Half-Life of Selected Isotopes			
Element	Isotope	Half-Life	Radiation Produced
hydrogen	$^{3}_{1}H$	12.3 years	β
carbon	$^{14}_{6}C$	5730 years	β
cobalt	$^{60}_{27}Co$	30 years	β, γ
iodine	$^{131}_{53}I$	8.07 days	β, γ
lead	$^{212}_{82}Pb$	10.6 hours	β
polonium	$^{194}_{84}Po$	0.7 seconds	α
polonium	$^{210}_{84}Po$	138 days	α, γ
uranium	$^{235}_{92}U$	7.1×10^{8} years	α, γ
uranium	$^{238}_{92}U$	4.51×10^{9} years	α, γ
plutonium	$^{236}_{94}Pu$	2.85 years	α
plutonium	$^{242}_{94}Pu$	3.79×10^{5} years	α, γ

9. A sample of 1.0 g of tritium, $^{3}_{1}H$, is produced. What will be the mass of the tritium remaining after 24.6 years?

   24.6 years = 2(12.3 years),

   which is 2 half-lives. Since

   $\frac{1}{2} \times \frac{1}{2} = \frac{1}{4}$, **there will be**

   (1.0 g) $\left(\frac{1}{4}\right)$ **= 0.25 g remaining**

10. The isotope $^{238}_{93}Np$ has a half-life of 2.0 days. If 4.0 g of neptunium is produced on Monday, what will be the mass of neptunium remaining on Tuesday of the next week?

    Amount remaining = (original

    amount) $\left(\frac{1}{2}\right)^{N}$ **where N is the number**

    of half-lives elapsed. Since

    $N = \frac{8 \text{ days}}{2.0 \text{ days}} = 4$

    Amount remaining = (4.0 g) $\left(\frac{1}{2}\right)^{4}$

    = 0.25 g

11. A sample of polonium-210 is purchased for a physics class on September 1. Its activity is 2×10^{6} Bq. The sample is used in an experiment on June 1. What activity can be expected?

The half-life of $^{210}_{84}Po$ is 138 days.

There are 273 days or about 2 half-lives between September 1 and June 1. So the activity

$= \left(2 \times 10^{6} \frac{\text{decays}}{\text{s}}\right)\left(\frac{1}{2}\right)\left(\frac{1}{2}\right)$

$= 5 \times 10^{5}$ Bq

12. Tritium, $^{3}_{1}H$, was once used in some watches to produce a fluorescent glow so that the watches could be read in the dark. If the brightness of the glow is proportional to the activity of the tritium, what would be the brightness of such a watch, in comparison to its original brightness, when the watch is six years old?

    From Table 30–1, 6 years is approximately 0.5 half-life for tritium. Since Figure 30–5 indicates that approximately $\frac{11}{16}$ of the original nuclei remain after 0.5 half-life, the brightness will be about $\frac{11}{16}$ of the original.

30.2 The Building Blocks of Matter
pages 701–712

page 708

13. The mass of a proton is 1.67×10^{-27} kg.

    a. Find the energy equivalent of the proton's mass in joules.

    $E = mc^{2}$

    $= (1.67 \times 10^{-27} \text{ kg})(3.00 \times 10^{8} \text{ m/s})^{2}$

    $= 1.50 \times 10^{-10}$ J

    b. Convert this value to eV.

    $E = \frac{1.50 \times 10^{-10} \text{ J}}{1.60 \times 10^{-19} \text{ J/eV}}$

    $= 9.38 \times 10^{8}$ eV

    $= 938$ MeV

    c. Find the smallest total γ ray energy that could result in a proton-antiproton pair.

    The energy will be

    (2)(938 MeV) = 1.88 GeV

Copyright © by Glencoe/McGraw-Hill

Chapter Review Problems

pages 714–715

page 714

Section 30.1

Level 1

18. An atom of an isotope of magnesium has an atomic mass of about 24 u. The atomic number of magnesium is 12. How many neutrons are in the nucleus of this atom?

    $A - Z$ = neutrons

    24 − 12 = 12 neutrons

    12 neutrons $^{24}_{12}$Mg

19. An atom of an isotope of nitrogen has an atomic mass of about 15 u. The atomic number of nitrogen is 7. How many neutrons are in the nucleus of this isotope?

    $A - Z$ = neutrons

    15 − 7 = 8 neutrons

20. List the number of neutrons in an atom of each of the following isotopes.

    a. $^{112}_{48}$Cd

    112 − 48 = 64 neutrons

    b. $^{209}_{83}$Bi

    209 − 83 = 126 neutrons

    c. $^{208}_{83}$Bi

    208 − 83 = 125 neutrons

    d. $^{80}_{35}$Br

    80 − 35 = 45 neutrons

    e. $^{1}_{1}$H

    1 − 1 = 0 neutrons

    f. $^{40}_{18}$Ar

    40 − 18 = 22 neutrons

21. Find the symbol for the elements that are shown by the following symbols, where X replaces the symbol for the element.

    a. $^{18}_{9}X$ b. $^{241}_{95}X$

    F   **Am**

    c. $^{21}_{10}X$ d. $^{7}_{3}X$

    Ne   **Li**

22. A radioactive bismuth isotope, $^{214}_{83}$Bi, emits a β particle. Write the complete nuclear equation, showing the element formed.

    $^{214}_{83}$Bi → $^{214}_{84}$Po + $^{0}_{-1}$e + $^{0}_{0}\bar{v}$

23. A radioactive polonium isotope, $^{210}_{84}$Po, emits an α particle. Write the complete nuclear equation, showing the element formed.

    $^{210}_{84}$Po → $^{206}_{82}$Pb + $^{4}_{2}$He

24. An unstable chromium isotope, $^{56}_{24}$Cr, emits a β particle. Write a complete equation showing the element formed.

    $^{56}_{24}$Cr → $^{56}_{25}$Mn + $^{0}_{-1}$e + $^{0}_{0}\bar{v}$

25. During a reaction, two deuterons, $^{2}_{1}$H, combine to form a helium isotope, $^{3}_{2}$He. What other particle is produced?

    $^{2}_{1}$H + $^{2}_{1}$H → $^{3}_{2}$He + $^{1}_{0}$n

26. On the sun, the nuclei of four ordinary hydrogen atoms combine to form a helium isotope, $^{4}_{2}$He. What particles are missing from the following equation for this reaction?

    4^{1}_{1}H → $^{4}_{2}$He + ?

    4^{1}_{1}H → $^{4}_{2}$He + 2^{0}_{1}e + $2^{0}_{0}\bar{v}$

27. Write a complete nuclear equation for the transmutation of a uranium isotope, $^{227}_{92}$U, into a thorium isotope, $^{223}_{90}$Th.

    $^{227}_{92}$U → $^{223}_{90}$Th + $^{4}_{2}$He

28. In an accident in a research laboratory, a radioactive isotope with a half-life of three days is spilled. As a result, the radiation is eight times the maximum permissible amount. How long must workers wait before they can enter the room?

    For the activity to fall $\frac{1}{8}$ its present amount, you must wait three half-lives, or 9 days.

Copyright © by Glencoe/McGraw-Hill

29. If the half-life of an isotope is two years, what fraction of the isotope remains after six years?

$$\left(\frac{1}{2}\right)^3 = \frac{1}{8}$$

30. The half-life of strontium-90 is 28 years. After 280 years, how would the intensity of a sample of strontium-90 compare to the original intensity of the sample?

280 years is 10 half-lives. $\left(\frac{1}{2}\right)^{10}$
is equal to 9.8×10^{-4} or
approximately 0.098%.

Level 2

31. $^{238}_{92}$U decays by α emission and two successive β emissions back into uranium again. Show the three nuclear decay equations and predict the atomic mass number of the uranium formed.

$$^{238}_{92}\text{U} \rightarrow {}^{234}_{90}\text{Th} + {}^{4}_{2}\text{He}$$
$$^{234}_{90}\text{Th} \rightarrow {}^{234}_{91}\text{Pa} + {}^{0}_{-1}\text{e} + {}^{0}_{0}\bar{v}$$
$$^{234}_{91}\text{Pa} \rightarrow {}^{234}_{92}\text{U} + {}^{0}_{-1}\text{e} + {}^{0}_{0}\bar{v}$$

A = 234

32. A Geiger-Mueller counter registers an initial reading of 3200 counts while measuring a radioactive substance. It registers 100 counts 30 hours later. What is the half-life of this substance?

3200 counts to 100 counts
represents 5 half-lives.

$$\frac{30\text{ h}}{5} = 6\text{ h}$$

page 715

33. A 14-g sample of $^{14}_{6}$C contains Avogadro's number, 6.02×10^{23}, of nuclei. A 5.0-g sample of C-14 will have how many nondecayed nuclei after 11 460 years?

$$\frac{6.02 \times 10^{23}\text{ nuclei}}{14\text{ g}} = \frac{N}{5.0\text{ g}}$$
$$N = \frac{(6.02 \times 10^{23}\text{ nuclei})(5.0\text{ g})}{14\text{ g}}$$
$$= 2.2 \times 10^{23}\text{ nuclei}$$

After 2 half-lives only $\frac{1}{4}$ of the nuclei are nondecayed.

$$\left(\frac{1}{4}\right)(2.2 \times 10^{23}\text{ nuclei})$$
$$= 5.5 \times 10^{22}\text{ nuclei}$$

34. A 1.00-μg sample of a radioactive material contains 6.0×10^{14} nuclei. After 48 hours, 0.25 μg of the material remains.

a. What is the half-life of the material?

48 h is two half-lives, therefore 24 h is one half-life.

b. How could one determine the activity of the sample at 24 hours using this information?

Determine the slope (at 24 hours) of the line of a graph of remaining nuclei versus time.

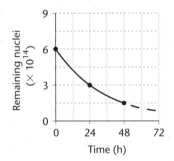

Section 30.2

Level 1

35. What would be the charge of a particle composed of three u quarks?

Each u quark has a charge of $+\frac{2}{3}$.
uuu $= 3\left(+\frac{2}{3}\right) = +2$ elementary charges

36. The charge of an antiquark is opposite that of a quark. A pion is composed of a u quark and an anti-d quark. What would be the charge of this pion?

$$u + \bar{d} = +\frac{2}{3} + \left[-\left(-\frac{1}{3}\right)\right]$$
$$= +1\text{ elementary charge}$$

Copyright © by Glencoe/McGraw-Hill

37. Find the charge of a pion made up of

a. u and anti-u quark pair.

$$u + \bar{u} = +\frac{2}{3} + \left[-\left(+\frac{2}{3}\right)\right] = 0 \text{ charge}$$

b. d and anti-u quarks.

$$d + \bar{u} = -\frac{1}{3} + \left[-\left(+\frac{2}{3}\right)\right] = -1 \text{ charge}$$

c. d and anti-d quarks.

$$d + \bar{d} = -\frac{1}{3} + \left[-\left(-\frac{1}{3}\right)\right] = 0 \text{ charge}$$

Level 2

38. The synchrotron at the Fermi Laboratory has a diameter of 2.0 km. Protons circling in it move at approximately the speed of light.

a. How long does it take a proton to complete one revolution?

$$v = \frac{d}{t}$$

so $t = \dfrac{d}{v} = \dfrac{\pi(2.0 \times 10^3 \text{ m})}{3.0 \times 10^8 \text{ m/s}}$

$$= 2.1 \times 10^{-5} \text{ s}$$

b. The protons enter the ring at an energy of 8.0 GeV. They gain 2.5 MeV each revolution. How many revolutions must they travel before they reach 400.0 GeV of energy?

$$\frac{(400.0 \times 10^9 \text{ eV}) \ 1 \ (8.0 \times 10^9 \text{ eV})}{2.5 \times 10^6 \text{ eV/revolution}}$$

$$= 1.6 \times 10^5 \text{ revolutions}$$

c. How long does it take the protons to be accelerated to 400.0 GeV?

$$t = (1.6 \times 10^5 \text{ rev})(2.1 \times 10^{-5} \text{ s/rev})$$

$$= 3.4 \text{ s}$$

d. How far do the protons travel during this acceleration?

$$d = vt = (3.0 \times 10^8 \text{ m/s})(3.4 \text{ s})$$

$$= 1.0 \times 10^9 \text{ m,}$$
$$\text{or about 1 million km}$$

Critical Thinking Problems

39. Gamma rays carry momentum. The momentum of a gamma ray of energy E_γ is equal to E_γ/c, where c is the speed of light. When an electron-positron pair decays into two gamma rays, both momentum and energy must be conserved. The sum of the energies of the gamma rays is 1.02 MeV. If the positron and electron are initially at rest, what must be the magnitude and direction of the momentum of the two gamma rays?

Because the initial momentum is zero, this must be the final momentum. Thus the two gamma rays must have equal and opposite momentum. So, each must have a momentum of $\frac{1}{2}$ (1.02 MeV)/c, and they move in opposite directions.

40. An electron-positron pair, initially at rest, also can decay into three gamma rays. If all three gamma rays have equal energies, what must be their relative directions?

The question becomes the following: how can three particles, each with the same momentum, have zero total momentum? The three gamma rays leave with angles of 120° between them on a plane.

Copyright © by Glencoe/McGraw-Hill

31 Nuclear Applications

Practice Problems

31.1 Holding the Nucleus Together
pages 718–721

page 720

Use these values to solve the following problems:

> *mass of proton = 1.007825 u*
>
> *mass of neutron = 1.008665 u*
>
> *1 u = 931.49 MeV*

1. The carbon isotope, $^{12}_{6}$C, has a nuclear mass of 12.0000 u.

   a. Calculate its mass defect.

6 protons = (6)(1.007825 u) =		**6.046950 u**
6 neutrons = (6)(1.008665 u) =		**6.051990 u**
	total	**12.098940 u**
mass of carbon nucleus		**−12.000000 u**
	mass defect	**−0.098940 u**

   b. Calculate its binding energy in MeV.

   −(0.098940 u)(931.49 MeV/u) = −92.162 MeV

2. The isotope of hydrogen that contains one proton and one neutron is called deuterium. The mass of its nucleus is 2.014102 u.

page 721

   a. What is its mass defect?

1 proton =		**1.007825 u**
1 neutron =		**1.008665 u**
	total	**2.016490 u**
mass of deuterium nucleus		**−2.014102 u**
	mass defect	**−0.002388 u**

   b. What is the binding energy of deuterium in MeV?

   −(0.002388 u)(931.49 MeV/u) = −2.222 MeV

3. A nitrogen isotope, $^{15}_{7}$N, has seven protons and eight neutrons. Its nucleus has a mass of 15.00011 u.

   a. Calculate the mass defect of this nucleus.

7 protons = 7(1.007825 u) =		**7.054775 u**
8 neutrons = 8(1.008665 u) =		**8.069320 u**
	total	**15.124095 u**
mass of nitrogen nucleus =		**−15.00011 u**
	mass defect =	**−0.12399 u**

Copyright © by Glencoe/McGraw-Hill

3. (continued)

    b. Calculate the binding energy of the nucleus.

    $-(0.12399\text{ u})(931.49\text{ MeV/u}) = -115.50\text{ MeV}$

4. An oxygen isotope, $^{16}_{8}\text{O}$, has a nuclear mass of 15.99491 u.

    a. What is the mass defect of this isotope?

8 protons = (8)(1.007825 u) =	8.062600 u	
8 neutrons = (8)(1.008665 u) =	8.069320 u	
total	16.131920 u	
mass of oxygen nucleus	−15.99491 u	
mass defect	−0.13701 u	

    b. What is the binding energy of its nucleus?

    $-(0.13701\text{ u})(931.49\text{ MeV/u}) = -127.62\text{ MeV}$

31.2 Using Nuclear Energy
pages 722–732

page 724

5. Use **Table F–6** of the Appendix to complete the following nuclear equations.

    a. $^{14}_{6}\text{C} \rightarrow ? + {}^{0}_{-1}\text{e}$

    $^{14}_{6}\text{C} \rightarrow {}^{14}_{7}\text{N} + {}^{0}_{-1}\text{e}$

    b. $^{55}_{24}\text{Cr} \rightarrow ? + {}^{0}_{-1}\text{e}$

    $^{55}_{24}\text{Cr} \rightarrow {}^{55}_{25}\text{Mn} + {}^{0}_{-1}\text{e}$

6. Write the nuclear equation for the transmutation of a uranium isotope, $^{238}_{92}\text{U}$, into a thorium isotope, $^{234}_{90}\text{Th}$, by the emission of an alpha particle.

    $^{238}_{92}\text{U} \rightarrow {}^{234}_{90}\text{Th} + {}^{4}_{2}\text{He}$

7. A radioactive polonium isotope, $^{214}_{84}\text{Po}$, undergoes alpha decay and becomes lead. Write the nuclear equation.

    $^{214}_{84}\text{Po} \rightarrow {}^{210}_{82}\text{Pb} + {}^{4}_{2}\text{He}$

8. Write the nuclear equations for the beta decay of these isotopes.

    a. $^{210}_{80}\text{Pb}$

    $^{210}_{82}\text{Pb} \rightarrow {}^{210}_{83}\text{Bi} + {}^{0}_{-1}\text{e}$

    b. $^{210}_{83}\text{Bi}$

    $^{210}_{83}\text{Bi} \rightarrow {}^{210}_{84}\text{Po} + {}^{0}_{-1}\text{e}$

    c. $^{234}_{90}\text{Th}$

    $^{234}_{90}\text{Th} \rightarrow {}^{234}_{91}\text{Pa} + {}^{0}_{-1}\text{e}$

    d. $^{239}_{93}\text{Np}$

    $^{239}_{93}\text{Np} \rightarrow {}^{239}_{94}\text{Pu} + {}^{0}_{-1}\text{e}$

page 731

9. Calculate the mass defect and the energy released for the deuterium-tritium fusion reaction used in the Tokamak, defined by the following reaction.

    $^{2}_{1}\text{H} + {}^{3}_{1}\text{H} \rightarrow {}^{4}_{2}\text{He} + {}^{1}_{0}\text{n}$

    Input masses
    2.014102 u + 3.016049 u

    = 5.030151 u.

    Output masses
    4.002603 u + 1.008665 u

    = 5.011268 u.

    Difference is −0.018883 u

    Mass defect: −0.018883 u

    Energy equivalent

    = −(0.018883 u)(931.49 MeV/u)

    = −17.589 MeV

Copyright © by Glencoe/McGraw-Hill

10. Calculate the energy released for the overall reaction in the sun where four protons produce one $^4_2$He, two positrons, and two neutrinos.

Positron mass = $(9.109 \times 10^{-31}$ kg$)\left(\dfrac{1\ u}{1.6605 \times 10^{-27}\ kg}\right)$ = 0.0005486 u

Input mass: 4 protons = 4(1.007825 u) = 4.031300 u

Output mass: $^4_2$He + 2 positrons = 4.002603 u + 2(0.0005486 u) = 4.003700

Mass difference = 0.027600 u

Energy released = (0.027600 u)(931.49 MeV/u) = 25.709 MeV

Chapter Review Problems

pages 734–735

Section 31.1

page 734

Level 1

21. A carbon isotope, $^{13}_6$C, has a nuclear mass of 13.00335 u.

a. What is the mass defect of this isotope?

6 protons = (6)(1.007825 u) =	6.046950	u
7 neutrons = (7)(1.008665 u) =	7.060655	u
total	13.107605	u
mass of carbon nucleus	−13.00335	u
mass defect	−0.10426	u

b. What is the binding energy of its nucleus?

−(0.10426 u)(931.49 MeV/u) = 97.117 MeV

22. A nitrogen isotope, $^{12}_7$N, has a nuclear mass of 12.0188 u.

a. What is the binding energy per nucleon?

7 protons = (7)(1.007825 u) =	7.054775	u
5 neutrons = (5)(1.008665 u) =	5.043325	u
total	12.098100	u
mass of nitrogen–12 nucleons	−12.0188	u
mass defect	−0.0793	u

binding energy:

−(0.0793 u)(931.49 MeV/u) = −73.9 MeV

binding energy per nucleon = $\dfrac{-73.9\ MeV}{12\ nucleons}$ = −6.16 MeV/nucleon

b. Does it require more energy to separate a nucleon from a $^{14}_7$N nucleus or from a $^{12}_7$N nucleus? $^{14}_7$N has a mass of 14.00307 u.

It requires more energy to remove a nucleon from nitrogen-14, 1.32 MeV/nucleon more.

Copyright © by Glencoe/McGraw-Hill

23. The two positively charged protons in a helium nucleus are separated by about 2.0×10^{-15} m. Use Coulomb's law to find the electric force of repulsion between the two protons. The result will give you an indication of the strength of the strong nuclear force.

$$F = \frac{K\,qq'}{d^2}$$

$$= \frac{(9.00 \times 10^9 \text{ N} \cdot \text{m}^2/\text{C}^2)(1.6 \times 10^{-19} \text{ C})(1.6 \times 10^{-19} \text{ C})}{(2.0 \times 10^{-15} \text{ m})^2} = 58 \text{ N}$$

Level 2

24. A $^{232}_{92}$U nucleus, mass = 232.0372 u, decays to $^{228}_{90}$Th, mass = 228.0287 u, by emitting an α particle, mass = 4.0026 u, with a kinetic energy of 5.3 MeV. What must be the kinetic energy of the recoiling thorium nucleus?

mass defect = (232.0372 u) − (228.0287 u + 4.0026 u) = 0.0059 u

total *KE* = (0.0059 u)(931.49 MeV/u) = 5.5 MeV

KE for thorium nucleus

= (5.5 MeV) − (5.3 MeV) = 0.2 MeV

25. The binding energy for $^4_2$He is 28.3 MeV. Calculate the mass of a helium nucleus in atomic mass units.

mass defect $\dfrac{28.3 \text{ MeV}}{931.49 \text{ MeV/u}} = 0.0304$ u

2 protons = (2)(1.007825 u) =	2.015650	u
2 neutrons = (2)(1.008665 u) =	2.017330	u
mass	4.032980	u
minus mass defect	−0.0304	u
	4.0026	u

Section 31.2

Level 1

26. The radioactive nucleus indicated in each of the following equations disintegrates by emitting a positron. Complete each nuclear equation.

a. $^{21}_{11}\text{Na} \rightarrow ? + {}^0_{+1}e + ?$

$^{21}_{11}\text{Na} \rightarrow {}^{21}_{10}\text{Ne} + {}^0_{+1}e + {}^0_0\nu$

b. $^{49}_{24}\text{Cr} \rightarrow ? + {}^0_{+1}e + ?$

$^{49}_{24}\text{Cr} \rightarrow {}^{49}_{23}\text{V} + {}^0_{+1}e + {}^0_0\nu$

27. A mercury isotope, $^{200}_{80}$Hg, is bombarded with deuterons, $^2_1$H. The mercury nucleus absorbs the deuteron and then emits an α particle.

a. What element is formed by this reaction?

Gold

b. Write the nuclear equation for the reaction.

$^{200}_{80}\text{Hg} + {}^2_1\text{H} \rightarrow {}^{198}_{79}\text{Au} + {}^4_2\text{He}$

28. When bombarded by protons, a lithium isotope, $^7_3$Li, absorbs a proton and then ejects two α particles. Write the nuclear equation for this reaction.

$^7_3\text{Li} + {}^1_1\text{H} \rightarrow 2\,{}^4_2\text{He}$

29. Each of the following nuclei can absorb an α particle, assuming that no secondary particles are emitted by the nucleus. Complete each equation.

a. $^{14}_7\text{N} + {}^4_2\text{He} \rightarrow ?$

$^{14}_7\text{N} + {}^4_2\text{He} \rightarrow {}^{18}_9\text{F}$

b. $^{27}_{13}\text{Al} + {}^4_2\text{He} \rightarrow ?$

$^{27}_{13}\text{Al} + {}^4_2\text{He} \rightarrow {}^{31}_{15}\text{P}$

Copyright © by Glencoe/McGraw-Hill

30. When a boron isotope, $^{10}_{5}B$, is bombarded with neutrons, it absorbs a neutron and then emits an α particle.

   a. What element is also formed?

   Lithium

   b. Write the nuclear equation for this reaction.

   $^{10}_{5}B + ^{1}_{0}n \rightarrow ^{7}_{3}Li + ^{4}_{2}He$

31. When a boron isotope, $^{11}_{5}B$, is bombarded with protons, it absorbs a proton and emits a neutron.

   a. What element is formed?

   Carbon

   b. Write the nuclear equation for this reaction.

   $^{11}_{5}B + ^{1}_{1}p \rightarrow ^{11}_{6}C + ^{1}_{0}n$

   c. The isotope formed is radioactive and decays by emitting a positron. Write the complete nuclear equation for this reaction.

   $^{11}_{6}C \rightarrow ^{11}_{5}B + ^{0}_{+1}e + ^{0}_{0}\nu$

Level 2

32. The isotope most commonly used in PET scanners is $^{18}_{9}F$.

   a. What element is formed by the positron emission of this element?

   Oxygen

page 735

   b. Write the equation for this reaction.

   $^{18}_{9}F \rightarrow ^{18}_{8}O + ^{0}_{+1}e + ^{0}_{0}\nu$

   c. The half-life of $^{18}_{9}F$ is 110 min. A solution containing 10.0 mg of this isotope is injected into a patient at 8:00 A.M. How much remains in the patient's body at 3:30 P.M.?

   The time is about 4.1 half-lives, so
   $\left(\frac{1}{4.1}\right)^{2}$**(10.0 mg) or 0.59 mg remains**

33. The first atomic bomb released an energy equivalent of 2.0×10^1 kilotons of TNT. One kiloton of TNT is the equivalent of 5.0×10^{12} J. What was the mass of the uranium-235 that underwent fission to produce this energy?

Energy = $(2.0 \times 10^1$ kilotons)

$\times (5.0 \times 10^{12}$ J/kiloton)

= 1.0×10^{14} J

$\dfrac{1.0 \times 10^{14} \text{ J}}{3.21 \times 10^{-11} \text{ J/atom}}$

= 3.1×10^{24} atoms

$\dfrac{3.1 \times 10^{24} \text{ atoms}}{6.02 \times 10^{23} \text{ atoms/mol}} = 5.1$ mol

$(5.1$ mol$)(0.235$ kg/mol$) = 1.2$ kg

34. Complete the following fission reaction.

   $^{239}_{94}Pu + ^{1}_{0}n \rightarrow ^{137}_{52}Te + ? + 3\,^{1}_{0}n$

   $^{239}_{94}Pu + ^{1}_{0}n \rightarrow ^{137}_{52}Te + ^{100}_{42}Mo + 3\,^{1}_{0}n$

35. Complete the following fission reaction.

   $^{235}_{92}U + ^{1}_{0}n \rightarrow ^{92}_{36}Kr + ? + 3\,^{1}_{0}n$

   $^{235}_{92}U + ^{1}_{0}n \rightarrow ^{92}_{36}Kr + ^{141}_{56}Ba + 3\,^{1}_{0}n$

36. Complete each of the following fusion reactions.

   a. $^{2}_{1}H + ^{2}_{1}H \rightarrow ? + ^{1}_{0}n$

   $^{2}_{1}H + ^{2}_{1}H \rightarrow ^{3}_{2}He + ^{1}_{0}n$

   b. $^{2}_{1}H + ^{2}_{1}H \rightarrow ? + ^{1}_{1}H$

   $^{2}_{1}H + ^{2}_{1}H \rightarrow ^{3}_{1}H + ^{1}_{1}H$

   c. $^{2}_{1}H + ^{3}_{1}H \rightarrow ? + ^{1}_{0}n$

   $^{2}_{1}H + ^{3}_{1}H \rightarrow ^{4}_{2}He + ^{1}_{0}n$

37. One fusion reaction is $^{2}_{1}H + ^{2}_{1}H \rightarrow ^{4}_{2}He$.

   a. What energy is released in this reaction?

   $(2)(2.014102$ u$) - (4.002603$ u$)$

   = 0.025601 u

   $(0.025601$ u$)(931.49$ MeV/u$)$

   = 23.847 MeV

   b. Deuterium exists as a diatomic, two-atom molecule. One mole of deuterium contains 6.022×10^{23} molecules. Find the amount of energy released, in joules, in the fusion of one mole of deuterium molecules.

   (23.847 MeV/molecule)

   $\times (6.022 \times 10^{23}$ molecules/mol)

   $\times (1.6022 \times 10^{-19}$ J/eV$)(10^6$ eV/MeV)

   = 2.301×10^{12} J/mol

Copyright © by Glencoe/McGraw-Hill

37. (continued)

c. When one mole of deuterium burns, it releases 2.9×10^6 J. How many moles of deuterium molecules would have to burn to release just the energy released by the fusion of one mole of deuterium molecules?

$$\frac{2.301 \times 10^{12} \text{ J}}{2.9 \times 10^6 \text{ J/mol}} = 7.9 \times 10^5 \text{ mol}$$

Critical Thinking Problems

38. One fusion reaction in the sun releases about 25 MeV of energy. Estimate the number of such reactions that occur each second from the luminosity of the sun, which is the rate at which it releases energy, 4×10^{26} W.

$1 \text{ eV} = 1.6022 \times 10^{-19}$ J

so

$25 \text{ MeV} = (25 \times 10^6 \text{ eV/reaction})$
$\times (1.6022 \times 10^{-19} \text{ J/eV})$
$= 4.0 \times 10^{-12} \text{ J/reaction}$

The total power is 4×10^{26} J/s, so the number of reactions occurring each second is

$$\frac{4 \times 10^{26} \text{ J/s}}{4.0 \times 10^{-12} \text{ J/reaction}}$$

$= 10^{38}$ reactions/s

39. The mass of the sun is 2×10^{30} kg. If 90 percent of the sun's mass is hydrogen, find the number of hydrogen nuclei in the sun. From the number of fusion reactions each second that you calculated in problem 38, estimate the number of years the sun could continue to "burn" its hydrogen.

The mass of a hydrogen atom is 1.674×10^{-27} kg, so the number of hydrogen atoms in the sun is

$$\frac{(0.90)(2 \times 10^{30} \text{ kg})}{(1.679 \times 10^{-27} \text{ kg/atom})}$$

$= 1 \times 10^{57}$ atoms

Each reaction consumes four protons, so the sun should burn a total of

$$\frac{10^{57} \text{ atoms}}{4 \times 10^{38} \text{ atoms/second}}$$

$= 2.5 \times 10^{18}$ s

Now there are about 3.2×10^7 s/year, so this is approximately 10^{11} years, or one-hundred billion years. Most estimates are about 1/10 of this value.

40. If a uranium nucleus were to split into three pieces of approximately the same size instead of two, would more or less energy be released?

Consider Figure 31–1. The binding energy per nucleon for U is about –7.4 MeV. When it splits in two, the binding energy for two nuclei each with $A = 118$ would be about –8.3 MeV, which agrees with the 200 MeV released. If it split into three, each nucleus would have A approximately 80, where the binding energy is most negative. Therefore the energy released would be larger.

Copyright © by Glencoe/McGraw-Hill

Appendix B
Extra Practice Problems

Chapter 2

1. Express the following numbers in scientific notation.

   a. 810 000 g

   8.1×10^5 g

   b. 0.000634 g

   6.34×10^{-4} g

   c. 60 000 000 g

   6×10^7 g

   d. 0.0000010 g

   1.0×10^{-6} g

2. Convert each of the following time measurements to its equivalent in seconds.

   a. 58 ns

   5.8×10^{-8} s

   b. 0.046 Gs

   4.6×10^7 s

   c. 9270 ms

   9.27 s

   d. 12.3 ks

   1.23×10^4 s

3. Solve the following problems. Express your answers in scientific notation.

   a. 6.2×10^{-4} m $+ 5.7 \times 10^{-3}$ m

   6.3×10^{-3} m

   b. 8.7×10^8 km $- 3.4 \times 10^7$ m

   8.4×10^8 km

   c. $(9.21 \times 10^{-5}$ cm$)(1.83 \times 10^8$ cm$)$

   1.69×10^4 cm^2

   d. $(2.63 \times 10^{-6}$ m$) \div (4.08 \times 10^6$ s$)$

   6.45×10^{-13} m/s

4. State the number of significant digits in the following measurements.

   a. 3218 kg

   4

   b. 60.080 kg

   5

   c. 801 kg

   3

   d. 0.000534 kg

   3

5. State the number of significant digits in the following measurements.

   a. 5.60×10^8 m

   3

   b. 3.0005×10^{-6} m

   5

   c. 8.0×10^{10} m

   2

   d. 9.204×10^{-3} m

   4

6. Add or subtract as indicated and state the answer with the correct number of significant digits.

   a. 85.26 g + 4.7 g

   90.0 g

   b. 1.07 km + 0.608 km

   1.68 km

   c. 186.4 kg − 57.83 kg

   128.6 kg

   d. 60.08 s − 12.2 s

   47.9 s

Copyright © by Glencoe/McGraw-Hill

7. Multiply or divide as indicated using significant digits correctly.

   a. $(5 \times 10^8 \text{ m})(4.2 \times 10^7 \text{ m})$

   $2 \times 10^{16} \text{ m}^2$

   b. $(1.67 \times 10^{-2} \text{ km})(8.5 \times 10^{-6} \text{ km})$

   $1.4 \times 10^{-7} \text{ km}^2$

   c. $(2.6 \times 10^4 \text{ kg}) \div (9.4 \times 10^3 \text{ m}^3)$

   2.8 kg/m^3

   d. $(6.3 \times 10^{-1} \text{ m}) \div (3.8 \times 10^2 \text{ s})$

   $1.7 \times 10^{-3} \text{ m/s}$

8. A rectangular room is 8.7 m by 2.41 m.

   a. What length of baseboard molding must be purchased to go around the perimeter of the floor?

   $P = 2l + 2w$

   $2(8.7 \text{ m}) + 2(2.41 \text{ m}) = 22.2 \text{ m}$

   b. What area must be covered if floor tiles are laid?

   $A = lw = (8.7 \text{ m})(2.41 \text{ m}) = 21 \text{ m}^2$

9. The following data table was established to show the total distances an object fell during various lengths of time.

Time (s)	Distance (m)
1.0	5
2.0	20
3.0	44
4.0	78
5.0	123

   a. Plot distance versus time from the values given in the table and draw a curve that best fits all points.

   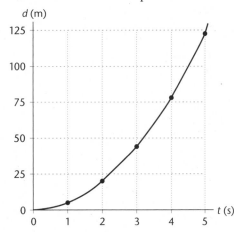

b. Describe the resulting curve.

   parabola; curve starts at origin and is concave upward

c. According to the graph, what is the relationship between distance and time for a free-falling object?

   The distance increases faster and faster with time.

10. The total distance a lab cart travels during specified lengths of time is given in the following table.

Time (s)	Distance (m)
0.0	0.500
1.0	0.655
2.0	0.765
3.0	0.915
4.0	1.070

    a. Plot distance versus time from the values given in the table and draw the curve that best fits all points.

    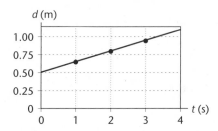

    b. Describe the resulting curve.

    straight line

    c. According to the graph, what type of relationship exists between the total distance traveled by the lab cart and the time?

    linear relationship

    d. What is the slope of this graph?

    $$M = \frac{\Delta y}{\Delta x} = \frac{1.070 \text{ m} - 0.655 \text{ m}}{4.0 \text{ s} - 1.0 \text{ s}}$$

    $$= 0.14 \text{ m/s}$$

    e. Write an equation relating distance and time for these data.

    $d = 0.50 + 0.14(t)$

Copyright © by Glencoe/McGraw-Hill

11. A cube has an edge of length 5.2 cm.

   a. Find its surface area.

   Area of one side

   $A = s^2 = (5.2)^2 = 27$ cm^2

   Total surface area

   $(27$ cm$^2)(6) = 160$ cm^2

   b. Find its volume.

   $V = s^3 = (5.2)^3 = 140$ cm^3

12. A truck is traveling at a constant velocity of 70 km/h. Convert the velocity to m/s.

   $$\frac{70 \text{ km}}{\text{h}} \cdot \frac{1000 \text{ m}}{\text{km}} \cdot \frac{\text{h}}{3600 \text{ s}} = 20 \text{ m/s}$$

13. The density of gold is 19.3 g/cm^3. A gold washer has an outside radius of 4.3 cm and an inside radius of 2.1 cm. Its thickness is 0.14 cm. What is the mass of the washer?

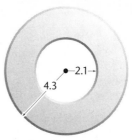

Volume of outside cylinder:

$V = \pi r^2 h = \pi(4.3)^2(0.14) = 8.1$ cm^3

Volume of inside cylinder:

$V = \pi r^2 h = \pi(2.1)^2(0.14) = 1.9$ cm^3

Volume of washer:

8.1 cm$^3 - 1.9$ cm$^3 = 6.2$ cm^3

$m = dV = (19.3$ g/cm$^3)(6.2$ cm$^3)$

$\quad = 120$ g

Copyright © by Glencoe/McGraw-Hill

CHAPTER 3

Create pictorial and physical models for the following problems. Do not solve the problems.

1. A sailboat moves at a constant speed of 2 m/s. How far does it travel every ten seconds?

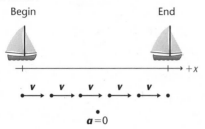

$v_0 = 2$ m/s

$t = 10$ s

$d = ?$ m

2. The putter strikes a golf ball 3.2 m from the hole. After 1.8 s, the ball comes to rest 15 cm from the hole. Assuming constant acceleration, find the initial velocity of the ball.

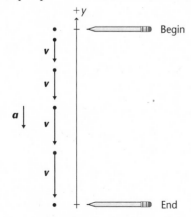

$d_1 = 3.2$ m

$d_2 = 0.15$ m

$v_2 = 0$ m/s

$t = 1.8$ s

$v_1 = ?$ m

3. How far above the floor would you need to drop a pencil to have it land in 1 s?

$d_2 = 0$ m

$v_1 = 0$ m/s

$a = -9.80$ m/s^2

$t = 1$ s

$d_1 = ?$ m

4. Two bikes 24 m apart are approaching each other at a constant speed. One bike is traveling at twice the speed of the other. If they pass each other in 4.3 s, how fast are they going?

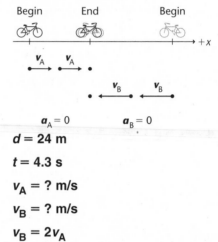

$d = 24$ m

$t = 4.3$ s

$v_A = ?$ m/s

$v_B = ?$ m/s

$v_B = 2v_A$

5. A sprinter accelerates from 0.0 m/s to 5.4 m/s in 1.2 s, then continues at this constant speed until the end of the 100-m dash. What time did the sprinter achieve for the race?

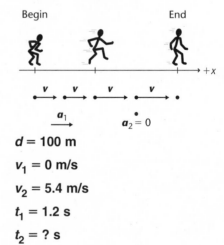

$d = 100$ m

$v_1 = 0$ m/s

$v_2 = 5.4$ m/s

$t_1 = 1.2$ s

$t_2 = ?$ s

Copyright © by Glencoe/McGraw-Hill

6. Toss your keys straight up at 1 m/s. How long will they stay aloft before you catch them?

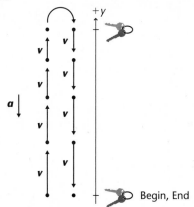

$v_0 = 1$ m/s

$a = -9.80$ m/s^2

$t = ?$ s

Copyright © by Glencoe/McGraw-Hill

CHAPTER 4

1. Bob walks 81 m and then he walks 125 m.

   a. What is Bob's displacement if he walks east both times?

   81 m + 125 m = 206 m

   b. What is Bob's displacement if he walks east then west?

   81 m − 125 m = −44 m

   c. What distance does Bob walk in each case?

   81 m + 125 m = 206 m

2. A cross-country runner runs 5.0 km east along the course, then turns around and runs 5.0 km west along the same path. She returns to the starting point in 45 min. What is her average speed? Her average velocity?

   average speed
   $$= \frac{\text{distance traveled during time interval}}{\text{time}}$$
   $$= \frac{5.0 \text{ km} + 5.0 \text{ km}}{45 \text{ min}}$$
   = (0.22 km/min)(60 min/h)
   = 13 km/h

   average velocity
   $$= \frac{\text{displacement during time interval}}{\text{time}}$$
   $$= \frac{+5.0 \text{ km} - 5.0 \text{ km}}{45 \text{ min}} = 0 \text{ km/min}$$
   = 0 km/h

3. Car A is traveling at 85 km/h while car B is at 64 km/h. What is the relative velocity of car A to car B

   a. if they both are traveling in the same direction?

   85 km/h − 64 km/h = 21 km/h

   b. if they are headed toward each other?

   85 km/h + 64 km/h = 149 km/h

4. Find θ for each of the following.

   a. tan θ = 9.5143

   θ = **84.00°**

   b. sin θ = 0.4540

   θ = **27.00°**

   c. cos θ = 0.8192

   θ = **35.00°**

   d. tan θ = 0.1405

   θ = **7.998°**

   e. sin θ = 0.7547

   θ = **49.00°**

   f. cos θ = 0.9781

   θ = **12.01°**

5. Find the value of each of the following.

   a. tan 28°

   0.5317

   b. sin 86°

   0.9976

   c. cos 2°

   0.9994

   d. tan 58°

   1.600

   e. sin 40°

   0.6428

   f. cos 71°

   0.3256

6. You walk 30 m south and 30 m east. Draw and add vectors representing these two displacements.

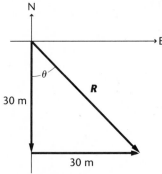

   $$\tan \theta = \frac{30 \text{ m}}{30 \text{ m}} = 1$$
   θ = **45°**

   So, the resultant is at
   45° + 270° = 315°.
   $$R^2 = (30 \text{ m})^2 + (30 \text{ m})^2$$
   $$R = 42 \text{ m}, 315° = 40 \text{ m}, 315°$$

Copyright © by Glencoe/McGraw-Hill

7. Solve for all sides and all angles for the
   following right triangles.

   a.

   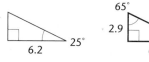

   b.

    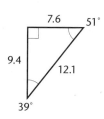

   c.

   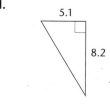 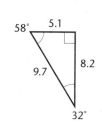

   d.

    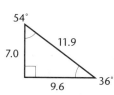

   e.

8. A plane flying at 90° at 1.00×10^2 m/s is
   blown toward 180° at 5.0×10^1 m/s by a
   strong wind. Find the plane's resultant
   velocity and direction.

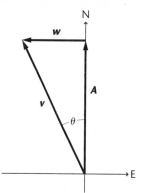

$A = 1.00 \times 10^2$ m/s, north

$w = 5.0 \times 10^1$ m/s, west

$$\tan \theta = \frac{5.0 \times 10^1 \text{ m/s}}{1.00 \times 10^2 \text{ m/s}} = 0.50$$

$\theta = 27°$

So the resultant is at $90° + \theta = 117°$.

$v^2 = A^2 + w^2$

$v = \sqrt{(1.00 \times 10^2 \text{ m/s})^2 + (5.0 \times 10^1 \text{ m/s})^2}$

$= 112 \text{ m/s} = 110 \text{ m/s}$

Thus, $v = 110$ m/s, 117°

9. A man hops a freight car 15.0 m long and
   3.0 m wide. The car is moving east at
   2.5 m/s. Exploring the surroundings, the
   man walks from corner A to corner B in
   20.0 s; then from corner B to corner C in
   5.0 s as shown. With the aid of a vector
   diagram, compute the man's
   displacement relative to the ground.

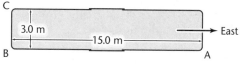

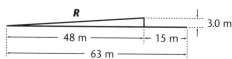

$d_{car} = vt = (2.5 \text{ m/s})(25.0 \text{ s}) = 63$ m

$d_E = 63 \text{ m} - 15.0 \text{ m} = 48$ m

$R^2 = (48 \text{ m})^2 + (3.0 \text{ m})^2$

$R = 48$ m

$$\tan \theta = \frac{3.0 \text{ m}}{48 \text{ m}} = 0.0625$$

$\theta = 3.6°$

Thus, $R = 48$ m, 3.6° N of E

Copyright © by Glencoe/McGraw-Hill

10. A plane travels on a heading of 40.0° for a distance of 3.00×10^2 km. How far north and how far east does the plane travel?

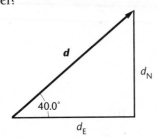

$d = 3.0 \times 10^2$ km at 40.0°

$d_N = d \sin \theta$

$\quad = (3.00 \times 10^2 \text{ km})(\sin 40.0°)$

$\quad = 1.93 \times 10^2$ km, north

$d_E = d \cos \theta$

$\quad = (3.00 \times 10^2 \text{ km})(\cos 40.0°)$

$\quad = 2.30 \times 10^2$ km, east

11. What are the x and y components of a velocity vector of magnitude 1.00×10^2 km/h and direction of 240°?

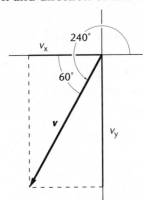

$v = 1.00 \times 10^2$ km/h at 240°

$v_x = v \cos \theta = (1.00 \times 10^2 \text{ km/h}) \cos 240°$

$\quad = -(1.00 \times 10^2 \text{ km/h} \cos 60°) = -50.0$ km/h

$v_y = v \sin \theta = (1.00 \times 10^2 \text{ km/h}) \sin 240°$

$\quad = -(1.00 \times 10^2 \text{ km/h}) \sin 60° = -86.6$ km/h

$v_x = -50.0$ km/h, $v_y = -86.6$ km/h

12. You are a pilot on an aircraft carrier. You must fly to another aircraft carrier, now 1.450×10^3 km at 45° of your position, moving at 56 km/h due east. The wind is blowing from the south at 72 km/h. Calculate the heading and air speed needed to reach the carrier 2.5 h after you take off. **Hint:** Draw a displacement vector diagram.

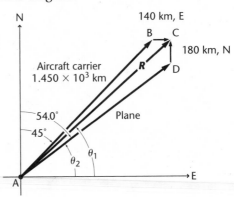

Position A: plane leaving aircraft carrier A, needing to reach carrier B 2.5 hr after takeoff

Position B: aircraft carrier B, which is 1.450×10^3 km at 45° from carrier A moving at $v_B = 56$ km/h, east

The distance components (east and north) of the aircraft carrier are

$d_E = 1.450 \times 10^3$ km cos 45° = 1025 km

$d_N = 1.450 \times 10^3$ km sin 45° = 1025 km

Position C: The position of aircraft carrier B in 2.5 h

The distance traveled by carrier B is

(56 km/h)(2.5 h) = 140 km, E

Solving for the resultant by the component method,

$R_E = 1025$ km + 140 km

$\quad = 1165$ km

$R_N = 1025$ km

Copyright © by Glencoe/McGraw-Hill

Chapter 4 (continued)

12. (continued)

$$\tan \theta_1 = \frac{1025 \text{ km}}{1165 \text{ km}}$$

So $\theta_1 = 41.3°$

$R = 1450 \text{ km}, 45° + 140 \text{ km}, 0°$

So $R^2 = (1165 \text{ km})^2 + (1025 \text{ km})^2$

$R = 1550 \text{ km}, 41.3°$

The wind will carry the plane north from position D to position C, a distance of (72 km/h)(2.5 h) = 180 km during the 2.5 h.

Therefore, with

d_1 **= distance the plane travels**

$d_1 + 180 \text{ km}, N = R = 1550 \text{ km}, 41.3°$

Comparing N and E components of the distance:

$d_{1E} + 0 = R_E = 1165 \text{ km}$

So $d_{1E} = 1165 \text{ km}$

$d_{1N} + 180 \text{ km} = R_N = 1025 \text{ km}$

So $d_{1N} = 845 \text{ km}$

$$\tan \theta_2 = \frac{845 \text{ km}}{1165 \text{ km}}$$

So $\theta_2 = 36.0°$

$d_1 = (1165 \text{ km})^2 + (845 \text{ km})^2$

$= 1440 \text{ km}$

So $d_1 = 1440 \text{ km}, 36.0°$

Heading = 0.0° − 36.0°

$= 54.0°$ E of N

$$\text{Air speed} = \frac{1440 \text{ km}}{2.5 \text{ h}} = 580 \text{ km/h}$$

Thus, the airspeed needed to reach the carrier 2.5 h after you take off is 580 km/h with heading 54.0° E of N.

13. An 80-N and a 60-N force act concurrently on a point. Find the magnitude of the vector sum if the forces pull

a. in the same direction.

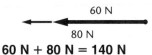

60 N + 80 N = 140 N

b. in opposite directions.

80 N − 60 N = 20 N

c. at a right angle to each other.

$R = \sqrt{(80 \text{ N})^2 + (60 \text{ N})^2} = 100 \text{ N}$

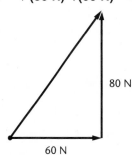

14. One force of 60.0 N and a second of 30.0 N act on an object at point **P.** Graphically add the vectors and find the magnitude of the resultant when the angle between them is as follows.

a. 0°

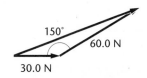

30.0 N + 60.0 N = 90.0 N

b. 30°

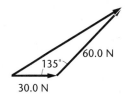

x-component: 30.0 N + 60.0 N cos 30°

= 82.0 N

y-component: 0.0 N + 60.0 N sin 30°

= 30.0 N

$R = \sqrt{(82.0 \text{ N})^2 + (30.0 \text{ N})^2} = 87.3 \text{ N}$

c. 45°

x-component: 30.0 N + 60.0 N cos 45°

= 72.4 N

y-component: 0.0 N + 60.0 N sin 45°

= 42.4 N

$R = \sqrt{(72.4 \text{ N})^2 + (42.4 \text{ N})^2} = 84.0 \text{ N}$

Copyright © by Glencoe/McGraw-Hill

14. (continued)

d. 60°

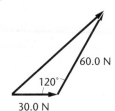

x-component: 30.0 N + 60.0 N cos 60°

= **60.0 N**

y-component: 0.0 N + 60.0 N sin 60°

= **52.0 N**

$R = \sqrt{(60.0 \text{ N})^2 + (52.0 \text{ N})^2} = \textbf{79.4 N}$

e. 90°

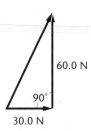

$R = \sqrt{(60.0 \text{ N})^2 + (52.0 \text{ N})^2} = \textbf{67.1 N}$

f. 180°

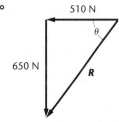

60.0 N − 30.0 N = 30.0 N

15. In tackling a running back from the opposing team, a defensive lineman exerts a force of 510 N at 180°, while a linebacker simultaneously applies a force of 650 N at 270°. What is the resultant force on the ball carrier?

$R^2 = (650 \text{ N})^2 + (510 \text{ N})^2$

$R = \textbf{830 N}$

$\tan \theta = \dfrac{650 \text{ N}}{510 \text{ N}}$

$\theta = 52°$

$180° + 52° = 232°$

$F = \textbf{830 N, 232°}$

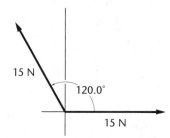

16. A water skier is towed by a speedboat. The skier moves to one side of the boat in such a way that the tow rope forms an angle of 55° with the direction of the boat. The tension on the rope is 350 N. What would be the tension on the rope if the skier were directly behind the boat?

$F_T = \textbf{(350 N)(cos 55°) = 2.0 × 10}^2$

17. Two 15-N forces act concurrently on point **P**. Find the magnitude of their resultant when the angle between them is

a. 0.0°

$\textbf{15 N + 15 N = 3.0 × 10}^1 \textbf{ N}$

b. 30.0°

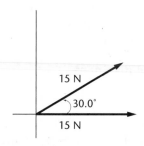

$F_h = \textbf{15 N + 15 N cos 30.0° = 28 N}$

$F_v = \textbf{0.0 N + 15 N sin 30.0° = 7.5 N}$

$F = \sqrt{(28 \text{ N})^2 + (7.5 \text{ N})^2} = \textbf{29 N}$

c. 90.0°

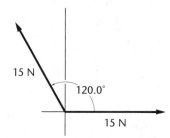

$F = \sqrt{(15 \text{ N})^2 + (15 \text{ N})^2} = \textbf{21 N}$

d. 120.0°

$F_h = \textbf{15 N + (15 N) cos 120.0°}$

= **15 N − 7.5 N = 7.5 N**

$F_v = \textbf{(15 N) sin 120.0° = 13 N}$

$F = \sqrt{(7.5 \text{ N})^2 + (13 \text{ N})^2} = \textbf{15 N}$

Copyright © by Glencoe/McGraw-Hill

17. (continued)

    e. 180.0°

      15 N + (−15 N) = 0 N

18. Kim pushes a lawn spreader across a lawn by applying a force of 95 N along the handle that makes an angle of 60.0° with the horizontal.

    a. What are the horizontal and vertical components of the force?

$$F_h = F\cos\theta = (95\text{ N})(\cos 60.0°)$$
$$= 48\text{ N}$$

$$F_v = F\sin\theta = (95\text{ N})(\sin 60.0°)$$
$$= 82\text{ N}$$

b. The handle is lowered so it makes an angle of 30.0° with the horizontal. Now what are the horizontal and vertical components of the force?

$$F_h = F\cos\theta = (95\text{ N})(\cos 30.0°)$$
$$= 82\text{ N}$$

$$F_v = F\sin\theta = (95\text{ N})(\sin 30.0°)$$
$$= 48\text{ N}$$

Copyright © by Glencoe/McGraw-Hill

CHAPTER 5

1. 0.30 s after seeing a puff of smoke rise from the starter's pistol, the sound of the firing of the pistol is heard by the track timer 1.00×10^2 m away. What is the velocity of sound?

$$v = \frac{\Delta d}{\Delta t} = \frac{1.00 \times 10^2}{0.30} = 33 \text{ m/s}$$

2. The tire radius on a particular vehicle is 0.62 m. If the tires are rotating 5 times per second, what is the velocity of the vehicle?

$$C = 2\pi R = 2\pi(0.62) = 3.9 \text{ m}$$

$$v = \left(\frac{3.9 \text{ m}}{\text{Rotation}}\right)\left(\frac{5 \text{ Rotations}}{\text{s}}\right)$$

$$= 20 \text{ m/s}$$

3. A bullet is fired with a speed of 720.0 m/s.

   a. What time is required for the bullet to strike a target 324 m away?

$$t = \frac{d}{v} = \frac{324 \text{ m}}{720.0 \text{ m/s}} = 0.450 \text{ s}$$

   b. What is the velocity in km/h?

$$v = \frac{(720.0 \text{ m/s})(3600 \text{ s/h})}{1000 \text{ km/h}}$$

$$= 2592 \text{ km/h}$$

4. Light travels at 3.0×10^8 m/s. How many seconds go by from the moment the starter's pistol is shot until the smoke is seen by the track timer 1.00×10^2 m away?

$$t = \frac{d}{v} = \frac{1.00 \times 10^2 \text{ m}}{3.0 \times 10^8 \text{ m/s}} = 3.3 \times 10^{-7} \text{ s}$$

5. You drive your car from home at an average velocity of 82 km/h for 3 h. Halfway to your destination, you develop some engine problems, and for 5 h you nurse the car the rest of the way. What is your average velocity for the entire trip?

$$\Delta d = \overline{v}\Delta t = (82)(3) = 246 \text{ km}$$

   Total distance traveled is 492 km.

   Total time is 8 hours.

$$\overline{v} = \frac{\Delta d}{\Delta t} = \frac{492 \text{ km}}{8 \text{ h}}$$

$$= 61.5 \text{ km/h} = 60 \text{ km/h}$$

6. The total distance a ball is off the ground when thrown vertically is given for each second of flight shown in the following table.

Time (s)	Distance (m)
0.0	0.0
1.0	24.5
2.0	39.2
3.0	44.1
4.0	39.2
5.0	24.5
6.0	0.0

   a. Draw a position-time graph of the motion of the ball.

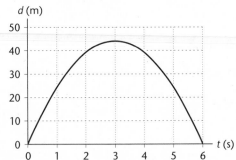

   b. How far off the ground is the ball at the end of 0.5 s? When would the ball again be this distance from the ground?

   13.5 m, 5.5 s

7. Use the following position-time graph to find how far the object travels between

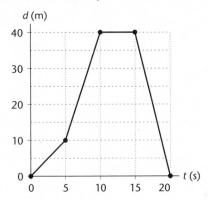

   a. t = 0 s and t = 5 s.

   10 m

   b. t = 5 s and t = 10 s.

   30 m

Copyright © by Glencoe/McGraw-Hill

7. (continued)

    c. $t = 10$ s and $t = 15$ s.

      0 m

    d. $t = 15$ s and $t = 20$ s.

      –40 m

    e. $t = 0$ s and $t = 20$ s.

      80 m of distance, but 0 displacement

8. Use the position-time graph from problem 7 to find the object's velocity between

    a. $t = 0$ s and $t = 5$ s.

      $v = \dfrac{\Delta d}{\Delta t} = \dfrac{10\text{ m}}{5\text{ s}} = 2$ **m/s**

    b. $t = 5$ s and $t = 10$ s.

      $v = \dfrac{30\text{ m}}{5\text{ s}} = 6$ **m/s**

    c. $t = 10$ s and $t = 15$ s.

      $v = \dfrac{0\text{ m}}{5\text{ s}} = 0$ **m/s**

    d. $t = 15$ s and $t = 20$ s.

      $v = \dfrac{-40\text{ m}}{5\text{ s}} = -8$ **m/s**

9. Two cars are headed in the same direction; the one traveling 60 km/h is 20 km ahead of the other traveling 80 km/h.

    a. Draw a position-time graph showing the motion of the cars.

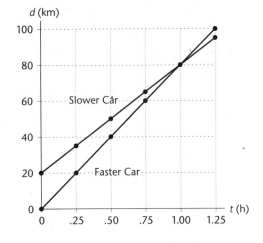

    b. Use your graph to find the time when the faster car overtakes the slower one.

      1.00 h

10. You head downstream on a river in an outboard. The current is flowing at a rate of 1.50 m/s. After 30.0 min, you find that you have traveled 24.3 km. How long will it take you to travel back upstream to your original point of departure?

    Downstream:

$$v_{\text{down}} = \frac{(24.3\text{ km})(1.00 \times 10^3\text{ m/km})}{(30.0\text{ min})(60\text{ s/min})}$$

      $= 13.5$ **m/s**

    $v_{\text{boat}} = v_{\text{down}} - v_{\text{current}}$

      $= 13.5$ m/s $- 1.50$ m/s

    $v_{\text{boat}} = 12.0$ **m/s**

    Upstream:

    $v_{\text{up}} = v_{\text{boat}} - v_{\text{current}}$

      $= 12.0$ m/s $- 1.50$ m/s

      $= 10.5$ **m/s**

    $v_{\text{up}} = \dfrac{d}{t}$

    So $t = \dfrac{d}{v_{\text{up}}}$

      $= \dfrac{2.43 \times 10^4\text{ m}}{10.5\text{ m/s}}$

      $= 2.31 \times 10^3$ **s** $= 38.5$ **min**

11. Use your graph from problem 6 to calculate the ball's instantaneous velocity at

    a. $t = 2$ s.

      ≈ 10 **m/s**

    b. $t = 3$ s.

      0 m/s

    c. $t = 4$ s.

      ≈ -10 **m/s**

Copyright © by Glencoe/McGraw-Hill

Chapter 5 (continued)

12. A plane flies in a straight line at a constant speed of +75 m/s. Assume that it is at the reference point when the clock reads $t = 0$.

a. Construct a table showing the position or displacement of the plane at the end of each second for a 10-s period.

Clock Reading t (s)	Position, d (m)
0	0
1	75
2	150
3	225
4	300
5	375
6	450
7	525
8	600
9	675
10	750

b. Use the data from the table to plot a position-time graph.

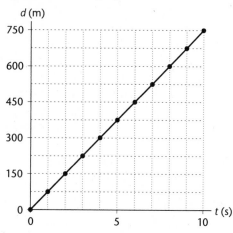

c. Show that the slope of the line is the velocity of the plane. Use at least two different sets of points along the line.

From d-t graph:

$$\text{slope 1} = \frac{(450 \text{ m} - 0 \text{ m})}{(6 \text{ s} - 0 \text{ s})} = 75 \text{ m/s,}$$

$$\text{slope 2} = \frac{(600 \text{ m} - 300 \text{ m})}{(8 \text{ s} - 4 \text{ s})} = 75 \text{ m/s}$$

d. Plot a velocity-time graph of the plane's motion for the first 6 s of the 10-s interval.

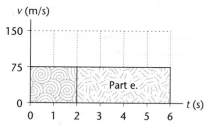

e. From the velocity-time graph, find the displacement of the plane between the second and the sixth period.

Shaded area under v-t graph is the displacement.

$$d = (75 \text{ m/s})(4 \text{ s}) = 300 \text{ m}$$

13. Shonda jogs for 15 min at 240 m/min, walks the next 10 min at 90 m/min, rests for 5 min, and jogs back to where she started at −180 m/min.

a. Plot a velocity-time graph for Shonda's exercise run.

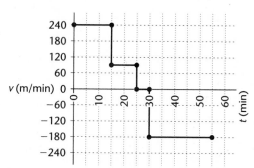

b. Find the area under the curve for the first 15 min. What does this represent?

Area = 240 m/min(15 min) = 3600 m

the distance jogged

c. What is the total distance traveled by Shonda?

3600 m + 900 m + 4500 m

= 9.0 × 10³ m

d. What is Shonda's displacement from start to finish?

4500 m − 4500 m = 0 m

Copyright © by Glencoe/McGraw-Hill

14. From the moment a 40.0 m/s fastball touches the catcher's mitt until it is completely stopped takes 0.012 s. Calculate the average acceleration of the ball as it is being caught.

$$a = \frac{v - v_0}{t} = \frac{0.0 \text{ m/s} - 40.0}{0.012 \text{ s}}$$

$$= -3.3 \times 10^3 \text{ m/s}^2$$

15. The following velocity-time graph describes a familiar motion of a car traveling during rush-hour traffic.

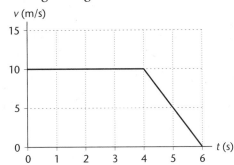

a. Describe the car's motion from $t = 0$ s to $t = 4$ s.

constant velocity of 10 m/s

b. Describe the car's motion from $t = 4$ s to $t = 6$ s.

slowing down to a stop

c. What is the average acceleration for the first 4 s?

0 m/s²

d. What is the average acceleration from $t = 4$ s to $t = 6$ s?

$$\frac{0 \text{ m/s} - 10 \text{ m/s}}{6 \text{ s} - 4 \text{ s}} = \frac{-10 \text{ m/s}}{2 \text{ s}} = -5 \text{ m/s}^2$$

16. Given the following table:

Time (s)	Velocity (m/s)
0.0	0.0
1.0	5.0
2.0	20.0
3.0	45.0
4.0	80.0

a. Plot a velocity-time graph for this motion.

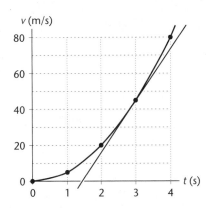

b. Is this motion constant velocity? Uniform acceleration?

no, no

c. Calculate the instantaneous acceleration at $t = 3.0$ s.

Slope of the tangent is ≈ 30 m/s².

17. Top-fuel drag racers are able to uniformly accelerate at 12.5 m/s² from rest to 1.00×10^2 m/s before crossing the finish line. How much time elapses during the run?

$$t = \frac{v - v_0}{a} = \frac{1.00 \times 10^2 \text{ m/s} - 0.00}{12.5 \text{ m/s}^2}$$

$$= 8.00 \text{ s}$$

18. A race car accelerates from rest at +7.5 m/s² for 4.5 s. How fast will it be going at the end of that time?

$$v = v_0 + at = 0.0 + (7.5 \text{ m/s}^2)(4.5 \text{ s})$$

$$= 34 \text{ m/s}$$

19. A race car starts from rest and is accelerated uniformly to +41 m/s in 8.0 s. What is the car's displacement?

$$d = \frac{(v + v_0)t}{2} = \frac{(41 \text{ m/s} + 0.0)(8.0 \text{ s})}{2}$$

$$= 160 \text{ m}$$

20. A jet plane traveling at +88 m/s lands on a runway and comes to rest in 11 s.

a. Calculate its uniform acceleration.

$$a = \frac{v - v_0}{t} = \frac{0.0 - 88 \text{ m/s}}{11 \text{ s}}$$

$$= -8.0 \text{ m/s}^2$$

Copyright © by Glencoe/McGraw-Hill

20. (continued)

   b. Calculate the distance it travels.

$$d = v_0t + \frac{1}{2}at^2$$

$$= (88 \text{ m/s})(11 \text{ s})$$

$$+ \left(\frac{1}{2}\right)(-8.0 \text{ m/s}^2)(11 \text{ s})^2$$

$$= 480 \text{ m}$$

21. A bullet accelerates at 6.8×10^4 m/s^2 from rest as it travels the 0.80 m of the rifle barrel.

   a. How long was the bullet in the barrel?

$$d = v_0t + \frac{1}{2}at^2$$

$$0.80 = (0.0 \text{ m/s})t + \frac{1}{2}(6.8 \times 10^4 \text{ m/s}^2)t^2$$

$$t = \sqrt{\frac{2(0.80)}{6.8 \times 10^4 \text{ m/s}}} = 4.9 \times 10^{-3} \text{ s}$$

   b. What velocity does the bullet have as it leaves the barrel?

$$v = v_0 + at$$

$$= 0.0 + (6.8 \times 10^4 \text{ m/s}^2)(4.9 \times 10^{-3} \text{ s})$$

$$= 3.3 \times 10^2 \text{ m/s}$$

22. A car traveling at 14 m/s encounters a patch of ice and takes 5.0 s to stop.

   a. What is the car's acceleration?

$$a = \frac{v - v_0}{t} = \frac{0.0 - 14 \text{ m/s}}{5.0 \text{ s}} = -2.8 \text{ m/s}^2$$

   b. How far does it travel before stopping?

$$d = \left(\frac{v + v_0}{2}\right)t = \left(\frac{0.0 + 14 \text{ m/s}}{2}\right)5.0 \text{ s}$$

$$= 35 \text{ m}$$

23. A motorcycle traveling at 16 m/s accelerates at a constant rate of 4.0 m/s^2 over 50.0 m. What is its final velocity?

$$v^2 = v_0^2 + 2ad$$

$$= (16 \text{ m/s})^2 + 2(4.0 \text{ m/s})(50.0 \text{ m})$$

$$= 656 \text{ m}^2/\text{s}^2$$

$$v = 26 \text{ m/s}$$

24. A hockey player skating at 18 m/s comes to a complete stop in 2.0 m. What is the acceleration of the hockey player?

$$a = \frac{v^2 - v_0^2}{2d} = \frac{0.0^2 - (18 \text{ m/s})^2}{2(2.0 \text{ m})}$$

$$= -81 \text{ m/s}^2$$

25. Police find skid marks 60.0 m long on a highway showing where a car made an emergency stop. Assuming that the acceleration was -10.0 m/s^2 (about the maximum for dry pavement), how fast was the car going? Was the car exceeding the 80 km/h speed limit?

$$v^2 = v_0^2 + 2ad$$

Since $v = 0$,

$$v_0^2 = -2ad$$

$$= -2(-10.0 \text{ m/s}^2)(60.0 \text{ m})$$

$$= 1.20 \times 10^3 \text{ m}^2/\text{s}^2,$$

$$v_0 = 34.6 \text{ m/s} = 125 \text{ km/h}.$$

Yes, the car was exceeding the speed limit.

26. An accelerating lab cart passes through two photo gate timers 3.0 m apart in 4.2 s. The velocity of the cart at the second timer is 1.2 m/s.

   a. What is the cart's velocity at the first gate?

$$d = \left(\frac{v + v_0}{2}\right)t$$

$$3.0 \text{ m} = \left(\frac{1.2 \text{ m/s} + v_0}{2}\right)4.2 \text{ s}$$

$$\frac{6.0 \text{ m}}{4.2 \text{ s}} = 1.2 \text{ m/s} + v_0$$

$$v_0 = 0.23 \text{ m/s}$$

   b. What is the acceleration?

$$a = \frac{v_f - v_0}{t}$$

$$a = \frac{1.2 \text{ m/s} - 0.23 \text{ m/s}}{4.2 \text{ s}}$$

$$a = 0.23 \text{ m/s}^2$$

Copyright © by Glencoe/McGraw-Hill

Chapter 5 (continued)

27. A camera is accidentally dropped from the edge of a cliff and 6.0 s later hits the bottom.

a. How fast was it going just before it hit?

$$v = v_0 + at$$
$$= 0.0 + 9.80 \text{ m/s}^2 (6.0 \text{ s}) = 59 \text{ m/s}$$

b. How high is the cliff?

$$d = v_0 t + \frac{1}{2}at^2$$
$$= 0.0(6.0 \text{ s}) + \frac{1}{2}(9.80 \text{ m/s}^2)(6.0 \text{ s})^2$$
$$= 1.8 \times 10^2 \text{ m}$$

28. A rock is thrown vertically upward with a velocity of 21 m/s from the edge of a bridge 42 m above a river. How long does the rock stay in the air?

To get back to bridge height

$$t = \frac{v - v_0}{a} = \frac{-21 \text{ m/s} - 21 \text{ m/s}}{-9.80 \text{ m/s}^2}$$
$$= 4.3 \text{ s}$$

Velocity before going into river

$$v^2 = v_0^2 + 2ad$$
$$= (21 \text{ m/s})^2 + 2(9.80 \text{ m/s}^2)(42 \text{ m})$$
$$= 1264.2 \text{ m}^2/\text{s}^2$$
$$v = 36 \text{ m/s}$$

Time to fall from bridge to river

$$t = \frac{v - v_0}{a} = \frac{36 \text{ m/s} - 21 \text{ m/s}}{9.80 \text{ m/s}^2} = 1.5 \text{ s}$$

Total time

$$4.3 \text{ s} + 1.5 \text{ s} = 5.8 \text{ s}$$

29. A platform diver jumps vertically with a velocity of 4.2 m/s. The diver enters the water 2.5 s later. How high is the platform above the water?

$$d = v_0 t + \frac{1}{2}at^2$$
$$= (4.2 \text{ m/s})(2.5 \text{ s})$$
$$+ \frac{1}{2}(-9.80 \text{ m/s}^2)(2.5 \text{ s})^2$$
$$= -2.0 \times 10^1$$

Diver is 2.0×10^1 m below starting point, so platform is 2.0×10^1 m high.

CHAPTER 6

1. A tow rope is used to pull a 1750-kg car, giving it an acceleration of 1.35 m/s². What force does the rope exert?

$$F_{net} = ma = (1750 \text{ kg})(1.35 \text{ m/s}^2)$$
$$= 2.36 \times 10^3 \text{ N, in the direction of the acceleration.}$$

2. A racing car undergoes a uniform acceleration of 4.00 m/s². If the net force causing the acceleration is 3.00×10^3 N, what is the mass of the car?

$$m = \frac{F_{net}}{a} = \frac{3.00 \times 10^3 \text{ N}}{4.00 \text{ m/s}^2}$$
$$= 7.50 \times 10^2 \text{ kg}$$

3. A 5.2-kg bowling ball is accelerated from rest to a velocity of 12 m/s as the bowler covers 5.0 m of approach before releasing the ball. What force is exerted on the ball during this time?

$$v^2 = v_0^2 + 2ad$$
$$a = \frac{v^2 - v_0^2}{2d} = (12 \text{ m/s})^2 - \frac{0.0^2}{2(5.0 \text{ m})}$$
$$= 14.4 \text{ m/s}^2$$
$$F_{net} = ma = (5.2 \text{ kg})(14.4 \text{ m/s}^2) = 75 \text{ N}$$

4. A high jumper, falling at 4.0 m/s, lands on a foam pit and comes to rest, compressing the pit 0.40 m. If the pit is able to exert an average force of 1200 N on the high jumper in breaking the fall, what is the jumper's mass?

$$v^2 = v_0^2 + 2ad$$
$$a = \frac{v^2 - v_0^2}{2d} = \frac{0.0^2 - (4.0 \text{ m/s})^2}{2(0.40 \text{ m})}$$
$$= -2.0 \times 10^1 \text{ m/s}^2$$

where the positive direction is downward.

$$F_{net} = W - F_{pit} = ma$$
$$mg - F_{pit} = ma$$
$$m = \frac{F_{pit}}{g - a}$$
$$= \frac{1200 \text{ N}}{(9.80 \text{ m/s}^2 - 2.0 \times 10^1 \text{ m/s}^2)}$$
$$= 4.0 \times 10^1 \text{ kg}$$

5. On Planet X, a 5.0×10^1-kg barbell can be lifted by exerting a force of only 180 N.

   a. What is the acceleration of gravity on Planet X?

   $$W = mg$$
   $$g = \frac{W}{m} = \frac{180 \text{ N}}{5.0 \times 10^1 \text{ kg}} = 3.6 \text{ m/s}^2$$

   b. If the same barbell is lifted on Earth, what minimal force is needed?

   $$W = mg$$
   $$= (5.0 \times 10^1 \text{ kg})(9.80 \text{ m/s}^2)$$
   $$= 4.9 \times 10^2 \text{ N}$$

6. A proton has a mass of 1.672×10^{-27} kg. What is its weight?

   $$W = mg$$
   $$= (1.672 \times 10^{-27} \text{ kg})(9.80 \text{ m/s}^2)$$
   $$= 1.6 \times 10^{-26} \text{ N}$$

7. An applied force of 21 N accelerates a 9.0-kg wagon at 2.0 m/s² along the sidewalk.

   a. How large is the frictional force?

   $$F_{net} = ma = (9.0 \text{ kg})(2.0 \text{ m/s}^2) = 18 \text{ N}$$
   $$F_f = F_{appl} - F_{net} = 21 \text{ N} - 18 \text{ N} = 3 \text{ N}$$

   b. What is the coefficient of friction?

   $$F_N = W = mg = (9.0 \text{ kg})(9.80 \text{ m/s}^2)$$
   $$= 88 \text{ N}$$
   $$\mu = \frac{F_f}{F_N} = \frac{3 \text{ N}}{88 \text{ N}} = 0.03$$

8. A 2.0-kg brick has a sliding coefficient of friction of 0.38. What force must be applied to the brick for it to move at a constant velocity?

   $$F_f = \mu F_N \text{ where}$$
   $$F_N = W = mg = (2.0 \text{ kg})(9.80 \text{ m/s}^2)$$
   $$= 19.6 \text{ N}$$
   Since $F_{net} = 0$ N, $F_{appl} = F_f$ and
   so $F_f = \mu F_N = (0.38)(19.6 \text{ N}) = 7.4$ N

Copyright © by Glencoe/McGraw-Hill

9. In bench pressing 1.0×10^2 kg, a weight lifter applies a force of 1040 N. How large is the upward acceleration of the weights during the lift?

$$W = mg = (1.0 \times 10^2 \text{ kg})(9.80 \text{ m/s}^2)$$
$$= 9.8 \times 10^2 \text{ N}$$
$$F_{net} = F_{appl} - W$$
$$= 1040 \text{ N} - 9.8 \times 10^2 \text{ N} = 60 \text{ N}$$
$$F_{net} = ma$$
$$a = \frac{F_{net}}{m} = 60 \text{ N}/1.0 \times 10^2 \text{ kg}$$
$$= 0.6 \text{ m/s}^2$$

10. An elevator that weighs 3.0×10^3 N is accelerated upward at 1.0 m/s². What force does the cable exert to give it this acceleration?

   The mass of the elevator is

$$m = \frac{W}{g} = \frac{+3.0 \times 10^3 \text{ N}}{+9.8 \text{ m/s}^2}$$
$$= 3.1 \times 10^2 \text{ kg}$$

   Now $ma = F_{net} = F_{appl} - W$, **so that**
$$F_{appl} = ma + W$$
$$= (3.1 \times 10^2 \text{ kg})(1.0 \text{ m/s}^2)$$
$$+ (3.0 \times 10^3 \text{ N})$$
$$= 3.3 \times 10^3 \text{ N}$$

11. A person weighing 490 N stands on a scale in an elevator.

   The basic equation to be applied is
$$ma = F_{net} = F_{appl} - W$$
   where the positive direction is taken upward and F_{appl} **is the force exerted by the scale. The mass of the person is**
$$m = \frac{W}{g} = \frac{490 \text{ N}}{9.80 \text{ m/s}^2} = 5.0 \times 10^1 \text{ kg}$$

   a. What does the scale read when the elevator is at rest?

   $a = 0$ **so** $F_{appl} = W = 490$ **N**

   b. What is the reading on the scale when the elevator rises at a constant velocity?

   $a = 0$ **so** $F_{appl} = W = 490$ **N**

c. The elevator slows down at −2.2 m/s² as it reaches the desired floor. What does the scale read?

$$F_{appl} = ma + W$$
$$= (5.0 \times 10^1 \text{ kg})(-2.2 \text{ m/s}^2)$$
$$+ 490 \text{ N}$$
$$= 380 \text{ N}$$

d. The elevator descends, accelerating at −2.7 m/s². What does the scale read?

$$F_{appl} = ma + W$$
$$= (5.0 \times 10^1 \text{ kg})(-2.7 \text{ m/s}^2)$$
$$+ 490 \text{ N} = 360 \text{ N}$$

e. What does the scale read when the elevator descends at a constant velocity?

   $a = 0$ **so** $F_{appl} = W = 490$ **N**

f. Suppose the cable snapped and the elevator fell freely. What would the scale read?

   $a = -g$ **so**
$$F_{appl} = ma + W = m(-g) + mg = 0 \text{ N}$$

12. A pendulum has a length of 1.00 m.

   a. What is its period on Earth?

$$T = 2\pi \sqrt{\frac{l}{g}}$$
$$T = 2\pi \sqrt{\frac{1.00 \text{ m}}{9.80 \text{ m/s}^2}} = 2.01 \text{ s}$$

   b. What is its period on the moon where the acceleration due to gravity is 1.67 m/s²?

$$T = 2\pi \sqrt{\frac{1.00 \text{ m}}{1.67 \text{ m/s}^2}} = 4.86 \text{ s}$$

13. The period of an object oscillating on a spring is

$$T = 2\pi \sqrt{\frac{m}{k}}$$

   where m is the mass of the object and k is the spring constant, which indicates the force necessary to produce a unit elongation of the spring. The period of a simple pendulum is

$$T = 2\pi \sqrt{\frac{l}{g}}$$

Copyright © by Glencoe/McGraw-Hill

13. (continued)

a. What mass will produce a 1.0-s period of oscillation if it is attached to a spring with a spring constant of 4.0 N/m?

$$T = 2\pi \sqrt{\frac{m}{k}}, \text{ so}$$

$$m = \frac{kT^2}{4\pi^2} = \frac{(4.0 \text{ N/m})(1.0 \text{ s})^2}{(4)(\pi^2)} = 0.10 \text{ kg}$$

b. What length pendulum will produce a period of 1.0 s?

$$T = 2\pi \sqrt{\frac{l}{g}}, \text{ so } l = \frac{gT^2}{4\pi^2}$$

$$l = \frac{(9.80 \text{ m/s}^2)(1.0 \text{ s})^2}{(4)(\pi^2)} = 0.25 \text{ m}$$

c. How would the harmonic oscillator and the pendulum have to be modified in order to produce 1.0-s periods on the surface of the moon where g is 1.6 m/s²?

No change is necessary for the harmonic oscillator. For the pendulum, because l is proportional to g,

$$l' = \frac{g'l}{g} = \frac{(1.6 \text{ m/s}^2)(0.25 \text{ m})}{9.80 \text{ m/s}^2}$$

$$= 0.041 \text{ m}$$

The pendulum must be shortened to 4.1 cm.

14. When a 22-kg child steps off a 3.0-kg stationary skateboard with an acceleration of 0.50 m/s², with what acceleration will the skateboard travel in the opposite direction?

$$F_{child} = ma = (22 \text{ kg})(0.50 \text{ m/s}^2)$$

$$= 11 \text{ N}$$

$$F_{child} = F_{skateboard}, \text{ so for the skateboard}$$

$$F = ma, \text{ or}$$

$$a = \frac{F}{m} = \frac{11 \text{ N}}{3.0 \text{ kg}} = 3.7 \text{ m/s}^2$$

15. A 10.0-kg mass, m_1, on a frictionless table is accelerated by a 5.0-kg mass, m_2, hanging over the edge of the table. What is the acceleration of the mass along the table?

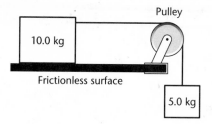

$F_{net} = ma$ where

$m = m_1 + m_2$

    = the total mass being accelerated

and $F_{net} = m_2g$ = the applied force

Thus,

$$m_2g = (m_1 + m_2)a$$

$$\text{or } a = \frac{m_2g}{m_1 + m_2} = \frac{(5.0 \text{ kg})(9.80 \text{ m/s}^2)}{5.0 \text{ kg} + 10.0 \text{ kg}}$$

$$= 3.3 \text{ m/s}^2, \text{ to the right}$$

16. A bricklayer applies a force of 100 N to each of two handles of a wheelbarrow. Its mass is 20 kg and it is loaded with 30 bricks, each of mass 1.5 kg. The handles of the wheelbarrow are 30° from the horizontal, and the coefficient of friction is 0.20. What initial acceleration is given the wheelbarrow?

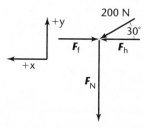

$m = 20 \text{ kg} + (1.5 \text{ kg})(30) = 65 \text{ kg}$

$F_N = -[(200 \text{ N}) \sin 30° +$

$\qquad (65 \text{ kg})(9.80 \text{ m/s}^2)]$

$\qquad = -737 \text{ N}$

$F_f = \mu F_N = (0.20)(-737 \text{ N}) = -147 \text{ N}$

$F_h = 200 \text{ N} \cos 30° = 173 \text{ N}$

$$a = \frac{F_{net}}{m} = \frac{(173 \text{ N} - 147 \text{ N})}{65 \text{ kg}}$$

$$= 0.4 \text{ m/s}^2$$

Copyright © by Glencoe/McGraw-Hill

CHAPTER 7

1. A 33-N force acting at 90.0° and a 44-N force acting at 60.0° act concurrently on point **P.** What is the magnitude and direction of a third force that produces equilibrium at point **P?**

F_1 = 33 N, 90.0°; F_2 = 44 N, 60.0°

Solution by component method.

F_{1h} = 0 N

F_{1v} = F_1 = 33 N

F_{2h} = (44 N) cos 60.0° = 22 N

F_{2v} = (44 N) sin 60.0° = 38 N

F_h = 0 N + 22 N = 22 N

F_v = 33 N + 38 N = 71 N

The resultant of the two given forces is

$F = \sqrt{(22\ N)^2 + (71\ N)^2}$ = 74 N

$\tan \theta = \dfrac{71\ N}{22\ N}$ = 3.23, θ = 73°

Equilibrant: 74 N, 253°

2. A person weighs 612 N. If the person sits in the middle of a hammock that is 3.0 m long and sags 1.0 m below the points of support, what force would be exerted by each of the two hammock ropes?

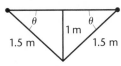

$\sin \theta = \dfrac{1}{1.5}$ = 0.6667

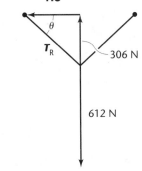

$\sin \theta = \dfrac{306\ N}{T_R}$

$T_R = \dfrac{306\ N}{\sin \theta} = \dfrac{306\ N}{0.6667}$ = 459 N

3. A bell ringer decides to use a bowling ball to ring the bell. He hangs the 7.3-kg ball from the end of a 2.0 m long rope. He attaches another rope to the ball to pull the ball back, and pulls it horizontally until the ball has moved 0.60 m away from the vertical. How much force must he apply?

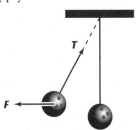

Angle pulled back from vertical given by $\sin \theta = \dfrac{0.60}{2.0}$ = 0.30, and θ = 17°
In equilbrium forces balance.

Vertical: $T \cos \theta$ = mg;

Horizontal: $T \sin \theta = F$, where T is the tension in the 2.0 m rope and F is the force on the horizontal rope.

Thus $\dfrac{F}{mg} = \tan \theta$, so

F = (7.3 kg)(9.80 m/s²)(0.31) = 22 N

4. A mass, M, starts from rest and slides down the frictionless incline of 30°. As it leaves the incline, its speed is 24 m/s.

a. What is the acceleration of the mass while on the incline?

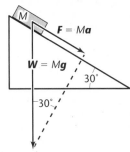

$F = W(\sin 30°)$

Ma = (sin 30°) Mg

a = (sin 30°) g = 4.90 m/s²

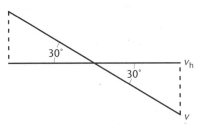

Chapter 7 (continued)

b. What is the length of the incline?

$$v_2 = v_0^2 + 2ad$$

$$d = \frac{v^2 - v_0^2}{2a} = \frac{(24 \text{ m/s})^2 - 0.0}{(2)(4.90 \text{ m/s}^2)}$$

$$d = \frac{576 \text{ m}^2/\text{s}^2}{(2)(4.90 \text{ m/s}^2)} = 59 \text{ m}$$

c. How long does it take the mass to reach the floor after it leaves the top of the incline?

$$a = \frac{\Delta v}{\Delta t} \text{, or}$$

$$\Delta t = \frac{\Delta v}{a} = \frac{24 \text{ m/s}}{4.90 \text{ m/s}^2} = 4.9 \text{ s}$$

5. A ball falls from rest from a height of 4.90×10^2 m.

a. How long does it remain in the air?

$$y = v_y t + \frac{1}{2} at^2 \text{ where } a = -g$$

Because initial vertical velocity is zero,

$$t = \sqrt{\frac{2y}{-g}} = \sqrt{\frac{(2)(-4.90 \times 10^2)}{-9.80 \text{ m/s}}}$$

$$= 10.0 \text{ s}$$

b. If the ball has a horizontal velocity of 2.00×10^2 m/s when it begins its fall, what horizontal displacement will it have?

$$x = v_x t$$
$$= (2.00 \times 10^2 \text{ m/s})(1.00 \times 10^1 \text{ s})$$
$$= 2.00 \times 10^3 \text{ m}$$

6. An archer stands 40.0 m from the target. If the arrow is shot horizontally with a velocity of 90.0 m/s, how far above the bull's-eye must she aim to compensate for gravity pulling her arrow downward?

$$t = \frac{x}{v_x} = \frac{40.0 \text{ m}}{90.0 \text{ m/s}} = 0.444 \text{ s}$$

$$d = v_y t + \frac{1}{2} at^2 \text{ where } a = g$$

$$= 0(0.444 \text{ s}) + \frac{1}{2}(9.80 \text{ m/s}^2)(0.444 \text{ s})^2$$
$$= 0.966 \text{ m (down is positive)}$$

7. A bridge is 176.4 m above a river. If a lead-weighted fishing line is thrown from the bridge with a horizontal velocity of 22.0 m/s, how far has it moved horizontally when it hits the water?

$$y = v_y t + \frac{1}{2} at^2 \text{ where } a = -g$$

Because initial vertical velocity is zero,

$$t = \sqrt{\frac{2y}{-g}} = \sqrt{\frac{(2)(-176.4 \text{ m})}{(-9.80 \text{ m/s}^2)}} = 6.00 \text{ s}$$

$$x = v_x t = (22.0 \text{ m/s})(6.00 \text{ s}) = 132 \text{ m}$$

8. A beach ball, moving with a speed of +1.27 m/s, rolls off a pier and hits the water 0.75 m from the end of the pier. How high above the water is the pier?

We need to know how long it takes the ball to hit the water in order to use

$$y = v_y t + \frac{1}{2} at^2, \text{ where } v_y = 0$$

to calculate pier height. This time is determined by the horizontal motion $x = v_x t$.

$$t = \frac{x}{v_x} = \frac{0.75 \text{ m}}{1.27 \text{ m/s}} = 0.59 \text{ s}$$

This gives a vertical displacement

$$y = \frac{1}{2} at^2 \text{ where } a = -g$$

$$= \left(\frac{1}{2}\right)(-9.80 \text{ m/s}^2)(0.59 \text{ s})^2 = -1.7 \text{ m}$$

and hence a pier height of 1.7 m.

9. Carlos has a tendency to drop his bowling ball on his release. Instead of having the ball on the floor at the completion of his swing, Carlos lets go with the ball 0.35 m above the floor. If he throws it horizontally with a velocity of 6.3 m/s, what distance does it travel before you hear a "thud"?

$$y = v_y t + \frac{1}{2} at^2 \text{ where } v_y = 0.$$

Make the downward direction positive so $a = g$. The time to hit the floor is

$$t = \sqrt{\frac{2y}{g}} = \sqrt{\frac{2(0.35 \text{ m})}{9.8 \text{ m/s}^2}} = 0.27 \text{ s}$$

So travel distance is

$$x = v_x t = (6.3 \text{ m/s})(0.27 \text{ s}) = 1.7 \text{ m}$$

Copyright © by Glencoe/McGraw-Hill

Chapter 7 (continued)

10. A discus is released at an angle of 45° and a velocity of 24.0 m/s.

    a. How long does it stay in the air?

$$v_y = v_i \sin 45° = (24.0 \text{ m/s}) \sin 45°$$

$$= 17.0 \text{ m/s}$$

So time to maximum height is

$$t = \frac{v_{top} - v_y}{a} = \frac{0.00 - 17.0 \text{ m/s}}{-9.80 \text{ m/s}}$$

$$= 1.735 \text{ s}$$

and by symmetry total time is 3.47 s.

    b. What horizontal distance does it travel?

$$v_x = v_i \cos 45° = (24.0 \text{ m/s}) \cos 45°$$

$$= 17.0 \text{ m/s}$$

$$\text{so } x = v_x t = 17.0 \text{ m/s}(3.46 \text{ s}) = 58.8 \text{ m}$$

11. A shot put is released with a velocity of 12 m/s and stays in the air for 2.0 s.

    a. At what angle with the horizontal was it released?

$$v_f = v_i + at \text{ where } v_f = 0 \text{ at maximum}$$
height and $v_i = v_y.$

Since time to maximum height is 1.0 s, $a = -g$, **and**

$$v_y = v_f - at = 0 - (-9.8 \text{ m/s}^2)(1.0 \text{ s})$$

$$= 9.8 \text{ m/s where upward is taken}$$

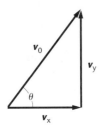

positive

$$v_y = 9.8 \text{ m/s}$$

$$v_0 = 12 \text{ m/s}$$

$$\sin \theta = \frac{v_y}{v_0} = \frac{9.8 \text{ m/s}}{12 \text{ m/s}} = 0.817$$

$$\theta = 55°$$

    b. What horizontal distance did it travel?

$$v_x = v_0 \cos 55° = (12 \text{ m/s}) \cos 55°$$

$$= 6.9 \text{ m/s}$$

$$\text{so } x = v_x t = (6.9 \text{ m/s})(2.0 \text{ s}) = 14 \text{ m}$$

12. A football is kicked at 45° and travels 82 m before hitting the ground.

    a. What was its initial velocity?

$$x = v_x t \text{ and } y = v_y t + \frac{1}{2} at^2$$
where $a = -g$

At end $y = 0,$

$$\text{so } 0 = v_y t - \frac{1}{2} gt^2 = t\left(\frac{v_y - gt}{2}\right) \text{ and}$$

$$t = \frac{-2v_y}{-g}$$

But $t = \frac{x}{v_x},$

$$\text{so } \frac{x}{v_x} = \frac{-2v_y}{-g} \text{ or } v_x v_y = +\frac{1}{2} xg$$

Now $v_x = v_0 \cos \theta$ **and** $v_y = v_0 \sin \theta$,

so $v_x v_y = v_0^2 \cos \theta \sin \theta$, **or**

$$v_0^2 = \frac{+\frac{1}{2} xg}{\cos \theta \sin \theta}$$

Here $v_0^2 = \dfrac{+(1/2)(82 \text{ m})(+9.80 \text{ m/s}^2)}{(\cos 45°)(\sin 45°)}$

$$= 804 \text{ m}^2/\text{s}^2$$

or $v_0 = 28 \text{ m/s}$

    b. How long was it in the air?

$$v_x = v_0 \cos 45° = (28 \text{ m/s}) \cos 45°$$

$$= 2.0 \times 10^1 \text{ m/s}$$

$$\text{so } t = \frac{x}{v_x} = \frac{82 \text{ m}}{2.0 \times 10^1 \text{ m/s}} = 4.1 \text{ s}$$

    c. How high did it go?

Maximum height occurs at half the flight time, so since

$$v_y = v_0 \sin 45° = (28 \text{ m/s}) \sin 45°$$

$$= 2.0 \times 10^1 \text{ m/s}$$

$$y = (2.0 \times 10^1 \text{ m/s})(2.1 \text{ s})$$

$$- \frac{1}{2}(+ 9.80 \text{ m/s}^2)(2.1 \text{ s})^2$$

$$= 2.0 \times 10^1 \text{ m}$$

13. A golf ball is hit with a velocity of 24.5 m/s at 35.0° above the horizontal. Find

    a. the range of the ball.

$$v_x = v_0 \cos \theta = (24.5 \text{ m/s})(\cos 35.0°)$$

$$= 20.1 \text{ m/s}$$

Copyright © by Glencoe/McGraw-Hill

13. a. (continued)

$$v_y = v_0 \sin \theta = (24.5 \text{ m/s})(\sin 35.0°)$$

$$= 14.1 \text{ m/s}$$

$$y = v_y t + \frac{1}{2} at^2 = t\left(v_y + \frac{1}{2} at\right)$$

where $a = -g$

When $y = 0$,

$$t = \frac{-2v_y}{-g} = \frac{-2(14.1 \text{ m/s})}{-9.80 \text{ m/s}^2} = 2.88 \text{ s}$$

so $x = v_x t = 57.9 \text{ m}$

b. the maximum height of the ball.

In half the flight time, $\left(\frac{1}{2}\right)$ (2.88 s), it falls

$$y = \left(\frac{1}{2}\right) at^2 \text{ where } a = -g$$

$$= \left(\frac{1}{2}\right)(-9.80 \text{ m/s}^2)(1.44 \text{ s})^2$$

$$= -10.2 \text{ m,}$$

so its maximum height is 10.2 m.

14. A carnival clown rides a motorcycle down a ramp and around a "loop-the-loop." If the loop has a radius of 18 m, what is the slowest speed the rider can have at the top of the loop to avoid falling? **Hint:** At this slowest speed, at the top of the loop, the track exerts no force on the motorcycle.

$F = ma$ and $F_{net} = W$, so

$$ma = mg$$

$$v = \sqrt{gr} = \sqrt{(9.80 \text{ m/s}^2)(18 \text{ m})}$$

$$= 13 \text{ m/s}$$

15. A 75-kg pilot flies a plane in a loop. At the top of the loop, where the plane is completely upside-down for an instant, the pilot hangs freely in the seat and does not push against the seat belt. The airspeed indicator reads 120 m/s. What is the radius of the plane's loop?

Because the net force is equal to the weight of the pilot, $ma = w$, or

$$\frac{mv^2}{r} = mg$$

or $r = \dfrac{v^2}{g} = \dfrac{(120 \text{ m/s})^2}{9.8 \text{ m/s}^2} = 1.5 \times 10^3 \text{ m}$

16. A 2.0-kg object is attached to a 1.5-m long string and swung in a vertical circle at a constant speed of 12 m/s.

a. What is the tension in the string when the object is at the bottom of its path?

$$F_{net} = \frac{mv^2}{r} = \frac{(2.0 \text{ kg})(12 \text{ m/s})^2}{1.5 \text{ m}}$$

$$= 1.9 \times 10^1 \text{ N}$$

$$W = mg = (2.0 \text{ kg})(9.80 \text{ m/s}^2)$$

$$= 2.0 \times 10^2 \text{ N}$$

$F_{net} = T - W$, so $T = F_{net} + W$

$$= 1.9 \times 10^2 \text{ N} + 0.20 \times 10^2 \text{ N}$$

$$= 2.1 \times 10^2 \text{ N}$$

b. What is the tension in the string when the object is at the top of its path?

$F_{net} = T + W$, so $T = F_{net} - W$

$$= 1.9 \times 10^2 \text{ N} - 0.20 \times 10^2 \text{ N}$$

$$= 1.7 \times 10^2 \text{ N}$$

17. A 60.0-kg speed skater with a velocity of 18.0 m/s comes into a curve of 20.0-m radius. How much friction must be exerted between the skates and ice to negotiate the curve?

$$F_f = F_{net} = \frac{mv^2}{r}$$

$$= \frac{(60.0 \text{ kg})(18.0 \text{ m/s})^2}{20.0 \text{ m}} = 972 \text{ N}$$

18. A 20.0-kg child wishes to balance on a seesaw with a child of 32.0 kg. If the smaller child sits 3.2 m from the pivot, where must the larger child sit?

$$m_1 g d_1 = m_2 g d_2$$

Because g is common to both sides,

$$(20.0)(3.2) = (32.0)(d_2), \text{ and } d_2 = 2.0 \text{ m}$$

2.0 m from the pivot

Copyright © by Glencoe/McGraw-Hill

CHAPTER 8

1. Comet Halley returns every 74 years. Find the average distance of the comet from the sun in astronomical units (AU).

$$\left(\frac{r_a}{r_b}\right)^3 = \left(\frac{T_a}{T_b}\right)^2, \text{ so}$$

$$r_a^3 = r_b^3 \left(\frac{T_a}{T_b}\right)^2 = (1.0 \text{ AU})^3 \left(\frac{74 \text{ y}}{1.0 \text{ y}}\right)^2 = 5.48 \times 10^3 \text{ AU}^3$$

so $r_a = 18$ AU or $18(1.5 \times 10^{11} \text{ m}) = 2.7 \times 10^{12}$ m

2. Area is measured in m^2, so the rate at which area is swept out by a planet or satellite is measured in m^2/s.

    a. How fast is area swept out by Earth in its orbit about the sun?

    $r = 1.49 \times 10^{11}$ m and

    $T = 3.156 \times 10^7$ s, so

    $$\frac{\pi r^2}{T} = \frac{\pi (1.49 \times 10^{11} \text{ m})^2}{(3.156 \times 10^7 \text{ s})} = 2.21 \times 10^{15} \text{ m}^2/\text{s}$$

    b. How fast is area swept out by the moon in its orbit about Earth. Use 3.9×10^8 m as the average distance between Earth and the moon, and 27.33 days as the moon's period.

    $$\frac{\pi (3.9 \times 10^8 \text{ m})^2}{2.36 \times 10^6 \text{ s}} = 2.0 \times 10^{11} \text{ m}^2/\text{s}$$

3. You wish to launch a satellite that will remain above the same spot on Earth's surface. This means the satellite must have a period of exactly one day. Calculate the radius of the circular orbit this satellite must have. **Hint:** The moon also circles Earth and both the moon and the satellite will obey Kepler's third law. The moon is 3.9×10^8 m from Earth and its period is 27.33 days.

    $$\left(\frac{T_s}{T_m}\right)^2 = \left(\frac{r_s}{r_m}\right)^3$$

    so $r_s^3 = \left(\frac{T_s}{T_m}\right)^2 r_m^3$

    $$= \left(\frac{1.000 \text{ dy}}{27.33 \text{ dy}}\right)^2 (3.9 \times 10^8 \text{ m})^3$$

    $$= 7.94 \times 10^{22} \text{ m}^3$$

    so $r_s = 4.3 \times 10^7$ m

4. The mass of an electron is 9.1×10^{-31} kg. The mass of a proton is 1.7×10^{-27} kg. They are about 1.0×10^{-10} m apart in a hydrogen atom. What gravitational force exists between the proton and the electron of a hydrogen atom?

    $$F = \frac{Gm_e m_p}{d^2} = \frac{(6.67 \times 10^{-11} \text{ N} \cdot \text{m}^2/\text{kg}^2)(9.1 \times 10^{-31} \text{ kg})(1.7 \times 10^{-27} \text{ kg})}{(1.0 \times 10^{-10} \text{ m})^2}$$

    $$= 1.0 \times 10^{-47} \text{ N}$$

Copyright © by Glencoe/McGraw-Hill

5. Two 1.00-kg masses have their centers 1.00 m apart. What is the force of attraction between them?

$$F_g = G\frac{m_1 m_2}{d^2} = \frac{(6.67 \times 10^{-11}\ \text{N}\cdot\text{m/kg}^2)(1.00\ \text{kg})(1.00\ \text{kg})}{(1.00\ \text{m})^2}$$

$$= 6.67 \times 10^{-11}\ \text{N}$$

6. Two satellites of equal mass are put into orbit 30 m apart. The gravitational force between them is 2.0×10^{-7} N.

a. What is the mass of each satellite?

$$F = G\frac{m_1 m_2}{r^2},\ m_1 = m_2 = m$$

$$m = \sqrt{\frac{Fr^2}{G}} = \sqrt{\frac{(2.0 \times 10^{-7}\ \text{N})(30\ \text{m})^2}{6.67 \times 10^{-11}\ \text{N}\cdot\text{m}^2/\text{kg}^2}} = \sqrt{2.698 \times 10^6\ \text{kg}^2} = 1.6 \times 10^3\ \text{kg}$$

b. What is the initial acceleration given to each satellite by the gravitational force?

$$F_{net} = ma$$

$$a = \frac{F_{net}}{m} = \frac{2.00\ \times 10^{-7}\ \text{N}}{1.6 \times\ 10\ \text{kg}} = 1.3 \times 10^{-10}\ \text{m/s}^2$$

7. Two large spheres are suspended close to each other. Their centers are 4.0 m apart. One sphere weighs 9.8×10^2 N. The other sphere has a weight of 1.96×10^2 N. What is the gravitational force between them?

$$m_1 = \frac{W}{g} = \frac{9.8 \times\ 10^2\ \text{N}}{9.8\ 0\ \text{m/s}^2} = 1.0 \times 10^2\ \text{kg}$$

$$m_2 = \frac{W}{g} = \frac{1.96 \times 10^2\ \text{N}}{9.80\ \text{m/s}^2} = 2.00 \times 10^1\ \text{kg}$$

$$F = G\frac{m_1 m_2}{d^2} = \frac{(6.67 \times 10^{-11}\ \text{N}\cdot\text{m}^2/\text{kg}^2)(1.0 \times 10^2\ \text{kg})(2.00 \times 10^1\ \text{kg})}{(4.0\ \text{m})^2}$$

$$= 8.3 \times 10^{-9}\ \text{N}$$

8. If the centers of Earth and the moon are 3.9×10^8 m apart, the gravitational force between them is about 1.9×10^{20} N. What is the approximate mass of the moon?

$$F = G\frac{m_1 m_2}{r^2}$$

$$m_m = \frac{Fr^2}{Gm_e} = \frac{(1.9 \times 10^{20}\ \text{N})(3.9 \times 10^8\ \text{m})^2}{(6.67 \times 10^{-11}\ \text{N}\cdot\text{m}^2/\text{kg}^2)(6.0 \times 10^{24}\ \text{kg})} = 7.2 \times 10^{22}\ \text{kg}$$

9. a. What is the gravitational force between two spherical 8.00-kg masses that are 5.0 m apart?

$$F = G\frac{m_1 m_2}{r^2} = \frac{(6.67 \times 10^{-11}\ \text{N}\cdot\text{m}^2/\text{kg}^2)(8.0\ \text{kg})(9.0\ \text{kg})}{(5.0\ \text{m})^2} = 1.7 \times 10^{-10}\ \text{N}$$

b. What is the gravitational force between them when they are 5.0×10^1 m apart?

$$F = G\frac{m_1 m_2}{r^2} = \frac{(6.67 \times 10^{-11}\ \text{N}\cdot\text{m}^2/\text{kg}^2)(8.0\ \text{kg})(8.0\ \text{kg})}{(5.0 \times 10^1\ \text{m})^2} = 1.7 \times 10^{-12}\ \text{N}$$

Copyright © by Glencoe/McGraw-Hill

Chapter 8 (continued)

10. A satellite is placed in a circular orbit with a radius of 1.0×10^7 m and a period of 9.9×10^3 s. Calculate the mass of Earth. **Hint:** Gravity is the net force on such a satellite. Scientists have actually measured the mass of Earth this way.

$$F_{net} = \frac{m_s v^2}{r} = \frac{Gm_s m_e}{r^2}$$

Since, $v = \frac{2\pi r}{T}$

$$\left(\frac{m_s}{r}\right)\left(\frac{4\pi^2 r^2}{T^2}\right) = \frac{Gm_s m_e}{r^2}$$

$$m_e = \frac{4\pi^2 r^3}{GT^2} = \frac{(4)(\pi)^2(1.0 \times 10^7 \text{ m})^3}{(6.67 \times 10^{-11} \text{ N} \cdot \text{m}^2/\text{kg}^2)(9.9 \times 10^3 \text{ s})^2}$$

$$m_e = 6.0 \times 10^{24} \text{ kg}$$

11. If you weigh 637 N on Earth's surface, how much would you weigh on the planet Mars? (Mars has a mass of 6.37×10^{23} kg and a radius of 3.43×10^6 m.)

$$m = \frac{W}{g} = \frac{637 \text{ N}}{9.80 \text{ m/s}^2} = 65.0 \text{ kg}$$

$$F = \frac{Gm_1 m_2}{d^2} = \frac{(6.67 \times 10^{-11} \text{ N} \cdot \text{m}^2/\text{kg}^2)(65.0 \text{ kg})(6.37 \times 10^{23} \text{ kg})}{(3.43 \times 10^6 \text{ m})^2} = 235 \text{ N}$$

12. Using Newton's variation of Kepler's third law and information from **Table 8–1,** calculate the period of Earth's moon if the radius of orbit was twice the actual value of 3.9×10^8 m.

$$T_p^2 = \left(\frac{4\pi^2}{GM_E}\right)(r^3) = \left(\frac{4\pi^2}{(6.67 \times 10^{-11} \text{ N} \cdot \text{m}^2/\text{kg}^2)(5.979 \times 10^{24} \text{ kg})}\right)(7.8 \times 10^8 \text{ m})^3$$

$$T_p = 6.85 \times 10^6 \text{ s or 79 days}$$

13. Use the data from **Table 8–1** to find the speed and period of a satellite that would orbit Mars 175 km above its surface.

$$r = R_m + 175 \text{ km} = 3.56 \times 10^6 \text{ m}$$

$$v = \sqrt{\frac{GM_m}{r}} = \sqrt{\frac{(6.67 \times 10^{-11} \text{ N} \cdot \text{m}^2/\text{kg}^2)(6.42 \times 10^{23} \text{ kg})}{3.56 \times 10^6 \text{ m}}}$$

$$v = 3.47 \times 10^3 \text{ m/s}$$

$$T = \sqrt{\frac{2\pi r^3}{GM_m}} = 2\pi \sqrt{\frac{(3.56 \times 10^6 \text{ m})^3}{(6.67 \times 10^{-11} \text{ N} \cdot \text{m}^2/\text{kg}^2)(6.42 \times 10^{23} \text{ kg})}}$$

$$T = 6.45 \times 10^3 \text{ s or 1.79 h}$$

14. What would be the value of g, acceleration of gravity, if Earth's mass was double its actual value, but its radius remained the same? If the radius was doubled, but the mass remained the same? If both the mass and radius were doubled?

$$g = \frac{GM_e}{R_e^2}$$

$2M_e \Rightarrow g = 19.6 \text{ m/s}^2$

$2R_e \Rightarrow g = 2.45 \text{ m/s}^2$

$2M_e$ and $2R_e \Rightarrow g = 4.90 \text{ m/s}^2$

Copyright © by Glencoe/McGraw-Hill

Physics: Principles and Problems

Problems and Solutions Manual **275**

15. What would be the strength of Earth's gravitational field at a point where an 80.0-kg astronaut would experience a 25% reduction in weight?

$W = mg = (80.0 \text{ kg})(9.80 \text{ m/s}^2) = 784 \text{ N}$

$W_{reduced} = (784 \text{ N})(0.75) = 588 \text{ N}$

$g_{reduced} = \dfrac{W_{reduced}}{m} = \dfrac{588 \text{ N}}{80.0 \text{ kg}} = 7.35 \text{ m/s}^2$

16. On the surface of the moon, a 91.0-kg physics teacher weighs only 145.6 N. What is the value of the moon's gravitational field at its surface?

$W = mg,$

So $g = \dfrac{W}{m} = \dfrac{145.6 \text{ N}}{91.0 \text{ kg}} = 1.60 \text{ m/s}^2$

Copyright © by Glencoe/McGraw-Hill

CHAPTER 9

1. Jim strikes a 0.058-kg golf ball with a force of 272 N and gives it a velocity of 62.0 m/s. How long was the club in contact with the ball?

$$\Delta t = \frac{m\Delta v}{F} = \frac{(0.058 \text{ kg})(62.0 \text{ m/s})}{272 \text{ N}}$$

$$= 0.013 \text{ s}$$

2. A force of 186 N acts on a 7.3-kg bowling ball for 0.40 s.

   a. What is the bowling ball's change in momentum?

   $$\Delta p = F \Delta t = (186 \text{ N})(0.40 \text{ s}) = 74 \text{ N} \cdot \text{s}$$

   b. What is its change in velocity?

   $$\Delta v = \frac{\Delta p}{m} = \frac{74 \text{ N} \cdot \text{s}}{7.3 \text{ kg}} = 1.0 \times 10^1 \text{ m/s}$$

3. A 5500-kg freight truck accelerates from 4.2 m/s to 7.8 m/s in 15.0 s by applying a constant force.

   a. What change in momentum occurs?

   $$\Delta p = m \, \Delta v$$

   $$= (5500 \text{ kg})(7.8 \text{ m/s} - 4.2 \text{ m/s})$$

   $$= 2.0 \times 10^4 \text{ kg} \cdot \text{m/s}$$

   b. How large of a force is exerted?

   $$F = \frac{\Delta p}{\Delta t} = \frac{2.0 \times 10^4 \text{ kg} \cdot \text{m/s}}{15.0 \text{ s}}$$

   $$= 1.3 \times 10^3 \text{ N}$$

4. In running a ballistics test at the police department, Officer Rios fires a 6.0-g bullet at 350 m/s into a container that stops it in 0.30 m. What average force stops the bullet?

   $$\Delta p = m \, \Delta v = (0.0060 \text{ kg})(-350 \text{ m/s})$$

   $$= -2.1 \text{ kg} \cdot \text{m/s}$$

   $$t = d\left(\frac{2}{v + v_0}\right)$$

   $$= (0.30 \text{ m})\left(\frac{2}{0.0 \text{ m/s} + 350 \text{ m/s}}\right)$$

   $$= 1.7 \times 10^{-3} \text{ s}$$

   $$F = \frac{\Delta p}{\Delta t} = \frac{-2.1 \text{ kg} \cdot \text{m/s}}{1.7 \times 10^{-3} \text{ s}}$$

   $$= -1.2 \times 10^3 \text{ N}$$

5. A 0.24-kg volleyball approaches Zina with a velocity of 3.8 m/s. Zina bumps the ball, giving it a velocity of –2.4 m/s. What average force did she apply if the interaction time between her hands and the ball is 0.025 s?

   $$F = \frac{m\Delta v}{\Delta t}$$

   $$= \frac{(0.24 \text{ kg})(-2.4 \text{ m/s} - 3.8 \text{ m/s})}{0.025 \text{ s}}$$

   $$= -6.0 \times 10^1 \text{ N}$$

6. A 0.145-kg baseball is pitched at 42 m/s. The batter hits it horizontally to the pitcher at 58 m/s.

   a. Find the change in momentum of the ball.

   Take the direction of the pitch to be positive

   $$\Delta p = mv - mv_0 = m(v - v_0)$$

   $$= (0.145 \text{ kg})[-58 \text{ m/s} - (+42 \text{ m/s})]$$

   $$= -14.5 \text{ kg} \cdot \text{m/s}$$

   b. If the ball and bat were in contact 4.6×10^{-4} s, what would be the average force while they touched?

   $$F \Delta t = \Delta p,$$

   $$F = \frac{\Delta p}{\Delta t} = \frac{-14.5 \text{ kg} \cdot \text{m/s}}{4.6 \times 10^{-4} \text{ s}}$$

   $$= -3.2 \times 10^4 \text{ N}$$

7. A 550-kg car traveling at 24.0 m/s collides head-on with a 680-kg pick-up truck. Both vehicles come to a complete stop upon impact.

   a. What is the momentum of the car before collision?

   $$p = mv = (550 \text{ kg})(24.0 \text{ m/s})$$

   $$= 1.3 \times 10^4 \text{ kg} \cdot \text{m/s}$$

   b. What is the change in the car's momentum?

   -1.3×10^4 kg · m/s, because car stops on impact

   c. What is the change in the truck's momentum?

   1.3×10^4 kg · m/s, by conservation of momentum

Copyright © by Glencoe/McGraw-Hill

7. (continued)

    d. What is the velocity of the truck before collision?

$$v = \frac{p}{m} = \frac{-1.3 \times 10^4 \text{ kg} \cdot \text{m/s}}{680 \text{ kg}}$$

$$= -19 \text{ m/s}$$

8. A truck weighs four times as much as a car. If the truck coasts into the car at 12 km/h and they stick together, what is their final velocity?

    Momentum before: (4 m)(12 km/h)

    Momentum after: (4 m + 1 m)v, so

    $v = (4 \text{ m}/5 \text{ m})(12 \text{ km/h}) = 9.6 \text{ km/h}$

---

9. A 50.0-g projectile is launched with a horizontal velocity of 647 m/s from a 4.65-kg launcher moving in the same direction at 2.00 m/s. What is the velocity of the launcher after the projectile is launched?

$$p_{A1} + p_{B1} = p_{A2} + p_{B2}$$

$$m_A v_{A1} + m_B v_{B1} = m_A v_{A2} + m_B v_{B2}$$

$$\text{so } v_{B2} = \frac{(m_A v_{A1} + m_B v_{B1} - m_A v_{A2})}{m_B}$$

Assuming projectile (A) is launched in direction of launcher (B) motion,

$$v_{B2} = \frac{(0.0500 \text{ kg})(2.00 \text{ m/s}) + (4.65 \text{ kg})(2.00 \text{ m/s}) - (0.0500 \text{ kg})(647 \text{ m/s})}{4.65 \text{ kg}}$$

$$v_{B2} = -4.94 \text{ m/s, or } 4.94 \text{ m/s backwards}$$

---

10. Two lab carts are pushed together with a spring mechanism compressed between them. Upon release, the 5.0-kg cart repels one way with a velocity of 0.12 m/s while the 2.0-kg cart goes in the opposite direction. What velocity does it have?

$$m_1 v_1 = m_2 v_2$$

$$(5.0 \text{ kg})(0.12 \text{ m/s}) = (2.0 \text{ kg})(v_2)$$

$$v_2 = 0.30 \text{ m/s}$$

11. A 12.0-g rubber bullet travels at a velocity of 150 m/s, hits a stationary 8.5-kg concrete block resting on a frictionless surface, and ricochets in the opposite direction with a velocity of -1.0×10^2 m/s. How fast will the concrete block be moving?

Momentum of bullet before collision:

$$p_B = (0.0120 \text{ kg})(150 \text{ m/s})$$

$$= 1.80 \text{ kg} \cdot \text{m/s}$$

Momentum of bullet and block after collision:

$$p_A = (0.0120 \text{ kg})(-1.0 \times 10^2 \text{ m/s})$$
$$+ (8.5 \text{ kg})(v)$$

$$p_B = p_A$$

$$1.80 \text{ kg} \cdot \text{m/s}$$

$$= (0.0120 \text{ kg})(-1.0 \times 10^2 \text{ m/s})$$
$$+ (8.5 \text{ kg})(v)$$

$$v = \frac{3.0 \text{ kg} \cdot \text{m/s}}{8.5 \text{ kg}} = 0.35 \text{ m/s}$$

12. A 6500-kg freight car traveling at 2.5 m/s collides with an 8000-kg stationary freight car. If they interlock upon collision, find their velocity.

$$m_1 v_1 + m_2 v_2 = (m_1 + m_2)v$$

$$(6500 \text{ kg})(2.5 \text{ m/s}) + (8000 \text{ kg})(0 \text{ m/s})$$

$$= (6500 \text{ kg} + 8000 \text{ kg})v$$

$$v = 1.1 \text{ m/s} = 1 \text{ m/s}$$

Copyright © by Glencoe/McGraw-Hill

13. Miko, mass 42.00 kg, is riding a skateboard, mass 2.00 kg, traveling at 1.20 m/s. Miko jumps off and the skateboard stops dead in its tracks. In what direction and with what velocity did she jump?

$$(m_1 + m_2)v_B = m_1 v_A + m_2 v_A$$

$$(42.00 \text{ kg} + 2.00 \text{ kg})(1.20 \text{ m/s})$$

$$= (42.00 \text{ kg})(v_A) + 0$$

v_A = 1.26 m/s in the same direction as she was riding.

14. A cue ball, mass 0.16 kg, rolling at 4.0 m/s, hits a stationary eight-ball of similar mass. If the cue ball travels 45° above its original path, and the eight-ball at 45° below, what is the velocity of each after collison?

$$p_{before} = (0.16 \text{ kg})(4.0 \text{ m/s})$$

$$= 0.64 \text{ kg} \cdot \text{m/s}$$

$$p_8 = p_C$$

$$\cos 45° = \frac{p_8}{0.64 \text{ kg} \cdot \text{m/s}}$$

$$p_8 = 0.45 \text{ kg} \cdot \text{m/s}$$

$$v = \frac{0.45 \text{ kg} \cdot \text{m/s}}{0.16 \text{ kg}} = 2.8 \text{ m/s}$$

15. Two opposing hockey players, one of mass 82.0 kg skating north at 6.00 m/s and the other of mass 70.0 kg skating east at 3.00 m/s, collide and become tangled.

a. Draw a vector momentum diagram of the collision.

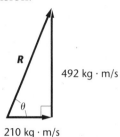

R

492 kg · m/s

θ

210 kg · m/s

$$p_N = 82.0 \text{ kg} (6.00 \text{ m/s}) = 492 \text{ kg} \cdot \text{m/s}$$

$$p_E = 70.0 \text{ kg} (3.00 \text{ m/s})$$

$$= 2.10 \times 10^2 \text{ km} \cdot \text{m/s}$$

b. In what direction and with what velocity do they move after collision?

$$\tan \theta = \frac{492}{2.10 \times 10^2}, \theta = 66.7°$$

$$R^2 = (492^2 + 2.10 \times 10^2)\text{kg}^2 \cdot \text{m}^2/\text{s}^2$$

$$R = 535 \text{ kg} \cdot \text{m/s}$$

$$v = \frac{535 \text{ kg} \cdot \text{m/s}}{152 \text{ kg}} = 3.52 \text{ m/s, } 66.7°$$

Copyright © by Glencoe/McGraw-Hill

CHAPTER 10

1. After scoring a touchdown, an 84.0-kg wide receiver celebrates by leaping 1.20 m off the ground. How much work was done by the player in the celebration?

   $W = Fd = mgd$

   $= (84.0 \text{ kg})(9.80 \text{ m/s}^2)(1.20 \text{ m})$

   $= 988 \text{ J}$

2. During a tug-of-war, Team A does 2.20×10^5 J of work in pulling Team B 8.00 m. What force was Team A exerting?

   $F = \dfrac{W}{d} = \dfrac{2.20 \times 10^5 \text{ J}}{8.00 \text{ m}} = 2.75 \times 10^4 \text{ N}$

3. To keep a car traveling at a constant velocity, 551 N of force is needed to balance frictional forces. How much work is done against friction by the car in traveling from Columbus to Cincinnati, a distance of 161 km?

   $W = Fd = (551 \text{ N})(1.61 \times 10^5 \text{ m})$

   $= 8.87 \times 10^7 \text{ J}$

4. A weightlifter raises a 180-kg barbell to a height of 1.95 m. How much work is done by the weightlifter in lifting the barbells?

   $W = mgh$

   $= (180 \text{ kg})(9.80 \text{ m/s}^2)(1.95 \text{ m})$

   $= 3.4 \times 10^3 \text{ J}$

5. A wagon is pulled by a force of 38.0 N on the handle at an angle of 42.0° with the horizontal. If the wagon is pulled in a circle of radius 25.0 m, how much work is done?

   $F_x = (\cos 42.0°)(38.0 \text{ N})$

   $F_x = 28.2 \text{ N}$

   $C = 2\pi r = 2\pi (25.0 \text{ m}) = 157 \text{ m}$

   $W = F_x d = (28.2 \text{ N})(157 \text{ m})$

   $= 4.43 \times 10^3 \text{ J}$

6. A 185-kg refrigerator is loaded into a moving van by pushing it up a 10.0-m ramp at an angle of inclination of 11.0°. How much work is done by the pusher?

   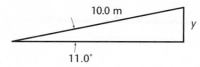

   $y = (10.0 \text{ m})(\sin 11.0°)$

   $y = 1.91 \text{ m}$

   $W = Fd = (185 \text{ kg})(9.80 \text{ m/s}^2)(1.91 \text{ m})$

   $= 3.46 \times 10^3 \text{ J}$

7. A lawn mower is pushed with a force of 88.0 N along a handle that makes an angle of 41.0° with the horizontal. How much work is done by the pusher in moving the mower 1.2 km in mowing the yard?

   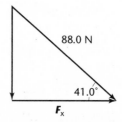

   $F_x = (\cos 41.0°)(88.0 \text{ N}) = 66.4 \text{ N}$

   $W = F_x d = (66.4 \text{ N})(1200 \text{ m})$

   $= 8.0 \times 10^4 \text{ J}$

8. A 17.0-kg crate is to be pulled a distance of 20.0 m, requiring 1210 J of work being done. If the job is done by attaching a rope and pulling with a force of 75.0 N, at what angle is the rope held?

   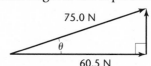

   $F_x = \dfrac{W}{d} = \dfrac{1210 \text{ J}}{20.0 \text{ m}} = 60.5 \text{ N}$

   $\cos \theta = \dfrac{60.5}{75.0} = 0.807$

   $\theta = 36.2°$

Copyright © by Glencoe/McGraw-Hill

9. An elevator lifts a total mass of 1.1×10^3 kg, a distance of 40.0 m in 12.5 s. How much power does the elevator demonstrate?

$$P = \frac{W}{t}$$

$$= \frac{(1.1 \times 10^3 \text{ kg})(9.80 \text{ m/s}^2)(40.0 \text{ m})}{12.5 \text{ s}}$$

$$= 3.4 \times 10^4 \text{ W}$$

10. A cyclist exerts a force of 15.0 N in riding a bike 251 m in 30.0 s. What is the cyclist's power?

$$P = \frac{W}{t} = \frac{(15.0 \text{ N})(251 \text{ m})}{30.0 \text{ s}} = 126 \text{ W}$$

11. A 120-kg lawn tractor goes up a 21° incline of 12.0 m in 2.5 s. What power is developed by the tractor?

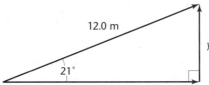

$$y = (12.0 \text{ m})(\sin 21°) = 4.3 \text{ m}$$

$$W = Fd = (120 \text{ kg})(9.80 \text{ m/s}^2)(4.3 \text{ m})$$

$$= 5.1 \times 10^3 \text{ J}$$

$$P = \frac{W}{t} = \frac{5.1 \times 10^3 \text{ J}}{2.5 \text{ s}} = 2.0 \times 10^3 \text{ W}$$

12. What power does a pump develop to lift 35 L of water per minute from a depth of 110 m? (A liter of water has a mass of 1.00 kg.)

$$P = \frac{W}{t} = \frac{mgd}{t}$$

$$\frac{m}{t} = (35 \text{ L/min})(1.00 \text{ kg/L})$$

$$= 35 \text{ kg/min}$$

Thus,

$$P = (35 \text{ kg/min})(1 \text{ min/60 s})(9.80 \text{ m/s}^2)$$

$$\times (110 \text{ m})$$

$$= 0.63 \text{ kW}$$

13. A force of 1.4 N is exerted through a distance of 40.0 cm on a rope in a pulley system to lift a 0.50-kg mass 10.0 cm.

a. Calculate the MA.

$$MA = \frac{F_r}{F_e} = \frac{(0.50 \text{ kg})(9.80 \text{ m/s}^2)}{1.4 \text{ N}}$$

$$= \frac{4.9 \text{ N}}{1.4 \text{ N}}$$

$$= 3.5$$

b. Calculate the IMA.

$$IMA = \frac{d_e}{d_r} = \frac{40.0 \text{ cm}}{10.0 \text{ cm}} = 4.00$$

c. What is the efficiency of the pulley system?

$$EFF = \frac{MA}{IMA} \times 100$$

$$= \frac{3.5}{4.00} \times 100 = 88\%$$

14. A student exerts a force of 250 N through a distance of 1.6 m on a lever in lifting a 150-kg crate. If the efficiency of the lever is 90%, how far is the crate lifted?

$$F_r = (150 \text{ kg})(9.80 \text{ m/s}^2) = 1470 \text{ N}$$

$$MA = \frac{F_r}{F_e} = \frac{1470 \text{ N}}{250 \text{ N}} = 5.9$$

$$IMA = \frac{(MA)(100)}{EFF} = \frac{(5.9)(100)}{90\%}$$

$$= 6.6$$

$$d_r = \frac{d_e}{IMA} = \frac{1.6 \text{ m}}{6.6} = 0.24 \text{ m}$$

15. Luis pedals a bicycle with a gear radius of 5.00 cm and wheel radius of 38.6 cm. What length of chain must be pulled through to make the wheel revolve once?

$$IMA = \frac{GR}{WR} = \frac{5.00 \text{ cm}}{38.6 \text{ cm}} = 0.130$$

$$d_r = 2\pi r = 2\pi (38.6 \text{ cm}) = 242.5 \text{ cm}$$

$$d_e = IMA(d_r) = (0.130)(242.5 \text{ cm})$$

$$= 31.5 \text{ cm}$$

Copyright © by Glencoe/McGraw-Hill

CHAPTER 11

1. Calculate the kinetic energy of a proton, mass 1.67×10^{-27} kg, traveling at 5.20×10^7 m/s.

$$K = \frac{1}{2}\, mv^2$$

$$= \frac{1}{2}(1.67 \times 10^{-27}\text{ kg})(5.20 \times 10^7\text{ m/s})^2$$

$$= 2.26 \times 10^{-12}\text{ J}$$

2. What is the kinetic energy of a 3.2-kg pike swimming at 2.7 km/h?

$$2.7\text{ km/hr}\left(\frac{1000\text{ m}}{\text{km}}\right)\left(\frac{\text{hr}}{3600\text{ s}}\right)$$

$$= 0.75\text{ m/s}$$

$$K = \frac{1}{2}\, mv^2 = \frac{1}{2}(3.2\text{ kg})(0.75\text{ m/s})^2$$

$$= 0.90\text{ J}$$

3. A force of 30.0 N pushes a 1.5-kg cart, initially at rest, a distance of 2.8 m along a frictionless surface.

   a. Find the work done on the cart by this force.

   $$W = Fd = (30.0\text{ N})(2.8\text{ m}) = 84\text{ J}$$

   b. What is its change in kinetic energy?

   $$W = \Delta K = 84\text{ J}$$

   c. What is the cart's final velocity?

   $$v = \sqrt{\frac{2K}{m}} = \sqrt{\frac{2(84\text{ J})}{1.5\text{ kg}}} = 11\text{ m/s}$$

4. A bike and rider, 82.0-kg combined mass, are traveling at 4.2 m/s. A constant force of –140 N is applied by the brakes in stopping the bike. What braking distance is needed?

   $$K = \frac{1}{2}\, mv^2 = \frac{1}{2}(82.0\text{ kg})(4.2\text{ m/s})^2$$

   $$= 723\text{ J of } K \text{ is lost}$$

   $$(-140\text{ N})d = -723\text{ J}$$

   $$d = 5.2\text{ m}$$

5. A 712-kg car is traveling at 5.6 m/s when a force acts on it for 8.4 s, changing its velocity to 10.2 m/s.

   a. What is the change in kinetic energy of the car?

   $$K_{final} = \frac{1}{2}\, mv^2 = \frac{1}{2}(712\text{ kg})(10.2\text{ m/s})^2$$

   $$= 3.70 \times 10^4\text{ J}$$

$$K_{initial} = \frac{1}{2}\, mv_0^2$$

$$= \frac{1}{2}(712\text{ kg})(5.6\text{ m/s})^2$$

$$= 1.1 \times 10^4\text{ J}$$

$$\Delta K = K_{final} - K_{initial} = 2.6 \times 10^4\text{ J}$$

   b. How far did the car move while the force acted?

   $$d = \left(\frac{v + v_0}{2}\right) t$$

   $$= \left(\frac{10.2\text{ m/s} + 5.6\text{ m/s}}{2}\right)(8.4\text{ s})$$

   $$= 66.4\text{ m} = 66\text{ m}$$

   c. How large is the force?

   $$Fd = \Delta K$$

   $$F(66\text{ m}) = 2.6 \times 10^4\text{ J}$$

   $$F = 3.9 \times 10^2\text{ N}$$

6. Five identical 0.85-kg books of 2.50-cm thickness are each lying flat on a table. Calculate the gain in potential energy of the system if they are stacked one on top of the other.

   Height raised:

   book 1 none

   book 2 2.5 cm

   book 3 5.0 cm

   book 4 7.5 cm

   book 5 10.0 cm

    **25.0 cm total**

   $$\Delta U_g = mg\,\Delta h$$

   $$= (0.85\text{ kg})(9.80\text{ m/s}^2)(0.250\text{ m})$$

   $$= 2.1\text{ J}$$

7. Each step of a ladder increases one's vertical height 4.0×10^1 cm. If a 90.0-kg painter climbs 8 steps of the ladder, what is the increase in potential energy?

   $$(4.0 \times 10^1\text{ cm})(8) = 320\text{ cm}$$

   $$\Delta U_g = mg\,\Delta h$$

   $$= (90.0\text{ kg})(9.80\text{ m/s}^2)(3.2\text{ m})$$

   $$= 2.8 \times 10^3\text{ J}$$

Copyright © by Glencoe/McGraw-Hill

8. A 0.25-kg ball is dropped from a height of 3.20 m and bounces to a height of 2.40 m. What is its loss in potential energy?

$\Delta h = 2.40 \text{ m} - 3.20 \text{ m} = -0.80 \text{ m}$

$\Delta U_g = mg \, \Delta h$

$= (0.25 \text{ kg})(9.80 \text{ m/s}^2)(-0.80 \text{ m})$

$= -2.0 \text{ J}$

loss = 2.0 J

9. A 0.18-kg ball is placed on a compressed spring on the floor. The spring exerts an average force of 2.8 N through a distance of 15 cm as it shoots the ball upward. How high will the ball travel above the release spring?

$W = Fd = (2.8 \text{ N})(0.15 \text{ m}) = 0.42 \text{ J}$

$W = \Delta U_g = mg \, \Delta h$

$0.42 \text{ J} = (0.18 \text{ kg})(9.80 \text{ m/s}^2)(\Delta h)$

$\Delta h = 0.24 \text{ m}$

10. A force of 14.0 N is applied to a 1.5-kg cart as it travels 2.6 m along an inclined plane at constant speed. What is the angle of inclination of the plane?

$W = Fd = (14.0 \text{ N})(2.6 \text{ m}) = 36.4 \text{ J}$

$W = \Delta U_g = mg \, \Delta h$

$36.4 \text{ kJ} = (1.5 \text{ kg})(9.80 \text{ m/s}^2)(\Delta h)$

$\Delta h = 2.48 \text{ m}$

$\sin \theta = \dfrac{2.48 \text{ m}}{2.6 \text{ m}}$

$\theta = 73°$

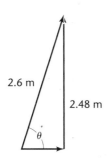

2.6 m 2.48 m θ

11. A 15.0-kg model plane flies horizontally at a constant speed of 12.5 m/s.

a. Calculate its kinetic energy.

$K = \dfrac{1}{2} mv^2$

$= \left(\dfrac{1}{2}\right)(15.0 \text{ kg})(12.5 \text{ m/s})^2$

$= 1.17 \times 10^3 \text{ J}$

b. The plane goes into a dive and levels off 20.4 m closer to Earth. How much potential energy does it lose during the dive? Assume no additional drag.

$\Delta U_g = mgh$

$= (15.0 \text{ kg})(9.80 \text{ m/s}^2)(20.4 \text{ m})$

$= 3.00 \times 10^3 \text{ J}$

c. How much kinetic energy does the plane gain during the dive?

$\Delta K = \Delta U_g = 3.00 \times 10^3 \text{ J}$

d. What is its new kinetic energy?

$K = 1.17 \times 10^3 \text{ J} + 3.00 \times 10^3 \text{ J}$

$= 4.17 \times 10^3 \text{ J}$

e. What is its new horizontal velocity?

$v = \sqrt{\dfrac{2K}{m}} = \sqrt{\dfrac{(2)(4170 \text{ J})}{15.0 \text{ kg}}}$

$= 23.6 \text{ m/s}$

12. A 1200-kg car starts from rest and accelerates to 72 km/h in 20.0 s. Friction exerts an average force of 450 N on the car during this time.

a. What is the net work done on the car?

$W = \Delta K = \dfrac{1}{2} mv^2$

$= \left(\dfrac{1}{2}\right)(1200 \text{ kg})(2.0 \times 10^1 \text{ m/s})^2$

$= 2.4 \times 10^5 \text{ J}$

Copyright © by Glencoe/McGraw-Hill

Chapter 11 (continued)

12 (continued)

b. How far does the car move during its acceleration?

$$d = \frac{(v + v_0)t}{2}$$

$$= \frac{(2.0 \times 10^1 \text{ m/s} + 0)(20.0 \text{ s})}{2}$$

$$= 2.0 \times 10^2 \text{ m}$$

c. What is the net force exerted on the car during this time?

$$W = Fd$$

$$F = \frac{W}{d} = \frac{2.4 \times 10^5 \text{ J}}{2.0 \times 10^2 \text{ m}} = 1.2 \times 10^3 \text{ N}$$

d. What is the forward force exerted on the car as a result of the engine, power train, and wheels pushing backward on the road?

$$F_{net} = F_{forward} - F_{friction}$$

$$F_{forward} = F_{net} + F_{friction}$$

$$= (1.2 \times 10^3 \text{ N}) + (450 \text{ N})$$

$$= 1.7 \times 10^3 \text{ N}$$

13. In an electronics factory, small cabinets slide down a 30.0° incline a distance of 16.0 m to reach the next assembly stage. The cabinets have a mass of 10.0 kg each.

a. Calculate the speed each cabinet would acquire if the incline were frictionless.

$$d_v = d \sin \theta = (16.0 \text{ m})(\sin 30.0°)$$

$$= 8.00 \text{ m}$$

$$\frac{1}{2} mv^2 = mgh$$

$$v = \sqrt{2gh} = \sqrt{(2)(9.80 \text{ m/s}^2)(8.00 \text{ m})}$$

$$= 12.5 \text{ m/s}$$

b. What kinetic energy would a cabinet have under such circumstances?

$$K = \frac{1}{2} mv^2$$

$$= \left(\frac{1}{2}\right)(10.0 \text{ kg})(12.5 \text{ m/s})^2$$

$$= 781 \text{ J}$$

14. An average force of 8.2 N is used to pull a 0.40-kg rock, stretching a sling shot 43 cm. The rock is shot downward from a bridge 18 m above a stream. What will be the velocity of the rock just before it enters the water?

Initial energy: $W + U_g$

$$= (8.2 \text{ N})(0.43 \text{ m})$$

$$+ (0.40 \text{ kg})(9.80 \text{ m/s}^2)(18 \text{ m})$$

$$= 3.5 \text{ J} + 70.6 \text{ J}$$

$$= 74.1 \text{ J}$$

Energy at water is kinetic energy:

$$K = \frac{1}{2} mv^2$$

$$v = \sqrt{\frac{2K}{m}} = \sqrt{\frac{2(74.1 \text{ J})}{0.40 \text{ kg}}} = 19 \text{ m/s}$$

15. A 15-g bullet is fired horizontally into a 3.000-kg block of wood suspended by a long cord. The bullet sticks in the block. Compute the velocity of the bullet if the impact causes the block to swing 1.0×10^1 cm above its initial level.

Consider first the collision of block and bullet. During the collision, momentum is conserved, so momentum just before = momentum just after

$$(0.015 \text{ kg})v_0 + 0 = (3.015 \text{ kg})v$$

where v_0 is the initial speed of the bullet and v is the speed of block and bullet after collision.

We have two unknowns in this equation. To find another equation, we can use the fact that the block swings 10 cm high. Therefore, choosing gravitational potential energy = 0 at the initial level of the block,

K just after collision = final U_g

$$\frac{1}{2}(3.015 \text{ kg})v^2$$

$$= (3.015 \text{ kg})(9.80 \text{ m/s}^2)(0.10 \text{ m})$$

$$v = 1.40 \text{ m/s}$$

$$v_0 = \frac{(3.015 \text{ kg})(1.40 \text{ m/s})}{0.015 \text{ kg}}$$

$$= 2.8 \times 10^2 \text{ m/s}$$

Copyright © by Glencoe/McGraw-Hill

CHAPTER 12

1. The boiling point of liquid chlorine is $-34.60°C$. Find this temperature in Kelvin.

$$K = °C + 273 = -34.60 + 273$$
$$= 238\ K$$

2. Fluorine has a melting point of 50.28 K. Find this temperature in degrees Celsius.

$$°C = K - 273 = 50.28 - 273$$
$$= -223°C$$

3. Five kilograms of ice cubes are moved from the freezing compartment of a refrigerator into a home freezer. The refrigerator's freezing compartment is kept at $-4.0°C$. The home freezer is kept at $-17°C$. How much heat does the freezer's cooling system remove from the ice cubes?

$$Q = mC\,\Delta T$$
$$= (5.0\ kg)(2060\ J/kg \cdot °C)[-4.0°C - (-17°C)]$$
$$= 1.3 \times 10^5\ J\ removed$$

4. How much thermal energy must be added to 124 g of brass at 12.5°C to raise its temperature to 97.0°C?

$$Q = mC\,\Delta T$$
$$= (0.124\ kg)(376\ J/kg \cdot C°)(84.5°C)$$
$$= 3.94 \times 10^3\ J$$

5. 2.8×10^5 J of thermal energy are added to a sample of water and its temperature changes from 293 K to 308 K. What is the mass of the water?

$$m = \frac{Q}{C\,\Delta T} = \frac{2.8 \times 10^5\ J}{(4180\ J/kg \cdot C°)(15°C)}$$
$$= 4.5\ kg$$

6. 1420 J of thermal energy are added to a 100.0-g block of carbon at $-20.0°C$. What final temperature will the carbon reach?

$$\Delta T = \frac{Q}{mC}$$
$$= \frac{1420\ J}{(710\ J/kg \cdot C°)(0.100\ kg)}$$
$$= 20.0°C$$

Final temperature is
$$-20.0°C + 20.0°C = 0.0°C$$

7. A gold brick, mass 10.5 kg, requires 2.08×10^4 J to change its temperature from 35.0°C to 50.0°C. What is the specific heat of gold?

$$C = \frac{Q}{m\,\Delta T} = \frac{2.08 \times 10^4\ J}{(10.5\ kg)(15.0°C)}$$
$$= 132\ J/kg \cdot °C$$

---

8. An 8.00×10^2-g block of lead is heated in boiling water, 100.0°C, until the block's temperature is the same as the water's. The lead is then removed from the boiling water and dropped into 2.50×10^2 g of cool water at 12.2°C. After a short time, the temperature of both lead and water is 20.0°C.

a. How much energy is gained by the cool water?

$$Q = mC\,\Delta T = (2.50 \times 10^{-1}\ kg)(4180\ J/kg \cdot °C)(20.0°C - 12.2°C) = 8.15 \times 10^3\ J$$

b. On the basis of these measurements, what is the specific heat of lead?

$$C_{lead} = \frac{Q}{m\,\Delta T} = \frac{-8.15 \times 10^3\ J}{(8.00 \times 10^{-1}\ kg)(20.0°C - 100.0°C)} = 1.27 \times 10^2\ J/kg \cdot °C$$

9. 250.0 g of copper at 100.0°C are placed in a cup containing 325.0 g of water at 20.0°C. Assume no heat loss to the surroundings. What is the final temperature of the copper and water?

$$Q_{loss} = Q_{gain}$$
$$(0.250\ kg)(385\ J/kg \cdot C°)(100.0°C - T_f) = (0.325\ kg)(4180\ J/kg \cdot C°)(T_f - 20.0°C)$$
$$9.63 \times 10^3 - 9.63 \times 10^1\ T_f = 1.36 \times 10^3\ T_f - 2.72 \times 10^4$$
$$1.46 \times 10^3\ T_f = 3.68 \times 10^4$$
$$T_f = 25.2°C$$

Copyright © by Glencoe/McGraw-Hill

10. A 4.00×10^2-g sample of methanol at $30.0°C$ is mixed with a 2.00×10^2-g sample of water at $0.00°C$. Assume no heat loss to the surroundings. What is the final temperature of the mixture?

$Q_{loss} = Q_{gain}$

$(4.00 \times 10^{-1} \text{ kg})(2450 \text{ J/kg} \cdot \text{C°})(30.0°C - T_f)$

$= (2.00 \times 10^{-1} \text{ kg})(4180 \text{ J/kg} \cdot \text{C°})(T_f - 0.00°C)$

$2.94 \times 10^4 - 9.80 \times 10^2 \, T_f = 8.36 \times 10^2 \, T_f$

$1.82 \times 10^3 \, T_f = 2.94 \times 10^4$

$T_f = 16.2°C$

11. How much heat is needed to change 50.0 g of water at $80.0°C$ to steam at $110.0°C$?

Step 1: Heat water:

$Q_1 = mC \, \Delta T = (0.0500 \text{ kg})(4180 \text{ J/kg} \cdot \text{C°})(20.0°C) = 4.18 \times 10^3 \text{ J}$

Step 2: Boil water:

$Q_2 = mH_v = (0.0500 \text{ kg})(2.26 \times 10^6 \text{ J/kg}) = 1.13 \times 10^5 \text{ J}$

Step 3: Heat steam:

$Q_3 = mC \, \Delta T = (0.0500 \text{ kg})(2020 \text{ J/kg} \cdot \text{C°})(10.0°C) = 1.01 \times 10^3 \text{ J}$

Total:

$Q_1 + Q_2 + Q_3 = 1.18 \times 10^5 \text{ J}$

12. The specific heat of mercury is $140 \text{ J/kg} \cdot \text{C°}$. Its heat of vaporization is $3.06 \times 10^5 \text{ J/kg}$. How much energy is needed to heat 1.0 kg of mercury metal from $10.0°C$ to its boiling point and vaporize it completely? The boiling point of mercury is $357°C$.

The amount of heat needed to raise mercury to its boiling point is:

$Q = mC \, \Delta T = (1.0 \text{ kg})(140 \text{ J/kg} \cdot \text{C°})(357°C - 10.0°C) = 4.9 \times 10^4 \text{ J}$

The amount of heat needed to vaporize the mercury is:

$Q = mH_v = (1.0 \text{ kg})(3.06 \times 10^5 \text{ J/kg}) = 3.1 \times 10^5 \text{ J}$

The total heat needed is

$(4.9 \times 10^4 \text{ J}) + (3.1 \times 10^5 \text{ J}) = 3.6 \times 10^5 \text{ J}$

13. 30.0 g of $-3.0°C$ ice are placed in a cup containing 104.0 g of water at $62.0°C$. All the ice melts. Find the final temperature of the mixture. Assume no heat loss to the surroundings.

$Q_{loss} = Q_{gain}$

$(0.1040 \text{ kg})(4180 \text{ J/kg} \cdot \text{C°})(62.0°C - T_f)$

$= (0.0300 \text{ kg})(2060 \text{ J/kg} \cdot \text{C°})(3.0°C) + (0.0300 \text{ kg})(3.34 \times 10^5 \text{ J/kg})$

$\qquad + (0.0300 \text{ kg})(4180 \text{ J/kg} \cdot \text{C°})(T_f - 0.0°C)$

$2.70 \times 10^4 - 4.35 \times 10^2 \, T_f = 1.85 \times 10^2 + 1.00 \times 10^4 + 1.25 \times 10^2 \, T_f$

$5.60 \times 10^2 \, T_f = 1.68 \times 10^4$

$T_f = 30.0°C$

Copyright © by Glencoe/McGraw-Hill

14. Water flows over a falls 125.0 m high. If the potential energy of the water is all converted to thermal energy, calculate the temperature difference between the water at the top and the bottom of the falls.

$$U_{loss} = Q_{gain}$$

$$mgh = mC\,\Delta T$$

$$\Delta T = \frac{gh}{C} = \frac{(9.80 \text{ m/s}^2)(125.0 \text{ m})}{4180 \text{ J/kg} \cdot \text{C}°}$$

$$= 0.293°C$$

15. During the game, the metabolism of basketball players often increases by as much as 30.0 W. How much perspiration must a player vaporize per hour to dissipate this extra thermal energy?

$$P = \frac{E}{t}$$

$$E = Pt = (30.0 \text{ W})(3600 \text{ s}) = 108\ 000 \text{ J}$$

$$m = \frac{Q}{H_v} = \frac{108\ 000 \text{ J}}{2260 \text{ J/g}} = 47.8 \text{ g}$$

Copyright © by Glencoe/McGraw-Hill

CHAPTER 13

1. How tall must a column of mercury, $\rho = 1.36 \times 10^4$ kg/m³, be to exert a pressure equal to the atmosphere?

$$1 \text{ atm} = 1.013 \times 10^5 \text{ Pa}$$

$$P = \rho h g$$

$$h = \frac{P}{\rho g}$$

$$= \frac{1.013 \times 10^5 \text{ Pa}}{(1.36 \times 10^4 \text{ kg/m}^3)(9.80 \text{ m/s}^2)}$$

$$= 0.760 \text{ m}$$

2. A dog, whose paw has an area of 12.0 cm², has a mass of 8.0 kg. What average pressure does the dog exert while standing?

$$\text{Total area} = 4(0.00120 \text{ m}^2)$$

$$= 0.00480 \text{ m}^2$$

$$P = \frac{F}{A} = \frac{mg}{A}$$

$$= \frac{(8.0 \text{ kg})(9.80 \text{ m/s}^2)}{0.00480 \text{ m}^2}$$

$$= 1.6 \times 10^4 \text{ Pa}$$

3. A crate, whose bottom surface is 50.4 cm by 28.3 cm, exerts a pressure of 2.50×10^3 Pa on the floor. What is the mass of the crate?

$$A = (0.504 \text{ m})(0.283 \text{ m}) = 0.143 \text{ m}^2$$

$$F = PA = (2.50 \times 10^3 \text{ Pa})(0.143 \text{ m}^2)$$

$$= 3.58 \times 10^2 \text{ N}$$

$$m = \frac{F}{g} = \frac{3.58 \times 10^2 \text{ N}}{9.80 \text{ m/s}^2} = 36.5 \text{ kg}$$

4. The dimensions of a waterbed are 2.13 m by 1.52 m by 0.380 m. If the frame has a mass of 91.0 kg and the mattress is filled with water, what pressure does the bed exert on the floor?

$$A = (2.13 \text{ m})(1.52 \text{ m}) = 3.24 \text{ m}^2$$

$$V = (2.13 \text{ m})(1.52 \text{ m})(0.380 \text{ m})$$

$$= 1.23 \text{ m}^3$$

$$m = \rho V = (1.00 \times 10^3 \text{ kg/m}^3)(1.23 \text{ m}^3)$$

$$= 1.23 \times 10^3 \text{ kg}$$

Total mass $= 1.23 \times 10^3$ kg $+ 91.0$ kg

$$= 1.32 \times 10^3 \text{ kg}$$

$$W = mg = (1.32 \times 10^3 \text{ kg})(9.80 \text{ m/s}^2)$$

$$= 1.29 \times 10^4 \text{ N}$$

$$P = \frac{F}{A} = \frac{1.29 \times 10^4 \text{ N}}{3.24 \text{ m}^2}$$

$$= 3.98 \times 10^3 \text{ Pa}$$

5. A rectangular block of tin, $\rho = 7.29 \times 10^3$ kg/m³, has dimensions of 5.00 cm by 8.50 cm by 2.25 cm. What pressure does it exert on a table top if it is lying on its side of

   a. greatest surface area?

$$V = lwh$$

$$= (0.0500 \text{ m})(0.0850 \text{ m})(0.0225 \text{ m})$$

$$= 9.56 \times 10^{-5} \text{ m}^3$$

$$m = \rho V$$

$$= (7.29 \times 10^3 \text{ kg/m}^3)$$

$$\times (9.56 \times 10^{-5} \text{ m}^3)$$

$$= 6.97 \times 10^{-1} \text{ kg}$$

$$F = mg = (6.97 \times 10^{-1} \text{ kg})(9.80 \text{ m/s}^2)$$

$$= 6.83 \text{ N}$$

$$A = (0.0500 \text{ m})(0.0850 \text{ m})$$

$$= 4.25 \times 10^{-3} \text{ m}^2$$

$$P = \frac{F}{A} = \frac{6.83 \text{ N}}{4.25 \times 10^{-3} \text{ m}^2}$$

$$= 1.61 \times 10^3 \text{ Pa}$$

   b. smallest surface area?

$$A = (0.0500 \text{ m})(0.0225 \text{ m})$$

$$= 1.125 \times 10^{-3} \text{ m}^2$$

$$P = \frac{F}{A} = \frac{6.83 \text{ N}}{1.125 \times 10^{-3} \text{ m}^2}$$

$$= 6.07 \times 10^3 \text{ Pa}$$

6. A rowboat, mass 42.0 kg, is floating on a lake.

   a. What is the size of the buoyant force?

$$F_{buoyant} = mg$$

$$= (42.0 \text{ kg})(9.80 \text{ m/s}^2)$$

$$= 412 \text{ N}$$

Copyright © by Glencoe/McGraw-Hill

Chapter 13 (continued)

6. (continued)

b. What is the volume of the submerged part of the boat?

$$V = \frac{F_{buoyant}}{\rho g}$$

$$= \frac{412 \text{ N}}{(1.00 \times 10^3 \text{ kg/m}^3)(9.80 \text{ m/s}^2)}$$

$$= 4.20 \times 10^{-2} \text{ m}^3$$

7. A hydraulic lift has a large piston of 20.00-cm diameter and a small piston of 5.00-cm diameter. What is the mechanical advantage of the lift?

$$MA = \frac{F_2}{F_1} = \frac{A_2}{A_1} = \frac{\pi r_2^2}{\pi r_1^2}$$

$$= \frac{\pi (10.00 \text{ cm})^2}{\pi (2.50 \text{ cm})^2} = 16.0$$

8. A lever on a hydraulic system gives a mechanical advantage of 5.00. The cross-sectional area of the small piston is 0.0400 m², and that of the large piston is 0.280 m². If a force of 25.0 N is exerted on the lever, what is the force given by the larger piston?

$$F_1 = (MA)(F_{lever})$$

$$= (5.00)(25.0 \text{ N}) = 125 \text{ N}$$

$$F_2 = \frac{F_1 A_2}{A_1} = \frac{(125 \text{ N})(0.280 \text{ m}^2)}{0.0400 \text{ m}^2}$$

$$= 875 \text{ N}$$

9. A piece of metal weighs 75.0 N in air and 60.0 N in water. What is the density of the metal?

$$\text{mass of metal} = \frac{W_m}{g} = \frac{75.0 \text{ N}}{9.80 \text{ m/s}^2}$$

$$= 7.65 \text{ kg}$$

weight of water displaced = 15.0 N

$$\text{mass of water displaced} = \frac{W_w}{g}$$

$$= \frac{15.0 \text{ N}}{9.80 \text{ m/s}^2}$$

$$= 1.53 \text{ kg}$$

volume of water displaced

$$V_w = \frac{m_m}{\rho_w} = \frac{1.53 \text{ kg}}{1.00 \times 10^3 \text{ kg/m}^3}$$

$$= 1.53 \times 10^{-3} \text{ m}^3$$

volume of metal is also 1.53×10^{-3} m³

$$\rho_m = \frac{m_m}{V_m} = \frac{7.65 \text{ kg}}{1.53 \times 10^{-3} \text{ m}^3}$$

$$= 5.00 \times 10^3 \text{ kg/m}^3$$

10. A river barge with vertical sides is 20.0 m long and 10.0 m wide. It floats 3.00 m out of the water when empty. When loaded with coals, the water is only 1.00 m from the top. What is the weight of the load of coal?

Volume of the water displaced

$$V_W = lwh = (20.0 \text{ m})(10.0 \text{ m})(2.00 \text{ m})$$

$$= 4.00 \times 10^2 \text{ m}^3$$

Mass of the water displaced

$$M_W = \rho_W V_W$$

$$= (1.00 \times 10^3 \text{ kg/m}^3)$$

$$(4.00 \times 10^2 \text{ m}^3)$$

$$= 4.00 \times 10^5 \text{ kg}$$

Mass of the coal is also 4.00×10^5 kg.

$$W = mg = (4.00 \times 10^5 \text{ kg})(9.80 \text{ m/s}^2)$$

$$= 3.92 \times 10^6 \text{ N}$$

11. What is the change in the length of a 15.0-m steel rail as it is cooled from 1535°C to 20°C?

$$\Delta L = \alpha L_i \Delta T$$

$$= (12 \times 10^{-6} {}^\circ C^{-1})(15.0 \text{ m})(-1515 {}^\circ C)$$

$$= -2.7 \times 10^{-1} \text{ m}$$

or −27 cm

12. A concrete sidewalk section 8.000 m by 1.000 m by 0.100 m at exactly 0°C will expand to what volume at 35°C?

$$V_i = (8.000 \text{ m})(1.000 \text{ m})(0.100 \text{ m})$$

$$= 0.800 \text{ m}^3$$

$$\Delta V = \beta V_i \Delta T$$

$$= (36 \times 10^{-6} {}^\circ C^{-1})(0.800 \text{ m}^3)(35 {}^\circ C)$$

$$\Delta V = 1.0 \times 10^{-3} \text{ m}^3$$

$$V_{final} = 0.800 \text{ m}^3 + 0.001 \text{ m}^3$$

$$= 0.801 \text{ m}^3$$

Copyright © by Glencoe/McGraw-Hill

13. An air-filled balloon of 15.0-cm radius at 11°C is heated to 121°C. What change in volume occurs?

$$V_i = \frac{4}{3}\pi r^3 = \frac{4}{3}\pi (15.0 \text{ cm})^3$$

$$= 1.41 \times 10^4 \text{ cm}^3$$

$$\Delta V = V_i \beta \Delta T$$

$$= (1.41 \times 10^4 \text{ cm}^3)(3400 \times 10^{-6}°\text{C}^{-1})$$
$$\times (110°\text{C})$$

$$\Delta V = 5.2 \times 10^3 \text{ cm}^3$$

14. A circular, pyrex watch glass of 10.0-cm diameter at 21°C is heated to 501°C. What change will be found in the circumference of the glass?

$$\Delta d = \alpha d_i \Delta T$$

$$= (3 \times 10^{-6}°\text{C}^{-1})(10.0 \text{ cm})(480°\text{C})$$

$$= 1.44 \times 10^{-2} \text{ cm}$$

$$\Delta C = \pi \Delta d$$

$$= \pi (1.44 \times 10^{-2} \text{ cm}) = 4.5 \times 10^{-2} \text{ cm}$$

15. A 200.0-cm copper wire and a 201-cm platinum wire are both at exactly 0°C. At what temperature will they be of equal length?

Length of Platinum = Length of Copper

$$L_P + \Delta L_P \alpha_P \Delta T = L_C + \Delta L_C \alpha_C \Delta T$$

$$201 \text{ cm} + (201 \text{ cm})(9 \times 10^{-6}°\text{C}^{-1})\Delta T$$

$$= 200.0 \text{ cm} + (200.0 \text{ cm})$$

$$(16 \times 10^{-6}°\text{C}^{-1})\Delta T$$

$$1.39 \times 10^{-3} \text{ cm} °\text{C}^{-1} \Delta T = 1 \text{ cm}$$

$$\Delta T = 719°\text{C}$$

Copyright © by Glencoe/McGraw-Hill

CHAPTER 14

1. A periodic transverse wave that has a frequency of 10.0 Hz travels along a string. The distance between a crest and either adjacent trough is 2.50 m. What is its wavelength?

   The wavelength is the distance between adjacent crests, or twice the distance between a crest and an adjacent trough.

   $\lambda = 2(2.50 \text{ m}) = 5.00 \text{ m}$

2. A wave generator produces 16.0 pulses in 4.00 s.

   a. What is its period?
   $$\frac{4.00 \text{ s}}{16.0 \text{ pulses}} = 0.250 \text{ s/pulse, so}$$

   $T = 0.250 \text{ s}$

   b. What is its frequency?
   $$f = \frac{1}{T} = \frac{1}{0.250 \text{ s}} = 4.00 \text{ Hz}$$

3. A wave generator produces 22.5 pulses in 5.50 s.

   a. What is its period?
   $$\frac{5.50 \text{ s}}{22.5 \text{ pulses}} = 0.244 \text{ s/pulse, so}$$

   $T = 0.244 \text{ s}$

   b. What is its frequency?
   $$f = \frac{1}{T} = \frac{1}{0.244 \text{ s}} = 4.10 \text{ Hz}$$

4. What is the speed of a periodic wave disturbance that has a frequency of 2.50 Hz and a wavelength of 0.600 m?

   $v = \lambda f = (0.600 \text{ m})(2.50 \text{ Hz})$

   $= 1.50 \text{ m/s}$

5. One pulse is generated every 0.100 s in a tank of water. What is the speed of propagation of the wave if the wavelength of the surface wave is 3.30 cm?

   $$v = \frac{\lambda}{T} = \frac{3.30 \text{ cm}}{0.100 \text{ s}} = 33.0 \text{ cm/s}$$

   $= 0.330 \text{ m/s}$

6. Five pulses are generated every 0.100 s in a tank of water. What is the speed of propagation of the wave if the wavelength of the surface wave is 1.20 cm?

   $$\frac{0.100 \text{ s}}{5 \text{ pulses}} = 0.0200 \text{ s/pulse, so}$$

   $T = 0.0200 \text{ s}$

   $$v = \frac{\lambda}{T} = \frac{1.20 \text{ cm}}{0.0200 \text{ s}} = 60.0 \text{ cm/s}$$

   $= 0.600 \text{ m/s}$

7. A periodic longitudinal wave that has a frequency of 20.0 Hz travels along a coil spring. If the distance between successive compressions is 0.400 m, what is the speed of the wave?

   $v = \lambda f = (0.400 \text{ m})(20.0 \text{ Hz})$

   $= 8.00 \text{ m/s}$

8. What is the wavelength of a water wave that has a frequency of 2.50 Hz and a speed of 4.0 m/s?

   $$\lambda = \frac{v}{f} = \frac{4.0 \text{ m/s}}{2.50 \text{ Hz}} = 1.6 \text{ m}$$

9. The speed of a transverse wave in a string is 15.0 m/s. If a source produces a disturbance that has a frequency of 5.00 Hz, what is its wavelength?

   $$\lambda = \frac{v}{f} = \frac{15.0 \text{ m/s}}{5.00 \text{ Hz}} = 3.00 \text{ m}$$

10. The speed of a transverse wave in a string is 15.0 m/s. If a source produces a disturbance that has a wavelength of 1.25 m, what is the frequency of the wave?

    $$f = \frac{v}{\lambda} = \frac{15.0 \text{ m/s}}{1.25 \text{ m}} = 12.0 \text{ Hz}$$

11. A wave has an angle of incidence of 24°. What is the angle of reflection?

    The angle of incidence is equal to the angle of reflection; thus, both are 24°.

Copyright © by Glencoe/McGraw-Hill

CHAPTER 15

1. The echo of a ship's foghorn, reflected from an iceberg, is heard 5.0 s after the horn is sounded. How far away is the iceberg?

   $d = vt$, where $t = \dfrac{5.0\ \text{s}}{2} = 2.5\ \text{s}$,

   because sound must travel to the iceberg and back.

   $d = vt = (343\ \text{m/s})(2.5\ \text{s})$

   $= 8.6 \times 10^2\ \text{m}$

2. What is the speed of sound that has a frequency of 250 Hz and a wavelength of 0.600 m?

   $v = \lambda f = (0.600\ \text{m})(250\ \text{Hz}) = 150\ \text{m/s}$

3. A sound wave has a frequency of 2000 Hz and travels along a steel rod. If the distance between successive compressions is 0.400 m, what is the speed of the wave?

   $v = \lambda f = (0.400\ \text{m})(2000\ \text{Hz})$

   $= 800\ \text{m/s}$

4. What is the wavelength of a sound wave that has a frequency of 250 Hz and a speed of 4.0×10^2 m/s?

   $\lambda = \dfrac{v}{f} = \dfrac{4.0 \times 10^2\ \text{m/s}}{250\ \text{Hz}} = 1.6\ \text{m}$

5. What is the wavelength of sound that has a frequency of 539.8 Hz?

   $\lambda = \dfrac{v}{f} = \dfrac{343\ \text{m/s}}{539.8\ \text{Hz}} = 0.635\ \text{m}$

6. What is the wavelength of sound that has a frequency of 320.0 Hz?

   $\lambda = \dfrac{v}{f} = \dfrac{343\ \text{m/s}}{320.0\ \text{Hz}} = 1.07\ \text{m}$

7. A stone is dropped into a mine shaft 250.0 m deep. How many seconds pass before the stone is heard to strike the bottom of the shaft?

   First find the time needed for the stone to strike the bottom of the shaft.

   $d = \dfrac{1}{2}\,gt_1^2$

   or $t_1 = \left(\dfrac{2d}{g}\right)^{1/2} = \left[\dfrac{2(250.0\ \text{m})}{9.80\ \text{m/s}^2}\right]^{1/2}$

   $= 7.14\ \text{s}$

The time needed for the sound to travel to the top of the shaft is

$t_2 = \dfrac{d}{v} = \dfrac{250.0\ \text{m}}{343\ \text{m/s}} = 0.729\ \text{s}$

The total time is thus

$t = t_1 + t_2 = 7.14\ \text{s} + 0.729\ \text{s} = 7.87\ \text{s}$

8. A rifle is shot in a valley formed between two parallel mountains. The echo from one mountain is heard after 2.00 s and from the other mountain 2.00 s later. What is the width of the valley?

   Distance to first mountain:

   $d_1 = vt_1 = (343\ \text{m/s})(2.00\ \text{s}/2) = 343\ \text{m}$

   Distance to second mountain:

   $d_2 = vt_2 = (343\ \text{m/s})(4.00\ \text{s}/2) = 686\ \text{m}$

   Width of valley:

   $w = d_2 + d_1 = 686\ \text{m} + 343\ \text{m}$

   $= 1.030 \times 10^3\ \text{m}$

9. Sam, a train engineer, blows a whistle that has a frequency of 4.0×10^2 Hz as the train approaches a station. If the speed of the train is 25 m/s, what frequency will be heard by a person at the station?

   For the Doppler shift,

   $f' = f\left(\dfrac{v - v_d}{v - v_s}\right)$, **where v_d is the speed of the detector and v_s is the speed of the source.**

   $f' = (400\ \text{Hz})\left(\dfrac{343\ \text{m/s} - 0\ \text{m/s}}{343\ \text{m/s} - 25\ \text{m/s}}\right)$

   $= 430\ \text{Hz}$

Copyright © by Glencoe/McGraw-Hill

Chapter 15 (continued)

10. Shawon is on a train that is traveling at 95 km/h. The train passes a factory whose whistle is blowing at 288 Hz. What frequency does Shawon hear as the train approaches the factory?

$$f' = f\left(\frac{v - v_d}{v - v_s}\right), \text{ where}$$

$$v_d = (-95 \text{ km/h})\left(\frac{1 \text{ h}}{3600 \text{ s}}\right)\left(\frac{1000 \text{ m}}{k}\right)$$

$$= -26 \text{ m/s}$$

v_d **is negative because its direction is opposite to that of the sound wave.**

$$f' = (288 \text{ Hz})\left[\frac{343 \text{ m/s} - (-26 \text{ m/s})}{343 \text{ m/s} - 0 \text{ m/s}}\right]$$

$$= 310 \text{ Hz}$$

11. What is the sound level of a sound that has a sound pressure one tenth of 90 dB?

When the sound pressure is multiplied by one-tenth, the sound level decreases by 20 dB, so the sound level = 90 dB − 20 dB = 70 dB.

12. What is the sound level of a sound that has a sound pressure ten times 90 dB?

When the sound pressure is multipled by ten, the sound level increases by 20 dB, so the sound level = 90 dB + 20dB = 110 dB.

13. A tuning fork produces a resonance with a closed tube 19.0 cm long. What is the lowest possible frequency of the tuning fork?

The longest wavelength occurs when the length of the closed pipe is one-fourth the wavelength, so

$$\frac{\lambda}{4} = 19.0 \text{ cm, or}$$

$$\lambda = 4(19.0 \text{ cm}) = 76.0 \text{ cm}$$

The longest wavelength corresponds to the lowest frequency,

$$f = \frac{v}{\lambda} = \frac{343 \text{ m/s}}{0.760 \text{ m}} = 451 \text{ Hz}$$

14. How do the frequencies of notes that are an octave apart compare?

The higher note has a frequency twice that of the lower note.

15. Two tuning forks of 319 Hz and 324 Hz are sounded simultaneously. What frequency of sound will the listener hear?

beat frequency

= 324 Hz − 319 Hz = 5 Hz

= 5 beats/s

16. How many beats will be heard each second when a string with a frequency of 288 Hz is plucked simultaneously with another string that has a frequency of 296 Hz?

beat frequency = 296 Hz − 288 Hz

= 8 Hz = 8 beats/s

17. A tuning fork has a frequency of 440.0 Hz. If another tuning fork of slightly lower pitch is sounded at the same time, 5.0 beats per second are produced. What is the frequency of the second tuning fork?

The second tuning fork has a lower frequency than the first.

$$f_1 - f_2 = 5.0 \text{ Hz, or}$$

$$f_2 = f_1 - 5.0 \text{ Hz} = 440.0 \text{ Hz} - 5.0 \text{ Hz}$$

$$= 435.0 \text{ Hz}$$

Copyright © by Glencoe/McGraw-Hill

CHAPTER 16

1. The wavelength of blue light is about 4.5×10^{-7} m. Convert this to nm.

$$(4.5 \times 10^{-7} \text{ m}) \left(\frac{10^9 \text{ nm}}{1 \text{ m}} \right)$$

$$= 4.5 \times 10^2 \text{ nm}$$

2. As a spacecraft passes directly over Cape Canaveral, radar pulses are transmitted toward the craft and are then reflected back toward the ground. If the total time interval was 3.00×10^{-3} s, how far above the ground was the spacecraft when it passed over Cape Canaveral?

   Round trip distance

   $$d = vt$$

   $$= (3.00 \times 10^8 \text{ m/s})(3.00 \times 10^{-3} \text{ s})$$

   $$= 9.00 \times 10^5 \text{ m}$$

   So distance is 4.50×10^5 m

3. It takes 4.0 years for light from a star to reach Earth. How far away is this star from Earth?

   $$d = vt = (3.00 \times 10^8 \text{ m/s})(4.0 \text{ yr})$$

   $$\left(\frac{365 \text{ days}}{\text{yr}} \right) \left(\frac{24 \text{ h}}{\text{day}} \right) \left(\frac{3600 \text{ s}}{\text{h}} \right)$$

   $$= 3.8 \times 10^{16} \text{ m}$$

4. The planet Venus is sometimes a very bright object in the night sky. Venus is 4.1×10^{10} m away from Earth when it is closest to Earth. How long would we have to wait for a radar signal from Earth to return from Venus and be detected?

   Round trip distance

   $$d = 2(4.1 \times 10^{10} \text{ m}) = 8.2 \times 10^{10} \text{ m}$$

   $$t = \frac{d}{v} = \frac{8.2 \times 10^{10} \text{ m}}{3.00 \times 10^8 \text{ m/s}}$$

   $$= 2.7 \times 10^2 \text{ s}$$

5. The distance from Earth to the moon is about 3.8×10^8 m. A beam of light is sent to the moon and, after it reflects, returns to Earth. How long did it take to make the round trip?

   Round trip distance

   $$d = 2(3.8 \times 10^8 \text{ m}) = 7.6 \times 10^8 \text{ m}$$

   $$t = \frac{d}{v} = \frac{7.6 \times 10^8 \text{ m}}{3.00 \times 10^8 \text{ m/s}} = 2.5 \text{ s}$$

6. A baseball fan in a ball park is 101 m away from the batter's box when the batter hits the ball. How long after the batter hits the ball does the fan see it occur?

   $$t = \frac{d}{v} = \frac{101 \text{ m}}{3.00 \times 10^8 \text{ m/s}}$$

   $$= 3.37 \times 10^{-7} \text{ s}$$

7. A radio station on the AM band has an assigned frequency of 825 kHz (kilohertz). What is the wavelength of the station?

   $$\lambda = \frac{c}{f} = \frac{3.00 \times 10^8 \text{ m/s}}{825 \times 10^3 \text{ Hz}} = 364 \text{ m}$$

8. A short-wave, ham, radio operator uses the 6-meter band. On what frequency does the ham operate?

   $$f = \frac{c}{f} = \frac{3.00 \times 10^8 \text{ m/s}}{6 \text{ m}}$$

   $$= 5 \times 10^7 \text{ Hz} = 50 \text{ MHz}$$

9. Find the illumination 8.0 m below a 405-lm lamp.

   $$E = \frac{P}{4\pi d^2} = \frac{405 \text{ lm}}{4\pi(8.0 \text{ m})^2}$$

   $$= 0.50 \text{ lm/m}^2 = 0.50 \text{ lx}$$

Copyright © by Glencoe/McGraw-Hill

10. Two lamps illuminate a screen equally. The first lamp has an intensity of 12.5 cd and is 3.0 m from the screen. The second lamp is 9.0 m from the screen. What is its intensity?

$$\frac{P}{4\pi} = I, \text{ so } E = \frac{P}{4\pi d^2} = \frac{I}{d^2}$$

$$E_1 = E_2, \text{ or } \frac{I_1}{d_1^2} = \frac{I_2}{d_2^2}, \text{ so}$$

$$I_2 = I_1\left(\frac{d_2}{d_1}\right)^2 = (12.5 \text{ cd})\left(\frac{9.0 \text{ m}}{3.0 \text{ m}}\right)^2$$

$$= (12.5 \text{ cd})(9.0)$$

$$= 1.1 \times 10^2 \text{ cd}$$

11. A 15-cd point source lamp and a 45-cd point source lamp provide equal illuminations on a wall. If the 45-cd lamp is 12 m away from the wall, how far from the wall is the 15-cd lamp?

$$E = \frac{I}{d^2} \text{ and } E_1 = E_2, \text{ so } \frac{I_1}{d_1^2} = \frac{I_2}{d_2^2}, \text{ or}$$

$$d_1^2 = I_1 d_2^2 = \frac{(15 \text{ cd})(12 \text{ m})^2}{45 \text{ cd}} = 48 \text{ m}^2$$

$$d_1 = 6.9 \text{ m}$$

12. What is the name given to the electromagnetic radiation that has a wavelength slightly longer than visible light?

infrared

13. What is the name given to the electromagnetic radiation that has a wavelength slightly shorter than visible light?

ultraviolet

14. If a black object absorbs all light rays incident on it, how can we see it?

The black object stands out from other objects that are not black. It is also illuminated by some diffuse reflection.

15. What is the appearance of a red dress in a closed room illuminated only by green light?

The dress appears black, because red pigment absorbs green light.

16. A shirt that is the color of a primary color is illuminated with the complement of that primary color. What color do you see?

black

Copyright © by Glencoe/McGraw-Hill

CHAPTER 17

1. A ray of light strikes a mirror at an angle of incidence of 28°. What is the angle of reflection?

    The angle of reflection is equal to the angle of incidence, or 28°.

2. A ray of light passes from an unknown substance into air. If the angle in the unknown substance is 35.0° and the angle in air is 52.0°, what is the index of refraction of the unknown substance?

    $n_i \sin \theta_i = n_r \sin \theta_r$,

    $$n_i = \frac{n_r \sin \theta_r}{\sin \theta_i}$$

    $$= \frac{(1.00)(\sin 52.0°)}{\sin 35.0°} = 1.37$$

3. A ray of light has an angle of incidence of 25.0° upon the surface of a piece of quartz. What is the angle of refraction?

    $n_i \sin \theta_i = n_r \sin \theta_r$,

    $$\sin \theta_r = \frac{n_i \sin \theta_i}{n_r} = \frac{(1.00)(\sin 25.0)}{1.54}$$

    $$= 0.274$$

    $$\theta_r = 15.9°$$

4. A beam of light passes from water into polyethylene, index of refraction = 1.50. If the angle in water is 57.5°, what is the angle in polyethylene?

    $n_i \sin \theta_i = n_r \sin \theta_r$,

    $$\sin \theta_r = \frac{n_i \sin \theta_i}{n_r} = \frac{(1.33)(\sin 57.5°)}{1.50}$$

    $$= 0.748$$

    $$\theta_r = 48.4°$$

5. Mi-ling makes some hydrogen sulfide, index of refraction = 1.000 644. If Mi-ling measures an angle of 85.000° in the hydrogen sulfide, what angle will Mi-ling measure in air if the index of refraction of air is 1.000 292 6?

    $n_i \sin \theta_i = n_r \sin \theta_r$

    $$\sin \theta_r = \frac{n_i \sin \theta_i}{n_r}$$

    $$= \frac{(1.000\ 644)(\sin 85.000°)}{1.000\ 292\ 6}$$

    $$= 0.996\ 544\ 7$$

    $$\theta_r = 85.235°$$

6. Luisa submerged some ice in water and shined a laser beam through the water and into the ice. Luisa found the angle in ice was larger than the angle in water. Which material has a larger index of refraction?

    $n_i \sin \theta_i = n_r \sin \theta_r$

    $$n_i n_r = \frac{\sin \theta_r}{\sin \theta_i}$$

    $\theta_r > \theta_i$, so $\dfrac{n_i}{n_r} = \dfrac{\sin \theta_r}{\sin \theta_i} > 1$, or

    $n_i > n_r$, **and water (the incident material) has the larger index of refraction**

7. A ray of light enters a triangular crown glass prism perpendicular to one face and it emerges from an adjacent side. If the two adjacent sides meet at a 30.0° angle, what is the angle the light ray has in the air when it comes out?

    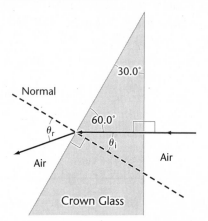

    $\theta_i = 180.0° - 60.0° - 90.0° = 30.0°$

    $n_i \sin \theta_i = n_r \sin \theta_r$

    $$\sin \theta_r = \frac{n_i \sin \theta_i}{n_r} = \frac{(1.52)(\sin 30.0°)}{1.00}$$

    $$= 0.760$$

    $$\theta_r = 49.5°$$

Physics: Principles and Problems

Copyright © by Glencoe/McGraw-Hill

Chapter 17 (continued)

8. Make a drawing to scale of the side of an aquarium in which the water is 12.0 cm deep. From a single point on the bottom, draw two lines upward, one vertical and the other 5.0° from the vertical. Let these two lines represent two light rays that start from the same point on the bottom of the tank. Compute the directions the refracted rays will travel above the surface of the water. Draw in these rays and continue them backward into the tank until they intersect. At what depth does the bottom of the tank appear to be if you look into the water? Divide the apparent depth into the true depth and compare it to the index of refraction.

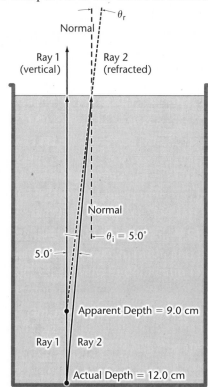

For ray 1, $\theta_r = \theta_i = 0°$

For ray 2, $n_i \sin \theta_i = n_r \sin \theta_r$

$$\sin \theta_r = \frac{n_i \sin \theta_i}{n_r} = \frac{(1.33)(\sin 5.0°)}{1.00}$$

$$= 0.116,$$

$$\theta_r = 6.7°$$

The refracted rays appear to intersect 9.0 cm below the surface; this is the apparent depth.

$$\frac{\text{apparent depth}}{\text{true depth}} = \frac{9.0 \text{ cm}}{12.0 \text{ cm}} = 0.75$$

Also, $\frac{n_{air}}{n_{water}} = \frac{1.00}{1.33} = 0.75$

Therefore,

$$\frac{\text{apparent depth}}{\text{true depth}} = \frac{n_{air}}{n_{water}}$$

9. Find the speed of light in water.

$$v_s = \frac{c}{n_s} = \frac{3.00 \times 10^8 \text{ m/s}}{1.33}$$

$$= 2.26 \times 10^8 \text{ m/s}$$

10. Find the speed of light in antimony trioxide if it has an index of refraction of 2.35.

$$v_s = \frac{c}{n_s} = \frac{3.00 \times 10^8 \text{ m/s}}{2.35}$$

$$= 1.28 \times 10^8 \text{ m/s}$$

11. The speed of light in a special piece of glass is 1.75×10^8 m/s. What is its index of refraction?

$$n_s = \frac{c}{v_s} = \frac{3.00 \times 10^8 \text{ m/s}}{1.75 \times 10^8 \text{ m/s}}$$

$$= 1.71$$

12. Glenn gently pours some acetic acid, index of refraction = 1.37, onto some antimony trioxide, index of refraction = 2.35. What angle will Glenn find in the acetic acid if the angle in the antimony trioxide is 42.0°?

$$n_i \sin \theta_i = n_r \sin \theta_r$$

$$\sin \theta_r = \frac{n_i \sin \theta_i}{n_r} = \frac{(2.35)(\sin 42.0°)}{1.37}$$

$$= 1.15$$

No angle because $\sin \theta_r$ cannot exceed 1. Therefore, total internal reflection occurs.

13. Marcos finds that a plastic has a critical angle of 40.0°. What is the index of refraction of the plastic?

$$\sin \theta_c = \frac{1}{n_i}$$

$$n_i = \frac{1}{\sin \theta_c} = \frac{1}{\sin 40.0°} = 1.56$$

14. Aisha decides to find the critical angle of arsenic trioxide, index of refraction = 2.01, which is very toxic. What angle did Aisha find?

$$\sin \theta_c = \frac{1}{n_i} = \frac{1}{2.01} = 0.498$$

$$\theta_c = 29.8°$$

15. A light source is in a cylindrical container of carbon dichloride, index of refraction = 1.500. The light source sends a ray of light parallel to the bottom of the container at a 45.0° angle from the radius to the circumference. What will the path of the light ray be?

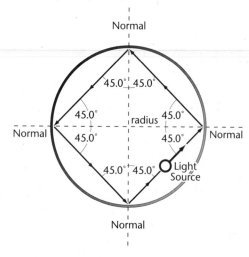

The ray from the light source is incident on the circumference at an angle of 45.0°

$$n_i \sin \theta_i = n_r \sin \theta_r$$

$$\sin \theta_r = n_i = \frac{(1.500)(\sin 45.0°)}{1.00}$$

$$= 1.06$$

This is impossible, because $\sin \theta_r$ cannot exceed 1. Therefore, total internal reflection occurs and the path of the light ray is a diamond, as shown.

16. With a square block of glass, index of refraction = 1.50, it is impossible, when looking into one side, to see out of an adjacent side of the square block of glass. It appears to be a mirror. Use your knowledge of geometry and critical angles to show that this is true.

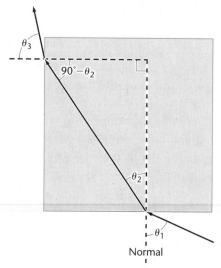

Say the light ray enters the glass at an angle θ_1, and is refracted to an angle θ_2.

$$n_{air} \sin \theta_1 = n_{glass} \sin \theta_2$$

$$\sin \theta_2 = \frac{n_{air} \sin \theta_1}{n_{glass}} = \frac{1.0 \sin \theta_1}{1.5}$$

For the light ray to leave an adjacent side, $(90° - \theta_2) < 42°$, or $\theta_2 > 48°$.

Recall that $\sin \theta_2 = \dfrac{1.0 \sin \theta_1}{1.5}$, so $\sin \theta_2$ and θ_2 are largest when θ_1 is 90°. In this case, $\sin \theta = \dfrac{1.0}{1.5} = 0.67$, or $\theta_2 = 42°$. But we found above that θ_2 must be greater than 48° for the light ray to leave an adjacent side. Because this is impossible, we conclude that one cannot see out of an adjacent side of a block of glass.

Copyright © by Glencoe/McGraw-Hill

Chapter 17 (continued)

17. The index of refraction for red light in arsenic trioxide is 2.010, and the index of refraction for blue light is 2.023. Find the difference between the angles of refraction if white light is incident at an angle of 65.0°.

$$n_i \sin \theta_i = n_r \sin \theta_r$$

$$\sin \theta_r = \frac{n_i \sin \theta_i}{n_r}$$

For red light,

$$\sin \theta_r = \frac{(1.00)(\sin 65.0°)}{2.010} = 0.451$$

$$\theta_r = 26.8°$$

For blue light,

$$\sin \theta_r = \frac{(1.00)(\sin 65.0°)}{2.023} = 0.448$$

$$\theta_r = 26.6°$$

Difference = 26.8° − 26.6° = 0.2°

18. The index of refraction for red light in a diamond is 2.410, and the index of refraction for blue light is 2.450. Find the difference in the speed of light in diamond.

$$v_s = \frac{c}{n_s}$$

For red light,

$$v_s = \frac{2.998 \times 10^8 \text{ m/s}}{2.410}$$

$$= 1.244 \times 10^8 \text{ m/s}$$

For blue light,

$$v_s = \frac{2.998 \times 10^8 \text{ m/s}}{2.450}$$

$$= 1.224 \times 10^8 \text{ m/s}$$

Difference

$$= (1.244 \times 10^8 \text{ m/s}) - (1.224 \times 10^8 \text{ m/s})$$

$$= 0.020 \times 10^8 \text{ m/s} = 2.0 \times 10^6 \text{ m/s}$$

Copyright © by Glencoe/McGraw-Hill

CHAPTER 18

1. Sally's face is 75 cm in front of a plane mirror. Where is the image of Sally's face?

   75 cm behind the mirror

2. A concave mirror has a focal length of 10.0 cm. What is its radius of curvature?

   $r = 2f = 2(10.0 \text{ cm}) = 20.0 \text{ cm}$

3. Light from a distant star is collected by a concave mirror that has a radius of curvature of 150 cm. How far from the mirror is the image of the star?

   $$f = \frac{r}{2} = \frac{150 \text{ cm}}{2} = 75 \text{ cm}$$

   $$\frac{1}{f} = \frac{1}{d_i} + \frac{1}{d_o}$$

   but d_o is extremely large, so

   $$\frac{1}{f} = \frac{1}{d_i} \text{ or } d_i = f = 75 \text{ cm}$$

4. An object is placed 25.0 cm away from a concave mirror that has a focal length of 5.00 cm. Where is the image located?

   $$\frac{1}{f} = \frac{1}{d_1} + \frac{1}{d_o}, \text{ so}$$

   $$d_i = \frac{d_o f}{d_o - f} = \frac{(25.0 \text{ cm})(5.00 \text{ cm})}{25.0 \text{ cm} - 5.00 \text{ cm}}$$

   $$= 6.25 \text{ cm}$$

   or 6.25 cm in front of the mirror

5. An object and its image as seen in a concave mirror are the same height when the object is 48.4 cm from the mirror. What is the focal length of the mirror?

   For a concave mirror, an object and its image have the same height when the object is two focal lengths from the mirror. Therefore,

   $48.4 \text{ cm} = 2f$, or $f = \dfrac{48.4 \text{ cm}}{2}$

   $= 24.2 \text{ cm}$

6. An object placed 50.0 cm from a concave mirror gives a real image 33.3 cm from the mirror. If the image is 28.4 cm high, what is the height of the object?

   $$m = \frac{h_i}{h_o} = \frac{-d_i}{d_o} = \frac{-33.3 \text{ cm}}{50.0 \text{ cm}} = -0.666$$

   So $h_o = \dfrac{h_i}{m} = \dfrac{-28.4 \text{ cm}}{-0.666} = 42.6 \text{ cm}$

   m is the negative, so the image is inverted and hi is negative.

7. An object, 15.8 cm high, is located 87.6 cm from a concave mirror that has a focal length of 17.0 cm.

   a. Where is the image located?

   $$\frac{1}{f} = \frac{1}{d_i} + \frac{1}{d_o}, \text{ so}$$

   $$d_i = \frac{d_o f}{d_o - f} = \frac{(87.6 \text{ cm})(17.0 \text{ cm})}{87.6 \text{ cm} - 17.0 \text{ cm}}$$

   $$= 21.1 \text{ cm}$$

   b. How high is the image?

   $$m = \frac{h_i}{h_o} = \frac{-d_i}{d_o} = \frac{-21.2 \text{ cm}}{87.6 \text{ cm}} = -0.242, \text{ so}$$

   $$h_i = mh_o = (-0.242)(15.8 \text{ cm})$$

   $$= -3.82 \text{ cm; inverted}$$

   The negative sign indicates an inverted image.

8. The image of the moon is formed by a concave mirror whose radius of curvature is 4.20 m at a time when the moon's distance is 3.80×10^5 km. What is the diameter of the image of the moon if the diameter of the moon is 3480 km?

   $$f = \frac{r}{2} = \frac{4.20 \text{ m}}{2} = 2.10 \text{ m}$$

   $$\frac{1}{f} = \frac{1}{d_i} + \frac{1}{d_o}, \text{ but } d_o \text{ is extremely large, so}$$

   $$\frac{1}{f} = \frac{1}{d_i}, \text{ or } d_i = f = 2.10 \text{ m}$$

   $$= 2.10 \times 10^{-3} \text{ km}$$

   $$m = \frac{h_i}{h_o} = \frac{-d_i}{d_o} = \frac{-(2.10 \times 10^{-3} \text{ km})}{3.80 \times 10^5 \text{ km}}$$

   $$= -5.53 \times 10^{-9}$$

   $$h_i = mh_o = (-5.53 \times 10^{-9})(3480 \text{ km})$$

   $$= -1.92 \times 10^{-5} \text{ km}$$

   $$= -1.92 \text{ cm; inverted}$$

   The negative sign indicates an inverted image.

Copyright © by Glencoe/McGraw-Hill

9. A shaving mirror has a radius of curvature of 30.0 cm. When a face is 10.0 cm away from the mirror, what is the magnification of the mirror?

    A shaving mirror is concave.

    $$f = \frac{r}{2} = (30.0 \text{cm})\backslash 2 \text{ cm} = 15.0 \text{ cm}$$

    $$\frac{1}{f} = \frac{1}{d_i} + \frac{1}{d_o} \text{ , so}$$

    $$d_i = \frac{d_o f}{d_o - f} = \frac{(10.0 \text{ cm})(15.0 \text{ cm})}{10.0 \text{ cm} - 15.0 \text{ cm}}$$

    $$= -30.0 \text{ cm}$$

    $$m = \frac{h_i}{h_o} = \frac{-d_i}{d_o} = \frac{-(-30.0 \text{ cm})}{10.0 \text{ cm}} = 3.00$$

    m is positive, so the image is erect.

10. A convex mirror has a focal length of −16 cm. How far behind the mirror does the image of a person 3.0 m away appear?

    $$\frac{1}{f} = \frac{1}{d_i} + \frac{1}{d_o} \text{ , so}$$

    $$d_i = \frac{d_o f}{d_o - f} = \frac{(3.0 \text{ m})(-0.16 \text{ m})}{3.0 \text{ m} - (-0.16 \text{ m})}$$

    $$= -0.15 \text{ m}$$

    or 15 cm behind the mirror.

11. How far behind the surface of a convex mirror, focal length of −6.0 cm, does a car 10.0 m from the mirror appear?

    $$\frac{1}{f} = \frac{1}{d_i} + \frac{1}{d_o} \text{ , so}$$

    $$d_i = \frac{d_o f}{d_o - f} = \frac{(10.0 \text{ m})(-0.060 \text{ m})}{10.0 \text{ m} - (-0.060 \text{ m})}$$

    $$= -0.060 \text{ m}$$

    or 6.0 cm behind the mirror.

12. A converging lens has a focal length of 25.5 cm. If it is placed 72.5 cm from an object, at what distance from the lens will the image be?

    $$\frac{1}{f} = \frac{1}{d_i} + \frac{1}{d_o} \text{ , so}$$

    $$d_i = \frac{d_o f}{d_o - f} = \frac{(72.5 \text{ cm})(25.5 \text{ cm})}{72.5 \text{ cm} - 25.5 \text{ cm}}$$

    $$= 39.3 \text{ cm}$$

13. If an object is 10.0 cm from a converging lens that has a focal length of 5.00 cm, how far from the lens will the image be?

    $$\frac{1}{f} = \frac{1}{d_i} + \frac{1}{d_o} \text{ , so}$$

    $$d_i = \frac{d_o f}{d_o - f} = \frac{(10.0 \text{ cm})(5.00 \text{ cm})}{10.0 \text{ cm} - 5.00 \text{ cm}}$$

    $$= 10.0 \text{ cm}$$

14. The focal length of a lens in a box camera is 10.0 cm. The fixed distance between the lens and the film is 11.0 cm. If an object is clearly focused on the film, how far must the object be from the lens?

    $$\frac{1}{f} = \frac{1}{d_i} + \frac{1}{d_o} \text{ , so}$$

    $$d_i = \frac{d_o f}{d_o - f} = \frac{(11.0 \text{ cm})(10.0 \text{ cm})}{11.0 \text{ cm} - 10.0 \text{ cm}}$$

    $$= 1.10 \times 10^2 \text{ cm}$$

15. An object 3.0 cm tall is placed 22 cm in front of a converging lens. A real image is formed 11 cm from the lens. What is the size of the image?

    $$m = \frac{h_i}{h_o} = \frac{-d_i}{d_o} = \frac{-(11 \text{ cm})}{22 \text{ cm}} = -0.50, \text{ so}$$

    $$h_i = mh_o = (-0.50)(3.0 \text{ cm})$$

    $$= -1.5 \text{ cm; inverted}$$

    The negative sign indicates an inverted image.

16. An object 3.0 cm tall is placed 20 cm in front of a converging lens. A real image is formed 10 cm from the lens. What is the focal length of the lens?

    $$\frac{1}{f} = \frac{1}{d_i} + \frac{1}{d_o} = \frac{1}{10 \text{ cm}} + \frac{1}{20 \text{ cm}}$$

    $$= \frac{3}{20 \text{ cm}}$$

    $$\text{so } f = \frac{20 \text{ cm}}{3} = 6.7 \text{ cm} = 7 \text{ cm}$$

17. What is the focal length of the lens in your eye when you read a book that is 35.0 cm from your eye? The distance from the lens to the retina is 0.19 mm.

    $$\frac{1}{f} = \frac{1}{d_i} + \frac{1}{d_o} \text{ , so}$$

    $$f = \frac{d_i d_o}{d_i + d_o} = \frac{(0.19 \text{ mm})(350 \text{ mm})}{0.19 \text{ mm} + 350 \text{ mm}}$$

    $$= 0.19 \text{ mm}$$

Copyright © by Glencoe/McGraw-Hill

18. When an object 5.0 cm tall is placed 12 cm from a converging lens, an image is formed on the same side of the lens as the object but the image is 61 cm away from the lens. What is the focal length of the lens?

$$f = \frac{d_i d_o}{d_i + d_o} = \frac{(-61 \text{ cm})(12 \text{ cm})}{-61 \text{ cm} + 12 \text{ cm}}$$

$$= 14.9 \text{ cm} = 15 \text{ cm}$$

19. When an object 5.0 cm tall is placed 12 cm from a converging lens, an image is formed on the same side of the lens as the object but the image is 61 cm away from the lens. What is the size of the image?

$$\frac{h_i}{h_o} = \frac{-d_i}{d_o}$$

$$h_i = h_o \left(\frac{-d_i}{d_o}\right) = 5.0 \text{ cm} \left(-\frac{-61}{12}\right)$$

$$= 25 \text{ cm; image is erect}$$

Copyright © by Glencoe/McGraw-Hill

CHAPTER 19

1. Monochromatic light passes through two slits that are 0.0300 cm apart and it falls on a screen 1.20×10^2 cm away. The first-order image is 0.160 cm from the middle of the center band. What is the wavelength of the light used?

$$\lambda = \frac{xd}{L}$$
$$= \frac{(1.60 \times 10^{-3} \text{ m})(3.00 \times 10^{-4} \text{ m})}{1.20 \text{ m}}$$
$$= 4.00 \times 10^{-7} \text{ m} = 4.00 \times 10^2 \text{ nm}$$

2. Green light passes through a double slit for which $d = 0.20$ mm and it falls on a screen 2.00 m away. The first-order image is at 0.50 cm. What is the wavelength of the light?

$$\lambda = \frac{xd}{L}$$
$$= \frac{(5.0 \times 10^{-3} \text{ m})(2.0 \times 10^{-4} \text{ m})}{2.00 \text{ m}}$$
$$= 5.0 \times 10^{-7} \text{ m} = 5.0 \times 10^2 \text{ nm}$$

3. Yellow light that has a wavelength of 6.00×10^2 nm passes through two narrow slits that are 0.200 mm apart. An interference pattern is produced on a screen 1.80×10^2 cm away. What is the location of the first-order image?

$$x = \frac{\lambda L}{d}$$
$$= \frac{(6.00 \times 10^{-7} \text{ m})(1.80 \text{ m})}{2.00 \times 10^{-4} \text{ m}}$$
$$= 5.40 \times 10^{-3} \text{ m} = 5.40 \text{ mm}$$

4. Violet light that has a wavelength of 4.00×10^2 nm passes through two slits that are 0.0100 cm apart. How far away must the screen be so the first-order image is at 0.300 cm?

$$L = \frac{xd}{\lambda}$$
$$= \frac{(3.00 \times 10^{-3} \text{ m})(1.00 \times 10^{-4} \text{ m})}{4.00 \times 10^{-7} \text{ m}}$$
$$= 0.750 \text{ m}$$

5. Two radio transmitters are 25.0 m apart and each one sends out a radio wave with a wavelength of 10.0 m. The two radio towers act exactly like a double-slit source for light. How far from the central band is the first-order image if you are 15.0 km away? (Yes, this really happens. Radio stations can and do fade in and out as you cross the nodals and the antinodals.)

$$x = \frac{\lambda L}{d}$$
$$= \frac{(10.0 \text{ m})(15.0 \times 10^3 \text{ m})}{25.0 \text{ m}}$$
$$= 6.00 \times 10^3 \text{ m} = 6.00 \text{ km}$$

6. Monochromatic light passes through a single slit, 0.500 mm wide, and falls on a screen 1.0 m away. If the distance from the center of the pattern to the first band is 2.6 mm, what is the wavelength of the light?

$$\lambda = \frac{xw}{L}$$
$$= \frac{(2.6 \times 10^{-3} \text{ m})(5.00 \times 10^{-4} \text{ m})}{1.0 \text{ m}}$$
$$= 1.3 \times 10^{-6} \text{ m}$$

7. Red light that has a wavelength of 7.50×10^2 nm passes through a single slit that is 0.1350 mm wide. How far away from the screen must the slit be if the first dark band is 0.9000 cm away from the central bright band?

$$L = \frac{xw}{\lambda}$$
$$= \frac{(9.000 \times 10^{-3} \text{ m})(1.350 \times 10^{-4} \text{ m})}{7.50 \times 10^{-7} \text{ m}}$$
$$= 1.62 \text{ m}$$

8. Microwaves with a wavelength of 3.5 cm pass through a single slit 0.85 cm wide and fall on a screen 91 cm away. What is the distance to the first-order band?

$$x = \frac{\lambda L}{w}$$
$$= \frac{(3.5 \times 10^{-2} \text{ m})(0.91 \text{ m})}{8.5 \times 10^{-3} \text{ m}}$$
$$= 3.7 \text{ m}$$

Copyright © by Glencoe/McGraw-Hill

9. Radio waves that are emitted by two adjacent radio transmitters behave like light waves coming from a double slit. If two transmitters, 1500 m apart, each send out radio waves with a wavelength of 150 m, what is the diffraction angle?

$\lambda = d \sin \theta$, so

$$\sin \theta = \frac{\lambda}{d} = \frac{150 \text{ m}}{1500 \text{ m}} = 0.100$$

$$\theta = 5.7°$$

10. What is the average distance between the lines of a diffraction grating if the number of lines per millimeter is 425?

$$\text{average distance} = \frac{\text{mm}}{425 \text{ lines}}$$

$$= 2.35 \times 10^{-3} \text{ mm/line}$$

11. A transmission grating with 5.85×10^3 lines/cm is illuminated by monochromatic light that has a wavelength of 492 nm. What is the diffraction angle for the first-order image?

$\lambda = d \sin \theta$

$$d = \frac{\text{cm}}{(5.85 \times 10^3 \text{ lines})}$$

$$= 1.71 \times 10^{-4} \text{ cm per line}$$

$$\sin \theta = \frac{\lambda}{d} = \frac{4.92 \times 10^{-27} \text{ m}}{1.71 \times 10^{-6} \text{ m}} = 0.288$$

$$\theta = 16.7°$$

12. Monochromatic light illuminates a transmission grating having 5900 lines/cm. The diffraction angle for a first-order image is 18.0°. What is the wavelength of the light in nanometers?

$\lambda = d \sin \theta$

$$d = \frac{\text{cm}}{5900 \text{ lines}}$$

$$= 1.695 \times 10^{-4} \text{ cm per line}$$

$$\lambda = (1.695 \times 10^{-4} \text{ cm})(\sin 18.0°)$$

$$= 5.24 \times 10^{-5} \text{ cm} = 524 \text{ nm}$$

13. A transmission grating, 5.80×10^3 lines/cm, is illuminated by a monochromatic light source that has a wavelength of 495 nm. How far from the center line is the first-order image if the distance to the grating is 1.25 m?

$$x = \frac{\lambda L}{d}$$

$$d = \frac{\text{cm}}{5.80 \times 10^3 \text{ lines}}$$

$$= 1.72 \times 10^{-4} \text{ cm per line}$$

$$x = \frac{(4.95 \times 10^{-7} \text{ m})(1.25 \text{ m})}{1.72 \times 10^{-6} \text{ m}}$$

$$= 0.360 \text{ m}$$

14. A pinhole camera uses a 1.5-mm hole instead of a lens to form an image. What is the resolution of this camera for green light, 545-nm wavelength, if the film is 6.0 cm behind the pinhole?

Use single-slit equation, $x = \frac{\lambda L}{w}$

$$x = \frac{(5.45 \times 10^{-7} \text{ m})(6.0 \times 10^{-2} \text{ m})}{1.5 \times 10^{-5} \text{ m}}$$

$$= 2.18 \times 10^{-5} \text{ m} = 2.2 \times 10^{-5} \text{ m}$$

So the resolution is 2.2×10^{-5} m.

Copyright © by Glencoe/McGraw-Hill

CHAPTER 20

1. Two charges, q_1 and q_2, are separated by a distance, d, and exert a force on each other. What new force will exist if d is doubled?

$$f' = \frac{Kq_1q_2}{d^2}$$

$$f' = \frac{Kq_1q_2}{(2d)^2} = \frac{Kq_1q_2}{4d^2} = \frac{f}{4}$$

2. Two charges, q_1 and q_2, are separated by a distance, d, and exert a force, f, on each other. What new force will exist if q_1 and q_2 are both doubled?

$$f = \frac{Kq_1q_2}{d^2}$$

$$f' = \frac{K(2q_1)(2q_2)}{d^2} = \frac{4Kq_1q_2}{d^2} = 4f$$

3. Two identical point charges are separated by a distance of 3.0 cm and they repel each other with a force of 4.0×10^{-5} N. What is the new force if the distance between the point charges is doubled?

$$F \propto \frac{1}{d^2}, \text{ so} \frac{F_2}{F_1} = \frac{d_1^2}{d_2^2}, \text{ or}$$

$$F_2 = \left(\frac{d_1}{d_2}\right)^2 F_1 = \left(\frac{3}{6}\right)^2 (4.0 \times 10^{-5} \text{ N}) = 1.0 \times 10^{-5} \text{ N}$$

4. An electric force of 2.5×10^{-4} N acts between two small equally charged spheres, which are 2.0 cm apart. Calculate the force acting between the spheres if the charge on one of the spheres is doubled and the spheres move to a 5.0-cm separation.

$$F = \frac{Kqq'}{d^2}, \text{ so } F_1 = \frac{Kq_1q_1'}{d_1^2}, \text{ and } F_2 = \frac{Kq_2q_2'}{d_2^2}, \text{ or } \frac{F_2}{F_1} = \left(\frac{q_2q_2'}{q_1q_1'}\right)\left(\frac{d_1}{d_2}\right)^2$$

From the problem statement, $q_2 = q_1$, $q_2' = 2q_1'$, and $\dfrac{d_1}{d_2} = \dfrac{2.0 \text{ cm}}{5.0 \text{ cm}} = 0.40$.

Therefore, $\dfrac{F_2}{F_1} = (2)(0.40)^2 = 0.32$, or

$$F_2 = 0.32F_1 = 0.32(2.5 \times 10^{-4} \text{ N}) = 8.0 \times 10^{-5} \text{ N}$$

5. How many electrons would be required to have a total charge of 1.00 C on a sphere?

$$(1.00 \text{ C}) \left(\frac{\text{electron}}{1.60 \times 10^{-19} \text{ C}}\right) = 6.25 \times 10^{18} \text{ electrons}$$

6. If two identical charges, 1.000 C each, are separated by a distance of 1.00 km, what is the force between them?

$$F = \frac{Kqq'}{d^2} = \frac{(9.0 \times 10^9 \text{ N} \cdot \text{m}^2/\text{C}^2)(1.000 \text{ C})^2}{(1.00 \times 10^3 \text{ m})^2} = +9.0 \times 10^3 \text{ N}$$

7. Two point charges are separated by 10.0 cm. If one charge is +20.00 μC and the other is −6.00 μC, what is the force between them?

$$F = \frac{Kqq'}{d^2} = \frac{(9.0 \times 10^9 \text{ N} \cdot \text{m}^2/\text{C}^2)(20.00 \times 10^{-6} \text{ C})(-6.00 \times 10^{-6} \text{ C})}{(0.100 \text{ m})^2}$$

$$= -1.1 \times 10^2 \text{ N; the force is attractive}$$

Copyright © by Glencoe/McGraw-Hill

8. The two point charges in the previous problem are allowed to touch each other and are again separated by 10.00 cm. Now what is the force between them?

If the charges touch, the two charges become equal and one half of the total charge:

$$q = q' = \frac{+20.00\ \mu C + (-6.00\ \mu C)}{2} = +7.00\ \mu C$$

$$F = \frac{Kqq'}{d^2} = \frac{(9.0 \times 10^9\ N \cdot m^2/C^2)(7.00 \times 10^{-6}\ C)^2}{(0.100\ m)^2} = +44\ N\ away$$

The force is repulsive.

9. Determine the electrostatic force of attraction between a proton and an electron that are separated by 5.00×10^2 nm.

$$F = \frac{Kqq'}{d^2} = \frac{(9.0 \times 10^9\ N \cdot m^2/C^2)(1.60 \times 10^{-19}\ C)(-1.60 \times 10^{-19}\ C)}{(5.00 \times 10^{-7}\ m)^2} = -9.2 \times 10^{-16}\ N$$

10. Find the force between two charged spheres 1.25 cm apart if the charge on one sphere is 2.50 μC and the charge on the other sphere is 1.75×10^{-8} C.

$$F = \frac{Kqq'}{d^2} = \frac{(9.00 \times 10^9\ N \cdot m^2/C^2)(2.50 \times 10^{-6}\ C)(1.75 \times 10^{-8}\ C)}{(1.25 \times 10^{-2}\ m)^2} = +2.52\ N$$

11. Two identical point charges are 3.00 cm apart. Find the charge on each of them if the force of repulsion is 4.00×10^{-7} N.

$$F = \frac{Kqq'}{d^2} = \frac{Kq^2}{d^2}\ \text{for identical charges.}$$

$$q^2 = \frac{Fd^2}{K} = \frac{(+4.00 \times 10^{-7}\ N)(0.0300\ m)^2}{9.0 \times 10^9\ N \cdot m^2/C^2} = +4.0 \times 10^{-20}\ C^2$$

$$q = \pm 2.0 \times 10^{-10}\ C$$

Either both of the charges are positive, or both are negative.

12. A charge of 4.0×10^{-5} C is attracted by a second charge with a force of 350 N when the separation is 10.0 cm. Calculate the size of the second charge.

$$F = \frac{Kqq'}{d^2}, \text{ so } q' = \frac{Fd^2}{Kq} = \frac{(-350\ N)(0.100\ m)^2}{(9.0 \times 10^9\ N \cdot m^2/C^2)(4.0 \times 10^{-5}\ C)} = -9.7 \times 10^{-6}\ C$$

13. Three particles are placed on a straight line. The left particle has a charge of $+4.6 \times 10^{-6}$ C, the middle particle has a charge of -2.3×10^{-6} C, and the right particle has a charge of -2.3×10^{-6} C. The left particle is 12 cm from the middle particle and the right particle is 24 cm from the middle particle. Find the total force on the middle particle.

First find the force that the right particle exerts on the middle particle.

$$F_r = \frac{Kq_m q_r}{d^2_{mr}} = \frac{(9.0 \times 10^9\ N \cdot m^2/C^2)(-2.3 \times 10^{-6}\ C)(-2.3 \times 10^{-6}\ C)}{(0.24\ m)^2}$$

= 0.83 N; the force is repulsive, or leftward.

Now find the force that the left particle exerts on the middle particle.

$$F_\ell = \frac{Kq_m q_\ell}{d^2_{m\ell}} = \frac{(9.0 \times 10^9\ N \cdot m^2/C^2)(-2.3 \times 10^{-6}\ C)(4.6 \times 10^{-6}\ C)}{(0.12\ m)^2}$$

= −6.6 N; the force is attractive, or leftward.

The total force is the sum of the two forces:

$$F_{total} = 0.83\ N\ (leftward) + 6.6\ N\ (leftward) = 7.4\ N,\ leftward$$

Copyright © by Glencoe/McGraw-Hill

14. The left particle in the previous problem is moved directly above the middle particle, still 12 cm away. Find the force on the middle particle.

The force exerted by the right particle is unchanged; it is 0.83 N leftward.

The force exerted by the particle above the middle particle is still 6.6 N, now directed upward.

The resultant force (F_R) has a magnitude of $F_R = [(6.6 \text{ N})^2 + (0.83 \text{ N})^2]^{1/2} = 6.7$ N; its direction is

$$\tan \theta = \frac{0.83 \text{ N}}{6.6 \text{ N}} \text{ , } \theta = 7.2° \text{ to the left of vertical}$$

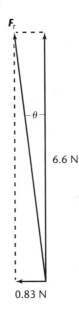

Copyright © by Glencoe/McGraw-Hill

CHAPTER 21

1. How strong would an electric field have to be to produce a force of 1.00 N if the charge was 1.000×10^3 μC?

$$E = \frac{F}{q} = \frac{1.00 \text{ N}}{1.000 \times 10^{-3}}$$

$$= 1.00 \times 10^3 \text{ N/C}$$

2. A positive charge of 7.0 mC experiences a 5.6×10^{-2} N force when placed in an electric field. What is the size of the electric field intensity?

$$E = \frac{F}{q} = \frac{5.6 \times 10^{-2} \text{ N}}{7.0 \times 10^{-3} \text{ C}}$$

$$= 8.0 \text{ N/C}$$

3. A positive test charge of 6.5×10^{-6} C experiences a force of 4.5×10^{-5} N. What is the magnitude of the electric field intensity?

$$E = \frac{F}{q} = \frac{4.5 \times 10^{-5} \text{ N}}{6.5 \times 10^{-6} \text{ C}}$$

$$= 6.9 \text{ N/C}$$

4. A charge experiences a force of 3.0×10^{-3} N in an electric field of intensity 2.0 N/C. What is the magnitude of the charge?

$$E = \frac{F}{q}, \text{ so}$$

$$q = \frac{F}{E} = \frac{3.0 \times 10^{-3} \text{ N}}{2.0 \text{ N/C}} = 1.5 \times 10^{-3} \text{ C}$$

$$= 1.5 \text{ mC}$$

5. What is the size of the force on an electron when the electron is in a uniform electric field that has an intensity of 1.000×10^3 N/C?

$$E = \frac{F}{q}, \text{ so}$$

$$F = qE = (-1.60 \times 10^{-19} \text{ C})$$

$$(1.000 \times 10^3 \text{ N/C})$$

$$= -1.60 \times 10^{-16} \text{ N}$$

6. Sketch the electric field lines around a -1.0-μC charge.

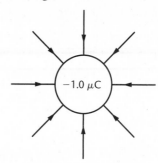

7. It takes 8.00 mJ to move a charge of 4.00 μC from point **A** to point **C** in an electric field. What is the potential difference between the two points?

$$\Delta V = \frac{W}{q} = \frac{8.00 \times 10^{-3} \text{ J}}{4.00 \times 10^{-6} \text{ C}}$$

$$= 2.00 \times 10^3 \text{ V}$$

8. How much work is required to move a positive charge of 2.5 μC between two points that have a potential difference of 60.0 V?

$$\Delta V = \frac{W}{q}, \text{ so}$$

$$W = q \Delta V$$

$$= (2.5 \times 10^{-6} \text{ C})(60.0 \text{ V})$$

$$= 1.5 \times 10^{-4} \text{ J} = 0.15 \text{ mJ}$$

9. A cloud has a potential difference relative to a tree of 9.00×10^2 MV. During a lightning storm, a charge of 1.00×10^2 C travels through this potential difference. How much work is done on this charge?

$$\Delta V = \frac{W}{q}, \text{ so}$$

$$W = q \Delta V$$

$$= (1.00 \times 10^2 \text{ C})(9.00 \times 10^8 \text{ V})$$

$$= 9.00 \times 10^{10} \text{ J}$$

Physics: Principles and Problems

Copyright © by Glencoe/McGraw-Hill

10. A constant electric field of 750 N/C is between a set of parallel plates. What is the potential difference between the parallel plates if they are 1.5 cm apart?

$$\Delta V = Ed = (750 \text{ N/C})(0.015 \text{ m}) = 11 \text{ V}$$

11. A spark will jump between two people if the electric field exceeds 4.0×10^6 V/m. You shuffle across a rug and a spark jumps when you put your finger 0.15 cm from another person's arm. Calculate the potential difference between your body and the other person's arm.

$$\Delta V = Ed = (4.0 \times 10^6 \text{ V/m})(0.0015 \text{ m})$$
$$= 6.0 \times 10^3 \text{ V}$$

12. A potential difference of 0.90 V exists from one side to the other side of a cell membrane that is 5.0 nm thick. What is the electric field across the membrane?

$$\Delta V = Ed, \text{ so}$$
$$E = \frac{\Delta V}{d} = \frac{0.90 \text{ V}}{5.0 \times 10^{-9} \text{ m}}$$
$$= 1.8 \times 10^8 \text{ V/m}$$

13. An oil drop having a charge of 8.0×10^{-19} C is suspended between two charged parallel plates. The plates are separated by a distance of 8.0 mm, and there is a potential difference of 1200 V between the plates. What is the weight of the suspended oil drop?

$$mg = Eq, \text{ and } \Delta V = Ed, \text{ or } E = \frac{\Delta V}{d},$$
$$\text{so}$$
$$mg = \left(\frac{\Delta V}{d}\right) q$$
$$= \left(\frac{1\ 200 \text{ V}}{8.0 \times \ 10^{-3} \text{ m}}\right)(8.0 \times 10^{-19} \text{ C})$$
$$= 1.2 \times 10^{-13} \text{ N}$$

14. A capacitor accumulates 4.0 µC on each plate when the potential difference between the plates is 100 V. What is the capacitance of the capacitor?

$$C = \frac{q}{\Delta V} = \frac{4.0 \times 10^{-6} \text{ C}}{100 \text{ V}}$$
$$= 4 \times 10^{-8} \text{ C/V} = 0.04 \text{ µF}$$

15. What is the voltage across a capacitor with a charge of 6.0 nC and a capacitance 7.0 pF?

$$C = \frac{q}{\Delta V}, \text{ so}$$
$$\Delta V = \frac{q}{C} = \frac{6.0 \times 10^{-9} \text{ C}}{7.0 \times 10^{-12} \text{ F}} = 8.6 \times 10^2 \text{ V}$$

16. How large is the charge accumulated on one of the plates of a 30.0-µF capacitor when the potential difference between the plates is 120 V?

$$C = \frac{q}{\Delta V}, \text{ so}$$
$$q = C\Delta V = (30.0 \times 10^{-6} \text{ F})(120 \text{ V})$$
$$= 3.6 \times 10^{-3} \text{ C}$$
$$= 3.6 \text{ mC}$$

Copyright © by Glencoe/McGraw-Hill

CHAPTER 22

1. How many amperes of current are in a wire through which 1.00×10^{18} electrons flow per second?

$$(1.00 \times 10^{18} \text{ e/s}) \left(\frac{1.60 \times 10^{-19} \text{ C}}{\text{e}} \right)$$
$$= 0.160 \text{ C/s} = 0.160 \text{ A}$$

2. A current of 5.00 A was in a copper wire for 20.0 s. How many coulombs of charge flowed through the wire in this time?

$I = \frac{q}{t}$, so

$q = It = (5.00 \text{ A})(20.0 \text{ s})$
$= 1.00 \times 10^2 \text{ C}$

3. What power is supplied to a motor that operates on a 120-V line and draws 1.50 A of current?

$$P = IV = (1.50 \text{ A})(120 \text{ V}) = 180 \text{ W}$$

4. An electric lamp is connected to a 110-V source. If the current through the lamp is 0.75 A, what is the power consumption of the lamp?

$$P = IV = (0.75 \text{ A})(110 \text{ V}) = 83 \text{ W}$$

5. A lamp is labeled 6.0 V and 12 W.

a. What is the current through the lamp when it is operating?

$$P = IV, \text{ so } I = \frac{P}{V} = \frac{120 \text{ W}}{6.0 \text{ V}} = 2.0 \text{ A}$$

b. How much energy is supplied to the lamp in 1.000×10^3 s?

$P = \frac{E}{t}$, so

$E = Pt = (12 \text{ W})(1.000 \times 10^3 \text{ s})$
$= 1.2 \times 10^4 \text{ J}$
$= 12 \text{ kJ}$

6. There is a current of 3.00 A through a resistor when it is connected to a 12.0-V battery. What is the resistance of the resistor?

$$R = \frac{V}{I} = \frac{12.0 \text{ V}}{3.00 \text{ A}} = 4.00 \text{ } \Omega$$

7. A small lamp is designed to draw a current of 3.00×10^2 mA in a 6.00-V circuit. What is the resistance of the lamp?

$$R = \frac{V}{I} = \frac{6.00 \text{ V}}{3.00 \times 10^{-1} \text{ A}} = 20.0 \text{ } \Omega$$

8. What potential difference is required if you want a current of 8.00 mA in a load having a resistance of 50.0 Ω?

$R = \frac{V}{I}$, so

$V = IR$
$\quad = (8.00 \times 10^{-3} \text{ A})(50.0 \text{ } \Omega) = 0.400 \text{ V}$

9. In common metals, resistance increases as the temperature increases. An electric toaster has a resistance of 12.0 Ω when hot.

a. What will be the current through it when it is connected to 125 V?

$$R = \frac{V}{I}, \text{ so } I = \frac{V}{R} = \frac{125 \text{ V}}{12.0 \text{ } \Omega} = 10.4 \text{ A}$$

b. When the toaster is first turned on, will the current be more or less than during operation?

When the toaster is first turned on, its temperature is low and its resistance is low, so the current is greater.

10. The resistance of a lamp is 230 Ω. The voltage is 115 V when the lamp is turned on.

a. What is the current in the lamp?

$$R = \frac{V}{I}, \text{ so } I = \frac{V}{R} = \frac{115 \text{ V}}{230 \text{ } \Omega} = 0.50 \text{ A}$$

b. If the voltage rises to 120 V, what is the current?

$$I = \frac{V}{R} = \frac{120 \text{ V}}{230 \text{ } \Omega} = 0.52 \text{ A}$$

11. What should the resistance of the lamp in part **a** of the previous problem be if the lamp is to draw the same current, but in a 230-V circuit?

$$R = \frac{V}{I} = \frac{230 \text{ V}}{0.500 \text{ A}} = 460 \text{ } \Omega$$

Copyright © by Glencoe/McGraw-Hill

12. A 110-W lamp draws 0.909 A. What is the lamp's resistance?

$P = I^2 R$, so

$$R = \frac{P}{I^2} = \frac{110\ W}{(0.909\ A)^2} = 133\ \Omega = 130\ \Omega$$

13. Each coil in a resistance box is capable of dissipating heat at the rate of 4.00 W.

What is the maximum current that should be allowed through a coil to avoid overheating if the coil has a resistance of

$P = I^2 R$, so $I^2 = \dfrac{P}{R}$, and $I = \sqrt{\dfrac{P}{R}}$.

a. 2.00 Ω?

$$I = \sqrt{\frac{P}{R}} = \sqrt{\frac{4.00\ W}{2.00\ \Omega}} = 1.41\ A$$

b. 20.0 Ω?

$$I = \sqrt{\frac{P}{R}} = \sqrt{\frac{4.00\ W}{20.0\ \Omega}} = 0.447\ A$$

14. What is the power supplied to a lamp that is operated by a battery having a 12-V potential difference across its terminals when the resistance of the lamp is 6.0 Ω?

$P = I^2 R$ and $R = \dfrac{V}{I}$, so $I = \dfrac{V}{R}$.

Therefore,

$$P = \left(\frac{V}{R}\right)^2 R = \frac{V^2}{R} = \frac{(12\ V)^2}{6.0\ \Omega} = 24\ W$$

15. How much does it cost to run a 2.00-W clock for one year (365.25 days) if it costs 3.53 cents/kWh?

$$Cost = \frac{3.53¢}{kWh}\ (2.00\ W)\left(\frac{kW}{1000\ W}\right)$$
$$\left(\frac{365.25\ dy}{1\ yr}\right)\left(\frac{24\ h}{1\ dy}\right)$$
$$= 62\ ¢/yr$$

16. A small electric furnace that expends 2.00 kW of power is connected across a potential difference of 120.0 V.

a. What is the current in the circuit?

$P = IV$, so

$$I = \frac{P}{V} = \frac{2.00 \times 10^3\ W}{120.0\ V} = 16.7\ A$$

b. What is the resistance of the furnace?

$$R = \frac{V}{I} = \frac{120.0\ V}{16.7\ A} = 7.19\ \Omega$$

c. What is the cost of operating the furnace for 24.0 h at 7.00 cents/kWh?

$$Cost = \frac{7.00¢}{kWh}\ (2.00\ kW)(24\ h) = \$3.36$$

Copyright © by Glencoe/McGraw-Hill

CHAPTER 23

1. The load across a 50.0-V battery consists of a series combination of two lamps with resistances of 125 Ω and 225 Ω.

   a. Find the total resistance of the circuit.

   $R_T = R_1 + R_2 = 125\ \Omega + 225\ \Omega$

   $= 3.50 \times 10^2\ \Omega$

   b. Find the current in the circuit.

   $V = IR$, so $I = \dfrac{V}{R} = \dfrac{50.0\ V}{3.50 \times 10^2\ \Omega}$

   $= 0.143\ A$

   c. Find the potential difference across the 125-Ω lamp.

   $V = IR = (0.143\ A)(125\ \Omega) = 17.9\ V$

2. The load across a 12-V battery consists of a series combination of three resistances that are 15 Ω, 21 Ω, and 24 Ω, respectively.

   a. Draw the circuit diagram.

   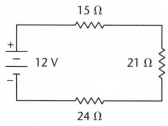

   15 Ω

   12 V   21 Ω

   24 Ω

   b. What is the total resistance of the load?

   $R_T = R_1 + R_2 + R_3$

   $= 15\ \Omega + 21\ \Omega + 24\ \Omega$

   $= 6.0 \times 10^1\ \Omega$

   c. What is the magnitude of the circuit current?

   $V = IR$, so $I = \dfrac{V}{R} = \dfrac{12\ V}{6.0 \times 10^1\ \Omega}$

   $= 0.20\ A$

3. The load across a 12-V battery consists of a series combination of three resistances R_1, R_2, and R_3. R_1 is 210 Ω, R_2 is 350 Ω, and R_3 is 120 Ω.

   a. Find the equivalent resistance of the circuit.

   $R_T = R_1 + R_2 + R_3$

   $= 210\ \Omega + 350\ \Omega + 120\ \Omega$

   $= 680\ \Omega$

   b. Find the current in the circuit.

   $V = IR$, so

   $I = \dfrac{V}{R} = \dfrac{12\ V}{680\ \Omega} = 1.8 \times 10^{-2}\ A$

   $= 18\ mA$

   c. Find the potential difference across R_3.

   $V = IR = (1.8 \times 10^{-2}\ A)(120\ \Omega) = 2.2\ V$

4. The load across a 40.0-V battery consists of a series combination of three resistances R_1, R_2, and R_3. R_1 is 240 Ω and R_3 is 120 Ω. The potential difference across R_1 is 24 V.

   a. Find the current in the circuit.

   $V = IR$, so $I = \dfrac{V_1}{R_1} = \dfrac{24\ V}{240\ \Omega} = 0.10\ A$

   b. Find the equivalent resistance of the circuit.

   $V = IR$, so $R = \dfrac{V}{I} = \dfrac{40.0\ V}{0.10\ A}$

   $= 4.0 \times 10^2\ \Omega$

   c. Find the resistance of R_2.

   $R_T = R_1 + R_2 + R_3$, so

   $R_2 = R_T - R_1 - R_3$

   $= 4.0 \times 10^2\ \Omega - 240\ \Omega - 120\ \Omega$

   $= 40\ \Omega$

5. Wes is designing a voltage divider using a 12.0-V battery and a 100.0-Ω resistor as R_2. What resistor should be used as R_1 if the output voltage is 4.75 V?

   $V_2 = \dfrac{VR_2}{R_1 + R_2}$,

   so $(R_1 + R_2)V_2 = VR_2$ and

   $R_1 V_2 = VR_2 - V_2 R_2$, so

   $R_1 = \left(\dfrac{V - V_2}{V_2}\right) R_2$

   $= \left(\dfrac{12.0\ V - 4.75\ V}{4.75\ V}\right) 100.0\ \Omega$

   $= 153\ \Omega$

Copyright © by Glencoe/McGraw-Hill

6. Two resistances, one 12 Ω and the other 18 Ω, are connected in parallel. What is the equivalent resistance of the parallel combination?

$$\frac{1}{R} = \frac{1}{R_1} + \frac{1}{R_2} = \frac{1}{12\ \Omega} + \frac{1}{18\ \Omega}$$

so $R = 7.2\ \Omega$

7. Three resistances of 12 Ω each are connected in parallel. What is the equivalent resistance?

$$\frac{1}{R} = \frac{1}{R_1} + \frac{1}{R_2} + \frac{1}{R_3}$$

$$= \frac{1}{12\ \Omega} + \frac{1}{12\ \Omega} + \frac{1}{12\ \Omega}$$

$$= \frac{3}{12\ \Omega} = \frac{1}{4.0\ \Omega}$$

so $R = 4.0\ \Omega$

8. Two resistances, one 62 Ω and the other 88 Ω, are connected in parallel. The resistors are then connected to a 12-V battery.

a. What is the equivalent resistance of the parallel combination?

$$\frac{1}{R} = \frac{1}{R_1} + \frac{1}{R_2} = \frac{1}{62\ \Omega} + \frac{1}{88\ \Omega}$$

so $R = 36\ \Omega$

b. What is the current through each resistor?

$$V = IR, \text{ so } I_1 = \frac{V}{R_1} = \frac{12\ V}{62\ \Omega} = 0.19\ A$$

$$I_2 = \frac{V}{R_2} = \frac{12\ V}{88\ \Omega} = 0.14\ A$$

9. A 35-Ω, 55-Ω, and 85-Ω resistor are connected in parallel. The resistors are then connected to a 35-V battery.

a. What is the equivalent resistance of the parallel combination?

$$\frac{1}{R} = \frac{1}{R_1} + \frac{1}{R_2} + \frac{1}{R_3}$$

$$= \frac{1}{35\ \Omega} + \frac{1}{55\ \Omega} + \frac{1}{85\ \Omega}$$

so $R = 17\ \Omega$

b. What is the current through each resistor?

$$V = IR, \text{ so } I_1 = \frac{V}{R_1} = \frac{35\ V}{35\ \Omega} = 1.0\ A$$

$$I_2 = \frac{V}{R_2} = \frac{35\ V}{55\ \Omega} = 0.64\ A$$

$$I_3 = \frac{V}{R_3} = \frac{35\ V}{85\ \Omega} = 0.41\ A$$

10. A 110-V household circuit that contains an 1800-W microwave, a 1000-W toaster, and an 800-W coffeemaker is connected to a 20-A fuse. Will the fuse melt if the microwave and the coffeemaker are both on?

$P = IV$, so

$$I = \frac{P}{V} = \frac{1800\ W}{110\ V} = 16.4\ A$$

$$= 16\ A \text{ (microwave)}$$

$$I = \frac{P}{V} = \frac{800\ W}{110\ V} = 7.27\ A$$

$$= 7\ A \text{ (coffeemaker)}$$

Total current of 23 A is greater than 20 A so the fuse will melt.

11. Resistors R_1, R_2, and R_3 have resistances of 15.0 Ω, 9.0 Ω, and 8.0 Ω respectively. R_1 and R_2 are connected in series, and their combination is in parallel with R_3 to form a load across a 6.0-V battery.

a. Draw the circuit diagram.

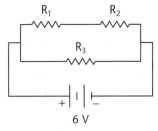

b. What is the total resistance of the load?

$$R_1 + R_2 = 15.0\ \Omega + 9.0\ \Omega = 24.0\ \Omega$$

$$\frac{1}{R_T} = \frac{1}{R_{12}} + \frac{1}{R_3} = \frac{1}{24.0\ \Omega} + \frac{1}{8.0\ \Omega}$$

so $R_T = 6.0\ \Omega$

c. What is the magnitude of the circuit current?

$$V = IR, \text{ so } I = \frac{V}{R} = \frac{6.0\ V}{6.0\ \Omega} = 1.0\ A$$

Copyright © by Glencoe/McGraw-Hill

11. (continued)

d. What is the current in R_3?

$V = IR$, so $I = \dfrac{V}{R_3} = \dfrac{6.0\text{ V}}{8.0\ \Omega} = 0.75\text{ A}$

e. What is the potential difference across R_2?

$I_T = I_2 + I_3$, so

$I_2 = I_T - I_3 = 1.0\text{ A} - 0.75\text{ A} = 0.25\text{ A}$

and $V_2 = I_2 R_2 = (0.25\text{ A})(9.0\ \Omega)$

$= 2.3\text{ V}$

12. A 15.0-Ω resistor is connected in series to a 120-V generator and two 10.0-Ω resistors that are connected in parallel to each other.

a. Draw the circuit diagram.

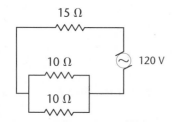

15 Ω

10 Ω 120 V

10 Ω

b. What is the total resistance of the load?

$\dfrac{1}{R_{12}} = \dfrac{1}{R_1} + \dfrac{1}{R_2} = \dfrac{1}{10.0\ \Omega} + \dfrac{1}{10.0\ \Omega}$

$= \dfrac{1}{5.0\ \Omega}$

so $R_{12} = 5.0\ \Omega$

$R_T = R_3 + R_{12} = 15.0\ \Omega + 5.0\ \Omega$

$= 20.0\ \Omega$

c. What is the magnitude of the circuit current?

$V = IR$, so $I = \dfrac{V}{R} = \dfrac{120\text{ V}}{20.0\ \Omega} = 6.00\text{ A}$

d. What is the current in one of the 10.0-Ω resistors?

The current would divide equally, so 3.0 A.

e. What is the potential difference across the 15.0-Ω resistor?

$V = IR = (6.0\text{ A})(15.0\ \Omega) = 9.0 \times 10^1\text{ V}$

13. How would you change the resistance of a voltmeter to allow the voltmeter to measure a larger potential difference?

increase the resistance

14. How would you change the shunt in an ammeter to allow the ammeter to measure a larger current?

decrease the resistance of the shunt

15. An ohmmeter is made by connecting a 6.0-V battery in series with an adjustable resistor and an ideal ammeter. The ammeter deflects full-scale with a current of 1.0 mA. The two leads are touched together and the resistance is adjusted so 1.0-mA current flows.

a. What is the resistance of the adjustable resistor?

$V = IR$, so

$R = \dfrac{V}{I} = \dfrac{6.0\text{ V}}{1.0 \times 10^{-3}\text{ A}} = 6.0 \times 10^3\ \Omega$

b. The leads are now connected to an unknown resistance. What external resistance would produce a reading of 0.50 mA, half full-scale?

$R = \dfrac{V}{I} = \dfrac{6.0\text{ V}}{0.50 \times 10^{-3}\text{ A}} = 1.2 \times 10^4\ \Omega$

and $R_T = R_1 + R_e$, so

$R_e = R_T - R_1$

$= 1.2 \times 10^4\ \Omega - 6.0 \times 10^3\ \Omega$

$= 6.0 \times 10^3\ \Omega$

Copyright © by Glencoe/McGraw-Hill

15. (continued)

    c. What external resistance would produce a reading of 0.25 mA, quarter-scale?

$$R = \frac{V}{I} = \frac{6.0 \text{ V}}{0.25 \times 10^{-3} \text{ A}} = 2.4 \times 10^4 \text{ }\Omega$$

and $R_e = R_T - R_1$

$$= 2.4 \times 10^4 \text{ }\Omega - 6.0 \times 10^3 \text{ }\Omega$$

$$= 1.8 \times 10^4 \text{ }\Omega$$

    d. What external resistance would produce a reading of 0.75 mA, three-quarter full-scale?

$$R = \frac{V}{I} = \frac{6.0 \text{ V}}{0.75 \times 10^{-3} \text{ A}} = 8.0 \times 10^3 \text{ }\Omega$$

and $R_e = R_T - R_1$

$$= 8.0 \times 10^3 \text{ }\Omega - 6.0 \times 10^3 \text{ }\Omega$$

$$= 2.0 \times 10^3 \text{ }\Omega$$

Copyright © by Glencoe/McGraw-Hill

CHAPTER 24

1. Assume the current in the wire shown in **Figure 24-24** on page 576 of your textbook goes in the opposite direction. Copy the wire segment and sketch the new magnetic field the current generated.

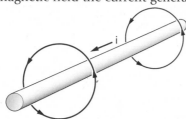

2. Assume the current shown in **Figure 24-25** on page 577 of your textbook goes into the page instead of out of the page. Copy the figure with the new current and sketch the magnetic field.

3. What happens to the strength of a magnetic field around a wire if the current in the wire is doubled?

   It doubles, because magnetic field strength is proportional to current.

4. What happens to the magnetic field inside the coil of **Figure 24–26** on page 577 of your textbook if the current shown was reversed?

   The direction of the magnetic field is also reversed.

5. What is the direction of the force on a current-carrying wire in a magnetic field if the current is toward the left on a page and the magnetic field is down the page?

   out of the page

6. A 0.25 m long wire is carrying a 1.25 A current while the wire is perpendicular to a 0.35-T magnetic field. What is the force on the wire?

   $F = BIL = (0.35 \text{ T})(1.25 \text{ A})(0.25 \text{ m})$

   $= 0.11 \text{ N}$

7. A 3.0-cm long wire lies perpendicular to a magnetic field with a magnetic induction of 0.40 T. Calculate the force on the wire if the current in the wire is 5.0 A.

   $F = BIL = (0.40 \text{ T})(5.0 \text{ A})(0.030 \text{ m})$

   $= 0.060 \text{ N}$

8. What is the force on a 3.5-m long wire that is carrying a 12-A current if the wire is perpendicular to Earth's magnetic field?

   $F = BIL = (5.0 \times 10^{-5} \text{ T})(12 \text{ A})(3.5 \text{ m})$

   $= 2.1 \times 10^{-3} \text{ N} = 2.1 \text{ mN}$

9. A wire, 0.50 m long, is put into a uniform magnetic field. The force exerted upon the wire when the current in the wire is 20 A is 3.0 N. What is the magnetic induction of the field acting upon the wire?

   $F = BIL$, so

   $B = \dfrac{F}{IL} = \dfrac{3.0 \text{ N}}{(20 \text{ A})(0.50 \text{ m})} = 0.3 \text{ T}$

10. What is the size of the current in a 35-cm long wire that is perpendicular to a magnetic field of 0.085 T if the force on the wire is 125 mN?

    $F = BIL$, so

    $I = \dfrac{F}{BL} = \dfrac{125 \times 10^{-3} \text{ N}}{(0.085 \text{ T})(0.35 \text{ m})} = 4.2 \text{ A}$

11. A galvanometer has a full-scale deflection when the current is 50.0 μA. If the galvanometer has a resistance of 1.0 kΩ, what should the resistance of the multiplier resistor be to make a voltmeter with a full-scale deflection of 30.0 V?

    $V = IR$, so

    $R = \dfrac{V}{I} = \dfrac{3.00 \text{ V}}{50.0 \times 10^{-6} \text{ A}}$

    $= 6.00 \times 10^{5} \ \Omega$

    $= 6.00 \times 10^{2} \text{ k}\Omega$

    $R_T = R_g + R_m$, so

    $R_m = R_T - R_g$

    $= 6.00 \times 10^{2} \text{ k}\Omega - 1.0 \text{ k}\Omega$

    $= 599 \text{ k}\Omega$

Copyright © by Glencoe/McGraw-Hill

Physics: Principles and Problems

12. A charged particle is moving to the right in a magnetic field whose direction is up the page. Show by diagram the direction of the force exerted by the magnetic field upon the particle if the particle is a positive proton.

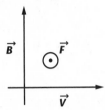

13. An electron beam moving horizontally away from you is deflected toward the right after passing through a certain region of space that contains a constant magnetic field. What is the direction of the magnetic field?

An electron beam moving away from you is the same as a positive beam moving toward you. The magnetic field is either up or down the page if the force is to the right. The right-hand rule shows the magnetic field must be down the page.

14. A beam of electrons moving left at 3.0×10^7 m/s passes at right angles to a uniform magnetic field that is down and in which the magnetic induction is 2.0×10^{-4} T. What force acts upon each electron in the beam?

$F = Bqv$

$= (2.0 \times 10^{-4}\text{ T})(1.60 \times 10^{-19}\text{ C})$

$\times (3.0 \times 10^7\text{ m/s})$

$= 9.6 \times 10^{-16}\text{ N}$

The right-hand rule gives a direction out of the page, but the force on an electron is in the opposite direction, into the page. So the force is 9.6×10^{-16} N into the page.

15. The electrons in a beam in a cathode ray tube are moving horizontally at 5.0×10^7 m/s and pass through a vertical magnetic field of 3.5×10^{-3} T. What size force acts on each of the electrons in the beam?

$F = Bqv$

$= (3.5 \times 10^{-3}\text{ T})(1.60 \times 10^{-19}\text{ C})$

$\times (5.0 \times 10^7\text{ m/s})$

$= 2.8 \times 10^{-14}\text{ N}$

16. An ion of oxygen having 2 elementary negative electric charges is moving at right angles to a uniform magnetic field for which $B = 0.30$ T. If its velocity is 2.0×10^7 m/s, what force is acting on the ion?

$F = Bqv$

$= (0.30\text{ T})(2)(1.60 \times 10^{-19}\text{ C})$

$\times (2.0 \times 10^7\text{ m/s})$

$= 1.9 \times 10^{-12}\text{ N}$

Copyright © by Glencoe/McGraw-Hill

CHAPTER 25

1. A north-south wire is moved toward the east through a magnetic field that is pointing down, into Earth. What is the direction of the induced current?

   north

2. A wire, 1.0 m long, is moved at right angles to Earth's magnetic field where the magnetic induction is 5.0×10^{-5} T at a speed of 4.0 m/s. What is the *EMF* induced in the wire?

   $EMF = BLv$

   $= (5.0 \times 10^{-5} \text{ T})(1.0 \text{ m})(4.0 \text{ m/s})$

   $= 2.0 \times 10^{-4} \text{ V} = 0.20 \text{ mV}$

3. An *EMF* of 2.0 mV is induced in a wire 0.10 m long when it is moving perpendicularly across a uniform magnetic field at a velocity of 4.0 m/s. What is the magnetic induction of the field?

   $EMF = BLv$, so

   $B = \dfrac{EMF}{Lv} = \dfrac{2.0 \times 10^{-3} \text{ V}}{(0.10 \text{ m})(4.0 \text{ m/s})}$

   $= 5.0 \times 10^{-3} \text{ T} = 5.0 \text{ mT}$

4. With what speed must a 0.20-m long wire cut across a magnetic field for which *B* is 2.5 T if it is to have an *EMF* of 10 V induced in it?

   $EMF = BLv$, so

   $v = \dfrac{EMF}{BL} = \dfrac{10 \text{ V}}{(2.5 \text{ T})(0.20 \text{ m})} = 20 \text{ m/s}$

5. At what speed must a wire conductor 50 cm long be moved at right angles to a magnetic field of induction 0.20 T to induce an *EMF* of 1.0 V in it?

   $EMF = BLv$, so

   $v = \dfrac{EMF}{BL} = \dfrac{1.0 \text{ V}}{(0.20 \text{ T})(0.50 \text{ m})}$

   $= 1.0 \times 10^1 \text{ m/s}$

6. A wire, 0.40 m long, cuts perpendicularly across a magnetic field for which *B* is 2.0 T at a velocity of 8.0 m/s.

   a. What *EMF* is induced in the wire?

   $EMF = BLv = (2.0 \text{ T})(0.40 \text{ m})(8.0 \text{ m/s})$

   $= 6.4 \text{ V}$

   b. If the wire is in a circuit having a resistance of 6.4 Ω, what is the size of the current through the wire?

   $V = IR$, so $I = \dfrac{V}{R} = \dfrac{6.4 \text{ V}}{6.4 \text{ }\Omega} = 1.0 \text{ A}$

7. A coil of wire, which has a total length of 7.50 m, is moved perpendicularly to Earth's magnetic field at 5.50 m/s. What is the size of the current in the wire if the total resistance of the wire is 5.0×10^{-2} mΩ?

   $EMF = BLv$ and $V = IR$, but $EMF = V$, so $IR = BLv$, and

   $I = \dfrac{BLv}{R}$

   $= \dfrac{(5.0 \times 10^{-5} \text{ T})(7.50 \text{ m})(5.50 \text{ m/s})}{5.0 \times 10^{-2} \text{ m}\Omega}$

   $= 4.1 \times 10^{-2} \text{ A} = 41 \text{ mA}$

8. A house lighting circuit is rated at 120 V effective voltage. What is the peak voltage that can be expected in this circuit?

   $V_{eff} = 0.707 \ V_{max}$, so

   $V_{max} = \dfrac{V_{eff}}{0.707} = \dfrac{120 \text{ V}}{0.707} = 170 \text{ V}$

9. A toaster draws 2.5 A of alternating current. What is the peak current through this toaster?

   $I_{eff} = 0.707 \ I_{max}$, so

   $I_{max} = \dfrac{I_{eff}}{0.707} = \dfrac{2.5 \text{ A}}{0.707} = 3.5 \text{ A}$

10. The insulation of a capacitor will break down if the instantaneous voltage exceeds 575 V. What is the largest effective alternating voltage that may be applied to the capacitor?

    $V_{eff} = 0.707 V_{max} = 0.707(575 \text{ V})$

    $= 406 \text{ V}$

Copyright © by Glencoe/McGraw-Hill

11. A magnetic circuit breaker will open its circuit if the instantaneous current reaches 21.25 A. What is the largest effective current the circuit will carry?

$$I_{eff} = 0.707 I_{max} = 0.707(21.25 \text{ A})$$
$$= 15.0 \text{ A}$$

12. The peak value of the alternating voltage applied to a 144-Ω resistor is 1.00×10^2 V. What power must the resistor be able to handle?

$P = IV$ and $V = IR$, so $I = \dfrac{V}{R}$ therefore,

$$P_{max} = \left(\frac{V}{R}\right)V = \frac{V^2}{R} = \frac{(1.00 \times 10^2 \text{ V})^2}{144 \text{W}}$$
$$= 69.4 \text{ W}$$

The average power is $P_{max}/2$ so the resistor must dissipate 34.7 W.

13. Shawn drops a magnet, S-pole down, through a vertical copper pipe.

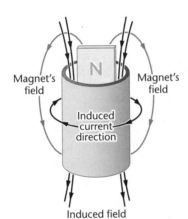

Magnet's field   Magnet's field

Induced current direction

Induced field

a. What is the direction of the induced current in the copper pipe as the bottom of the magnet passes?

Clockwise around the pipe, as viewed from above.

b. The induced current produces a magnetic field. What is the direction of the induced magnetic field?

Down the pipe, at the location of the S-pole of the magnet (or opposite the magnet's field).

14. The electricity received at an electrical substation has a potential difference of 240 000 V. What should the ratio of the turns of the step-down transformer be to have an output of 440 V?

$$\frac{N_s}{N_p} = \frac{V_s}{V_p} = \frac{440 \text{ V}}{240\,000 \text{ V}} = \frac{1}{545}$$

1 to 545

15. The CRT in a television uses a step-up transformer to change 120 V to 48 000 V. The secondary side of the transformer has 20 000 turns and an output of 1.0 mA.

a. How many turns does the primary side have?

$$\frac{N_s}{N_p} = \frac{V_s}{V_p}, \text{ so } N_s V_p = N_p V_s \text{, and}$$

$$N_p = \frac{N_s V_p}{V_s} = \frac{(20\,000)(120 \text{ V})}{48\,000 \text{ V}}$$
$$= 50 \text{ turns}$$

b. What is the input current?

$$V_s I_s = V_p I_p \text{, so}$$

$$I_p = \frac{V_s I_s}{V_p} = \frac{(48\,000 \text{ V})(1.0 \times 10^{-3} \text{ A})}{120 \text{ V}}$$
$$= 0.40 \text{ A}$$

Copyright © by Glencoe/McGraw-Hill

CHAPTER 26

1. A beam of electrons travels through a set of crossed electric and magnetic fields. What is the speed of the electrons if the magnetic field is 85 mT and the electric field is 6.5×10^4 N/C?

$$v = \frac{E}{B} = \frac{6.5 \times 10^4 \text{ N/C}}{85 \times 10^{-3} \text{ T}}$$

$$= 7.6 \times 10^5 \text{ m/s}$$

2. Electrons, moving at 8.5×10^7 m/s, pass through crossed magnetic and electric fields undeflected. What is the size of the magnetic field if the electric field is 4.0×10^4 N/C?

$$v = \frac{E}{B}, \text{ so}$$

$$B = \frac{E}{v} = \frac{4.0 \times 10^4 \text{ N/C}}{8.5 \times 10^7 \text{ T}}$$

$$= 4.7 \times 10^{-4} \text{ T} = 0.47 \text{ mT}$$

3. What effect does increasing the magnetic induction of the field have on the radius of the particle's path for a given particle moving at a fixed speed?

   It decreases the radius.

4. An electron is moving at 2.0×10^8 m/s in a constant magnetic field. How strong should the magnetic field be to keep the electron moving in a circle of radius 0.50 m?

$$\frac{q}{m} = \frac{v}{Br}, \text{ so}$$

$$B = \frac{mv}{qr}$$

$$= \frac{(9.11 \times 10^{-31} \text{ kg})(2.0 \times 10^8 \text{ m/s})}{(1.60 \times 10^{-19} \text{ C})(0.50 \text{ m})}$$

$$= 2.3 \times 10^{-3} \text{ T} = 2.3 \text{ mT}$$

5. A positively charged ion, having two elementary charges and a velocity of 5.0×10^7 m/s, is moving across a magnetic field for which $B = 4.0$ T. If the mass of the ion is 6.8×10^{-27} kg, what is the radius of the circular path it travels?

$$\frac{q}{m} = \frac{v}{Br}, \text{ so}$$

$$r = \frac{mv}{qB}$$

$$= \frac{(6.8 \times 10^{-27} \text{ kg})(5.0 \times 10^7 \text{ m/s})}{2(1.6 \times 10^{-19} \text{ C})(4.0 \text{ T})}$$

$$= 0.27 \text{ m}$$

6. A beam of electrons, moving at 2.0×10^8 m/s, passes at right angles to a uniform magnetic field of 41 mT. What is the radius of the circular path in which this beam will travel through the magnetic field?

$$\frac{q}{m} = \frac{v}{Br}, \text{ so}$$

$$r = \frac{mv}{qB}$$

$$= \frac{(9.11 \times 10^{-31} \text{ kg})(2.0 \times 10^8 \text{ m/s})}{(1.6 \times 10^{-19} \text{ C})(41 \times 10^{-3} \text{ T})}$$

$$= 0.028 \text{ m} = 2.8 \text{ cm}$$

7. An unknown particle is accelerated by a potential difference of 1.50×10^2 V. The particle then enters a magnetic field of 50.0 mT, and follows a curved path with a radius of 9.80 cm. What is the ratio of q/m?

$$\frac{q}{m} = \frac{2V}{B^2 r^2}$$

$$= \frac{2(1.50 \times 10^2 \text{ V})}{(50.0 \times 10^{-3} \text{ T})^2 (9.80 \times 10^{-2} \text{ m})^2}$$

$$= 1.25 \times 10^7 \text{ C/kg}$$

8. A beam of doubly ionized oxygen atoms is accelerated by a potential difference of 232 V. The oxygen then enters a magnetic field of 75.0 mT, and follows a curved path with a radius of 8.3 cm. What is the mass of the oxygen atom?

$$\frac{q}{m} = \frac{2V}{B^2 r^2}, \text{ so}$$

$$m = \frac{qB^2 r^2}{2V}$$

$$= \frac{2(1.6 \times 10^{-19} \text{ C})(75.0 \times 10^{-3} \text{ T})^2 (8.3 \times 10^{-2} \text{ m})^2}{2(232 \text{ V})}$$

$$= 2.7 \times 10^{-26} \text{ kg}$$

Copyright © by Glencoe/McGraw-Hill

9. If the atomic mass unit is equal to 1.67×10^{-27} kg, how many atomic mass units are in the oxygen atom in the previous problem?

$$2.7 \times 10^{-26} \text{ kg} \left(\frac{1\text{u}}{1.67 \times 10^{-27} \text{ kg}}\right) = 16 \text{ u}$$

10. A hydrogen ion is accelerated through an accelerating potential of 1.00×10^2 V and then through a magnetic field of 50.0 mT to standarize the mass spectrometer. What is the radius of curvature if the mass of the ion is 1.67×10^{-27}kg?

$$r = \frac{1}{B} \sqrt{\frac{2Vm}{q}}$$

$$= \frac{1}{50.0 \times 10^{-3} \text{ T}}$$

$$\sqrt{\frac{2(1.00 \times 10^2 \text{ V})(1.67 \times 10^{-27} \text{ kg})}{1.60 \times 10^{-19} \text{ C}}}$$

$$= 2.89 \times 10^{-2} \text{ m} = 2.89 \text{ cm}$$

11. What is the change in the radius of curvature if a doubly ionized neon atom, mass $= 3.34 \times 10^{-26}$ kg, is sent through the mass spectrometer in the previous problem?

$$r = \frac{1}{B} \sqrt{\frac{2Vm}{q}}$$

$$= \frac{1}{50.0 \times 10^{-3} \text{ T}}$$

$$\sqrt{\frac{2(1.00 \times 10^2 \text{ V})(3.34 \, 3 \, 10^{-26} \text{ kg})}{2(1.60 \, 3 \, 10^{-19} \text{ C})}}$$

$$= 9.14 \times 10^{-2} \text{ m}$$

diff $= 9.14 \times 10^{-2}$ m $- 2.89 \times 10^{-2}$ m

$$= 6.25 \times 10^{-2} \text{ m} = 6.25 \text{ cm}$$

12. An FM radio station broadcasts on a frequency of 94.5 MHz. What is the antenna length that would give the best reception for this radio station?

$$c = \lambda f, \text{ so } \lambda = \frac{c}{f}$$

$$= \frac{3.00 \times 10^8 \text{ m/s}}{94.5 \times 10^6 \text{ Hz}} = 3.17 \text{ m}$$

$$\frac{1}{2} \lambda = \frac{1}{2} (3.17 \text{ m}) = 1.59 \text{ m}$$

Copyright © by Glencoe/McGraw-Hill

CHAPTER 27

1. Consider an incandescent light bulb on a dimmer control. What happens to the color of the light given off by the bulb as the dimmer control is turned down?

    The light becomes more red.

2. What would the change in frequency of the vibration of an atom be according to Planck's theory if it gave off 5.44×10^{-19} J, while changing the value of n by 1?

    $E = nhf$, so

    $$f = \frac{E}{nh} = \frac{5.44 \times 10^{-19} \text{ J}}{(1)(6.627 \times 10^{-34} \text{ J/Hz})}$$

    $$= 8.21 \times 10^{14} \text{ Hz}$$

3. What is the maximum kinetic energy of photoelectrons ejected from a metal that has a stopping potential of 3.8 V?

    $$K = qV = (1 \text{ e})(3.8 \text{ V}) = 3.8 \text{ eV}$$

4. The stopping potential needed to return all the electrons ejected from a metal is 7.3 V. What is the maximum kinetic energy of the electrons in J?

    $$K = 7.3 \text{ eV} \left(\frac{1.60 \times 10^{-19} \text{ J}}{1 \text{ eV}} \right)$$

    $$= 1.2 \times 10^{-18} \text{ J}$$

5. What is the potential difference needed to stop photoelectrons that have a maximum kinetic energy of 8.0×10^{-19} J?

    $$K = 8.0 \times 10^{-19} \text{ J} \left(\frac{1 \text{ eV}}{1.60 \times 10^{-19} \text{ J}} \right)$$

    $$= 5.0 \text{ eV, so } 5.0 \text{ V}$$

6. The threshold frequency of a certain metal is 8.0×10^{14} Hz. What is the work function of the metal?

    $E = hf_0$

    $$= (6.627 \times 10^{-34} \text{ J/Hz})(8.0 \times 10^{14} \text{ Hz})$$

    $$= 5.3 \times 10^{-19} \text{ J}$$

7. If light with a frequency of 1.6×10^{15} Hz falls on the metal in the previous problem, what is the maximum kinetic energy of the photoelectrons?

    $K = hf - hf_0$

    $$= (6.627 \times 10^{-34} \text{ J/Hz})(1.6 \times 10^{15} \text{ Hz})$$

    $$- 5.3 \times 10^{-19} \text{ J}$$

    $$= 1.06 \times 10^{-18} \text{ J} - 5.3 \times 10^{-19} \text{ J}$$

    $$= 5.3 \times 10^{-19} \text{ J}$$

8. The threshold frequency of a certain metal is 3.00×10^{14} Hz. What is the maximum kinetic energy of the ejected photoelectrons when the metal is illuminated by light with a wavelength of 6.50×10^2 nm?

    $c = \lambda f$, so

    $$f = \frac{c}{\lambda} = \frac{3.00 \times 10^8 \text{ m/s}}{6.50 \times 10^{-7} \text{ m}}$$

    $$= 4.62 \times 10^{14} \text{ Hz}$$

    $K = hf - hf_0$

    $$= (6.627 \times 10^{-34} \text{ J/Hz})(4.62 \times 10^{14} \text{ Hz})$$

    $$- (6.627 \times 10^{-34} \text{ J/Hz})(3.00 \times 10^{14} \text{ Hz})$$

    $$= 3.06 \times 10^{-19} \text{ J} - 1.99 \times 10^{-19} \text{ J}$$

    $$= 1.07 \times 10^{-19} \text{ J}$$

9. What is the momentum of a photon of violet light that has a wavelength of 4.00×10^2 nm?

    $$p = \frac{h}{\lambda} = \frac{6.627 \times 10^{-34} \text{ J/Hz}}{4.00 \times 10^{-7} \text{ m}}$$

    $$= 1.66 \times 10^{-27} \text{ kg} \cdot \text{m/s}$$

10. What is the momentum of a photon of red light that has a wavelength of 7.00×10^2 nm?

    $$p = \frac{h}{\lambda} = \frac{6.627 \times 10^{-34} \text{ J/Hz}}{7.00 \times 10^{-7} \text{ m}}$$

    $$= 9.47 \times 10^{-28} \text{ kg} \cdot \text{m/s}$$

11. What is the wavelength associated with an electron moving at 3.0×10^6 m/s?

    $$\lambda = \frac{h}{mv}$$

    $$= \frac{6.627 \times 10^{-34} \text{ J/Hz}}{(9.11 \times 10^{-31} \text{ kg})(3.0 \times 10^6 \text{ m/s})}$$

    $$= 2.4 \times 10^{-10} \text{ m}$$

    $$= 0.24 \text{ nm}$$

Copyright © by Glencoe/McGraw-Hill

12. What velocity would an electron need to have a wavelength of 3.0×10^{-10} m associated with it?

$$\lambda = \frac{h}{mv}, \text{ so}$$

$$v = \frac{h}{m\lambda}$$

$$= \frac{6.627 \times 10^{-34} \text{ J/Hz}}{(9.11 \times 10^{-31} \text{ kg})(3.0 \times 10^{-10} \text{ m})}$$

$$= 2.4 \times 10^6 \text{ m/s}$$

13. An electron is accelerated across a potential difference of 5.0×10^3 V in the CRT of a television.

a. What is the velocity of the electron if it started from rest?

$$\frac{1}{2} mv^2 = qV, \text{ so}$$

$$v = \sqrt{\frac{qV}{\frac{1}{2} m}}$$

$$= \sqrt{\frac{(1.60 \times 10^{-19} \text{ C})(5.0 \times 10^3)}{\frac{1}{2}(9.11 \times 10^{-31} \text{ kg})}}$$

$$= 4.2 \times 10^7 \text{ m/s}$$

b. What is the wavelength associated with the electron?

$$\lambda = \frac{h}{mv}$$

$$= \frac{6.627 \times 10^{-34} \text{ J/Hz}}{(9.11 \times 10^{-31} \text{ kg})(4.2 \times 10^7 \text{ m/s})}$$

$$= 1.7 \times 10^{-11} \text{ m} = 0.017 \text{ nm}$$

Copyright © by Glencoe/McGraw-Hill

CHAPTER 28

1. A calcium atom drops from 5.16 eV above the ground state to 2.93 eV above the ground state. What is the frequency of the photon emitted by the atom?

$$E = hf$$

$$f = \frac{E}{h}$$

$$= \frac{(5.16 \text{ eV} - 2.93 \text{ eV}) \frac{1.60 \times 10^{-19} \text{ J}}{1 \text{ eV}}}{6.627 \times 10^{-34} \text{ J/Hz}}$$

$$= 5.38 \times 10^{14} \text{ Hz}$$

2. A calcium atom is in an excited state when the energy level is 2.93 eV, E_2, above the ground state. A photon of energy 1.20 eV strikes the calcium atom and is absorbed by it. To what energy level is the calcium atom raised? Refer to diagram at right.

$$E_2 = 2.93 \text{ eV} + 1.20 \text{ eV} = 4.13 \text{ eV} = E_3$$

3. A calcium atom is in an excited state at the E_6 energy level. How much energy is released when the atom dropped down to the E_2 energy level? Refer to diagram at right.

$$E_6 - E_2 = 5.16 \text{ eV} - 2.93 \text{ eV}$$

$$= 2.23 \text{ eV}$$

3. (continued)

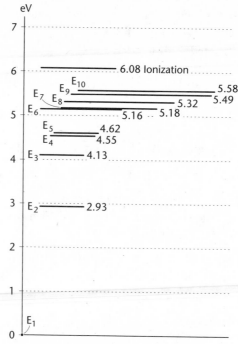

Energy Level Diagram for Calcium Atom

4. A photon of orange light, wavelength of 6.00×10^2 nm, enters a calcium atom in the E_6 excited state and ionizes the atom. What kinetic energy will the electron have as it is ejected from the atom?

$$E = \frac{hc}{\lambda} = \frac{(6.627 \times 10^{-34} \text{ J/Hz})(3.00 \times 10^8 \text{ m/s})}{6.00 \times 10^{-7} \text{ m}} = 3.314 \text{ J}$$

$$= 3.314 \text{ J} \left(\frac{1 \text{ eV}}{1.60 \times 10^{-19} \text{ J}} \right) = 2.07 \text{ eV}$$

Energy needed to ionize   6.08 eV

E_6 −5.16 eV

=   0.92 eV

Photon energy − ionization energy = kinetic energy

2.07 eV − 0.92 eV = 1.15 eV

5. Calculate the radius of the orbital associated with the energy level E_4 of the hydrogen atom.

$$r = \frac{h^2 n^2}{4\pi^2 Kmq^2} = \frac{(6.627 \times 10^{-34} \text{ J} \cdot \text{s})^2 (4)^2}{4\pi^2 (9.00 \times 10^{-31} \text{ kg})(9.11 \times 10^{-31} \text{ kg})(1.60 \times 10^{-19} \text{ C})^2}$$

$$= 8.48 \times 10^{-10} \text{ m} = 0.848 \text{ nm}$$

Copyright © by Glencoe/McGraw-Hill

6. Calculate the difference in energy associated with the E_7 and the E_2 energy levels of the hydrogen atom.

$$E_7 = -13.6 \text{ eV} \left(\frac{1}{n^2}\right)$$

$$= -13.6 \text{ eV} \left(\frac{1}{7^2}\right) = -0.278 \text{ eV}$$

$$E_2 = -13.6 \text{ eV} \left(\frac{1}{n^2}\right)$$

$$= -13.6 \text{ eV} \left(\frac{1}{2^2}\right) = -3.40 \text{ eV}$$

$$E_7 - E_2 = -0.278 \text{ eV} - (-3.40 \text{ eV})$$

$$= 3.12 \text{ eV}$$

7. What frequency photon is emitted from the hydrogen atom when the atom releases the energy found in the previous problem?

$E = hf$, so

$$f = \frac{E}{h} = \frac{(3.12 \text{ eV}) \left(\dfrac{1.60 \times 10^{-19} \text{ J}}{\text{eV}}\right)}{6.627 \times 10^{-34} \text{ J/Hz}}$$

$$= 7.53 \times 10^{14} \text{ Hz}$$

Copyright © by Glencoe/McGraw-Hill

CHAPTER 29

1. An LED, light-emitting diode, produces infrared radiation, wavelength 800.0 nm, when an electron jumps from the conduction band to the valence band. Find the energy width of the forbidden gap in this diode.

$$E = \frac{hc}{\lambda}$$

$$= \frac{(6.627 \times 10^{-34} \text{ J/Hz})(3.00 \times 10^8 \text{ m/s})}{8.000 \times 10^{-7} \text{ m}}$$

$$= 2.49 \times 10^{-19} \text{ J}$$

$$2.49 \times 10^{-19} \text{ J} \left(\frac{1 \text{ eV}}{1.60 \times 10^{-19} \text{ J}} \right)$$

$$= 1.55 \text{ eV}$$

2. How many free electrons exist in 1.00 cm³ of lithium? Its density is 0.534 g/cm³, atomic mass is 6.941 g/mole, and there is one free electron per atom.

$$\left(\frac{1 \text{ free } e^-}{1 \text{ atom}} \right) \left(\frac{6.02 \times 10^{23} \text{ atom}}{1 \text{ mole}} \right)$$

$$\times \left(\frac{1 \text{ mole Li}}{6.941 \text{ g}} \right) \left(\frac{0.534 \text{ g}}{1 \text{ cm}^3} \right)$$

$$= 4.63 \times 10^{22} \text{ } e^-/\text{cm}^3$$

3. The voltage drop across a diode is 0.70 V when it is connected in series to a 210-Ω resistor and a battery, and there is an 11-mA current. If the LED has an equivalent resistance of 70 Ω, what potential difference must be supplied by the battery?

$$R = R_r + R_D = 210 \text{ } \Omega + 70 \text{ } \Omega$$

$$= 280 \text{ } \Omega$$

and

$$V = IR = (11 \times 10^{-3} \text{ A})(280 \text{ } \Omega) = 3.1 \text{ V}$$

4. What resistor would replace the 210-Ω resistor in the previous problem if the current was changed to 29 mA?

$$V = IR, \text{ so}$$

$$R = \frac{V}{I} = \frac{3.1 \text{ V}}{29 \times 10^{-3} \text{ A}} = 107 \text{ } \Omega$$

$$R = R_r + R_D, \text{ so}$$

$$R_r = R - R_D = 107 \text{ } \Omega - 70 \text{ } \Omega = 37 \text{ } \Omega$$

$$= 40 \text{ } \Omega$$

5. What would the new current in the previous problem be if the leads on the battery were reversed?

Zero. The diode would stop the current.

Copyright © by Glencoe/McGraw-Hill

CHAPTER 30

1. What particles, and how many of each, make up an atom of $^{109}_{47}Ag$?

   47 electrons, 47 protons, 62 neutrons

2. A calcium ion has 20 protons and 20 neutrons. Write its isotopic symbol.

   $^{40}_{20}Ca$

3. What is the isotopic symbol of a zinc atom composed of 30 protons and 34 neutrons?

   $^{64}_{30}Zn$

4. Write the complete nuclear equation for the alpha decay of $^{210}_{84}Po$.

   $^{210}_{84}Po \rightarrow \, ^{4}_{2}He + \, ^{206}_{82}Pb$

5. Write the complete nuclear equation for the beta decay of $^{14}_{6}C$.

   $^{14}_{6}C \rightarrow \, ^{0}_{-1}e + \, ^{14}_{7}N + \, ^{0}_{0}\nu$

6. Complete the nuclear reaction:
   $^{225}_{89}Ac \rightarrow \, ^{4}_{2}He + \underline{\quad}$

   $^{225}_{89}Ac \rightarrow \, ^{4}_{2}He + \, ^{221}_{87}Fr$

7. Complete the nuclear reaction:
   $^{227}_{88}Ra \rightarrow \, ^{0}_{-1}e + \underline{\quad} + \underline{\quad}$

   $^{227}_{88}Ra \rightarrow \, ^{0}_{-1}e + \, ^{227}_{89}Ac + \, ^{0}_{0}\nu$

8. Complete the nuclear reaction:
   $^{65}_{29}Cu + \, ^{1}_{0}n \rightarrow \underline{\quad} \rightarrow \, ^{1}_{1}p + \underline{\quad}$

   $^{65}_{29}Cu + \, ^{1}_{0}n \rightarrow \, ^{66}_{29}Cu \rightarrow \, ^{1}_{1}p + \, ^{65}_{28}Ni$

9. Complete the nuclear equation:
   $^{235}_{92}U + \, ^{1}_{0}n \rightarrow \, ^{96}_{40}Zr + 3(^{1}_{0}n) + \underline{\quad}$

   $^{235}_{92}U + \, ^{1}_{0}n \rightarrow \, ^{96}_{40}Zr + 3(^{1}_{0}n) + \, ^{137}_{52}Te$

10. An isotope has a half-life of 3.0 days. What percent of the original material will be left after

    a. 6.0 days?

    $\dfrac{6.0 \text{ dy}}{3.0 \text{ dy}} = 2$ **half-lives, so** $\left(\dfrac{1}{2}\right)^2 = \dfrac{1}{4}$ **, so**

    25% is left.

    b. 9.0 days?

    $\dfrac{9.0 \text{ dy}}{3.0 \text{ dy}} = 3$ **half-lives, so** $\left(\dfrac{1}{2}\right)^3 = \dfrac{1}{8}$ **, so**

    12.5% is left.

    c. 12 days?

    $\dfrac{12 \text{ dy}}{3.0 \text{ dy}} = 4$ **half-lives, so** $\left(\dfrac{1}{2}\right)^4 = \dfrac{1}{16}$ **,**

    so 6.3% is left.

11. $^{211}_{86}Rn$ has a half-life of 15 h. What fraction of a sample would be left after 60 h?

    $\dfrac{60 \text{ h}}{15 \text{ h}} = 4$ **half-lives, so** $\left(\dfrac{1}{2}\right)^4 = \dfrac{1}{16}$

    is left.

12. $^{209}_{84}Po$ has a half-life of 103 years. How long would it take for a 100-g sample to decay so only 3.1 g of Po-209 was left?

    $\dfrac{100 \text{ g}}{3.1 \text{ g}} = 32 = 2^5$ **, so = 5 half-lives or**

    515 years.

13. The positron, $^{0}_{+1}e$, is the antiparticle to the electron and is the particle ejected from the nucleus in some nuclear reactions. Complete the nuclear reaction:
    $^{17}_{9}F \rightarrow \, ^{0}_{+1}e + $

    $^{17}_{9}F \rightarrow \, ^{0}_{+1}e + \, ^{17}_{8}O + \, ^{0}_{0}\nu$

Copyright © by Glencoe/McGraw-Hill

14. Complete the nuclear reaction:

$^{22}_{11}\text{Na} \rightarrow {}^{0}_{+1}\text{e} +$

$^{22}_{11}\text{Na} \rightarrow {}^{0}_{+1}\text{e} + {}^{22}_{10}\text{Ne} + {}^{0}_{0}\nu$

15. Find the charge of a π^+ meson made of a *u* and *anti-d* quark pair.

$$\text{u} + \bar{\text{d}} = +\frac{2}{3} + -\left(-\frac{1}{3}\right) = +1$$

16. Baryons are particles that are made of three quarks. Find the charge on each of the following baryons.

a. neutron; *d, d, u* quark triplet

$$\text{d} + \text{d} + \text{u} = \left(-\frac{1}{3}\right) + \left(\frac{2}{3}\right) = 0$$

b. antiproton; *anti-u, anti-u, anti-d* quark triplet

$$\bar{\text{u}} + \bar{\text{u}} + \bar{\text{d}}$$

$$= -\left(\frac{2}{3}\right) + -\left(\frac{2}{3}\right) + -\left(-\frac{1}{3}\right) = -1$$

Copyright © by Glencoe/McGraw-Hill

CHAPTER 31

1. The carbon isotope, $^{12}_{6}C$, has a nuclear mass of 12.000 000 u.

   a. What is the mass defect of this isotope?

   $6(^1_1p) = 6(1.007\ 825\ u) = \quad 6.046\ 950$ u

   $6(^1_0n) = 6(1.008\ 665\ u) = \quad \underline{6.051\ 990}$ u

   total mass of nucleus   12.098 940 u

   $^{12}_{6}C$ −12.000 000 u

   mass defect   −0.098 940 u

   b. What is the binding energy of its nucleus?

   E = (931.5 MeV/u)(0.098 940 u)

   = 92.16 MeV

2. The sulfur isotope, $^{32}_{16}S$, has a nuclear mass of 31.972 07 u.

   a. What is the mass defect of this isotope?

   $16(^1_1p) = 16(1.007\ 825\ u) =$ 16.125 20 u

   $16(^1_0n) = 16(1.008\ 665\ u) =$ $\underline{16.138\ 64}$ u

   32.263 84 u

   $^{32}_{16}S =$ 31.972 07 u

   $\underline{32.263\ 84}$

   mass defect −0.291 77 u

   b. What is the binding energy of its nucleus?

   E = (931.5 MeV/u)(0.291 77 u)

   = 271.8 MeV

3. The sodium isotope, $^{22}_{11}Na$, has a nuclear mass of 21.994 44 u.

   a. What is the mass defect of this isotope?

   $11(^1_1p) = 11(1.007\ 825\ u) =$ 11.086 08 u

   $11(^1_0n) = 11(1.008\ 665\ u) =$ $\underline{11.095\ 32}$ u

   22.181 40 u

   $^{22}_{11}Na =$ 21.994 44 u

   $\underline{22.181\ 40}$

   mass defect −0.186 96 u

   b. What is the binding energy of its nucleus?

   E = (931.5 MeV/u)(0.186 96 u)

   = 174.2 MeV

c. What is the binding energy per nucleon?

$$\frac{174.2\ MeV}{22\ nucleons} = 7.916\ MeV/nucleon$$

4. The binding energy for ^7_3Li is 39.25 MeV. Calculate the mass of the lithium-7 nucleus in atomic mass units.

   $3(^1_1p) = 3(1.007\ 825\ u) =$ 3.023 475 u

   $4(^1_0n) = 4(1.008\ 665\ u) =$ 4.034 660 u

   mass defect $= \dfrac{39.25\ MeV}{931.5\ MeV/u} =$ −0.042 14 u

   7.016 00 u

5. Write the complete nuclear equation for the positron decay of $^{132}_{55}Cs$.

   $^{132}_{55}Cs \rightarrow {}^0_{+1}e + {}^{132}_{54}Xe + {}^0_0\nu$

6. Complete the nuclear reaction:

   $^{14}_{7}N + {}^1_0n \rightarrow \underline{\quad} \rightarrow {}^1_1p + \underline{\quad}$

   $^{14}_{7}N + {}^1_0n \rightarrow {}^{15}_{7}N \rightarrow {}^1_1p + {}^{14}_6C$

7. Complete the nuclear reaction:

   $^{65}_{29}Cu + {}^1_0n \rightarrow \underline{\quad} \rightarrow {}^1_1p + \underline{\quad}$

   $^{65}_{29}Cu + {}^1_0n \rightarrow {}^{66}_{29}Cu \rightarrow {}^1_1p + {}^{65}_{28}Ni$

8. When a magnesium isotope, $^{24}_{12}Mg$, is bombarded with neutrons, it absorbs a neutron and then emits a proton. Write the complete nuclear equation for this reaction.

   $^{24}_{12}Mg + {}^1_0n \rightarrow {}^{25}_{12}Mg \rightarrow {}^1_1p + {}^{24}_{11}Na$

9. When oxygen-17 is bombarded by neutrons, it absorbs a neutron and then emits an alpha particle. The resulting nucleus is unstable and it will emit a beta particle. Write the complete nuclear equation for this reaction.

   $^{17}_{8}O + {}^1_0n \rightarrow {}^{18}_{8}O \rightarrow {}^4_2He + {}^{14}_6C$

   $\rightarrow {}^0_{-1}e + {}^{14}_7N + {}^0_0\nu$

10. Complete the following fission reaction:

    $^{239}_{94}Pu + {}^1_0n \rightarrow {}^{137}_{52}Te + 3({}^1_0n) + \underline{\quad}$

    $^{239}_{94}Pu + {}^1_0n \rightarrow {}^{137}_{52}Te + 3({}^1_0n) + {}^{100}_{42}Mo$

11. Complete the following fission reaction:

    $^{233}_{92}U + {}^1_0n \rightarrow {}^{134}_{55}Cs + 2({}^1_0n) + \underline{\quad}$

    $^{233}_{92}U + {}^1_0n \rightarrow {}^{134}_{55}Cs + 2({}^1_0n) + {}^{98}_{37}Rb$

Copyright © by Glencoe/McGraw-Hill

12. Complete the following fission reaction:
$^{235}_{92}U + ^1_0n \rightarrow ^{90}_{38}Sr + 10(^1_0n) + \underline{\quad}$

$$^{235}_{92}U + ^1_0n \rightarrow ^{90}_{38}Sr + 10(^1_0n) + ^{136}_{54}Xe$$

13. Strontium-90 has a mass of 89.907 747 u, xenon-136 has a mass of 135.907 221 u, and uranium-235 has a mass of 235.043 915 u.

a. Compute the mass defect in the previous problem.

$$\begin{aligned}
\text{Sr-90} &= 89.907\ 747 \ \text{u} \\
\text{Xe-136} &= 135.907\ 221 \ \text{u} \\
10(^1_0n) = 10(1.008\ 665 \ \text{u}) &= \underline{10.086\ 65} \ \text{u} \\
&= 235.901\ 62 \ \text{u} \\
^1_0n &= 1.008\ 665 \ \text{u} \\
\text{U-235} &= \underline{235.043\ 915} \ \text{u} \\
&= 236.052\ 580 \ \text{u}
\end{aligned}$$

mass defect $= 235.901\ 62 \ \text{u} - 236.052\ 58 \ \text{u}$

$\qquad = -0.150\ 96 \ \text{u}$

b. Compute the amount of energy released.

$E = (931.5 \ \text{MeV/u})(0.150\ 96 \ \text{u})$

$\quad = 140.6 \ \text{MeV}$

14. One of the simplest fusion reactions involves the production of deuterium, ^2_1H (2.014 102 u), from a neutron and a proton. Write the complete fusion reaction and find the amount of energy released.

$$^1_1p + ^1_0n \rightarrow ^2_1H$$

$$\begin{aligned}
1(^1_1p) = 1(1.007\ 825 \ \text{u}) &= 1.007\ 825 \ \text{u} \\
1(^1_0n) = 1(1.008\ 665 \ \text{u}) &= 1.008\ 665 \ \text{u} \\
& 2.016\ 490 \ \text{u} \\
^2_1H &= 2.014\ 102 \ \text{u} \\
& -2.016\ 490 \ \text{u} \\
\text{mass defect} &= -0.002\ 388 \ \text{u}
\end{aligned}$$

$E = (931.5 \ \text{MeV/u})(0.002\ 388 \ \text{u})$

$\quad = 2.224 \ \text{MeV}$

15. The fusion reactions most likely to succeed in a fusion reactor are listed below. Complete each fusion reaction.

a. $^2_1H + ^2_1H \rightarrow ^3_1H + \underline{\quad}$

$\qquad ^2_1H + ^2_1H \rightarrow ^3_1H + ^1_1H$

b. $^2_1H + ^2_1H \rightarrow ^3_2He + \underline{\quad}$

$\qquad ^2_1H + ^2_1H \rightarrow ^3_2He + ^1_0n$

c. $^2_1H + ^3_1H \rightarrow ^4_2He + \underline{\quad}$

$\qquad ^2_1H + ^3_1H \rightarrow ^4_2He + ^1_0n$

d. $^3_1H + ^3_1H \rightarrow ^4_2He + 2\underline{\quad}$

$\qquad ^3_1H + ^3_1H \rightarrow ^4_2He + 2(^1_0n)$

Copyright © by Glencoe/McGraw-Hill

Appendix D
Additional Topics in Physics

Topic 1 Falling Raindrops
Pages 811–816
Practice Problems

page 816

1. Use the spreadsheet model for objects with different terminal velocities. Would a larger raindrop fall a smaller or larger distance before reaching terminal velocity?

    Larger drops fall a greater distance before reaching terminal velocity.

2. A coffee filter falls with a terminal velocity of 1.2 m/s. Use the spreadsheet model to find how far it fell before it reached terminal velocity.

    It falls about 0.24 m before reaching terminal velocity.

Applying Concepts

1. Use the data given at the beginning of this lesson on the size and terminal velocities of raindrops. Does the drag force on raindrops of all sizes depend on the square of the velocity? Because such a drag force leads to a terminal velocity that is proportional to the square root of the radius, you can test this assumption by plotting the terminal velocity versus the square root of the radius, shown in Figure 6.

    The assumption is good for the three smaller drop sizes. If larger drops flatten into pancake-shaped drops as weather books suggest, then their cross-sectional area, A, would be larger than that calculated by the spherical model, reducing their terminal velocity.

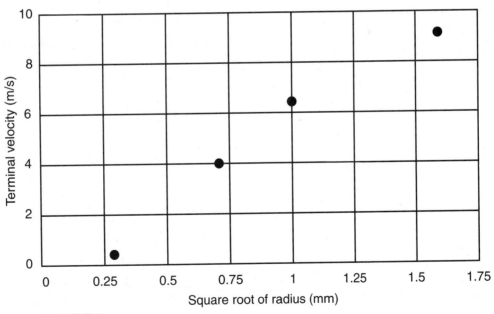

FIGURE 6

Copyright © by Glencoe/McGraw-Hill

Topic 1 (continued)

2. When you tried the demonstration that shows coffee filters experience a drag force proportional to the square of the velocity, you found that four filters fell 2 m in the same time one filter fell 1 m. You estimated that it took 1.5 s for the filters to fall. As you know, it takes some time for all objects to reach their terminal velocity, so the filters are not falling at constant speed during their entire fall. Use the spreadsheet model to estimate the actual time it would take the two sets of filters to fall. Does this result make the demonstration faulty? Explain.

A filter falling 1 m in 1.5 s has an average velocity of 2/3 m/s down. With the terminal velocity set at 0.667 m/s, the spreadsheet model indicates that the filter falls 1.0 m in 1.525 s. (Time interval is set at 0.025 s). The time the filter takes to accelerate to the terminal velocity (0.2 s) only has a small effect on the fall time.

The four filters fall 2 m in 1.5 s for an average velocity of 4/3 m/s down. The terminal velocity is now set at 1.333 m/s. These filters, according to the spreadsheet model, fall 2.0 m in 1.575 s. It takes almost 0.5 s for these filters to reach their terminal velocity.

The difference in fall time is only 0.05 s, which is too small to be detected in this experiment. Thus, the demonstration experiment gives the correct results.

Topic 2
Fundamentals of Rotation
Pages 817–824
Practice Problems

page 819

1. Describe the frequency of rotation of the hour, minute, and second hands of a clock.

   one revolution per 12 hours; one per hour; one per minute

2. **a.** What is the period of Earth's rotation in seconds?

   (24 h)(60 min/h)(60 s/min) = 86 400 s

   b. What is the frequency of Earth's rotation in rotations per second?

   1/(86 400 s) = 1.157 × 10⁻⁵ s⁻¹

3. What is the linear velocity of a person standing on Earth's surface at the equator, due only to the rotation of Earth?

   $v = r\omega$
   $= (6.38 \times 10^3 \text{ km})(7.27 \times 10^{-5} \text{ rad/s})$
   $= 0.463 \text{ km/s}$

4. What is the angular velocity in rad/s of the tip of the second hand of a watch?

   (2π rad)/(60 s) = 0.10 rad/s

5. The tip of a second hand of a watch is 11 mm from the axis. What is the velocity of the tip?

   (11 mm)(0.10 rad/s) = 1.1 mm/s

page 821

6. Your car has a flat tire. You get out your tools and find a lug wrench to take the nuts off the bolt studs. You find it impossible to turn the nuts. A friend suggests ways you might produce enough torque to turn them. What three ways might your friend suggest?

   Use as much force as you can safely apply with your arms. Exert the force at the end of the wrench as far from the nuts as possible. Exert the force at right angles to the wrench.

7. A bolt on a car engine is to be tightened with a torque of 35 N·m. If you have a 25-cm long wrench, what force should you exert?

   $F = \tau/s = (35 \text{ N·m})/(0.25 \text{ m}) = 1.4 \times 10^2 \text{ N}$

8. What mass would have a weight equal to the force needed in the above problem?

   $m = F_g/g$
   $= (1.4 \times 10^2 \text{ N})/(9.80 \text{ m/s}^2)$
   $= 14 \text{ kg}$

9. Mo, whose mass is 43 kg, sits 1.8 m from the center of a seesaw. Joe, whose mass is 52 kg, wants to balance Mo. Where should Joe sit?

Copyright © by Glencoe/McGraw-Hill

Topic 2 (continued)

$r_M F_M = r_J F_J$, so $r_J = r_M(F_M/F_J)$

$= r_M(m_M/m_J)$

$= (1.8 \text{ m})(43 \text{ kg})/(52 \text{ kg})$

$= 1.5 \text{ m on the other side}$

10. Jane (56 kg) and Joan (43 kg) want to balance on a 1.75-m long seesaw. Where should they place the pivot point?

Let x be the distance of the pivot from Jane's end.

$x(56 \text{ kg})(g) = (1.75 \text{ m} - x)(43 \text{ kg})(g)$

$x(56 \text{ kg}) = (1.75 \text{ m} - x)(43 \text{ kg})$

$x(56 \text{ kg}) = (1.75 \text{ m})(43 \text{ kg}) - x(43 \text{ kg})$

$x(56 \text{ kg}) + x(43 \text{ kg}) = (1.75 \text{ m})(43 \text{ kg})$

$x(56 \text{ kg} + 43 \text{ kg}) = (1.75 \text{ m})(43 \text{ kg})$

$x = \dfrac{(1.75 \text{ m})(43 \text{ kg})}{(56 \text{ kg} + 43 \text{ kg})}$

$x = 1.75 \text{ m} \left(\dfrac{43 \text{ kg}}{56 \text{ kg} + 43 \text{ kg}} \right)$

$x = 0.76 \text{ m}$

The pivot point should be 0.76 m from Jane's end.

page 822

11. Two disks have the same mass, but one has twice the diameter of the other. Which would be harder to start rotating? Why?

The larger one has a greater moment of inertia and would need a greater torque for the same angular acceleration.

12. When a bowling ball leaves the bowler's hand, it is not spinning, but after it has gone about half the length of the lane, it spins. Explain how its rotation rate is increased and why it does not continue to increase.

Torque is needed. The force is the force of the friction with the lane surface, and the lever arm is the radius of the ball. The angular velocity increases until there is no relative velocity between the ball and the lane. At this point, there is no more frictional force.

page 823

13. Two children first sit 0.3 m from the center of a seesaw. Assuming that their masses are much greater than that of the seesaw, by how much is the moment of inertia increased when they sit 0.6 m from the center?

It is increased by a factor of four.

14. Suppose there are two balls with equal diameters and masses. One is solid; the other is hollow, with all its mass near its surface.

a. Are their moments of inertia equal? If not, which is larger?

No, the hollow one has a larger moment of inertia.

b. Describe an experiment you could do to see if the moments of inertia are equal.

Give equal torque to the two; see if one gains rotational speed faster.

15. You buy a piece of 10-cm-square lumber, 2.44 m long. Your friend buys the same size piece, but has it cut into two lengths, each 1.22 m long. You each carry your lumber on your shoulders.

a. Which would be easier to lift? Why?

Neither, both have the same weight.

b. You apply a torque with your hand to keep the lumber from rotating. Which would be easier to keep from rotating? Why?

The longer ones would be easier to keep from rotating because they have a larger moment of inertia.

page 824

16. Where is the center of mass of a roll of masking tape?

The center of mass is at the center of the hole.

17. When you walk in a strong wind, why do you have to lean into the wind to avoid falling down? Hint: consider torque produced by wind.

Your pivot point is your feet. The wind exerts a force on your body, producing a backward torque. To balance it, you must move your center of mass forward so gravity exerts a forward torque.

Copyright © by Glencoe/McGraw-Hill

Topic 3 Applications of Rotation

Pages 825–832

Practice Problems

page 826

1. Why is a vehicle in storage with its body raised high on blocks less stable than a similar vehicle with its body at normal height?

   Because the center of mass is higher, less work is required to rotate the vehicle until its center of mass is beyond the edge of the base.

2. Circus tightrope walkers often carry long bars that sag so that the ends are lower than the center. Sometimes weights are attached to the ends. How does the pole increase the walker's stability? Hint: consider both center of mass and moment of inertia.

   The drooping pole lowers the center of mass, possibly even below the feet. The long bar with masses on the ends makes the inertia greater. Then the angular acceleration resulting from any torque, such as beginning to fall, is smaller and gives the walker time to respond.

page 828

3. The outer rim of a Frisbee is thick and heavy. Besides making it easier to catch, how would this affect its rotational properties?

   The heavy rim gives the Frisbee a large moment of inertia, which increases the gyroscope effect.

4. A gymnast first does giant swings on the high bar, holding her body straight and pivoting around her hands. She then lets go and grabs her knees with her hands in the tuck position. Finally, she straightens up and lands on her feet.

page 829

   a. In the second and final parts of the gymnast's routine, around what axis does she spin?

   She spins around an axis through her center of mass.

   b. Rank in order, from largest to smallest, her moments of inertia for the three positions.

   largest when swinging about her hands, smallest when in the tuck position, and middle when straightened up

   c. Rank in order her angular velocities in the three positions.

   smallest in first position, largest in second position, and middle in third position

5. A student, holding a bicycle wheel with its axis vertical, sits on a stool that can rotate without friction. He uses his hand to get the wheel spinning. Would you expect the student and stool to turn? Which direction? Explain.

   Yes, you would expect them to turn because angular momentum must be conserved in the absence of outside torques. Before the wheel is spinning, there is no angular momentum. After the wheel is spinning, the wheel has angular momentum, so the student and stool must rotate in the opposite direction to produce zero net angular momentum.

6. The diameter of a bicycle wheel is 71.5 cm. The mass of the rim, tire, and inner tube is 0.925 kg.

   a. Find the moment of inertia of the wheel (ignoring the spokes and hub).

   $$I = mr^2 = (0.925 \text{ kg})(0.715 \text{ m})^2$$
   $$= 0.473 \text{ kg·m}^2$$

   b. When the bike is moving at 9.0 m/s, what is the angular velocity of the wheel?

   $$\omega = v/r = (9.0 \text{ m/s})/0.375 \text{ m}$$
   $$= 25.2 \text{ rad/s}$$

Copyright © by Glencoe/McGraw-Hill

Topic 3 (continued)

c. What is the rotational kinetic energy of the wheel?

$$K = \frac{1}{2}I\omega^2$$

$$= \frac{1}{2}(0.473 \text{ kg·m}^2)(25.2 \text{ rad/s})$$

$$= 150.2 \text{ J}$$

page 830

7. When a spinning ice skater pulls in her arms, by conservation of angular momentum, her angular velocity increases. What happens to kinetic energy? We write $K = \frac{1}{2}I\omega^2 = \frac{1}{2}L\omega$. Thus, if L is constant and ω increases, K increases. But if kinetic energy increases, work must have been done. What did work on the skater?

The skater did work on herself by pulling her arms in.

page 832

8. While riding a merry-go-round, you toss a key to a friend standing on the ground. For your friend to catch the key, should you toss it a second or two before you reach your friend's position or wait until your friend is directly behind you? Explain.

Toss the key just before you reach your friend. You and the key both have an angular velocity in the direction of rotation. If you wait until you are beside your friend, the angular velocity will carry the key past him or her.

9. People sometimes say that the moon stays in its orbit because the "centrifugal force just balances the centripetal force, giving no net force." Explain why this idea is wrong.

If the moon has no net force on it, it would move in a straight line. Earth's gravitational force is the force that causes the centripetal acceleration it has in a circular orbit.

Topic 4 Statics

Pages 833–839
Practice Problems

page 836

1. Determine the tension in the rope supporting the pivoted lamp pole shown in **Figure 3** below. The pole weighs 27 N, and the lamp, 64 N. **Table 2** shows the torque caused by each force.

a Sketch

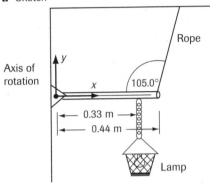

b Free-body diagram

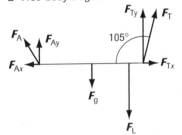

c Torque diagrams

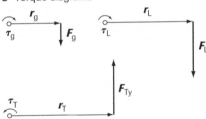

TABLE 2		
Clockwise Torque		
Lever arm	Force	Torque
$r_g = 0.22$ m	$F_g = 27$ N	$\tau_g = 5.9$ N · m
$r_L = 0.33$	$F_L = 64$ N	$\tau_L = 21$ N · m
		Total $\tau_{cw} = 27$ N · m
Counterclockwise Torque		
Lever arm	Force	Torque
0.44 m	F_{Ty}	$\tau_T = (0.44$ m$)$ F_{Ty}
		Total $\tau_{ccw} = (0.44$ m$)$ F_{Ty}

Copyright © by Glencoe/McGraw-Hill

Topic 4 (continued)

$$\tau_{ccw} = \tau_{cw}$$

$$(0.44 \text{ m})F_{Ty} = 27 \text{ N·m}$$

$$F_{Ty} = \frac{27 \text{ N·m}}{0.44 \text{ m}}$$

$$F_{Ty} = 61 \text{ N}$$

$$F_T = \frac{F_{Ty}}{\sin 105.0°} = \frac{61 \text{ N}}{0.966} = 63 \text{ N}$$

The tension in the rope is 63 N.

page 839

2. What is the force of friction acting on a 1.7-m wooden plank weighing 145 N propped at an angle of 65° from the horizontal? There is friction only between the plank and the ground.

$$F_f = \frac{1}{2}F_g \frac{\cos \theta}{\sin \theta} = \frac{1}{2}F_g \cot \theta$$

$$= \frac{1}{2}(145 \text{ N})\cot 65°$$

$$F_f = 33.8 \text{ N}$$

3. What coefficient of friction is needed to keep the plank propped up?

$$\mu_s \geq F_f/F_g$$

$$\mu_s \geq (\cot \theta)/2$$

$$\mu_s \geq (\cot 65°)/2$$

$$\mu_s \geq 0.233$$

Reviewing Concepts

1. Why can you ignore forces that act on the axis of rotation of an object in static equilibrium when determining the net torque?

    A force on the axis of rotation has no lever arm because the distance from the force to the axis is zero. Therefore, its torque is zero.

2. In solving problems about static equilibrium, why is the axis of rotation often placed at a point where one or more forces are acting on the object?

    If the axis of rotation is placed at this point, the torque caused by each force is zero. Therefore, the solution equation has fewer variables.

Topic 5 Gas Laws
Pages 841–853
Practice Problems

page 845

1. The volume of a cylinder with a movable piston is 0.063 m³. It exerts 236 kPa on a certain amount of air. While the temperature is held constant, the pressure is increased to 354 kPa. What is the new volume of the air?

$$P_1V_1 = P_2V_2$$

$$V_2 = \frac{P_1V_1}{P_2} = \frac{(236 \text{ kPa})(0.063 \text{ m}^3)}{354 \text{ kPa}}$$

$$V_2 = 0.042 \text{ m}^3$$

2. A pressure of 235 kPa holds neon gas in a cylinder whose volume is 0.0500 m³. The volume increases to 0.125 m³. What pressure is now exerted on the gas?

$$P_1V_1 = P_2V_2$$

$$P_2 = \frac{P_1V_1}{V_2} = \frac{(235 \text{ kPa})(0.0500 \text{ m}^3)}{0.125 \text{ m}^3}$$

$$P_2 = 94.0 \text{ kPa}$$

3. The volume of a helium-filled balloon is 2.0 m³ at sea level. The balloon rises until its volume is 6.0 m³. What is the pressure in kPa at this height?

$$P_1V_1 = P_2V_2 \text{ where } P_1 = 101.3 \text{ kPa, the atmospheric pressure at sea level}$$

$$P_2 = \frac{P_1V_1}{V_2} = \frac{(101.3 \text{ kPa})(2.0 \text{ m}^3)}{6.0 \text{ m}^3}$$

$$P_2 = 33.8 \text{ kPa} = 34 \text{ kPa}$$

4. A diver works at a depth of 52 m in fresh water. A bubble of air with a volume of 2.0 cm³ escapes from her mouthpiece. What is the volume of the bubble just as it reaches the surface of the water?

    From an earlier example problem, each 10.4 m of water depth exerts 1 atm of pressure so that the pressure at the diver's depth is

Copyright © by Glencoe/McGraw-Hill

Topic 5 (continued)

$$P_1 = 1.0 \text{ atm} + \frac{52 \text{ m}}{10.4 \text{ m/atm}} = 6.0 \text{ atm}$$

$$P_1 V_1 = P_2 V_2$$

$$V_2 = \frac{P_1 V_1}{P_2} = \frac{(6.0 \text{ atm})(2.0 \text{ cm}^3)}{1.0 \text{ atm}}$$

$$V_2 = 12 \text{ cm}^3$$

page 846

5. A 30.0-m^3 volume of argon gas is heated from 20.0°C to 293°C under constant pressure. What is the new volume of the gas?

$$\frac{V_1}{T_1} = \frac{V_2}{T_2} \text{ with } T_1 = 20.0°C + 273°C$$

$$= 293 \text{ K and } T_2 = 293°C + 273°C$$

$$= 566 \text{ K}$$

$$V_2 = \frac{T_2 V_1}{T_1} = \frac{(566K)(30.0 \text{ m}^3)}{293K} = 58.0 \text{ m}^3$$

6. Thirty liters of oxygen gas are cooled from 20.0°C to −146°C under constant pressure. What is the new volume?

$$\frac{V_1}{T_1} = \frac{V_2}{T_2} \text{ with } T_1 = 20.0°C + 273°C$$

$$= 293 \text{ K and } T_2 = -146°C + 273°C$$

$$= 127 \text{ K}$$

$$V_2 = \frac{T_2 V_1}{T_1} = \frac{(127 \text{ K})(3.0 \times 10^1 \text{ L})}{293 \text{ K}} = 13 \text{ L}$$

7. The volume of a sample of krypton gas at 60.0°C is 0.21 liters. Under constant pressure, it is heated to twice its original volume. To what temperature (in Celsius degrees) is it heated?

$$\frac{V_1}{T_1} = \frac{V_2}{T_2} \text{ with } T_1 = 60.0°C + 273°C$$

$$= 333 \text{ K and}$$

$$V_2 = 2V_1$$

$$T_2 = \frac{V_2 T_1}{V_1} = \frac{(2V_1)(333 \text{ K})}{V_1} = 666 \text{ K}$$

$$T_C = 666 \text{ K} - 273 \text{ K} = 393°C$$

8. The volume of a balloon of helium is 63 liters at 20.0°C. At what temperature would its volume be only 19 liters?

$$\frac{V_1}{T_1} = \frac{V_2}{T_2} \text{ with } T_1 = 20.0°C + 273°C$$

$$= 293 \text{ K}$$

$$T_2 = \frac{V_2 T_1}{V_1} = (19 \text{ L})(293 \text{ K})\backslash 63 \text{ L} = 88 \text{ K}$$

$$T_C = 88 \text{ K} - 273 \text{ K} = -185°C$$

page 849

9. A tank of helium gas used to inflate toy balloons is at 15.5×10^6 Pa pressure at 293 K. Its volume is 0.020 m^3. How large a balloon would it fill at 1.00 atmosphere and 323 K?

$$\frac{P_1 V_1}{T_1} = \frac{P_2 V_2}{T_2}; \text{ so, } V_2 = \frac{T_2 P_1 V_1}{P_2 T_1}$$

$$1 \text{ atm} = 101.3 \times 10^3 \text{ Pa}$$

$$V_2 = \frac{(323 \text{ K})(15.5 \times 10^6 \text{ Pa})(0.020 \text{ m}^3)}{(101.3 \times 10^3 \text{ Pa})(293K)}$$

$$V_2 = 3.4 \text{ m}^3$$

10. What is the mass of helium gas in Practice Problem 9? The mass of helium is 4.00 grams per mole.

$$PV = nRT; \text{ so}$$

$$n = \frac{PV}{RT} = \frac{(15.5 \times 10^6 \text{ Pa})(0.020 \text{ m}^3)}{(8.31 \text{ Pa·m}^3/\text{mol·K})(293 \text{ K})}$$

$$n = 127.3 \text{ mol}$$

$$m = (127.3 \text{ mol})(4.00 \text{ g/mol}) = 509 \text{ g}$$
$$= 510 \text{ g}$$

11. Two hundred liters of hydrogen gas at 0°C are kept at 156 kPa. The temperature is raised to 95°C and the volume is decreased to 175 L. What is the pressure of the gas now?

$$\frac{P_1 V_1}{T_1} = \frac{P_2 V_2}{T_2} \text{ with } T_1 = 273 \text{ K and}$$

$$T_2 = 95°C + 273°C = 368 \text{ K}$$

$$P_2 = \frac{T_2 P_1 V_1}{V_2 T_1}$$

$$= \frac{(368 \text{ K})(156 \text{ kPa})(2.0 \times 10^2 \text{ L})}{(175 \text{ L})(273 \text{ K})}$$

$$P_2 = 240 \text{ kPa}$$

12. The molecular weight of air is about 29 grams/mole. What is the volume of one kilogram of air at standard atmospheric pressure and 20°C?

Copyright © by Glencoe/McGraw-Hill

Physics: Principles and Problems

Problems and Solutions Manual **337**

Topic 5 (continued)

$PV = nRT$; so $V = \dfrac{nRT}{P}$

where $n = (1.0 \times 10^3 \text{ g})/(29 \text{ g/mol})$

$= 34.5 \text{ mol}$

$V =$
$\dfrac{(34.5 \text{ mol})(8.31 \text{ Pa·m}^3/\text{mol·K})(293 \text{ K})}{(101.3 \times 10^3 \text{ Pa})}$

$V = 0.83 \text{ m}^3$

page 850

Reviewing Concepts

1. If you made a barometer and filled it with a liquid one-third as dense as mercury, how high would the level of the liquid be on a day of normal atmospheric pressure?

   1 atm = 760 mm = 0.760 m

   height = 0.760 m × 3 = 2.28 m

2. What happens when the pressure acting on a gas is held constant but the temperature of the gas is changed?

   The volume of a gas varies directly with the temperature.

3. What happens when the temperature of a gas remains constant and pressure is changed?

   The volume of a gas varies inversely with the pressure.

4. If a balloon filled with air is at rest, then the average velocity of the particles is zero. Does that mean the assumptions of the kinetic theory are not valid? Explain.

   The average velocity is zero, but the average speed is not.

5. What causes atmospheric pressure?

   The weight of the air causes it.

6. State standard atmospheric pressure in four different units.

   1 atm = 1.013 × 10³ N/m² = 101.3 mb = 760 Torr = 1.013 kPa

7. Why does air pressure in tires increase when a car is driven on a hot day?

   The temperature increases, and at constant volume, pressure varies directly with absolute temperature.

8. When an air cylinder with a movable piston is placed in a refrigerator, the volume inside the cylinder shrinks. How could you increase the volume to its original size without removing the piston from the refrigerator?

   decrease the pressure

9. Describe how a real gas differs from an ideal gas. What are some of the consequences of these differences?

   Unlike an ideal gas, the particles of a real gas have mass and volume and attract each other. Real gases do not follow the $PV = nRT$ equation at low temperatures and high pressures, and can be liquefied.

Applying Concepts

10. **a.** Explain why liquid rises in a straw when you drink a soda.

    Suction lowers the air pressure inside the straw. Air pressure on the soda then pushes it up the straw.

    b. What would be the longest soda straw you could use? Assume you could remove all air from the straw.

    10.4 m; the height of a column of water supported by atmospheric pressure

11. You lower a straw into water and place your finger over its top. As you lift the straw from the water, you notice water stays in it. Explain. If you lift your finger from the top, the water runs out. Why?

    As you lift the straw, the volume of air trapped inside the straw increases because a little water runs out. Because its volume increases, its pressure decreases. The pressure of the trapped air on the surface of the water in the straw is less than atmospheric pressure pushing on the surface of the water on the open end of the straw. The difference in pressure exerts an upward force on the water equal to the weight of water in the straw. When your finger is released, the air pressure on both surfaces of the water is the same. So, there is no net upward force. The force of gravity pulls the water out.

Copyright © by Glencoe/McGraw-Hill

Topic 5 (continued)

12. Explain why you could not use a straw to drink a soda on the moon.

    There is no atmospheric pressure to push the liquid up the straw.

13. A tornado produces a region of extreme low pressure. If a house is hit by a tornado, is it likely to explode or implode? Why?

    Explode; the pressure is greater inside the house, which pushes the walls outward.

14. Suppose real gas particles had volume but no attractive forces. How would this real gas differ from an ideal gas? How would it differ from other real gases?

    At high pressure, its volume would shrink more slowly than for an ideal gas; but at low temperatures, it would behave like an ideal gas. It would never liquefy.

page 851

15. Explain how Charles's experiments with gases predicted the value of the absolute zero of temperature.

    At constant pressure, all gases expand the same amount for a given temperature change. By graphing changes in volume versus Kelvin temperature, Charles arrived at a temperature for which the volume would be equal to zero.

16. Suppose you are washing dishes. You place a glass, mouth downward, over the water and lower it slowly.

    a. What do you see?

    The division between the water and air moves up toward the bottom of the inverted glass.

    b. How deep would you have to push the glass to compress the air to half its original volume? Try part a. Do not try part b.

    Volume decreases to half when pressure doubles. At the surface, the pressure on the air in the glass is 1 atmosphere. To double the

pressure to 2 atmospheres, the glass would have to be pushed to a depth of 10.4 m.

17. Once again at the sink, you lift a filled glass above the water surface with the mouth below the surface and facing downward.

    a. The water does not run out. Why?

    Air pressure on the water surface pushed the water up the glass.

    b. How tall would the glass have to be to keep the water from running out?

    greater than 10.4 m (Water runs out till the level equals 10.4 m above the sink.)

Problems

18. Weather reports often give atmospheric pressure in inches of mercury. The pressure usually ranges between 28.5 and 31.0 inches. Convert these two values to Torr, millibars, and kPa.

    28.5 in = 724 Torr = 965 mb = 96.5 kPa

    31.0 in = 787 Torr = 1050 mb = 105 kPa

19. a. Find the force exerted by air at standard atmospheric pressure on the front cover of your textbook.

    $A = (0.20 \text{ m})(0.26 \text{ m}) = 0.052 \text{ m}^2$

    $P = \dfrac{F}{A}$; so, $F = PA$

    $F = (101.3 \text{ kN/m}^2)(0.052 \text{ m}^2)$

    $= 5.3 \times 10^3 \text{ N}$

    b. What mass would exert the same force?

    $m = \dfrac{F}{g} = \dfrac{5.3 \times 10^3 \text{ N}}{9.80 \text{ m/s}^2} = 5.4 \times 10^2 \text{ kg}$

20. A tire gauge at a service station indicates a pressure of 32.0 psi (lb/in^2) in your tires. One standard atmosphere is 14.7 psi. What is the absolute pressure of air in your tires in kPa?

    32.0 psi = 2.18 atm

    Thus, absolute pressure is 3.18 atm.

    1 atm = 101.3 kPa

    $3.18 \text{ atm} \times \dfrac{101.3 \text{ kPa}}{1 \text{ atm}} = 322 \text{ kPa}$

Copyright © by Glencoe/McGraw-Hill

Topic 5 (continued)

page 852

21. How high a column of alcohol (density 0.9 that of water) could be supported by atmospheric pressure?

$$\frac{h_1}{h_2} = \frac{\rho_2}{\rho_1}$$

$$h_2 = \frac{h_1 \rho_1}{\rho_2} = \frac{(10.4 \text{ m})(1.0 \text{ g/mL})}{0.90 \text{ g/mL}}$$

$$= 12 \text{ m}$$

22. Two cubic meters of gas at 30.0°C are heated at constant pressure until the volume is doubled. What is the final temperature of the gas?

$$\frac{V_1}{T_1} = \frac{V_2}{T_2} \text{ with } T_1 = 30.0°C + 273°C$$

$$= 303 \text{ K}$$

$$T_2 = \frac{V_2 T_1}{V_1} = \frac{(4.00 \text{ m}^3)(303 \text{ K})}{2.0 \text{ m}^3} = 606 \text{ K}$$

$$T_C = 606 - 273° = 333°C$$

23. The pressure acting on 50.0 m³ of air is 1.01×10^5 Pa. The air is at −50.0°C. The pressure acting on the air is increased to 2.02×10^5 Pa. Then the air occupies 30.0 m³. What is the temperature of the air at this new volume?

$$\frac{P_1 V_1}{T_1} = \frac{P_2 V_2}{T_2}$$

with $T_1 = -50.0°C + 273°C = 223$ K

$$T_2 = \frac{P_2 V_2 T_1}{P_1 V_1}$$

$$T_2 = \frac{(2.02 \times 10^5 \text{ Pa})(30.0 \text{ m}^3)(223 \text{ K})}{(101.3 \times 10^3 \text{ Pa})(50.0 \text{ m}^3)}$$

$$T_2 = 267 \text{ K}, T_C = 267 \text{ K} - 273 \text{ K} = -6°C$$

24. The pressure acting on 50.0 cm³ of a gas is reduced from 1.2 atm to 0.30 atm. What is the new volume of the gas if the temperature does not change?

$$P_1 V_1 = P_2 V_2$$

$$V_2 = \frac{P_1 V_1}{P_2} = \frac{(1.2 \text{ atm})(50.0 \text{ cm}^3)}{0.30 \text{ atm}}$$

$$V_2 = 2.0 \times 10^2 \text{ cm}^3$$

25. A tank containing 30.0 m³ of natural gas at 5.0°C is heated at constant pressure by the sun to 30.0°C. What is its new volume?

$$\frac{V_1}{T_1} = \frac{V_2}{T_2} \text{ with } T_1 = 5.0°C + 273°C$$

$$= 278 \text{ K and}$$

$$T_2 = 30.0°C + 273°C = 303 \text{ K}$$

$$V_2 = \frac{V_1 T_2}{T_1} = \frac{(30.0 \text{ cm}^3)(303 \text{ K})}{278 \text{ K}}$$

$$= 32.7 \text{ cm}^3$$

26. Fifty liters of gas are cooled to 91.0 K at constant pressure. Its new volume is 30.0 liters. What was the original temperature?

$$\frac{V_1}{T_1} = \frac{V_2}{T_2}$$

$$T_2 = \frac{V_2 T_1}{V_1} = \frac{(91.0 \text{ K})(50.0 \text{ L})}{30.0 \text{ L}} = 152 \text{ K}$$

27. Suppose the lungs of a scuba diver are filled to a capacity of 6.0 liters while the diver is 8.3 m below the surface of a lake. To what volume would the diver's lungs (attempt to) expand if the diver suddenly rose to the surface?

$$P_1 = 1.0 \text{ atm} + \frac{8.3 \text{ m}}{10.4 \text{ m/atm}} = 1.8 \text{ atm}$$

$$P_1 V_1 = P_2 V_2$$

$$V_2 = \frac{P_1 V_1}{P_2} = \frac{(1.8 \text{ atm})(6.0 \text{ L})}{1.0 \text{ atm}} = 11 \text{ L}$$

28. A bubble of air with volume 0.050 cm³ escapes from a pressure hose at the bottom of a tank filled with mercury. When the air bubble reaches the surface of the mercury, its volume is 0.500 cm³. How deep is the mercury?

For mercury, pressure increases 1.0 atm per 0.760 m of depth increase

$$P_1 V_1 = P_2 V_2; \text{ so, } \frac{P_2 V_2}{V_1}$$

$$P_1 = \frac{(1.00 \text{ atm})(0.500 \text{ cm}^3)}{0.050 \text{ cm}^3} = 10.0 \text{ atm}$$

$$\text{depth} = (10.0 \text{ atm} - 1.0 \text{ atm}) \times$$

$$(0.760 \text{ m/atm})$$

$$\text{depth} = 6.8 \text{ m}$$

Physics: Principles and Problems

Copyright © by Glencoe/McGraw-Hill

29. At 40.0 K, 0.100 m³ of helium is at 408 kPa. The pressure exerted on the helium is increased to 2175 kPa while its volume is held constant. What is the temperature of the helium now?

$$\frac{P_1}{T_1} = \frac{P_2}{T_2}$$

$$T_2 = \frac{P_2 T_1}{P_1} = \frac{(2175 \text{ kPa})(40.0 \text{ K})}{408 \text{ kPa}} = 213 \text{ K}$$

30. A 20-L sample of neon is at standard atmospheric pressure at 300°C. The sample is cooled in dry ice to −79°C at constant volume. What is its new pressure?

$$\frac{P_1}{T_1} = \frac{P_2}{T_2} \text{ with } T_1 = 300°C + 273°C$$

$$= 573 \text{ K and}$$

$$T_2 = -79°C + 273°C = 194 \text{ K}$$

$$P_2 = \frac{P_1 T_1}{T_2} = \frac{(1.00 \text{ atm})(194 \text{ K})}{573 \text{ K}}$$

$$= 0.3 \text{ atm}$$

31. A 50.0-cm³ sample of air is at standard pressure and −45.0°C. The pressure on the gas sample is doubled and the temperature adjusted until the volume is 30.0 cm³. What is the temperature?

$$\frac{P_1 V_1}{T_1} = \frac{P_2 V_2}{T_2} \text{ with } T_1$$

$$= -45.0°C + 273°C = 228 \text{ K}$$

$$T_2 = \frac{P_2 V_2 T_1}{P_1 V_1}$$

$$T_2 = \frac{(2.00 \text{ atm})(30.0 \text{ cm}^3)(228 \text{ K})}{(1.00 \text{ atm})(50.0 \text{ cm}^3)}$$

$$T_2 = 274 \text{ K}, \, T_C = 274 \text{ K} - 273 \text{ K} = 1°C$$

32. At 40.0 K, 10.0 m³ of nitrogen is under 4.0×10^2 kPa pressure. The pressure acting on the nitrogen is increased to 2000 kPa. Its volume stays the same. What is the temperature of the nitrogen?

$$\frac{P_1}{T_1} = \frac{P_2}{T_2}; \text{ so, } T_2 = \frac{P_2 T_2}{P_1}$$

$$T_2 = \frac{(2000 \text{ kPa})(40.0 \text{ K})}{4.0 \times 10^2 \text{ kPa}} = 200 \text{ K}$$

33. The markings on a thermometer are worn off, so a student creates new degree markings, which she calls °S. She then measures the volume of a gas held at constant pressure at three temperatures, finding 30 L at 90°S, 45 L at 120°S, and 60 L at 150°S. What is absolute zero on the S scale?

Her values extrapolate to zero at 30°S, which is absolute zero on the S scale.

34. How many particles are in one cubic centimeter of air (6.02×10^{23} particles/mole) at standard pressure and 20°C temperature?

$$PV = nRT \text{ with } T = 20°C + 273°C = 293 \text{ K}$$

$$n = \frac{PV}{RT}$$

$$= \frac{(1.01 \times 10^5 \text{ Pa})(1.00 \times 10^{-6} \text{ m}^3)}{(8.31 \text{ Pa·m}^3/\text{mol·K})(293 \text{ K})}$$

$$= 4.15 \times 10^{-5} \text{ mol}$$

$$4.15 \times 10^{-5} \text{ mol} \times$$

$$\frac{6.02 \times 10^{23} \text{ particles}}{1 \text{ mol}}$$

$$= 2.50 \times 10^{19} \text{ particles}$$

35. Physicists can, with proper equipment, obtain vacuums with pressures of 1.0×10^{-11} Torr.

a. What fraction of atmospheric pressure is this?

$$(1.0 \times 10^{-11} \text{ Torr})\left(\frac{1 \text{ atm}}{760 \text{ Torr}}\right)$$

$$= 1.3 \times 10^{-14} \text{ atm}$$

b. Using the results from Problems 34 and 35a, find the number of particles in a cubic centimeter of this vacuum.

$$(2.50 \times 10^{19} \text{ particles/atm})(1.3 \times 10^{-14} \text{ atm}) = 3.3 \times 10^5 \text{ particles}$$

Copyright © by Glencoe/McGraw-Hill

36. Two hundred grams of argon (39.9 grams/mole) are sold in a bottle at 5.0 atm and 293 K. How many liters are in the bottle?

$PV = nRT$; so, $V = \dfrac{nRT}{P}$

$n = (2.00 \times 10^2 \text{ g})(1 \text{ mol}/39.9 \text{ g}) = 5.01 \text{ mol}$

$V = \dfrac{(5.01 \text{ mol})(8.31 \text{ Pa·m}^3/\text{mol·K})(293 \text{ K})}{(5 \text{ atm})(101.3 \times 10^3 \text{ Pa/atm})}$

$V = 0.024 \text{ m}^3 \times \dfrac{1 \text{ L}}{1 \times 10^{-3} \text{ m}^3} = 24 \text{ L}$

37. A 2.00 L-tank of gas is designed to hold gas at 20.0 atm and 50.0°C. What mass of methane (16.0 grams/mole) can be put into the tank?

$PV = nRT$ with $T = 50.0°\text{C} + 273°\text{C}$
$= 323 \text{ K}$

$2.00 \text{ L} \times \dfrac{1 \times 10^{-3} \text{ m}^3}{1 \text{ L}} = 2.00 \times 10^{-3} \text{ m}^3$

$n = \dfrac{PV}{RT}$

$20.0 \text{ atm} \times \dfrac{101.3 \times 10^3 \text{ Pa}}{1 \text{ atm}}$
$= 2.026 \times 10^6 \text{ Pa}$

$n = \dfrac{(2.026 \times 10^6 \text{ Pa})(2.00 \times 10^{-3} \text{ m}^3)}{(8.31 \text{ Pa·m}^3/\text{mol·K})(323 \text{ K}) \, n}$
$= 1.51 \text{ mol}$

$m = (1.51 \text{ mol})(16.0 \text{ g/mol}) = 24.2 \text{ g}$

38. The pressure on 20.0 liters of gas is 120.0 kPa. If the temperature is 23.0°C, how many molecules are present?

$PV = nRT$ with $T = 23°\text{C} + 273°\text{C} = 296 \text{ K}$

$V = (20.0 \text{ L})(1.00 \times 10^{-3} \text{ m}^3/\text{L}) = 0.0200 \text{ m}^3$

$n = \dfrac{PV}{RT} = \dfrac{(120.0 \times 10^3 \text{ Pa})(0.0200 \text{ m}^3)}{8.31 \text{ Pa·m}^3/\text{mol·K})(296 \text{ K})}$
$= 0.976 \text{ mol}$

$n = 0.976 \text{ mol} \times \dfrac{6.02 \times 10^{23} \text{ molecules}}{1 \text{ mol}}$
$= 5.88 \times 10^{23} \text{ molecules}$

39. The specific gravity of mercury is 13.6; that is, mercury is 13.6 times more dense than water. If a barometer were constructed using water rather than mercury, how high (in meters) would the water rise under normal atmospheric pressure?

$\dfrac{h_1}{h_2} = \dfrac{\rho_2}{\rho_1}$

$h_2 = \dfrac{h_1 \rho_1}{\rho_2} = \dfrac{(0.760 \text{ m})(13.6 \text{ g/mL})}{1.00 \text{ g/mL}}$
$= 10.3 \text{ m}$

Topic 6 Radio Transmissions
Pages 855–860
Practice Problems

page 856

1. Find the frequency, period, and wavelength of a sound wave produced by a source vibrating at 440 Hz. The speed of sound in air at 20°C is 343 m/s.

$f = 440 \text{ Hz}$

$T = \dfrac{1}{f} = \dfrac{1}{440 \text{ Hz}} = 2.3 \times 10^{-3} \text{ s}$

$v = \lambda f$

$\lambda = \dfrac{v}{f} = \dfrac{343 \text{ m/s}}{440 \text{ Hz}} = 0.78 \text{ m}$

2. Find the frequency, period, and wavelength of an electromagnetic wave generated by a 440-Hz signal. Recall that an electromagnetic wave moves at the speed of light.

$f = 440 \text{ Hz}$

$T = \dfrac{1}{f} = \dfrac{1}{440 \text{ Hz}} = 2.3 \times 10^{-3} \text{ s}$

$v = \lambda f$

$\lambda = \dfrac{v}{f} = \dfrac{3.0 \times 10^8 \text{ m/s}}{440 \text{ Hz}} = 6.8 \times 10^5 \text{ m}$

3. The optimum antenna height is half the wavelength of the electromagnetic wave it is designed to receive. What optimum antenna height would be needed to receive electromagnetic waves produced by a 440-Hz signal?

The length is 3.4×10^5 m, which is half the wavelength of 6.8×10^5 m.

page 860

Reviewing Concepts

1. How does the signal affect the carrier wave in an AM radio transmitter?

The amplitude of the signal wave at each instant multiplies the amplitude of the carrier wave at that instant.

Copyright © by Glencoe/McGraw-Hill

Topic 6 (continued)

2. How does the signal affect the carrier wave in an FM radio transmitter?

The amplitude of the signal wave at each instant determines the change in frequency of the carrier wave at each instant.

Applying Concepts

3. Suppose a modulator adds the signal and carrier waves instead of multiplying them.

a. Using the signal and carrier waves shown in **Figure 3b** and **Figure 3c**, sketch the wave that this modulator would produce.

The resulting wave should have the higher frequency wave, the carrier wave, in the pattern of the signal wave. Thus, it should appear as a rapidly oscillating wave moving in another, slower-oscillating wave. Note that the wave has been shifted up due to the constant potential in the signal, so the resulting wave does not drop much below zero potential difference.

b. How does the wave produced by adding the signal and carrier waves compare to the wave produced by multiplying the signal and carrier waves?

The wave produced by adding does not have the beatlike pattern that the wave produced by multiplying has. The wave produced by multiplying is still centered around a potential difference of zero, while the wave produced by summing is centered around a positive potential difference.

4. Devices such as microphones and loudspeakers are classified as energy converters, that is, they convert the input energy to another form.

a. What are the forms of the input and output energy of a microphone?

The input energy is mechanical energy (sound waves), and the output energy is electrical (signal).

b. What are the forms of the input and output energy of a loudspeaker?

The input energy is electrical energy (signal), and the output energy is mechanical (sound waves).

5. Which type of modulation allows the transmitter to generate radio signals at maximum power? Recall from Chapter 25 that the average power dissipated in an AC circuit is proportional to the square of the amplitude of the voltage.

FM allows the transmitter to generate radio waves at maximum power because the amplitude (voltage) of the FM carrier wave does not vary, and therefore, the power does not vary, unlike AM carrier waves.

6. Television signals modulate the carrier at frequencies as high as 4 MHz. Could TV be broadcast in the AM band? Explain.

No. You can't modulate a carrier wave with a frequency higher than the frequency of the carrier wave. Thus, TV must be broadcast at much higher frequencies. (Channel 2, the lowest frequency signal, is above 56 MHz.)

7. Interpret the importance of wave behaviors and characteristics in the radio industry.

Student answers may vary. Students should include the importance of amplitude in AM waves, frequency in FM waves, and modulation in both AM and FM. Students should also discuss the ability of radio waves to travel through a vacuum.

8. Compare the characteristics of electromagnetic waves used in radio with sound waves and their characteristics.

They are the same in some ways. They have a frequency and amplitude. The modulated waves are more complex than simple waves, but sound waves can be complex as well. But, electromagnetic waves are transverse waves, and sound waves are longitudinal waves.

Copyright © by Glencoe/McGraw-Hill

Topic 7 Relativity

Pages 861–871

Reviewing Concepts

page 869

1. State the two postulates of relativity.

   The laws of physics are the same for all reference frames moving at constant relative velocity. The speed of light is a constant in every such frame.

2. A spaceship moves at half the speed of light and shines one laser beam forward and another beam backward. As seen by an observer at rest, does the beam shining forward appear to move faster than the one shining backward? Explain.

   No; the speed of light does not depend on the motion of the source. It is always c.

3. One student travels in a plane moving to the left at 100 m/s. A student on the ground drives a car to the right at 30 m/s. A third student is standing still. Identify and describe the relative motion between the students. What is the speed of light for each reference frame?

   To the student standing still, the student in the plane is traveling to the left at 100 m/s, while the student in the car is traveling to the right at 30 m/s. To the student in the car, it could appear, by ignoring the background scenery and the fact that the student's legs aren't moving, that the student on the ground is moving 30 m/s to the left, and the student in the plane is moving 130 m/s to the left. To the student in the plane, the student on the ground could appear to be moving at 100 m/s to the right (again ignoring scenery and non-moving legs), while the student in the car moves 130 m/s to the right. The speed of light is the same in all frames.

4. Suppose, in another world, the speed of light were only 10 m/s, the speed of a fast runner. Describe some effects on athletes in this world.

   Sprinters would have extremely hard times reaching high speeds. Distance runners would think the race times were shorter. Starting events at the same time or finding out who got to a finish line first would be difficult. High jumpers and pole-vaulters would think the bars were lower, but then the bars would also shrink.

page 870

5. In the world of question 4, a contestant rides a bicycle. Would she see the bicycle as shorter than it was at rest? What would stationary people who are observing the bicycle see?

   No; to her the bicycle would be the same length, but to those who were at rest, it would look shorter.

6. An airplane generates sound waves. When it flies at the speed of sound, it catches up with the waves, producing a sonic boom.

   a. Could an object radiating light in a vacuum ever catch up with its waves? Explain.

   No; nothing can accelerate to the speed of light, and, to a moving object, the light moves away at the speed of light.

   b. Suppose the object moves at 90% the speed of light in a vacuum. Then it enters water. If its speed did not change, could it catch up with the light waves it emits in water? Explain.

   Yes; the speed of light in water is 3/4 its speed in a vacuum, so the object is now going faster than the speed of light in the water. It would produce the equivalent of a sonic boom, called Cerenkov radiation. This is the source of the blue light produced by radioactive material put in water baths.

7. An astronaut aboard a spaceship has a quartz watch, a meterstick, and a mass on a spring. What changes would the astronaut observe in these items as the spaceship moves at half the speed of light? Explain.

   None; the astronaut is moving with the items.

Copyright © by Glencoe/McGraw-Hill

Topic 7 (continued)

8. The astronaut in question 7 measures the period of an oscillator consisting of a mass on a spring. Would the frequency of oscillation change? Explain.

   No; the laws of physics do not change.

9. Under what circumstances could a 40-year-old man have a 50-year-old daughter?

   If the man, following the birth of his daughter, had gone on a long space trip at very high speed and then returned to Earth (twin effect).

10. Science books often say that "matter can never be created or destroyed." Is this correct? If not, how should it be modified?

    No; the sum of matter and energy can never be created or destroyed.

Problems

11. A rocket, 75 m long, moves at $v = 0.50c$. What is its length as measured by an observer at rest?

    $$L = L_0 \sqrt{1 - \frac{v^2}{c^2}} = 75 \text{ m} \sqrt{1 - \frac{(0.50c)^2}{c^2}}$$

    $$L = 65 \text{ m}$$

12. A spaceship traveling at $v = 0.60c$ passes near Earth. A 100.0-m long soccer field lies below its path. What is the length of the field as measured by the crew aboard the ship?

    $$L = L_0 \sqrt{1 - \frac{v^2}{c^2}}$$

    $$= 100.0 \text{ m} \sqrt{1 - \frac{(0.60c)^2}{c^2}}$$

    $$L = 8.0 \times 10^1 \text{ m}$$

13. A certain star is 30.0 light-years away. One light-year is the distance light travels in one year. From the point of view of a person on Earth, how long would it take a spaceship traveling at $v = 0.866c$ to make the one-way trip? Ignore the time needed for acceleration and braking.

    $$t = \frac{d}{v} = \frac{(30.0 \text{ y})(c)}{0.866c} = 34.6 \text{ y}$$

14. From the point of view of the astronauts in the spaceship in question 13, how long would the round-trip require?

$$t = t_0 \sqrt{1 - \frac{v^2}{c^2}}$$

$$= (2)(34.6 \text{ y}) \sqrt{1 - \frac{(0.866c)^2}{c^2}}$$

$$t = 34.6 \text{ y}$$

page 871

15. A spaceship is 98 m long. How fast would it have to be moving to appear only 49 m long?

    $$L = L_0 \sqrt{1 - \frac{v^2}{c^2}} \text{ ; so,}$$

    $$\frac{L}{L_0} = \sqrt{1 - \frac{v^2}{c^2}}$$

    $$\left(\frac{L}{L_0}\right)^2 = 1 - \left(\frac{v}{c}\right)^2$$

    $$\frac{v}{c} = \sqrt{1 - \left(\frac{L}{L_0}\right)^2} = \sqrt{1 - \left(\frac{49 \text{ m}}{98 \text{ m}}\right)^2} = 0.87$$

    $$v = (0.87)c = (0.87)(3.0 \times 10^8 \text{ m/s})$$

    $$= 2.6 \times 10^8 \text{ m/s}$$

16. The lifetime of a pion at rest is 2.6×10^{-8} s. What is the lifetime, measured by an observer at rest, of a pion traveling at $0.80c$?

    $$t = \frac{t_0}{\sqrt{1 - \frac{v^2}{c^2}}} = \frac{2.6 \times 10^{-8} \text{ s}}{\sqrt{1 - \frac{(0.80c)^2}{c^2}}}$$

    $$= 4.3 \times 10^{-8} \text{ s}$$

17. The rest energy of a pion is 140 MeV. What is its kinetic energy when it moves at $0.80c$? Its total energy?

    $$K = mc^2 \left(\frac{1}{\sqrt{1 - \frac{v^2}{c^2}}} - 1 \right)$$

    $$= 140 \text{ MeV} \left(\frac{1}{\sqrt{1 - \frac{(0.80c)^2}{c^2}}} - 1 \right)$$

    $$K = 93 \text{ MeV}$$

    $$E = K + E_0 = 93 \text{ MeV} + 140 \text{ MeV}$$

    $$= 233 \text{ MeV}$$

Copyright © by Glencoe/McGraw-Hill

Topic 7 (continued)

18. When a pion decays, it emits a muon. If the pion decays at rest, the muon is emitted at velocity 0.80c. If the pion is moving at 0.50c, and the muon is emitted in the same direction as the pion, what is the velocity of the muon as seen by an observer at rest?

$$v' = \frac{v + u}{1 + \dfrac{uv}{c^2}} = \frac{0.50c + 0.80c}{1 + \dfrac{(0.50c)(0.80c)}{c^2}}$$

$$v' = \frac{1.30c}{1.40} = 0.93c$$

19. A spaceships is moving at velocity 0.40c. A meteor is moving toward it at 0.60c, as measured by the crew on the ship. What is the speed of the meteor as measured by an observer at rest?

$$v' = \frac{v + u}{1 + \dfrac{uv}{c^2}} = \frac{0.40c + 0.60c}{1 + \dfrac{(0.40c)(0.60c)}{c^2}}$$

$$v' = \frac{1.00c}{1.24} = 0.81c$$

20. What is the equivalent energy in joules of 1.0 kg of apples?

$$E_0 = mc^2 = (1.0 \text{ kg})(3.0 \times 10^8 \text{ m/s})$$
$$E_0 = 9.0 \times 10^{16} \text{ J}$$

Copyright © by Glencoe/McGraw-Hill